DAVIES, CROALL AND TYRER'S CRIMINAL JUSTICE

Fifth Edition

DAVIES, CROALL AND TYRER'S CRIMINAL JUSTICE

Malcolm Davies

PEARSON

Harlow, England • London • New York • Boston • San Francisco • Toronto • Sydney
Auckland • Singapore • Hong Kong • Tokyo • Seoul • Taipei • New Delhi
Cape Town • São Paulo • Mexico City • Madrid • Amsterdam • Munich • Paris • Milan

Pearson Education Limited
Edinburgh Gate
Harlow CM20 2JE
United Kingdom
Tel: +44 (0)1279 623623
Web: www.pearson.com/uk

First published 1995 (print)
Second edition 1998 (print)
Third edition 2005 (print)
Fourth edition 2009 (print and electronic)
Fifth edition published 2015 (print and electronic)

ISBN: 978–1–408–28305–9 (print)
      978–1–408–28308–0 (PDF)
      978–1–292–00343–6 (eText)

British Library Cataloguing-in-Publication Data
A catalogue record for the print edition is available from the British Library

Library of Congress Cataloguing-in-Publication Data
Davies, Malcolm, 1946- author.
  [Criminal justice]
  Davies, Croall and Tyrer on criminal justice / Malcolm Davies, Hazel Croall, Jane Tyrer. -- Fifth edition.
    pages cm
  Revision of the author's Criminal justice.
  Includes bibliographical references and index.
  ISBN 978-1-4082-8305-9
  1. Criminal justice, Administration of--England. I. Croall, Hazel, 1947- author.
  II. Tyrer, Jane, 1951- author. III. Title.
  KD7876.D38 2015
  364.942--dc23
                                                                        2014048761

ARP impression 98

Print edition typeset in 9/12pt Stone Ser ITC Std by 35

Printed by Ashford Colour Press Ltd

NOTE THAT ANY PAGE CROSS REFERENCES REFER TO THE PRINT EDITION

We should like to dedicate this book to Michael Molyneux (1929–2005) for his inspiration as a teacher to generations of students and colleagues at Ealing Law School.

Brief contents

Contents

PART B CRIMINAL JUSTICE PROCESS: LAW ENFORCEMENT

Preface

It is nearly twenty years since the first edition of *Criminal Justice* was published in 1995. This fifth edition continues with the task of describing the operation of, and the changes to, the criminal justice system in England and Wales from the end of the twentieth century to the early decades of the twenty-first.

The changes described in the preceding four editions were many. Some were designed to give the appearance of modernisation. Some were the results of the pressure created by the single-issue pressure groups. Others were the consequences of new crimes, media attention and public outcry. There was a noted shift in emphasis from a system that sought to respond to crimes to one that also sought to increase the efforts to prevent crime by reducing criminal opportunities, enhance the coordination and collaboration between the agencies, increase surveillance by use of CCTV and electronic monitoring of offenders, and adopt strategies to counter anti-social behaviour in crime-prone communities and families.

The criminal justice system that emerged from the nineteenth and twentieth centuries was built on commendable principles to ensure the state and its agencies did not have all its own way. The constraints on the powerful were intended and enforceable through a range of principles and agencies that set limits on those whose duty it was to respond to crime. The most notable of these was that the agencies of criminal justice and the agents of law enforcement and prosecution were not above the rules of law.

Furthermore, in dealing with those accused of crime the determination of guilt for serious crimes was a matter of lay juries reaching decisions based only on the evidence heard in court.

In addition, the trial dice were loaded in our adversarial system of justice in favour of the defendant in two ways: first, with the 'burden of proof' principle whereby it is the prosecutor who needs to gather relevant and admissible evidence while the defendant does not need to provide evidence or account for their behaviour, and; second, by the 'standard of proof' criteria used in criminal cases whereby the jury are instructed that the decision to either convict or not convict, should be based on a standard that is 'beyond reasonable doubt', or as it is sometimes translated, the jurors had to be fairly certain the defendant did what had been claimed by the prosecution.

When talking about the principles and practice in a field of study such as criminal justice we refer to the dominant perspectives and theories that are taken for granted and underpin the work of institutions and the agencies. We call this a paradigm; defined as, 'A mode of viewing the world which underlies the theories and methodology of science in a particular period of history'.

What is the shift in the criminal justice paradigm in the early twenty-first century and to what extent have we moved away from a system defined primarily in terms of principles that focused on the rights of the defendant?

The era of the ECHR and its focus on the human rights of the criminal and prisoner probably reached its zenith in the first decade of the twenty-first century with demands for prisoners to have the right to vote regardless of their crimes or the extent of their anti-social behaviour. One key development for clarifying and finessing these issues on human rights was the establishment in 2008 of the Supreme Court for the UK.

The early twenty-first century has seen a paradigm shift as a consequence of shifting sympathies which has seen, first a move towards the victims of crime, and second, a major refocus on the basics of criminal justice, i.e. public safety, as different types of organised criminal groups took full opportunity to operate globally.

Hence, two key drivers of change in the last decade have been the continued increase in victims' rights at home, and the enhanced perceived threat to the public from global crimes. This latter concern is dismissed by some as yet another example of a 'moral panic', a concept that has gained in popularity but stumbles over a key element of having no guide as to how the public, media and governments – castigated for 'overreacting' to an outbreak of crime – should react to new manifestations of criminality.

This rebalance in the system reflected the growing influence of the victims' movement and is illustrated by the series of trials held in 2014 of media celebrities, mainly radio and television presenters, who were accused of sexual crimes, usually involving younger victims. These resulted in historic prosecutions; in some cases going back to allegations made in the 1960s.

The status of the victim of crime has continued to advance and in 2013 the Victims' Right of Review (VRR) was introduced to give victims the right to challenge a decision by the Crown Prosecution Service not to prosecute an offender. This was a further example of a series of incremental reforms giving the victim more say in the system and followed on from the Victims Charter, Victim Support, victim compensation, victim impact statements and victim surcharge.

Developments in public accountability, illustrated the shift in the criminal justice paradigm, by giving the individual victim a greater voice, and also in addition by giving the public at large a chance to influence law enforcement at the local level by the introduction in 2012 of elected Police and Crime Commissioners.

On the international scene the impact of crime was to involve much soul searching and questioning of basic assumptions as to what is the purpose of the criminal justice system. Those who reiterated the shibboleths of liberty, and protecting the rights of the accused, were to be challenged and unsettled by the growing reality that we were in a global encounter whereby the parochial features of traditional jurisdictions with proud distinctions and trusted assumptions were somewhat inadequate when facing the dramatic nature of crimes being carried out by criminals operating on a global scale.

Cyber fraud is one example of criminals exploiting new technologies that are unhindered by international distances and, indeed, often protected by jurisdictional differences with regard to extradition and national laws that impeded cross-jurisdictional collaboration between police forces and prosecutors.

New horror stories emerged to do with cross-jurisdictional crimes that included human trafficking, people smuggling, slavery and terrorism.

Terrorist acts from around the world resulted in long lists of victims. These included: Kenyans and Tanzanians office workers and US embassy officials (1998, killed 200 and 1,000 injured), office workers in the Twin Towers in New York City (2001, killed 2,999), Bali holidaymakers (2002, killed 202 and 240 injured),

Spanish commuters on the Madrid Railway (2004, killed 191 and 1,800 injured), London Underground and bus passengers (2005, 52 killed and 70 injured), hotel guests and workers in Mumbai (2008, killed 164 and 308 injured), Lee Rigby, a soldier, hacked to death in a street in south London (2013) and cartoonists, publishers, shoppers and police officers in Paris (January 2015, 17 killed and 1 wounded).

The link between the national and international world is clearly evident in the new reality of global crime. It is also evident in the economic context of criminal justice in England and Wales, as from 2008 the global recession has resulted in a prolonged period of economic austerity and fiscal pruning that led to cutbacks to services and manpower and stimulated the search for more cost-efficient solutions such as increasing the number of services contracted out, i.e. switched from the public to the commercial and voluntary sector.

Some things, however, do not change. It is still a point of uniqueness that the criminal justice system in England and Wales relies on a very high proportion of tasks and decisions being undertaken by volunteers, independent professionals and lay participants, and this is in contrast to other countries where government employees and public officials undertake most of the tasks of delivering criminal justice services.

I trust you find this fifth edition helpful.
Cordially yours,
Professor Malcolm Davies

List of figures

List of tables

Chronology of key dates in the development of criminal justice in England and Wales

The following gives a list of significant dates referred to in the text. Added comments indicate key developments in the criminal justice system in England and Wales.

1717 Transportation Act
1779 Penitentiary Act
1784 Transportation Act
1816 Millbank penitentiary opened in London
1823 Gaol Act
1824 Vagrancy Act
1829 Metropolitan Police Improvement Act. The Metropolitan Police Force was established
1833 Factory Act
1842 Pentonville prison opened
1853 Penal Servitude Act. Ends short terms of transportation and Parkhurst Prison opens with a regime designed for young offenders
1854 Reformatory School Act
1856 County and Borough Police Act
1861 Offences Against the Person Act
1867 End of transportation
1877 Prison Act. The Prison Commission was established with responsibility for all prisons in the country: the first chairman was Sir Edmund Du Cane
1878 Criminal Investigation Department (CID) of the Metropolitan Police was established
1879 Prosecution of Offences Act
1895 Gladstone Committee Report on prisons
1883 Trial of Lunatics Act allowed juries to bring in a guilty but insane verdict
1898 Prison Act
1898 Criminal Evidence Act
1901 Borstal experiment introduced
1907 Probation of Offenders Act
1908 Prevention of Crime Act. Borstal system and preventive detention introduced
1908 Children Act. Restrictions on the imprisonment of children
1913 Mental Deficiency Act. Mentally deficient persons were diverted out of the prison system
1919 Police Act followed the Police Strike and the formation of the Police Federation
1925 Criminal Justice Act
1933 Children and Young Persons Act. Reformatories and industrial schools were replaced by approved schools

1936 Open prison was established near Wakefield
Prison Officers' Association was founded
End to arrows on uniforms and treadmills
1936 Public Order Act
1948 Criminal Justice Act. Abolished penal servitude, prison with hard labour and whipping. Introduced corrective training, preventive detention and detention centres
1949 Royal Commission on Capital Punishment
1957 Homicide Act
1961 Criminal Justice Act. Minimum age of imprisonment was raised from 15 to 17. Greater use was encouraged of borstal training instead of prison for offenders under 21
1962 Royal Commission on the Police
1963 Prison Commission abolished and replaced by the Prison Department
1964 Criminal Procedure (Insanity) Act
1964 Police Act
1965 Murder (Abolition of Death Penalty) Act
1966 Mountbatten Report. Following the escape of the Russian spy George Blake from Wormwood Scrubs prison, Earl Mountbatten conducted an inquiry into prison security
1967 Criminal Justice Act. Introduction of the suspended sentence and discretionary parole. Courts were empowered to suspend any sentence of imprisonment not exceeding two years. Parole allowed an inmate to apply for parole after serving one-third of their sentence. Abolition of preventive detention and corrective training and corporal punishment in prisons. Introduction of majority jury verdicts
1968 Firearms Act
1968 Criminal Appeal Act
1969 Children and Young Persons Act. Introduced care and supervision orders and replaced approved schools and remand homes with community homes
1971 Misuse of Drugs Act
1971 Courts Act. Abolished Assizes and Quarter Sessions and established the Crown Court
1972 Road Traffic Act. Introduced the breathalyser
1972 Criminal Justice Act. Introduced community service orders
1974 Juries Act
1974 Rehabilitation of Offenders Act
1976 Bail Act
1977 Criminal Law Act. Allowed the court to suspend a sentence of imprisonment in part
1979 Report of the May Committee on the Prison Services. A policy of positive custody was advocated
1980 Magistrates' Courts Act
1981 Scarman Report on riots in Brixton
1981 Contempt of Court Act
1981 Royal Commission on Criminal Procedure

1982 Criminal Justice Act. Reduction of the parole eligibility criteria from 12 to 6 months. Statutory criteria for sentencing young offenders to a custodial sentence. Borstal training replaced by youth custody

1983 Mental Health Act

1984 Police and Criminal Evidence Act. Introduced the PACE Codes to cover police stop and search, questioning of suspects and detention in police custody

1985 Prosecution of Offences Act. Established the Crown Prosecution Service

1986 Public Order Act

1986 Drug Trafficking Offences Act made laundering of cash derived from the sale of drugs illegal and allowed confiscation of money made through drug dealing

1988 Criminal Justice Act. Extension of statutory criteria for custodial sentences for young offenders

1988 Legal Aid Act

1988 Road Traffic Act

1990 White Paper, *Crime, Justice and Protecting the Public*

1990 Criminal Justice (International Cooperation) Act introduced a new power for police and customs officers to seize cash discovered on import or export which is reasonably suspected of being derived from or intended for use in drug trafficking and enabled the UK to request and provide assistance to all countries

1991 Criminal Justice Act. Introduced the combination order, unit fine and a sentencing framework

1991 Report on the Prison Disturbances of April 1990 (chairman, Lord Justice Woolf). It recommended wide-ranging changes to the nature of prison regimes and the need for greater coordination throughout the criminal justice system

1991 Criminal Procedure (Insanity and Unfitness to Plead) Act

1993 Royal Commission on Criminal Justice (chairman, Lord Runciman)

1993 Bail (Amendment) Act

1993 Criminal Justice Act repealed the unit fine

1994 Sexual Offences Act

1994 Criminal Justice and Public Order Act. Secure training order, revised bail law, right to silence redefined, new offences relating to collective trespass, raves and squatters; new offence of male rape and reduction in the age of homosexual consent to 18

1994 Police and Magistrates' Courts Act. New process of funding and monitoring police performance and changed the organisation and funding of magistrates' courts. Home Secretary was given the power to set the objectives for the Police Service which have to be included in the local policing plan

1995 Criminal Appeal Act established the Criminal Cases Review Commission to review and investigate possible miscarriages of justice in England, Wales and Northern Ireland. It became operational on 31 March 1997 and it took over the powers formerly exercised by the Home Secretary to refer a conviction or sentence on indictment to the Court of Appeal

1995 Learmont report on prison security

1996 Criminal Procedure and Investigations Act introduced new rules on the disclosure of evidence and the timing of the plea. Restored committal proceedings to replace the unimplemented transfer proceedings and introduced plea before venue

1997 Firearms (Amendment) Act outlawed ownership of handguns above .22 calibre

1997 Protection from Harassment Act

1997 Sex Offenders Act established the Sex Offender Register

1997 Crime (Sentences) Act introduced mandatory life sentence for adults convicted of a second serious offence such as rape or robbery with the use of a firearm, and minimum custodial sentences of seven years for those reconvicted of trafficking in Class A drugs

1997 White Paper, *No More Excuses,* proposed a range of proposals to improve the effectiveness of the youth court in preventing offending by children and young people. This became the principal aim of the youth justice system

1998 White Paper, *Modernising Justice*

1998 Consultation Paper, *Joining Forces to Protect the Public*

1998 Crime and Disorder Act introduced Drug Treatment and Testing Orders and the Sentencing Advisory Panel

1999 Access to Justice Act. Legal Service Commission established to oversee reformed legal aid scheme. Introduces Criminal Defence Service (CDS). The purpose of the Criminal Defence Service (CDS) is to secure the provision of advice, assistance and representation, according to the interests of justice, to people suspected of a criminal offence or facing criminal proceedings

1999 Criminal Cases Review (Insanity) Act

1999 Youth Justice and Criminal Evidence Act. Introduced a referral order for the youth court for young people convicted for the first time and its primary aim is to prevent reoffending. A youth offender panel will work with the young offender to establish a programme of behaviour for the young offender. Introduced reforms to the process of giving evidence to help young, disabled, vulnerable or intimidated witnesses give evidence in criminal proceedings such as use of screens, live link CCTV and the use of pre-recorded interviews; changes to the conduct of trials in rape cases

2000 *National Standards for the supervision of offenders in the community,* revised version came into force on 1 April 2000

2000 Criminal Justice and Court Services Act. Created the National Probation Service for England and Wales and the Children and Family Court Advisory and Support Service. Community orders were renamed: probation order became a community rehabilitation order. Extended the use of electronic monitoring and stricter enforcement. Measures to prevent unsuitable people from working with children. Sex offenders not to be eligible for the Home Detention Curfew scheme. Introduced new powers for the compulsory drug testing of offenders and alleged offenders at various points in their contact with the criminal justice system and allows a court considering the question of bail to take into account any drug misuse by the defendant

2000 Powers of Criminal Courts (Sentencing) Act. This was a consolidation Act that brought together all existing legislation on sentencing

2001 Sir Robin Auld's *Review of the Criminal Courts in England and Wales*. A comprehensive review of criminal procedure and the criminal courts

2001 Anti-terrorism, Crime and Security Act. In response to the 11 September terrorist attacks on New York and Washington DC. Introduced powers to cut off terrorist funds, allow government departments and agencies to collect and share information on terrorist activities, and provisions to improve the security of nuclear facilities that may be targeted by terrorists and enhanced police powers when detainees in police custody refuse to cooperate with the police as to their identity

2001 Criminal Justice and Police Act. Introduced on-the-spot penalties for disorderly behaviour and measures to prohibit the consumption of alcohol in designated public places

2001 Criminal Defence Service (Advice and Assistance) Act. Sets out the extent of the duty of the Criminal Defence Service to provide advice, assistance and representation

2001 International Criminal Court Act. The International Criminal Court (ICC) in The Hague, was established to try individuals for genocide, crimes against humanity and war crimes

2001 White Paper *Policing a New Century: A Blueprint for Reform*

2002 Police Reform Act. The Home Secretary will be required to produce an annual National Policing Plan. The Police Complaints Authority is replaced with a new body, the Independent Police Complaints Commission (IPCC)

2002 White Paper *Justice for All*

2002 Proceeds of Crime Act. Provides for powers to confiscate from convicted defendants the financial benefits criminals have made from their criminal activity. Confiscation orders are available following a conviction

2003 White paper *Respect and Responsibility – taking a stand against anti-social behaviour*

2003 Courts Act. Abolished Magistrates' Courts Committees (MCCs), and established courts boards. This Act abolishes commission areas and petty sessions areas and replaces them with local justice areas. It establishes a new HM Inspectorate of Court Administration

2003 Crime (International Cooperation) Act. Implements European Union police and judicial cooperation and provides for a database to store criminal information from all participating countries; cooperation to locate banking accounts and information relating to criminal investigations. Implements measures for combating terrorism. Implements the mutual recognition of driving disqualifications

2003 Anti-social Behaviour Act. It provides sanctions and powers for police, local authorities and housing associations to tackle anti-social behaviour in local communities and in social housing, including provisions aimed at dealing with noise nuisance. It provides a means for schools, local authorities and youth offending teams to work with the parents of children. Powers to tackle the problem of premises used for drug dealing; young people with air weapons, banning the possession of imitation guns and air guns in public; new powers of the police to impose conditions on public assemblies, deal with illegal raves and to deal with unauthorised encampments

2003 European Union (Accessions) Act. The Accession Treaty provides for the accession of 10 new states to join the existing 15 countries in the European Union on 1 May 2004

2003 Sexual Offences Act. Redefines main sexual offences

2003 Criminal Justice Act. The Act introduced a major reform of sentencing including many of the reforms proposed by the Auld and Halliday reports on court process and sentencing. It established the Sentencing Guidelines Council and introduced a generic community sentence and a new indeterminate public protection sentence. For the first time it set out the aims of sentencing in a statute. Changes are made to pre-trial and trial process and the law governing evidence and juries.

2004 Domestic Violence, Crime and Victims Act. This introduced a new offence of causing or allowing the death of a child or vulnerable adult (to deal in particular where one of two people must be responsible for a death, but it is uncertain which). It makes common assault an arrestable offence, and makes provisions for victims and witnesses of crime.

2005 Constitutional Reform Act. Establishes the Supreme Court of the UK to replace the judicial appeal role of the House of Lords

2005 Prevention of Terrorism Act. Introduces control orders putting constraints on suspected terrorists who are not in custody awaiting trial

2005 Mental Capacity Act. Clarifies the law with regard to persons who have a 'lack of capacity' to take responsibility for their own actions.

2005 Serious Organised Crime and Police Act. Established the Serious Organised Crime Agency. Provided methods of recovering the proceeds of crime and preventing money laundering

2006 Criminal Defence Service Act. Created the Criminal Defence Service (CDS)

2006 Police and Justice Act. This dealt with reforms to police authorities and set up a mechanism for establishing police reforms via the National Police Improvement Agency (NPIA); introduced a standard set of powers for PCSOs. Punitive conditions may now be attached to conditional cautions. A new definition of computer hacking was provided

2006 Identity Card Act. Provides for a National Identity Register and the powers to issue ID cards and sets out the role of the National Identity Scheme Commissioner

2006 Terrorism Act. This Act increased the period of pre-charge detention to allow the police to question terrorist suspects from 14 to 28 days.

2007 Offender Management Act. This allows the Government to subcontract probation services from the public, private or voluntary sector

2007 UK Borders Act. This allows for the automatic deportation of foreign criminals who have been sentenced in the UK to a period of 12 months in prison

2007 Mental Capacity Act. This amends the Mental Health Act 1983 which governs the compulsory treatment of people with a mental disorder, and the Mental Capacity Act 2005 (MCA), and defines the circumstances in which a person with a mental disorder can be compulsorily detained for treatment.

2007 Serious Crimes Act. This introduced the Serious Crime Prevention Orders for those aged over 18 after a convicted for a serious crime in order to protect the public, based on the same principle as an ASBO or a Sex Crime Prevention Order, i.e. it is a civil order but failure to comply carries a maximum sentence of five years' custody. The Asset Recovery Agency (ARA) is abolished and its work incorporated into the Serious Organised Crime Agency (SOCA)

2008 Criminal Evidence (Witness Anonymity) Act. This Act follows the House of Lords judgment in *R* v. *Davis* [2008] UKHL 36 of 18 June 2008. A decision which restricted the use of anonymous witnesses in trials under the common law. The new Act defines the statutory power for the courts to grant witness anonymity orders in criminal trials

2008 Criminal Justice and Immigration Act. Introduced a Youth Rehabilitation Order – a generic community sentence for children and young offenders and replaces all exiting community penalties available for younger offenders and a Youth Conditional Caution for 16 and 17 year old offenders. In both cases this brings the procedures in line with those applicable to adults. It set out the purposes of sentencing in the youth justice system. It created Violent Offender Orders. It created a presumption that trials in magistrates' courts will proceed if the defendant does not attend

2008 Counter-Terrorism Act. This Act gave authorities further powers to gather and share information to prevent terrorism; it created a requirement on the part of anyone convicted of a terrorist offence to regularly notify police of their whereabouts for a minimum period of ten years following release from prison. It enabled the police to take fingerprints and DNA samples from individuals subject to control orders as well as to register and monitor their movement. The Act amended the definition of terrorism by inserting a reference to a racial cause

2008 Children and Young Persons Act. Legislation to improve standards for children and young people in care and those leaving care, including new regulations for care agencies and powers for chief inspectors to fine failing agencies

2009 Policing and Crime Act. Places a duty on police authorities to seek out the public's views on policing in their area; amends police powers to deal with children drinking alcohol in public; introduces stricter provisions for people who sell alcohol to children; and provides for the mutual recognition of football banning orders between Scotland, Northern Ireland and England and Wales. The Act also introduces a specific injunction intended to reduce gang-related violence. It strengthens the arrangements for recovery of assets obtained through criminal means; there are new arrangements for judicial cooperation in relation to extradition. It made 'reduction of reoffending' a statutory responsibility of the crime and disorder reduction partnerships

2009 Coroners and Justice Act. It clarified the homicide laws with respect to diminished responsibility. It abolished the defence of provocation and replaced it with a new defence of 'loss of self-control'. It allows courts to grant anonymity to vulnerable or intimidated witnesses, and to those who assist certain gun and knife crime cases. It creates powers to seize profits made by criminals from publications about their crimes. The Act creates a National Coroner Service, led by a new Chief Coroner. The Act also amends sentencing laws and guidelines, by replacing the Sentencing Advisory Panel and the Sentencing Guidelines Council with a new Sentencing Council for England and Wales. The courts can give indeterminate sentences for certain terrorist offences in the name of public protection. It provides for live video links and screens around the witness box in order to help vulnerable and intimidated witnesses give evidence

2009 Borders, Citizenship and Immigration Act. It extended powers to take fingerprints from foreign criminals liable to automatic deportation

2010 Crime and Security Act. Provided new PACE rules by reducing the reporting requirements with regards to stop and search powers; provided additional powers to take fingerprints and DNA samples from those convicted of serious sexual and violent offences overseas; and rules for the destruction and use of DNA and fingerprints. Introduced a new power called a Domestic Violence Protection Notice (DPVN)

2010 Terrorist Asset-Freezing (Temporary Provisions) Act. This Act enables the Treasury to freeze assets belonging to anyone believed to be involved in terrorist activities

2010 Bribery Act. Created a new offence of failing to prevent acts of bribery. It is specific to commercial organisations and requires the organisations to take verifiable steps to prevent acts of bribery

2010 Identity Documents Act. Repealed the Identity Cards Act 2006

2010 Anti-Slavery Day Act. Introduced a national day (18 October) to raise awareness of the need to eradicate all forms of slavery, human trafficking and exploitation

2011 Police Reform and Social Responsibility Act. It transferred the accountability of police forces from police authorities to elected Police and Crime Commissioners (PCCs). The first elections of PCCs were held in November 2012. Elections will take place every four years

2011 Terrorism Prevention and Investigation Measures (TPIM) Act. Replacing control orders, the Act introduced Terrorism Prevention and Investigation Measures (TPIMs) with an aim to protect the public from individuals believed to have participated in terrorist activities but who cannot be brought before the court or deported. The notices are imposed by the Home Secretary, can last up to two years and include a number of restrictions

2011 Police (Detention and Bail) Act. This changed the sections in PACE 1984 which refer to the way police calculate the maximum permitted detention period without charge, so that if at the point of releasing a suspect without charge there is unexpired detention time remaining, the police may recall and detain the suspect for further questioning until the total period of detention has expired

2012 Domestic Violence, Crime and Victims (Amendment) Act. It introduced new provisions related to the protection of victims of crime, particularly domestic violence. It also amended provisions for trials without jury, introduced new regulations for trials regarding the death of a child or vulnerable adult and permitted bailiffs to use force when entering homes

2012 Legal Aid, Sentencing and Punishment of Offenders (LASPO) Act. Abolished the sentence of Imprisonment for Public Protection (IPP) and Extended Sentence for Public Protection (EPP). Introduced a new Extended Determinate Sentence (EDS) imposable on those which would have formerly received an IPP or EDP. It extends the period covered by a suspended sentence order up to two years rather than 12 months; it gives courts new powers to allow curfews to be imposed for more hours in the day (currently a maximum of 12) and for up to 12 months rather than the current six. It imposes a new test for bail and if there is 'no real prospect' of a custodial sentence, the offender should be granted bail. Revised Prison Rules allows for deductions from prisoners' pay, in order to finance victim reparations. It creates a new offence, and a mandatory minimum sentence, of threatening with an offensive weapon, with a minimum sentence of six months' imprisonment for persons over 18 found guilty

2012 Prisons (Interferences with Wireless Telegraphy) Act. The Act permits the blocking and capture of electronic communications data sent and received within prisons, young offenders' institutions and secure training centres located in England, Wales and Scotland

2012 The Protection of Freedoms Act. This Act brings in new laws regarding police retention of fingerprints and DNA data. It introduced a code of practice for surveillance camera systems (CCTV) and makes a new requirement to obtain judicial approval for certain surveillance activities by local authorities. It introduces revised rules to stop and search persons and vehicles reasonably suspected of being involved in terrorist activities as well as anyone within a specified area on terrorist alert. It reduces the maximum period of detention without charge for terrorist suspects from 28 to 14 days

2013 Prevention of Social Housing Fraud Act. It provided enhanced investigatory powers of local authorities and introduced new criminal penalties for sub-letting or parting with possession, without permission, of social housing

2013 Mental Health (Discrimination) Act. It amended the Juries Act 1974 by removing the ban on 'mentally disordered persons' undertaking jury service

2013 Justice and Security Act. Its provisions include an oversight of intelligence and security matters of the Security Service (MI5), the Secret Intelligence Service (MI6) and the Government Communications Headquarters (GCHQ). It made the Intelligence and Security Committee (ISC) a statutory Committee of Parliament providing it with greater powers and enhancing its remit. The Act established closed material procedures (CMP) in relation to certain civil proceedings

2013 Crime and Courts Act. The Act abolished the Serious Organised Crime Agency (SOCA), the National Policing Improvement Agency (NPIA), the Child Exploitation and Online Protection Centre (CEOP) and the National Cyber Crime Unit (NCCU) by incorporating and consolidating their operational activities into a new National Crime Agency (NCA)

2013 Victims 'Right to Review' (VRR) was introduced allowing a victim the right to appeal against a decision of the CPS not to prosecute a suspect

2014 Offender Rehabilitation Act amends the period after which a criminal conviction or caution becomes spent, and provides supervision in the community for those released after a short prison sentence. Before those sentenced to less than 12 months in prison did not receive supervision on release

2014 Anti-Social Behaviour, Crime and Policing Act introduced new community trigger and community remedy empowering victims and communities by giving them a greater say in how agencies respond to their complaints. The Act abolishes Anti-Social Behaviour Orders (ASBOs) and replaces them with Crime Prevention Injunctions (CPIs), that can be granted against a person aged ten or over when the court is satisfied on the balance of probabilities that the person has engaged or will engage in anti-social behaviour

Author's acknowledgement

As usual an author is helped by many people and the following are those that I would wish to express my gratitude and thanks for their contribution to the fifth edition:

Emma Grove and Milena Beata Wzietek for their assiduous efforts to update the data, undertake research and edit the drafts for the new edition;

The editorial team at Pearson, in particular the ever patient Cheryl Cheasley;

My colleagues and students at Ealing Law School and in particular Donley Jack, Phil Ells, Mohamed Ramjohn, Khalid Butt, Dr Philipp Elliot-Wright, and Mark Roycroft for his help with the chapter on policing, and of course Marlesha Robinson Brown who provided a continuous source of loyal support with calmness, charm and complete professionalism;

Judge Tan Ikram for his contribution to the chapter on youth justice;

Finally, I must acknowledge the vital part that Professor Hazel Croall and Jane Tyrer played in the project as co-authors on the first four editions of *Criminal Justice* and without whom there wouldn't have been a textbook.

Publisher's acknowledgement

We are grateful to the following for permission to reproduce copyright material:

Figures

Figure on page 59 from *Criminal Justice Statistics, Quarterly Update to March 2013 England and Wales Ministry of Justice. Statistics bulletin. Published 22 August 2013, Figure 7* Ministry of Justice (2013) p. 12, Minstry of Justice, Contains public sector information licensed under the Open Government Licence v1.0.; Figure on page 62 from *Crime in England and Wales, year ending September 2012. Statistical Bulletin.*, Office for National Statistics: London p. 3, © Crown copyright 2013, Source: Office for National Statistics licensed under the Open Government Licence v.2.0.; Figure on page 79 from Percentage of BCS respondents by area type who were victims of household crime in 2010/11, https://www.gov.uk/government/uploads/ . . . data/file/ . . . /hosb1011-tabs.xls, GOV.UK, Contains public sector information licensed under the Open Government Licence v3.0.; Figure on page 114 from The Conservative Party; Figure on page 217 from Earprint identification, *The Times*, 21/02/1998, Times Newspapers Ltd; Figure on page 244 from http://www.ons.gov.uk/ons/taxonomy/index.html?nscl=Crime+in+England+and+Wales, ONS, Source: Office for National Statistics licensed under the Open Government Licence v.2.0.; Figure on page 312 from Crown Prosecution Service Annual Report and Accounts 2011–12 (for the period April 2011–March 2012), https://www.cps.gov.uk/publications/docs/cps_annual_report_and_accounts_2012.pdf, © Crown copyright 2012, Contains public sector information licensed under the Open Government Licence (OGL) v2.0. http://www.nationalarchives.gov.uk/doc/open-government-licence.; Figure on page 313 from https://www.cps.gov.uk/publications/docs/cps_annual_report_and_accounts_2012.pdf, HMSO, Contains public sector information licensed under the Open Government Licence (OGL) v2.0. http://www.nationalarchives.gov.uk/doc/open-government-licence.; Figures on page 390, page 391 from https://www.gov.uk/government/publications/criminal-justice-statistics--2, GOV.UK, Contains public sector information licensed under the Open Government Licence (OGL) v2.0. http://www.nationalarchives.gov.uk/doc/open-government-licence/version/2/; Figure on page 413 from https://www.gov.uk/government/statistics/criminal-justice-statistics--2, GOV.UK, Contains public sector information licensed under the Open Government Licence (OGL) v2.0. http://www.nationalarchives.gov.uk/doc/open-government-licence/version/2/; Figure on page 432 from http://www.msgc.state.mn.us/guidelines/grids/grid_2008.pdf, Minnesota Sentencing Guidelines Commission; Figure on page 484 from *The Works of Jeremey Bentham, IV* (Bowering I. 1843) pp. 172–3, © The British Library Board (X9/4127).

Tables

Table on page 29 adapted from *The Framework of Criminal Justice*, London: Croom Helm (King, M. 1981) p. 13, Routledge; Table on page 60 from Proportion of incidents reported to the police, www.ons.gov.uk/ons/dcp171778_273169.pdf, ONS, Source: Office for National Statistics licensed under the Open Government Licence v.2.0.; Table on page 65 from Police recorded crime by type of crime, 2011/12, https://www.gov.uk/government/publications/police-recorded-crime-open-data-tables, GOV.UK, Contains public sector information licensed under the Open Government Licence v3.0.; Table on page 153 from *Crime Prevention and Community Safety: Politics, policies and practices*, Longman: London (Crawford, A. 1998) p. 19, Pearson Education; Table on page 245 from Criminal Justice Statistics Quarterly Update to September 2012p16 Tab Q1.5, https://www.gov.uk/government/uploads/system/uploads/attachment_data/file/220090/criminal-justice-stats-sept-2012.pdf, © Crown copyright, Contains public sector information licensed under the Open Government Licence v3.0.; Table on page 276 from Convictions in January 2007 National Summary, http://www.cps.gov.uk/publications/performance/case_outcomes/2007_01/index.html, © Crown copyright, Contains public sector information licensed under the Open Government Licence v3.0.; Table on page 279 from Persons aged 10–17 arrested for notifiable offences by offence group, 2010/11 in England and Wales Sheet AO8, https://www.gov.uk/government/uploads/system/uploads/attachment_data/file/186815/ppp-arrests-1112-tabs.xls, © Crown copyright, Contains public sector information licensed under the Open Government Licence v3.0.; Table on page 279 from Number and proportion of persons aged 18–20 arrested for notifiable offences by offence group, 2010/11 in England and Wales. Sheet A09, https://www.gov.uk/government/uploads/system/uploads/attachment_data/file/186815/ppp-arrests-1112-tabs.xls, © Crown copyright, Contains public sector information licensed under the Open Government Licence v3.0.; Table on page 328 from 2013 Judicial Diversity statistics – Gender, Ethnicity1, Profession and Age, http://www.judiciary.gov.uk/publications/diversity-statistics-and-general-overview-2013, © Copyright Judiciary 2014, Contains public sector information licensed under the Open Government Licence v3.0.; Table on page 404 from The rate of Victim Surcharge in 2014 for those aged over 18 years. http://sentencingcouncil.judiciary.gov.uk/sentencing/victim-surcharge.html, © Crown copyright, Contains public sector information licensed under the Open Government Licence v3.0.; Table on page 482 from *A Just Measure of Pain: The Penitentiary in the Industrial Revolution 1750–1850*, Macmillan, London (Ignatieff M. 1978) Palgrave Macmillan; Table on page 495 from : Ministry of Justice, Prison Population Figures, http://www.justice.gov.uk/statistics/prisons-and-probation/prison-population-figures, © Crown copyright, Contains public sector information licensed under the Open Government Licence v3.0.; Table on page 496 from International Centre for Prison Studies World Prison Brief website, http://www.prisonstudies.org/, ICPS; Table on page 539 from Proven Re-offending Statistics Quarterly Bulletin, October 2009 to September 2010, England and Wales, Ministry of Justice, 24 July 2012, https://www.gov.uk/government/uploads/system/uploads/attachment_data/file/225090/proven-reoffending-oct10-sep11.pdf, © Crown copyright, Contains public sector information licensed under the Open Government Licence v3.0.; Table on page 540 from Criminal Justice Statistics, Quarterly Update to March 2012, Ministry of Justice Statistics bulletin, September 2012, https://www.gov.uk/government/uploads/system/uploads/attachment_data/file/217641/criminal-justice-stats-march-2012.pdf, © Crown copyright,

Contains public sector information licensed under the Open Government Licence v3.0.

Text

Extract on page 18 from Guilt or innocence?, *The Times*, 12/08/1994 (Zander, M.), Times Newspapers Ltd., © Zander M., News Syndication 12/08/1994; Quote on page 124 adapted from Tony Blair at Labour Party conference, Blackpool, October 2002 Tony Blair; Extract on pages 178–9 from Broken Windows: The police and neighborhood safety *The Atlantic Monthly*, pp. 29–37 (Wilson J.Q. and Kelling G.L. 1982), The Atlantic Monthly Group; Newspaper Headline on page 224 from 'The Law that lets off a self-confessed killer'. *The Sunday Times*, 28/10/2012, p. 6 (Brennan Z.), Sunday Times, © Brennan Z., News Syndication 28/10/2012; Extract on page 355 from Is the cab-rank rule worth saving?, *The Times*, 01/05/2008 (Gibb, F.), The Times, © Gibb F., News Syndication 01/05/2008; Extract on page 377 from Jury changed verdict after hearing antecedents Regina v Bills, *The Times* 01/03/1995, The Times, © News Syndication 01/03/1995; Extract on pages 382–3 from *Wigs and Wherefores: A biography of Michael Sherrard.* Wildy, Simmonds & Hill Publishing (2008) pp. 103–4, Wildy & Sons Ltd; Extract on page 438 from Kiosk theft justifies jail Regina v Decino *The Times*, 10/05/1993, The Times, © News Syndication 10/05/1993; Extract on page 439 from Sentencing in cases of incest, *The Times*, 22/02/1989, The Times, © News Syndication 22/02/1989; Extract on page 440 from Punishment for perjury, *The Times*, 04/02/1984, The Times, © News Syndication 04/02/1984.

In some instances we have been unable to trace the owners of copyright material, and we would appreciate any information that would enable us to do so.

Table of cases

INTRODUCTION TO CRIMINAL JUSTICE

Chapter 1

What is criminal justice?

Learning objectives

After reading the chapter you should be able to:

1. Describe the agencies and processes of the criminal justice system in England and Wales
2. Define the purpose of the criminal justice system
3. Explain the principles of criminal justice
4. Understand the system of criminal justice and its key sub-systems
5. Explain the **paradigms** and models of criminal justice
6. Outline recent legislation and current policy developments

Key statistics

- The number of police officers fell from 141,925 in 2007 to 128,351 in 2014
- Between 11.9.2001 (New York City bombing of the Twin Towers) and 30.6.2013, 332 individuals were convicted in England and Wales for terrorism offences, including murder, illegal possession of firearms and explosives offences. 2,465 people have been arrested under the Terrorism Act during this period
- In 2014, there were 240 magistrates' courts and 76 Crown Court Centres in England and Wales. The number of lay magistrates declined from 28,300 in 2007 to 23,401 in 2014
- Total number of Security Industry Association (SIA) licensed qualifications held by individuals in January 2014 was 339,940
- On 31 march 2014 there were 10,749 prisoners aged over 50 (12%) of the prison population
- 16% of all prisoners in 2014 were held in private prisons
- The number of Victim Support volunteers rose from 1,700 in 2007 to 5,600 in 2014

Introduction

Criminal justice systems change over time. New agencies appear and some disappear. New crimes appear and some older ones disappear such as blasphemy (decriminalised in 2008 in the UK); many crimes continue as new versions of the old sins of greed, intimidation, violence and theft. The criminal justice system (CJS) in the twenty-first century has had to adapt to crimes, both ancient and modern, from both domestic and global sources.

The CJS has many parts – as with the blindfolded men who were asked to describe an animal by touch, perspectives vary and depend on whether one starts at the front or back end of the animal, which in this case was an elephant.

Criminal justice, like the elephant, has many parts. There are numerous agencies, procedures and personnel, and in recent years in England and Wales – under the 'New Labour' Government from 1999 to 2010, and the Coalition Government since 2010 – we have seen new agencies and players emerge; these have included the elected justice commissioners, a National Crime Agency, Resettlement Prisons, Community Rehabilitation Companies, the UK Supreme Court and a Sentencing Council.

Is the elephant getting smaller? During the Coalition Government era of 2010 to 2015, the actions of government was dominated by the worldwide recession and an economic climate of austerity and financial stringency. Cutting the cost of the system was paramount as demonstrated by cuts to budgets and a decline in court, police, probation and prison staff numbers. Over the period from 2009 to 2013 the average cost of imprisonment per inmate fell from £45,000 to £36,808.

However, unlike the elephant, with a criminal justice system there is regular debate as to how it can be made to work more effectively. Reducing costs and increasing efficiency have become a major theme of policy discourse in criminal justice along with the policy debates on 'what is it for?'

The policy reform agenda pursued under the Coalition Government included issues of accountability, as illustrated by the new Parliamentary Intelligence and Security Committee, that was established to oversee the security services; and a civil liberties agenda with ID cards being abolished before they were introduced, less restriction on terrorist suspects with the abolition of control orders, and a limit on **CCTV** usage. The advance of the commercial sector continued as evidenced by the privatisation of probation and prison services, such that 16% of the prison population was held in private prisons in 2014.

A criminal justice system should be more than the sum of its parts, but only if it is coordinated to achieve commonly agreed goals. The question, 'does it work?' depends on what you want it to do. Hence the policy debates as to the aims of the system and answers to the question of 'what is it for?' Without understanding its purposes it is difficult to make a reasoned response to the question as to whether it is effective or not. Thus, the absence of a comprehensive overview of the logic and purpose of the criminal justice system allows the self-interested, the single-issue pressure groups, the mischievous, the misguided and the malevolent to misrepresent it.

So what is the CJS for? To answer this we should learn the lessons of history that includes recent events such as the urban riots of August 2011 that started in Tottenham, North London and spread across a number of English cities over the subsequent week. The riots, although untypical, brought fear and anxiety to everyday life as shops and workplaces were burnt and looted, people attacked and robbed, and four people were known to have been killed by rioters.

Not everyone is aware of the second sea adventure of Robinson Crusoe who had the misfortune to be shipwrecked for the second time in his life on what looked like another desert island. Crusoe could not believe his bad luck and he became very depressed thinking of the forthcoming isolation and fear of the unknown. Having decided to explore the island he climbed a hill and to his great relief he declared, 'Thank god. Civilisation', as there on the crest of the hill was a scaffold.

This symbol of punishment, considered barbaric to some, meant there were people, authority and laws: necessary conditions of a stable and ordered society. This was the lesson that Thomas Hobbes wrote about in *Leviathan* during the English civil war in seventeenth century England. Law with order requires individuals to accept some loss of liberty in order to achieve public protection from government. Without that protection, the potential for a state of anarchy increases and in Hobbes's words, 'the life of man becomes nasty, brutish and short'.

The riots of 2011 reminded people of a fundamental reality that had been taken for granted in the human rights era of the late twentieth century, when discussions turned to voting rights for prisoners – without law and order, the right to vote and the chance of being a prisoner would be greatly diminished if frightened people turned to self-protection and vigilante-style responses to perceived threats from criminals to themselves, their businesses and their homes. The absence of the police on the streets during the riots of 2011 reminded those caught up in them, including the most 'stout hearted of citizens' (a phrase used in the *Blackshaw* Court of Appeal sentencing guideline case on the riots) that the fundamental human right to life and liberty requires an effective criminal justice system.

Not all crimes are as dramatic as rioting. In fact, routine crimes continued, but there were fewer of them. The results of the Crime Survey for England and Wales and the police crime statistics showed steady reductions in the number of high-frequency crimes committed, such as burglary and theft. The number of overall crimes recorded by the police have been dropping each year since 2002/3.

Other crimes that have dominated the headlines since 2010, included phone tapping and illegal electronic snooping in the newspaper industry leading to the closure of the *News of the World* and imprisonment of its editor.

The **Metropolitan Police**'s investigation in 2014, called 'Operation Yewtree', examined historic allegations of sexual crimes going back to the 1960s made against high-profile TV, media and radio celebrities that included Max Clifford, Rolf Harris and Freddie Starr. The allegations started when complaints were made against Jimmy Savile who died in 2011. An investigation was set up to look into 11 allegations of sexual abuse by Savile at the high-security psychiatric hospital at Broadmoor between 1968 and 2004.

Meanwhile, crime threats from abroad continued; most notably from terrorist activities linked with global conflicts in Islamic counties such as Syria and Iraq.

Electronic innovation provided new means to commit newly named crimes such as cyber-fraud and cyber-stalking. Globalisation of criminal opportunities is also apparent with organised criminal groups operating across Europe and engaged in activities such as smuggling people, drugs and weapons. The emergence of human trafficking in recent decades has led the UK to pass the Anti Slavery Day Act in 2010 to highlight the existence of modern styles of slavery. The UK Parliament passed the Abolition of Slavery Act in 1807. Then and now the global nature of crime is apparent and the need to deal with British citizens convicted of crimes abroad and foreign nationals convicted of crimes in the UK has meant that special arrangements have been set up for detaining and deporting foreign national offenders.

In 2014, foreign nationals in prison in England and Wales accounted for 12% of the total prison population in England and Wales. Originating from 159 countries, over half were from the following ten countries: Albania, India, Ireland, Jamaica, Lithuania, Nigeria, Pakistan, Poland, Romania and Somalia (**Ministry of Justice quarterly bulletin October to December 2014**). In 2012, 4,765 foreign national offenders were deported or removed (**Hansard, HC, 25 November 2013**).

Global television and radio meant that crimes and criminal trials could now be instantaneously seen around the world and provide a source of documentary cum news cum entertainment as with the coverage of the trial of Oscar Pistorius on a charge of murder in South Africa in 2014. The media and global circus surrounding this trial was reminiscent of the trial in 1995 of another celebrity sportsman O J Simpson in California, for the murder of his wife and her friend. Yet another sportsman celebrity seized the world's media attention in 2014 during the football World Cup in Brazil when the Uruguayan player Luis Suarez bit an Italian player on the shoulder, a type of assault that he had committed at least twice before on other players during his footballing career.

'Footballer bites opponent' could have remained the headline were it not for the pronouncements of Oscar Tabarez, the Uruguayan football coach at a press conference, angry at the four-month footballing ban on Luis Suarez. He said:

> 'I have been a teacher in my life and I present the theory of the scapegoat: you know about the psychology of it all. When giving a punishment to someone who commits a transgression – not a crime – so that the whole group will know what is good, what is bad, what is wrong, what is correct, what ought to be done, and what shouldn't.'
>
> (*The Independent*, 27 June 2014)

This brings an important insight into the nature of punishment in a criminal justice system. Even if the term of scapegoat is wrongly used by the coach in this example, he was right to point out that high-profile, anti-social and deviant acts stimulate discussion in the wider community that help to clarify behaviour that is right from that which is wrong.

Hence, a final lesson for those studying criminal justice is the realisation that crime affects everyday life in many ways: this includes the responses that in a practical way help to reduce crime opportunities and protect citizens against crime, as well as responses that come to shape the moral discourse and prompt demands for 'new laws' or 'tougher penalties' that are stimulated in the community by the well-publicised transgressions of Pistorius, Simpson and Suarez, *et al*.

Crime is a feature of all societies and criminal justice is the response to it. The response to crime will include practical and instrumental aspects of protecting the citizens from everyday threats to their safety, such as by ensuring dangerous and persistent offenders are monitored effectively when in the community and imprisoned when necessary. It also generates moral debate about defining expectations as to types of behaviour that is unacceptable. In response to concrete acts of unacceptable behaviour the criminal justice system plays its part in the moral drama of society. By censuring breaches of the law, and the consequent confirmation or re-examination of moral boundaries, we come to define and shape civic expectations; hence, our response to crime comes to define what type of society we want to live in.

1.1 Criminal justice in England and Wales

Objective 1

Describe the agencies and processes of the criminal justice system in England and Wales

There are three distinctive criminal justice systems with separate procedures and agencies in the UK: England and Wales, Scotland, and Northern Ireland. The organisation and jurisdictional limits of criminal justice in England and Wales are determined by constitutional distinctions within the UK and increasingly by the need to respond to issues of crime in the outside world, especially in light of the acts of terrorism in New York City and Washington DC on 11 September 2001 and in London in July 2005. Membership of the European Union has also meant that on some constitutional, policy and everyday regulations we are no longer an isolated island in the sea of criminal justice. To varying extents the agencies of criminal justice in the UK have had to comply with aspects of harmonisation, integration and greater cooperation with our European partners (28 member countries since 2013).

Within the UK, different government departments are responsible for criminal justice in the three jurisdictions – the Home Office and the Ministry of Justice for England and Wales, the Justice Department in Scotland, and the Northern Ireland Office. Other government departments such as the Attorney General's Office are involved in the administration of criminal justice. Local councils have a statutory duty to establish a Social Services Department employing qualified social workers to deal with children in trouble with the criminal law. Criminal investigations are not made exclusively by the police but also by many other agencies such as investigators for HM Customs and Revenue and various local government bodies such as the Environmental Health and Trading Standards departments.

▶ Agencies

In England and Wales, criminal justice agencies such as the police, prisons and probation are funded primarily by central government. Policy is established in part by civil servants who advise ministers and by legislation enacted by Parliament. For administrative purposes agencies are divided into regional areas. The main agencies are briefly described below.

- *Police.* There are 43 regional police forces, each under the direction of a chief constable and, except for the Metropolitan Police and the City of London police, local police authorities. Forces vary in size – the biggest being the Metropolitan Police with 30,417 uniformed officers available for duty, and one of the smaller is Warwickshire with 979. Across England and Wales in 2013 there were 128,351 police supplemented by 18,351 Specials, 13,552 Police Community Support Officers and civilian employees. The **Home Office** is the government department responsible for the police and counter-terrorism services.

- *Prosecutors*. The **Crown Prosecution Service** was established in 1985 and is divided into 42 areas which in 2007 were formed into 14 regional groups outside London. The **Attorney General** is answerable in Parliament for the Crown Prosecution Service, which is headed by the **Director of Public Prosecutions**. In 2013/14 the CPS employed 6,163 people and dealt with 640,657 prosecutions in the magistrates' courts and 94,617 in the Crown Courts, plus it dealt with 304,982 pre-charge review decisions and 10,358 appeals from the Crown Court.

- *Criminal Defence Service*. Oversees the system of legal support for those accused of a crime by advice, assistance and representation in court through a combination of full-time public defenders and contracted private sector lawyers.

- *Courts*. Of the total of criminal cases, 97 per cent begin and end in the magistrates' courts although more serious cases are ultimately dealt with in the Crown Courts. Officials in these courts include judges, **recorders, magistrates**. The criminal courts come under the authority of the Ministry of Justice.

- *Ministry of Justice*. Came into being in 2007 with the merger of the **Department for Constitutional Affairs** and part of the Home Office and is responsible for: Her Majesty's Courts Service; National Offender Management Service; Her Majesty's Prison Service; Probation Service; **Parole Board; Youth Justice Board; Criminal Injuries Compensation Authority**; the **Sentencing Guidelines Council**; Legal Services Board; and the **Law Commission**.

- *Probation*. The Probation Service is responsible for preparing pre-sentence reports for courts, supervising community orders and helping prisoners adapt to community life following release. Legislation in 2000 established the National Probation Service.

- *Prisons*. The Prison Service is an executive agency, with policy direction from the Ministry of Justice. With probation they constitute the **Correctional Services** and are also part of the National Offender Management Service (NOMS) with the responsibility of managing offenders from sentence to resettlement in the community.

- *Youth Justice*. The Youth Justice Board is a central board that monitors the work of the youth justice system and the work of the **Youth Offending Teams** (YOTs). Established across England and Wales in 2000, YOTs are local authority multi-agency teams that coordinate the effort of the agencies and volunteers working with young offenders.

Smaller agencies and bodies

- *Coroners*. Officials who investigate suspicious or unusual deaths.
- *Criminal Injuries Compensation Authority*. Compensates the victims of some forms of crime. The scheme, initially introduced in 1965, is now governed by the Criminal Injuries Compensation Act 1995.
- **Forensic Science Service**. A scientific support service for the investigation of crime and the evaluation of evidence. In 2008 it had a database of 4.5 million DNA samples.

- *HM Inspectorate.* There are different inspectors who are semi-autonomous of government who inspect and report on the work of the police, courts, probation, prison and the CPS. They report to the government and Parliament on the efficiency and effectiveness of the specific service for which they have responsibility.
- *Parole Board.* This decides on the release and recall of prisoners where the sentence has an indeterminate aspect.
- **Victim Support.** An independent agency that organises 5,600 volunteers in 2014 to provide support for victims of crime and also runs the Court Witness Service.

▶ Civil society and the private sector

As well as the professions and officials in these agencies, many private citizens are involved in criminal justice on a voluntary basis. These include lay visitors to police stations, neighbourhood watch groups, victim support volunteers, members of juries, Independent Monitoring Boards in prisons, and over 23,401 lay magistrates in 2014.

There is also a growing army of employees in private security firms, of which G4S (Group 4 originally), Pinkerton's, Securicor and Wells Fargo are the best known. There are also many smaller businesses, such as private detectives, locksmiths, bailiffs and credit investigation and information services. Although it is extremely difficult to estimate the total number of employees in this sector, some have estimated the number to be as high as 400,000. The total number of private security guards outnumbers the police. The private sector plays a major and growing role in crime prevention. It is also becoming increasingly involved in other sectors of the system. In November 1991, Group 4 signed a contract to run the first private prison, the Wolds Remand Prison in Humberside; others include Blakenhurst, a local prison, Doncaster which opened in 1994, Altcourse, a category A local prison, Parc, a local male prison, Lowdham Grange, a category B prison, and Buckley Hall for category C prisoners.

Finally, the legal professions are a vital part of criminal justice. **Barristers** and **solicitors** are the two branches of this powerful professional group that is independent of government. Barristers are primarily court advocates, whereas solicitors advise clients on a variety of matters and deal with clients prior to **trial**. The majority of advocacy in the Crown Court is done by barristers, and the higher courts have only recently been open to solicitors as advocates. Both solicitors and barristers have the right to appear and represent clients, i.e. they have **rights of audience**, in the magistrates' court, where much of the work is undertaken by solicitors. A member of the public cannot directly seek advice from a barrister without first instructing a solicitor. In 2009 there were 12,000 practising barristers based in 350 chambers (most are in London), most of whom will have represented criminal clients in their career, and 2,800 members of the Criminal Bar Association who specialise in criminal cases.

▶ Expansion of the criminal justice system personnel

Whether we assess growth by expenditure, output or number of employees, the agencies making up the criminal justice system in England and Wales have

Table 1.1 Employees and volunteers in the criminal justice system 2007 and 2013

	2007	2013
Police		
Police officers	141,925	128,351
Special constables	14,547	18,068
Civilian employees of the Police Service	80,209	64,961
PCSOs	15,557	13,552
Numbers working in the private sector who are licensed by the SIA		
Vehicle immobilisers with licences	1,934	94
Security guards with licences	127,598	93,664
CCTV operators with licences	20,475	43,149
Door supervisors with valid licences	139,172	221,926
Close protection bodyguards with licences	5,175	13,412
Cash transit guards with licences	10,862	9,873
	Total 305,216	Total 382,377
Forensic Science Industry	2,400 (FSS)	8,947
Crown Prosecution Service	8,351	6,163
Victim Support volunteers	1,700	5,600
Judiciary		
Lay magistrates	28,300	23,401
District Judges	171	142
Circuit Judges and Recorders	1,771	1,850
Her Majesty's Courts Service	21,000	18,269
Corrections		
Prison Service staff	49,571	39,510
Probation Service	21,000	16,297
Independent Monitoring Boards	1,762	1,850

undergone change and general expansion over the last 50 years. Numbers involved in 2007 and 2013 are set out in Table 1.1.

In addition to the quantitative growth of this occupational sector, a qualitative change is also occurring as pressure mounts for greater professionalisation through degree level entry and an increasing emphasis on training. This is most evident in the police, prison and court services. This demand for greater professionalism reflects the greater complexity of the work of criminal justice employees in the twenty-first century. It is recognised, for example, that officials need to be responsive to the changing demands of society and the increasing complexities of the system. Social change and community demands have resulted in continual reviews and a re-examination of the function and practice of many agencies and professions. The implications of greater European and international cooperation lead to both procedural and substantive changes. The introduction of new technology has increased demands for a more highly trained and flexible workforce.

The volume of recent legislation, government reports and commissions on aspects of criminal justice, which will be referred to throughout this book, reflects this state of change. Throughout the 1990s and into the twenty-first century we have seen a steady flow of legislation on matters to do with criminal justice (**see the chronology section**). Virtually every aspect of the system has recently undergone, or is currently undergoing, change – partly as a result of new problems such as terrorism and the expansion of 'electronic crime', partly because of the consequences of EU harmonisation and partly because of the steady rate of reform introduced by governments since the 1990s.

The criminal justice system in England and Wales is extensive and widespread, but what is it for? To answer these questions the subsequent sections of this chapter will examine the definitions of criminal justice, its principles and models. It will explain, by reference to flow charts, the processes and throughputs of the system of justice and finally look at some of the key policy directions as illustrated by legislative changes since 1990.

1.2 Criminal justice defined: functions and form

Objective 2

Define the purpose of the criminal justice system

How can a criminal justice system be defined and described? Criminal justice is about society's formal response to crime and is defined more specifically in terms of a series of decisions and actions taken by a number of agencies in response to a specific crime or criminal, or crime in general. Following the recognition of a crime-like incident, or in seeking to prevent lawless behaviour, criminal justice agencies become involved. There are four key sub-systems of criminal justice:

- Law enforcement: involving the police and prosecuting agencies.
- Courts: making decisions about pre-trial detention, **adjudication** on the guilt of the **defendant**, deciding on the sentence for those convicted and ensuring that the rights of the defendant are respected.
- Penal system: involves probation, prisons and other agencies that punish and incarcerate and/or seek to monitor, control and reduce offending behaviour.
- Crime prevention: involves the above agencies who deal with individual offenders along with a wider group of agencies, some private, others governmental, who plan crime-free environments or seek to change the conditions that lead to criminal behaviour.

People are exposed in everyday life to images and realities of crime and criminal justice as victims, witnesses, professionals, offenders and as onlookers. We develop ideas about and images of the way the different agencies, such as the police, prosecutors, courts, prisons, probation, local authorities and private security agencies respond to crime or its perceived threats. We are made aware through the media, official statements and political debates about the issues of crime and justice. In an effort to become more analytical in our approach to these issues, ideas and images, it is possible to conceptualise the criminal justice system in the following terms:

- Substantive law: The content of the criminal law provides the starting point of the criminal justice system by defining behaviour that is to be regulated through the use of the criminal law.

- Form and process: Who is given the task of responding to crime and what procedures must they follow?
- Functions: What are the intended consequences and aims of the system?
- Modes of punishment: What sentences are available to the courts?
- Criminal justice paradigms: What are the dominant ways of thinking about issues of crime, criminals and justice?

When we look at other countries we can see differences in the definitions of criminality in the criminal law, the procedures in the courts, the types of sentences, and the ways of thinking about crime and punishment (penal paradigms). The purpose of the criminal justice system will be very different when a secular society is contrasted with a religious one. It becomes apparent that cultural factors are a major influence on the operation of a criminal justice system.

The O J Simpson trial in the United States and the investigation into the disappearance of Madeleine McCann in Portugal generated immense interest about differing systems of criminal investigation and prosecution, and led to discussion as to how such cases would be dealt with in this country. A trip around the world would show that many aspects of law, procedure and punishment vary considerably. In Scotland the age of criminal responsibility starts at 9 while in Finland it is 15. In France the law demands that a bystander must intervene to help a person being attacked. The legal system in California found O J Simpson responsible for killing his wife in the civil court while the criminal court found him not guilty. Barbados, Jamaica and Trinidad & Tobago have threatened to leave the Commonwealth because the Privy Council in London reprieved all death penalty cases. Nearly all the former colonies of the Caribbean retained the Privy Council as the final Court of Appeal. South Africa abolished the death penalty in 1995 at a time when many US states were about to implement it. In Saudi Arabia beheading is regarded as an appropriate mode of punishment, and two nurses found guilty of the murder of an Australian colleague were subject to bartering for their lives. People living in different jurisdictions are subject to different sets of laws. In Saudi Arabia there is no concept of rape within a marriage and alcohol is prohibited by law.

We use these illustrations from around the globe, firstly, to demonstrate the many variations in the way issues of crime, guilt and punishment are approached in different jurisdictions; secondly, so that students of criminal justice should be conscious of this diversity of approach. It follows that an awareness of different legal systems is required for those who wish to understand the complexities of other jurisdictions and the differences in the definitions of crimes and criminal procedures. Thirdly, we use these illustrations to show that beyond the legal details are issues of morality, politics and ethics that might require a strong stomach and a willingness to understand that issues of criminal justice raise many fundamental questions about the nature of humanity and society.

❯ Content of the criminal law: what is penalised?

In most countries, particular kinds of behaviour are criminalised through the criminal law, formulated in some countries by a penal code. As we will see in **Chapter 2**, there is no simple way of defining what behaviour is criminal, and this may vary between different countries and over time. Nonetheless, in most Western societies similar kinds of behaviour are considered to be criminal including **homicide, rape,** arson, kidnapping, **robbery, burglary, assault, theft,** fraud and motoring offences. Thus, according to Knut Sveri, 'if a person does something which is considered to be a crime in Sweden, it will practically always be considered to be a crime in New York' (**Sveri 1990**).

▶ Form and process: criminal procedure and criminal justice agencies

Different countries have very different ways of investigating and prosecuting criminal cases, based on different principles and rules. Varying procedures and regulations govern such matters as the investigation of crime, the arrest and interrogation of suspects, prosecution decisions, bail procedure, trial procedures, rules of evidence and the role of the jury, if there is one. There are also differences in how courts decide on the guilt or otherwise of defendants.

This is in part because other countries have different agencies dealing with these matters. In France an investigating magistrate, the *juge d'instruction*, conducts investigations into serious crime and embraces a policing, prosecutorial and judicial role, in contrast to the UK where the police, prosecutors and judiciary have distinct responsibilities. In Germany the public prosecutor, the *staatsanwalt*, has overall responsibility for pre-trial proceedings and advises the examining judge on bail and remand decisions. There is no equivalent in England and Wales to the Scottish **Procurator Fiscal** who also has an investigating and prosecuting role, and can issue a Fiscal fine. Across the USA, each of the 50 states has its own penal code and each county within a state has its own criminal justice agencies such as district attorneys and sheriffs, in addition to the state and federal agencies.

It is important to appreciate how criminal justice agencies define and interpret their role and legal responsibilities. *The criminal law does not enforce itself.* To understand a system we need to consider how law enforcers, prosecutors, lawyers, magistrates, judges, probation officers and prison officers perceive their job and their function within the system. How they work will not only be affected by their official role but by political, financial, organisational and cultural influences. While Parliament and judges may create and interpret the criminal law, they do not implement it on a day-to-day basis. An appreciation of the everyday world of those who translate the law as described in books into the law in action is therefore essential to an understanding of how criminal justice agencies operate.

▶ Functions and aims of the criminal justice system

In exploring what a criminal justice system aims to do, we need to distinguish between the goals of the system as a whole, and the functions of the different agencies who make up the system. Agency-specific functions are shown below. Cross-system goals include:

- Public protection: by preventing and deterring crime and terrorism, by rehabilitating offenders and incapacitating others who constitute a persistent threat to the community.

- Justice and the rule of law: upholding and promoting the rule of law and respect for the law, by ensuring due process and proper treatment of suspects, arrestees, defendants and those held in custody, successfully prosecuting criminals and acquitting innocent people accused of a crime.
- Public order: maintaining law and order.
- Punishment: sentencing criminals with regard to the principles of just deserts.
- Denunciation: registering social disapproval of censured behaviour of criminal acts.
- Victim services: aiding and advising the victims of crime.
- Public confidence: maintaining public confidence so that the public system of criminal justice is perceived as dealing effectively and fairly with the threats to the public from criminals such that citizens do not feel the need to engage in private acts of vengeance and vigilantism.

◗ Mode and distribution of punishment

Finally, variations between systems include differences in the modes and distribution of punishment, recognising that societies punish offenders in diverse ways. If one point of distinction in defining a criminal justice system is to establish what is punished, another is to describe the types or mode of punishment used.

The main penal sanctions or court sentencing options are imprisonment, fines, probation, community penalties, discharges, admonitions and cautions. The death penalty for murder was abolished in this country in 1965, and has also been abolished in most European countries, although it is still in use in some US states and in most African and Asian countries.

The most noticeable difference between countries, however, is not merely in the mode of punishment but in the distribution of punishment, that is the range of sentences routinely given for particular offences. What is acceptable to a Swedish, British or American court in terms of typical sentencing practice varies greatly.

Agency-specific functions

Police

- Investigating crime
- Preventing crime
- Arresting and detaining suspects
- Maintaining public order
- Protecting the public from terrorist threats
- Traffic control
- Responding to criminal and non-criminal emergencies

Some of these tasks are also carried out by private and other public law enforcement agencies such as HMRC and environmental health and trading standards departments of local authorities.

Prosecution

- Filtering out weak cases
- Deciding on charges and preparing cases for prosecution
- Prosecuting cases in the magistrates' courts
- Preparing cases for trial in the Crown Court by liaising with barristers for the prosecution before and throughout a trial

Criminal Defence Service

- Advising and defending those charged with criminal offences

Courts

- Handling and processing cases efficiently
- Deciding on **bail, remands**, and **mode of trial**
- Protecting the rights of the defendant
- Deciding on guilt
- Passing sentence
- Hearing **appeals** against conviction and sentence
- Providing a public arena so that justice can be seen to be done

Prisons

- Holding persons **remanded in custody** by the courts
- Holding sentenced offenders
- Maintaining proper conditions for those held in custody
- Preparing inmates for release
- Attempting to **rehabilitate** offenders

Probation

- Preparing pre-sentence reports
- Providing bail facilities for and information to the courts on offenders' appropriateness for bail
- Working with offenders given a probation, community service, or combination order
- Running probation centres
- Supervising released prisoners and pre-release work with inmates in custody

In different cultures, ideas as to what constitutes an appropriate punishment will differ. A good illustration of this is provided in the following extract from the *Daily Telegraph*, which looks at differences within Australia between the European and Aboriginal attitude towards punishment and distinctive examples of the criminal justice paradigm.

Tribal elders punish Aborigine car thieves

Six Aborigines have been beaten for stealing cars after Northern Territory police let their elders handle the matter in a traditional way.

The six, aged 15–25, were beaten with rubber hoses in front of the local council chambers in an Aboriginal community near Darwin.

Since the incident three months ago, only one minor offence of theft has been committed in the town.

It was not the first time Aborigines in the Territory have been handed over to elders by the Australian justice system for tribal punishment.

Earlier this year, Mr Brian Martin, the Chief Justice of the Territory, asked the Department of Correctional Services to monitor the tribal 'payback' spearing through both thighs of Wilson Jagamara Walker, an Aboriginal convicted of manslaughter. Mr Martin's decision was influenced by petitions from the man's tribal council and a group of senior women at Yuendumu, 150 miles southwest of Alice Springs, who warned him that innocent members of the man's family would be speared instead of him if he was jailed.

Taking this into account, the judge released Walker on a bond and asked that correctional services report on whether the spearing took place.

However, the judicial outcome remained unclear after officials said that the victim's family had decided not to proceed with the spearing even though Walker was prepared to submit to the punishment.

Mr Martin gave Walker a three-year suspended jail term and allowed six months, which expires in August, for the payback to occur. In the ritual, the convicted man will be speared through the thighs in front of the tribe by the younger brother of a man he stabbed to death in Alice Springs in a family feud last year.

Walker, who has accepted the tribal law and is said to be happy with the judge's decision, is now being cared for by relatives at an isolated settlement. He is said to be ready to return to Yuendumu for the spearing when preliminary tribal ceremonies have been completed.

My Kevin Kitchener, a barrister with the North Australian Aboriginal Legal Aid Service, said: 'Maybe we should go back to the old traditional ways. They seem to work.' Mr Kitchener, who related the beating incident to a conference on Aboriginal justice issues in Townsville, Queensland, said the youths had been surrounded in the street by Aboriginal male adults. They had not been seriously hurt because the adults knew how to beat them without causing permanent injuries.

'It sounds barbaric', he said, 'but the instant justice had an important further deterrent effect. They know that if they get into trouble again the same thing will happen. But next time women will be wielding the rubber hoses, which will give them an even greater sense of shame.'

Mr Kitchener said the day before the public beating another group of Aboriginal youths had been arrested in Darwin for similar offences.

They told friends they were very glad to be facing white man's justice – not one of them wanted to face Aboriginal punishment,' he said.

(by Geoffrey Lee Martin in Sydney)

Source: 'Tribal elders punish Aborigine car thieves',
Daily Telegraph, 18 June 1994, (Martin, G.),
Telegraph Group Limited, © Telegraph Media Group Limited 1994

1.3 Principles of criminal justice

Objective 3

Explain the principles of criminal justice

Unlike many other countries, England and Wales have no written penal code or definitive statement of the principles of criminal justice. Nonetheless some important principles guide criminal justice procedure. A crucial feature of criminal justice in England and Wales is the adversarial principle, which determines how guilt should be established. A central aspect of this is that the individual has rights; whether as a suspect, defendant or convicted person.

▶ Adversarial justice

The main principle that underpins the system of criminal justice in England and Wales is **adversarial justice**. Vital are the ideas of the burden of proof and the standard of proof. The burden of proof requires the police to identify a suspect from the evidence available and, if there is sufficient evidence against him or her, to prosecute that person and establish his or her guilt. An adversarial system does not seek to establish what happened or the truth about an incident, that is sometimes left to inquiries; the adversarial system requires the police and prosecutor to identify a person, called a suspect. The logic of adversarial justice, however, requires that the police and the prosecutors will not continue to prosecute a case even if they are convinced that they know who committed a crime, until they have sufficient evidence to show beyond reasonable doubt that the person they accused of the crime did it. They will have to convince the magistrates in a **summary trial**, or a **jury** in the Crown Court. There is no burden on the defendant to establish their innocence as this is not a question raised in an adversarial courtroom in England and Wales.

'Beyond reasonable doubt' is a high standard of proof and this not only protects the innocent against wrongful conviction but also protects the guilty where the evidence is not available or exists but is not admissible. The adversarial system does not presume that all people arrested are innocent, otherwise no one would be arrested or remanded in custody. The presumption of innocence is a rule that governs the conduct of the trial stage. It means in effect that the prosecutor must convince a jury or magistrates of the fact that the person accused of the crime did it by reference to evidence rather than assertion. The trial procedure is based on the assumption that the defendant is innocent and it is up to the prosecutor to demonstrate by evidence that the person is guilty beyond reasonable doubt. The trial and the system of appeals never establish the innocence of the accused. Because a person is acquitted does not mean he or she was innocent in the commonsense meaning of the word.

The image of adversarial justice is of ranks of bewigged and articulate barristers using argument and evidence and cross-examination to establish the guilt or otherwise of the offender accused of a crime. This image is unrealistic, as most defendants admit their guilt for an offence rather than have it established by trial.

It is therefore arguable whether the adversarial nature of criminal justice is the dominant feature of a system in which only a small proportion of defendants exercise their right to trial. However, it is still accurate to describe the system as adversarial because the possibility of a trial, and the onus of having to prove beyond reasonable doubt the guilt of an offender, affects many parts of the system – particularly the way the police and prosecutors conduct their business. The police will need evidence that might be exposed to the full glare of a trial. A prosecutor's reputation will be adversely affected if he or she allows a case to proceed that does not meet the standards set in the Code for Crown Prosecutors for evidential sufficiency, which means the evidence must be admissible, credible and reliable such that it is likely to convince a jury that the person was guilty beyond reasonable doubt.

In adversarial systems, therefore, a trial does not establish whether the accused is innocent of the offence he or she has been charged with, but whether the evidence is sufficient, beyond reasonable doubt, to establish guilt. Criminal appeals examine the same issue, a point explained by Professor Michael Zander in the context of a Court of Appeal decision that overturned the conviction of Winston Silcott for the murder of PC Blakelock during the Broadwater Farm riot of October 1985.

In a letter to *The Times*, Zander explains the key logic of the adversarial system:

Guilt or innocence?

Sir, In writing about compensation for Winston Silcott (August 3) Janet Daley says, 'He has now been declared innocent of one particular crime'. This commonly held view is incorrect.

Mr Silcott, whose conviction for another murder still stands, had his conviction for murder in the case of PC Blakelock quashed by the Court of Appeal. This no more represents a declaration of innocence than does acquittal by a jury.

A jury acquittal means that in the jury's view the prosecution have not proved beyond reasonable doubt, or that even if guilt has been established they are unwilling to convict. The quashing of a conviction by the Court of Appeal means that for one of a large number of possible reasons the conviction cannot stand. Very often the reason is that the judge directed the jury wrongly on law. In the Silcott case, the reason related to documents which the Court of Appeal considered had been tampered with.

Many people, including many commentators in the media, have confused these issues.

The question of whether someone is innocent is not one that is addressed in a criminal trial in our legal system [emphasis added].

(M. Zander, letter to *The Times*, 12 August 1994)

In the same way as the trial questions whether guilt has been established on the basis of evidence presented, an appeal after conviction considers whether the trial process was flawed. In neither case does the court ask, 'Is the defendant innocent?'

Principles, other than adversarial, can be found in policy statements by parliamentary bodies such as the Select Committee on Home Affairs and in the written aims of separate agencies in the system (**see Chapter 11**). General statements can also be found in policy documents such as **white papers** or as preambles to legislation. The Home Office and the Ministry of Justice have overall responsibility for many aspects of the criminal justice system, but unlike other more centralised systems, a policy document from these departments is not regarded as a definitive statement of policy to be followed slavishly. This is partly because this would conflict with other principles such as the independence of the judiciary, professional autonomy and divisions of responsibility for the management and funding of criminal justice (**see Chapter 4**).

In contrast to our system, some countries have penal codes that contain clearly stated principles. An example of this is Finland where the basic principles of the criminal justice system were set out in the Penal Code of 1889. Although these have been amended over the century, the Finnish Ministry of Justice identifies the fundamental principles in Finnish criminal law and procedure:

Today, the fundamental principles in criminal law include the principles of legality, equality, predictability and proportionality. Among the consequences of the strict interpretation given the principle of *legality* in Finland is that the court may not impose forms of punishment that are not specified for the offence in question. *Equality* demands that all cases falling within a specific category are dealt with in the same way. *Predictability* demands that it is possible to assess, in advance, the certainty and level of punishment for a given act. Predictability increases if the law is simple and legal practice is uniform. *Proportionality* requires that the sanction for an offence is in proportion to its blameworthiness. This principle, which also requires that consideration be taken of all official and un-official penal and non-penal consequences of an offence, establishes the maximum punishment. It is not seen to prevent mitigation of punishment where this is deemed reasonable.

In Finland, as in all of the Nordic countries, it is generally felt that punishments primarily have, and should have, a general preventive effect. General prevention can be enhanced by two components, the *certainty* and *severity* of punishment. Finnish criminal policy emphasises certainty, but not severity. General prevention also involves the maintenance of standards of morality through the public disapproval that punishment directs at criminal behaviour. Individual prevention, as a primary goal of punishment, has been rejected. The coercive rehabilitation of offenders was found to be based on flawed arguments and to raise problems with legal safeguards and the control of discretion.

(Joutsen 1990: 2)

▶ Rule of law

Without a penal code or its equivalent, the principles that govern criminal justice in England and Wales evolve from the system of parliamentary sovereignty and the principles of the rule of law. The system of parliamentary sovereignty means that Parliament is the supreme authority and the final arbiter of legality as defined by the enacted laws of the land. In recent years, since the Treaty of Rome, Parliament has not been the only source of rules and regulations and some aspects of the sovereignty of the British Parliament have been ceded to European institutions.

The basic principles of the rule of law were articulated by A V Dicey, who wrote:

No man is punishable or can be lawfully made to suffer in body or goods except for a distinct breach of law established in the ordinary legal manner before the ordinary courts of the land.

➡

> ...no man is above the law, but ...every man, whatever be his rank or condition, is subject to the ordinary law of the realm and amenable to the jurisdiction of the ordinary tribunals.
>
> ...the general principles of the constitution (as for example the right to personal liberty, or the right to public meeting) are with us as the result of judicial decisions determining the rights of private persons in particular cases brought before the courts.
>
> (Dicey 1959: 188–95)

The rights of the defendant, and the victim and the public at large, are derived from the provisions enacted by Parliament and interpretations of the ordinary courts. A primary principle of the rule of law is that everyone is subject to the law including those who enforce it. They can claim no special status unless given by the law and must always be answerable to the law.

In England and Wales official objectives are typically expressed in Home Office documents, such as *Criminal Justice: A Working Paper* (**Home Office 1984**). In the foreword the then Home Secretary, Leon Brittan, specified four objectives for criminal justice, which would contribute towards sustaining the principle of the rule of law:

> A fair and effective criminal justice system marks the distinction between a civilised society and anarchy. If it works well, we as citizens can live our lives peacefully, and enjoy the rewards of our labours; if it works badly, many of us – particularly the elderly and the vulnerable – will have our lives marred by the fear, and sometimes the experience, of crime ...
>
> We needed a strategy ...
>
> The central objectives of this strategy are to sustain the rule of law:
>
> a. by preventing crime wherever possible;
>
> b. when crimes are committed, by detecting the culprit;
>
> c. by convicting the guilty and acquitting the innocent;
>
> d. by dealing adequately and appropriately with those who are guilty and by giving proper effect to the sentences or orders which are imposed.

Principles of criminal justice, whether set out in penal codes, legislation or policy documents, attempt to capture a complex set of issues in grand statements which are supposed to guide the policies and actions of participants in the system. However, the world of human behaviour is not so easily captured into a few phrases and reality is necessarily more complex. The presumption of innocence, for example, sounds simple but raises complex questions. One of these is how many guilty criminals are we prepared to allow to escape apprehension and punishment in order to ensure that no innocent person is unjustly arrested and punished? We could punish those whom we are absolutely certain have committed an offence, but victims may feel aggrieved when cases fall on seeming technicalities and the release of too many apparently guilty persons could encourage vigilantism. Then the chances of justice being done would be even less likely.

Principles of criminal justice are abstractions which portray what ought to happen. Anecdotal insights, be they from police officers, solicitors, barristers, probation officers or recidivists, are frequently stories of the way the system failed to work as it is supposed to. Empirical studies by criminologists and social scientists in recent years have given credence to some of these insights by revealing the gap between principles and reality.

It is very important for a student of criminal justice not to treat the principles as facts, but to regard them instead as criteria by which to judge the performance and practices of a criminal justice system.

1.4 Systems approach and criminal justice sub-systems

Objective 4

Understand the system of criminal justice and its key sub-systems

We have used the term 'criminal justice system' and must now look at what this implies. The term 'system' is often used to describe a designed unit such as a central heating or a recording system, or a natural phenomenon such as the solar system. It has also been used by social reformers who applied the term to the education or welfare systems and talked in terms of social engineering. The word 'system' conveys an impression of a complex object with interconnected parts and sub-divisions with a flow from beginning to end.

Would it be accurate to describe criminal justice as a system? Certainly looking at the flow charts in Figures 1.1–1.3, it could well appear that there is a system at work which has a beginning and a number of predictable stages. The agencies in the criminal justice system are interdependent. One agency's output is another agency's input. Those who leave the courts with a custodial sentence become the intake into the prisons at the back-end of the system. The role of each agency depends on its particular function in the overall scheme of things. For instance, policing cannot be fully understood without an awareness of the role of the police in the overall context of the system. The system may therefore be seen as greater than the sum of its parts.

It is also useful to view criminal justice as a system when considering planning, organisation and policy. During the 1980s, for example, there were a number of attempts to encourage a systems approach towards criminal justice. The then Home Secretary, Leon Brittan, in evidence to the **Home Affairs Committee** of the House of Commons, declared:

> . . . on taking office I decided that we needed a strategy which would enable us to establish and pursue our priorities and objectives in a deliberate and coherent way . . . Our principal preoccupation is, and I believe it ought to be, the criminal justice system which, incidentally, I wish to see treated in all that we do as a system.
>
> (Home Affairs Select Committee, 23 January 1984)

There are several implications of regarding criminal justice as a system. It recognises that agencies are interdependent. Hence, the work of the prison and probation services depends on the work of the courts which, in turn, depend on the filtering role of the Crown Prosecution Service, the generation of cases by the police and initially by the activities of lawbreakers. It is very important for financial and resource planning and is particularly crucial when considering reforms to

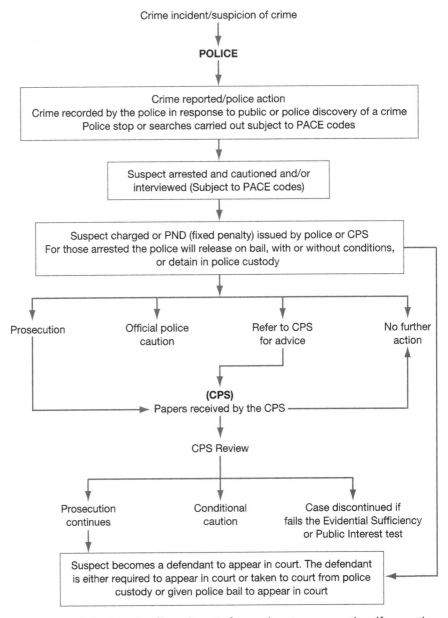

Figure 1.1 Criminal justice flow chart 1: from crime to prosecution (for routine cases involving adults)

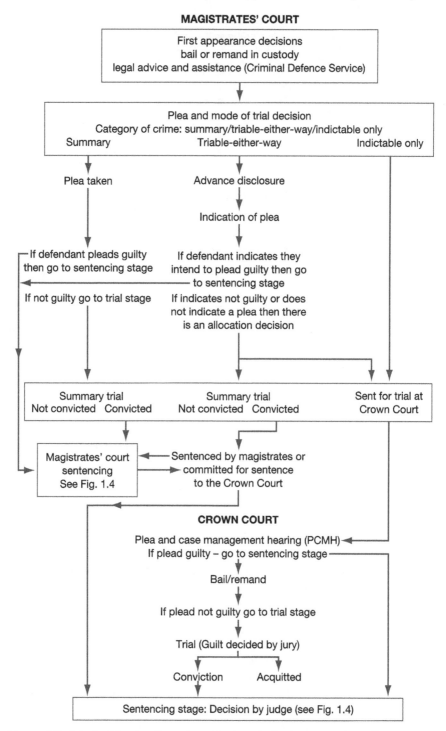

Figure 1.2 Criminal justice flow chart 2: the criminal courts – from first court appearance to conviction (for routine cases involving adults)

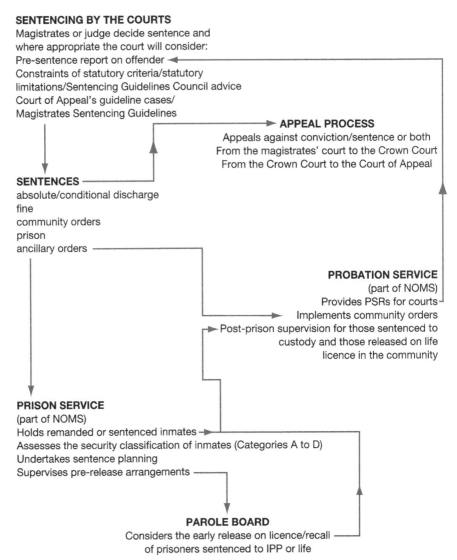

SENTENCING BY THE COURTS
Magistrates or judge decide sentence and
where appropriate the court will consider:
Pre-sentence report on offender
Constraints of statutory criteria/statutory
limitations/Sentencing Guidelines Council advice
Court of Appeal's guideline cases/
Magistrates Sentencing Guidelines

APPEAL PROCESS
Appeals against conviction/sentence or both
From the magistrates' court to the Crown Court
From the Crown Court to the Court of Appeal

SENTENCES
absolute/conditional discharge
fine
community orders
prison
ancillary orders

PROBATION SERVICE
(part of NOMS)
Provides PSRs for courts
Implements community orders
Post-prison supervision for those sentenced to
custody and those released on life
licence in the community

PRISON SERVICE
(part of NOMS)
Holds remanded or sentenced inmates
Assesses the security classification of inmates (Categories A to D)
Undertakes sentence planning
Supervises pre-release arrangements

PAROLE BOARD
Considers the early release on licence/recall
of prisoners sentenced to IPP or life

Figure 1.3 Criminal justice flow chart 3: interrelationship of agencies in the
penal system (for routine cases involving adults)

recognise the interdependency of the system. Thus, reforms proposed for one part
of the system will often have an impact on other agencies not directly involved in
the proposed changes.

This can be seen by considering how the prison population can be affected by
changes in the law. The advent of the motor car has created the need for more
regulation by the criminal law, as cars not only provide opportunities for theft,
but also necessitate regulation of driving if others are not to be endangered or
inconvenienced. This increases the number of people brought to court, which in
turn affects the number in prison. Motoring offences have resulted in a rise in the
number of receptions into prisons of those convicted of serious motoring offences

such as causing death by dangerous driving, along with a few fine defaulters initially convicted of a motoring offence.

A systems approach also encourages inter-agency consultation and cooperation. One recommendation from the Woolf Inquiry into the series of prison riots during 1990 was the need for greater cooperation and liaison between agencies in the criminal justice system. Thus, prisons cannot be effectively managed without the fullest cooperation of all agencies responsible for dealing with offenders. The report recommended that a Criminal Justice Consultative Council (CJCC) be set up. This was done in 1991 and includes senior members of most of the agencies. Since then, 24 local committees have been formed. The aim of establishing Area Committees was to encourage better communications between agencies and to improve strategic planning by identifying common areas of concern, receive reports, collect and distribute information on agency and cross-agency activities, disseminate information regarding available resources and be a forum for addressing strategic developments that affect all agencies (see Chapter 4).

Greater cooperation between criminal justice agencies and external organisations was also encouraged during the 1980s and the idea of joined-up government has stimulated greater coordination in areas such as youth justice since 1997. With respect to crime prevention, many partnerships were set up, encouraged by the Home Office, involving links between official criminal justice agencies, local government and the voluntary and business sectors.

How systematic is criminal justice in England and Wales? It must be recognised that the multiple and competing aims of the system mean that different goals may be simultaneously pursued by different participants. These aims are not easy to reconcile, either in the system as a whole or within specific agencies. For example, should the judge give a sentence that deters the future lawbreaker or one that rehabilitates past lawbreakers?

These multiple aims also affect how those working in agencies see their role, and how, over time, they have developed their own ways of working within conflicting constraints. Thus, agencies have developed what can be described as a distinctive working culture or professional ideology. One example of these kinds of conflicts can be found in the implementation of parts of the Criminal Justice Act 1991, which enacted **curfew** orders and electronic monitoring but did not provide details as to how or when they were to come into effect. These new sanctions were not popular with some sections of the probation service who regarded themselves as a profession whose aim is to help or care for offenders, rather than to supervise or control them. So the central problem of describing criminal justice as a system is to recognise the practical implications of these conflicting goals.

Another problem may arise where agencies are expected to cooperate with each other. There may, for example, be competition between agencies over the allocation of responsibilities or funding. Different working cultures which derive from different perceptions of the goals of the system may lead to mistrust between agencies. Differing models, as described below, may be followed: the police, who have traditionally been seen as following a crime control model, may have difficulties in communicating with lawyers whose role derives from the due process model, or with social workers, who may be more committed to a rehabilitative model.

A certain level of conflict is designed into the system by the *adversarial* nature of criminal trials. It is the duty of the prosecution to prove the guilt of the accused 'beyond reasonable doubt', whereas it is the duty of the defence lawyer to plant that 'reasonable doubt' in the minds of the magistrates or the jury and so secure an acquittal. This adversarial nature of criminal trials has important and pervasive consequences for other parts of the system. It affects the way the police, prosecutors and the probation service perceive and discharge their respective roles.

As we have seen, the trial seeks not to establish the truth, but provides a process for the conviction or acquittal of the accused which affects the kind of evidence the police must secure. The logic of the adversarial style of trial explains why the defence lawyer may cross-examine victims of crime, for example in rape cases, in a way that appears at times to be brutal and insensitive.

▶ Flow charts of the criminal justice system

The interrelationships between agencies and stages in the system can be represented in flow charts which provide a helpful snapshot of the process to enhance understanding of the jigsaw of interrelationships. Figures 1.1–1.3 illustrate the flow and stages of the criminal justice system from crime to prosecution, in the courts, and in the penal system.

Flow charts, however, provide a misleadingly simplistic picture of a system that involves encounters between human beings, all coming into the system with their own motives, be they criminals, victims or criminal justice officials. Each encounter involves an individual story, and has significance in the overall drama of society's response to crime. The drama, morality and social consequences of crime and punishment cannot be portrayed easily in such charts. In addition, while they show some of the ways in which agencies and the stages of the system interrelate, they cannot always reflect the complexities of how one decision, taken by one agency at a particular point in the system, affects later decisions.

Some prefer to see criminal justice as a process – through which a case or a defendant passes. In this process all stages, each governed by a set of discrete rules, are interrelated and affect the eventual outcome. Whether a defendant pleads guilty or not guilty for example affects not only whether he or she is convicted, but whether and how evidence must be prepared, whether he or she is given bail, and it will almost certainly affect any sentence. At the same time, defendants' decisions about whether or not to plead guilty and, if so, when to plead guilty, will be affected by what might happen at later stages.

1.5 Paradigms and models of criminal justice

Objective 5

Explain the paradigms and models of criminal justice

In what ways are issues of crime and justice thought about in public debates and in everyday life? Are criminals regarded as an evil minority or just as ordinary people? Should the police be more concerned with strategies to prevent crime or to capture criminals? Should we spend more money on probation to help offenders or more on prison to punish them? Are the courts effective in ensuring fair trials and preventing miscarriages of justice? Should the phrase 'miscarriage of justice' apply only to those who are wrongly convicted of a crime they did not commit, or should it also apply to those who committed a crime but were not convicted through a lack of evidence caused by witness intimidation? Should it even apply to those who avoid conviction although they have committed a criminal act? These questions and issues will depend on a number of assumptions and views about the nature and extent of the problems of crime and the justice and injustices associated with the way the agencies which operate on behalf of society go about their business.

In this book we have included chapters about images of, and the extent of, crime and in this opening chapter we introduce the reader to some of the key principles of criminal justice, current policy shifts brought about by legislation, models of criminal justice, and flow diagrams that provide ways of thinking about the criminal justice system in England and Wales, or elsewhere. The sum of these different institutional arrangements and ways of thinking about crime and criminal justice is referred to as the criminal justice paradigm.

❱ Models of criminal justice

Models of criminal justice are essentially different perspectives on, or different ways of looking at, criminal justice, derived from the work of writers from a variety of legal, sociological, or administrative backgrounds. They provide a way of looking at criminal justice in terms of some general characteristics, principles or themes of a system. They help the person new to a system to come to terms with its complexities and to make some sense of it. But it should be remembered that, like all models, they are a scaled-down version of the real thing and will not capture all its complexities.

Herbert Packer first identified two alternative models – a **crime control model** which stressed the role of criminal justice in terms of the efficient controlling of crime (the conveyor belt), and a **due process** model (the obstacle course), which stressed the importance of the rule of law and procedural safeguards (**Packer 1968**). These ideas were extremely influential, and later writers identified further models, for example Michael King who outlined six such models (**King 1981**).

The *first model*, originally developed by Packer, is the *due process* model, which represents an idealised version of how the system should work derived from the ideas inherent in the rule of law. It encompasses the principles of the defendant's rights found in textbooks and constitutional documents. It incorporates principles conveyed in well-known phrases such as the presumption of innocence, the defendant's right to a fair trial, equality before the law and that justice should be seen to be done. These phrases embody principles that underlie and allow us to interpret the many rules surrounding both the trial and the pre-trial processes. They protect defendants in order that the innocent may be acquitted and only the guilty convicted.

With the Human Rights Act 1998 this model has come to the foreground of public attention as the implications for basic aspects of policing, criminal procedure and sentencing were subject to considerable scrutiny and challenges from the human rights and due process perspective.

The *second model* is the *crime control* model identified by Packer and earlier explored by Jerome Skolnick in his book *Justice Without Trial* (Skolnick 1966). This stresses the role of the system in reducing, preventing and curbing crime by prosecuting and punishing those who are guilty of offences. It also stresses the importance of protecting citizens and serving the public by crime reduction. Thus, the police and prosecution agencies may interpret their role primarily as crime fighters responsible for ensuring that the guilty are brought to justice. However, problems arise if this aim is pursued regardless of rules protecting the rights of the suspect. Fabricating evidence or neglecting to use search **warrants** could be seen as justifiable in order to ensure that an offender whom the police 'know' to be guilty is found guilty. This problem underlies many laws governing police procedure, seen most recently in legislative reforms of the 1980s. The Police and Criminal Evidence Act 1984 (commonly referred to as **PACE**) introduced the procedure under which the police tape recorded interviews with suspects in police stations, and the Prosecution of Offences Act 1985 led to the establishment of a prosecution agency independent of the police – the Crown Prosecution Service.

For many decades it has been accepted that offenders may not be wholly responsible for their own actions but that their criminality may spring from individual characteristics or social factors. These may be psychological disturbance or problems related to their family circumstances or the social environment. It may make little sense to punish such offenders without at the same time attempting to deal with these underlying issues. This is reflected in King's *third model*, that of *rehabilitation*, which has affected many parts of the criminal justice process. Under this model one of the major considerations at each stage is how best to deal with the individual offender, assuming that their criminality can be reduced by taking a rehabilitative approach. Thus, it might be more desirable for the police to divert some offenders, especially young offenders, from the system, in circumstances where they feel that no benefit will be served by prosecution. The police have powers to caution offenders and refer them to social work agencies which may also help adult offenders. Social workers and probation officers become involved at the sentencing stage, by preparing pre-sentence reports on the offender's circumstances and outlining sentencing options, which may involve counselling and treatment rather than punishment.

Rehabilitation therefore individualises decisions, requiring that the needs of the offender are taken into account. It gives all agencies far greater amounts of discretion. This may well conflict with other goals – for example with those of due process which seek to ensure that all offenders are treated equally, or with the crime control model which stresses the need to punish the guilty.

King's *fourth model* reflects the pressure on criminal justice officials to implement rules and procedures within the many constraints imposed by limited resources and public pressure to solve crimes. Agencies must therefore establish measures of *bureaucratic efficiency*. They must ensure that defendants are tried and sentenced as speedily and efficiently as possible. If defendants spend too long in prison before they come to trial, if trials take too long and are too costly, or if it is argued that too many defendants are acquitted or that there are miscarriages of justice, agencies and courts will come under considerable criticism. The cost-effectiveness of law enforcement and court administration has become a major concern of the government since the 1990s.

Balancing the interests of due process with those of crime control and bureaucratic efficiency is not always easy. It is difficult for example to subject abstract

Table 1.2 Models of criminal justice

Social function	Process model	Features of court
1 Justice	Due process model	a. Equality between parties b. Rules protecting defendants against error c. Restraint of arbitrary power d. Presumption of innocence
2 Punishment	Crime control model	a. Disregard of legal controls b. Implicit presumption of guilt c. High conviction rate d. Unpleasantness of experience e. Support for police
3 Rehabilitation	Medical model (diagnosis, prediction, and treatment selection)	a. Information collecting procedures b. Individualisation c. Treatment presumption d. Discretion of decision-makers e. Expertise of decision-makers or advisers f. Relaxation of formal rules
4 Management of crime and criminals	Bureaucratic model	a. Independence from political considerations b. Speed and efficiency c. Importance of and acceptance of records d. Minimisation of conflict e. Minimisation of expense f. Economical division of labour
5 Denunciation and degradation	Status passage model	a. Public shaming of defendant b. Court values reflecting community values c. Agents' control over process
6 Maintenance of class domination	Power model	a. Reinforcement of class values b. Alienation of defendant c. Deflection of attention from issues of class conflict d. Differences between judges and judged e. Paradoxes and contradictions between rhetoric and performance
7 Just deserts	Justice model	a. Punishment of the deserving b. Proportionality principles: relate to seriousness of the offence c. Only deserved by the culpable
8 Offender control	Management model	a. Offender instrumental b. Monitoring, surveillance and control c. Range of intervention strategies

Source: Adapted from King (1981: 13)

principles such as justice to tests of cost-effectiveness. How many defendants should be acquitted? How many should be tried rather than plead guilty? There are no straightforward answers to these questions – no yardstick against which to assess the efficiency of the system. Indeed in some instances the interests of justice may conflict with those of efficiency – as can be seen in the example of not guilty pleas. If the defendant pleads not guilty, the prosecution and the defence have to prepare a case which may involve collecting evidence, summoning witnesses and preparing the many documents involved in a trial. If the defendant pleads guilty, much of this work can be avoided. Guilty pleas are, therefore, cost-effective and save the time of victims, witnesses, police, courts and the Crown Prosecution Service. But any pressure on defendants to plead guilty could deprive them of their right to trial. However, if more defendants insisted on their right to trial the system could become overloaded and more costly.

On the other hand, the police might not have sufficient admissible evidence to proceed against a person they suspect is guilty. The due process model would result in no action being taken. However, there may be some concern about the resources expended on an investigation with no result. The tension between these models will result in a difficult decision on whether to charge the person and hope that he or she pleads guilty or to drop the case.

Some would argue that offenders should be publicly tried and sentenced in order to reflect the community's moral disapproval of offending behaviour. This is reflected in the *fifth model* identified by King – the **denunciation** *and degradation* model. In this model, public trial and punishment are necessary to underlie the law-abiding values of the community. Some sociologists have argued that the criminal justice system serves an important social function in reinforcing social values. While this may conflict with the aims of rehabilitation, it can be argued that such public punishment and expression of society's disapproval can in itself be rehabilitative, as it may induce feelings of shame in offenders – a prerequisite for rehabilitation. John Braithwaite argues in favour of re-integrative shaming – offenders should feel ashamed of their offences but shaming should not be so extreme that it stigmatises offenders to a point where they cannot be re-integrated into the community (**Braithwaite 1989**).

Exploring the potentially repressive nature of criminal justice systems also raises questions about who makes the law and whose interests are served by the criminal justice system. This is reflected in King's *sixth model*, the *power* model. Some, using a Marxist or conflict perspective, argue that criminal justice systems essentially reinforce the role of the powerful – those who make the laws and who are served by the many agencies of the system. Thus, criminal law and its enforcement are influenced, it is argued, by the interests of dominant classes, which may also include elements of patriarchy and colonialism, thus affecting the treatment of women and minority ethnic groups. The state is regarded in this model as acting in the interest of the dominant group, who use the criminal law to further these interests. Advocates of this approach point to the over-representation of those from poorer sections of the community as defendants in the criminal justice system.

To King's six models of criminal justice we would add two more models. A *seventh* would be the **just deserts** model. Combining elements of retribution for offenders with a notion of proper respect for the treatment of the accused or defendant, this model stresses the importance of punishing offenders in terms of their blameworthiness and the seriousness of their offence, not through crude revenge or incapacitation, but in response to the wrongfulness of their act. This brings together the principles of respect for the offender as a human being with certain rights, the need to establish the offender's **culpability** for the offence so as to punish only the guilty, and the right of society to exact retribution from those who have done wrong. This links punishment and crime to issues of morality and control.

An *eighth model, managing offender behaviour,* is a second model added by us to recognise the focus on instrumental-offender strategies that are broader than rehabilitation and, while encompassing efforts to change behaviour, also monitor and control criminals depending on the level of risk and record of offending. Intensive supervision and surveillance programmes for juveniles and electronically monitored curfews are examples of a strategy of intervention that relies on surveillance and supervision to reduce crime. Here we see the crime control model being extended beyond policing into the correctional stage, blending rehabilitative practice with surveillance and control.

How useful are these models of criminal justice? To an extent they focus on and magnify one feature of the system. They do, however, illustrate different ways of looking at the system and indicate very different influences on policy and practice. Most of these models have been developed by different academic disciplines such as criminology, sociology or law, and more recently from systems analysis utilised by experts in management and auditing techniques. Not surprisingly these disparate disciplines provide different snapshots of bits of the system from their own perspective. Lawyers focus mainly on procedures before and during trial. Sociologists put emphasis on the informal influences that can lead to inequalities and injustice. Criminologists focus on crime statistics and explanations of crime. Systems analysts trace the aggregate flow of cases through the system, management consultants look at problems of accountability and effectiveness, while accountants examine the cost-effectiveness of the entire system and agencies within it. This has led to the development of management by objectives and the use of auditing techniques in the criminal justice system.

These different models reflect the many different influences that come to shape practice and policy in criminal justice. A different emphasis is seen by the Human Rights Act 1998, which highlights the *due process model.* These shifts in emphasis are at times determined by events such as the terrorist bombings in London on 7 July and 21 July 2005, leading to a greater concern with *crime control.* In this last section of this introductory chapter on criminal justice we will look at recent changes brought about by legislative reforms as an indicator of the way British lawmakers perceive the need for change to the criminal justice system. Underpinning these reforms will be shifts in the way different aspects of the system are being balanced in the light of changing circumstances, such as attempts to control new crimes (cross-European crime), modernisation and efficiency, efforts to protect human rights, and a shifting political and economic environment, be it greater public concern about crime in the UK or the consequences of greater integration across the enlarged European Union of 28 countries in 2014. These changing circumstances and concerns are embodied in the history of recent legislation in the UK.

1.6 Recent legislation and policy developments

Objective 6

Outline recent legislation and current policy developments.

'The first five Criminal Justice Acts of the century were spaced out over nearly 50 years, from 1925 to 1972, whereas the last five have come in less than 20 years since 1972 and the current Act is the third in only five years.' **Wasik and Taylor** wrote this in 1991, since when there has been at least one piece of criminal justice legislation in every year since 1993.

Some legislative reforms focus on one aspect of the system. The Proceeds of Crime Act 2002 attempts to deal with money obtained illegally and money laundering, be it to do with drug dealing, terrorist groups, organised crime, or tax and social security fraud. One consequence has been to change the way solicitors deal with clients they suspect of having obtained money illegally. Other statutes have a broader impact, such as the Criminal Justice Act 2003, resulting in changes across many aspects of the criminal justice process.

This section aims to outline briefly the numerous developments in legislation since 1990, reflecting the continually shifting governmental and public priorities in relation to the conflicting goals and models (**examined in section 1.5**) of the criminal justice system.

We start with the Criminal Justice Act of 1991, which was intended to create a systematic and principled approach to sentencing, after a thorough review of the sentencing framework.

❯ Criminal Justice Act 1991

The Criminal Justice Act (CJA 1991) was preceded by an unprecedented amount of research, planning, consultation and training. An experiment on unit fines was carried out in magistrates' courts in Hampshire, and extensive training was given to those who were to enforce the Act. But despite the research and consultation that went into the Act, within seven months of its implementation the Home Secretary announced that amendments were to be made to it.

The CJA 1991 was hailed as a far-reaching systematic reform of sentencing, although it reflected many existing shifts in penal philosophy and sentencing policy. The underlying themes of this change were expressed in the 1990 White Paper, **Crime, Justice and Protecting the Public (Home Office 1990a)** and included the need for more consistency in sentencing policy and for sentences to be proportionate to the offence. In addition it introduced what has come to be known as a 'twin track' approach to sentencing, making a clearer distinction between property offences and violent crime. The former were to be dealt with by a greater use of punishment in the community, while the latter, with a view to crime prevention, could result in longer prison sentences. The overall framework for sentencing otherwise was provided by a philosophy of 'just deserts': punishing in accordance with the current offence, rather than past crimes or possible future ones.

Vociferous criticism was made of the unit fine and another aspect of the sentencing reforms introduced by the CJA 1991. Section 29 had prevented judges and magistrates taking into account past convictions when sentencing except in limited circumstances. Furthermore, they could only take into account two offences when assessing seriousness for a person convicted of multiple incidents. Thus, the burglar convicted of 20 burglaries would actually be sentenced on the basis of the worst two burglaries. Sentencers felt unable to reflect in their disposals the frequency and history of offending.

▶ Criminal Justice Act 1993

Most of the provisions of the CJA 1991 came into effect on 1 October 1992. By Easter 1993, Kenneth Clarke, the then Home Secretary, announced that the unit fine system was to be abandoned. Legislation to this effect was added to the Criminal Justice Bill already before Parliament. Thus, the CJA 1993, which dealt primarily with measures to combat anti-terrorist acts, drug trafficking and insider dealing, was used to amend the CJA 1991. Section 65 abolished the two main planks of the 1991 Act, unit fines and section 29. The later Act provided that sentencers must take account of means when fining, and adjust fines up or down as appropriate, but without imposing a framework for doing so. In addition, the court could consider all offences before the court, and offenders' previous convictions or any failure to respond to earlier sanctions could be used by the courts when deciding on a sentence.

▶ Criminal Justice and Public Order Act 1994

Major changes included:

- The introduction of a secure training order for 12–14-year-old persistent offenders. The first half of this order is to be spent in secure training units, and the second half to be spent under compulsory supervision in the community.
- The ability of a court to draw inferences from a defendant's silence during police questioning or in court.
- Bail not to be granted to defendants charged with or convicted of homicide or rape or who have a previous conviction for such an offence. Section 26 provided that persons accused or convicted of committing an offence while on bail need not be given bail (see Chapter 9).
- Pilot projects for curfew orders and electronic monitoring.
- With regard to discounts for guilty pleas, it required the courts to take account of the timing and circumstances of a guilty plea.
- Tougher powers against trespassers and unauthorised camping were directed at New Age travellers and rave parties of more than 100 people.
- Changes to the laws in relation to obscenity to incorporate child pornography produced on computers and some restrictions on the classification of video recordings were directed against what are commonly known as 'video nasties'.
- Rape was redefined to include the offence commonly known as 'male rape', and the age of consent lowered for homosexual acts from 21 to 18.

◗ Crime and Disorder Act 1998

An array of measures were introduced to permit intervention at an early stage and allow for a response to anti-social and criminal behaviour of children, including: a local child curfew scheme, parenting orders, **action plan orders**, and police reprimands and final warnings. Youth offending teams were established on a multi-disciplinary basis to coordinate crime prevention and responses to youth crime.

New sentences for young offenders were introduced: the reparation order and the detention and training order replaced the secure training order. Secure training centres for those aged from 12 to 14 were placed under the authority of a new Youth Justice Board. Tougher community protection laws with respect to sex offenders and anti-social behaviour and a new category of racially aggravated offence were created.

In the courts, procedural changes included speeding up the process of dealing with cases by imposing time limits, and ending committal proceedings for indictable-only offences. Reform of the CPS enabled lay employees to conduct pre-trial procedure such as bail hearings.

◗ Youth Justice and Criminal Evidence Act 1999

The Act introduced a new sentencing disposal for the **youth court**. A Referral order was a new sentence of referral to a youth offender panel. Referral is available for young people convicted for the first time and its primary aim is to prevent reoffending. The youth offender panel works with the young offender to establish a programme of behaviour for the young offender to follow. The programme is guided by the following three principles of restorative justice: making restoration to the victim; achieving reintegration into the law-abiding community; and taking responsibility for the consequences of offending behaviour.

◗ Criminal Justice and Courts Services Act 2000

This created the National Probation Service for England and Wales and the Children and Family Court Advisory and Support Service. It aims to prevent unsuitable people from working with children, with a **statutory** ban enforced by criminal sanctions. It increases the maximum penalties for offences relating to indecent photographs of children and raises the age of the child protected from under 14 to under 16. Community orders were renamed: **probation orders** became **community rehabilitation orders**, community service orders and combination orders.

◗ Anti-terrorism, Crime and Security Act 2001

In response to the 11 September 2001 terrorist attacks on New York and Washington DC, new powers to counter the threat to the UK were enacted to cut off terrorist funding, and the Act allows government departments and agencies to collect and share information required for countering the terrorist threat; streamline relevant immigration procedures; protect the security of the nuclear and aviation industries; improve the security of dangerous substances that may be targeted or used by terrorists, and enhance police powers when detainees in police custody refuse to cooperate with the police as to their identity.

▶ Criminal Justice and Police Act 2001

This Act introduced penalty notices as a way of responding to a range of low-level anti-social offending associated with disorderly conduct such as consuming alcohol in a public place. Penalty notices may be issued on the spot or at a police station for a range of disorder offences.

▶ Police Reform Act 2002

This Act requires the Home Secretary to produce an annual National Policing Plan, and introduces a new system for handling complaints against the police. The **Independent Police Complaints Commission (IPCC)** replaces the Police Complaints Authority.

▶ Proceeds of Crime Act 2002

This provided powers to confiscate from convicted defendants the financial benefits of their crime and attempts to prevent money laundering by organised crime, drug cartels and terrorist groups.

▶ Crime (International Cooperation) Act 2003

The Act implements police and judicial cooperation within the EU by adopting the mutual legal assistance provisions of the 1985 Schengen Convention, the Convention on Mutual Assistance in Criminal Matters 2000, and other agreements on terrorism and driving offences. The Schengen Convention was designed to facilitate the free movement of persons by removing internal border controls. The Act implements the obligations for participating countries to respond to requests for assistance with locating banking accounts and to provide banking information relating to criminal investigations. It implements measures against terrorism and the mutual recognition of driving disqualifications.

▶ Anti-Social Behaviour Act 2003

Following on from the 2003 report *Respect and Responsibility – taking a stand against anti-social behaviour* the Act extended the strategy started with the **ASBOs** that were introduced in 1998 to close down premises being used for drug selling, increased landlord and local authorities powers where there was anti-social or nuisance neighbours on social housing estates and added a parenting order for situations where children had been issued with ASBOs.

▶ Criminal Justice Act 2003

The Act introduced a major reform of sentencing including many of the reforms proposed by the Auld and Halliday reports on court process and sentencing. It established the Sentencing Guidelines Council and introduced a generic community sentence and a new indeterminate public protection sentence. For the first time it set out the aims of sentencing in a statute.

▶ Constitutional Reform Act 2005

The measure established the Supreme Court of the UK to replace the judicial appeal role of the House of Lords.

▶ Prevention of Terrorism Act 2005

This Act introduced control orders putting constraints on suspected terrorists who are not in custody awaiting trial or deportation.

▶ Police and Justice Act 2006

It set up a mechanism for police reforms via the **National Policing Improvement Agency (NPIA)** and introduced a standard set of powers for PCSOs. Punitive conditions may now be attached to conditional cautions. A new definition of computer hacking was provided.

▶ Serious Crime Act 2007

This measure introduced the Serious Crime Prevention Orders for those aged over 18 after a conviction for a serious crime in order to protect the public, based on the same principle as an ASBO or a Sex Crime Prevention Order, i.e. it is a civil order but failure to comply carries a maximum sentence of five years' custody. The **Asset Recovery Agency** (ARA) was abolished and its work incorporated into the **Serious Organised Crime Agency (SOCA)**.

▶ Criminal Justice and Immigration Act 2008

It set out the purposes of sentencing in the youth justice system and introduced a Youth Rehabilitation Order – a generic community sentence for children and young offenders and replaces all existing community penalties available for **younger offenders** and a Youth Conditional Caution for 16- and 17-year-old offenders. It created a Violent Offender Orders.

The Act clarified the law of self-defence. It created a presumption that trials in magistrates' courts will proceed if the defendant does not attend. For more serious offenders it introduced a minimum tariff of two years for prisoners serving indeterminate public protection sentences.

▶ Policing and Crime Act 2009

The Act strengthens the voice of local communities in that the police authorities should reflect the local communities' views in the routines of police work. The Act makes it easier to recover criminal assets and to ensure international judicial cooperation. Powers granted by the Act allow the UK Border Agency to question travellers and to require the production of passports and travel documents for customs purposes. It introduces gang injunctions (or gangbos) which is a civil injunction against a person, on the civil standard of proof, when the court thinks the person has been involved in gang-related violence. Makes football banning orders in England and Wales enforceable in Scotland and Northern Ireland.

▶ Coroners and Justice Act 2009

Reforms the law on homicide with respect to the defence of diminished responsibility. The old defence of provocation contained in section 3 of the Homicide Act 1957 has been abolished and replaced with the loss of self-control as a new partial defence to murder.

Established a new Sentencing Council for England and Wales, with a strengthened remit to promote consistency in sentencing practice. Created a new national coroner service, led by a new chief coroner. Enables the courts to pass an indeterminate sentence for public protection for certain terrorist offences.

▶ Crime and Security Act 2010

The Act reduced the reporting requirements on the police when they stop and search individuals and gives additional powers to the police to take fingerprints and DNA samples from people who have been arrested, charged or convicted in the UK, and from those convicted overseas of serious sexual and violent offences. It provided the police with the power to issue an alleged perpetrator of an offence relating to domestic violence with a Domestic Violence Protection Notice (DVPN).

Following the European Court of Human Rights judgment in the case of *S and Marper* v. *United Kingdom* [2008] ECHR 1581, the Act also sets out a statutory framework for the retention and destruction of biometric material, including DNA samples, DNA profiles and fingerprints, that has been taken from an individual as part of the investigation of a recordable offence.

The Act amended the Private Security Industry Act 2001 to enable the Security Industry Authority (SIA) to introduce a licensing regime for private security businesses, in particular vehicle immobilisation businesses. Wheel clamping firms will no longer be able to operate without a SIA issued licence.

▶ Terrorism Prevention and Investigation Measures Act 2011

These new measures are an attempt to deal with the risk to protect the public from persons believed to have engaged in terrorism-related activity abroad, but who cannot be prosecuted nor deported, and to provide protection with the abolition of control orders. They are ordered by the Home Secretary and include restrictions such as overnight residence at a specified address, electronic tagging, reporting requirements and restrictions on travel, association, communication, finances, work and study.

▶ Police Reform and Social Responsibility Act 2011

This Act transfers the control of police forces from police authorities to elected Police and Crime Commissioners. The first police commissioner elections were held in November 2012. Elections will take place every four years. The next is due in May 2016.

▶ Legal Aid, Sentencing and Punishment of Offenders Act 2012

New release and recall provisions for **determinate sentence** prisoners, and abolishes the sentence of Imprisonment for Public Protection (IPP) and Extended Sentences for Public Protection (EPPs). These are replaced by a new Extended Determinate Sentence (EDS) which will be used for offenders who previously would have received an IPP or an extended sentence under the 2003 Act.

▶ Crime and Courts Act 2013

Created a new nationwide crime fighting unit called the United Kingdom National Crime Agency (NCA), which incorporated the duties of the abolished Serious Organised Crime Agency, the Child Exploitation and Online Protection Centre and the National Cyber Crime Unit. The National Policing Improvement Agency is abolished.

▶ Justice and Security Act 2013

Provides for oversight by the Parliamentary Intelligence and Security Committee (ISC) of the Security Service (MI5), the Secret Intelligence Service (MI6) and the Government Communications Headquarters (GCHQ) on intelligence or security matters.

▶ Offender Rehabilitation Act 2014

Under the CJA 2003 those serving a sentence of 12 months or less were released from custody at the halfway point of their sentence without any further supervision (e.g. after three months for a six-month sentence and release without supervision) but there will now be a period of supervision following release from prison, other than for those sentenced to one day in prison. Short-term prisoners will serve their whole sentence in a new 'resettlement prison' with greater integration of pre- and post-release supervision and support. The majority of those serving longer sentences will be moved to a resettlement prison at least three months before the end of their time in custody. This will mean the majority of offenders should be released from prisons in, or close to, the area in which they will live.

There are new rules governing when convictions and cautions are spent. Under the new regime the only circumstances in which a conviction will never be spent are those where an individual receives a custodial sentence of over four years or has received a public protection sentence for sexual and violent offences.

There will be 21 new Community Rehabilitation Companies (blending voluntary and private resources with rewards based on successful rehabilitation, as measured by recidivism rates) to work with low- and medium-risk offenders. The National Probation Service will concentrate on high-risk offenders and the stated purpose of the reforms in the statute is to seek the rehabilitation of offenders.

Conclusion

In this chapter, we have suggested that to understand how a criminal justice system operates it is necessary to identify its many aims, to be able to describe its procedures, modes of punishment and the behaviour criminalised, and to appreciate the interdependencies between agencies, which at a minimum allow us to call it a system. We have also indicated through the models of criminal justice many of the influences and principles that guide criminal justice agencies and placed this into the context of the political, economic and cultural factors that shape participants' views and actions, be they offenders, judges, police or probation officers. Finally, we have illustrated how models of criminal justice help us to come to terms with the tensions between the formal goals, principles and the real practices that go on in the world of those who enforce, interpret and implement the criminal law. That world is complex, given its many manifestations, aspirations and everyday encounters, and no one theory, model or principle will do justice to that reality. This book will attempt to reflect these many issues as we look at specific agencies and stages of the system.

Review question

1. Identify and outline the characteristics of the eight models of criminal justice defined in this chapter.

Discussion questions

1. Visit a local magistrates' court for a morning session and then work through the eight models of criminal justice and give examples of each model based on your observations from your visit.

2. Identify current issues and controversies affecting criminal justice (for example a current case, issue or debate in Parliament, statement by politicians or other public figures) and consider:

   a. To what extent these reveal the conflicting goals of the criminal justice system.
   b. How these would be approached by the different models of criminal justice outlined above.

3. Examine the range of recent statutes referred to above and identify the model or models of criminal justice that appear to influence their approach.

Further reading

Ashworth A and Redmayne M (2010) *The Criminal Process* (4th edn), Oxford University Press: Oxford

King M (1981) *The Framework of Criminal Justice*, Croom Helm: London

McConville M and Wilson G (2002) *The Handbook of the Criminal Justice Process*, Oxford University Press: Oxford

Muncie J and Wilson D (2004) *Student Handbook of Criminal Justice and Criminology*, Routledge-Cavendish: London

Packer H L (1968) *The Limits of Criminal Sanction*, Stanford University Press: Stanford, CA

Weblinks

Information about the system for citizens: **www.cjsonline.org/home.html**

Website of the Ministry of Justice: **www.justice.gov.uk/**

Main government department responsible for policing and law enforcement: **www.homeoffice.gov.uk/**

Information provided by the Metropolitan Police Service in London: **www.met.police.uk**

Current and recent legislation in Parliament: **www.publications.parliament.uk**

Chapter 2

What is crime?

Learning objectives

After reading the chapter you should be able to:

1. Define the meaning of 'crime'
2. Distinguish between the different legal categories of criminal offences
3. Understand how crime is measured
4. Describe and explain crime trends
5. Describe different types of criminal offences

Key statistics

- In the 12 months ending March 2013, the Crime Survey for England and Wales (CSEW) estimated that there were 8.6 million crimes against individuals in England and Wales – the lowest since the survey began in 1981
- The police recorded 3.7 million offences in total in the year ending June 2013
- In 2013 victim-based crime accounted for 83 per cent of all offences recorded by the police, the rest were crimes with no specific victims
  - The CSEW does not include crimes committed in the workplace or commercial premises such as **vandalism**, burglary, assaults, theft and fraud. The Commercial Victimisation Surveys (CVS) states that from 2002 to 2012 there were 14.5 million fewer crimes against wholesale and retail business premises in 2012 than in 2002 (down from a total of around 21.5 million to around 7 million)
  - The police recorded 2.4 million incidents of anti-social behaviour in the year ending September 2012

- In 2012/13 there were 532 recorded homicides
- One event, or one criminal, can change the criminal data trends when the numbers are relatively small as with homicide numbers each year that are normally less than 1,000 pa in England and Wales. The number of homicides initially recorded by the police in 2002/03 was 1,048; this includes 173 murders committed by Harold Shipman. The total homicide figure of 766 in 2005/06 includes 52 homicide victims of the 7 July London terrorist bombings

Introduction

What is crime? This is not such an easy question to answer as it might at first appear, because a number of different meanings are associated with the words crime and criminal. In this chapter we will look at the differing ways in which criminal behaviour is defined and perceived. We look at the legal conception of crime used to establish a person's liability for criminal conduct; the different categories of crime in criminal law; and the attempts to measure the extent of different types of crime.

In addition to the legal notions of criminal culpability, we discuss the popular images of crime and we offer a model of understanding and analysing crime based on three elements required for crime to exist in the formal system of criminal justice; a model that distinguishes between behaviour, rules and enforcement.

2.1 Defining crime

Objective 1

Define the meaning of 'crime'

Legally, a crime is any act or omission proscribed by the criminal law and thus punishable by the state through the criminal justice process. The criminal law and its associated punishments are used against a very wide range of behaviour – from **murder**, rape and assault to driving with excess alcohol, parking on a yellow line and failing to comply with a plethora of health and safety regulations. While few would dispute that murder is and should be an offence, not all members of the public would think of someone who drives with excess alcohol in their blood as a criminal.

The public have a commonsense view of what they regard as crime. Behaviour which people disapprove of is often described as criminal to emphasise its seriousness and unacceptability. These common sense images tend to be associated with the deliberate infliction of physical harm, often involving a confrontation between an offender and a victim. Dishonesty, cheating or theft are also a key part of these commonsense notions of crime. Everyday conceptions of the criminal carry connotations of a wrongdoer who should be stigmatised. Stigma means that a person is not considered normal, or is deviant and should be censured as a person who behaves badly.

Yet not all activities proscribed by the criminal law are necessarily regarded as crimes, or their perpetrators as criminal. In the workplace, for example, employees may regularly fiddle the books or engage in petty pilfering. These activities are described euphemistically as perks or fiddles rather than as theft or fraud. Members of the public may inflate insurance claims or fail to disclose their full earnings to the tax authority without regarding themselves as criminals, or being viewed as such by others. Drivers may regularly infringe road traffic laws without considering their behaviour as deviant. Different groups therefore may have different conceptions of where to draw the line between acceptable behaviour and crime.

Although there is considerable overlap between legal and everyday conceptions of crime there is no necessary equation between the two. Public tolerance of different activities changes over time and legal categories are subject to change. The criminal law in our society is not based on a fundamentalist or absolutist conception of morality but shifts according to changes in public attitudes. This is reflected in political pressures to change legislation that defines crime. Thus over the last 50 years the way in which the law has dealt with drunk driving, homosexuality, prostitution, marital rape and criminal damage has changed. Changes in the public's tolerance of activities leads to campaigns to criminalise some behaviours and to decriminalise others. Parts of the Criminal Justice and Public Order Act 1994 aimed to curb the activities of New Age travellers and organisers of raves, while lowering from 21 to 18 years the age at which men may lawfully perform homosexual acts in private.

Hence, the legal conception of crime is subject to change and depends, in a parliamentary democracy, on political as well as moral considerations. However, if the criminal law did not express and reflect public morality and concerns about harm to the community the public would have little regard for the law – it would lose its legitimacy. Furthermore, it would be seen as unduly oppressive – as an instrument of social control and political domination. Such laws are unlikely to inspire public trust, confidence or legitimacy. They would be difficult to enforce and would undermine confidence in the criminal justice process.

▶ Three aspects of the concept of crime

To avoid confusion between the more technical and legal conception of crime used by lawyers and its everyday usage, we suggest the following definition of a criminal:

> A person whose behaviour is in breach of legally prescribed rules which renders that person liable to criminal proceedings.

As a starting point this definition is useful because it focuses on the three elements that are indispensable if we are to understand and explain crime. They are: behaviour, breach of rules and the possibility of enforcement and punishment.

Behaviour

Criminal law is essentially concerned with the regulation of behaviour. This may involve prohibitions on some kinds of behaviour, such as stealing another person's property or harming them deliberately. Some criminal laws may require a specific action, such as having insurance when driving a car, or complying with regulations. In some instances it is the combination of behaviour with a particular situation that defines a crime, such as the offence of being drunk in a public place. In others it is the combination of status with behaviour, such as the purchase of alcohol by someone under 18 years of age.

Illegality covers a multitude of actions, responsibilities, circumstances and statuses and hence the diversity of acts that may be characterised as criminal is considerable. Thus it is impossible to offer a simple explanation of why someone acts criminally. Furthermore, people do not act in an identical fashion. Some people are more prone to self-indulgence, others are more violent in character.

The causes of criminal behaviour are complex and multiple. They are multiple because crime does not relate to only one form of action. For instance, the causes of domestic violence by a woman may not be the same as when committed by a man. The causes that lead a teenager to commit arson may be very different from those that lead an old-age pensioner to fraud. Therefore, we should not expect to find a single cause for all types of criminality.

Furthermore, the complexity is apparent when we look at the range of factors used to explain delinquency. Contributing to the debate are criminologists, sociologists, psychologists, penologists, economists, biologists, geneticists, psychiatrists, town planners, architects, social workers, doctors, nutritionists, teachers and theologians. The potential list of causes is long: biological predisposition, inconsistent and irresponsible parenting, failure at school, truancy, labelling, violent videos, hyperactivity, over stimulating foods, drugs, glue, alcohol, masculinity, testosterone, repressed sexuality, underdeveloped super ego, lack of discipline, peer influence, television, lack of moral training, racism, lack of legitimate opportunities and too many illegal opportunities.

Some accounts of criminal conduct seek to identify the cause, or causes, that lead to behaviour that is distinctively deviant and untypical, such as the murders of two children committed by Ian Huntley in Soham or the murder by Steve Wright of five prostitutes in Ipswich in 2006. In contrast, other theories of criminal behaviour focus on the types of motives that might affect anyone, such as greed, envy, lust and jealousy, as causes of bad behaviour. We will discuss some of these explanations later in this book as well as the importance that the theories about the causes of crime have in determining society's responses in terms of both the prevention and punishment of crime.

Rules

The rules which determine whether or not behaviour is criminal are found in legislation passed by Parliament or in decisions of the courts. These form the starting point for understanding crime as they provide the legal definition of criminal acts. As we have seen, these rules may change over time, and the number of potentially illegal acts may increase as new areas and types of behaviour are criminalised. For example, under the Firearms Amendment Act 1996, pistol owners were required to hand over to the police, before midnight on 30 September 1997, any hand guns over .22 calibre they possessed or face up to 10 years' imprisonment. In 1997, what had become known as stalking was made an offence by the Protection from Harassment Act. The development of the internet and behaviour associated with it led to the formulation of offences dealing with the storage and retrieval of obscene computer images of children. Equally, however, conduct can cease to be criminal by virtue of legislation, such as abortion and homosexual acts.

There are two sources of law in England and Wales: legislation and law based on decided cases. Legislation consists of Acts of Parliament (statutes) and statutory instruments (often called subordinate legislation). **Case law** is law that has been built up over the years by decisions of the courts in individual matters: these may include decisions on the meaning of statutes. The law of England and Wales is thus based on the accumulation of previous cases and is described as a **common law** system, which distinguishes it from European systems which are based on codes established by legislation. Although the sources of the law are as above, since the enactment of the Human Rights Act 1998 all statutes and indeed the common law have to be interpreted in line with the Act, so that in a sense European human rights jurisprudence is now affecting English law. Although many offences are now governed by, or were created by, statute, the general principles of criminal law are still matters of the common law, which also still governs some of the most serious crimes: for example, murder. The idea that the common law evolves from the piecemeal interpretation of the law by judges is an integral part of the legal tradition in England and Wales. Nevertheless, in order for behaviour to be defined and recognised as criminal, it must be in breach of some rule laid down in case law or legislation.

Enforcement and criminal proceedings

Behaviour is not self-defining, nor are rules self-enforcing. Laws do not have an impact unless they are enforced, or unless there is the anticipation of enforcement. How, then, is behaviour interpreted as breaking the rules? By whom and how are rules interpreted and applied? The criminal law specifies who can enforce the law and what procedures are necessary to investigate and prosecute crime, adjudicate on guilt and decide on an appropriate sentence. Enforcement is the responsibility of specialist agencies or organisations specifically given the right to enforce the law, such as the police, HM Revenue and Customs officers and Crown Prosecutors. Although the basic procedures and guidelines for law enforcement are set out in statutes and case law, it is inevitable that these cannot cover every situation. That is why it is important to understand that many factors in addition to legal rules influence the way the criminal law is put into action.

Resources are required to fund the agencies and organisations that enforce the law. To learn how these agencies operate, it is necessary to establish how they deploy these resources and how they interpret their formal goals and objectives. Professional loyalties, training and commonsense notions of crime and the crime problem will influence the way officials decide on priorities and interpret their responsibilities. Also, as officials in criminal justice agencies do not normally come from outside the society in which they work, many of the taken-for-granted prejudices of the wider culture also influence how they see their role.

Edwin Schur wrote, 'Once we recognise that crime is defined by the criminal law and is therefore variable in content, we see quite clearly that no explanation of crime that limits itself to the motivation and behaviour of individual offenders can ever be a complete one' (**Schur 1969: 10**).

The three elements that constitute a criminal act – behaviour, rules and the enforcement of rules – are further refined by the concept of **criminal liability**. Not all actions by a person that might appear to be in breach of the criminal law are necessarily criminal because there may be an excuse or acceptable reason for their behaviour. In commonsense terms and in a legal sense they may not be blameworthy or culpable. Establishing the culpability of a defendant is therefore central to the criminal process and explains the central role of the **trial** as the mechanism of establishing criminal liability.

▶ Legal liability and the elements of a crime

One of the most fundamental principles of criminal law is that a person should not be punished unless he or she has both committed the act or omission in question and is blameworthy. This means that in order to be considered culpable, it must be established that an offender has not only committed an offence but is responsible for it. These two aspects are usually referred to as the **actus reus**, the guilty act, and the **mens rea**, the guilty mind. Both the guilty act and the guilty mind are generally required before someone is deemed to be guilty of a crime.

Some crimes, called crimes of strict or absolute liability, do not require a guilty mind. These include offences such as speeding, drinking and driving, and applying a false trade description to goods. These types of crimes tend not to attract the same level of blame or culpability as offences that involve intention and are largely concerned with commerce and public welfare. To illustrate the concepts of *actus reus* and *mens rea*, it is useful to analyse the offence of theft, which is now defined by section 1 of the Theft Act 1968:

A person is guilty of theft if he dishonestly appropriates property belonging to another with the intention of permanently depriving that other of it.

It can be seen that two different elements make up the offence: first, the act of appropriating property belonging to another person; and, second, the mental element of dishonesty and the intent to permanently deprive another person. If either of these elements is missing, the offence is not committed.

Someone is guilty of murder if that person kills another person either intending to do so, or intending to cause him or her serious harm. Killing means causing the death of. So, if a person shoots someone dead, the pulling of the trigger and the consequent death constitutes the *actus reus*. The *actus reus* relates to the events and consequences. Despite the fact that someone died, the person with the gun might not be guilty of murder. In addition to the act, *mens rea* is necessary: the person who fired the gun must have intended to kill or cause really serious injury. If, for example, the gun was fired by mistake while it was being cleaned at home, or the victim was shot accidentally while straying onto a grouse moor, the person who fired the gun would not be guilty of murder: they did not have the relevant intent.

The significance of the concept of intent can be illustrated by the problem of dealing with those who take cars but abandon them after use. The takers never intended to keep the car, thus they cannot be guilty of theft, having no 'intention to permanently deprive'. Therefore, a different offence had to be created if this conduct was to be punished as a crime. The offence, now in section 12 of the Theft Act 1968, is 'taking a conveyance without the owner's consent'. This provision states:

> . . . a person shall be guilty of an offence if, without having the consent of the owner or other lawful authority, he takes any conveyance for his own or another's use or, knowing that any conveyance has been taken without authority, drives it or allows himself to be carried in or on it.

Different offences relating to similar behaviour – for example, assault – may reflect different levels of intent and seriousness of injury. This can be illustrated by examining the different crimes relating to offences of violence, the seriousness of which is determined both by the injury inflicted and the level of intention, thereby combining an assessment of *actus reus* and *mens rea* in determining culpability.

Common assault is the least serious, and can be tried only in the magistrates' court; it is punishable by up to six months' imprisonment. It is defined as the intentional or reckless causing of another to fear immediate unlawful violence. More serious is the offence of occasioning **actual bodily harm** under section 47 of the Offences Against the Person Act 1861 (OAPA 1861). This can be tried either in the magistrates' court or the Crown Court and is punishable with a maximum sentence of five years' imprisonment. It is not necessary to establish that the accused intended the kind of injury that occurred. Actual bodily harm means any physical harm.

Another offence, higher up the ladder of seriousness, although attracting the same maximum penalty, is the offence under section 20 of the OAPA 1861, of unlawfully and maliciously wounding or inflicting **grievous bodily harm**. Grievous bodily harm means really serious harm. More serious still, triable only on indictment, and attracting up to life imprisonment, is the offence under section 18 of the OAPA 1861, of malicious wounding or causing grievous bodily harm with intent to do grievous bodily harm.

The most serious offence known to the criminal law is murder, which is punishable with a mandatory life sentence. This means that once a conviction is recorded, only a life sentence can be passed by the judge. However, the law has long recognised that deaths can be caused, even intentionally, in many different circumstances, not all equally blameworthy. This is reflected in three categories of homicide: murder, **manslaughter** and infanticide. Murder is described as unlawful killing involving intention to kill or cause grievous bodily harm.

Prior to the Coroners and Justice Act 2009, murder could have been reduced to manslaughter (for which the sentence is variable) because of 'provocation' by virtue of section 3 of the Homicide Act 1957 (now abolished). This recognised that, under pressure, people may lose control, and provocation related to a 'sudden temporary loss of self-control'. This provision has been the subject of much criticism. Particularly problematic has been the situation of women who have been systematically brutalised by partners and have planned to kill them. Decisions where such women have been prosecuted have underlined the requirement that the defence of provocation will be successful only if there is a sudden explosion of emotions so that the person is temporarily out of control as a result of a particular trigger such as a remark or incident. Sara Thornton, who was prosecuted for murder, stabbed her husband while he was in a drunken stupor and did not succeed with the defence that she had been provoked. Kiranjit Ahluwalia was convicted of the murder of her husband and sentenced to life imprisonment in 1989 despite claiming she was 'provoked' by 10 years of abuse at his hands.

The defence of provocation has been replaced by a new defence, entitled 'loss of control', and the subsequent changes noted in section 54–56 of the Coroners and Justice Act 2009. In the context of domestic violence it was thought by the Law Commission that the notion of provocation is a vague notion too readily used in courts as a defence by those who kill after losing their temper, and that this should be replaced by two more specific partial defences that act to reduce the level of culpability, where a death is caused either in response to 'a fear of serious violence; and/or circumstances of an extremely grave character, giving rise to a justifiable sense of being seriously wronged'. The new provisions of the Coroners and Justice Act 2009, that came to force on 4 October 2010, provide that it will no longer matter whether the loss of control was sudden, and instead allow to run the 'slow-burn' defence in the circumstance in which a person has been subjected to a long-term abuse. Section 55 of the Act defines a number of situations (the 'qualifying triggers') which must be present for the defence of loss of control to be considered.

Murder is currently reduced to manslaughter when killing takes place as a result of diminished responsibility, defined as an abnormality of mind which impairs the mental processes, or under a suicide pact. Both these circumstances are referred to as voluntary manslaughter, where the intent was to kill but in less blameworthy circumstances. Some abused women have succeeded in arguing that they should be convicted of manslaughter rather than murder as a result of diminished responsibility brought on by the abuse. Kiranjit Ahluwalia's conviction was thus reduced to manslaughter on appeal in 1992. The Coroners and Justice Bill 2009 proposes to abolish the partial defence to murder of diminished responsibility and replace it with a defence that is based on the killer suffering from an abnormality of mental functioning which arises from a recognised medical condition or a substantially impaired mental ability.

Manslaughter includes all other forms of unlawful killing when there was a lesser degree of responsibility than that required for murder. Manslaughter is therefore committed when death results as a result of an unlawful and dangerous act – for example, any assault – and in other circumstances where neither death nor serious harm was actually intended but results from a high degree of **negligence**. Many different combinations of circumstances can be envisaged and have come before the courts: the defendants who threw a brick from a motorway bridge to deter a 'blackleg' (*R* v. *Hancock and Shankland* (1986)) and the defendant who played 'Russian Roulette' with tragic consequences for his stepfather (*R* v. *Maloney* (1985)).

The role of the law is to develop rules that reflect moral blameworthiness. But, as the following case illustrates, it is not always easy to apply these principles in cases involving the deliberate commission of a dangerous act resulting in death. In one case the Court of Appeal, seeking to clarify the application of principles, listed the kinds of situation in which this type of killing, sometimes called involuntary manslaughter, arises (*R* v. *Sulman and Others* (1993)). This particular case arose after a patient died following a negligently conducted operation. There had been negligence – did that create a criminal offence? Negligent inattention in the sense of mere inadvertence does not create criminal liability; the degree of fault has to be gross negligence, such as:

- indifference to a known risk;
- foresight of a risk which is nevertheless undertaken;
- appreciation of the risk, and an intention to avoid it, but coupled with a high degree of negligence in the attempted avoidance;
- inattention to a serious and obvious risk.

Infanticide is also recognised as a special case by the law, which provides that a different offence, less culpable than murder or manslaughter, is committed where a woman kills her child in the first year of its life, when the balance of her mind is affected by the birth.

Another situation recognised by the law is where death occurs as a result of a road accident. Legislation has taken a variety of approaches to these situations, the current position being that there are four different offences, which reflect changing public and political concerns.

It is an offence to cause death by dangerous driving or to cause death by careless driving while under the influence of drink or drugs. New offences of causing death by careless driving and causing death while driving without a licence or while uninsured were introduced in 2008. An offence introduced in the Legal Aid, Sentencing and Punishment of Offenders Act 2012 (LASPO) is that causing serious injury by dangerous driving in 2012. Dangerous driving is defined as driving at a standard far below that of a competent and careful driver and where it would be obvious to such a driver that driving in that way would be dangerous, while careless driving is at a standard below that of a competent and careful driver, and would include a driver's momentary inattention.

The introduction of new offences, and the increase in penalties available for the longer established ones, reflected public concern about cases where an otherwise relatively trivial offence resulted in death, or where those who should never have been driving at all caused a death. The offences also reflect the complex relationship between assessing the seriousness of crimes by a combination of their level of culpability and the effect of the action.

Thus culpability under the criminal law stretches from those who deliberately set out to commit criminal acts such as a planned robbery, through those who behave recklessly and cause harm, to those who have no intention at all but nevertheless are guilty of a crime of strict liability. Failure to take steps to prevent harm can result in guilt: an offence of omission. The Court of Appeal upheld the decision of North Shields magistrates' court that convicted Mark Greener under the Dangerous Dogs Act 1991 because he did not take sufficient steps to prevent his Staffordshire bull terrier from straying into a nearby garden and biting a young child's face (*Greener* v. *DPP* (1996)).

▶ Criminal defences

In criminal trials, the defence may argue that although the defendant did commit the act he or she had an excuse for so doing. These excuses reflect an acceptance that in certain circumstances the defendant could not help acting in a particular way, was somehow forced into the action, or could not control his or her behaviour and is, therefore, not to blame. The *mens rea* element of the criminal trial focuses on blameworthiness or moral culpability and the defence **counsel** may use principles of criminal defences in an attempt to show that the defendant was not responsible or blameworthy for the act he or she did indeed commit, and, therefore, not liable to punishment.

There are two categories of people who cannot be liable for criminal offences because they are not seen as responsible for their acts:

- children under the age of criminal responsibility;
- those certified as insane within a legal – rather than a medical – definition.

In the first category, children under 10 in England and Wales are, by law, deemed unable to commit offences: in other words they cannot be criminally liable. This is often referred to as being **doli incapax** (incapable of crime). The mentally ill are not held responsible in law for their actions and if they do stand trial at all will be found not guilty by reason of insanity **(see Chapter 7)**.

There are, however, other situations where, although the accused cannot escape liability because of age or mental incapacity, circumstances may provide a complete defence. If the defence applies and is accepted, the person is found not guilty. These circumstances are as follows:

- **Duress***:* where people are compelled by threats or circumstances to do something criminal. In these circumstances, although the act is deliberate and intended, the offender is regarded as not responsible for the act committed. The threat or danger must be severe – such as death or serious personal injury. This would excuse all offences other than murder and treason.
- **Automatism***:* where a person is not in control of his or her physical actions, such as during an epileptic fit.
- *Self-defence:* defendants are seen as not blameworthy and therefore not criminally liable when, in responding to another person's aggression, they cause injury (or even death) in the process of defending themselves. The scriptures might require a person to turn the other cheek; the law does not, provided that their response is in proportion to the threat to them.

In other situations, the defendant may be held less responsible or blameworthy, by relying on partial defences. A partial defence, as its name suggests, will partly exonerate the defendant. Whereas a successful complete defence means that the defendant is found not guilty of any offence at all, a partial defence means that, if successful, the defendant will be found not guilty of the major offence but guilty of a lesser offence. The situation arises only in the case of murder, where a successful defence of diminished responsibility or loss of control will result in the accused being found guilty of manslaughter rather than murder.

A situation commonly found in criminal acts is that the defendant was affected by alcohol or drugs. The mere fact of being drunk is not a defence, even although it is recognised that drinking may reduce inhibitions. It may, however, be a defence where the alcohol or drugs had the effect that the offender did not in fact form the intent required for the commission of the crime, such as murder or wounding 'with intent'.

❿ Sentencing mitigation

Even where a legal defence – which removes all blame – is not available or has not been accepted by the jury or magistrates, other factors may reduce culpability. After a defendant has been found guilty or has pleaded guilty, the defence may offer a plea in **mitigation** to the court. This will introduce factors suggesting that the seriousness of the offence is not as great as it might be, or that the offender is less blameworthy.

Mitigation may relate to the offence: that the offender played a limited part, was led into the offence by others, or that it happened almost by accident. Defendants may claim they forgot to renew a licence or their motor vehicle insurance. Mitigation might also relate to the personal circumstances of the offender. It may be argued that an offender is in such difficult circumstances that he or she should not be blamed or punished any more than has already happened because he or she might have lost his or her job or have been deserted by his or her family. If you sit in court for any length of time you might be surprised to hear the same mitigation repeated, such as the number of recently convicted people who are starting a job next week or whose girlfriend has just discovered she is pregnant. This part of the criminal process allows the convicted person the opportunity to minimise their culpability for the offence and so increase their chance of a more lenient sentence.

The court will take mitigating factors into account in passing sentence, which may mean that individual sentencing decisions are unpopular. Some sentencing decisions cause outrage and public anxiety and have been widely criticised in the press, in Parliament or on the radio and television. It is important to appreciate that members of the public may have very different perceptions of criminal responsibility from those of the court. Questions of crime and criminal responsibility generate many strong opinions and public conceptions may well conflict with legal concerns. Public views of crime are not necessarily informed by the somewhat narrow legal conceptions of culpability and blameworthiness outlined above, nor do the public always appreciate the technicalities of requirements to prove intent or to focus on the act rather than the result. Public discussion tends to be more general than legal discussion.

2.2 Legal categories of criminal offences

Objective 2

Distinguish between the different legal categories of criminal offences

Legal categories also indicate in a variety of ways the level of blame and the level of severity accorded to a particular crime. This is in part achieved by the way the crime is defined, as discussed above, partly by the maximum sentence able to be imposed by courts and partly by the procedural and organisational categories into which all offences are divided. Criminal offences are divided into three categories as follows:

* summary offences
* offences triable on indictment only
* offences triable either way, i.e. summarily or on indictment.

The latter two categories together constitute the category of **indictable** offences (i.e. offences which are capable of being tried on indictment). These divisions define the procedures and, in particular, the methods and place of trial for each type of offence. The categorisation is made by statute.

Cases **triable only on indictment** must be tried at the Crown Court. An **indictment** is the formal document used in a Crown Court trial setting out the charges against the defendant. The magistrates' court has power to hear **summary offences** and offences that are **triable either way** where a decision has been made to try them summarily, that is in the magistrates' court. In 2012, 1.66 million defendants were proceeded against in magistrates' courts, of which:

* 356,480 were indictable
* 624,540 were summary non-motoring
* 490,712 were summary motoring.

The time and place at which the alleged offence was committed can also affect where it is heard. Magistrates' courts can try only offences committed in their area and normally proceedings for summary offences must be started within six months of the commission of the offence. Indictable offences may be tried in any Crown Court and there is generally no time limit for the commencement of proceedings except in a few cases such as some Revenue and Customs offences where there is a 20-year time limit.

▶ Classification of offences: summary and indictable

Summary offences are comparatively less serious crimes. Most motoring offences are summary, including driving with excess alcohol, but there is a wide variety of other summary offences, including common assault, assaulting a police officer, and taking a motor vehicle without the owner's consent. All summary offences are made so by statute.

Generally speaking, the maximum penalty for a summary offence is six months' imprisonment or a fine or both, but many summary offences carry much lower maximum penalties, and many are not imprisonable at all. The maximum financial penalties are determined in accordance with a range of levels established by

Parliament and set out by the Sentencing Council but the former limit of £5,000 on fines issued in the magistrates' court has been abolished in LASPO 2012.

Offences triable only on indictment are very serious matters, including murder, rape, blackmail, robbery, and wounding with intent. For those convicted of murder the only sentence available to the court is life imprisonment. Maximum penalties for other offences are laid down by statute and may include a discretionary life sentence or a simple term of years. For example, 14 years is the maximum custodial penalty for blackmail and burglary of a dwelling, while 10 years is the maximum for burglary of a non-dwelling. Financial penalties for offences tried on indictment have no limit, but fines are rarely imposed for such serious offences.

Triable-either-way (TEW) offences include theft, burglary, assault occasioning actual bodily harm, and unlawful wounding. This category covers many offences where the offence's relative seriousness can vary tremendously depending on the facts. Theft, for example, includes stealing a bottle of milk from a doorstep, shoplifting and stealing from an employer. The seriousness of these matters is affected by the value of the theft and all the circumstances surrounding it, including the relationship between thief and victim.

Criminal damage is another offence where the circumstances can vary tremendously. The offence is committed when someone knowingly or recklessly inflicts damage on the property of another person and it is generally a TEW offence. However, in criminal damage cases not involving threat to life or arson, and where the value of the damage inflicted is £5,000 or less, the charge is regarded as summary with a maximum penalty of three months' custody or a £2,500 fine. When the value of the damage is over £5,000 the offence remains triable either way.

Successive Acts have attempted to reduce the number of TEW offences, in part to reduce costs and to spread the work more efficiently between the courts. An offence which was reclassified in response to changing legislative and public perceptions of seriousness was taking a vehicle without the owner's consent, an offence under section 12 of the Theft Act 1968. This, in its original form, was a TEW offence. In the Criminal Justice Act 1988 it, along with common assault and driving while disqualified, became triable in summary proceedings only. The early 1990s saw an increase in public concern about offences involving a number of widely reported incidents where such cars were used to commit robberies, or resulted in the deaths of the drivers or bystanders. Vivid newspaper reports about ramraiders fuelled political disquiet. In response Parliament created a new indictable offence, 'aggravated vehicle-taking', to cover the situation in which a car, taken without the owner's consent, was involved in an accident or crime. Changing views of what should be criminalised, and changing definitions of what is criminalised, can cloud our understanding of crime. The first problem is how to measure the amount and type of crime that is committed.

2.3 Measuring crime

Objective 3
Understand how crime is measured

We have seen above how difficult it is to define crime and establish that an offence has been committed – difficulties which also affect how crime can be measured. Before behaviour is dealt with and counted as crime, it must be considered to be 'criminal' and be brought to the attention of a law enforcer, who must then establish whether it is indeed against the criminal law and what kind of offence it is. It was pointed out in **Chapter 1** that criminal justice can be viewed as a process, with many factors affecting how an incident or a suspected offender proceeds to a criminal conviction. Official statistics reflect different stages of this process, producing different figures as cases proceed. Therefore, criminal statistics must be interpreted with considerable caution, although they are often taken as a barometer of crime from which the media, politicians and the public shape their ideas about crime. This in turn affects criminal justice policy. It is important to realise, however, that these statistics are likely to be at considerable variance with the actual incidence of crime and that all attempts to calculate the crime figure are no more than estimates. Thus the Home Office *Digest 2: Information on the Criminal Justice System in England and Wales* commented that 'no-one knows the true extent of crime in this country' (**Barclay 1995: 1**).

Recent years have seen an 'explosion' (**Maguire 2007**) of information about crime and the criminal justice system, with statistics now being routinely available on the internet, along with more detailed studies of particular kinds of crime. The main sources of information about crime include statistics based on records of crimes reported to and investigated by the police and victim, or crime surveys which ask samples of the general population about their experiences of crime. The following section will explore these sources of information and look at how they are created, what their main limitations are and how they can be best interpreted. Later sections will consider what they tell us about trends in crime, different groups of offences and information about offenders.

▶ Government statistics on crime

The government publishes many different statistics on crime and the criminal justice process, which have changed considerably in recent years. The most definitive source of official statistics is the publication *Criminal Statistics England and Wales* formerly published by the Home Office and now available on the Ministry of Justice website. From 2002, a widely used source has been the publication *Crime in England and Wales*, published annually, which incorporates information from police records and the **British Crime Survey** (BCS) which will be described below, and takes account of some of the many criticisms levelled against **criminal statistics** over the years, such as that they failed to provide any information about crime which victims did not report. Summaries, such as *Crime in England and Wales 2006/7: A Summary of the Main Figures* (available from www.homeoffice. gov.uk/rds) and supplementary information in the form of Statistical Bulletins are also published, such as the Statistical Bulletin *Crimes Detected in England and Wales, 2006/7* (**Mitchell and Babb 2007**). This follows the review of national crime statistics carried out by Professor Adrian Smith, which reported in 2006.

The official Home Office web address from which the statistics and the report on 'Crime in England and Wales' is www.gov.uk or www.ons.gov.uk (Office for National Statistics [crime survey]) and the statistics are available from www. justice.gov.uk/statistics (Ministry of Justice). From 1 April 2012, national statistics on crime, previously published by the Home Office, have been published by the Office for National Statistics.

These crime and criminal justice data sources contain extensive tables along with analyses of many facets of crime including the extent of and trends in crime and specific forms of crime that are invaluable for those interested in understanding crime and the criminal justice system in England and Wales.

Information about offenders and sentencing are now available via the Ministry of Justice whose publications include information about race and the criminal justice system; arrests; recorded crime (notifiable offences) and police powers under PACE; women and the criminal justice system; and the average time from arrest to sentence for persistent young offenders. They also include information about courts and sentencing, such as judicial and court statistics and sentencing statistics; prison and probation, such as offender management caseload statistics, details of the population in custody and statistics relating to mentally disordered offenders along with figures relating to the reoffending of adults and juveniles.

Information about offenders is also gathered in the Home Office's Offender Index.

Taken together, all of these statistics contain a wealth of information about the number and kinds of offences and offenders dealt with by the police and the courts. Full details of statistics published both by the Home Office and the Ministry of Justice can be found on their websites, and include:

- numbers of offences recorded by the police, along with breakdowns of different groups of offences such as violent offences, sexual offences and property crime;
- increases and decreases in these categories;
- comparisons with information from the Crime Survey for England and Wales ([CSEW]; formerly British Crime Survey [BCS]);
- information about 'repeat victimisation';
- public perceptions of crime;
- geographic patterns of recorded crime.

Official statistics refer to many different categories of offences. The main statistics refer to **notifiable offences** recorded by the police. This covers most serious crimes including indictable offences, along with some summary offences. While notifiable offences are often seen as inherently more serious, legal categories may hide the real level of seriousness. For example, many indictable offences involve relatively small sums of money or damage, whereas some summary offences – such as, for example, driving after consuming alcohol or drugs – are counted as relatively serious (**Maguire 2007**). Considerations such as this have led to periodic changes in which offences are considered to be notifiable – leading, for example, to the inclusion in 1997 and 1998 of some summary offences (e.g. common assault and assault on a constable), which increased the number of offences in the category of violence against the person and produced an apparent increase in 'violent crime' (ibid.).

The criminal statistics bring together data from many agencies including the 43 police forces, and they provide much detailed information about crime and the activities of the criminal justice agencies. Nevertheless, many offences are not included. They omit, for example, offences recorded by police forces outside the ambit of the Home Office, such as the British Transport Police, the Ministry of Defence Police and the UK Atomic Energy Authority Police. Many other offences are dealt with by agencies other than the police, some of whom may not prosecute some offences where they feel that there are more appropriate courses of action. Thus, HM Revenue & Customs and the Department for Work and Pensions (formerly DSS) deal with a variety of offences, many of which are not prosecuted, as do the many regulatory agencies involved with public health, pollution or trading standards offences. Many of these are summary offences and statistics are less readily available.

In addition, many potential offences may not be perceived by those involved as criminal or reported to the police. Some kinds of offences are less likely to come to the attention of the police than others, including the following:

- Offences which are not often brought to the attention of the police by the victim, including those offences which take place in private – for example, domestic violence, sexual offences and some offences in the workplace.

- Offences with no discernible victim, often called victimless crimes – for example, prostitution, pornography, illegal gambling or drug abuse. These involve an exchange of illegal commodities between consumers and suppliers who are unlikely to report themselves to the police.

- Offences where victims are unaware that they have been a victim of a crime. Many frauds, for example, depend on victims not noticing that they have been defrauded. Other offences, such as the failure of businesses to comply with health, safety or environmental regulations, involve dangers which cannot readily be detected.

Many offences are not included in the criminal statistics. Criminologists have long recognised that there is a large **hidden or 'dark figure' of crime** and that official crime rates reflect only those crimes reported to the police. Variations in crime rates, therefore, could be the result, not of differences between the real rates of offending, but of variations in reporting.

Even when crimes are reported to the police, they may not subsequently be recorded and counted as crimes 'known to the police'. In some cases the police may decide to take 'no further action' or decide that 'no crime' has been committed. This may happen, for example, where police are called to an incident such as a pub brawl and resolve it without arresting or charging someone, or where items are reported missing but it is unclear whether they are lost or stolen. Police have a high amount of discretion, as will be seen in **Chapter 6**, and not all incidents reported to them are considered as 'crimes' or worth recording or investigating as such. In addition, different police organisations may use different recording practices. Changes in reporting and recording practices can produce apparent increases in different kinds of crime.

In an attempt to systematise how the police record crime a National Crime Recording Standard (NCRS) was introduced in April 2002, which effectively asks the police to take at face value what a person reports (**Maguire 2007**). This had the effect of increasing the figures for some kinds of crime, making rises and falls difficult to interpret, although they have been taken account of in estimates of crime trends (see, e.g., **Simmons and Dodd 2003**).

Statistics relating to offenders also have limitations. Many offenders escape detection as the police clear up only a proportion of crimes reported. Some crimes are easier to detect than others, which accounts for variations by offence in the clear-up rates given in the statistics. For example, many victims of assault know their assailant, leading to almost automatic clear-up. If a fraud is discovered its perpetrator may be self-evident. In total, the proportion of recorded crimes cleared up in 2007/8 by what is described as a 'sanctioned detection' was 28 per cent compared with 26 per cent in 2006/7 (**Babb and Ogunbor 2008**). The proportion of offenders detected becomes even smaller when the large volume of unreported crimes is taken into account. Thus, only a small proportion of offenders are caught or brought to court.

To provide a clearer picture of crime and improve data presentation, from April 2013 a number of changes have been made to the presentation of data:

- Fraud offences are separated from other recorded crimes. Fraud data is now recorded by Action Fraud, a national reporting centre that records incidents from the public and organisations.

- Victim and victimless crimes: Separating the recorded crime into two broad categories – offences with a specific identifiable victim referred to as 'victim-based crime' and **crimes without a direct victim** referred to as 'other crimes against society'.

- A new Theft offences category, which brings together offences such as burglary, theft from a person and shoplifting under one single category.

We know from the data that the majority of offences are not cleared up and even when there is a known suspect the police or the Crown Prosecution Service may decide not to proceed with a case. The police have discretion and may decide to take no further action, to caution offenders rather than bring a formal charge, not to proceed with the case because they consider they have insufficient evidence, or to proceed with the case and pass the papers on to the Crown Prosecution Service.

The way in which clear-up rates are calculated changed in an attempt to produce greater consistency, and figures are now given for numbers of 'sanction' detections (detections which have criminal justice outcomes) and 'non-sanction' detections (covering cases which have been cleared up but in which no further action is taken because, for example, the offender is ill, the victim refuses or is unable to give evidence or the offender is under the age of criminal responsibility) (**Mitchell and Babb 2007**).

In effect, therefore, official statistics tell us which crimes the public choose to report and how those crimes are dealt with by the police. The data produced by the police will tell us as much about the method of policing as it does about the amount of crime. The report on the first British Crime Survey commented that:

> Variations over time or place in recorded crime rates can reflect the processes by which the statistics are compiled as much as the condition they are intended to depict.
>
> (Hough and Mayhew 1983)

This is illustrated in Table 2.1 and Figures 2.1 and 2.2, showing the drop in numbers at each stage of the process. Figure 2.1 illustrates the large gap between recorded and detected crime, the number of persons proceeded against and the number of offenders found guilty or cautioned for indictable offences. The steep rise in recorded offences is shown in the graphs from 1950 to 2000, and the subsequent drop in the last few years, which will be discussed later in the chapter. Finally, the statistics may tell us about the numbers of different offences reported to the police, but little about how serious these offences are or the situations in which they occur. Many offence groups include vastly different kinds of offences. Thus, categories of theft include very minor thefts along with serious ones, and frauds may involve very trifling sums or millions of pounds. In addition, as Maguire points out, a long-standing criticism of official statistics is that they cannot indicate changing patterns of crime – there may, for example, be changes in the kinds of typical thefts or robberies which are not reflected in broad classifications (**Maguire 2007**). More information about these kinds of issues can be found in crime surveys, which will be described below. Figure 2.1 is an example of an 'Attrition Table' that shows the flows through the system and how the numbers decline at each stage of the process.

❭ Crime Survey for England and Wales (previously the British Crime Survey)

One way of finding out more about crime is to ask the public what kinds of crime they have been the victims of and whether or not they have reported this to the police. This is done in what are called **victim surveys** such as the Crime Survey for England and Wales ([CSEW]; formerly British Crime Survey [BCS]) which was first carried out in 1981. This survey has become a regular feature of the criminological scene, with further surveys during the 1980s and 1990s; and since 2001/2 surveys have been annual, with upwards of 40,000 interviews of people aged 16 or over taking place each year. The survey relates only to England and Wales and since 1 April 2012 is known as the Crime Survey for England and Wales (CSEW) to better reflect its geographical coverage. Separate surveys have been carried out in Scotland and Northern Ireland. Respondents are selected randomly and asked how often they have been a victim of a specific offence in a specified time period. The scope of the questionnaire is extensive, with around 200 questions to elicit information on many aspects of crime, including the following:

• what kinds of crime people have been victims of;
• what proportions of these offences are reported to the police;
• why some offences are not reported;
• what kinds of crime people are most worried about.

Since 2009, interviews have included children. The sample size includes 35,000 aged over 16, and 3,100 children aged 10 to 15 years.

The information obtained can be compared with police statistics to ascertain the difference between crimes known to the police and those experienced by victims. This data can be charted over time to give a more accurate picture of crime trends. Thus the survey estimated that the crime rate in the 1980s rose at a

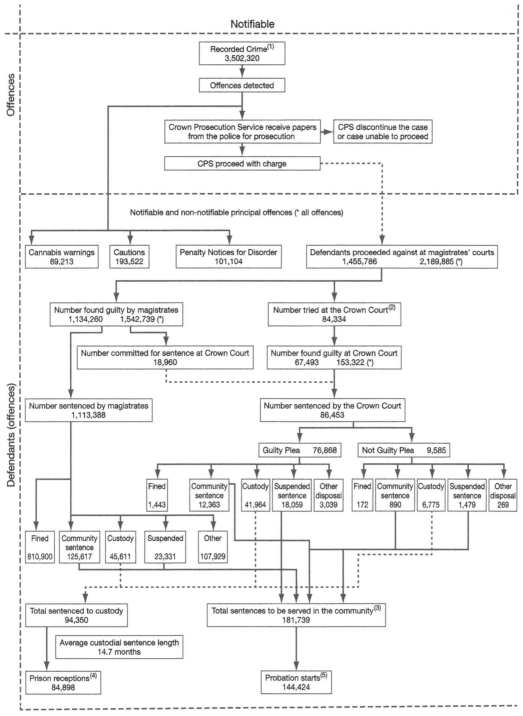

Figure 2.1 Flows through the criminal justice system, 12 months ending March 2013

(1) Covers all indictable offences, including triable either way, plus a few closely associated summary offences.
(2) Defendants tried at the Crown Court in a given year may have been committed for trial by a magistrate in a previous year.
(3) Includes community sentences and suspended sentence orders.
(4) Receptions for offenders given a custodial sentence (figures include fine defaulters).
(5) Offenders starting Community Order or Suspended Sentence Order supervision by the Probatin Service.
* Total number of all offences in comparison with the total number of defendants on a principal offence basis.

Source: Criminal Justice Statistics, Quarterly Update to March 2013 England and Wales Ministry of Justice. Statistics Bulletin. Published 22 August 2013, Figure 7

slower rate than that suggested by recorded police statistics. Between 1981 and 1991, for the subset of crimes covered by the BCS, the police recorded a 96 per cent increase in crime, in contrast to a 49 per cent increase reported in the survey. However, between 1991 and 1993, the British Crime Survey indicated an 18 per cent rise in crime compared with a 7 per cent increase recorded by the police, and between 1993 and 1995 recorded crime fell by 8 per cent, whereas BCS figures for equivalent offences rose by 2 per cent (**Home Office 1994; Mirrlees-Black *et al.* 1996**). Nonetheless, while the overall trends suggested by the two sources of information remained the same, there have been divergences, particularly in relation to violent crime, since the mid-1990s (**Maguire 2007; Newburn 2007**). These, which are related to the changes in the 'counting rules' referred to above, will be discussed below.

High rates of reporting car theft and burglary reflect the higher losses typical of these kinds of crime along with the need for victims to report these offences for insurance purposes. The main reason why victims do not report a crime to the police is that they consider the incident to be too trivial, and in many cases there is no loss. In addition victims often feel that the police cannot do much about it. These reasons accounted for 72 per cent of cases in 2006/7 with a further 16 per cent considering that the incident was a private matter which they would deal with themselves (**Nicholas *et al.* 2007**).

Crime surveys can also provide information about which kinds of crime people are most worried about, and about the risks of victimisation for different groups such as the young and ethnic minorities and how these risks vary by neighbourhood. The surveys can thus capture information on aspects of crime which escape official attention and indicate the types of crime that give the public most concern.

While producing much valuable information, the survey has important limitations. It includes only private households and therefore does not include crimes committed in organisations and businesses (such as shoplifting and theft by employees) and thus greatly underestimates the amount of theft committed. Many of the offences or incidents reported to the interviewers do not conform easily to legal classifications of crime, creating difficulties when comparing with police statistics. For example, if someone reports an assault, how is it to be classified? Respondents' information may be inaccurate. They may forget some incidents or exaggerate others. In some circumstances they may be unwilling to reveal to interviewers offences that cause them embarrassment. Respondents may

Table 2.1 Proportion of incidents reported to the police

Theft of vehicle	94%
Burglary with loss	81%
Robbery	55%
Bicycle theft	44%
Theft from vehicle	38%
Wounding	65%
Common assault	33%
Theft from the person	32%
Vandalism	34%

Source: Crime Survey for England and Wales 2011/12

misunderstand a question or the meaning of a word. Victim surveys cannot cover crimes of which victims are unaware, such as consumer fraud or those which have no direct victims – for example, drug offences. Some groups, such as the homeless, are less likely to be on the personal address files which are the basis of the sample. Despite these limitations, however, the CSEW has become an invaluable source of information about the extent of some crimes.

2.4 Crime trends

Objective 4

Describe and explain crime trends

What can be deduced from these official sources of data about crime? A major question of interest to governments, the media and the public alike has been whether crime can be said to have 'risen' or fallen in any given period of time. Any estimates have, however, to be treated with caution bearing in mind variations in reporting and recording practices. Analysis is also dependent on which years are taken for comparison (**Maguire 2007**).

Between 1876 and 1920, the annual recorded figure that was stable at around 100,000 recorded crimes a year. There was a dramatic rise in recorded crime from 1950 to 2003/4, from 0.5 million offences a year to 6 million, in recent years, there has been a steady decline to 3.7 million recorded offences in 2012/13.

While in general the BCS and more recently the CSEW indicate a much higher rate of crime than police figures, it also suggests that increases in crime have been less dramatic than these figures suggest – **Maguire (2002)**, for example, points out that for the sub-set of offences which are comparable between the BCS and police figures, BCS figures showed a less steep increase. Between 1981 and 1991 for example, recorded crime increased by 78 per cent, whereas those reported to the BCS rose by only 37 per cent. The surveys showed that the level of offending for some crimes peaked in the mid-1990s and has been followed by falls since that period, suggesting, for example, a 44 per cent decrease between 1995 and 2005/6 (**Maguire 2007**) and a 25 per cent decrease between 2001/2 and 2011/12. Crime figures indicate an increase of 9 per cent over this period – which has become the subject of considerable debate. While some of these increases can be explained by the counting changes referred to above, some discrepancies remain. While both sets of figures show a decline in burglary, differences are greater for violent crime which rose for 2002/03 by 2 per cent even after taking account of the effects of recording changes (**Simmons and Dodd 2003**). In April 2004 the police recorded crime statistics showed that the serious violent crimes of homicide and serious wounding rose by 13 per cent between the last quarter of 2002 and the same period in 2003. The BCS showed that the category of robbery increased by 28 per cent in 2001/2 (Home Office, *Crime in England and Wales 2001/2*: 47). Further rises took place up to 2005/6, which according to the Home Office, were largely due to counting changes and other extraneous factors such as increased reporting on the part of victims and more accurate police recording. Others argue, however, that this, along with the clear preference shown for the BCS figures by the Home Office and their combination in publications such as *Crime in England and Wales*, can amount to political 'explaining away' of rises in violent crime (**Maguire 2007;**

Number of offences (000s)

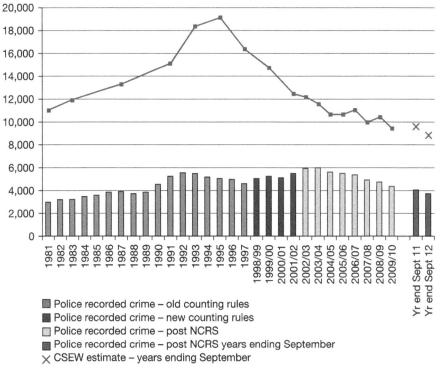

Police recorded crime – old counting rules
Police recorded crime – new counting rules
Police recorded crime – post NCRS
Police recorded crime – post NCRS years ending September
× CSEW estimate – years ending September

Figure 2.2 Trends in police recorded crime and CSEW, 1981 to year ending September 2012

Source: Crime in England and Wales, year ending September 2012. Statistical Bulletin Office for National Statistics: London. 24 January 2013, page 3

Newburn 2007). It is apparent, therefore, that it is not always accurate to speak in terms of 'the (single) crime trend', as trends may be crime-specific and subject to very different and contested interpretations.

A number of considerations thus have to be borne in mind when interpreting overall rises and falls in crime rates. Taking the twentieth century as a whole, the population itself has grown and a less dramatic growth in crime rates is indicated when population figures are taken into account. Methods of recording crime have also changed, as have categories and definitions of crime, with new crimes emerging. Furthermore, the Home Office has helped to promote more reliable and consistent data collection methods. Crime statistics may also be affected by the growth of the police – if there are more police to record and investigate crime, this will produce higher rates of recorded crime.

Changes in the crime rate can also be affected by wider changes in society as a whole. For example, mass car ownership in the twentieth century resulted in the creation of new offences, such as careless or dangerous driving, along with driving without a licence or insurance. Motor cars parked in streets have created many opportunities for theft, both of the cars themselves and of accessories such as radios and spare parts. In 1997, vehicle crime accounted for around one-quarter of all notifiable crimes recorded by the police. Economic factors such as rising unemployment, a growth in casual employment and a decline in manufacturing industries have had a major impact on society and, many argue, on patterns of crime. More recent years have seen the growth of new offences related to consumerism such as fraudulent use of credit cards and theft of mobile phones. It is therefore important to consider different kinds of crime, rather than looking at crime as a whole.

Crimes of the century

Recorded crime

During the first two decades of the twentieth century the police in England and Wales recorded an average of 90,000 indictable offences each year, a figure which increased to over 500,000 during the 1950s.

The crime rate consequently quadrupled from 250 crimes per 100,000 people in 1901 to 1,000 by 1950.

But the history of crime in the twentieth century is dominated by the even sharper rise in offences recorded by the police since the late 1950s. During the 1960s there was acceleration in recorded crime: it was the only decade in the century where crime doubled. Crime continued to rise according to this measure for much of the remainder of the twentieth century, with an average of over one million crimes recorded each year in the 1960s, increasing to two million during the 1970s, and 3.5 million in the 1980s.

There is no simple answer as to why crime rates increased so markedly in the second half of the century. Over the period, there were significant changes to the types of offences recorded as crime, and how they are counted, making it difficult to accurately assess underlying trends in 'real' crime. Recorded crime levels have also been affected by the behaviour of the public in reporting crimes to the police. An increase in the number of burglaries reported, for example, may partly be due to the relatively recent need to inform the police in order to make an insurance claim, rather than an indication of any real increase in the level of burglary.

New inventions, creating new opportunities for misdemeanour, a growth in the value of ordinary people's personal property, and the criminalisation of drug use have had real effects on crime levels during the twentieth century. The most obvious example of an invention that has spurred crime is the motorcar: by 1991, a car was being reported stolen on average once every minute across England and Wales. Aeroplanes made international transport and smuggling easier, while the growing use of computers has created new kinds of offences.

The puzzle for today's criminologists is to explain falling crime. Recorded offences reached six million in 2003, and a steady decline has since been seen in most kinds of recorded crime, with particularly steep falls in some offences such as burglary. Some argue that improvements in security, particularly modern systems to prevent vehicle intrusion, have significantly reduced the opportunities for committing crime. Others contend that imprisonment, policing or demographic factors play the most important role.

Figure 2.3 shows recorded offences per 100,000 people in England and Wales during the twentieth century.

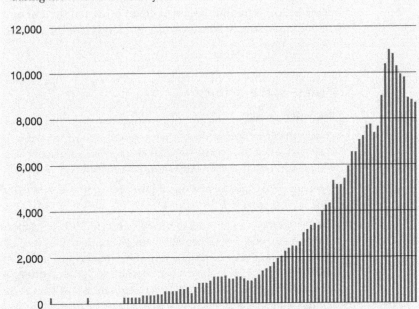

Figure 2.3 Recorded offences per 100,000 people in England and Wales during the twentieth century

Source: Gavin Thompson, Oliver Hawkins, Aliyah Dar, Mark Taylor *et al.* (2012) *Olympic Britain: Social and Economic change since the 1908 and 1948 London Games,* House of Commons Library

2.5 Types of offence

Objective 5

Describe different types of criminal offences

Looking at different kinds of crime can correct some of the misleading images which result from the tendency of the press, for example, to focus on more dramatic and newsworthy offences. Table 2.2 indicates the percentages of different kinds of crime recorded by the police in 2011/12. This illustrates that violent crime, which includes sexual offences, often represented as a major crime problem, accounts for a relatively small proportion of the total, with property crime including different kinds of theft, vehicle crime and burglary dominating the figures. Some of these categories will be explored below.

❱ Violent crime

Violent crime, which usually includes violence against the person from minor assaults up to murder and sexual crimes and robbery, accounted for 19 per cent of recorded crime in 2011/12. As seen above, there were increases in reported violent

Table 2.2 Police recorded crime by type of crime, 2011/12

Burglary	13%
Offences against vehicles	10%
Other thefts	28%
Fraud and forgery	4%
Violence against the person	19%
Drug offences	6%
Sexual offences	1%

Police recorded crime 2013. Available from: https://www.gov.uk/government/publications/police-recorded-crime-open-data-tables

crime up to a peak in the mid-1990s, since when BCS figures, on which there is an increasing reliance, show a consistent overall decline, while recorded crime figures show an increase in some forms of violent crime (**Jansson** *et al.* **2007**). Of the violent offences reported to the most recent CSEW in 2011/12, just over half (56 per cent) did not result in any injury and an overwhelming majority consisted of the least serious grouping of violent crime – indicating that much of what is counted as violent crime is not as serious as often imagined. Some features of the main categories of violent offences are summarised below.

Homicide

A general category covering the offences of murder, manslaughter and infanticide, and attracting a lot of public attention. Many of the most notorious criminal incidents that enter public consciousness relate to horrific cases, often involving multiple or child killings, such as the Moors murderers Ian Brady and Myra Hindley, Peter Sutcliffe (the Yorkshire Ripper) and Frederick West, the Gloucester builder who committed suicide in prison in 1995 while awaiting trial for the murder of 12 people. The case of Harold Shipman, the Manchester doctor who was found to have killed hundreds of his elderly patients, had a major effect on homicide figures; and the murder of Holly Wells and Jessica Chapman in Soham in April 2003, and the subsequent trial and conviction of Ian Huntley in December that year, dominated the media, with some papers offering 'pull-out supplements' once the case had been completed. Stranger murders of children are relatively rare, however, and children under the age of one are most at risk of being killed by their parents (**Newburn 2007**). In many homicides relatives and acquaintances rather than strangers kill each other – of 4,123 homicides in England and Wales between 1997 and 2001, 1,287 or 31 per cent could be classified as 'domestic', involving parents and children and current or former spouses and lovers along with sexual rivals (**Brookman 2005**). A further 22 per cent were classified as 'confrontational homicides' occurring through fighting, and males are more likely to be the victims of all homicides – 70 per cent between 1997 and 2001.

Individual incidents may have a significant effect on these figures. A total of 1,048 deaths were initially recorded as homicide in 2002/3, with 172 being victims of Harold Shipman – following the official inquiry a number of deaths not initially recorded as homicide were entered as homicides during 2002/3. Although not all the murders were carried out in 2002/3 the statistics are based on the year that the offence is recorded rather than when it was committed. Once these are accounted for there was no significant increase in the number of homicides (**Povey and Allan 2003**). A total of 532 homicides were recorded in 2012/13, the smallest in a decade. Deaths caused by terrorist bombings are also included in this category, with the figures for 2005/6 including the 52 victims of the London bombings of 7 July 2005.

Domestic violence

In the 2001 BCS, 4 per cent of women surveyed reported domestic violence compared with 2 per cent of men (**Walby and Allen 2004**), and domestic violence remains the only category of violence for which women have a higher risk than men (0.6 per cent in 2006/7 for women compared to 0.3 per cent for men), although overall rates have been showing a consistent decline (**Jansson *et al.* 2007**). More difficult to calculate is the number of children and the elderly who are also affected by violence in the home.

Assaults

The picture which has emerged from victim and crime surveys is that many reported assaults take place in and around leisure sites such as pubs and clubs, with the category of officially recorded assaults dominated by fights, largely between young men, who form the highest risk category. Thus young men between 16 and 24 are most at risk of violence, and people who visit pubs or wine bars more than once a week are at higher risk of violent crime (6 per cent) than those who visit such places less than once a week or not at all (2.2 per cent). Single people are more at risk – particularly of stranger and acquaintance violence.

Figures for assault have undergone some reporting changes, with violent offences being divided so that 'most serious violence against the person' is distinguished from assaults without injury and less serious wounding. The most serious violence category includes murder, serious wounding and other acts endangering life, representing 1 per cent of all violent offences. CSEW figures for 2011/12 show that 24 per cent of reported violence involved wounding, 21 per cent involved assaults with minor injury and 42 per cent involved no injury – figures which show no significant changes since 2010/11.

While small in proportion to other forms of recorded crime, it is important to recognise that many violent incidents are not recorded, particularly where victims and offenders know each other – only one-third of domestic violent offences reported to the BCS in 1995 were reported to the police compared with two-thirds of muggings (**Mirrlees-Black *et al.* 1996**). In addition, while many violent incidents do not result in injury, threats of violence and harassment, where no actual assault takes place, can for some people be more psychologically damaging than occasional incidents of actual violence. This might happen particularly within families, among neighbours or with persistent racial harassment which may involve verbal abuse, threats of violence, vandalism and daubing racist slogans on the homes or businesses of members of minority ethnic groups. To the catalogue of violence could also be added 'road rage' and threatening or aggressive driving.

▶ Sexual offences

The offences recorded by the police in this category include those defined as most serious sexual crime which includes rape, sexual assault and unlawful sexual intercourse with a person under 16. The category of 'other sexual offences' includes soliciting, exploitation of prostitution and other unlawful sexual activity between consenting adults. In 2011/12, a total of 53,664 most serious sexual offences were recorded by the police, which represented a fall of 5 per cent from the previous year. Rape of a female constituted 14,767 of these offences, an increase of 2 per cent from a previous year and 15 per cent since 2006/7. There were 1,276 male rapes recorded.

Many victims and offenders are known to each other – one survey carried out by the Home Office found that nearly two-thirds of rapes, three-quarters of indecent assaults on males and two-thirds on females involved family members. About one-quarter of rapes involved strangers, with one-third involving spouses, lovers, parents and other family members and another one-third involving acquaintances (**Watson 1996**). As seen above, women outnumber men as victims – one BCS estimate suggests that 17 per cent of women compared with 2 per cent of men have been sexually assaulted at least once since they were 16 with 4 per cent of women having been raped and 1 per cent having experienced a form of serious sexual assault (**Walby and Allen 2004**).

In 2012 and 2013 a number of allegations were made of past sexual misconduct of BBC disc jockeys and employees, included allegations relating to the 1960s and 1970s involving sexual assaults against females and children. The most prominent allegations were made against Jimmy Savile, who was dead by then, but others were sent to trial including Dave Lee Travis. Other media celebrities were sent to trial and acquitted. William Roache, the *Coronation Street* actor was acquitted of rape and sexual assault charges brought by five women.

▶ Property crime

As seen in Table 2.2, property crime dominates officially recorded crime. The general category of property crime includes criminal damage and vandalism, which accounts for around 70 per cent of the total of crimes recorded by the police, and what is now described as 'acquisitive crime', which covers all household crime where items are stolen such as burglary, vehicle-related thefts, thefts from/in dwellings and bicycle thefts (**Taylor *et al.* 2007**). Overall, recent figures confirm that there has been a fall in all forms of property crime since the peak of the mid-1990s. Theft, which together with handling stolen goods accounts for around half of all recorded crimes, includes shoplifting, theft by an employee and theft from the person – many of which may involve relatively trivial amounts although their total cost is considerable. Property crimes also include burglary, vehicle theft and fraud and forgery.

Burglary

The CSEW estimated that 2.6 per cent of households in 2012/13 experienced an actual or attempted burglary. There has been some change in the most common items stolen. In 1995 these were jewellery, video equipment and cash (**Mirrlees-Black** *et al.* 1996), whereas the 2002/3 BCS indicated an increase in burglaries of computer equipment and bags, credit cards and mobile phones (**Simmons and Dodd 2003**). Risks of burglary vary, with having security measures in place being strongly related to lower levels of victimisation (**Taylor** *et al.* 2007).

Vehicle theft

This category includes thefts of, and thefts from, cars. Thefts from cars, which include the theft of external items such as wheels and badges and the theft of audio equipment, account for the largest proportion in this category. Thefts of cars include so-called joyriding and thefts of cars for economic gain – with the latter having been estimated to have risen in the early 1990s (**Webb and Laycock 1992**). There has, however, been a consistent decrease in vehicle-related theft since 1997 (**Taylor** *et al.* 2007).

Fraud and forgery

This accounts for around 3 per cent of recorded crime, although it is generally assumed to be undercounted – many frauds are not detected by victims and data is collected from different sources such as the police and financial institutions, who use different methods of counting (**Taylor** *et al.* 2007; **Levi** *et al.* 2007). Particularly wide disparities are evident in relation to credit card fraud where the UK Payments Association records much higher figures than the frauds recorded by the police. This constitutes the largest category of recorded frauds, with the BCS estimating that 4 per cent of 'plastic card' users were a victim in the previous 12 months, although much business and financial fraud is either not detected or dealt with by agencies other than the police. Much public concern has surrounded so-called identity fraud, which is however very difficult to measure. According to the BCS, 2 per cent of adults reported the use of their personal details without their consent – although many more may be unaware of this offence (**Taylor** *et al.* 2007).

▶ Organised and white-collar crime

Any snapshot of recorded crime must also acknowledge the extent of many forms of crime which are less likely to appear in official statistics. These include organised and **white-collar crime** – sometimes referred to as 'economic' or 'business' crime. Taken together, these kinds of crime would add enormously to the extent and impact of officially recorded offences, as the following examples indicate:

- *Professional and organised crime.* In contrast to one-off, occasional and opportunistic crimes the term 'professional and organised' refers to the structured and businesslike approach of those involved, for example, in local and global businesses involving drugs, money laundering and a host of illegal enterprises (**Levi** *et al.* 2007). Thus, **organised crime** involves the sale of illegitimate goods and services or the illegal sale of otherwise legitimate goods in order, for example, to avoid revenue: there are major trades, for instance, in 'bootleg' or 'contraband' cigarettes and alcohol. Other illegal trades, many of them global, involve dealing in arms, pornography, gambling, art works, protected wildlife, stolen goods, 'people trafficking' (the transportation of illegal immigrants), 'sex trafficking' and the manufacture of counterfeit goods such as designer clothes, sports equipment, audio and video cassettes. Often these are fuelled by the need to launder or disguise the profits of illegal activities.

* *White-collar and corporate crime.* In contrast to the category above, these crimes are committed by people already engaged in legitimate enterprises in business or the professions who use their position to commit offences such as financial or pensions frauds. The collapse of major international corporations such as Enron and Worldcom amidst revelations of a host of fraudulent business practices and the association of major household names in pensions 'mis-selling' have recently highlighted these kinds of offences. These crimes can also affect the public service: the Healthcare Financial Management Association, for example, once estimated that 'tens of millions of pounds are being lost by prescriptions frauds and false claims of payment by doctors, dentists, pharmacists and opticians' (*The Guardian*, **24 June 1997: 8**). Frauds on the European Union are also said to be widespread, and to involve both legitimate and illegitimate business enterprises. While it is notoriously difficult to estimate the extent of these kinds of crime, many argue that, if known, their cost would far outstrip the costs of burglaries, robberies and other forms of property crime (**Croall 2001**). The category of corporate crime also includes breaches of health, safety and consumer legislation on the part of companies which, while such offences may endanger and on occasion take lives, are not included as notifiable offences. Information about these is less readily available in the criminal statistics but can be obtained on the websites of enforcement agencies such as the Health and Safety Executive or the Environment Agency.

▶ Offenders

The Criminal Statistics give details of the age and gender of offenders found guilty of or cautioned for offences. Young men tend to dominate the figures. It should also be borne in mind that many young offenders caught for the first time may not be formally cautioned, but are given an informal warning and that 'young offender crime' such as vandalism and criminal damage is considerably under-reported. The 'gender gap' between male and female offenders has been a consistent feature of the statistics, not only in England and Wales but across Europe and America. Female offenders also show a different pattern of offending, being less involved in violent offences and proportionately more involved in theft. While it has been argued that some of this difference could be due to a greater reluctance on the part of criminal justice agencies to take action against girls or women, most now accept that girls and women do commit fewer offences than boys and men.

Statistics do not give breakdowns of offenders by ethnic groups, and information on this matter is somewhat inconclusive, having been gathered by a number of different research studies using only partial information. Broadly speaking, figures indicate that black people tend to be arrested, convicted and imprisoned in higher proportions than would be expected from their overall representation in the population (**Bowling and Phillips 2007**). However, these figures are extremely difficult to interpret and could be affected by a variety of factors. For example, black people tend to be more concentrated in areas where more street crime occurs, and, compared to the white population, the black population has higher proportions of young people, who, as we have seen, feature prominently as offenders. Thus it might be expected that higher proportions of black youths would appear as offenders although many argue that there is also discrimination against black people at different stages in the criminal justice process (**see, for example, Chapter 6**).

These breakdowns may, of course, be affected by unreported crime. Fewer offences of domestic violence, fraud and white-collar and organised crime are likely to be reported or detected, so it could be argued that males over 21 are under-represented in the statistics. Although the majority of convicted offenders are from lower socio-economic backgrounds, the relative absence of white-collar offenders from reported crime means that we cannot necessarily conclude that the majority of offences are committed by lower class individuals. On the other hand, acts of vandalism are estimated to be one of the least reported offences and, as seen above, many young people may be dealt with informally or diverted from the system (**see also Chapter 8**).

Conclusion

This chapter has explored many dimensions of crime. We have identified the three interrelated elements that are vital to understand crime: behaviour, rules and their enforcement. The legal conception of crime defined in terms of *actus reus* and *mens rea* focuses on the need of the criminal justice system to establish the blame or degree of blame with respect to behaviour either proscribed or required by the criminal law. Hence the importance of criminal defences such as self-defence or duress which might absolve a person of an act otherwise deemed criminal, and the mitigation statements put forward for those convicted in order to diminish their culpability for an offence. The different legal categories of crime have been explored and we have also seen that everyday conceptions of crime may differ from legal definitions, affecting which behaviour people consider to be 'criminal' and that what is legally a crime changes over time.

This means that crime is a concept subject to change and ambiguity and the second part of the chapter has indicated that it is also not easy to measure with precision. The vast amount of information now available about crime based on police statistics and victim surveys can give only a partial picture of the real extent of crime. In effect it may tell us more about what the public define as crime and what the police and other agencies choose to process.

Exploring how these statistics are created has several implications for a consideration of criminal justice agencies and policy. In the first place, it shows that the actions of the public and the police have an important impact on the crime figures. It is therefore important, in examining the role of criminal justice agencies, also to examine how they contribute to overall estimates of the extent of crime and how offenders are selected for subsequent stages. There is considerable discretion at all stages in the process. In addition, the public can be affected by the images of crime portrayed in the media. If, for example, they learn that there has been an increase in a particular kind of crime, they may be more likely to report it. They may come to be more afraid of this kind of crime and take action to prevent it.

The analysis of crime figures also shows that public pressure and policy may be directed against a limited and atypical group of crimes – those which receive most attention in the media. Many offences are relatively trivial; many more never reach the attention of the police and many offenders remain undetected. Therefore those going through the criminal justice system may be a small and unrepresentative group of offenders. This raises important questions in relation to the role of criminal justice. How far can it seek to prevent crime, when it deals with only a proportion of those who commit it? A common response to a **moral panic** or a seeming spate of offences reported in the media is often to institute tougher penalties. However, if so many offenders remain undetected, how effective are these strategies likely to be? Should the system not focus on attempting to catch more offenders rather than punishing the ones that are caught? Or should it aim to do both? How much can sentencing policy really affect the volume of crime? These considerations underlie the current emphasis on crime prevention. The impact that sentencing makes on crime is discussed in **Chapters 12** and **13** and depends on whether it can deter some criminals, incapacitate others or rehabilitate those capable of change.

However, the criminal justice system exists not only to reduce crime – from the 'just deserts' and denunciatory perspectives it is important to punish wrongdoers regardless of their numbers. This directs us to the harm which crime causes. So far we have examined crime as an objective, definable, measurable concept but have not yet considered its impact on those most specifically affected: the victims. The impact on individuals is the focus of the next chapter.

Review questions

1. How would you define a criminal?

2. List the ways in which the criminal law reflects a concern with blameworthiness.

3. List the factors involved in the process of attrition charted in Figure 2.1.

4. Explain the main difficulties in assessing crime trends.

Discussion questions

1. Discuss the factors which might explain why men are convicted of more offences than women and young offenders are convicted in different proportions from adults.

2. See also Appendix 1, Practical Exercises 1 and 2.

Further reading

Babb P and Ogunbor I (2008) 'Detection of crime' in Kershaw C *et al.* (eds) *Crime in England and Wales 2007/8*, Home Office: London

ONS (2013) *Crime in England and Wales, year ending September 2012.* Statistical Bulletin Office for National Statistics: London

Coleman C and Moynihan J (1996) *Understanding Crime Data: Haunted by the Dark Figure*, Open University Press: Buckingham

Croall H (1998) *Crime and Society in Britain*, Longman: London

Kershaw C *et al.* (eds) (2008) *Crime in England and Wales 2007/8*, Home Office: London

Maguire M (2007) 'Crime Data and Statistics', in Maguire M, Morgan R and Reiner R (eds) *The Oxford Handbook of Criminology* (4th edn), Clarendon Press: Oxford

Mitchell, H and Babb, P (2007) *Crimes Detected in England and Wales 2006/7*, Home Office Statistical Bulletin 15/07

Muncie, J, McLaughlin, E and Langan, M (eds) (1999) *Criminological Perspectives*, Sage: London

Taylor P and Bond S (eds) (2012) *Crimes detected in England and Wales 2011/12*, Home Office: London

Weblinks

www.ons.gov.uk

www.gov.uk/government/collections/crime-statistics

www.citizensreportuk.org/reports/murders-fatal-violence-uk.html

www.justice.gov.uk/publications/criminalannual.htm

Chapter 3

Victims and the impact of crime

Learning objectives

After reading the chapter you should be able to:

1. Outline the cost and impact of crime
2. Describe those who are most likely to become the victims of crime
3. Explain the history of the victim in the criminal justice system
4. Describe how victims are compensated
5. Describe the aspects of support for victims
6. Explain the part played by victims in the criminal justice system

Key statistics

- 21.5% of people annually are victims of some sort of crime
- 3.1% of people experience violent crime
- Victims of domestic violence are highly likely to experience the crime more than once: 73% of all domestic violence incidents are repeat incidents; 44% of British Crime Survey (BCS) respondents were victimised more than once and 24% were victimised three or more times
- Of all crimes, the one which victims are most likely to report to the police is vehicle theft
- The risk of being a victim of household crime has dropped from a high of 32.5% in 1995 to 16.3% in 2010/11
- People most at risk of being a victim of crime are those who are aged 16–24 (31.8%), those who are unemployed (29.8%), those who are students (31.4%), those of mixed ethnic background (29.5%), those who are single (27.9%), or those

who visit nightclubs once a week (38.7%), compared to the average across all characteristics (21.5%)

- Adults with a combined household income of £50,000 or more, are most likely to be a victim of household crime (20.6%) compared with those who have a combined household income of less than £10,000 (14.4%)
- Terraced houses are most likely to be targeted for household crime (20.1%) while detached houses are the least likely (12.9%)
- 70% of crime victims say that they are very or fairly satisfied with the way their cases were handled by police

(Statistics taken from *Crime in England and Wales 2010/11*)

Introduction

In recent decades, the victim has become a key stakeholder in the criminal justice system. The growing intolerance of crime among the public has resulted in a shift in perceptions as to who is regarded as the client of the criminal justice system. There was a time when the victim was the forgotten player and the offender was the main focus; the probation service before 1990 used the term client when referring to offenders under its supervision. The victim lobby is now influential and in recent years we have seen the growth in services such as Victim Support. Other victim-focused changes in policy can be seen with the development of restitution and compensation for victims at time of sentencing whereby monetary compensation is sought for victims of crime. There is a government-funded tariff of payments for victims injured by crime and delivered by the Criminal Injuries Compensation Authority (CICA).

Other policy changes include changes to the victim facilities at the courts which mean that victims do not have to share facilities with the defendants and defendants' friends during the trial. Victims are now kept better informed about the progress of their case and **Victim Personal Statements** (VPS, but known elsewhere as Victim Impact Statements) are used in courts to inform the sentencing judges and magistrates about the impact a crime has had on the victim's life.

In the past, victim was described as the 'forgotten' player in the criminal justice process. This is in part because of an adversarial system of justice and the requirement to establish the guilt of an offender. Hence, the victim is an essential part of this process: without victims to act by way of reporting crime, providing information and giving evidence in court, the system of criminal justice will not work. The system requires the prosecution to establish guilt beyond reasonable doubt, and this is difficult for many crimes without the active participation of the victim. Individual victims suffer financially, physically and emotionally from crime; and families, communities and society as a whole are also affected. The first section of this chapter will focus on this impact, drawing from the victim surveys described in **Chapter 2**. The risk of becoming a victim is not evenly spread throughout society, and the following section will explore how the risks of crime vary according to geographic and socio-economic factors along with gender, age and race.

The latter decades of the twentieth century saw what has been described as the 'rediscovery' of the victim, with a range of studies revealing victims' needs for support, advice and practical help, and dissatisfaction with their experiences of the criminal justice process. For some victims, particularly victims of violent and sexual crimes, the experience of reporting crime and giving evidence could amount to secondary victimisation. In what has been described as a victim 'movement', outlined in the third section of the chapter, a range of groups called for more attention to be given to these issues. This led to the development of a number of policies to assist victims, to successive Victims' Charters, and, across Europe and other jurisdictions, to statements about victims' needs and rights. We will look at the ways in which the victim has become more 'centre stage' in recent years, with policies that aim to help victims deal with the consequences of crime and also to make their participation in the criminal justice system more tolerable.

Subsequent sections of the chapter will look at how victims are compensated, at the various ways in which they are supported and at their role in the criminal justice process – in relation to, for example, reporting crime, giving evidence and their role in sentencing and restorative justice. The chapter will conclude by considering some of the issues raised by these developments. How far do they represent a real improvement for victims? To what extent do victims, like offenders, have 'rights' in relation to criminal justice? To what extent can or should the criminal justice processes incorporate the victim?

First, it is important to look briefly at the concept of the victim, which, like the concept of crime, requires some exploration. We have seen that victims play a key role in defining crime, and victimisation must also be defined. In order to be considered or consider themselves as a victim of crime, citizens have to be aware that they have suffered harm from an incident which they consider to be criminal. Thus, in both commonsense and legal terms the notion of victim is linked to notions of crime and it is also subject to different social conceptions. If, for example, victims have been seen to have provoked an offence they will be seen as less 'deserving' than if they are perceived to be 'innocent'. These notions are also related to social perceptions of the situations in which a crime occurs and the characteristics of offenders and victims. The elderly person set upon by an attacker or the child victim of a murder are perceived to be vulnerable and innocent, whereas the woman appearing to invite rape by her dress or demeanour, or the victim of an assault who has been involved in provoking a fight, are seen as less deserving of sympathy.

Early **victimologists** hypothesised that some groups, such as children, the elderly, the weak or the depressed, were particularly prone to being victims and others argued that some victims precipitated offences, particularly in cases of murder and rape (see, for example, **von Hentig 1948; Walklate 1989**). Amir, for example, surveying police records, stated that 19 per cent of rapes were 'victim precipitated' in that women had initially agreed to sex but later changed their mind or had not resisted strongly enough (**Amir 1971**).

Later victimologists focused more specifically on how people's lifestyles were related to victimisation, arguing, for example, that victimisation was related to the amount of time spent in public places where crimes were more likely to occur. If these situations can be identified then high-risk lifestyles can be better avoided and the cost and impact of crime reduced.

3.1 The cost and impact of crime

Objective 1

Outline the cost and impact of crime

All members of the public are affected by crime. They pay for crime through taxes which pay for the criminal justice system. They also pay higher insurance premiums to protect themselves from the financial losses incurred by insurance fraud. Prices in shops include an amount to take account of theft by customers and employees, and the costs of the health service also increase as a result of violent crime.

We know that the cost and impact of crime can be great and widely felt, yet obtaining an accurate measure is more difficult. In 1982, the Home Office introduced the British Crime Survey (BCS), ostensibly to obtain a more realistic count of actual crime than that which is reported to the police. It was also expected to help identify risk factors in victimisation and understand how people felt about crime and the police. However, since its conception, it has become a useful tool for examining long-term trends in crime. In March 2012, the BCS which formerly covered England, Wales and Scotland, was renamed the Crime Survey for England and Wales (CSEW), while Scotland developed its own survey. The Crime Survey and other studies are helpful for estimating the impact and cost of crime among victims and wider society and have informed much of what we know about these matters, but still it is not easy to calculate the costs of crime. A Home Office study (**Brand and Price 2000**) estimated the cost of selected notifiable offences including violence, sexual offences, robbery, burglary, thefts, fraud and forgery and criminal damage, with cost estimates based on information from the BCS and commercial victimisation surveys. The total cost of crime in the UK was estimated by **Chambers *et al.* (2009)** at £78 billion, although this does not include the impact on the victim's, or the public's, quality of life.

The Home Office in 2000, concluded that estimated costs include approximately a third for the cost of the stolen or damaged property, a third on the treatment of victims of crime and another third on the cost of law enforcement and criminal justice. This is not a full figure as the study excluded a number of offences such as drug trafficking, handling stolen goods, public order offences, fare evasion and many summary offences.

An attempt to estimate costs (at 2003 prices) for crimes covered by the BCS plus sexual offences and homicides included costs to the criminal justice system and costs to the victim, including, for example, costs of lost income; adverse health effects; and any property stolen. It also takes into account the more intangible costs of the reduction in the quality of a victim's life as well as the more easily calculated economic costs. On these calculations, homicide unsurprisingly emerges as the crime with greatest costs – estimated as £1,310,000 to victims and £1,460,000 in total. Sexual and violent offences have higher costs than property offences, with, for example, the total costs of sexual offences being estimated at £31,400 and serious wounding being estimated at £7,280 compared to the total cost of theft of a vehicle (the highest figure of all property offences) estimated at £4,410, domestic burglary at £3,270 and other thefts at £634 (**Thorpe** *et al.* **2007**).

The impact of criminal damage through graffiti might be considered a minor offence but repairing damage to railway trains and carriages from spray painting is estimated as costing over a million pounds between 2004 to 2006. At Southwark Crown Court in July 2008, one such culprit was given a two-year prison sentence, three were given 18 months, and one other 15 months.

While these figures are not complete, they do indicate the many ways in which crime affects victims and society as a whole. Crime not only has financial costs but affects our daily lives – people worry about crime and take steps to avoid it. Houses must be locked and protected and many people are scared to go to certain areas through fear of being mugged, raped or assaulted. Valuable items are post-coded and car windows have numbers etched on them.

However, what has been called the 'fear of crime' is not the same as the actual risks of crime, with the 2010/11 CSEW showing that, as in previous years, there is a disparity between perceived likelihood and actual prevalence of crime. For example, 13 per cent of respondents thought that they were very likely or fairly likely to be a victim of violent crime in the next 12 months, compared with three per cent who reported having actually been a victim of such a crime in the year before interview. Most people imagine that crime is rising despite not seeing any evidence of that in their own areas: the 2010/11 data showed that 60 per cent of people thought that crime in the country as a whole had increased over the last few years, but only 28 per cent of people thought the same about crime in their local area. However, overall fear of crime has fallen over the years: the 2010/11 results show that across all three headline measures of burglary, car crime and violent crime, the perceived likelihood of being a victim of crime was lower compared with 2009/10.

The analyses of public perceptions of victimisation in **Scribbins** *et al.* **(2010)** and **Moon and Flatley** *et al.* **(2011)** provide some interesting information about the demographics associated with public perceptions of the risk of crime: those living in multicultural areas perceived a higher risk of crime than those living in more homogenous areas; women are more likely to worry about being a victim of crime and often avoid going out alone at night, although it is actually men who experience more crime than women; a higher proportion of those who read tabloid newspapers think that the likelihood of their being a victim of crime is 'likely' or 'very likely' than those who read broadsheet newspapers (19 per cent compared to 12.2 per cent in 2009/10).

As seen above, the impact of crime affects individual victims financially, phys-ically and emotionally and varies according to the circumstances of the offence and the situation of the victim – some victims are not greatly affected by offences, with more severe effects being found among victims of wounding, burglary, and vehicle theft (**Nicholas and Wood 2003**). While some property offences involve trivial amounts, others, as seen above, involve considerable financial costs, particularly those involving cars. Burglary also has emotional effects as it can give rise to feelings that privacy has been invaded and to anger and annoyance. In the 2002/3 BCS, for example, 83 per cent of burglary victims reported an emotional reaction, which was more likely if entry had been gained. Anger and annoyance were the most common reactions with fear, loss of confidence and difficulty sleeping being reported by around one-quarter of victims. 37 per cent felt 'very much' affected by burglary. In addition to financial losses and injury, many offences cause inconvenience – reports have to be made to the police, lost goods replaced or damaged items and houses repaired – effects felt most severely by the poorest victims who cannot easily replace goods and may not be insured (**Croall 2007**).

Offences may also have indirect effects – most particularly in cases of murder and serious injury, but also in cases of burglary. Children in houses which have been burgled have been found to suffer from sleeplessness and bedwetting (**Morgan and Zedner 1992**). Witnesses to crime, particularly violent crime, may be emotionally affected and also have to suffer the inconvenience of giving statements to the police or attending court. In more general terms the quality of life of entire communities may be affected by high rates of crime, which may lead to the general 'decline' of an area.

In contrast to Europe, Gavin Lockhart (**Chambers 2009**) states, 'England and Wales have a recorded-crime rate twice that of the European average.' A report by Policy Exchange states, 'Britain has the fourth highest rate of recorded crime in 39 European countries, at around five million.' The higher than average crime rate in England and Wales compared with the rest of Europe is confirmed by the International Crime Victimisation Survey (ICVS).

3.2 Who are the victims of crime?

Objective 2

Describe those who are most likely to become the victims of crime

While all of us are affected by crime and are at risk of being its victims, risks and effects are spread differentially among the population. Geographical location, lifestyles, socio-economic factors, gender, age and race and ethnicity all affect patterns of victimisation. These factors are interrelated. For example, neighbourhoods tend to contain people of similar socio-economic status, and different groups have different lifestyles – young people are likely to go out more than older people, which affects their risk of being a victim of street crime. A brief exploration of some aspects of differential victimisation follows.

▶ Geographical area

Risks of victimisation tend to be higher in urban than rural areas. According to the 2010/11 CSEW, just 1.3 per cent of people in rural areas were victims of burglary compared with 2.9 per cent in urban areas, and similar patterns were also found in relation to vandalism, vehicle-related theft and violent crime.

Figure 3.1 shows the percentage of victims of household crime in urban and rural areas in 2010/11. Recorded crime rates per 1,000 members of the population

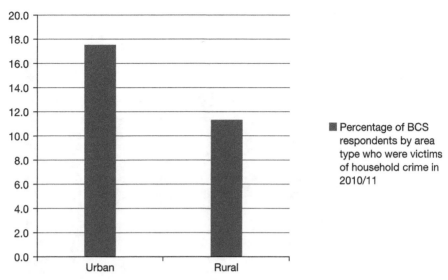

Figure 3.1 Percentage of respondents by area type who were victims of household crime in 2010/11
Source: Crime in England and Wales 2010/11, Data Tables

for personal and household crime by region are provided in Figure 3.2, illustrating that London has the highest rates of both types of crime. Figure 3.3 breaks down these figures into more detail, showing that the highest rates of violence against the person, sexual offences, robbery, offences against vehicles and other theft offences are found in London. However, London has the lowest rate of criminal damage. According to police records, the East of England and the South West had the lowest rates of overall recorded crime. The North East had the lowest rate of violence against the person, robbery, burglary, vehicle crime and fraud and forgery. Separate figures for Wales show that overall, England has higher rates of all recorded crime than Wales, except for criminal damage, for which rates in Wales are higher. Police-recorded robberies and offences involving a knife were found to be mostly concentrated in just 3 of the 10 police force regions: Metropolitan (London), Greater Manchester and the West Midlands.

Geographical area is also linked to socio-economic status, and the ACORN (A Classification of Residential Neighbourhoods) classifications used by the CSEW incorporate measurements of economic, demographic and housing characteristics of areas, classified by postcode. The risks of burglary have consistently been found to be highest in 'rising' and 'striving' areas (**Aitchison and Hodgkinson 2003**), now described as areas of 'urban prosperity' and 'hard pressed' (**Higgins and Budd 2007**), the former being characterised by young, professional couples and singles and the latter being council estates with higher numbers of elderly, single parents and unemployed residents along with multi-ethnic, low-income areas. Rates for these areas are highest for all kinds of crime.

This reflects a variety of factors. Some kinds of houses are more ready targets for burglars – burglary is higher, for example, in flats than in houses, in terrace-type houses than in detached houses, and in rented accommodation. While lower-income

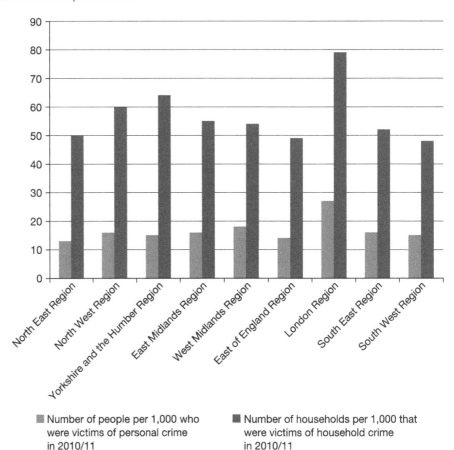

Number of people per 1,000 who were victims of personal crime in 2010/11

Number of households per 1,000 that were victims of household crime in 2010/11

Figure 3.2 Recorded personal and household crime figures per 1,000 of the population by region[1][2]

Source: *Crime in England and Wales 2010/11*, Data Tables
Note: [1] Personal crime includes: Violence against the person, sexual offences and robbery
Note: [2] Household crime includes: Burglary, offences against vehicles, other theft offences, fraud and forgery, criminal damage, drug offences, other offences.

groups have high rates of victimisation, the more affluent may also make attractive targets especially to car thieves, as they have more worth stealing.

Crime mapping details of crimes reported and their location became available in 2011. It was possible to see street-level crime maps with details of crime reported and the streets where they occurred. For access go to the following website: www.police.uk/

▶ Lifestyle

Lifestyle (or what some call 'routine activities') also affects the risk of victimisation. Factors such as age, gender, socio-economic status and ethnicity naturally influence lifestyle, and consequently the risk of victimisation. As pointed out above, those who go out more often or travel through areas characterised by high

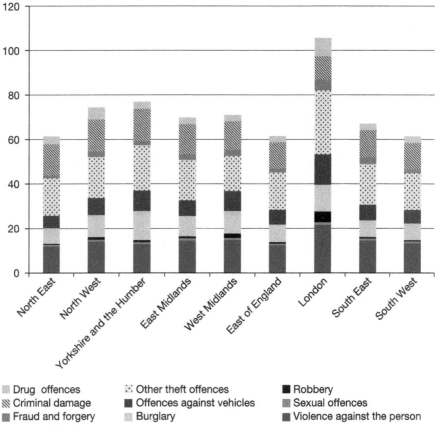

Figure 3.3 Recorded personal and household crime per 1,000 of the population by region and type 2010/11

Source: Crime in England and Wales 2010/11, Data Tables

rates of crime are more at risk. Young men aged between 16 and 24 are most at risk of violent crime, much of which takes place in or around places where people have been drinking. The 20010/11 CSEW indicated for example that those who had visited a bar once a week or more in the past month had a higher risk of victimisation for all CSEW crime and more than twice the risk of personal crime compared to those who had not visited a bar at all (**Parfrement-Hopkins 2011**), and it has been shown that this demographic are particularly likely to experience stranger violence (**Hoyle and Zedner 2007**).

▶ **Socio-economic status**

While the above figures indicate that 'rising' and 'striving' areas carry high risks of victimisation many argue, on the basis of closer analysis of patterns of victimisation and considerations of its impact, that 'survey data has constantly identified that those most likely to be victimised by crime in Britain are often the most marginalised social groups living in the poorest areas' (**Davies et al. 2003: 13**). The relationship between victimisation and socio-economic status is a complex one as, put quite simply, the rich have more to steal and present more attractive targets. At the same time however they have greater resources to protect themselves from victimisation by purchasing security and buying houses in low crime areas (**Croall 2007**). **Hope (2001)**, summarising analyses of BCS data which take into account repeated victimisation, points to how crime can be concentrated in a small number of areas – thus he found that:

- around one-fifth of victims of household property crime live in the 10 per cent of residential areas with highest crime rates and experience more than one-third of household property crime;

- over half of all property crime, and over one-third of all property crime victims, are likely to live in only one-fifth of communities of England and Wales; conversely, the 50 per cent of communities with the lowest crime rates suffer merely 15 per cent of household property crime, spread between a quarter of victims;

- victims who are multiply or repeatedly victimised are more likely to live in high crime rate areas than those less frequently victimised;

- concentrations of crime risks coincide with concentration of the 'poor' – 20 per cent of communities with the highest crime rates have higher numbers of the 'poor' than the 'rich'.

◗ Gender

Chapter 2 outlined some variations in victimisation rates by gender. Young men are more likely to be the victims of public and street violence, whereas women are more likely to be victimised in the home. Overall, however, men are more likely to be victims of violent crime (**Hoyle and Zedner 2007**). A major thrust in the victim movement was the attention drawn by women's groups to the high rates of violence against women in the home. This has been recognised as more difficult to capture in standard victim surveys as victims may not wish to reveal this to interviewers. One survey, based on a sample of 1,000, indicates that 24 per cent of married women and 59 per cent of divorced or separated women had been hit by their spouses (**Painter and Farrington 1998**), and a more recent survey revealed that 2 per cent of men and 4 per cent of women had been subject to physical domestic violence in the previous year (**Walby and Allen 2004**). Figure 3.4 shows that generally, men have higher rates of victimisation than women, except those aged between 45 and 54; the higher rate of crime experienced by women of this age group can be mainly attributed to domestic violence. Some forms of violence are what can be described as gender specific, with women being subject to a continuum of sexual offences ranging from verbal harassment through to physical and sexual threats and sexual assaults.

◗ Age

Age is related to victimisation in different ways, with both 'innocent' children and the elderly being perceived as particularly vulnerable victims. While cases of robbery or mugging against elderly victims receive much public attention – understandable in terms of the callousness of the crime – the elderly have lower rates of victimisation from violent crime than younger age groups. The chance of

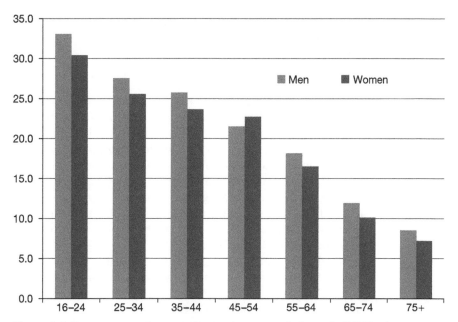

Figure 3.4 Percentage of respondents who were victims of all BCS crime once or more by age and gender, 2010/11

Source: Crime in England and Wales 2010/11, Data Tables

being a victim is in fact much higher between the ages of 16 and 24 than any other age (see Figure 3.4). This may be a result of different lifestyles, and any effects of age on victimisation also interact with socio-economic status and geographical location – as **Pain (2003)** points out, old people are not a homogeneous group and affluent old age pensioners living in the country have a low risk of being a victim. On the other hand, elderly people by virtue of being elderly can be the victims of 'elder abuse' in the home and in institutions, and of stone throwing and harassment in local neighbourhoods (ibid.). They may also be targeted by investment fraud and the predatory sales tactics of, for example, the suppliers of burglar alarms where salespeople prey on their fear of crime (**Croall 2001**).

While young people are often more associated than other age groups with committing crime, they are also the group most at risk of being victims. A range of studies have revealed considerable victimisation among school students (**Anderson *et al*. 1994; Hartless *et al*. 1995**), often excluded from national surveys such as the BCS.

Since 2009 the BCS has been conducting ongoing research into the extent and type of crime experienced by this age group. Figures from the 2010/11 BCS show there were an estimated 878,000 crimes experienced by children aged 10 to 15. Of this number, two-thirds were violent crimes (576,000) while most of the remaining crimes were thefts of personal property (275,000). A much smaller number of children experienced vandalism of personal property (27,000).

Much crime in this age group, which includes bullying, theft and violence, involves young people stealing from other young people, as the recurrent stories indicate of youths being '**mugged**' for mobile phones and designer clothes. Young people may be scared to report these crimes as it can lead parents to curtail their activities, and they fear that they may be treated by the police as suspects rather than victims.

▶ Race and ethnicity

Racial or minority ethnic status may also affect victimisation. More recent sweeps of the BCS have taken 'booster samples' of minority ethnic groups, finding that both Afro-Caribbean and Asians are more at risk of household and personal offences than whites. The CSEW results for 2010/11 demonstrate that adults living in households in areas classified as predominantly 'multicultural' experienced a higher rate of crime than those in any other type of area: 21 per cent as opposed to 17.7 per cent of those living in 'blue-collar communities', 18.2 per cent of those in 'city living' areas and 10.5 per cent of those living in the countryside. By 2000, rates for Afro-Caribbean and whites for household crime had converged, whereas Indians, Pakistanis and Bangladeshis had a greater risk. Black respondents reported higher rates of personal crimes (**Phillips and Bowling 2002**). Many of these differences can be explained by socio-economic factors, although for some, especially Asian groups, it remains significant and these groups also perceive more crime to be racially motivated.

Some offences are specifically directed at ethnic minorities and are described as 'racially motivated' (ibid.). These can include verbal harassment and abuse, damage to property and various offences involving racist graffiti, throwing stones, eggs or other items at people or their property. While individual incidents may be trivial, their accumulation can have a serious impact on victims, not always recognised in surveys which record individual incidents. Reports of racially motivated offences have increased considerably since figures were first collected but this probably reflects an increase in reporting and recording; and the definition of a racially motivated crime changed to be defined by the victims' or witness's perception following the Macpherson inquiry into the murder of Stephen Lawrence.

British Crime Survey information indicates that in 1999, 2 per cent of black, 4 per cent of Pakistani and Bangladeshi, and 4 per cent of Indian respondents reported racial victimisation. Police-recorded crime data from 2010/11 indicates that during the last decade racially or religiously aggravated violent crime has consistently accounted for between 3 and 4 per cent of all police-recorded violent crime. The volume of racist incidents is higher in areas with concentrations of ethnic minority populations and in the North of England, and there have also been findings that attacks are most frequent in areas with small but growing ethnic minority populations (ibid.). Since 9/11 and the terrorist bombings in London on 7 July 2005, there have been claims by Islamic pressure groups about the growing volume of harassment and victimisation experienced by those assumed to be Muslim.

3.3 The rediscovery of the victim

Objective 3

Explain the history of the victim in the criminal justice system

Having moved from being the 'forgotten player' in the criminal justice process, victims are now often seen to occupy 'centre stage' of criminal justice policy, such has been the growth of strategies and policies to support them and to address their needs in the criminal justice process. First, during the period 1960 to 1975, compensation schemes for crime victims were developed. Second, from 1975 to 1980, following women's campaigns on the part of the victims of rape and domestic violence and the rise of support services for the victims of violent and property crimes, a range of support services grew up including shelters for female victims of domestic violence, specialist suites in police stations for the victims of rape, and a range of voluntarily staffed support services under the auspices of Victim Support. This organisation, whose role will be described below, has, in addition to providing support services, conducted research and acted to advocate policies in relation to victims. Third, from the 1980s there were repeated calls for justice for victims and improvements in their experiences of criminal justice, and throughout the 2000s victims featured very strongly in what has been described as New Labour's 'victim-orientated justice' (**Mawby 2007**). After the general election in 2010, the newly allied Coalition Government continued this trend with a special focus on domestic violence victims. In 2012, the Home Office began a £28 million investment programme to help victims of domestic and sexual violence, with £225,000 of funding for male victims of domestic violence, and nearly £1 million invested in nine new rape support centres across the UK.

Victims of major crimes have perhaps been afforded a higher profile in recent years as a result of victims themselves and their families becoming more adept at using the media to help their cause. Gerry and Kate McCann, the parents of the missing four-year-old Madeleine, are probably the most famous example of 'celebrity' victims. When their daughter was abducted from a Portugal hotel in 2007, they immediately made the international press their closest confidant, hiring a PR officer to manage their public campaign to 'Find Maddie'. Even today, Madeleine's wide brown eyes are probably still familiar to anyone who glanced at a newspaper front page in the years following her abduction. Eight years on, her parents run a charity dedicated to raising funds to enable them to continue their search, as well as a sophisticated website dedicated to finding Madeleine and her abductor. The website has an online shop where once can purchase 'holiday packs' of stickers and luggage tags bearing the website's name, 'findmadeleine. com', 'Look for Madeleine' wristbands and 'Don't give up on me' T-shirts.

The media, and the concerned public, gave so much attention to the victims of Madeleine's abduction that the case inspired a copycat mother, Karen Matthews, to organise the false kidnapping and imprisonment of her nine-year-old daughter, Shannon, in 2008. The child was discovered, 24 days later, hidden in the base of a divan bed in the home of her mother's boyfriend's uncle. The conspiring adults had been planning to 'find' the child after surreptitiously releasing her, then claim the £50,000 reward offered by *The Sun* newspaper.

Liaisons between victims and media are not always so cynical: the use of the internet and social networking sites can enable victims to gain publicity and thereby clout. The murder of Ben Kinsella, the 17-year-old boy stabbed to death in London in 2008, gained huge publicity partly because Kinsella's family and friends used the social networking site Facebook to spread word of a vigil and demonstration in Ben's name to highlight the prevalence and problem of knife-crime. After Kinsella's murderers were sentenced for a minimum of 19 years each, the victim-led campaign in newspapers and online for longer tariffs for murders committed with a knife. In 2010, a new minimum sentence of 25 years replaced the 15 years' tariff for murders committed with a knife.

▶ Victims' needs

The increasing use of victim surveys along with studies of particular groups of victims revealed more about the impact of crime along with the considerable problems which many victims encountered following a crime (see for example, **Shapland *et al*. 1985; Maguire and Pointing 1988**). Victims reported, for example, that they needed immediate help in coping with practical matters, such as repairing damage from a burglary or making insurance claims, along with, in the most serious cases, help to overcome emotional problems. They also reported frustration at not being given information about the progress of their case and what would happen next. Many felt confused and uncertain about what was expected of them when giving evidence in court, which could be an intimidating experience, as they could face cross-examination from the defence in an attempt to discredit their evidence – problems also found among witnesses. Inside and outside the courtroom, victims could also be brought face to face with the offender. If the case did not go to court, particularly if it was discontinued, victims could feel 'let down' and were often not informed about why decisions had been made; and victims reported disappointment where they felt, particularly in relation to a **discontinuance** or what they saw as a lenient sentence, that the impact of the offence was not being taken seriously. In some cases, victims feared retaliation from offenders and felt that they were offered inadequate protection.

Several high-profile cases in the 1980s and 1990s, which revealed the extent of physical and sexual child abuse both in the home and in institutions, influenced the range of services available to children. Organisations such as Childline, set up following such cases, highlighted the problems of detecting, prosecuting and obtaining convictions. Giving evidence in court, especially against parents or those previously close to them, could be particularly harrowing for children who were obliged to speak in open court and be examined by strangers.

A range of policies and solutions were introduced to resolve these issues and by the start of the 1990s more support was available for victims and there was some official recognition of victims' needs. There was, however, no coherent strategy, and the implementation of policies was limited by what **Shapland (1988)** described as a tendency for agencies in the criminal justice process to resist change to protect their 'fiefdoms'; and **Newburn (2003)** comments that political parties pursued half-formed and half-hearted policies in relation to victims. Since the 1990s there has been a series of statements about what victims can and should expect from the criminal justice process and a series of major policy changes.

What are the main needs of victims? In 1995, Victim Support produced a paper, *The Rights of the Victims of Crime* (**Victim Support 1995**), which argued that the state should exercise responsibilities grouped under five main principles which summarise the key concerns of victims:

- *Compensation:* victims should be entitled to compensation which leaves them in approximately the same financial position as they were in before the crime.

- *Protection:* victims and witnesses should be protected in any way necessary including psychological protection by, for example, protecting their privacy.
- *Services:* victims have the right to respect, recognition and support, to receive services from an organisation dedicated to their needs and to be treated with respect by all the agencies they come into contact with.
- *Information:* victims have the right to receive information about the progress of their case, the procedures being followed and about their role in the process and their rights. This includes receiving an explanation of any decisions and the opportunity to give a statement about the full financial, physical and emotional consequences of the crime.
- *Responsibility:* victims should be free of the burden of decisions relating to the offender, decisions which lie with the state.

Since then, there have been a variety of Victims' Charters and statements from other jurisdictions about what victims can and should expect. Looking across the globe, **Goodey (2004: 130)** identifies a common 'checklist' of core 'rights':

- Compassion and respect
- Information on proceedings and rights
- Presentation of victims' views
- Legal aid
- Swift case processing
- Protection of privacy and identity
- Protection from retaliation and intimidation
- Compensation from the offender and the state
- Recognition of victims with special needs.

In England and Wales during the 1990s, two Victims' Charters had spelt out what victims should expect, including information and some levels of support. These Charters were not, however, expressed as 'rights', nor were they legislative requirements – an important point in evaluating victim-centred policy. Distinctions can be drawn, for example, between lists of victims' 'needs' – 'service standards' which detail what victims should be able to expect – and 'rights' – which imply the possibility of legal redress should they not be implemented (**Davies *et al.* 2003; Hoyle and Zedner 2007; Walklate 2007; Goodey 2004**). The charters of the 1990s, argues **Goodey (2004)**, were a product of their time, reflecting the view prevalent in England and Wales that victims are a group to which the criminal justice system owes some services, but not rights. Many argue, for example, that despite the charters and the implementation of policies, there remained no cohesive policy towards victims (**Davies 2003; Newburn 2003**) and that victims have few enforceable 'rights'. They did, however, apply standards of good practice across the criminal justice process (**Mawby 2007**) although many policies were unevenly implemented, with many victims remaining unaware of their entitlements to compensation and support; and reports by victims of feeling intimidated by their experiences of criminal justice are still common.

A key part of New Labour's criminal justice strategy was to 'rebalance' the criminal justice process towards the victim, expressed in key policy statements and legislation. A Home Office review of the Victim's Charter in 2001 argued that victims should have more rights, the Home Office *Justice for All* White Paper of 2002 set out a number of proposals and the Domestic Violence, Crime and Victims Act of 2004 widened the opportunities for victims to provide and be given information in cases involving a prison sentence. The Protection from Harassment Act 1997 allows the courts to impose a restraining orders following conviction for any offence or on acquittal, if it is considered necessary to protect a named person from harassment in the future.

The Domestic Violence, Crime and Victims Act 2004 established a Commissioner for Victims and Witnesses, a post which was taken up by Louise Casey in 2010 and has been held by Baroness Helen Newlove since December 2012. The Act also introduced the 'victim surcharge' **(see details later in Chapter 11)**.

Finally the Act set out a Code of Practice for Victims of Crime (Home Office 2005) which describes, for many agencies within the criminal justice process, the minimum level of services that victims should expect and introduces a complaints system to be used if agencies fail to deliver an appropriate standard of service. It sets targets for how and when criminal justice agencies must respond. Some of these provisions will be discussed below in relation to specific agencies. While this is more extensive than previous legislation, critics argue that it does not provide for legal redress, thus falling short of giving victims 'rights' (**Walklate 2007**).

The Coalition Government, on taking office in May 2010, agreed that there was 'more to be done' when it came to focusing on victims. In the Coalition's *Programme for Government*, the section on 'justice' makes explicit reference to 'overhauling the system of rehabilitation to . . . provide greater support and protection for the victims of crime'. The Prime Minister, David Cameron, and his Deputy, Nick Clegg, went on to briefly set out their vision of helping victims: a percentage of prisoners' earnings would be channelled into the Victims' Fund; proceeds from the Victims' Surcharge would be channelled into rape support centres, and Legal Aid would undergo a thorough review to maximise efficiency. Already, several of these objectives have been or are currently being met.

The Prisoners' Earnings Act 1996, was intended to ensure that prisoners make financial reparations to victims and communities by transferring up to 40 per cent of wages of low-risk prisoners with jobs in the community to Victim Support in order to fund services which support victims of crime. A new levy came into force in September 2011 – and by the end of May 2012 had raised £383,724 in its first six months. The Minister for Justice, Crispin Blunt, was quoted as describing the Prisoners' Earnings Act as 'the start of Government getting the balance right'. The Legal Aid, Sentencing and Punishment of Offenders (LASPO) Act which came into force in May 2012 makes it mandatory for courts to consider demanding that convicted offenders pay compensation directly to their victims. The latest policy on victims was informed by the results of two major consultations: 'Breaking the Cycle' in 2011 and 'Getting it right for victims and witnesses' in 2012. Several of the sentencing reforms that formed part of the former consultation were incorporated into LASPO 2012, while the latter resulted in the reform of the Criminal Injuries Compensation Authority (CICA), discussed in more detail below.

3.4 Compensating victims

Objective 4

Describe how victims are compensated

One of the rights advocated by Victim Support is financial compensation, and victims can be financially compensated in three ways: first, by the state through the Criminal Injuries Compensation Authority (CICA); second, by offenders, through the imposition by the court (at the time of sentencing) of compensation orders; and third, by receiving support from specific services paid for by the victims' fund, which in turn is funded by the victim surcharge.

▶ State compensation

In the early part of the twentieth century there was no formal means by which the victims of crime could be compensated by the state, and a range of penal reformers, including, prominently, Margery Fry from the Howard League for Penal Reform, argued that victims' needs should be recognised by the introduction of a state compensation scheme. The Criminal Injuries Compensation Board was set up in Britain in 1964 and was later renamed the Criminal Injuries Compensation Authority. This did not recognise a 'right' of victims to compensation, and restricted compensation to 'deserving' victims – while those who had failed to report crimes to the police, could be seen to have provoked a crime, or were related to offenders were not deemed eligible (**Newburn 2003**). It not only compensates those who suffered injuries as a result of the criminal activities of others, but also compensates those bereaved by crime. The impetus for this scheme came largely from penal reformers and political parties and did not arise from any campaigning by or consultation with victims themselves (**Davies *et al*. 2003; Newburn 2003**).

CICA is now well established and has compensated a large number of victims. The CICA Annual Report and Accounts of 2011/12 states that the 'Authority settled total compensation awards of £449.4 million to blameless victims of violent crime during 2011–12', and resolved 57,480 claims in 2011/12 compared to 64,768 in 2010/11: the number of applications fell last year, due to changes to the scheme outlined below, which limit eligibility.

CICA makes awards of between £1,000 to £500,000, which excludes the majority of victims of minor assaults and robberies (**Dignan 2004**), and victims' campaigners have argued that a much smaller award could be of considerable benefit to those on a low income.

In 2012, the former Justice Secretary Kenneth Clarke, announced an overhaul of the CICA scheme as one of several initiatives intended to reduce government costs. The CICA budget has been reduced by around five per cent and, in terms of access to the scheme, has undergone some major changes which are expected to save money in some areas and create it elsewhere. For example, CICA now reserves compensation payments for those most seriously injured, while removing less serious injuries like sprains from the scheme. Previous levels of compensation were based on 25 bands, ranging from band one, which attracted a payout of £1,000, to the most serious band, 25, at £250,000. People could claim for multiple injuries with the total amount payable capped at £500,000. The lower five bands have now been removed and no longer attract any compensation; payouts for bands six to twelve have been reduced by as much as 50 per cent; while the top 13 bands – the most serious – remain unchanged. Claimants with criminal convictions, who hitherto have been able to benefit from the scheme, will now find it much more difficult to claim successfully.

The changes will reduce the overall cost of the scheme in the long-term but during the changeover period in 2011/12 the value of awards paid out surged to £449.4 million as CICA attempted to clear the backlog of 'pre-tariff' claims – i.e. those submitted before the changes were introduced and still qualifying for compensation under the old rules. New liabilities arising during 2011/12 totalled £219.6 million. When assessing the amount that different injuries should attract, consideration is given to which part of the body is affected, the extent of the injury, whether the injury causes temporary or permanent disability, and whether it will affect the victim's ability to work (see Table 3.1). For instance, when assessing injury to a thumb or forefinger, the scheme allows one set of tariffs for fracture or dislocation, and another set for the loss or partial loss of the thumb or forefinger. If the injury affects a thumb, payments will be greater than if it affects an index finger, while injury to any finger other than the index will attract the lowest pay-out. The tariff system also takes account of whether the injury has occurred on just one hand or both, whether one or more digits are affected, and if the finger or thumb in question makes a substantial recovery or causes significant continuing disability. Hence, an award for an injury of this kind ranges from £1,000 (for partial loss of one thumb or finger, or for continuing significant disability caused by fracture or dislocation of two or more fingers other than an index finger on one hand) to £55,000 (for complete loss of both thumbs).

Where victims cannot work after 28 weeks they may be recompensed for loss of earnings, excluding those who are unable to work for less than that period. In a report **Victim Support (2003)** argues that it discriminates against some victims. If, for example, victims are dependent on means-tested benefits such as income support and an award takes their savings over certain thresholds, their benefits can be reduced or cut.

▶ Victim surcharge

The victim surcharge was introduced in 2011 and helps to fund CICA. It contributed £800,000 in the first year of operation to funds for victim and witness support services. From October 2012, the scope of offences to which the victim surcharge is applied was expanded to include more offences, as well as court sentences that previously did not attract a fine. Any adult receiving a court fine must now pay 10 per cent of the fine amount, with a minimum of £20 to a maximum of £120, as a victim surcharge. Adults given a Suspended Sentence Order will pay £80 and those given Community Orders will pay £60. There is a separate tariff for younger offenders, the proceeds of which would be channelled into a 'victims' fund' which would be used to help pay compensation to victims of crime.

▶ Compensation orders

Compensation orders, first introduced in 1972, can be ordered by the court and form part of the sentence. This was until recently a matter of court discretion, but

Table 3.1 Criminal Injuries Compensation Scheme

Levels of compensation	Example of qualifying injury	Value
	Part A: PHYSICAL AND MENTAL INJURIES	
Level A1	Sprained wrist lasting 13 weeks or more	£1,000
Level A2	Bone fracture in foot with substantial recovery	£1,500
Level A3	Permanent partial deafness in one ear	£1,800
Level A4	Partial loss of nose (at least 10%)	£2,400
Level A5	Detached retina in one eye	£3,500
Level A6	Fracture or dislocation of two or more fingers (other than index finger) causing significant disability on both hands	£4,600
Level A7	Injury to abdomen requiring surgical repair of three or more organs	£6,200
Level A8	Loss of kidney	£11,000
Level A9	Epilepsy which is partially controlled on medication	£13,500
Level A10	Minor brain damage lasting 6 months to 2 years	£16,500
Level A11	Severe impaired speech	£19,000
Level A12	Loss of sight in one eye	£22,000
Level A13	Severe burns (causing more than minor disfigurement) to face	£27,000
Level A14	Loss of one leg below the knee	£33,000
Level A15	Loss of tongue	£44,000
Level A16	Loss of fertility	£55,000
Level A17	Paralysis of or equivalent loss of function of both arms	£82,000
Level A18	Loss of, or equivalent loss of function of both hands	£110,000
Level A19	Complete paraplegia	£175,000
Level A20	Very serious brain injury resulting in no useful physical movement etc., and the need for full-time nursing care	£250,000
	Part B: SEXUAL/PHYSICAL ABUSE AND OTHER PAYMENTS	
Level B1	Minor abuse of children consisting of isolated or intermittent assaults resulting in weals, hair pulled from scalp etc	£1,000
Level B2	Minor non-penetrative frequent sexual physical acts over clothing	£1,500
Level B3	Serious abuse of children	£2,000
Level B4	Severe sexual assault consisting of non-penile penetrative or oral genital act(s)	£3,300
Level B5	Two or more incidents of sexual assault involving one or more of non-penile penetrative or oral genital acts	£4,400
Level B6	Pregnancy / Loss of foetus	£5,500
Level B7	Persistent pattern of severe abuse of an adult over period of more than 3 years	£6,600
Level B8	Severe abuse of children consisting of persistent pattern of repetitive violence resulting in significant multiple injuries	£8,200
Level B9	Fatal criminal injury to a single relative	£11,000
Level B10	Penile penetration by two or more attackers in one incident	£13,500
Level B11	Pattern of repetitive incidents (any age) involving penile penetration (whether by one or more attackers) over a period of up to 3 years	£16,500
Level B12	Infection with one or more of HIV, Hepatitis B or Hepatitis C	£22,000
Level B13	Sexual assault (any age) resulting in resulting in permanently disabling severe mental illness	£27,000
Level B14	Sexual assault (of a child or mentally incapacitated adult) resulting in serious internal bodily injury with permanent disabling moderate mental illness	£33,000
Level B15	Penile penetration (any age) resulting in serious internal bodily injury with permanent disabling severe mental illness	£44,000

Source: *The Criminal Injuries Compensation Scheme 2012 Index to Tariff of Injuries*, London: Ministry of Justice 2012

as of May 2012, the Legal Aid, Sentencing and Punishment of Offenders Act now compels the court to consider imposing a compensation order. From 1988, courts have been required to consider a compensation order in cases involving death, injury, loss or damage and to provide reasons in cases where an order is not made. Payment is now deducted at source from state benefits. Orders are widely used – in 1999, for example, 43 per cent of offenders sentenced for violent offences, 27 per cent for burglary, 45 per cent for robbery, 31 per cent for fraud and forgery, and 51 per cent for criminal damage were ordered to pay compensation. Failure to pay compensation can result in imprisonment. The Home Office issues magistrates with a table of injuries which indicates typical amounts of compensation. This type of compensation is limited. As only a small number of offences result in the conviction of an offender, awards are restricted to a small proportion of victims and are also limited by offenders' ability to pay. Where offenders have small incomes or are reliant on state benefits, victims may receive small amounts over a long period of time – which may prolong the financial and emotional effects of the offence (**Davies 2003; Reeves and Mulley 2002**). Victim Support has called for victims to be compensated immediately by the courts, with offenders having to pay instalments to the court (**Reeves and Mulley 2002**). While many victims therefore do receive compensation it applies to only a small proportion of victims and may not fully recompense them for the impact of offences.

3.5 Victim support

Objective 5
Describe the aspects of support for victims

There is now an extensive network of support available for victims. Victim Support provides a range of services, and criminal justice agencies and women's groups have addressed the needs of particular groups of victims such as rape victims, women who have suffered from domestic violence and support for the bereaved after murder and manslaughter (SAMM). The activities of Victim Support have already been referred to and they now offer help to over one million crime victims per year. Victim support schemes were first set up in Bristol in 1974 and were nationally regulated by the National Association of Victim Support Schemes (NAVSS), which received financial support from the government. By 2000, there were 386 schemes throughout England, Wales and Northern Ireland staffed by over 17,000 volunteers. Victim Support, as it is now known, is a charity which, in addition to providing individual support for victims, aims to influence the provision of services for victims and campaigns on matters relating to compensation and provision for the victim in court. It has established itself as the major victim-based organisation and has, argues **Goodey (2005: 105)**, assumed a 'quasi-official' status, being routinely consulted about changes to victim-orientated policy.

The major role of victim support is to provide services, on a voluntary basis, to individual victims at the local level. Each victim support scheme is run by a management committee, and a coordinator collects details of victims from the police. Under local agreements the police give the local victim support scheme information about victims, including their name and address, unless the victim asks them not to. These details are then distributed to a pool of volunteers who contact victims either by letter, telephone or doorstep visits.

Schemes provide help with practical matters or the provision of information. The emphasis of victim support has mainly been on short-term help and support on a 'good neighbour' principle by providing a shoulder to cry on (**Gill and Mawby 1990**). The original emphasis was mainly on victims of burglary, robbery or theft; although it has now expanded its work to include more long-term work with the victims of sexual and violent crime, the families of murder victims, and some schemes include a service for those involved in serious motor accidents. It aims to provide a comprehensive service to all victims of crime, and to ensure that victims have access to services and that they can talk freely to an outsider, and also now runs a witness service to support those giving evidence. It also emphasises working closely with criminal justice agencies and is politically neutral, factors which have arguably contributed to its success (**Newburn 2003**).

In addition to Victim Support, a range of services address the needs of particular groups of victims, particularly women and children. As seen above, an important part of the victims' movement was played by women's groups who also initiated support mechanisms. In 1972 in Chiswick, Erin Pizzey established the first refuge for victims of domestic violence. Rape crisis centres were also developed during the 1970s, and by 1988 there were 40 such centres. These, staffed mainly by volunteers, offer a helpline and a 24-hour counselling service. A Home Office Circular (69/1986) to chief police officers offered advice on achieving better treatment for victims of rape and domestic violence, including the provision of private facilities for the examination of victims, reference to advice and coun-selling services, and police training. Many police forces developed specialist units to provide a better service for women and child victims, and some set up special interview suites in police stations staffed by trained teams of female officers.

In addition, the CJA 1988 contained tougher provisions to ensure the anonym-ity of rape victims. The woman's identity is safeguarded, subject to the oversight of the courts, from the moment of allegation, whether or not any proceedings follow, and for the rest of her life. Other measures, described below, have now been introduced to assist rape victims in court. In January 2009, Sara Payne, the mother of eight-year-old Sarah Payne who was murdered in 2008, was appointed to a new one-year post of Victims' Champion. Her role was to listen to the con-cerns of victims, represent their views to government, to urge further reforms of criminal justice practices and to work with Victim Support and learn from the organisation's experience. The appointment was designed to lay the foundations for the development of a post of Commissioner for Victims and Witnesses from 2010. Louise Casey, who served as the first from 2010–2011, emphasised the disappointment she felt at the distinct failure of the criminal justice system to meet 'the very real needs of a victim or their families'. Casey described the victim as 'the poor relation' in the criminal justice system and spoke with fervour about the state having to fulfil their part of 'the deal' – i.e. ensure that justice against the victim's perpetrator is served. Making sure that justice is done involves more than simply sentencing the perpetrator, however: Casey's annual report cited poor communication – the failure of the law agencies to keep families informed about ongoing cases or offenders' release dates – as being the most common cause of distress among victims. Before vacating the post, Casey made a plea to introduce a 'victims' law', which would give victims legally enforceable rights, rather than a charter or a code of practice (**Casey 2011**). The post remained vacant until December 2012, when Baroness Newlove, the widow of a man who was murdered in 2007 by a gang of car vandals whom he had apprehended, was appointed as the new commissioner.

It has been suggested that recent technological advances could help to transform the victim's experience of dealing with the criminal justice system by allowing them to track their cases online, view real-time crime maps for their areas and open up the lines of communication between victims and the police, the courts and the Crown Prosecution Service. In June 2012, the think tank IPPR, published a study entitled *Empowering victims through Data and Technology*, which proposed that every police force in England and Wales should develop a crime-tracking app to enable all victims in their area to follow their case through the system, and that criminal justice agencies should systematically refer victims to online peer support networks or Victim Support, and that the courts should become more accessible and transparent by publishing details online of the cases they are dealing with (**Muir 2012**).

3.6 Victims and criminal justice

Objective 6

Explain the part played by victims in the criminal justice system

Criminal justice agencies require cooperation from victims to provide information and evidence, and yet the relationship between victims and the criminal justice process can be problematic. Criminal justice agencies deal primarily with offenders, and may not take victims' interests or needs into account. As seen above, victims may require protection and support and desire information about the progress of their case. Yet, as Davies has commented:

> . . . realistically . . . the police and criminal justice system have nothing tangible to offer the victim. There are no guarantees that property will be returned, that the offender/s will be caught or that justice will be done.
>
> (Davies 2003: 13)

Complex issues also arise when considering the appropriate role of the victim in a criminal justice process which has as its primary aim establishing the elements of the offence and securing a fair balance between the conviction of those guilty of a crime and the rights of defendants to fair proceedings at all stages. Addressing victims' needs and involving the victim in the process may conflict with defendants' rights, particularly in relation to giving evidence and sentencing. This section will look at the role of the victim in some key areas of criminal justice, starting with the first stage at which victims come into contact – reporting crime.

▶ Reporting crime and the role of the police

It was seen in **Chapter 2**, that not all victims report crime to the police as many feel that the police would do little or might not take them seriously, yet the police are reliant on victims to report crime and to provide information which may help them construct a case against an offender.

We have seen that some victims experience particular difficulties, including victims of rape and domestic violence. In addition, victims of racially motivated crime have complained that the police fail to take account of racial motivation. Indeed, once new instructions were issued, reporting rates for many of these crimes increased. Nevertheless, some victims remain reluctant to report some crimes and, in general terms, the police and victims may have different priorities. While the primary concern for the police is detecting and prosecuting the offender, victims may want reassurance, protection, advice and information.

Following the Victims' Charters, the police role widened. They are expected to provide victims with more information and a leaflet about support services and compensation and to refer victims to Victim Support, which in itself is heavily reliant on the police for referrals. The provision of such information has been found to vary, and the ability of the police to provide support and advice may be limited by the demands of their other work. **Reeves and Mulley (2000)** give the example of the treatment of rape victims. Some police stations have set up a 'chaperone' system in which one specialist officer deals with the victim. After a period of time, however, the victim may still need support and help, whereas the dedicated officer must move on to other cases.

Following the second Victims' Charter, a pilot project described as 'One Stop Shop' (OSS) was developed in six police force areas. Under this initiative, victims of selected crimes could opt into a scheme in which they were kept informed by the police about whether a suspect is cautioned or charged, whether the charge is altered, the date of the trial, verdict and sentence.

Another major initiative arising out of the Victim's Charter was the introduction of pilot schemes of Victim Statements (VS), in which victims have a chance to describe the physical, emotional, financial and other effects of the offence. These, now known as Victim Personal Statements (VPS), are initiated by the police and passed on to the CPS – their use will be discussed below in relation to sentencing.

The 2005 Code of Practice contains four pages of detailed statements about police obligations in relation to victims, along with providing time limits by which certain kinds of information must be given to victims (**Home Office 2005; Mawby 2007**). These include, for example, requirements to advise victims where no investigation will be pursued, provide them with information about support services, pass on their details to Victim Support and notify the victim on at least a monthly basis about progress in cases. They must advise victims about any investigations which have not led to the detection of a suspect, and must inform victims about any arrests, the release of offenders on bail and any bail conditions. Despite its detail, however, it deals largely with information and less with the way in which the police interact with victims – for example, whether they are treated sympathetically or not (**Mawby 2007**).

Victims' satisfaction with the police forms a specific section of the British Crime Survey. In 2010/11, 38 per cent of those who had been a victim of a crime and had been in contact with the police about it said that they were very satisfied with the contact, 32 per cent were fairly satisfied and 30 per cent were not satisfied. Longer-term trends show between 2007/08 and 2010/11, the proportion of victims very satisfied with the contact they had with the police increased by 12 percentage points (**Innes, 2011**).

▶ Victims in court

Without victims to act as willing witnesses the successful prosecution of criminals is difficult. The burden and the standard of proof tilts the system of justice in favour of the defendant. It is not as in a civil case where the judge has to decide which side to believe. In criminal cases the defendants do not have to explain themselves, as they are presumed innocent, and therefore the active role in a case is given to the prosecution to explain what happened, to identify who was culpable and to demonstrate this beyond reasonable doubt. This is difficult and in many cases impossible without victims willing to act as witnesses in court, which means undergoing the process of adversarial justice whereby the victim's version of events is frequently challenged by the defence. For many, this adds to the outrage of being a victim.

Giving evidence and being subjected to cross-examination can be intimidating and it can be time-consuming, incur loss of earnings, and emotionally stressful as it involves reliving an unpleasant experience. It has also been seen that these problems are particularly marked for victims of violent and sexual offences whose credibility may be challenged. Despite the many improvements which have been made, **Newburn (2003)** cites a study by **Spencer and Stern (2002)** who found that around two-fifths of witnesses felt so intimidated by appearing in court and being cross-examined that they would not wish to give evidence again.

Victim Support has also been involved with the provision of schemes to help victims in court, arising out of victims' complaints about their experiences. Initially a number of pilot schemes were set up. One such scheme was described by **Rock (1991)**, who found that the main role of volunteers was to offer 'companionship and solace' during the long periods of waiting and confusion. All Crown Court centres now have a witness service run by Victim Support which includes advice about what might happen in court, and victims and witnesses should receive a leaflet about their roles. By 2002, services were also available in magistrates' courts.

Rape victims and child witnesses have had their particular difficulties recognised. Child witnesses may have their evidence pre-recorded on video tape, be cross-examined by TV-link from outside the court and may not be cross-examined by the accused personally. Rape victims are prevented from being asked about their sexual experience with people other than the defendant. The Youth Justice and Criminal Evidence Act 1999 contained a range of further provisions for such witnesses including screening witnesses from the accused, giving evidence by a live link, the removal of barristers' and judges' wigs and gowns, the opportunity to give evidence in private, video-recording of cross- and re-examinations of witnesses, examination through intermediaries and aids to communication for young or incapacitated witnesses.

These measures aim to assist victims to provide evidence and successive Labour governments have placed a very high priority on maximising the extent to which victims and witnesses are prepared to give evidence in court, believing that this is a crucial factor in maximising conviction rates (**Mawby 2007**). This has led to the 'No Witness, No Justice' initiative and to the setting up of new Witness Care Units, jointly run by the local police and CPS, working closely with Victim Support and the Witness Service. They provide for a single point of contact for victims and the identification of any problems which victims and witnesses have with attending court. The tasks of these Witness Care Units are spelt out in the 2005 Code of Practice and include the provision of a full needs assessment with victims, the provision of information such as the 'Witness in Court' or 'Young Witness in Court' leaflets, the date of criminal hearings and information about court hearings.

The Code also specifies responsibilities for the CPS including:

- liaising with the police in relation to this information;
- explaining, in certain cases, why a decision to proceed has been made;
- introducing themselves to victims and witnesses and explaining and answering questions about proceedings and sentences;
- arranging for the prompt payment of expenses.

Court staff should, where possible, liaise with Witness Care Units, ensure that victims have a separate waiting area from the defendants' family and friends, should not have to wait more than two hours and should have access to information. They should also, as far as is possible, ensure the availability of special measures for vulnerable victims.

While few dispute that victims should be assisted in this way, and that special provision should be made for vulnerable victims, there remain issues about how far the protection of witnesses and providing them with assistance may interfere with defendants' rights to question those making accusations against them – a fundamental right in the adversarial system of justice. Moreover, many defendants may also find the court an intimidating setting in which to present their version of events.

▶ Victims and sentencing

There is considerable controversy over what role, if any, victims should play in sentencing, other than being compensated through compensation orders. So far policy in England and Wales has fallen short of so-called 'victim allocation models' practised in some jurisdictions which provide some measure of victim empowerment, and a role in prosecution and sentencing decisions (**Walklate 2007**). In the United States of America, for example, there are provisions in some states for victim impact statements to precede the court's consideration of compensation and sentencing. In some cases victims may state an opinion about the sentence. In California the courts and the parole boards must listen to representation by victims, their relatives or legal representatives at the time of sentencing or in hearings regarding early prison release.

These ideas have some strength but also raise significant issues. **Ashworth (2000)**, for example, points out that victims have been wronged by the crime and allocation allows them to express their thoughts, although there may be other ways of achieving what is seen as a therapeutic effect. As seen above, the criminal justice system needs the cooperation of victims and it may be appropriate to make them feel that they have a role – in this sense victim participation can act, according to Ashworth, as a 'sweetener'. On the other hand, he, along with others, queries whether victims want this degree of involvement and it is also pointed out that it is the state's responsibility to make decisions about offenders. Other arguments against the use of impact statements are that it may be difficult to test the accuracy of the claims made and that it is questionable whether the court should take account of what may be the unforeseen effects of the offence on victims. While therefore it may be appropriate to use victim statements when deciding on compensation or reparation, it is less appropriate to use them in other aspects of sentencing. Victims' involvement in sentencing also conflicts with other principles of sentencing – it may for example introduce elements of inconsistency as victims may differ in their attitudes and victims may be present in some cases but not others.

While falling short of allocution some measures have introduced an element of victim involvement into sentencing considerations. As seen above, in 2001 a Victim Personal Statement (VPS) Scheme was introduced which, according to a Practice Direction, was to play a limited role in sentencing – the statement could be used to provide information about the impact of the offence. While some victims welcomed this opportunity, many were disappointed as they did not know what use had been made of their statement. These are optional and the take-up of the option has been very low (**Sanders and Jones 2007**).

Since 2006, the relatives of victims of manslaughter and murder have been entitled to make a statement regarding the death of their relative. These statements should be limited to the effect of a death and it should not give an opinion on possible punishments. One family impact statement, written by the bereaved mother of a murder victim, was recently censored for referring, however obliquely, to a possible sentence by stating that the murderer 'should never be allowed freedom out of jail to be able to do it again, he should rot in prison'.

In August 2014, a Crown Court judge's comment caused controversy, when following an impact statement from a murder victim's parents – Colin McGinty was stabbed to death and his murderer convicted – who made an impact statement about their feelings and grief at the loss of their son. They did so via a video link. Judge Graham White, thought the video link was closed when he commented, 'I feel sorry for these families. They make these statements thinking they are going to make a difference [to the sentence], but they make no difference at all.'

Critics have questioned the extent to which it privileges the families of homicide victims at the expense of those victims who have been seriously harmed but not killed (ibid.). The journalist Marcel Berlins argued that victim and family statements give unfair gravitas to 'the articulate, the educated and the attractive' compared to 'those with lesser advantages – and whose loved ones could not be painted in saintly colours' ('Why victim impact statements should be axed', Marcel Berlins, *The Guardian*, 4 December 2006), while Jan Moir, another voluble columnist, agreed with Berlins, adding that the statements would be better suited to a group therapy session than a British courtroom, and that the impact statements do not, in fact, always seem to garner the effect on sentencing that the victim would perhaps like to see ('Victim impact statements have no place in the UK', Jan Moir, *Daily Telegraph*, 24 October 2007).

Recent research into victim personal statements suggests that only a minority of those who submit impact statements are seeking to influence sentencing. In 2011, the Victims' Commissioner requested researchers at the University of Oxford to examine data collected by the Witness and Victim Experience Survey (WAVES) over the preceding three years (i.e. from 2008 to 2011) and to conduct a review into victim personal statements. The researchers reported that the majority of statements are intended by the victim to communicate a message to the court and the offender, not to influence the severity of the sentence.

▶ Mediation and restorative justice

Victims have also been involved in the growth of schemes falling under the general heading of restorative justice which are linked to mediation and reparation, and the involvement of victims is a key part in the government's efforts to 'rebalance' the criminal justice system. Restorative justice involves a variety of strategies which aim to bring the offender and victim together, sometimes in 'conferencing' schemes, with a view to encouraging the offender to recognise the harm done by the offence and to make some direct reparation. There has also been a growth in mediation schemes, which involve meetings between offenders and victims, by which some form of compensation might be agreed. Such schemes can operate as an alternative to the formal trial process, as part of a community sentence, or while the offender is in custody. While in theory restorative justice is supposed to involve and empower victims, in practice schemes have been criticised as offender-centred and there have been both theoretical and practical difficulties in involving victims – particularly individual victims as opposed to the wider 'community'. A further problem with the participation of victims in restorative justice is that the extent to which it benefits primarily offenders or victims can be questioned. It can, as **Reeves and Mulley (2000)** argue, become a burden as it is not clear how much victims genuinely want to be involved and many schemes are primarily directed towards educating and rehabilitating offenders. One critic, **Dignan (2007: 323)** argues that the government's rhetoric has not been matched by a commitment to promote the development of 'restorative justice initiatives specifically for the benefit of victims'.

Some schemes have been introduced which contain restorative elements involving victims. The Crime and Disorder Act 1998 introduced a new reparation order which can be a sentence on its own or combined with other disposals, and which requires the young offender to make reparation to the victim. This can involve mediation but evaluations have found that only 9 per cent of cases resulted in mediation between victims and offenders (**Dignan 2007**). The Youth Justice and Criminal Evidence Act 1999 set up **youth offender panels** (YOPs) in which victims may be involved and which can be an alternative to prosecution. There have, however, been difficulties in involving victims and victim participation rates are low, although this may be due to the patchy implementation of schemes (**Newburn 2003; Zedner 2002**).

There are a number of reasons for the low take-up of these options by victims. Some are largely bureaucratic, relating to the length of time cases take to proceed through the system and difficulties of sharing information between agencies such as the police and Young Offender Teams. In addition, however, there are problems with the focus of youth justice on offenders – members of YOPs for example may find it difficult to accept their role in relation to the victim as well as the offender (**Dignan 2007**).

The Restorative Justice Council (RJC) is a campaign group for wider take-up of restorative justice. The Ministry of Justice supports its work through funding and the results of a seven-year-long pilot programme funded by the government revealed that 85 per cent of the victims who took part in a restorative justice programme were satisfied with the outcome.

Conclusion

We have seen, therefore, that crime has a considerable impact on its individual victims, on communities and on the quality of life of all citizens, an impact which may fall particularly heavily on specific groups and is also likely to have a widespread consequence on communities at large in terms of feeling safe in their neighbourhoods. This directs our attention to the need to look carefully at where crime has a more severe impact and at strategies aimed to prevent crime **(which will be the subject of Chapter 5)**, and at the role that sentencing can play in reassuring the public and in reducing criminality **(in Chapter 11, and Chapter 12 on sentencing and penal policy)**.

We have also seen that, having formerly been largely neglected by the criminal justice process and in legislation, much greater attention is now paid to the needs and interests of victims, and a wide range of policies have undoubtedly improved the experiences of victims in the criminal justice process. Despite the large volume of legislation and policies dealing with victims, however, there are still major issues to be addressed, including the culture of criminal justice agencies which may not fully recognise the needs of victims. Further problems lie in the extent to which these many initiatives and the extensive requirements of, for example, the Code of Practice, have added to the responsibilities of criminal justice agencies such as the police, the CPS and the probation service. 'Integrating a victim's perspective' **(Crawford and Goodey 2000)** into the criminal justice process involves a major rethinking of the roles of agencies, which in turn involves a cultural change within them.

This is related to the often-made point that traditionally our adversarial criminal justice system has focused on offenders as suspects and defendants, which means that a balance must be drawn between the rights of defendants and those of victims, and the appropriate role of victims in the sentencing process. Victims' interests may also, as **Reeves and Mulley (2000)** argue, be 'hijacked' by the criminal justice agenda. Emphasising the assumed needs or interests of victims can be used by those who argue for more severe sentences – thus, **Ashworth (2000)** points to the dangers of victims being used in the 'service of severity'. He also argues that they can be used in the 'service of offenders': for example, when they are involved in restorative justice schemes, which, as seen above, Victim Support also identifies as a potential burden for victims. There are dangers, therefore, of what Ashworth describes as 'victim prostitution' and there are also dangers of victims being used by politicians keen to demonstrate that they are doing something about crime.

Review questions

1. What do victim surveys tell us about which groups of people are most likely to be the victims of crime and which are least likely? Provide some examples of this kind of evidence.

2. List the different ways in which victims can be supported or involved at each stage of the criminal justice process.

Discussion questions

1. Consider how far victims should have 'rights' in the criminal justice process. Can victims' rights conflict with offenders' rights?

2. Examine the Victim Support website and identify a current issue affecting victims. What are the key concerns?

Further reading

Davies P, Greer C and Francis P (eds) (2007) *Victims, Crime and Society*, Sage: London

Goodey J (2004) *Victims and Victimology: Research, Policy and Practice*, Pearson Longman: Harlow

Walklate S (2007) *Imagining the Victim of Crime*, Open University Press: Maidenhead

Walklate S (ed) (2007) *Handbook of Victims and Victimology*, Willan Publishing: Cullompton

Weblinks

Criminal Injuries Compensation Authority: **www.cica.gov.uk/**

Victim Support: **www.victimsupport.org.uk/**

Restorative Justice Council: **www.restorativejustice.org.uk/**

Crime Survey for England and Wales: **crimesurvey.co.uk/**

Chapter 4

Governmental, political and administrative context of criminal justice in England and Wales

Learning objectives

After reading the chapter you should be able to:

1. Explain the role of law and policy making
2. Describe the importance of government on criminal justice policy and practice
3. Understand the political context of criminal justice in England and Wales
4. Describe aspects of 'Globalisation' and cross-jurisdictional and international responses to crime
5. Explain the influences from Europe on criminal justice policy
6. Understand the complexities of implementing criminal justice policy
7. Describe the ways by which the system is monitored and is accountable to the public

Key statistics

- The criminal justice system costs over £20 billion pounds a year. (Estimate from Ministry of Justice (July 2012) *Swift and Sure Justice: The Government's Plans for Reform of the Criminal Justice System*)
- Up to 100 magistrates' courts are now sitting on Saturdays and Bank Holidays in England and Wales
- The Ministry of Justice is responsible for 500 courts and tribunals and 133 prisons

- From 2009 to July 2013, European Arrest Warrants (EAW) were issued in 5,184 cases resulting in 4,005 people (77%) being returned to the issuing country
- From 2009 to July 2013 the EAW was used to extradite from the UK 57 suspects for child sex offences, 86 for rape and 105 for murder; in the same period, 63 suspects for child sex offences, 27 for rape and 44 for murder were extradited back to Britain to face charges

Introduction

Protecting the public is a major theme in political rhetoric that legitimates, or justifies, the very existence of government. While the provision of schools, hospitals and roads is important, they become secondary when citizens fear for their safety in the communities where they live. As Thomas Hobbes pointed out in the seventeenth century in *Leviathan* (1650), there are limits to the extent to which individuals can protect themselves and therefore one of the major responsibilities and purposes of government is to provide security against threats to personal safety from others. Thus criminal justice systems are expected to protect both the citizen and their property; and in the early twenty-first century the sense of personal security and fear of crime requires a governmental response that encompasses a global as well as a domestic perspective.

In a democratic society there may be differences of opinion as to how public protection, and the process of reassurance that goes with this, can best be achieved. Since the late eighteenth century we have seen a steady growth of interest in all aspects of criminal justice. With this have come innovative modes of intervention:

- the development of professionals such as the police, psychiatrists and social workers;
- new institutions such as borstals, youth courts and detention centres;
- use of technologies for crime prevention, investigation and offender monitoring such as fingerprints, electronic tagging, **DNA** and CCTV;
- a succession of paradigms about how best to curb crime, deal with criminals, maintain law and order, and provide due process to ensure justice for those accused of a crime.

It is evident that ideas about these issues are subject to change and today's plethora of legislation, which would have been inconceivable by Parliaments and governments for much of the twentieth century, illustrates that we live in a society where

103

the response to crime is a major feature of government and politics. One aspect of the section on politics includes a look at the approach of the New Labour Government, in power from 1997 to 2010 following 18 years of Conservative governments (1979–1997). Reforms include those to the hallowed and traditional role of the Lord Chancellor, new rules on detaining terrorist suspects, measures to prevent criminals living off the proceeds of crime, and interventions and experiments to curtail crime by use of neighbourhood curfews on children on the street after 9 p.m. New Labour cannot be accused of complacency as every aspect of criminal justice underwent review and reform.

In this chapter, we will identify the main features of the administrative, political and policy-making context of the criminal justice system in England and Wales. Key players are to be found in Whitehall and Westminster but we will be looking beyond the United Kingdom to the increasing internationalisation of crime policy, particularly the growth in European cooperation, and further fuelled since 11 September 2001 by fears of international terrorism; a fear that had a local impact in July 2005 when terrorist bombs killed 52 people travelling on London Transport buses and tube trains.

We will examine issues to do with the implementation of criminal justice policy such as the problems of coordination between agencies, the increasing role played by private industry and the continuing and considerable role played by the lay and voluntary sector. Pragmatic and political issues are raised by the system for evaluating and monitoring the effectiveness of agencies through such innovations as performance indicators. Despite greater efforts to clarify objectives and assess performance, the issue of accountability is still relevant as it affects public confidence in the system and whether it is believed to work to protect people's safety and property. The political and public reaction to crime policy will involve issues of how crime is represented in the media and the attitudes of the public to issues of crime and punishment. This leads on to the role that the public may play in responding to crime, through initiatives such as Crime and Disorder Reduction Partnerships. The public might also become involved as victims of crime, and we will discuss some of the recent reforms that focus on victims (**see also Chapter 3**). Ideas change and policy experiments and initiatives do not wait for legislation but enter the fray of public discourse. Fashions change about the proper way to respond to crime, and new theories, policies and slogans may become encapsulated in crime strategies and new policy directions.

4.1 Law and policy making

▶ Who makes crime policy?

Objective 1

Explain the role of law and policy making

The most fundamental statement of criminal justice policy is to be found in legislation. Acts of Parliament provide both the starting point for defining many crimes and also the criminal justice agencies' powers and responsibilities in their response to crime.

In the United Kingdom, central government plays the dominant role in legislative reforms. Laws may start out as ideas in ministerial speeches, parliamentary statements and election manifestos. After a period of 18 years in opposition the newly formed Labour Government set out its approach to crime in the Crime and Disorder Act 1998. At other times the government may be responding to a new or newly perceived problem as a result of a single incident which reflects wider public anxiety. Following the stabbing of headmaster Philip Lawrence outside his school in Maida Vale in 1995 the law was changed to prohibit children under 16 from buying knives. The murders of Jessica Chapman and Holly Wells in Soham in 2003, prompted calls to change police vetting procedures and raised questions about the misuse and misunderstandings of the Data Protection Act. The murder of Stephen Lawrence in 1993 prompted far-reaching analyses of policing (**discussed in Chapter 6**) and led to a change to the law to allow for a retrial, previously regarded as infringing the double jeopardy rule (Criminal Justice Act 2003). Concerns over identifying which one of a couple was responsible for the death of a child in their care led to provisions in the Domestic Violence, Crime and Victims Act 2004. The terrorist bombings in London in 2005, along with a general concern about terrorism, led to controversial proposals to increase the period that terrorist suspects can be detained. The fatal stabbing of Ben Kinsella in 2008 led to longer minimum sentences for knife-murders. The response to the protesters encamped in Parliament Square in 2011, was to ban such encampments in the Police Reform and Social Responsibility Act 2011. The Ministry of Justice publication of 2010, *Breaking the Cycle: effective punishment, rehabilitation and sentencing of offenders* led to the Legal Aid, Sentencing and Punishment of Offenders Act 2012 (LASPO).

Where legislation is approaching the planning stage, the government may issue a **Green Paper**, a general discussion document inviting comment on particular ideas or proposals. Subsequently, a White Paper may be published which gives firm detailed proposals taking account of the feedback from the Green Paper. The White Paper is the most definitive statement of the government's policy and usually forms the basis of subsequent bills, although many bills are introduced without this preliminary process of deliberation. All bills must go through a number of stages in both the House of Commons and the House of Lords before being transformed into an Act of Parliament. This process is not a formality and parliamentary debate may lead to amendments to the original details set out in the bill.

Policy can emerge in forms other than legislation and can be influenced not only by ministers or other politicians. Permanent officials in government departments will also have a departmental view on such issues as prison reduction and police powers. Policy statements are not always embodied in statute, and innovations such as the introduction of the office of the Prison Ombudsman and providing cautioning *in lieu* of prosecution by the police had no statutory basis but emerged from decisions within the Home Office. Documents published by the Home Office are most influential on a range of matters concerning the police, law enforcement and terrorism. The Ministry of Justice (formerly the Lord Chancellor's Department and the Department for Constitutional Affairs) is important on matters relating to the judiciary, the courts, prisons and probation.

Whitehall – a term that refers to both ministers and civil servants – is not the only source of policy statements. The work of the Home Affairs Committee at Westminster is important, as are the views of the senior members of the judiciary in the House of Lords who have spoken strongly against proposals for mandatory prison sentences for those reconvicted of serious violent or sexual offences, drug trafficking and for those convicted for a third time of burglary of a domestic dwelling. They were very critical of Michael Howard when he was Home Secretary, and claimed he was pandering to public opinion in introducing tougher penalties that would increase the prison population.

It would be simplistic to think that policymaking is restricted to Whitehall and Westminster. Policy is also found in the many documents defining the role and approach of the various agencies and professional and voluntary bodies that make up the criminal justice system. The process of policy making is very complex and reflects the fact that government is only one of a number of key players in the system. Other influential players in the process of consultation are professional groups, pressure groups and lay participants, who have a unique role in criminal justice in this country when compared with others. The Magistrates' Association, for instance, has played an important role in developing sentencing guidelines.

Professional bodies are of considerable influence in England and Wales, and include the following:

- **Association of Chief Police Officers (ACPO)**
- **Police Federation** (represents the ordinary police officer)
- National Association of Probation Officers (NAPO)
- Prison Officers' Association (POA)
- Prison Governors' Association
- Bar Council and the Criminal Bar Association (represent barristers)
- **Law Society** (represents solicitors)
- Justices' Clerks Society.

The most powerful of professions on matters of criminal law, procedure and prosecution are the lawyers, represented by the Bar Council, Criminal Bar Association and Law Society, and the judiciary (judges) both individually and through bodies such as the Council of Circuit Judges and the Judicial Studies Board. The judiciary, although small in number, is powerful in defence of the principle of its independence, and is regularly consulted about new legislation. Lawyers' views are sought and listened to by the major government departments such as the Office of the Attorney General – responsible for the Crown Prosecution Service – and the Ministry of Justice, which is responsible for constitutional matters, the appointment and training of judges, and the administration of the courts through the Courts and Tribunals Service.

▶ Parliament and the Select Committee on Home Affairs

A system of select committees was introduced in 1979, allowing for committees of the House of Commons to monitor the work of government departments. The aim was to provide a forum by which parliamentary committees could monitor and scrutinise the work of government departments. The Select Committee on Home Affairs has over the years held public hearings and issued reports on a number of criminal justice topics such as improving the machinery for investigating complaints against the police (1981), administration of the prison service (1981) and the state and use of prisons (1987). Similar topics have been revisited over time: police disciplinary codes and complaints procedure (1997–8), and the use of custody in 1998. The committee's agenda is heavily influenced by the legislative proposals and reports of the Home Office. It also returned once again to a topic that has arisen several times since 1979 and is no doubt related to the activities of the pressure groups such as Nacro: that is the rehabilitation of prisoners and the effectiveness of prisons in reducing reoffending.

In 1997, Frederick Crawford, chairman of the new Criminal Cases Review Commission, gave evidence about the work of the Commission, and the then Lord Chancellor, Lord Irvine, gave evidence about the work of the Lord Chancellor's Department. In 2007 it published reports on the use of surveillance and counter-terrorism; in 2008 on policing and forced marriages, while in 2009 it investigated knife crime, managing migration, human trafficking and wheel clamping. In 2011, the Home Affairs Committee turned its attention to the subject of phone-hacking allegations against the *News of the World* newspaper and the 'unauthorised tapping into or hacking of mobile communications'. In early 2012, it published a report to determine the roots of terrorist movements in the UK linked to Islamic fundamentalism, Irish dissident republicanism and domestic extremism, reviewing the appropriateness of the government's current preventative approaches to violent radicalisation. The committee can set its own agenda and may develop its own particular perspective on issues. Its prison reductionist agenda has been apparent for some time, regardless of the party in government. The committee inquired into the use of custody and alternatives to prison sentences with the aim of seeking 'to reduce the prison population' (Home Affairs Committee, Press Notice, 31 July 1997).

In January 1998, the committee published a critical report of the existing procedure for dealing with complaints against the police (**outlined in Chapter 6**). Its 43 recommendations included proposals to improve the system of dealing with corruption by police officers and to reform the complaints and disciplinary system. The report sought a change to the rules in disciplinary hearings involving police officers, moving away from the existing standard of proof, beyond reasonable doubt, as used in criminal court cases, to the civil court standard based on the balance of probabilities. Furthermore, an officer acquitted in a criminal case would not face subsequent disciplinary charges. While open to criticism on the ground of **double jeopardy**, the report recommended the possibility of further action when an officer is found not guilty in court. Other recommendations related to holding disciplinary meetings in public and making it easier to sack police officers guilty of serious misconduct. The Home Secretary accepted the report and produced reforms to the way the police complaints and disciplinary system works (**see Chapter 6**).

Established parliamentary lobby groups also work within Westminster. The All-Party Parliamentary Penal Affairs Group (APPPAG) started in 1979 and was aided by a clerk, Paul Cavadino, who worked as the senior information officer for Nacro, and later became chief executive of the organisation. This lobby group has a close relationship with the Prison Reform Trust and has led the prison reductionist argument in Parliament with considerable success. For example, the introduction of statutory criteria for the use of custody for those under 21 in the Criminal Justice Act 1982 led to a substantial drop in the use of custody for those offenders. Other campaigns have not been so successful, such as attempts to reform the mandatory life sentence for murder. Reformers have persuaded Parliament to take a lead on some criminal justice issues such as the abolition of the death penalty, against the wishes of the majority of the voting public. Since the Murder (Abolition of the Death Penalty) Act 1965, the House of Commons has held 14 debates and votes between 1969 and 1994 and each time there was a clear majority against the restoration of capital punishment. Public opinion has consistently shown about a 70 to 30 per cent divide in favour of the death penalty, but, despite this, MPs have consistently voted against its restoration. This is possibly because the government of the day has not regarded this issue as a matter of government or party political policy but left it to a 'free vote' in which MPs are asked to follow their conscience.

4.2 Government and administration

▶ Home Office

Objective 2

Describe the importance of government on criminal justice policy and practice

The Home Office was for many years the major government department with respect to criminal justice policy. As a source of ideas and funding, its role is pivotal in determining reforms of the criminal law and the direction of criminal justice policy. Until 2007, the Home Office had responsibilities for the police, prisons, probation, reviewing the criminal law, crime prevention and victim support. It has other non-criminal duties regarding the fire service, immigration control, dangerous dogs, national security, licensing of gambling and sales of alcohol, passports and applications for British citizenship. In 2007, responsibility for prisons, probation, the Parole Board and sentencing policy was transferred to the new Ministry of Justice.

While it is wrong to suggest that there is only one source of influence on criminal justice policy in England and Wales, the Home Office was until 2007 the government agency with an overall view of the system. Issues of public confidence in the system of justice in terms of effectiveness, efficiency and fairness would now normally be regarded as the responsibility of both the Home Office and the new Ministry of Justice.

The Home Office has responsibilities regarding the criminal justice system in the following areas:

- public safety and responding to public disasters;
- responding to terrorism;
- policy, funding, training and the efficiency of the police service, including setting performance indicators and vetting senior appointments;
- forensic services (an executive agency of the Home Office since 1991);
- exercising the prerogative of mercy;
- dealing with foreign jurisdictions on matters of common policy, for example Europol, and individual decisions regarding the extradition of suspects and the transfer of convicted prisoners;

- mentally disordered persons subject to restriction orders;
- producing annual statistics on the work of the criminal justice agencies and commissioning and conducting research into policy developments;
- providing information to Parliament in response to parliamentary questions about activities under its control and providing information for government inquiries and Royal Commissions on criminal justice topics;
- promoting crime prevention policy;
- conducting the Crime Survey for England and Wales.

The responsibilities and duties of the Home Office have frequently changed to reflect changing policy and political concerns. For example, the administration and control of prisons between 1877 and 1963 was the responsibility of the Prison Commission. In 1964, prisons came under the direct control of the Prison Department in the Home Office. The Permanent Secretary at the Home Office at that time, Charles Cunningham, believed the advantage of amalgamating the Prison Service into the Home Office was that it would bring the key law enforcement and crime control agencies under one roof to allow for a more integrated approach to crime prevention and permit better planning of the forces available to the state to combat crime. The idea of coordinating the work of criminal justice agencies and involving the voluntary and business communities in multi-agency approaches will be discussed later in this chapter, and it is clear that in the 1980s the Home Office gave a lead on this issue in the field of crime prevention.

However, by the 1990s it was also clear that government was attempting to devolve and diversify responsibilities for the day-to-day running of criminal justice agencies and the courts. In 1993, the Prison Service became an executive agency. This signalled the beginning of a fundamental change in the administration of powers and budgets and management responsibilities. In 2007 after a series of problems which called into question the fitness for purpose of the Home Office, responsibility for prisons was transferred to the Ministry of Justice. It was argued at the time that the remit of the Home Office was too wide; thus a rebalancing was undertaken.

▶ Home Secretary

The Home Secretary is one of the major political figures in government. He/she is responsible for promoting criminal law reform and has a general responsibility for the criminal justice system, though this is now shared with the Ministry of Justice. During the 18-year period of previous Conservative governments, from 1979 to 1997, influential figures were appointed to the post: William Whitelaw, Leon Brittan, Douglas Hurd, David Waddington, Kenneth Baker, Kenneth Clarke and Michael Howard. In 1997, Jack Straw became the first Labour Party Home Secretary since Merlyn Rees in 1979, followed by David Blunkett in 2001. He was followed in quick succession by Charles Clarke, John Reid and in 2007 by the first female Home Secretary, Jacqui Smith, who was in turn followed by Alan Johnson in 2009. When the Coalition Government formed its Cabinet in May 2010, Theresa May took over the post. It is a demanding office to hold, and regarded as potentially disastrous for those who have further political ambitions, despite being one of the three great Offices of State, along with the Chancellor of the Exchequer and the Foreign Secretary. Only two twentieth-century Home Secretaries, Winston Churchill (1910–11) and Jim Callaghan (1967–70), went on to become Prime Minister.

Some of the momentum for reforms that laid the foundations for new agencies in the system of criminal justice came from influential nineteenth-century Home Secretaries. Robert Peel (1822–27 and 1828–30) played a vital role in the foundation of the Metropolitan Police Force. Lord Palmerston (1852–55) introduced a number of penal reforms during his period at the Home Office, abolishing transportation and substituting the sentence of penal servitude (The Penal Servitude Act 1853), and introducing reform schools (The Reformatory Schools Act 1854). Palmerston's responsibilities on matters of policing meant that a political row blew up when the political refugee, Louis Kossuth was exiled to London. He was a radical who led the independence movement to free the Magyars from the Austrian Empire. His activities were investigated by plain-clothed policemen and he was implicated in a plot to manufacture arms and send them to Hungary for use in an uprising. Parliamentary questions, threats of prosecution and press coverage, particularly in *The Times*, led to the type of high-profile public controversy that most Home Secretaries can expect to have to deal with.

Home Secretaries are vulnerable to the type of political rows that get front page press coverage. They are expected to respond to public disquiet following major crime stories such as those about Jack the Ripper in 1880 or Peter Sutcliffe in Yorkshire a century later. Murders particularly attract media coverage, no more so than when the victims are numerous (Fred and Rosemary West) or vulnerable, such as patients murdered by their doctor (Harold Shipman), or are children (Thompson and Venables, and Ian Huntley). Very emotive issues have to be considered, such as claims for the restoration of the death penalty, deaths in custody, and appropriate responses following miscarriages of justice, corruption within the police force, disasters such as those at Hillsborough and Dunblane, prison escapes such as those by the Great Train Robber, Ronnie Biggs, the KGB spy, George Blake and IRA terrorists.

They also have to consider what to do with terrorist or murder suspects who are wanted for crimes in jurisdictions where they are likely to receive the death penalty. The European Convention bars **extradition** of those who might be executed. So when the radical Muslim cleric, Abu Hamza Al-Mazri was arrested by police acting on a US extradition order for terrorism-related charges – i.e. helping al-Qaeda – the UK could not surrender him if the death penalty was a possibility. Likewise, the inability of the UK to deport terror suspect Abu Qatada to Jordan after his release from prison in February 2012 on human rights grounds caused huge public controversy. Theresa May faced immense pressure to personally persuade the Jordanian government to guarantee that, Abu Qatada would not face torture if deported. In the meantime the terror suspect was living in London on state benefits, much to the outrage of the general public.

Eventually, the Home Secretary secured a promise with regard to torture from the Jordanian government. Now that the Home Office was in a position to legally deport him, without contravening the ruling of the European Court of Human Rights, Theresa May jubilantly declared on 17 April 2012 that his deportation was now underway, and that as the three-month deadline for Abu Qatada's lawyers to lodge an appeal with the European Court of Human Rights against his deportation was believed to have passed, there was no way that Qatada could prevent this. The following day, among much derision from the opposition and the press, it emerged that the three-month deadline was in fact 24 hours later than when Theresa May had understood it to be, giving Qatada's lawyers 24 hours to lodge an appeal within the legal timeframe, which they duly did. The question of Abu Qatada's deportation was thus put on hold for several more months, pending the European Court's decision. Although the deportation was eventually granted in July 2013, the government's apparent inefficiency in dealing with such an important case has certainly damaged public confidence. The legal battle prompted proposals for reforms to human rights laws to make it easier to extradite foreign offenders from the UK. Such issues of great moral concern and public interest require the Home Secretary to provide leadership at times of heightened public anxiety about the safety of UK citizens from both domestic and overseas threats. In addition to the potential political rows following major crime and related incidents, the Home Secretary has a minefield to tread in the area of civil liberties. Unlike other government departments where the minister is responsible for the broad issues of policy, the Home Secretary has discretionary powers to make decisions affecting individuals in a number of ways, such as in deportation cases. Charles Clarke lost his post in a Cabinet reshuffle in May 2006 after a series of what were seen as Home Office blunders in relation to the loss of electronic data, the failure to consider over 1,000 foreign prisoners for deportation before the end of their sentences, and problems over the introduction of identity cards.

The Home Secretary exercises the prerogative of mercy on matters of reprieves and pardons. In the period before the death penalty was abolished in 1965, the Home Secretary made decisions as to whether to reprieve condemned persons or let them hang. Chuter Ede, the Home Secretary in 1950, decided that the case against Timothy Evans was strong enough to allow him to hang for the murder of his wife and daughter, in spite of Evans's not-guilty plea and his insistence that the murders had in fact been committed by his neighbour, John Reginald Christie. A later Home Secretary in 1966, Roy Jenkins, granted Evans a posthumous pardon in the light of new evidence against Christie, who was subsequently hanged for the murder of at least six women whose bodies were found in the house at 10 Rillington Place in 1953. There were many other high-profile cases involving the death penalty and much subsequent public discussion and disquiet, particularly in the cases of Derek Bentley, James Hanratty and Ruth Ellis. Ellis was the last woman to be hanged in this country, on 13 July 1955, provoking the headline in the *Daily Mirror*, 'Should Hanging be Stopped?'

Despite its abolition, death penalty cases continue to involve the Home Secretary and in 1992, Kenneth Clarke announced that he had rejected the application for a posthumous pardon for Derek Bentley who was hanged aged 19 in 1953 for the murder of PC Sydney Miles. Bentley and an accomplice, Christopher Craig, had broken into a warehouse in Tamworth Road, Croydon. They had been seen climbing over the gate and the police were alerted. As the murder was a joint enterprise, the execution was legal although by today's standards considered harsh as Craig, who was by law too young at 16 to be executed, had pulled the trigger that had killed the police officer. Craig was released from prison in 1963 but the campaign by Bentley's sister to get him pardoned continued and the case was submitted to the newly formed **Criminal Cases Review Commission** in 1997 and was heard by the **Court of Appeal** in 1998, when the **conviction** was overturned.

▶ Department for Constitutional Affairs (2003–2007)

The Department for Constitutional Affairs (DCA) emerged in June 2003 not so much as a fully fledged Department of Justice – as found in the United States of America and Europe – but as a consequence of a number of influences, one of which was the desire to reform the office and role of the Lord Chancellor. Announced as part of a Cabinet reshuffle, the new department was given the task of taking on responsibility for constitutional matters as well as the work of everyday matters concerning the judiciary: the appointment of new judges and overseeing the effectiveness and efficiency of the courts. The new department provided part of the answer to the problem of a Lord Chancellor who combined many roles: head of the judiciary, senior member of the executive with a place in the Cabinet, and a role in the Lords equivalent to the Speaker in the House of Commons. In short the role brought together an office holder who was at one and the same time a key player in the judicial, executive and legislative branches of government. With European jurisprudence in mind and the principle of the 'separation of powers' it was thought desirable for the protection of liberty that the three aspects of government be kept clearly demarcated, as they are in the constitution of the United States of America. Reform of the Lord Chancellor's Office also reflected New Labour's wish to be seen as a modernising party willing to forsake English tradition in the cause of efficiency, fairness and innovation. Lord Irvine was Lord Chancellor from 1997 to 2003.

The first head of the DCA, Lord Falconer, combined the offices of Secretary of State for Constitutional Affairs and Lord Chancellor. His role was to reform the administration of the courts' system in line with the Courts Act 2003 whereby the old Petty Sessions and Magistrates' Courts Committees were abolished with the creation of a single, unified court service in England and Wales. Responsibility for the magistrates' courts was transferred from the Home Office to the DCA. The DCA set up an independent **Judicial Appointments Commission** for appointment of judges, free from the claim that they are political appointments.

The DCA also had broader responsibility for matters of constitutional reform. To meet the separation of powers principle the DCA was responsible for creating a new Supreme Court to replace the role played by the Law Lords in the House of Lords.

In March 2007, responsibility for the penal agencies (NOMS, Prison and Probation Services) was transferred from the Home Office to the DCA.

▶ Ministry of Justice

In May 2007, the DCA was renamed the Ministry of Justice and the new ministry took over part of the responsibility of the Home Office.

Ministry of Justice: responsibilities

- The National Offender Management Service: administration of correctional services in England and Wales through Her Majesty's Prison Service and the Probation Service, under the umbrella of the National Offender Management Service;

- Youth Justice and sponsorship of the Youth Justice Board;

- Parole Board;

- Her Majesty's Inspectorates of Prison and Probation, Independent Monitoring Boards and the Prison and Probation Ombudsmen;

- Criminal, civil, family and administrative law: criminal law and sentencing policy, including sponsorship of the Sentencing Council for England and Wales and the Law Commission;

- The Office for Criminal Justice Reform: hosted by the Ministry of Justice but working with the Home Office and Attorney General's Office;

- Her Majesty's Courts Service: administration of the civil, family and criminal courts in England and Wales;

- The Tribunals Service: administration of tribunals across the UK;

- Legal Aid and the wider Community Legal Service through the Legal Aid Agency (formerly Legal Services Commission);

- Support for the judiciary: judicial appointments via the newly created Judicial Appointments Commission, the Judicial Office and Judicial Communications Office;

- Supreme Court of the United Kingdom (opening in October 2009 as a result of the Constitutional Reform Act 2005);

- Constitutional affairs: civil and human rights, freedom of information and data protection.

Source: Ministry of Justice (www.justice.gov.uk)

In the next section we will explore the political dimensions and context of the representation and polarisation of opinion around matters of crime and justice in England and Wales.

4.3 Political context

▶ Politics

Objective 3

Understand the political context of criminal justice in England and Wales

Policy cannot be divorced from politics and crime is a salient issue on the political agenda in the United Kingdom. As seen in the earlier section of this chapter, the Home Secretary plays a high-profile role in the politics of law and order and in influencing policy developments. Politicians quite properly talk about issues which worry the public and there can be little doubt that crime is a major election topic.

But who do the politicians listen to? We can see from the previous section of this chapter that, on the issue of the restoration of the death penalty, politicians chose to disregard public opinion. However, they cannot completely ignore the public mood among voters and the fact that they can afford to do this at all illustrates the nature of the system of parliamentary government. Political office, and hence influence on decision making, depends on the fortunes of political parties in which voters primarily focus upon deciding which political party they wish to see in office. The democratic process means that politicians are at the centre of a number of influences and ideas about how best to respond to crime.

Politicians can provide leadership on issues such as hanging but will follow the public mood on other matters. They also have to negotiate their position within the party and the annual party conference. Politicians are answerable to their party activists and even ministers may feel embarrassed by the need to explain themselves and their policies to the annual party conference. William Whitelaw, a Conservative Party Home Secretary (1979–83), regarded as a liberal on sentencing matters, wrote that he 'dreaded and disliked the prospect of the law and order debate, for the atmosphere was so strangely hostile and so different from that accorded to one's colleagues' (**Whitelaw 1989**).

There was a time when crime policy was not at the centre of party political disagreement, with a cross-party consensus about many aspects of criminal justice policy, but in the 1950s and 1960s crime issues started becoming more politicised. There are those who blame right-wing politicians for exploiting the fear of crime issues by presenting their opponents as soft on crime. Another factor was the level of public interest in the death penalty. The moves towards abolition in 1957 and 1965 involved parliamentary debates that generated considerable media coverage and public interest. What it highlighted, of course, was the strong division between parliamentary opinion, as represented by MPs who voted for abolition, and the public who then, as now, wish to retain the death penalty. It seems likely that public interest in matters of law and order may well have been stimulated initially by the high profile given to the death penalty debate, as well as by the steady rise in recorded crime from 1950 to 1990.

In the 1979 General Election, the Conservative Party was able to represent the Labour Party as soft on crime and the criminal (see the poster reproduced in Figure 4.1.) In recent elections the Labour Party has sought to change its image as

MUGGING UP 204%*
CRIMINAL DAMAGE UP 135%†
ROBBERY UP 88%†

Labour's record on crime is criminal. Crime is one of the few things in Britain that is booming under Labour.

In England and Wales last year, over 800,000 more crimes were recorded than in 1973. That's a rise of almost 50%. And yet since Labour came to power, police strength has risen by a mere 7%.

Perhaps if Labour had been more concerned with creating wealth rather than redistributing it, they might have found it easier to be able to afford to increase policemen's pay. But it's not just more pay our policemen need.

The Government have a duty to be seen to support law and order, to protect people and property.

It certainly doesn't make the police's job any easier when some Labour Ministers are seen associating themselves with potentially violent situations, as they did at Grunwick last year.

The police are doing a difficult job, in difficult times-and they need the support of all the people-and that includes Government Ministers.

Many policemen feel there's only one way they can make the Government understand their plight. And that's by leaving the force.

IS IT SAFE TO VOTE FOR ANOTHER LABOUR GOVERNMENT?
VOTE CONSERVATIVE X

*Figure for London between 1973–1977. † Home Office Annual Criminal Statistics for England and Wales between 1973–1977.

Figure 4.1 Conservative Party publicity on crime in the 1979 general election

being the softer party on matters of crime. In 1994, the Labour Party spokesperson for Home Affairs, Tony Blair, popularised the slogan that a Labour Government would be 'tough on crime and tough on the causes of crime'.

Political controversy is likely to continue even though the ideological gap between the parties has narrowed dramatically on the issue of crime. There has been, for example, considerable political disagreement over the extent to which rising crime can be attributed to greed or badness on the part of individuals, to family problems or problem families, or whether it is related to wider social factors such as unemployment. The Conservative Party expressed the following view during the 1987 General Election:

> The origins of crime lie deep in society in families where parents do not support or control their children; in schools where discipline is poor and in the wider world where violence is glamourised and traditional values are under attack.

Suggestions of a link between crime and unemployment, poverty or deprivation were dismissed as, in effect, excusing crime. In 1988, Margaret Thatcher commented that:

> If anyone else is to blame it is the professional progressives among broadcasters, social workers and politicians who have created a fog of excuses in which the mugger and burglar operate.
>
> (Loveday 1992: 302)

The link between poverty and crime was rejected in a Conservative Political Centre pamphlet in 1994. David Hunt, the Employment Secretary at the time, wrote:

> . . . some of the so-called cultures springing up in our country reject all decency and civilised values . . . the bulk of thieving today, of course, has nothing to do with poverty. It is the result of wickedness and greed.
>
> (*The Guardian*, 21 March 1994)

▶ New Labour and criminal justice reforms – a plethora of change

Between 1997 and 2004, the Home Office launched over 120 consultation papers, introduced 44 bills and commissioned major reviews of the criminal justice system such as the Auld Report on the courts and Halliday on sentencing. Its successor organisations have continued the rate of change or proposals for change. Centuries-old traditions have been swept away, such as the Petty Session administrative units of the magistrates' courts and the role of the Lord Chancellor. New criminal justice roles were created, with Police Community Support Officers (PCSOs), the Serious Organised Crime Agency (SOCA), Youth Offender Teams

(YOTs) and Community Safety Officers (CSOs), and initiatives to combat crime from neighbourhood curfews, anti-social behaviour orders and parenting orders. New bodies were established such as the Sentencing Guidelines Council (now the Sentencing Council of England and Wales) and the Youth Justice Board. The names of community penalties have been changed at least twice with a probation order becoming a community rehabilitation order in 2000 and under the CJA 2003 becoming a community order with supervision requirements. Proposals were made in 2003/4 to change prisons and probation to Correctional Services and subsequently to the National Offender Management Service.

With New Labour in power, the 'right wing tough on crime, and left wing soft on crime' polarity no longer applied. No one would regard New Labour as soft on crime as its directives sent record numbers to prison. Tony Blair's 'Tough on crime, tough on the causes of crime' manifesto was intended to demonstrate that New Labour would not only deal appropriately with those who broke the law, but that they understood there were deeper problems that had to be tackled alongside. As Blair told the Labour Party Conference in 2002, 'the problem is not just crime. It is disrespect. It is anti-social behaviour. It is the drug dealer at the end of the street and no one seems to be able to do anything about it.' David Blunkett's views on crime and asylum seekers did not match the 'old' Labour Home Secretaries' views, such as Roy Jenkins who introduced laws perceived as liberal, including laws on abortion and homosexuality, and abolition of the death penalty.

New Labour held onto its liberal credentials by its introduction of data protection and freedom of information laws, the Human Rights Act 1998, the reclassification of some Class B drugs and the speed with which it complied, unlike other European governments, with rulings from the European Court of Human Rights. Some people felt that the reforms brought in under New Labour were made to demonstrate that the government was doing something about the crime problem. Andrew Rawnsley, writing in *The Observer* newspaper in 2002 about the government's 'frantic' creation of new powers, wrote that it was 'not surprising that the department of law enforcement is so pathological about wanting to give itself more and more laws to enforce. What it finds acutely challenging is creating laws that actually work.'

▶ 2010 General Election – the Coalition Government

Under Labour, official crime figures showed a year-on-year decline in the number of recorded crimes. People were still concerned about crime, but in early 2010, as a general election loomed, crime itself did not take political centre-stage. National debt, taxes, pensions, MPs expenses, the NHS and immigration were making bigger headlines and sparking bigger rows. For the three main parties, crime came further down the agenda. Labour proposed to allow the takeover of failing police forces by successful ones. Alcohol rehabilitation programmes would be trebled and young disaffected people would be 'reached' by street teams of ex-offenders. They wanted to see more restorative justice schemes. The Liberal Democrats vowed to halt the Labour-generated creation of new criminal offences. They proposed to scrap ID cards, as well as Labour's prison building programme to pay for 3,000 more police officers. They wanted to see more use of community sentences and an end to anti-terrorist control orders. They hoped to make prisoners work and contribute to a victims' fund. The Conservatives' crime manifesto was less about specific targets or changes to the law. It was set to the backdrop of one recurrent theme: Britain's 'broken society'. David Cameron commented:

> It is not just the crime. It is a whole stew of violence, anti-social behaviour, debt, addiction, family breakdown, educational failure, poverty and despair . . . I am certain that government is a big part of the problem – its size has now reached a point where it is actually making our social problems worse . . . There is, I believe, only one way out of this national crisis – and that is what I have called the Big Society . . . It requires, I believe, drawing on the deepest values of Conservatism, giving power to people not the state, strengthening families, encouraging responsibility, common sense and rigour, and applying these values to the key aims of improving the lives of people in our country – especially the very poorest.
>
> ('Let's mend our broken society', speech delivered by David Cameron at the Centre for Social Justice in London, 27 April 2010)

When polling day came, it was a close-run thing. Voters delivered a hung Parliament, with the Tories holding the highest number of seats but not enough to govern alone. After several days of deliberation in Parliament and frenzied speculation in the press, the Liberal Democrats agreed to join the Conservatives in government.

The Coalition Government took over on 12 May 2010. David Cameron, the Conservative Prime Minister, and Nick Clegg, his Liberal Democrat Deputy, tore up their election manifestos and sat down together to find some common ground. The main and absolutely clear primary policy concern of the new government in 2010 was the economy, which was in a state of recession, and government finances, which were overstretched with a national debt at a level of 52% of GDP.

On other matters the Conservatives wanted to reduce bureaucracy, 'red tape' and 'wasteful expenditure'. The Liberal Democrats sought to empower the individual and increase citizens' rights and abolish control orders for terrorists suspects. The 'Big Society' and not 'Big Government' was promoted as a theoretical framework within which the government could mobilise people. However, for a few days in August 2011, an outburst of criminal activity and violence seemed to take over urban centres across Britain,

▶ The Riots of 2011

The August Riots of 2011 came as a shock to the nation. What started out as a peaceful protest on 6 August against the police-killing of a black man named Mark Duggan (on 4 August) spiralled rapidly out of control as the protesters in Tottenham clashed with the police. Police cars were overturned, fires were started and shops were looted. The use of social media such as Twitter and in particular – because of its greater security facilities at the time – Blackberry Messenger enabled news of the unrest to travel with unprecedented speed and within hours the rioting had spread from Tottenham to Hackney, Croydon and Peckham. High street shops suffered huge damage as people smashed windows and helped themselves to trainers, televisions and bottles of spirits. The lure of a free shopping spree tempted others out onto the streets. Within 48 hours, stories and images of similar rioting and criminal behaviour were emerging from other urban centres including Bristol, Manchester and Birmingham.

The disorder was not limited to shoplifting. Minimal police presence in some areas emboldened the mob and for a couple of days England seemed to be governed by a spirit of lawlessness. Homes and businesses were burnt to the ground. Witnesses reported extreme levels of violence some of them were caught on camera, later becoming some of the most iconic images associated with the disorder. A Malaysian youth studying in London, injured with a broken jaw following a robbery when his bike was stolen and sitting in a pool of blood was robbed by a group of men pretending to help him to his feet. A 68-year-old man in Ealing died from head wounds after being thrown to the ground when he intervened when youths were setting fire to a street rubbish bin. A 26-year-old man was shot dead in Croydon. Three men, Haroon Jahan, Shazad Ali and Abdul Musavir, died in Birmingham as they tried to protect shops in Winson Green from looters; they were killed when a man drove his car directly into them.

One story told by Alison Saunders from the CPS illustrates the degree of lawlessness of one rioter:

> It started from one end of Croydon High Street, where we had a picture of him, to the other end, where we had his DNA . . . In between those two points he committed 16 different offences. Either burglary, robbery, violent disorder or egging on the crowd . . . He had no previous convictions. There was no excuse for his behaviour at all. It has nothing to do with 'He doesn't trust the police, he doesn't like the police.'

What was evident, however, from the subsequent prosecutions and convictions of participants of the riots was the very high proportion with previous cautions and convictions for crimes. It was as if those who were committed to non-lawful lifestyles, including gangs, plus the opportunist thieves had found the riots as a good cover to engage in violence, looting and criminal acts because for a period of time it was clear that the police were unable or unwilling to contain the rioters.

Ministry of Justice data of 28 June 2012 showed that 3,051 of those arrested during the disturbances had appeared before the courts by June 2012. The data on those arrested showed a predictable pattern of rioter profile: predominantly male (89%), and younger than the normal population with just over half aged under 21 (27% were aged between 10 to 17 years, 26% between 18 to 20). Of the older rioters, 41% were aged 21 to 39, and 6% were aged above 40.

Burglary was the most common offence charged in relation to the riots. It accounted for 50% of charges, compared with violent disorder 22%, and theft 16%. Deprivation indices were high: 35% of adults were claiming work benefits, and the ethnic profile showed the following distribution: white 36%, black 34%, Asian 6%, mixed or other 15%. Crucially, the arrestee profile showed a key fact: 76% of those who appeared before the courts by 28 September 2011 had on average 14 previous convictions or cautions. Half of the adult males (that is those aged 18 or above) had 6 or more previous convictions or cautions; 21% of adult males had 15 to 49 previous convictions or cautions; 5.9% of adult males and 6.9% adult females arrested had 50 or more previous convictions of cautions (Ministry of Justice data as of 1 February 2012). Many of the rioters were already committed to a lifestyle of crime.

Parliament was recalled and emergency measures were hurried in to deal with the turmoil. As the wave of crime subsided, David Cameron made one of his most famous speeches at a youth centre in Witney, Oxfordshire. He told the 400 youths gathered there that it was time to start 'the fight back'.

> Do we have the determination to confront the slow-motion moral collapse that has taken place in parts of our country these past few generations?
>
> Irresponsibility. Selfishness. Behaving as if your choices have no consequences.
>
> Children without fathers. Schools without discipline. Reward without effort.
>
> Crime without punishment. Rights without responsibilities. Communities without control.
>
> . . .
>
> In my very first act as leader of this party I signalled my personal priority: to mend our broken society. That passion is stronger today than ever . . . So yes, the broken society is back at the top of my agenda.
>
> . . .
>
> First and foremost, we need a security fight-back . . . That starts with a stronger police presence . . . Let me be clear: under this government we will always have enough police officers to be able to scale up our deployments in the way we saw last week.
>
> . . . For years we've had a police force suffocated by bureaucracy, officers spending the majority of their time filling in forms and stuck behind desks.
>
> . . . Our reforms mean that the police are going to answer directly to the people.
>
> . . . Elected police and crime commissioners are part of the answer: they will provide that direct accountability so you can finally get what you want when it comes to policing.
>
> The point of our police reforms is not to save money, not to change things for the sake of it – but to fight crime.
>
> And in the light of last week it's clear that we now have to go even further, even faster in beefing up the powers and presence of the police.
>
> Already we've given backing to measures like dispersal orders, we're toughening curfew powers, we're giving police officers the power to remove face coverings from rioters, we're looking at giving them more powers to confiscate offenders' property – and over the coming months you're going to see even more.
>
> . . . It's time for something else too. A concerted, all-out war on gangs and gang culture.
>
> . . . It is a major criminal disease that has infected streets and estates across our country.
>
> Stamping out these gangs is a new national priority . . . We will fight back against gangs, crime and the thugs who make people's lives hell and we will fight back hard.

The last front in that fight is proper punishment.

On the radio last week they interviewed one of the young men who'd been looting in Manchester. He said he was going to carry on until he got caught. This will be my first arrest, he said. The prisons were already overflowing so he'd just get an ASBO, and he could live with that. Well, we've got to show him and everyone like him that the party's over . . . I am determined we sort it out and restore people's faith that if someone hurts our society, if they break the rules in our society, then society will punish them for it. And we will tackle the hard core of people who persistently reoffend and blight the lives of their communities.

. . . But we need much more than that. We need a social fight-back too, with big changes right through our society.

. . . Team-work, discipline, duty, decency: these might sound old-fashioned words but they are part of the solution to this very modern problem of alienated, angry young people.

. . . This social fight-back is not a job for government on its own.

. . . There is no 'them' and 'us' – there is us. We are all in this together, and we will mend our broken society – together.

(David Cameron, Speech on the fight-back after the riots, Witney, 15 August 2011)

More than a month later, when the Shadow Home Secretary gave her speech to the Labour Party Conference, the riots were still one of the biggest topics on the crime agenda.

'For four nights thousands of people took to the streets to loot and to pillage.

Burning police cars, looting shops and torching homes. Putting people's lives as well as livelihoods at risk. This country must never again tolerate such lawlessness. Never again should criminals be allowed take control of the streets, and they cannot be allowed to get away with it. But it took 16,000 officers to quell the madness on London streets – officers from Norfolk, South Wales, Hampshire, Cumbria, all joining the Met to bring the streets back under control.

. . .

Next week at the Tory Party conference, we'll hear a lot of tough talk from David Cameron about broken Britain, cracking down on crime and gangs. Tough talk from a Prime Minister who is still cutting the police, still cutting police powers, still pushing up unemployment and has barely mentioned crime since he started in the job. He says it now. He hasn't done it before.

Prime Minister. It shouldn't take a riot.

. . . We know in the Labour Party how much it matters to cut crime . . . We know crime is still too high. We want crime to fall further.'

(Speech by Yvette Cooper, Shadow Home Secretary, Labour Party
Conference, Blackpool, September 2011)

◗ Pressure and interest groups

Political parties are not the only representative groups to engage in debates about crime. A number of other bodies representing professional interests also contribute to discussions of crime policy. They may participate officially in Royal Commissions, appear on current affairs programmes or contribute newspaper articles. These bodies include, as we stated earlier in the chapter, the **Police Federation**, ACPO, NAPO, POA, the Bar Council, the Law Society, and the Justices' Clerks Society. Voluntary groups such as the Magistrates' Association and Victim Support also contribute in this way.

Pressure groups also have an important role in shaping attitudes about penal policy. The Howard League for Penal Reform, the Prison Reform Trust and the National Association for the Care and Resettlement of Offenders (Nacro) have played a key role in changing opinions. Nacro, for example, carries out research, sponsors projects, runs conferences and provides much useful information to its members, along with schools, colleges, journalists, policy makers, politicians and academics. Nacro aims to ensure that the case for improved prison conditions and less frequent use of custodial sentences is put effectively both in Parliament and in the mass media. An example of lobbying involving a fusion of interest groups and pressure groups is revealed in *The Times* headline 'Crisis in Britain's Jails' (16 April 2014); this headline might be a contestant for the most overused headlines by home affairs correspondents in the British press over the last half century. The story on the front page quotes the Chairman of the Prison Governor's Association who refers to a 'perfect storm' of conditions for prison riots over the summer due to the prison population numbers and staff shortages. This view is not unsurprisingly supported by the view of the General Secretary of the Prison Officers' Association who claims that they have also been warning ministers about the potential dangers of staff voluntary redundancy schemes aimed to reduce the cost and numbers of prison officers. This view from professional interest groups is added to the constant theme of the prison reform groups, such as the Howard League who tend to claim – whatever is the actual numbers of offenders incarcerated – that the number in prison is too high and a 'penal crisis' is yet again predicted.

In a study of the impact of pressure groups on penal policy, **Ryan (1978)** describes the history of the Howard League and the considerable influence exercised by its representatives Margery Fry and George Benson MP, during the 1950s and 1960s, in Whitehall and Westminster. It was an acceptable pressure group: reliable, practical and trusted. In contrast, Ryan outlines the fate of RAP (Radical Alternatives to Prison), which did not have status as an acceptable pressure group in its campaign to abolish all prisons. The differences in resources, contacts, access and the degree of ideological congruence between lobbyists and officials are important if a group is to have an influence on public policy.

The mass media have considerable influence on the way policies are presented. The opportunity for making political gains is evident if a good sound bite or slogan can be found. In the 1979 General Election campaign the Conservative Party, on advice from Saatchi and Saatchi, ran a poster campaign on the theme of crime and whether it was safe to vote for Jim Callaghan's Labour Government. The poster, shown in Figure 4.1, made use of official statistics to highlight the growth of mugging, robbery and criminal damage.

▶ Media

Some people find out about crime and form views on the basis of their own experiences or those of their family, friends or neighbours. In large part, however, their views are also influenced by information in newspapers or on television. This may include coverage of individual cases, and some may follow discussions on crime by politicians and commentators.

Most people are influenced to some extent by the mass media – newspapers, television, books or films. This is because the majority of the public have limited first-hand knowledge about crime or the criminal justice system unless they are victims or perpetrators. Newspapers and television coverage of crime stories will influence people's knowledge about crime and may deepen their fear of becoming a victim. Media coverage in itself may affect people's behaviour – women and the elderly, for example, are often scared to walk the streets at night for fear of being raped or mugged, and parents may be frightened to let their children out of the house alone through fear of kidnapping, sexual assault or murder.

Crime is, of course, a popular subject in the mass media and, as many point out, crime, especially sexual crime, sells newspapers (see, for example, **Schlesinger and Tumber 1994; Soothill and Walby 1991; Jewkes 2004**). Crime dramas are also extremely popular, as seen in the high ratings given to TV detectives such as Inspectors Morse, Taggart, Wexford or Barnaby. Few, of course, believe that drama gives a real picture of crime or policing – otherwise the murder rate in Oxford, Glasgow, Kingsmarkham or the Midsomer villages would be the subject of national concern and police **clear-up rates** would be vastly improved! Luckily for the residents of rural England the focus of TV murders has in recent years been transferred to Scandinavia.

Television documentaries such as *Crimewatch*, in which the police provide information and CCTV photographs to encourage the public to telephone in with information about crimes and suspects, have become popular in recent years. Police videos are broadcast on television that shows drivers at their worst, as in *Police, Camera, Action!* or *Police Interceptors* or *Traffic Cops*. As a result, information blends with entertainment.

High-profile cases such as the trials of Ian Huntley and Maxine Carr provide a fascination that might be untypical and could lead people to draw general conclusions based on limited knowledge. Frederick West, Derek Bentley and Myra Hindley were to become household names because of the interest taken by the mass media. But the focus on these selective and unusual cases may not provide a reliable impression of the crime problem: a very unrepresentative picture of crime may be given by the media. From all the possible news stories about crime, the media can select only a small number. This selection will depend on decisions as to whether or not such stories are newsworthy. Thus cases reported in newspapers are likely to be unusual or have elements capable of providing drama or titillation (**Chibnall 1977; Soothill and Walby 1991**). Most researchers would appear to agree, for example, that sexual and violent crimes, which play on the public's fear, are more likely to be reported than more common kinds of crime such as theft or vandalism (**Ditton and Duffy 1983**). In addition, these kinds of crime are also selectively reported with an overemphasis on, for example, serial killers or rapists (**Soothill 1993**). Many have argued that the reporting of rape tends to focus on the 'sex fiend' who attacks women in public places, whereas in reality women are more likely to be raped in private places, by people they know (ibid.).

Newspaper reports also tend to simplify crime stories, providing little by way of extended analysis (**Schlesinger and Tumber 1994**). News reports about crimes are necessarily abbreviated accounts of events, focusing on those aspects considered likely to attract the public's attention. This is also the case when the criminal statistics are reported. Although these are complex documents requiring careful interpretation, reports in the media tend to focus on simple questions about whether some kinds of crime have risen or fallen.

The media may also set in train what is called a moral panic about a particular kind of crime (**Cohen 1980**). This happens where a spectacular incident or series of incidents – for example, a riot, a series of child abuse cases, or cases of gang, gun or knife crime – alerts the public to a particular problem. The media may effectively create a new form of crime, as the example of 'road rage' demonstrates. 'Road rage' was a term coined to describe violent incidents between motorists triggered by a dispute over such things as parking, driving styles or accidents.

The press are blamed by some criminologists for generating public anxiety in order to sell newspapers. However, many of these stories are newsworthy not just because they are printed in the papers but because they capture a fascination about a bizarre or horrific event that would be in itself of public interest. Deviancy, as the sociologist Emile Durkheim pointed out, provides a community with a concrete example of unacceptable and censored behaviour and thus gives a collective focus to re-evaluate and rethink its values. The press might also justify their coverage as campaigning newspapers when the criminal justice system appears to let victims down or wrongly convicts an innocent person. Campaigning programmes on the television and reports in the press have helped to clear innocent people and convict guilty ones. Frustration with the lack of action in the murder inquiry following the death of the black teenager Stephen Lawrence (**discussed in Chapter 6**) led the *Daily Mail* to take the unprecedented step of printing the names of five men they believed responsible for his death under the headline, 'Murderers'. The *Daily Mail* commented:

> We are naming them because, despite a criminal case, a private prosecution and an inquest, there has still been no justice for Stephen . . . One or more of the five may have a valid defence to the charge which has been repeatedly levelled against them. So far they have steadfastly refused every opportunity to offer such a defence.
>
> (*Daily Mail*, 14 February 1997)

4.4 'Globalisation': cross-jurisdictional and international responses to crime

Objective 4

Describe aspects of 'Globalisation' and cross-jurisdictional and international responses to crime

The nightmare pictures of aeroplanes flying into the World Trade Centre, killing 3,000 civilians in New York City and Washington DC on 11 September 2001 heralded a growing consciousness of the global threat of crime at the beginning of the twenty-first century. The global terrorist threat is not the only concern as the potential for internet-based fraud becomes more apparent and the networks of organised crime from Russia to China operate on a worldwide scale to move drugs, weapons and people around in a world where there is greater mobility and opportunities to exploit. In the wake of the 'credit crunch' and evidence of major international frauds, governments are keen to toughen up regulations to control the use of tax havens which cost billions of pounds to governments across the world. Free movement of people in the enlarged European Union means that criminals have a wider market to deal in and more places to hide both themselves and their assets.

In response, a number of regional and world developments have emerged and a greater insight into both the nature of crime and of other criminal justice systems as law enforcement agencies try to share information, and attempt to harmonise with and accommodate each other's systems and procedures. International agreements on extradition and cooperation between jurisdictions were evident after September 2001.

The mood of interdependency was captured in 2002 in a speech by the then Prime Minister, Tony Blair:

The paradox of the modern world is this:

We've never been more interdependent in our needs; and

We've never been more individualist in our outlook.

Globalisation and technology open up vast new opportunities but also cause massive insecurity.

. . .

Interdependence is obliterating the distinction between foreign and domestic policy.

It was the British economy that felt the aftermath of 11 September.

Our cities who take in refugees from the 13 million now streaming across the world from famine, disease or conflict.

Our young people who die from heroin imported from Afghanistan.

It is our climate that is changing.

. . .

Interdependence is the core reality of the modern world.

It is revolutionising our idea of national interest.

It is forcing us to locate that interest in the wider international community.

(Speech by Tony Blair, Prime Minister, Labour Party conference, Blackpool, October 2002)

▶ Global terrorism and the dilemma of the Coalition Government

The debate on how to control the threat of terrorism in the UK has been a major dilemma since the Coalition Government was formed in 2010. There was a major rift between the Liberal Democrats and their commitment to human rights of the terrorist suspects and the Conservative partner's concern with public protection.

The Prime Minister is claimed to have said in 2010 that the Coalition Government was heading for a 'car crash' over the use of control orders with terrorist suspects because of the contrasting views of the Liberal Democrats, headed by Deputy Prime Minister Nick Clegg, and the Conservative Home Secretary Theresa May. Over the period of the Coalition Government the Liberal Democrat partners, with the support of some Conservative MPs, seem to have won out, as successive legislation has limited the powers to deal with terrorist suspects in the name of traditional freedoms and modern conceptions of human rights.

However, the debate is far from over, especially since the spectre of terrorist acts in the UK was raised by Prime Minister David Cameron and the security services following the conflict between Islamic ethnic groups in Syria in 2013 and Iraq in the summer of 2014, with British volunteers participating in the conflicts in both countries; 25 people were arrested and 14 passports withheld to stop people travelling to Syria in 2013 and 40 people were arrested in the first three months of 2014 for activities linked to Syria. David Cameron said in June 2014 that it was vital to halt ISIS (radical Sunni group in Iraq renamed Islamic State or IS) and insisted: 'I disagree with those people who think that having some sort of extreme Islamist regime in the middle of Iraq will not affect us – because it will.'

The history of recent legislation on terrorism reflects this dilemma of contrasting views as to how to balance the risk to the public and the rights of a terrorist suspect. The introduction in 2005 of control orders to replace detention in prison reflected the first concession in the debate towards less restrictive conditions for monitoring the terrorist suspect, and over the period from 2011, the Coalition Government reforms have continued in this direction as evidenced by the history of legislation aimed to curtail terrorism in the twenty-first century.

Terrorism Act 2000

The Terrorism Act 2000 outlawed some groups espousing terrorist activities and provided the legal basis for prosecuting terrorists and proscribing (banning) organisations from operating in the UK. It also included provisions on police counter-terrorist powers. The Act reformed previous counter-terrorist legislation, originally created in response to terrorism related to Northern Ireland and extended some of its provisions to a number of categories of international terrorism.

Anti-Terrorism, Crime and Security Act 2001

This Act was introduced in the aftermath of the Twin Towers attack in New York City on September 11. It allowed for the detention of foreign suspects of terrorist acts abroad. This was criticised particularly by the Liberal Democrats and human rights groups as an infringement of the traditional right to a trial. The response to this criticism was that this ignored the reality of global terrorism and the restrictions imposed by the European Court of Human Rights (ECHR) on the British legal system not to send suspects back to countries either for trial or for punishment if they could receive the death penalty, or be potentially liable to torture. The terrorist suspects were wanted by foreign countries following acts of terrorist violence abroad. The tension between the rights of a suspect under a democratic society and the rights of the general public to be protected by government was clearly demonstrated in the two sides of the argument.

The human rights lobby groups referred to the ECHR whereby governments cannot deprive person of their liberty without due process of law. This process must include informing the person of the accusation made against him, allowing him access to legal assistance to prepare his defence and giving him the right to have his case heard and decided in public before a competent court. This was difficult when suspected terrorists had fled from countries where they were convicted or suspected with terrorist offences but the evidence was not available in British courts.

Prevention of Terrorism Act 2005

The Act introduced control orders to replace detention in prison of foreign terrorist suspects who could not be extradited because of the ECHR forbidding the extradition of suspects to countries where they were subject to possible torture or execution.

Control orders were used to deal with terror suspects who cannot be deported or tried. Control orders were made by the Home Secretary on the basis of intelligence provided primarily by the Security Services. Following this Act, ten detainees under the Anti-Terrorism, Crime and Security Act 2001 were released from Belmarsh prison and were immediately subject to control orders. Between 2005 and 2011, 48 individuals were subject to control orders. This meant they were subject to a form of house arrest with the following restrictions: electronic tagging, curfews, restrictions on visitors, surrender their passport, restrict, no internet access, monitoring daily by phone and reporting to the police.

The Joint Parliamentary Committee on Human Rights published critical reports on control orders, and some led to legal challenges and court cases. In 2006, a High Court judge released a statement declaring that section 3 of the Act was incompatible with the right to a fair trial under Article 6 of ECHR. Finally, the Act was repealed in 2011 replacing the control orders with Terrorism Prevention and Investigation Measures (TPIM Act 2011).

Terrorism Act 2006

This Act increased the period of pre-charge detention to allow the police to question terrorist suspects from 14 to 28 days.

Counter-Terrorism Act 2008

The Act gave powers to take fingerprints and DNA samples from those subject to control orders.

Terrorism Prevention and Investigations Measures Act (TPIM) 2011

This Act abolished control orders and introduced new Terrorism Prevention and Investigation Measures (TPIMs). Ten people have been subject to TPIMs since

2012, nine of whom were British citizens and all believed to have been involved in al-Qaeda terrorist activities.

The Home Secretary may issue a TPIM notice that could include electronic tagging, overnight residence at a specified address, reporting requirements and other restrictions such as foreign travel bans, association, finances, work and study. Individuals subject to the TPIM measures cannot be 'relocated' to an unfamiliar area. The restrictions under the TPIM scheme (e.g. on electronic communication and curfew) are also lighter than the ones under the control order regime.

The problem of less restrictive surveillance means that it became easier to disappear.

Two TPIMs subjects have absconded: Ibrahim Magag on 26 December 2012 and Mohammed Ahmed Mohamed on 1 November 2013. The latter cut off his electronic surveillance bracelet and walked out of a mosque disguised in a burka. This raises questions about the effectiveness of TPIMs to provide effective control over potential terrorists.

Protection of Freedoms Act 2012

The Act repealed the anti-terrorism stop and search powers (referred to as section 44 of the Terrorism Act 2000) and reduced the maximum period of detention of terrorist suspects, before they are charged or released, from 28 to 14 days.

Justice and Security Act 2013

The Act created a new Intelligence and Security Committee of Parliament (ISC) to replace the Intelligence and Security Committee created by the Intelligence Services Act 1994. The statutory remit of the ISC was expanded to oversee the government's intelligence community. Parliament and the courts were given a greater role in monitoring cases involving national security.

One thing is clear, and that is that attempts to monitor, curb or prevent terrorist activities rely heavily on global collaboration between the law enforcement and security services. We will discuss aspects of this in the next section.

▶ International cooperation

One reform that preceded the terrorist attacks on the United States of America in 2001 came about as a result of world abhorrence at the genocide in Rwanda and Kosovo. This led to the foundation of the International Criminal Court (ICC). This court, situated in The Hague, now tries individuals for genocide, crimes against humanity and war crimes. Not all countries have agreed to be subject to the ICC but the United Kingdom did with the passing of the International Criminal Court Act 2001. The Act provides for international cooperation in terms of identifying, arresting and extraditing suspects and collecting evidence; and it enables cooperation with ICC investigations into the proceeds of crimes.

The Anti-terrorism, Crime and Security Act 2001 established new powers to: cut off terrorist funding; allow government departments and agencies to collect and share information required for countering the terrorist threat; streamline relevant immigration procedures; protect the security of the nuclear and aviation industries; improve the security of dangerous substances that may be targeted or used by terrorists; and enhance powers when detainees in police custody refuse to cooperate with the police as to their identity.

Following a new *National Security Strategy* published by the government in October 2010, new initiatives were taken to counter the terrorism threats both in the UK and overseas, including the passing of the Terrorism Prevention and Investigation Measures Act 2011. Within the Home Office, the Office for Security and Counter-Terrorism (OSCT) was set up to coordinate anti-terrorist activities. During this period the human rights lobby groups worked to reform the constraints on suspected terrorists. The maximum detention period for terrorist suspects before they are charged or released, was reduced from 28 to 14 days under the Protection of Freedoms Act 2012; and new stop and search powers were introduced to ensure the counter-terrorism stop and search powers were not abused by the police and a new code of practice was implemented for this purpose in July 2012. The Justice and Security Act 2013 clarified public accountability and oversight of the Security Service (MI5), the Secret Intelligence Service (MI6) and the Government Communications Headquarters (GCHQ). It also provides a public immunity protection for information that the government considers to be a threat to public security if disclosed in public; the closed material procedures (CMP) was introduced for this purpose.

Other forms of cooperation include bilateral agreements between two countries to combat crime and these indicate the greater cross-jurisdictional awareness among governments of the need to cooperate to deal with a problem that is not restricted within national boundaries. Successful criminals have exploited the differences in the law and legal procedures to avoid detection or, if discovered, prosecution.

Bilateral international cooperation has been given a lead by the United States of America. The UK/US Drugs Agreement of 1988 provides for cooperation in the investigation of drug-trafficking offences, the freezing and confiscation of the proceeds of drug-related crimes, providing for the exchange of documents and banking evidence, allows for the transfer of prisoners with their consent to give evidence, and carrying out requests to search and seize property. On 27 February 1997, Poland and the United Kingdom signed a mutual cooperation agreement to work together to deal with the illegal distribution of weapons and drugs and with organised crime. This allows for swifter extradition orders, intelligence gathering on illegal arms and drug sales, and powers to confiscate the proceeds of crime that have been moved between the jurisdictions. Poland signed a similar agreement with the United States in 1996.

International cooperation involved the Forensic Science Service (FSS) conducting DNA tests in 1992 in response to the Russian Government's approach to check the remains of a group of people, thought to be those of the Romanov family, the Russian royal family that disappeared, presumed murdered, on the night of 16 July 1918 or soon after. Using bone material the FSS concluded that the DNA test supports the view that the family found in the mass grave was the Romanovs.

International cooperation is increasingly evident between the 190 member countries of Interpol. Within the National Criminal Intelligence Service (NCIS) later merged into Serious Organised Crime Agency, Customs and Excise manage a network of Drugs Liaison officers (DLOs) who work with their counterparts in Europe and around the world. The success of the policing of Euro 96, when between one-quarter and half a million foreign football supporters came to England, was due in part to the role played by the NCIS who helped to plan the policing of this event by putting together a team of experts on football **hooliganism** from different forces across the country, and liaison officers from each of the competing countries, as well as relying on information from Interpol.

The NCIS are also involved in the efforts to combat international crime gangs, which were originally set out in the White Paper *One Step Ahead: A 21st Century Strategy to Defeat Organised Criminals* (2004). The paper contained details about the Serious Organised Crime Agency (SOCA), announced by the Home Secretary in February 2004. SOCA was eventually established in 2008 with its principle duty to tackle serious organised crime such as Class A drugs, people-smuggling and human-trafficking, major gun crime, fraud, computer crime and money laundering.

SOCA was replaced in October 2013 by the National Crime Agency (NCA). It intends to broaden the responsibilities of the agency to include the Child Exploitation and Online Protection Centre and parts of the National Policing Improvement Agency (NPIA). The first director was Keith Bristow, a former Chief Constable of Warwickshire Police. The Home Office website describes the NCA as a 'powerful body of crime-fighters' that will 'tackle organised crime, defend our borders, fight fraud and cyber crime, and protect children and young people'. Criminal organisations are rarely confined to one country alone and to defeat it requires international collaboration, thus one of the most important areas for the NCA will be maintaining the cooperative global network of partners already built up by SOCA in its role as the UK's national bureau for international crime partnerships including Interpol, Europol and the Strategic Alliance Group (SAG).

4.5 European influences on criminal justice policy

Objective 5

Explain the influences from Europe on criminal justice policy

The European Union has 28 member states. Originally based in western Europe, it now encompasses many central and eastern states such as the Czech Republic, Estonia, Cyprus, Latvia, Lithuania, Hungary, Croatia, Malta, Poland, Slovenia and Slovakia. The increasing interdependency of the European states has meant that many policy developments are no longer the sole responsibility of Parliament in the United Kingdom; and today policy is shaped by a need to take account of other jurisdictions, most notably those in the European Union. Apart from the gradual process of European harmonisation, the exploitation of relaxed border controls and new forms of crime have prompted the governments of Europe to take initiatives to combat cross-jurisdictional crimes such as drug trafficking and international fraud. Cross-jurisdictional cooperation has become essential given the limitations of crime policy based on the nation state and its restricted geographical boundaries.

Countries take it in turn to hold the presidency of the European Union for a six-month period and crime issues feature large in the rhetoric of each country's agenda for the period. Jack Straw, as Home Secretary, declared that, 'Organised crime is no respecter of borders and it is crucial that we recognise that reality' (*Daily Telegraph*, 29 December 1997). The areas of primary concern were identified as paedophiles, drug trafficking, money laundering, electronic fraud, and industrial and political espionage. Priority was given to improving arrangements for the extradition of suspects, introducing video links to interview suspects and witnesses, and greater powers to intercept messages sent via the internet, referring to the cyber-criminals such as terrorist groups and paedophiles who use modern technology, especially coded email messages, to organise their criminal activity.

In 1995, all members of the European Union agreed to the establishment of Europol. The United Kingdom became the first country in the European Union to ratify the Europol Convention in December 1996, which provided for a pan-European law enforcement organisation for the exchange and analysis of crime intelligence on drug trafficking, unregulated dealing in nuclear and radioactive substances, illegal immigrant smuggling, motor vehicle crime and terrorism.

In January 1997, Michael Howard, the then Home Secretary, met the Russian Interior Minister in Moscow to discuss greater cooperation to deal with organised crime. He commented:

> Serious, dangerous criminals do not respect national borders . . . Organised criminals run their operations across the whole of Europe, including Russia. We need to find their ring-leaders and bring them to justice. The UK has helped set up Europol – for the exchange and analysis of criminal intelligence which will help catch and convict international villains.
>
> (Home Office press release, 25 January 1997)

The Crime (International Cooperation) Act 2003 implements police and judicial cooperation between EU countries in response to the attacks of 11 September 2001, with the purpose of ensuring that all EU member states have effective terrorist legislation in place. There is also agreement regarding a database storing criminal information from all participating countries and procedures for sharing banking information and tracing illegal money. On another level is the mutual recognition of driving disqualifications so that motorists resident in one member state of the European Union who are disqualified from driving in another member state will also be disqualified in their state of residence.

Another aim is the approximation of the laws and regulations of the member states, which means in the future there will be other EU-wide agreements and cooperation, and where possible the harmonisation of laws, as is currently the case with crimes concerning counterfeiting the euro.

In 2008, EU member states agreed to take account of convictions given in other EU countries. This mutual recognition of criminal offences mean that a conviction and criminal record in an EU country will come to have the same effect as a previous conviction given by a court in England and Wales.

4.6 Implementing criminal justice policy

▶ Coordinating criminal justice

Objective 6

Understand the complexities of implementing criminal justice policy

Developments within the international community to improve cooperation on matters of crime have helped bring attention to the need to do more to promote better coordination within the criminal justice system in England and Wales. This has many parts and has many different agencies with distinctive functions and styles of operating. This fragmentation leads to 'discorrespondence' in two senses of the word: in that agencies do not always communicate effectively with each other; and that the work of different agencies does not always fit together to provide for an efficient system. The origins of the fragmentation are complex and are concerned with the distinctive constitutional, political and cultural histories of the agencies and professions, each having a unique agenda of interests and concerns. The judiciary in England and Wales come from a strong profession with deep traditional roots that are well embedded in the system of power and influence in this country. Thus, when issues of policy such as a proposal for a sentencing commission are perceived as threatening the independence of the judiciary we can be sure that much pressure will be brought to reformulate the proposal. Traffic wardens and PCSOs, in contrast, do not have this degree of influence.

Coordination between agencies has also been a problem because of the principles inherent in our adversarial system, which puts the offender at centre stage with defence counsel and probation officers taking a pro-defendant line and the police and prosecutors doing their best to convict the accused. The combative nature of the contest encourages strategies among the participants, such as appealing to prejudice, lack of frankness regarding the facts, and undermining the confidence of a witness, which may have more to do with winning the case rather than discovering the truth, with public interest and justice sometimes taking second place. Different working cultures add to the difficulties of getting better cooperation between the agencies.

Until the 1950s, governments took an interest in but did not seek directly to intervene on routine matters best left to judges and other professional groups. A more interventionist role for government on matters of crime control was revealed in the White Paper, *Penal Practice in a Changing Society*, published in 1959:

> The Government's responsibility does not end with ensuring that the efficiency of the police is maintained and that the courts are equipped with adequate machinery. Behind these front lines of defence the counter-attack on crime must be mounted. It is to the development of the means of dealing with the individual offender who has been sentenced by the courts to some form of detention that this Paper is principally directed.
>
> (Home Office 1959: s.16)

It was the Home Office who took on the task of organising and planning an approach to crime control that was more comprehensive than maintaining law-enforcement agencies and punishment options. This task involves the need to develop strategies at a number of levels, provide adequate funding and, most difficult to achieve, coordination between the differing agencies involved both on the 'front line' and in the 'counter-attack on crime'.

Since Leon Brittan's period at the Home Office (1983–5) there has been a more concerted effort to generate greater attention to inter-agency consultation and regard for the general objectives of the criminal justice system as a whole. This has involved two developments, in which the government has come to take a more central and corporatist role to crime and widened its approach by moving from a **reactive** to a preventative approach to crime; and, secondly, by taking the initiative to coordinate the activities of the different criminal justice agencies, which because of their own institutional histories have tended to regard themselves as not part of a system.

The problems of coordination are threefold: first, getting agencies performing the same tasks to work together (e.g., will the Metropolitan Police cooperate with an investigation originating from the Merseyside Police?); secondly, getting the different agencies in a region to work more cooperatively together (e.g., the probation and prison services having an integrated post-release supervision programme for prisoners before and after release); and, thirdly, ensuring that the regional work of the agencies operates within a framework of priorities that reflect national and, nowadays, internationally established objectives.

One solution to improve the collaboration between the agencies that in the past have worked with different regional areas was to introduce co-terminosity, which is to have similar district and regional alignments across all the agencies. To this end, the 13 Crown Prosecution Service areas were brought into line with the 43 police forces in England and Wales (the London area CPS to cover the work of the Metropolitan and the City of London police).

Awareness of the way that administrative boundaries provide potential hindrance to crime prevention and investigation is revealed in a survey of 39 police forces in England and Wales: *Tackling Cross Border Crime* (**Porter 1997**). Its main recommendations were to encourage neighbouring forces to establish collaborative arrangements, such as regional crime groups to share intelligence on crime and criminals, and appointing inter-force liaison officers and joint operation teams.

Another report, *Getting to Grips with Crime – A New Framework for Local Action* (**Home Office 1997b**), led to a new statutory duty on the local authority to take into account the impact of crime when making decisions on planning, housing, social services and locating schools. The intention was to make the police and local authorities jointly responsible for crime prevention. Targets for crime prevention were set by the Home Office and the police and local authorities were expected to provide leadership for a cooperative community-wide approach to crime.

This area of crime prevention (**as described further in Chapter 5**) has seen a great deal of change over the last decade, specifically with regard to the amount of discretion enjoyed by the police and Local Authorities. Under the bureaucracy-reduction strategy introduced by the Home Office since 2010, the number of directives and targets set by Whitehall has been cut so as to allow for a more localised approach to community crime. The government has also introduced directly elected Police and Crime Commissioners for each police area, who will be responsible for producing an annual action plan, a budget and will also play a role in appointing a Chief Commissioner. It is expected that as a result there will be wide regional variation between the approaches and prioritisation of different police forces. **This is discussed in more detail in Chapter 6.**

At the national level the National Criminal Intelligence Service (NCIS) was established in 1992 to coordinate the approaches of law enforcement agencies. It provided nationwide and international intelligence to law enforcement agencies by collecting and analysing information about serious and organised crime. The Police Act 1997 provided for another new agency, the National Crime Squad to deal with crime across police areas in England and Wales. The two organisations were brought together under the Serious Organised Crime Agency (SOCA) in February 2004, which in October 2013 was replaced by the National Crime Agency (NCA). **(See Chapter 6 for further discussion.)**

The Criminal Justice Consultative Council (CJCC) was established in 1991 to promote a greater awareness between agencies of their common purpose. The first recommendation of the Woolf Report on prison unrest in 1990 was the need for closer cooperation between the different parts of the criminal justice system, and it proposed a national forum and local committees. The CJCC was given the task of improving communications, cooperation and coordination by improving consultation and information sharing. To help to do this it publishes an annual report. It was set up with 23 area committees and membership is drawn from the judiciary, police, social services, criminal justice agencies and government departments. In 1997, the chairman, Lord Justice Rose, said that the CJCC provided a unique opportunity to promote 'a greater awareness between agencies of their common purpose'. It has looked at video evidence, fast-tracking cases involving child witnesses and race issues, and standardising definitions in child abuse cases.

More recent attempts to provide greater coordination between the agencies were seen in the approach to dealing with offenders through the introduction of the National Offender Management Service, or NOMS to better integrate the prison and probation services from sentence to resettlement. In 2008, NOMS became responsible for commissioning and delivering prison and probation services across England and Wales. The two services remain distinct in terms of function but they are both overseen by the NOMS so as to enable 'joined up thinking' on offending. The key purpose of NOMS's involvement is that they ensure an integrated approach across the whole range of prison and probation services to support effective offender management in all settings. NOMS also works closely with the courts, local authorities, police and the voluntary sector. NOMS had to contend with a cut to its budget of £90 million – or 37 per cent of its total central budget – for the period 2011–2015.

The Courts Act 2003 instructed the Courts Boards to work with Her Majesty's Courts and Tribunal Service to ensure the efficient running of the courts in England and Wales. However, the Courts Boards were abolished by the Public Bodies (Abolition of Courts Boards) Order 2012, and the service they performed – that of advising the courts on how to improve their service for the specific community they serve. In 2011, the administration of courts came under the sole jurisdiction of Her Majesty's Courts and Tribunals Service.

Finally, if the agencies are to work better together on common tasks in agreed geographical localities it would also be helpful if they shared common IT systems, but this proves to be easier said than done. There are ongoing efforts to unite the IT systems for all users of the criminal justice system. This is naturally an area of great importance which has enormous potential for information sharing. Common electronic case files was one of the ambitions of the Auld Report, with files being sent onwards from one agency to another. However, attempts to wire up a single agency has proved difficult, as was seen with the failure of a huge project in 2001 to put all the nation's magistrates' courts on one computer system, and more recently by the mishandling of the C-NOMIS development project, which was abandoned on the grounds of escalating costs and running years over its deadline.

The attempt to have a single integrated offender management IT system was examined by the National Audit Office in March 2009, in its publication, *The National Offender Management Information System*. The report recommends the abandonment of a single integrated system and the development of five separate databases, as listed in the following extract.

Offender management: shared IT system cancelled

In June 2004, the newly-created National Offender Management Service (NOMS), then part of the Home Office, now within the Ministry of Justice, initiated the National Offender Management Information System project (C-NOMIS) to implement a single offender management IT system across prison and probation services by January 2008. C-NOMIS was intended to support a new way of working, known as end-to-end offender management, and to replace existing prison inmate and local probation area offender case management systems with one integrated system, allowing prison and probation officers and others to access shared offender records in real time.

. . .

The aim of one integrated information system was to improve information sharing about offenders; address the lack of continuity and follow up of interventions with offenders as they move within the prison system and between prison and the community; and to provide a clearer alignment of prison and probation work with offenders.

. . .

Rather than introducing a single shared database with interfaces to other criminal justice systems, the programme now consists of five separate projects:

1. replacement of several current prison systems with the C-NOMIS application;
2. creation of a national probation case management system based on an existing package called Delius;
3. the introduction of a read-only data share facility between prison and probation;
4. the creation of a single offender risk assessment system; and
5. replacement of the current Prison Inmate Information System.

(National Audit Office 2009)

The Ministry of Justice recently put £300 million into creating an information, communication and technology (ICT) system for NOMS – a complicated job as in order to work effectively NOMS must guarantee secure but straightforward access to millions of offenders' details, including offences and sentences. Efforts to modernise and integrate criminal justice databases is progressing but it is not always easy to implement, and requires expensive investment in new IT systems. In contrast to the costly development of ever-larger information systems, the historically unique use of lay volunteers in criminal justice in the UK continues as a cost-effective way to involve members of the public in the response to crime.

▶ Lay participation

An unprecedented role in criminal justice in England and Wales is played by unpaid volunteers who contribute in many different ways. There are 26,000 **lay magistrates** who play a vital role in pre-trial procedure and in making decisions about guilt and sentencing (**seen in Chapter 10**). It was seen in **Chapter 3** that Victim Support is a charity that provides practical and emotional support to victims of crime. There are special constables and lay visitors (custody visitors) to police stations, and independent monitoring boards for each prison. Custody visitors are independent members of the local community appointed by the Police Authority to visit police stations to observe, comment and report on the welfare of people detained in police custody; conditions in which they are held; and the operation of the rules governing their detention. It is charitable organisations that provide the bulk of services available to offenders leaving prison, which aid their resettlement in the community.

Independent watchdogs based in all prisons and immigration removal centres are now known as Independent Monitoring Boards (IMBs). All prisons and immigration removal centres have boards of volunteers who monitor conditions and report to ministers and the general public. Previously known as Boards of Visitors in prisons and Visiting Committees in Immigration Removal Centres, IMBs operate through 1,850 volunteers.

Another role for volunteers is as an 'appropriate' adult because of the requirements of the Police and Criminal Evidence Act 1984. This requires an appropriate adult to be present before the police can begin interviewing a young person in custody. Normally a family member would act in this role but for some young people this is not always possible, so volunteer appropriate adults are used. Their role is to ensure that the rights, interests and welfare of young people, aged 10–17 years old, in custody are safeguarded. Appropriate adult volunteers must be aged 18 or over and cannot be employed by the police.

The significance of lay participants has to be understood in terms of a political culture in which society has not wanted to become over-reliant on state functionaries and professional elites. This aspect of civil liberties is often misunderstood by those who question the representativeness of magistrates. They represent decision makers who do not have to take orders from government or follow the strictures of professional interest. They represent the laity and are expected to bring a common sense to the process of decision making. This may not lead to better decisions but it might at important times represent another point of view independent of the latest orthodoxy as laid down by government or professions.

There are over 30 Independent Monitoring Boards (IMBs) in England and Wales, one for each prison and young offender institution. These were established under the Prison Act 1952, and each has on average 15 lay members who receive no payment. They are independent of the Prison Service and must provide an annual report to the Home Secretary on the running of the prison; members visit the prison regularly and hear complaints from prisoners and have a general concern for the treatment of inmates. The report from the (then) Board of Visitors at Whitemoor Prison correctly predicted future security problems before the escape from their maximum security unit in 1994. The 1997 annual report of the Board of Visitors at Wormwood Scrubs Prison referred to allegations of abuse and assaults of inmates by prison officers, leading to the trial and conviction of prison officers. The Chief Inspector of Prisons made an unannounced inspection of Wormwood Scrubs in 1999 and among the options in his report was the possibility of closure or privatisation because of the failure to respond to a previous visit and a critical report about the standards in the prison. The IMB report of 2011 (*Behind Closed Doors*) highlights cell sanitisation, the inhabitation of cells by more people than they were constructed for, the quality of meat served to prisoners, voting rights for prisoners, late-night transfers between institutions, segregation practices at high-security establishments, access of Independent Monitors to high-security prisons, and information-sharing between institutions and agencies for women prisoners as areas of concern.

Lay or custody visitors to police stations are volunteers aged between 18 and 70, but Justices of the Peace, retired police officers and people convicted of a serious crime cannot be appointed. Lay visitors have the right to visit police stations to check on the treatment of people held in custody. They may arrive unannounced, and usually in pairs, and the police must allow them immediate access to custody areas of the police station. They will typically ask the custody officer how many detainees are being held and are then shown around the cells, escorted by an officer. Cells that are occupied will be opened and the officer will tell the detainees the reason for the visit and ask whether they will talk with the visitors. If they agree they will be asked questions such as how long they have been held by the police, have they contacted a solicitor, do their relatives know they are here, and whether they have received food and drink. If any of the detainees are drunk, violent or hostile the visitors may talk to them through the grill in the cell door. Lay visitors are expected to talk with all those detained in police custody, and they prepare a report. The report is sent to the secretary of the lay visitor panel and a copy to the officer in charge of the police station. If they find anything wrong in their visits they should talk directly with the officer in charge of the station and expect an immediate response.

▶ Under new management: privatisation and agency status

The political economy of crime control changed in a very obvious sense in the 1990s, during which a shift from the public to the commercial sector took place. Some prisons are now run by G4S (Group 4), Securicor, Wackenhut Corporation and UK Detention Service Ltd; and a private security industry at least the size of the police service provides security for paying clients. Business interests are evident in other ways such as sponsorship of Safer City and Crime Concern projects.

Finance and auditing methods have changed for those agencies remaining within the public sector. The Prison Service is now an executive agency with control over the budget allocated to it. The Police Service must now charge the economic costs for activities such as maintaining order at football matches.

In addition to the greater privatisation and commercialisation of the sector and the devolution of budgets, there has been an associated change in the culture of management in which a more aggressive accounting approach is adopted by management, with performance indicators used to assess efficiency. The Conservative governments of the 1980s were determined to tackle what was regarded as a corporatist and overly intrusive system of government that generated a bureaucratic and costly approach to public sector funding and management. By 1990 reform ideas were emerging by which the public sector agencies had to cope with objectives that could be measured by performance indicators relating objectives to funding.

The Police and Prison Service were to undergo radical organisational and managerial reforms. The Prison Service had been involved in a long-running battle with the Prison Officers' Association over the way prisons were managed. In 1978, the *Committee of Inquiry into the United Kingdom Prison Service* (**Home Office 1979**) was set up following 'a long period of deteriorating industrial relations, especially in England and Wales' (para. 1). A new pay structure was established under the Fresh Start programme in 1987 but industrial conflict was to continue. In this historical context the late 1980s and 1990s saw the introduction of initiatives to save money and undermine traditional styles of doing business that included: private prisons, new funding initiatives such as the Private Finance Initiative (PFI) to raise capital from the private sector, financial targets, Key Performance Targets, and structural reforms that included redesignating the prison service as an executive agency, and the contracting-out of prison escort work. They bore the hallmarks of the new management culture.

▶ Management and administration of the courts

Sir Robin Auld's Review of the Criminal Courts in England and Wales, 2001 recommended that a single centrally funded agency, as part of the **Lord Chancellor's Department** (later the Department for Constitutional Affairs), should replace the Courts Service and the Magistrates' Courts Committees (MCCs) – these are the benches, or the basic unit of local magistrates' court organisation. In the 2002 White Paper *Justice for All*, the government accepted the recommendation for a single courts' organisation. The Courts Act 2003 abolished the MCCs and replaced them with Courts Boards, setting up a new executive agency with community links through the boards which would include least one judge; at least two lay magistrates; at least two other members who appear to have knowledge or experience of the work of the courts in the area; and at least two members who appear to be representative of local people in the area. The then DCA was to take over responsibility for the magistrates' courts. The Act abolished petty sessions areas and replaced them with local justice areas. Lay magistrates were to be appointed nationally rather than to local petty sessional divisions.

The Crown Court and county courts are organised into six circuits and 18 groups. A Circuit Administrator heads each circuit. Below circuit level, Group Managers are responsible for the Crown Court centres and county courts within their areas. Group boundaries are aligned to the 42 criminal justice system (CJS) areas.

In March 2009, the National Audit Office reported on the Crown Court and examined the role of HM Courts Service in administering the Crown Court and looked at the practical issues of buildings, staffing and information technology. The report, entitled *National Audit Office Report – Administration of the Crown Court*, made the following conclusions:

NAO Report 2009: Administration of Crown Court

In 2007, the Crown Court received 136,000 criminal cases, including the most serious cases such as murder and rape. The Crown Court sits in almost 100 locations in England and Wales. It is administered by HM Courts Service, which is an executive agency of the Ministry of Justice. HM Courts Service is organised into six regions, and Wales and has 24 areas which are responsible for the day-to-day management of Crown Court locations and other courts within their boundaries. HM Courts Service calculates that in 2007–08 the cost of operating the Crown Court was around £382 million.

. . .

Between 2008–09 and 2010–11, HM Courts Service plans to spend around £100 million a year on new Crown Court and other court buildings and major refurbishments to existing court buildings. Of this spending, the Service has allocated, or earmarked, a total of £120 million to projects which will increase the number of Crown Court rooms by 30 (or around 6 per cent) by the end of 2012.

. . .

The Crown Court has two main information technology systems. CREST is a case management system that is used for tracking case progression, and facilitates the allocation of cases to court rooms. XHIBIT provides real-time information on the progress of hearings to interested parties outside the court room and records the outcome of court proceedings, including any sentence.

(National Audit Office, 2009)

The report highlighted the need for new court rooms in the Crown Courts and identified the problems of the 20-year-old CREST system, and as with the earlier ambitious IT schemes to link up the data systems such as Libra in the magistrates' courts and the National Offender Management Information System (NOMIS), the coordinated single information systems have yet to overcome the technical problems of transferring files between different agencies and the logistical difficulties of agencies working with different protocols and agendas.

4.7 Monitoring, accountability and complaints

Objective 7

Describe the array of ways that the system is monitored, and is accountable to the public

By the 1990s, the new management culture went hand in hand with new ideas about monitoring performance and the accountability of the services. The political agenda on accountability had moved on from the political issues raised about who controls police work and how it is to be accountable to the local community, to monitoring in a very different sense in terms of auditing performance targets set centrally but delivered locally. The agencies had to meet specific criteria established by key performance indicators (KPIs) and respond to a new breed of HM Inspectors who monitored regimes in prisons and the performance of the probation and the police services. Key performance indicators provide targets by which agency performance can be measured. For the Probation Service, KPI 1 aims 'to lower the actual reconviction rates for all types of order and achieve rates lower than those predicted'. This is monitored by the Home Office.

▶ Key performance indicators: police

Police forces must monitor their performance against five performance targets set by the Home Secretary. Theresa May, the Home Secretary in 2010 commented that KPIs are to be abandoned but have continued to be published. The key objectives for policing issued in 1995 were as follows:

Policing objectives and KPIs (in brackets)

1. To maintain and if possible increase the number of detections for violent crimes (KPI: number of violent crimes detected per 100 officers).
2. To increase the number of detections for burglaries of people's homes (KPI: number of burglaries of dwellings detected per 100 officers).
3. To target and prevent crimes which are a particular problem in partnership with the public and other local agencies (no KPI).
4. To provide high-visibility policing so as to reassure the public (KPIs: public satisfaction with the levels of foot and mobile patrols/number of police officers available for ordinary duty per 1,000 population/proportion of uniformed constables' time spent in public).
5. To respond promptly to emergency calls from the public (KPIs: percentage of 999 calls answered within the local target time/the percentage of responses within the local target time to incidents requiring immediate response).

The local forces establish their own targets. For instance, in the case of objective 5 they have to decide their local target time for answering 999 calls, and the time to reach the incident in the case of an emergency call requiring an immediate response. They will then, at the end of the year, calculate what proportion of calls are answered within that target time. West Yorkshire police, for example, have published their targets for the year 2012/2013 for several KPIs on their website. Their aim is to 'reduce the level of acquisitive crime (house burglary, robbery and vehicle crime)' from a predicted 43,500 to 43,053, and increase 'the proportion of residents who believe the police do an excellent or good job' from a predicted 55 per cent to 55.6 per cent.

▶ Key performance indicators: the criminal courts

The following is a list of some of the key performance indicators that were set for Her Majesty's Courts Service for 2010/2011. The actual performance for the period is also shown.

Her Majesty's Courts Service key performance indicators 2010–2011

- To commence 78% of cases in the Crown Court within the target period. In 2010–11, only 77% of cases commenced within the target period.

- To maintain the 2009–10 ineffective trial rate in the Crown Court at the 13.0% baseline figure for 2009–10. The rate of ineffective trials increased to 13.5% in 2010–11.

- To increase the proportion of days jurors overall sit on Crown Court trials during their period of service from the 2009–10 baseline figure of 67.2% to 70%. In 2010–11, the figure increased by 1.1 percentage point to 68.3%.

- To decrease the average number of hearings held for each magistrates' court case from the 2009–10 baseline of 2.26 to 2.25. The average for 2010–11 was 2.17.

- To produce and send to police 95% of the results from the magistrates' courts within three working days and 100% within six working days. Performance improved compared to 2009–10, when the respective percentages were 83.9% and 95.7%, to 86.5% and 97.1% in 2010–11.

- To ensure that 85% of financial penalties imposed by the court are enforced. This is an adjustment from the 2009–10 rate of 85.8%. The performance in 2010–11 was well above target, with 93.2% of financial penalties collected.

Source: HMCS Annual Report 2010–11

▶ Her Majesty's Inspectors

There is a system of inspection for magistrates' courts, prisons, police and probation. Her Majesty's Inspectors provide independent expert advice to the Secretary of State. They may publish detailed reports on specific inquiries conducted and are required to produce an annual report for Parliament on the efficiency and effectiveness of the organisations for which they have responsibility.

- Her Majesty's Inspectorate of Constabulary was established in 1865. It is not primarily a policy-making body and its main function is monitoring, although it offers a source of consultation and advice on objectives, performance indicators, and senior police appointments. It helps to disseminate good practice throughout the 43 forces in England and Wales. The annual report provides a source of information on the overall picture of police work in England and Wales. The report provides basic information about the size of the 43 forces and their performance against the Home Secretary's objectives. Home Office policies on policing and local targets are set out in the police authority's policing plans.

- The probation service inspectorate was established in 1936. The current system of inspection was established in 1985 and given a statutory role in the Criminal Justice Act 1991. The first annual report from **Her Majesty's Inspectorate of Probation** was published in 1994.

- Her Majesty's Inspector of Prisons for England and Wales has the responsibility to visit and report to the government on conditions for and treatment of those in prison, young offender institutions and immigration detention facilities. Reports may be on specific aspects (themes) of operations within a prison or on general issues affecting prisons. The focus is on management practice, spreading good practice and identifying bad practice. The Chief Inspector is appointed –

from outside the Prison Service – for a term of five years. In December 1995, David Ramsbotham was appointed Chief Inspector of Prisons, followed in August 2001 by Anne Owers, whose position was renewed twice until she left the post in 2010. The incumbent in 2014 was Nick Hardwick.

- Her Majesty's Magistrates' Courts Service Inspectorate (MCSI) started in 1995 and was given statutory authority by the Police and Magistrates' Courts Act 1994. Its task is to inspect and report on the organisation and administration of courts for each magistrates' courts committee area. It is not involved in considering the judicial process or decision making. The Courts Act 2003 established a new HM Courts Service Inspectorate.

▶ Complaints: Prisons and Probation Ombudsman

The Prison Ombudsman was set up in 1994 following the recommendations of the Woolf Report 1991. The report referred to the importance 'of a proper balance between security and control on the one hand and humanity and justice on the other' (**Home Office 1991a: para. 10.44**). It went on specifically to recommend an independent complaints adjudicator to investigate individual grievances and act as the final avenue of appeal against findings of disciplinary hearings (para. 14.347). The government accepted the need for an independent element in the complaints procedure and the 1991 White Paper, *Custody, Care and Justice* (**Home Office 1991c**) stated, 'there should be an independent avenue of appeal against disciplinary findings once avenues within the prison service have been exhausted' and 'appeals against decisions made in response to complaints should also be considered by the same independent body' (para. 8.8).

In 2002, the role was extended to include complaints from those serving community sentences under the Probation Service or under post-release supervision or parole or licence and on matters concerned with pre-sentence and other reports.

Complaints must first have been aired through the internal complaints system of either the Prison Service or the National Probation Service. The Prisons and Probation Ombudsman will take a fresh look at the complaint and decide whether it has been dealt with fairly. If the Ombudsman upholds the complaint, he will make recommendations to the Prison Service or the National Probation Service to put things right.

The Ombudsman is able to investigate nearly all matters for which the Prison Service is currently responsible with respect to individual prisoners, including contracted-out prisons and contracted-out services within a prison.

The Prison Ombudsman only takes complaints from prisoners or their legal representative acting on their behalf; he does not act on complaints from relatives, neighbours or friends. The range of complaints typically cover food, assault, loss of property and complaints against adjudication decisions. Prisoners are not denied the right to go to court – they can still sue in the civil courts and can still seek judicial review. Most complaints are from long-term prisoners.

Complaints that are investigated and upheld will lead to a recommendation for action that is sent to the prisoner and the Prison Service. They are not made public. The Prison Ombudsman's remit is not to investigate prisons as a whole, as that is the responsibility of the Prison Inspectorate; he deals solely with grievances from individual prisoners who have written to him.

The Prison Ombudsman may make the following types of recommendation. For instance, if there is negligence regarding a prisoner's property that gets lost, he may recommend compensation. If there is a complaint about a transfer from one prison to another, he may suggest returning the prisoner to the original situation or, if it is too late, may recommend a written apology from the Prison Service. He may recommend changes or review of a prisoner's security classification.

▶ Independent Police Complaints Commission (IPCC)

On 1 April 2004, a new system for dealing with police complaints in England and Wales was introduced. The new system, operated by the Independent Police Complaints Commission, was designed to raise standards, cut delays, increase public confidence and transform the way police forces handle complaints from the public. It was intended to ensure that complaints are handled in an open, efficient and fair way. The Commission consists of 18 independent commissioners who cannot have worked for the police. They and their staff are organised in four regional offices and are involved in running or supervising investigations and from these identifying areas for improvements and best practice. Much emphasis is placed on the rights of complainants to be kept informed of progress.

One particularly high-profile case of recent times is that of Mark Duggan, the victim of a fatal police shooting on 4 August 2011. The IPCC investigation began immediately after the shooting and within days of the shooting, the IPCC was compelled to respond to complaints made by Mark Duggan's family that they had not received enough support or information. A further report on 9 August by the IPCC which published all the known details of the shooting was blamed for inflaming the situation on the streets by claiming a shot had been fired prior to the police shooting Duggan. Later on during the investigation, the IPCC and the Metropolitan Police again received widespread criticism in the media for the perceived lack of contact with and concern in February 2012 that Mark Duggan's family had not been formally informed about his death. Both the Metropolitan Police and the IPCC apologised for this.

In April 2012, the BBC received footage from an anonymous witness to the aftermath of the shooting which appeared to show a police officer bending down to retrieve something, possibly vital evidence, from the ground. The witness also verbally reported that he had heard officers shouting 'Put it down, put it down' to Mark Duggan before shooting at him. The IPCC expressed disappointment that the BBC had withheld this potentially invaluable and inflammatory footage from the IPCC, while simultaneously appearing to suggest in its report that the IPCC was struggling to obtain evidence from witnesses. The IPCC has had to repeatedly respond to comments made about the case and details surrounding it reported in the press and appeal for calm and patience while it conducts its investigation.

The campaign group claimed that Mark Duggan had been executed by the police and this rumour started the August riots in Tottenham that subsequently spread across several cities of England resulting in arson, murder, manslaughter, robbery, burglary, criminal violence, criminal damage and looting.

The police account was supported when it became known that Mark Duggan was a member of a north London gang, and was supplied with a BBM Bruni Modal handgun 15 minutes before he was killed by the police. The gun was supplied by

Kevin Hutchinson-Foster who was convicted by a jury on 23 February 2013 – following a retrial – of supplying a firearm to Mark Duggan, and given a prison sentence of 11 years.

Then on 8 January 2014 the jury at a **Coroner's Inquest** concluded that Duggan had been lawfully killed by the police. At the time of the shooting Duggan had been under surveillance by Metropolitan Police officers attached to Operation Trident, a group, which was set up to investigate and reduce gun and knife crime among the black communities in London. In January 2014, the IPPC issued an apology to the Duggan family for erroneously claiming a shot had been fired before the police shot Duggan. The IPCC as of June 2014 had yet to complete its report on the shooting.

The previous system, under the auspices of the Police Complaints Authority (PCA), where complaints were conducted by the police themselves (**see also Chapter 6**) was criticised as lacking in independence and objectivity. However, the PCA had been critical of police work in some very high-profile case inquiries. For example, the inquiry conducted for the PCA by the Deputy Chief Constable of Kent, Robert Ayling, into the police handling of the investigation of the murder of the black teenager, Stephen Lawrence, aged 18, in Eltham in April 1993, found that the Metropolitan Police Force was insufficiently thorough in its investigation.

Complaints about the police do not prevent individuals who have been subject to unlawful acts at the hands of the police from using the civil court procedure to seek compensation. In serious miscarriages of justice, compensation may be awarded against, or offered by, the police. In 1997, George Lewis received £200,000 in compensation after serving 5 years of a 10-year sentence for burglary and robbery after the police, he claimed, had concocted the evidence. The police officer involved, Detective Constable John Perkins, was a member of the West Midlands Crime Squad and had been cited in 23 cases where fabricated evidence had led to convictions, including the arrests and imprisonment of those convicted of killing Carl Bridgewater.

On 22 July 2005, Jean Charles de Menezes, a 27-year-old Brazilian electrician, was mistaken for a terrorist suspect and was shot by police marksmen in a London Underground train that he had just boarded at Stockwell station in south London. The shots were fired by two police officers who thought he would blow up the train, killing many people, as had happened a fortnight earlier in London.

The police were hunting four suspected suicide bombers who had attempted to blow up tube trains and a bus a day before in what was a follow-up attack to the 7 July attacks, in which 52 people died and more than 700 were injured on London buses and the Tube.

A surveillance team had been monitoring a block of flats in Tulse Hill, south London, where Mr Menezes lived, in the belief that he was a suspect who had been involved with the previous day's attempted suicide bombings.

Following this shooting, there was an IPCC inquiry and from this the CPS concluded that no police officers were to be prosecuted over the fatal shooting as there was 'insufficient evidence' to prosecute any individual over the death. However, the Metropolitan Police was charged under section 3 of the Health and Safety at Work Act 1974 and on 1 November 2007 the courts found they had acted in breach of this law, even though, once again, they did not identify any one officer as having acted in an illegal manner. The Metropolitan Police was given a £175,000 fine and ordered to pay £385,000 in costs.

There are many ways the police are accountable to the public through the criminal and civil courts, the IPCC, Police Authorities and Her Majesty's Inspectorate of Constabulary but it is unlikely that the legislators of 1974 ever intended that a law to promote safety on building sites and in factories should apply to the emergency services such as the police and the fire service where officers and firefighters regularly put themselves at risk to protect the public.

Conclusion

The government, administration and political aspects of criminal justice are likely to continue to grow in complexity, if for no other reason than because we will be encompassing a more worldwide view of the crime problem and crime responses as a result of world terrorism, membership of the European Union and the global significance of the internet and movement of people as tourists and migrants. The public will look to the political leadership to provide solutions and this is bound to lead to demands for more effective crime prevention strategies and more responsibilities on the police. These topics are looked at in the next two chapters.

Review questions

1. Below is a list of Home Secretaries over the last 75 years. Use the index to identify the Home Secretary when the following occurred:

   - introduction of detention centres
   - execution of Derek Bentley
   - abolition of the term 'borstal training'
   - introduction of the term 'Young Offender Institution'
   - publication of the Woolf report
   - Abolition of Control Orders for Terrorist suspects detained in the UK

Home Secretaries

Year	Home Secretary	Year	Home Secretary
1940–1945	Herbert Morrison	1979–1983	William Whitelaw
1945	Donald Somervell	1983–1985	Leon Brittan
1945–1951	James Chuter Ede	1985–1989	Douglas Hurd
1951–1954	David Maxwell-Fyfe	1989–1990	David Waddington
1954–1957	Gwilym Lloyd-George	1990–1992	Kenneth Baker
1957–1962	Richard (Rab) Butler	1992–1993	Kenneth Clarke
1962–1964	Henry Brooke	1993–1997	Michael Howard
1964–1965	Frank Soskice	1997–2002	Jack Straw
1965–1967	Roy Jenkins	2002–2004	David Blunkett
1967–1970	Jim Callaghan	2004–2006	Charles Clarke
1970–1972	Reginald Maudling	2006–2007	John Reid
1972–1974	Robert Carr	2007–2009	Jacqui Smith
1974–1976	Roy Jenkins	2009–2010	Alan Johnson
1976–1979	Merlyn Rees	2010–	Theresa May

2. The Criminal Justice Consultative Committee, established in 1991, has the task of improving awareness and cooperation between the different agencies in the criminal justice system. In what ways could the work of this committee be extended? Answer this by indicating which of the following key words and phrases indicate the type of coordinating role you would think desirable for the criminal justice system in England and Wales. Think initially in terms of the impact of greater cooperation between agencies working in the same field such as policing. Secondly, how might these key words apply to cross-agency cooperation between different functioning agencies, for instance probation and prisons?

Information exchange

Consultation

Data-sharing

Cross-agency computerisation of data

Joint operations

Exchange of personnel

Establishing common definitions

Agreeing to cross-agency common objectives

Mergers of local units into regional units

Merger of regional units into nationwide units

Merger of national units into European-wide agencies

None of these.

Discussion questions

1. The Private Security Industry Act 2001 established the Security Industry Authority (SIA). Explore the SIA's website and list the types of firms regulated.

2. Consider the two statements below about the response to the de Menezes shooting and the use of Health and Safety laws in this context. Do you think the doubts raised about the use of this legislation are justified?

> We must remember an innocent man died during the course of a Met police operation – this is damning enough. Our thoughts continue to be with the Menezes family and friends, together with those of the other victims.
>
> . . .
>
> The police are not above the law but the MPA have always had reservations about whether bringing a case against the MPS for a breach of the Health and Safety at Work Act 1974 was the most appropriate course to take.
>
> (Len Duvall, Chair of the Metropolitan Police Authority)

In considering this judgment we should not lose sight of the heavy burden which falls on the police to weigh risks and take decisions, often under extreme pressure and in difficult circumstances, in order to carry out their work effectively. While the service does not shy away from public scrutiny, during counter-terrorism operations, situations will inevitable arise whereby legislation such as the Health and Safety at Work Act of 1974 is a wholly inappropriate standard against which police actions should be judged. This is especially true where intelligence-led activity is involved.

(ACPO President Ken Jones)

Further reading

Jewkes Y (2004) *Media and Crime*, Sage: London

Newburn T (2003) *Crime and Criminal Justice Policy* (2nd edn), Pearson: London

Ryan M (2003) *Penal Policy and Political Culture in England and Wales: Four essays on policy and process*, Waterside Press: Winchester

Windlesham, Lord (1993/2001) *Responses to Crime* (4 vols), Clarendon Press: Oxford

Weblinks

Civitas: the Institute for the Study of Civil Society **www.civitas.org.uk**

HMCS: **www.hmcourts-service.gov.uk**

Home Office: **homeoffice.gov.uk**

Ministry of Justice: **www.justice.gov.uk**

NOMS: **www.hmprisonservice.gov.uk/abouttheservice.noms**

Policy Exchange (think tank): **www.policyexchange.org.uk/**

Prisons and Probation Ombudsman: **www.hmprisonservice.gov.uk**

Chapter 5

Crime prevention and reduction

Learning objectives

After reading the chapter you should be able to:

1. Define the concept and categories of crime prevention
2. Explain the theoretical basis of crime prevention
3. Describe the growth of crime prevention
4. Describe the emergence of CCTV
5. Distinguish and define the concepts of situational and social crime prevention
6. Understand the concepts of broken windows, zero tolerance policing and anti-social behaviour
7. Discuss the various issues in crime prevention

Key statistics

- Between 1 June 2010 and 31 December 2011 there were 1,414 Anti-Social Behaviour Orders (ASBOs) issued at all courts in England and Wales confirming a steady decline from a peak of 4,122 in 2005
- 27% of all ASBOs administered between 1 June 2010 and 31 December 2011 were given to young people (aged 10 to 17) within which the breach rate in the age group of 12 to 14 was the highest among all age groups, reaching 74%
- There were 625 Drinking Banning Orders (DBOs) issued between 31 August 2009 and 20 June 2012
- In July 2013, the British Security Industry Authority (BSIA) reported between 4.9 and 5.9 million CCTV cameras in the UK
- The Anti-social Behaviour, Crime and Policing Act, intended to tackle anti-social behaviour and provide better protection for victims and communities, received Royal Assent in March 2014

Introduction

How central to a criminal justice system is the goal of preventing crime? The formal process of adversarial justice described in later chapters of this book is based on responding to the offender as suspect, defendant, convicted, sentenced and sometimes as prisoner. A central concern of this system is to ensure that the innocent are acquitted and the guilty are convicted and given a deserved penalty. Some sentences aim at rehabilitating, incapacitating or deterring offenders, and thereby reducing crime, but their impact on overall levels of offending has been uncertain. There was, during the latter part of the twentieth century, a disillusionment with rehabilitative methods and a general pessimism that 'Nothing worked' **(see Chapters 11 and 12)** – a climate in which interest in the victim of crime rose as the system was seen as being too 'offender centred' **(as seen in Chapter 3)**. The limitations of the criminal justice system as far as reducing crime is concerned were also illustrated in **Chapter 2** where we saw that most crimes are not reported and, of those that are, the majority do not result in a conviction. Furthermore, some factors determining the crime rate such as economic or cultural forces are outside the control of the formal system, which further limits its effects – for example, the tenfold increase in the crime rate from the 1950s to the 1990s does not suggest that the criminal justice system alone could reduce crime. Of course this might in part be a consequence of growing affluence and/or cultural attitude changes since the 1960s; or the lenient and liberal sentencing approach of the judges in the 1970s may in part have been responsible for the growth in crime **(Davies 1997)**. Whatever it did, the criminal justice system did not appear able to do much about the growth in crime in the second half of the twentieth century.

This general pessimism led to a reorientation in thinking about strategies to reduce crime. At the level of the formal system debates on crime policy tended to swing between calls to be tougher on crime (e.g. more police, less bail, tougher penalties) or doing more to change offenders' behaviour in a rehabilitative sense (e.g. counselling, therapy, education, training, drug-use reduction, anger control strategies). Others looked to strategies which, rather than centring on the predispositions and motivation of offenders, focused instead on the situations in which crime was committed in an attempt to reduce any opportunities for crime which existed in the immediate situation. While the police had always had a role in advising on crime prevention, this was seen as a more peripheral activity than detecting or prosecuting crime.

From the 1980s, however, different forms of crime prevention focusing on communities, such as Safer Cities and Neighbourhood Watch, were developed and crime reduction became central to the approach of New Labour governments from 1997 **(described in Chapter 4)**. This is evident in a range of policies including the growth of CCTV, the development of **Crime and Disorder Reduction Partnerships** (CDRPs; later called Community Safety Partnerships [CSPs]). There was a focus on pre-criminal intervention such as neighbourhood child curfews, parenting orders and anti-social behaviour schemes – many of which involve a wide range of agencies coming together in an attempt to make local communities safer. The aim of building 'safer, stronger communities' had become a key element in political rhetoric in relation to criminal justice. This changing focus led us to suggest in **Chapter 1** that we need an additional model of criminal justice, one that takes account of this new focus on controlling offenders in a way that is more systematic and comprehensive than the rehabilitative model. The introduction of the Serious Crime Prevention Order is another example of the growth of the offender management model. It was introduced in the Serious Crime Act 2007 and came into force in 2008. It is for those aged over 18 who have been convicted of a serious crime, and used in order to protect the public. It is similar to an ASBO or a Sex Crime Prevention Order, in that it is a civil order but failure to comply carries the potential of a prison sentence (maximum of five years).

Finally, the widespread use of mobile phones has put new technology in the hands of victims and witnesses, and thus the potential aggressors and thieves, who want to avoid detection, might think twice before confronting a victim who can contact the police in an instance, sometimes with a photograph of the criminal.

5.1 What is crime prevention?

Objective 1

Define the concept and categories of crime prevention

Crime prevention is defined as:

> . . . any action taken or technique employed by private individuals or public agencies aimed at the reduction of damage caused by acts defined as criminal by the state.
>
> (Hughes in McLaughlin and Muncie 2001: 63)

The definition focuses on crime reduction so as to distinguish between the actions of public agencies and private citizens with a focus on physical measures to prevent crime, but as many point out, it is the intermediate agencies of civil society (such as family, school, churches) that may be of most influence in reducing crime in the long run. Crime prevention includes everyday actions which we all take, from locking doors or concealing money to redesigning buildings to make them more secure, redesigning products to make them more difficult to steal or to use after they have been stolen, or redesigning the urban environment. It can involve strategies which aim, by changing offenders' attitudes and life circumstances, to turn them away from crime – thus the formal criminal justice system can also be part of crime prevention. As thinking about crime prevention and a range of policies developed, its description altered. A range of crime prevention policies were introduced during the 1980s, and the 1990s saw the emphasis widening to include communities – both as places where crime had its greatest impact and as sites of many different policies involving different agencies. During this period, the term Community Safety, reflecting a broader focus than crime prevention, became more widely used and there was a growth of 'Community Safety Officers' (**Pease 2002; Hughes 2002**). More recently the phrase 'crime reduction' has been more prominent although this can be used more or less interchangeably with 'crime prevention' (**Pease 2002**). It may, however, signal a narrower approach, focusing on policies which address clearly defined targets for reducing crime. As will be seen below, many of these policies involve Criminal Justice Agencies, working in partnership with other community based agencies in an attempt to reduce crime.

As outlined above, there are many different forms of crime prevention, often grouped into primary, secondary and tertiary approaches.

- *Primary crime prevention* refers to strategies aiming to prevent crime before it happens and involves all the social, physical and other strategies to prevent crime. It may involve making a target more difficult to steal (e.g. by installing better locks on doors). At a more general level it involves socialisation, the processes through which people learn the dominant moral values of civic society and their responsibilities as citizens. It thus involves families, schools, community and other organisations. The criminal justice system also plays a part here, particularly in the denunciatory function of affirming and reinforcing the dominant moral code as a justification for punishing those who infringe against it.

- *Secondary crime prevention* identifies 'at risk' people and situations. It involves policies which target people considered to be at risk of becoming offenders – such as young people in areas known for high levels of offending; or situations where crime is likely to occur. Thus a variety of educational and sports schemes aim to divert youth in high crime areas from criminal activity. The focus is on 'at-risk' neighbourhoods, schools and families. An important role is played by health, educational, welfare and medical staff to spot those at risk of committing a crime, or of being a victim. Thus nurses question children who come into hospital with signs of violent injury. Teachers check on pupils they suspect of playing truant. Recent policies have addressed the sale of alcohol in areas associated with anti-social behaviour and curfews for young people under 15.

- *Tertiary crime prevention* deals with known criminals and crime situations. It aims to prevent those already convicted of crime from continuing with their criminal careers, mainly through the sentences of the court. Parenting orders and drug abstinence orders have been introduced and several recent criminal justice policies have aimed to secure greater cooperation and mergers of agencies dealing with offenders, set out in *Reducing Crime, Changing Lives*. One aim of the National Offender Management Service (NOMS) is to ensure that offenders are managed throughout the whole of their sentences, whether in custody or in the community. Other examples of more joined-up approaches to responding to known offenders are Youth Offender Teams, Local **Criminal Justice Boards**, CDRPs and **Drug Action Teams**.

Some advocates of crime prevention do so because of an ideological disposition against punishment and imprisonment. However, one major function of imprisonment is to keep criminals away from the public simply by removing the offender from society – also works as a preventative measure in these cases. Indeed, there are certain criminal justice commentators who see prison as the only reliable means of preventing known criminals from committing further crime. Prison's incapacitative effect and crime reduction possibilities are spelt out in a letter to *The Times* on 24 October 2009:

Sir,

While it may be true that many ex-prisoners reoffend, it is not true to say that putting people in prison does nothing to reduce crime. As a Neighbourhood watch co-ordinator who produced a month newsletter that went to 30 local schemes. I had regular meetings with the local police and was given detailed local crime figures as well as information as to whom among local criminal fraternity had been put away and who had just come out. It was noticeable that when certain notorious burglars were locked up the rate of burglary in the area declined substantially. And when they came out of prison it went back up again. Prisons may not be a deterrent, but it certainly provides some relief for the general public.

Barry Richardson (Isham, Northants)

Another way of looking at different forms of crime prevention is to distinguish between policies which focus largely on the immediate situational aspects of crime, and those that attempt to target the broader social aspects of crime. Thus, many refer to situational and social crime prevention.

- *Situational crime prevention*, sometimes referred to as 'physical' crime prevention, involves altering the situational or spatial characteristics either to make offending more difficult or detection easier (**Crawford 1998**).
- *Social crime prevention* is based more on the social factors associated with crime such as living conditions, relative deprivation and social disorganisation. This may include what is often described as 'community crime prevention' and may involve community regeneration.

While primary crime prevention is often equated with situational crime prevention, the relationships between these different forms are more complex – a combination of these different ways of classifying crime prevention is suggested by **Crawford (1998)** (see Table 5.2). **Van Dijk and de Waard (1991)** developed the threefold typology set out in Table 5.1 and focused on the three different targets of the offender, victim and potential crime situations.

5.2 The theoretical basis of crime prevention

Objective 2

Explain the theoretical basis of crime prevention

Crime reduction policies are implicitly or explicitly based on theories about why crime occurs. These can focus on different elements of crime. Some theories focus on individual offenders – seeking to establish, for example, if there are any characteristics which distinguish offenders from the rest of the population and whether offenders are 'predisposed' to commit crime. Crime is committed, however, in a cultural context, and sociologists have long pointed to the thrill and excitement provided by crime (**Hayward and Young 2007**) while other sociologists focus on features of the social structure said to influence crime, such as social deprivation or the impact of social change. Crime prevention policies, as seen above, signalled a different approach by arguing that another means of reducing crime was to explore the situations in which criminal events occur – it is easier, for example, to commit a crime successfully in situations in which there is less chance of being observed or being caught. As **Pease (2002)** explains, crime can be related to psyche, structure or circumstance. While it is not possible to explore these theories fully as is done in criminology texts (see, for example, **Carrabine** *et al.* **2004**; **Newburn 2007; Lilly** *et al.* **2010**), a brief exploration is important to understand the theoretical bases of crime prevention.

Table 5.1 Typology of crime prevention

	Primary: General interventions	**Secondary: Focus on at-risk groups and situations**	**Tertiary: Responding to known criminal activities and offenders**
Offender	School socialisation on civic responsibilities	Youth employment training project in high crime area	Restorative justice mediation between offender and victim
	Educational and deterrent strategy of a media campaign about the effects and possible consequences of drink and driving	Curfews on those suspected of anti-social behaviour	Electronic tagging of offender
Situations	All cars manufactured with anti-theft devices	CCTV in city centre areas where rowdy behaviour is predicted	CCTV situated outside public houses where there have been disturbances
	Gun control laws	Identity checks on people coming into the country to combat terrorism	
		Identity cards to reduce likelihood of credit card fraud	
Victims	Media campaign to warn the public to be aware of growing incidence of a particular crime such as credit card fraud	Surveillance of homes of those who have received threats or are likely targets of artifice burglary such as homes for the elderly	Repeat victims of burglary offered security advice and grants for locks

Source: Adapted from van Dijk and de Waard (1991)

Table 5.2 A process/target two-dimensional typology of crime prevention

	Primary	Secondary	Tertiary
Social	Education and socialisation, public awareness and advertising campaigns, neighbourhood watch	Work with those 'at risk' of offending: youths, the unemployed, community regeneration	Rehabilitation, confronting offending behaviour, aftercare, diversion, reparation
Situational	Target-hardening, surveillance, opportunity reduction/removal, environmental design, general deterrence	Target-hardening and design measures for 'at risk' groups, risk prediction and assessment, deterrence	Individual deterrence, incapacitation, assessment of dangerousness and 'risk'

Source: Crawford (1998) *Crime Prevention and Community Safety: Politics, policies and practices,* Longman: London, p. 19

What is generally known as **positivist** criminology, which developed from the late nineteenth century, was extremely influential. Basically this represented an attempt to establish scientifically the causes of crime, in order to develop a 'cure'. Offenders were believed to have some form of 'pathology' and researchers looked for characteristics which differentiated offenders from the rest of the population. These characteristics could be biological, psychological or environmental. Early criminologists focused on biological characteristics: the Italian criminologist Cesare Lombroso, for example, studied the physical characteristics of convicts in prisons, and claimed that criminal men were distinguished by what he called 'physical stigmata', which included long arms, shifty glances, droopy eyelids, bushy eyebrows, large ears, twisted noses and abnormal mouths and skulls (**Lombroso 1897**). His theories were later discredited, particularly as many similar characteristics were found in the general population, but they stimulated further research relating criminality to physical and genetic characteristics such as body shapes, chromosome abnormalities or biochemical factors such as vitamin deficiencies or food allergies.

While much interesting research has been produced, attributing crime to biological characteristics has been found to have limited applicability as few characteristics clearly differentiate offenders from so-called 'non-offenders'. Moreover, crime is a form of behaviour which contravenes rules made by society (**as seen in Chapter 2**). Even if we could assume that people could inherit a propensity to behave aggressively, such aggression could have legitimate and illegitimate outlets. Criminality involves issues of morality, a choice between right and wrong, learnt within the social environment. Thus, it is very difficult to establish the extent to which characteristics are a result of genetic inheritance or socialisation.

Another line of enquiry has been to explore psychological factors. Criminal behaviour, like any other form of behaviour, is learnt during the socialisation process and learning theories have considerable potential in establishing how criminality is learnt. Other psychological approaches have focused on links between personality traits such as extroversion, neuroticism and psychoticism with crime (**Eysenck 1977**), while others have looked at the possible relationship between criminality and mental illness. While these factors are related to some individual offences, mental illness, for example, is found only in a minority of offenders and, in addition, the majority of people considered to be suffering from mental illness do not commit crime.

Individuals are also affected by their immediate environment, particularly the family, and much research has explored the relationship between offending and family background. Parental discipline has been seen as important, with inconsistent and erratic discipline in the home having been found to be more likely to be associated with crime than lax or strict discipline (**West and Farrington 1973, 1977**). Much attention has been paid to the quality of parental supervision, and one Home Office study found that supervision was strongly related to offending, with higher numbers of those who were not closely supervised admitting offending. Around one-third of boys who were closely supervised had offended compared with over half of those who were not closely supervised (**Graham and Bowling 1995**). The structure of families may also be important – some studies have found that fewer offenders come from families living with two natural parents, but there is no evidence to suggest that divorce, separation or single parenthood are criminogenic factors as these are widespread throughout society and not always related to crime (**Utting** *et al.* **1993; Graham and Bowling 1995**).

The quality of relationships within the family is particularly important (**Graham and Bowling 1995**) and the conflict surrounding separation or divorce may be more significant than family breakdown (**Rutter 1985**); a single-parent home may provide the child with a more caring and affectionate environment than one in which two parents are constantly in dispute and have little time to pay attention to their children (**Utting** *et al.* **1993**).

Sociologists have focused on the relationship between crime and the wider social structure and on the adverse effects of social and economic change. To Emile Durkheim, for example, writing at the end of the nineteenth century amidst rapid social change, social and economic changes following the Industrial Revolution had led to the decline of communities and religion which provided people with guidance about morality and standards of behaviour. This could lead, he argued, to the development of anomie, or normlessness, in which individuals lacked such guidance. In addition, the growth of materialism led to people developing what he called 'boundless aspirations' which often could not be met (**Durkheim 1970**). These ideas were taken up by the American sociologist Robert Merton. In American society, he argued, goals of material success predominated, and socially approved norms provided guidelines to achieve these goals by legitimate means such as hard work and educational achievement, but not all who work hard would achieve the goals. This strain could produce anomie, in which the norms of hard work are no longer relevant, especially to those at the bottom of the ladder (**Merton 1938**). Many theories developed out of this anomie paradigm, and while its original formulation had many limitations, the view that crime can be interpreted as a 'solution' to the problems of blocked aspirations has continued to influence sociological approaches.

Anomie points to the significance of a culture which values and promotes the pursuit of success and achievement, and sociologists have long pointed to the role of subcultures in society in which achievement and status may be gained from illegitimate pursuits, among for example groups of young people, drug takers or **joyriders**. These might emerge, for example, out of the strain faced by young people confronted with the difficulties of achieving culturally approved goals such as employment, material success or consumption. Participation in crime may be a 'deviant solution', particularly in the presence of what has been described as the structure of illegitimate opportunities of a particular neighbourhood (**Cloward and Ohlin 1960**), where youth can learn how to engage in activities such as burglary or theft and where there is a pre-existing criminal economy.

Contemporary culture continues to place a high value on young people's consumption of, for example, 'must haves' such as designer goods and clothes, the latest technology and expensive leisure activities, along with values such as speed, risk and thrills (**Hayward and Young 2007**). The urban rioting which dominated the headlines in August 2011 was blamed on precisely this set of circumstances having come to a head: a generation influenced by the glamorisation of criminal culture, without fear of detection, charged with material and consumer desires they were unable to satisfy through legitimate means (**Hall 2012**). Crime itself, argue some, has become a saleable commodity with many products such as books, TV, newspapers and computer games being dominated by crime and violence. These attractions of crime, many argue, must be recognised as they may limit the success of policies which seek to reduce crime – indeed overcoming technological barriers and being given ASBOs may in themselves become part of the risk taking and status associated with illegitimate activities. These cultures have often been associated with economic deprivation, social exclusion and, as **Lea and Young (1992)** argued, with relative deprivation. If people expect and feel entitled to achieve a certain standard of living, they will feel more frustrated if they are denied the opportunity, particularly if they can see others succeeding. This may be exacerbated by the impact of the major social changes of the twentieth century which have led to the decline of traditional industries and, for many, of permanent employment. In communities affected by these changes young people can no longer expect stable full-time employment, which affects their ability to undertake financial and other commitments, such as buying a house or getting married. Many of the most affected communities are also geographically isolated, some in peripheral estates outside towns and cities. This has led to what some see as a situation in which groups and whole communities are effectively excluded from participation in society. This exclusion is not, however, total, and those from excluded areas pass through areas of affluence in which their relative deprivation is made starkly clear (**Young 2005**).

These theories suggested many avenues for reducing crime, and, as will be seen in later chapters, for a large part of the twentieth century the belief that individual offenders could be rehabilitated or 'cured' was a crucial part of criminal justice policy. This criminological 'project', however, came to be questioned as it was found that many rehabilitative programmes had less effect than was assumed and that, as some research suggested, 'nothing works'. Sociological approaches were also questioned by the continuing rise in crime rates despite the development of the welfare state and rising affluence – all of which should theoretically have reduced crime. New approaches were sought which moved away from looking at how offenders might be 'predisposed' to crime and focused on trying to stop crime before it happened – on prevention rather than cure. Attention was thus directed at the third factor identified above: the situations or circumstances in which crime occurred.

This involved a different approach to offenders' motivation and it was argued that individuals make rational choices whether or not to commit an offence. They may weigh up, for example, the gain they might derive from the crime against their chances of being caught and punished. Thus, crime depends on this evaluation of risk and the opportunities provided by the situation (see, for example, **Clarke 1980**). Faced with an open till in an empty shop, a potential thief is more likely to steal than if the shop is crowded and has publicised video surveillance. Much crime, it was argued, is therefore opportunistic, rather than being related to individual pathologies or sub cultural motivation.

This led to more attention being paid to the relationship between crime and what Felson has described as 'routine activities' (**Felson 2002**). Simply put, this involves looking at crime as involving a triangular relationship between an offender, a victim and a location; change one and the crime will not take place. As Pease explains:

> In a pub (location), someone (offender) assaults someone else (victim) in an argument about whose turn it was to be served. The offender could be banned, the victim may choose to drink in another pub, or the licensee may be encouraged to change bar arrangements or train staff so as to make such disputes less likely. Each option could resolve the problem.
>
> (Pease 2002: 950)

Crime prevention was also related to the work of **Oscar Newman (1972)** who argued that the physical design of estates and public buildings can hamper the community's surveillance of social space and thus reduce its ability to control crime. High-rise buildings and estates that are built so that windows do not overlook public spaces, and buildings with many corridors and exits, help to create conditions conducive to crime because they do not provide the opportunity to be able to see or respond to anti-social behaviour. Thus redesigning housing schemes may produce more 'defensible space' – space which people occupy and feel responsibility for. This prevents crime as it means that strangers can be more readily observed and, therefore, deterred. In any situation in which a crime may occur, levels of surveillance are crucial. Surveillance can be increased informally by altering the design of buildings to ensure greater surveillance by employees or residents, or formally by employing security guards or installing video cameras.

5.3 The growth of crime prevention

Objective 3

Describe the growth of crime prevention

While people have always taken steps to prevent victimisation, institutional responsibility for crime prevention was, until the mid-twentieth century, largely restricted to police crime prevention units; and the police have always had crime prevention as part of their role, albeit a small and often unrewarded one. Crime Prevention Panels were set up in 1966, although it was not until the 1980s that crime prevention 'took off' (**Tilley 2002**) as a major part of governmental policy. Since then, there has been a large volume of research and different policy initiatives, CCTV has become widespread and partnership arrangements between criminal justice agencies and local authorities have been institutionalised. There were many reasons for this rapid growth, some of which have already been outlined (**Hughes 2002; Crawford 1998 and 2007; Tilley 2002; Newburn 2003**). Rising crime rates created an 'overload' for the criminal justice system, and increased its costs. There was also a rising political and public concern about crime, to which governments wished to respond. In the face of the growing recognition of the limits of the criminal justice system to reduce crime, crime prevention offered an attractive, and relatively inexpensive, means of reducing crime. As Tilley comments:

'where cure appears unavailable, and containment is very expensive, prevention looked extremely attractive in the face of a high-profile problem like crime.'

(Tilley 2002: 16)

A major role in the rising focus on crime prevention was played by the development of the Home Office Research and Planning Unit, under Ron Clarke. In an influential publication it detailed the potential of a variety of measures (**Mayhew** *et al.* **1976**) which had had some success, and in 1983 the Crime Prevention Unit was set up. Many different research projects, focusing largely on situational crime prevention, were undertaken to establish which strategies affected which crimes in specific circumstances. It was also recognised that crime prevention necessarily involved a range of agencies other than the police, and was best achieved through 'multi agency' working and collaborative partnerships. At governmental level, crime prevention was also encouraged. In 1983, the Home Office Standing Conference on Crime Prevention was strengthened by having a Home Office Minister in the Chair, and a circular in 1984 stated clearly that:

The primary objective of the police has always been the prevention of crime. However, since some of the factors affecting crime lie outside the control or direct influence of the Police, crime prevention can not be left to them alone. Every individual citizen and all those agencies whose policies and practices can influence the extent of crime should make their contribution. Preventing crime is a task for the whole community.

This, argues **Crawford (1998: 36)**, was a crucial symbolic milestone and following this, central government policy became clearly fixed around the partnership approach.

By the late 1980s many new initiatives had been launched. In 1988, Crime Concern, a charity funded partly by the Home Office and partly by private enterprise, was launched. This organisation has been responsible for a large number of crime prevention projects in conjunction with both commercial and public organisations. The Crack Crime campaign was also launched in 1988. In 1993, a National Board for Crime Prevention was established to bring together representatives of central and local government, business, voluntary agencies, the media, the police and the Probation Service.

A major development was the Safer Cities programme, launched in 1988 with the aim of reducing crime, lessening the fear of crime and creating safer cities where 'economic enterprise and community life can flourish' (**Tilley 1993**). It incorporated not only crime prevention but a concern with other related aspects of community safety. It included the growing concern for crime victims and recognised that crime was related to economic enterprise and community life. If crime rates are high in a particular area and the population has a high fear of crime, people will avoid public places, local shops and community activities. The *Annual Safer Cities Progress Report of 1992/3* stated that, up to 1993, more than 3,300 crime prevention and community safety measures had been initiated involving £20.4 million in Home Office funding. The wide variety of activities included (**Home Office 1993: 7**):

- projects to improve security in homes, businesses and public facilities;
- helping young people as potential offenders, offenders and victims of crime;
- schemes to tackle domestic violence and other women's safety issues;
- action on car crime and racial harassment.

While representing a major development in crime prevention and incorporating many multi-agency groups, the Safer Cities initiative had limitations; it was somewhat ad hoc and was implemented only in selected areas (**Newburn 2003**) and projects often lacked resources. Taken together with other developments of the 1980s, it did not represent a national strategy for crime prevention and, while partnership working was encouraged, there was no clear idea of which agency should take the lead in developing local community safety strategies.

Another major development was **Neighbourhood Watch**, which emerged in the early 1980s, based on the principle that the police and the community can work together to prevent crime. Located in local areas, schemes involve the public looking out for and reporting anything suspicious – being the 'eyes and ears' of the police. By 1988, as many as 14 per cent of households were members (**Mayhew et al. 1989**) and by 1996 there were 150,000 Neighbourhood Watch schemes with five million members.

The organisation of individual schemes has varied enormously; however, they normally involve groups of residents with a local coordinator. Members produce and distribute newsletters and leaflets giving general crime prevention advice, often supported by local businesses. Some schemes encourage property marking and security surveys, and members are asked to display their membership by stickers on doors.

Despite its popularity the success of Neighbourhood Watch has been limited. One problem is that schemes are easier to set up and operate more effectively in areas in which they are least needed. Thus the British Crime Survey found that schemes were most common in affluent suburban areas, with members being drawn from high status and higher income groups (ibid.). The population in multi-racial areas and the poorest council estates, on the other hand, were least likely to join. This survey also found that areas where membership was lower also tended to be those where burglary risks were higher. This may have the effect that schemes divert police resources from high-crime to low-crime areas (**Heal and Laycock 1986**).

In addition, membership of a Neighbourhood Watch scheme may in reality mean very little and involvement often falls off after initial launch meetings (**Bennett 1990**). Three-quarters of members interviewed by the British Crime Survey had put stickers or posters in their windows but 21 per cent had neither attended progress meetings nor knew the name of their coordinator. Many members found it difficult to pinpoint any specific benefits of schemes although there are some indications that burglary risks were lower after joining Neighbourhood Watch. Displacement, discussed above, is also a problem as a successful scheme might prevent crime in one group of streets, but crime may rise in an adjoining area without a scheme. It might well be that the benefit of schemes such as Neighbourhood Watch is to reassure the community that someone is trying to do something about crime.

In 1991, the report of a review carried out by the Standing Conference on Crime Prevention (the Morgan Report) made several recommendations. Local authorities, it was argued, should be given statutory responsibility, working with the police, for the development of community safety and crime prevention. Voluntary groups and businesses should also be involved. New legislation should be monitored by a national body and a community safety strategy group should be set up at the highest tier of local government. There should be a local action group to formulate objectives and a strategic plan, consulting many local and neighbourhood-based groups. This would have provided a coherent structure (**Crawford 1998**), although it was never fully implemented, partly due to the then Conservative Government's reluctance to enhance the role of local authorities. It did, however, highlight the importance of partnership-working and underline the role which local authorities and local agencies could play (**Tilley 2002**). In the event many local community safety partnerships were formed.

Government strategy in the early to mid-1990s was largely dominated by a concern with tough penal strategies, although it continued to advocate the partnership approach and encouraged people to be 'active citizens' by becoming involved in Neighbourhood Watch schemes; and there were plans to increase the use of voluntary special constables (**Newburn 2003**). There was also encouragement for the use of CCTV, and, in 1995, the National Board for Crime Prevention became the National Crime Prevention Agency, whose task was to focus on and coordinate the national agenda, to disseminate good practice and to develop strategies for preventing and reducing crime. It had representation from the Home Office, the Police, Crime Concern and other individuals but no representatives from local government. It was not an independent body, as envisaged by the Morgan Report, nor did it have any agenda-setting powers compared to other National Crime organisations such as those in Sweden, France or the Netherlands (**Crawford 1998**).

▶ Crime and Disorder Reduction Partnerships/Community Safety Partnerships

The Crime and Disorder Act (CDA) 1998 established a more structured approach to crime prevention, and emphasised principles of partnership and collective responsibility between local authorities and chief police officers to work in cooperation with probation committees and health authorities to implement a 'strategy for the reduction of crime and disorder in the area'. Before doing so, the responsible authorities, known as Crime and Disorder Partnerships, were to be required to carry out a review of the levels and patterns of crime and disorder in the area; prepare an analysis of the results of that review; publish a report of this analysis; and obtain views of relevant authorities. Strategies were to contain 'objectives to be pursued by the responsible authorities, and long term and short term performance targets'. The Act also required local authorities, police authorities, joint authorities, National Parks Authorities and Broads Authorities to take crime consequences into account in their practices and policies. Local Partnerships had to undertake this work in a three-year cycle, advised by, among others, the Home Office Crime Reduction website which includes a 'knowledge base', 'toolkits' made up from evaluated best practice, a discussion forum and a strategy statement (**Pease 2002**). By November 2000, 376 statutory Crime and Disorder Partnerships in England and Wales were implementing their first three-year strategy to reduce crime and disorder (**Phillips 2002**).

Partnerships were to set five-year targets, with annual milestones for the reduction of vehicle crime, burglary and robbery under the government's **Crime Reduction Programme** (**Newburn 2003**). Performance monitoring regimes were also put in place. All nine regional government offices now have Regional Crime Reduction Directors, high-ranking civil servants whose task is to facilitate, inform and catalyse increased and improved attention to crime reduction in their areas (**Tilley 2002**). This is in line with the managerialist characteristic of many areas of criminal justice and social policy. According to **Tilley (2002: 23)** they involve 'new rules, roles, committees, tiers of authority, accountability mechanisms and reporting hierarchies'. Community safety officers and departments became part of the local authority structure and are being professionalised through a process of training and accreditation. A National Community Safety Network had around 200 members by 2000 (**Hughes 2002**) and there is a growing research literature, aimed at producing evidence-based community safety policies.

Some of the problems faced by partnerships, which would themselves be subject to review, were revealed by a Home Office Research project into three crime and disorder partnerships (**Phillips 2002**). This found that some agencies, particularly health authorities, were more difficult to engage due to a lack of resources and a lack of clarity about their role. Businesses were also found to have a limited role. While not seen as police 'takeovers', the leading roles of the police and local authorities could make some smaller voluntary and community organisations feel marginalised. All partners faced time and resource limitations and the setting of nationally determined five-year targets placed pressure on partnerships and could conflict with what they saw as local priorities. The report identified a danger that the pressure of performance management could encourage partnerships to opt for the 'quick wins' associated with situational crime prevention rather than longer-term measures.

The Crime Reduction Programme, while representing a major financial commitment and incorporating a large variety of interventions, only ran for three years, until 2003. It faced many problems (**Maguire 2004**). Many projects failed to be fully implemented and cooperation between different criminal justice agencies, as required by the CDA, was not easy to implement. **Maguire (2004)**, for example, argues that it was difficult to secure the full participation of agencies for whom crime was not a primary responsibility and **Crawford (2007)** talks of the conflicting interests, priorities and cultural assumptions of different agencies. Government ministers, keen to see quick results, set increasingly unrealistic targets which also led to a tension between government-based central targets and local priorities. In addition, academic research did not provide the evidence to lead the policies to the extent that had been hoped for (**Maguire 2004**).

This led to a review of CDRPs following the publication of the 2004 White Paper *Building Communities, Beating Crime.* In addition, a National Community Safety Plan (**Home Office 2005**) signalled the incorporation of the National Policing Plan within a wider community safety agenda and the aim of creating a more coordinated national approach by requiring ministers to prioritise community safety policies and consider community safety dimensions of new and existing policies (**Crawford 2007**).

A review of CDRPs was published in 2006. It acknowledged a number of problems in relation to strategic direction, information-sharing and local consultation and also found that some of these difficulties were related to the continual changes which had been instituted. A number of changes were built into the Police and Justice Act of 2006. These included the removal of the requirement to audit communities every three years and a requirement that local three-year community safety plans should be refreshed every year and should be integrated with other local strategies and plans using Local Area Agreements. Community consultation and information gathering was directed to be conducted through both formal and informal feedback and updated every six months using the National Intelligence Model. The section 17 duty on local authorities to consider the crime and disorder implications in all decisions was extended to include anti-social behaviour, substance misuse and behaviour which adversely affect the environment, and the power to share information under section 115 of the Crime and Disorder Act became a duty among the three statutory agencies and probation. National Standards were subsequently introduced. The changes attempted to coordinate local activities using new National Frameworks and Local Strategic Agreements to integrate policing and community safety plans and they also reflected the increased emphasis being placed on disorder and anti-social behaviour (**Newburn 2007**).

Stephen Rimmer, Director General of the Crime and Policing Group in the Home Office, wrote in a letter to all Crime and Disorder Reduction Partnerships in August 2009 that the localised approach was working. In particular, the Home Office team, having examined the work being done by different partnerships, were encouraged by the increase from 45 per cent to 49 per cent in the proportion of the public who believed that police and local agencies were dealing effectively with the anti-social behaviour and crime issues that matter.

From 1 March 2010, Community and Disorder Reduction Partnerships were rebranded Community Safety Partnerships (CSPs), apart from in Wales, where they were already known as such. There was no immediate change to the responsibilities or capabilities of partnerships, although in 2011, the Crime and Disorder (Formulation and Implementation of Strategy) (Amendment) repealed some of the regulations for CSPs in order to free up more time for direct action. The Probation Service joined the partnerships as a key statutory member responsible for reducing reoffending. The main role of CSPs is to ensure that offenders are targeted effectively, that victims are offered immediate support and that local public spaces are safe. The CSPs are expected to respond to the communities in which they operate in, rather than central government, for advice on what crime issues to prioritise.

❱ Safer Neighbourhoods

A National Community Safety Plan (NCSP) for the years 2006–2009, published by the Home Office in 2007, listed the six 'key themes' of community safety as: making communities stronger and more effective, reducing crime and anti-social behaviour and building a culture of respect, preventing extremism and countering terrorism, creating safer environments, protecting the public and building confidence, and improving people's lives so they are less likely to commit offences or reoffend. For each theme, the plan lists 10 or more priorities and sets itself targets for specific years, such as 'establish neighbourhood policing teams in every community by April 2008' and 'bring 1.25 million offences to justice by 2007–8 through improved performance on sanction detections, especially in relation to more serious crime'. CDRPs were listed as one of 12 'key partners', led by the police, striving to achieve the NCSP targets.

As promised by the NCSP, the Safer Neighbourhoods project – which allows fora dedicated local policing team in each ward to focus on improving relations with the community – was rolled out across the UK by 2008. Most neighbourhoods in England and Wales now have their own team made up of one sergeant, two constables and three police community support officers. The teams' responsibilities are to deal with local people's concerns about community safety and anti-social behaviour. (Their work is reviewed in more detail in **Chapter 6**.)

Crime prevention (and its associated structural framework) has, as a result, grown considerably in a short space of time – what, therefore, does it consist of and how can it be evaluated? The following sections will look at some of its major forms, and at some issues of evaluation.

5.4 CCTV

Objective 4

Describe the emergence of CCTV

A major feature of crime prevention has been the use of CCTV in a variety of areas including high streets, shopping malls, housing estates, organisations, schools, hospitals and individual retail establishments. From a mere two local authority schemes in 1987, there were around 440 town centre schemes by 1998. The government provided £37 million to fund the introduction of schemes between 1994 and 1997, and during that period it took up around 78 per cent of the crime prevention budget. A further

£170 million was made available in 1999 (**Coleman and Norris 2000**). **Norris and Armstrong (1999)** point out, it is now virtually impossible in Britain to move through public and private space without being subject to surveillance – as they comment:

> As consumers we are monitored by the routine use of cameras in retail outlets; whether in the supermarket, department store or corner shop. When we leave the store our image, in all probability, will be captured by high street, town centre and shopping mall camera systems. On our journey home, traffic cameras will monitor our compliance with speed and red light restrictions and, if we travel by rail, cameras at stations and along platforms will ensure a record of our presence. In other roles, whether it be as workers on the factory floor or at the office, as students, from kindergarten to university, as hospital patients, football fans or even customers at a local restaurant, cameras are probably watching over us. Put simply, in urban Britain . . . in almost every area to which the public have access we are under surveillance from CCTV.
>
> (Norris and Armstrong 1999: 1)

It is widely believed that CCTV performs a number of functions and its use was highlighted in 1993 by the filming of the abduction of Jamie Bulger, the small child later killed. Its use may reduce the fear of crime by making people feel safer. A survey of losses from shops and retailers in 1994/5 showed a decrease in cheque fraud, down 53 per cent. This might be explained as customers switch to plastic cards. It is interesting to note that fraud using plastic cards was down 60 per cent and might reflect the methods of the use of CCTV (**Brooks and Cross 1996**). It is assumed that it can act as a deterrent to crime, as it means that an offence may be captured on camera and the perpetrator identified. It is thus seen as having the ability to prevent crime and to assist detection; as the August 2011 civil disorder demonstrated in terms of the numbers of rioters and looters brought to courts.

The Home Secretary stated in 1995:

> CCTV catches criminals. It spots crimes, identifies law breakers and helps convict the guilty. The spread of this technology means that more town centres, shopping precincts, business centres and car parks around the country will become no-go areas for the criminal . . . CCTV is a wonderful technological supplement to the police.
>
> (**cited in Coleman and Norris 2000: 151**)

CCTV is now ubiquitous and its use has grown particularly in the following areas (see, for example, **Norris and Armstrong 1999**):

- *In residential areas.* Many will be familiar with 'concierge' systems which monitor communal areas of housing estates and multi-storey blocks. It can be used to monitor those coming into areas to protect residents' safety but can also be used to monitor residents – against, for example, anti-social behaviour, vandalism and drug dealing in residential estates.

- *In schools.* Schools were previously vulnerable to intruders and vandals, and there were also concerns about assaults on teachers within schools. Many schools now have CCTV equipment. This can protect against intruders, verify the identity of people coming to collect children and identify the cause of possible accidents. CCTV cameras in schools can also be used to monitor the behaviour of pupils, checking, for example, for drug dealing in playgrounds.

- *On the road.* Since 1992, speed cameras, which have caused considerable controversy, have been employed and used in the enforcement of traffic legislation, as well as for popular entertainment shows. Vehicle licence plates can be recorded to assist catching thieves of stolen cars and also to assist in combating terrorism.

- *In car parks and petrol stations.* There has been a considerable increase in video surveillance of car parks which has been claimed to have dramatically cut the numbers of vehicles stolen and vandalised. In addition, most major petrol stations now have CCTV installed to prevent robbery and theft.

- *Railways and trains.* Most stations now have CCTV monitoring and during the 1990s London Underground installed CCTV across its 250 stations. Drivers also have 'track to train' systems which allow them to receive pictures of the platform at each station and see pictures of the side of the train to monitor door and passenger safety (ibid.).

- *In shops.* Most shops, whether small corner shops or large supermarkets, chain and high street stores have CCTV. These protect against shoplifting, assaults on staff and robberies. In large stores they are also used covertly to monitor staff behaviour – to prevent theft but also to control behaviour – one Parcel Force employee was sacked after being filmed playing frisbee during working hours (ibid.).

- *In hospitals.* Publicised cases of babies being stolen and staff and patients being victimised by threatened and actual violence highlight the importance of security in hospitals, and this is now widespread.

- *In town and city centres.* During the 1980s and 1990s, CCTV spread to public as well as private spaces – starting with, in 1985, a system covering the promenade in Bournemouth. The government funding referred to above led to a situation in which all major cities had city centre schemes by around 1996, and many smaller and medium-sized towns by 1998 (ibid.).

Advances in digital and wireless technology are constantly improving the quality of CCTV footage. Many CCTV cameras are now able to capture audio as well as 'follow' the action with the use of remote control. In 2009, for example, 95 per cent of Scotland Yard's murder cases used CCTV coverage as evidence (**Barrett 2013**). The British Security Industry Association (BSIA), reported in July 2013 – based on a two-year survey – that there are between 4.9 and 5.9 million CCTV cameras in the UK, and this figure excluded traffic system cameras and those in private households. There were more than 300,000 cameras in public sector schools, with an average of 10 per school. BSIA commented that there is more extensive use of cameras in the UK than in other European countries and that there is widespread public support for their use in the UK.

The success or otherwise of CCTV is not easy to evaluate. Any reduction in crime may be the result, not of CCTV, but of other factors – crime rates, for example, fluctuate in any event, and the police might patrol areas covered by CCTV more intensively (**Coleman and Norris 2000**). Displacement, which will be discussed below, is also a problem. Its success may also be affected by the kind of systems in use and the extent to which, even if a crime is on camera, an operator is watching and can do anything about the offence. Research results have been somewhat contradictory, with some showing a reduction in crime after the installation of cameras, whereas others show little reduction, and yet others have indicated displacement. A variety of factors may affect the extent to which CCTV might work. For example, in order to be deterred by surveillance, a potential offender has to be aware of it, yet many people may not be aware of the system in operation. Discussing apparently contradictory results between studies in Airdrie, in Scotland, and Glasgow, **Ditton and Short (1999)** point out that Airdrie is a small town and the existence of cameras was well known. In addition, if offenders were filmed they could be readily identified. In Glasgow, however, many were unaware of the cameras and offenders were less easy to identify. **Coleman and Norris (2000: 168)** conclude that the 'criminological evidence is far from straightforward: the effects are neither universal nor consistent', and **Ditton and Short (1999: 217)** argue that 'open-street CCTV can "work in limited ways" . . . in different ways in different situations'. As with other forms of situational crime prevention, CCTV also raises issues of the intrusiveness of surveillance, which will be discussed below.

5.5 Situational and social crime prevention

▶ Situational crime prevention

Objective 5

Distinguish and define the concepts of situational and social crime prevention

As seen above, situational crime prevention measures focus on the circumstances in which crime takes place, rather than on offenders. Measures commonly involve 'the design of products, services, environments or systems to make them crime resistant' (**Ekblom in Muncie and McLaughlin 2001: 263**). It may involve making sure that an area is subject to surveillance by, for example, householders, residents or employees, and its methods include simple strategies such as the use of anti-climb paint on drainpipes to prevent burglars or vandals. It focuses very specifically on the opportunities to commit crime – as **Clarke (2005)** points out, opportunity is crucial:

- criminally disposed individuals will commit more crimes if they encounter more criminal opportunities;
- regularly encountering these opportunities could lead to them seeking more opportunities;
- individuals without pre-existing dispositions can be drawn into criminal behaviour by a proliferation of opportunities;

- law-abiding citizens might be drawn into crime by regularly encountering easy opportunities.

What is sometimes described as 'opportunity reduction' (**Crawford 1998, 2007**) can take three main forms:

1. Increasing the effort involved in crime, often known as 'target hardening', examples of which are installing speed humps on roads to prevent speeding, or introducing physical protection to targets such as locks and bolts.

2. Increasing the risks of detection, which involves increasing surveillance by, for example, redesigning buildings, introducing concierges or installing CCTV cameras.

3. Reducing the rewards of crime by, for example, making sure that a stolen item can be traced through property marking, or 'target removal', an example of which is replacing coin-operated meters or boxes with those which require a swipe card (**Crawford 1998**).

To this, **Crawford (2007)** adds two further dimensions to answer observations that situational crime prevention is only about nuts and bolts. These are:

4. Reducing provocation by reducing stress and frustration, for instance with efficient queuing arrangements, police service and soothing music. Disputes should be avoided by separating rival football fans, for instance, and temptations and arousals avoided, by banning racial slurs and controls on pornography. Advertising campaigns can be targeted at activities such as drugs and drinking and driving, and imitation can be discouraged by rapidly repairing damaged property and abandoned vehicles.

5. Removing excuses by reminders and exhortations about the rules, such as, for example, public campaigns and clear notices about 'Private Parking'. Compliance can be made easier by, for instance, providing sufficient waste bins and toilets.

There have now been many 'success stories' associated with situational crime prevention and, as **Pease (2002)** argues, the literature demonstrating their effectiveness is now extensive. Since the mid-2000s, for example, when the use of chip and pin credit and debit cards became widespread, card fraud has dropped dramatically, from £504million in 2004 to £341million in 2011 (information from the UK Payments Administration Ltd (UKPA) website, formerly APACS, the Association for Payment Clearing Services). An early example of the success of such measures was not related to crime but to the reduction of suicide by the replacement of toxic town gas with non-toxic natural gas (**Crawford 1998; Pease 2002**). This led to a fall in suicide rates in England and Wales from 5,700 to under 3,700 between 1963 and 1975, at a time when suicide rates were increasing across Europe. Suicide by domestic gas virtually disappeared, whereas it had previously accounted for 40 per cent of suicides. An important feature of this is that those wishing to commit suicide are highly motivated and might be assumed to look for alternative methods – thus showing the potential of preventative measures. Other successes have included the following:

- The introduction of steering locks in cars has been found to reduce car theft. In West Germany, where steering locks were introduced in all cars, rates fell dramatically, whereas in Britain, where they were introduced only to new cars from 1971, theft may have been 'displaced' to cars without steering locks.

- Improved street lighting provides a good example of the more subtle effects of crime prevention measures (**Pease 2002**). Some have claimed that improved street lighting reduces the incidence of assault, car crime and threats, with **Painter (1988)** having claimed a 75 per cent decrease in a period of six weeks. Theoretically, argues Pease, it could be assumed that this 'works' by increasing surveillance and would be most effective at night, whereas it also appears to reduce crime during daylight! Its effect, therefore, may lie more in an increased pride in the community and community cohesion, although not all research confirms its effect on crime reduction (**Crawford 1998**). It does, however, appear to reduce people's fear of crime and increase feelings of safety.

- The Kirkholt Project: an extremely influential project was targeted at repeat victimisation from burglary on a housing estate in Kirkholt near Rochdale, which had a rate of burglary double that which would be expected, and high rates of repeat victimisation. A range of interventions included the installation of window locks and strengthened doors, the removal of coin-fed meters, neighbourhood watch schemes and support for burglary victims. Repeat victimisation declined by 80 per cent within seven months and within three years burglary rates had fallen by around one-quarter. The scheme became a model, although it was subsequently difficult to establish which of the many measures might have contributed to the decline of burglary (**Crawford 1998; Pease 2002**).

These examples demonstrate the considerable promise of situational crime prevention but also indicate some of the difficulties of evaluating it. It is difficult, for example, to pinpoint the factors which have led to a reduction in crime and further difficulties are raised by the problem, common to all forms of crime prevention, that crime may have been displaced elsewhere. Displacement can take several forms, outlined by **Crawford (1998)**:

- Spatial or geographic displacement – the same crime is committed in a different place.

- Temporal displacement – the same crime is committed against the same target at a different time.

- Tactical displacement – the same crime is committed against the same target but in a different way or by a different means.

- Target displacement – the same type of crime is committed but a new target is selected, for example increasing bank security may have led to robbers moving to post offices and then to garages or other, easier targets.

- Type of crime displacement – a change in nature of criminal activities, for example moving from robbing post offices to street mugging.

- Perpetrator displacement – new offenders fill the vacuum.

Displacement is clearly a major problem in evaluating crime prevention schemes and often features in criticisms of them. It may not, however, always be negative; as Crawford argues, it can be malign if it involves a shift to more serious offences, but it can also be benign if lesser consequences result. There can also be, for example, a diffusion of benefits (**Clarke 2005**), as seen above in relation to street lighting where another study also found that crime declined in a nearby estate to the one which had increased lighting, and Clarke also discusses 'anticipatory benefits' where potential offenders anticipate that crime prevention measures will have been brought in.

Other limitations of situational crime prevention include issues concerning how sustainable improvements may be (**Pease 2002**) – there may be, for example, an initial reduction followed by an 'escalation' (**Crawford 1998**), in which one set of measures is overcome by offenders which necessitates the introduction of a further set of measures. The introduction of increased security measures may also adversely affect the quality of life in an area, and perversely heighten people's concern about crime rather than reducing it. (Other issues surrounding situational and other forms of crime prevention will be discussed later in the chapter.) Nevertheless most accept that many forms of situational crime prevention do reduce some offences in some circumstances and, as **Pease (2002)** argues, looking at their sustainability and identifying precisely 'how' they work are important issues for the future.

▶ Social crime prevention

As seen above, social crime prevention targets those considered most likely to commit crime and intervenes before crime occurs. It can be generally divided into interventions that target individual motivations, often referred to as developmental crime prevention, and those that seek to change 'communal interactions or collective processes of control', often referred to as community crime prevention (**Crawford 2007: 882**).

Developmental crime prevention

Young people are often the targets of social crime prevention as they feature so prominently among offenders, and there has always been a general belief that the pursuit of a criminal career can be prevented by 'nipping it in the bud'. A wide range of research has attempted to identify factors that place young people at risk of offending and to develop policies, following the trend towards evidence-based policy, which address these. Risk factors, which should not be confused with causes, include, according to **Newburn (2007: 584)**:

- low income and poor housing;
- living in dilapidated inner-city areas;
- a high degree of impulsiveness and hyperactivity;
- low intelligence and low school attainment;
- poor parental supervision and harsh and erratic discipline;
- parental conflict and broken families.

A wide variety of schemes have been introduced both in the United States and in England and Wales, and **Newburn and Souhami (2005)** describe some of these, along with the results of such evaluations as there have been. They include cognitive-behavioural interventions based on attempting to change offenders' thinking patterns, or 'consequentialist thinking'. Some research has suggested that young offenders participating in such schemes in the UK did have lower reconviction rates, but many offenders did not complete the programmes and results over a two-year period were less encouraging. Later programmes, run by the Youth Justice Board, focused on moral reasoning, problem-solving and self-management and aimed at 'encouraging offenders to understand the impact of their offending and to equip them with the skills and knowledge they need to go on to lead law-abiding lives' (ibid.: 369). Results, however, were not encouraging – many failed to complete the projects, particularly persistent offenders, and of those for whom data was available, the overall reconviction rate was over 60 per cent, rising to 80 per cent for persistent offenders.

Some community-based schemes are targeted at the risk factors outlined above, particularly those relating to social deprivation and exclusion. The Youth Inclusion Programme run by the Youth Justice Board provides an example of this kind of intervention which was targeted at the 'top 50' young people between 13 and 16 years of age considered to be at risk of offending. This aimed to include these young people into mainstream activities 'by offering support to them to overcome a variety of social problems' (ibid.). Interventions involved for example education and training, sports, motor projects, family projects and outreach and detached work. While there was some decrease in the frequency of arrests for some of the participants and an indication that it led to less serious offending, crime rates in the neighbourhoods concerned increased, and it appeared that the schemes had not recruited the more persistent offenders. As Newburn and Souhami (ibid.: 370) comment, 'community based preventive interventions are by their very nature difficult both to implement and to evaluate'.

Community crime prevention

Other forms of social crime prevention involve what is sometimes referred to as 'community crime prevention' – involving individuals and institutions in a community or neighbourhood and mobilising community resources. While the word 'community' is often used, it has many meanings – although it is often employed generally and rather vaguely as implying something positive and may involve nostalgia for a better time when communities were more involved. It is, therefore, sometimes unclear in what sense 'community' is being used – does it refer, for example, to some rather idealised notion of 'community', to a geographical neighbourhood, or to groupings or partnerships between individuals and organisations within this neighbourhood?

Many schemes involving community crime prevention have been based in the United States and have had varying degrees of success, and in general the UK has been slower to adopt and, more particularly, to evaluate innovative schemes. **Newburn and Souhami (ibid.)** detail some of these initiatives. Considerable promise would appear to attach to, for example, recreational schemes, which attempt to provide alternative facilities and opportunities based on the assumption that involvement in criminal activities is related to an absence of legitimate leisure opportunities – particularly for young people who cannot afford private leisure provision. Unfortunately, few schemes have been fully evaluated although some have indicated positive effects.

Another form of community crime prevention is mentoring schemes in which older people 'mentor' younger groups considered to be at risk. Results from the United States have not, however, been uniformly positive, although again they suggest some potential benefits. An evaluation of a project called Mentoring Plus, for example, found that there were substantial reductions in offending behaviour although this also decreased among non-participants in the programme. It is not, therefore, easy to assess the effectiveness of many of these programmes and there is a generally acknowledged need for more thorough evaluative research.

5.6 Broken windows, zero tolerance policing and anti-social behaviour

Objective 6

Understand the concepts of broken windows, zero tolerance policing and anti-social behaviour

Related to community crime prevention, but focusing on the responses to actual crimes, is the influence of ideas which suggest a tough approach to what is perceived to be a growing problem of anti-social behaviour involving a range of incivilities, with policies being related to the influential broken windows thesis associated with the ideas of **Wilson and Kelling (1982)**. This states that if minor incivilities, such as drunkenness, vandalism, begging, litter, graffiti and disorderly behaviour go unchecked then an atmosphere is encouraged in which more serious crime will flourish. Incivilities, it is argued, encourage a more general fear of crime. Graffiti might be seen by some as the exploration of artistic talent, whereas others might see it as a sign of urban disorder which drives away respectable citizens and attracts anti-social elements.

This thinking was extremely influential in the United States and became associated with the approach generally known as **zero tolerance** policing, coined first within the New York Police Department (NYPD) to indicate that there would be no tolerance of police officers' involvement in drug taking and corrupt behaviour. If the NYPD could be cleaned up, then why not New York City? This more aggressive approach to policing low-level street crime, allowing more local autonomy to police commanders, using local neighbourhood intelligence and crucially not ignoring minor acts of anti-social behaviour, was associated with William Bratton in Boston and New York City where he was appointed Police Commissioner in 1994. Bratton empowered local commanders but with instructions to concentrate on the types of crime that were conducive to public anxiety, including those that the police had been ignoring or tolerating in the past. The police were told to have a more visible profile on the streets and not to ignore minor infringements. Performance targets were introduced for local precincts. Considerable success was claimed for this method of policing. In 1997, Bratton reported that 'over the past three years, the City's crime rate has dropped by 37 per cent. The homicide rate has plummeted over 50 per cent' (**Bratton 1997: 29**). These claims, however, have been subsequently contested, particularly as a number of other features could have been associated with reduced crime levels, and the practices of zero tolerance policing had little impact in the UK.

The emphasis of zero tolerance policing was not only to reduce crime but also to restore citizen confidence in New York as a safe place by showing that the police and not the criminals are in control of the streets. Part of the idea is to 'Prevent anti-social elements developing the feeling that they are in charge' (**Dennis in Bratton 1997: 3**). Norman Dennis wrote:

> Zero-tolerance policing is based on three ideas. One is the simple principle, 'nip things in the bud'. Prevent anti-social elements developing the feeling that they are in charge. Prevent a broken-down and ugly environment of neglect becoming a breeding ground for crime and disorder.
>
> (Dennis in Bratton 1997: 3)

The broken windows thesis, referred to above, has been related to the growth, from the late twentieth century, of measures to curb anti-social behaviour. Anti-social Behaviour Orders (ASBOs) were introduced in the CDA of 1998, but were slow to be taken up, in part due to delays in processing applications and to poor communication between agencies. They were, however, seen as central to government policy and a series of measures sought to strengthen them. In 2003, a White Paper was published outlining proposals for tackling anti-social behaviour, *Respect and Responsibility – taking a stand against anti-social behaviour*, followed by the introduction of what has come to be known as the 'respect agenda'. The subsequent Anti-social Behaviour Act 2003 (ASBA 2003) introduced several secondary crime prevention measures to help deal with younger offenders and their parents as well as social nuisances, such as graffiti. It provided a means for schools, local authorities and youth offending teams to work with the parents of children who are behaving anti-socially.

ASBA 2003 also extended the measures that can be taken to remove graffiti, and restricted the sale of aerosol paint to children. As seen above, the Police and Justice Act 2006 placed anti-social behaviour within the remit of CDRPs. There was a considerable growth in the use of ASBOs at first, but after a review of ASBOs announced in July 2010, it was established that between 2005 and 2011 its use had dropped by more than half, as the Home Office stopped explicitly encouraging local areas to use it. It was surmised that this was partly because of the sheer number of options (19) available to the authorities in the 'toolkit', including **Acceptable Behaviour Agreements** and some interventions specifically related to social housing such as Notices Seeking Possession, and the fact that practitioners tended to use not necessarily the intervention that was most appropriate, but the one with which they were most familiar. Not only had the take-up rate of ASBOs dropped, but the compliance rate had dropped too, with 56 per cent of ASBOs breached in 2009, as opposed to 40 per cent in 2003 (*More Effective Responses to Anti-Social Behaviour*, Home Office, February 2011).

Following this review, the Coalition Government presented a public consultation document in February 2011, outlining a series of proposals for tackling anti-social behaviour, and announced that ASBOs would be phased out.

The Home Secretary, Theresa May, commented critically on the wide range of different types of anti-social behaviour powers introduced in the previous decade:

... the ISO, the ASBI, the ASBO and the CRASBO. Crack house closure orders; dog control orders; graffiti removal orders, litter and noise abatement orders, housing injunctions and parenting orders. (And that's not even all of them!) These sanctions were too complex and bureaucratic ... Such a centralised approach, imposed from Whitehall, can never be the best way to deal with an inherently local problem. Rather than part of the solution, the previous government's focus on anti-social behaviour became part of the problem. The multitude of central government initiatives and gimmicks meant that people expected the government to deal with these issues ... They waited for the slow machine of the state to crank up and intervene, rather than getting on, getting out there and doing it themselves.

We need to re-establish that sense of personal and social responsibility.

We need to make anti-social behaviour what it once was – unusual, abnormal and something to stand up to – instead of what it has become – frequent, normal and tolerated ... For 13 years, politicians told us that the government had the answer; that the ASBO was the silver bullet that would cure all society's ills ... But too often with the old approach, sanctions were not followed through. Ineffective orders were issued, then breached. Fines were issued, but not enforced. People got away with it – and the victims knew it ... Just this morning, the latest ASBO statistics have shown that breach rates have yet again increased – more than half are breached at least once, 40% are breached more than once and their use has fallen yet again, to the lowest ever level.

It's time to move beyond the ASBO.

The Home Secretary outlined some of the planned policy changes that were expected to reduce anti-social behaviour instead. These included the introduction of elected Police and Crime Commissioners, the launch of the 101 non-emergency phone service, tightening alcohol licensing laws and banning below-cost alcohol sales.

We need a complete change in emphasis, with communities working with the police and other agencies to stop bad behaviour escalating that far ... Local authority workers; social landlords; health and education professionals; social services – they all need to work together, and to work with the police, to tackle anti-social behaviour in whatever form it takes ... But crucially, we also want communities to come up with their own ideas of what they are going to do.

It's not just the police, it's not just social landlords, or councils – it's the whole of society that needs to come together and work together to tackle anti-social behaviour. Because fundamentally this is a local problem, and the answers to it can only come from local people who are close enough to understand the root causes.

Speech by Home Secretary Theresa May, 'Moving beyond the ASBO', 28 July 2010

Following the consultation, the government presented a White Paper in May 2012 outlining the introduction of six new measures, shown in Table 5.3, to prevent anti-social behaviour including Criminal Behaviour Orders (CBOs), already dubbed by some as 'crimbos'. These do not replace ASBOs directly, but will allow police and local authorities, either on the grounds of their own intelligence or in response to reports from members of the community about 'low-level nuisance', to apply to the courts to impose a CBO on an individual, the requirements of which will vary depending on the nature of the behaviour. Breach of the order will be a criminal offence, with a range of sanctions available to the court and a maximum sentence of five years in custody. Police will also have an explicit duty to take action on anti-social behaviour if it has been reported by five different

Table 5.3 New measures to prevent anti-social behaviour

Existing system	Proposed changes
ASBO on conviction ASBO Interim ASBO ASB Injunction Individual Support Order(ISO) Intervention Order	**'Criminal Behaviour Order'** – available on conviction for any criminal offence, and including both prohibitions and support to stop future behaviour likely to lead to further anti-social behaviour or criminal offences.
	'Crime Prevention Injunction' – a purely civil order with a civil burden of proof, making it much quicker and easier to obtain. The injunction would also have prohibitions and support attached, and a range of civil sanctions for breach.
Crack House Closure Order Premises Closure Order Brothel Closure Order Designated Public Place Order Special Interim Management Order Gating Order Dog Control Order	**Community Protection Order (Level 2)** – a local authority/police power to restrict use of a place or apply to the courts to close a property linked with persistent anti-social behaviour.
Litter Clearing Notice Noise Abatement Notice Graffiti/Defacement Removal Notice	**Community Protection Order (Level 1)** – a notice issued by a practitioner to stop persistent anti-social behaviour that is affecting quality of life in an area or neighbourhood, with a financial penalty for non-compliance, or other sanctions where relevant e.g. the seizure of noise-making equipment.
Direction to Leave Dispersal Order	Police 'Direction' power – a power to direct any individual causing or likely to cause crime or disorder away from a particular place, and to confiscate related items.

Source: More Effective Responses to Anti-Social Behaviour, London: Home Office, 2011

people, known as the 'community trigger', a safeguard inserted to prevent a repeat of the tragic case of Fiona Pilkington, who took her own life and that of her mentally disabled daughter Francesca Hardwick, in 2007 after years of victimisation by local youths despite more than thirty attempts by Fiona Pilkington and her family to get police to intervene.

Similar to ASBOs are Drinking Banning Orders (DBOs). They are available through the provisions of the Violent Crime Reduction Act 2006 and have been in force since 31 August 2009. DBOs intend to tackle *alcohol-related* anti-social and disorderly behaviour, such as public order offences, criminal damage, minor and serious assaults, violent offences as well as traffic offences. In England and Wales, DBOs can be issued to individuals aged 16 or over and the order would typically prohibit an individual from entering particular streets or areas. Such restrictions are deemed necessary for the protection of persons from disorderly or criminal conduct that the individual may commit under the influence of alcohol. Other prohibitions may include, where both necessary and proportionate, exclusion from consuming alcohol in public places, exclusion from a single or number of licensed premises as well as exclusion from purchasing alcohol. Each DBO is different and is decided by the magistrates who must consider nature and circumstances of the offence in question. A period specified in the order must be not less than two months and not more than two years, and a breach of the order, considered a criminal offences, carries a maximum fine of £2,500 (**Home Office, 2010**).

Finally, the Anti-social Behaviour, Crime and Policing Act 2014 makes provisions about protecting the public from serious anti-social behaviour by enabling the police forces to 'adjust their approach' to the needs of the area they serve in and to ensure accountability to local citizens for their decisions. The Bill is expected to achieve this by the provision of new 'Community Trigger' and 'Community Remedy', allowing victims and communities to have a greater say in how complaints of anti-social behaviour and out-of-court disposals are handled by the authorities (**Home Office 2013**).

5.7 Issues in crime prevention

Objective 7

Discuss the various issues in crime prevention

Crime prevention has, therefore, been a growth industry involving a 'mixed economy' of government, private sector, local authorities, criminal justice agencies and private citizens and there is a growing recognition that crime prevention should be taken into account by a wide range of agencies, and is not an activity restricted to criminal justice. There have been successes but there are also a number of issues associated with this growth. Some critics claim that successes are often short-term and limited to situational crime prevention while leaving the social structural roots of crime relatively untouched, and that it also neglects other features associated with crime such as emotions. In addition, there are a number of concerns about the overall impact of crime prevention strategies.

As seen above, the Crime and Disorder Act 1998 required a range of local bodies to consider crime and disorder by, for example, considering the impact on crime prevention in the designing of new homes, the provision of public transport, lighting and the licensing of pubs and clubs. Nevertheless, there remain areas where such a consciousness of crime prevention could usefully be developed and some talk of the 'greening' of crime prevention where the potential for crime could be incorporated into many more aspects of design and organisation (**Pease 2002; Tilley 2002**). As Pease points out, central government is not included in these requirements, nor is the private sector; and crime reduction practitioners report frustration at commercial practices such as the reluctance to add photographs to cheque guarantee cards. Pease argues that product designers should be required to look at the 'criminogenic capacity' of a product. Mobile phone designers have already begun to build crime prevention components into their products, and the handset of the future will most likely carry a biometric identification module as a matter of course, preventing anyone other than the phone-owner from using it, which will render it valueless to any potential thief. Crime prevention should also be considered by a number of 'place managers' such as landlords, whose neglect of property may assist burglary and drug dealing, licensees whose poor management allows pubs to be used for the sale of stolen goods and transport companies whose poorly lit stations and badly constructed bus shelters may encourage theft and vandalism. The implications of the growth of e-commerce should also take crime prevention into account.

Whatever the future developments of crime prevention may be, many point to some of the dangers inherent in some of the current strategies and in what is seen as an overemphasis on crime reduction. Some, for example, point to the danger of creating a 'fortress society' organised around crime reduction (**Crawford 2007; Tilley 2002**) which may have an adverse effect on the quality of life and on social relationships. Locks, bolts, bars and entry phones in housing developments may deter intruders but may also limit normal social interaction. An extreme form is the 'gated community' with perimeter security. These kinds of schemes and the ever-present surveillance from CCTV may, as seen above, increase people's fear of crime and feelings of insecurity. They can also be experienced as invasive and as a threat to privacy.

Moreover, some measures may exacerbate social divisions. Tilley (ibid.), for example, talks of the creation of a society divided into safe and unsafe areas with whole groups of people, perceived to pose a danger, being excluded. There are also dangers of stigmatising communities, families and groups of young people picked out for their risk of becoming involved in crime. Social divisions may also be exacerbated by the ability of financially better off citizens to pay for security, whereas those with fewer resources cannot so do. Security, argue some, has become a 'commodity' and some talk of private security 'clubs' (**Hope 2000**). Moreover, the crime displaced from the more affluent may be displaced onto those who are already the subject of repeat victimisation (**Crawford 1998; Hughes 2002**).

Other criticisms hinge around the faith placed in the 'technological fix' of situational crime prevention and the consequent neglect of the social conditions which may be associated with crime. This limits the potential effectiveness of crime reduction measures while also diverting attention from these social conditions. This may be exacerbated by the tendency to prioritise crime reduction in areas of social policy. In what is described as the 'criminalisation of social policy', critics argue that community safety can be associated with the marginalisation of fundamental public issues except in so far as they are related to their criminogenic qualities (**Hughes 2002**).

Developmental crime prevention strategies also raise important issues about civil rights, privacy and equity. How early, for example, should policies aim to target children deemed to be 'at risk' and how are these risk factors to be determined? As Crawford argues:

> ideas of 'nipping crime in the bud' have pushed criminological concern further and earlier into child – and even foetal – development . . . The impact of this logic is to expand the range and reach of state interventions deeper into the social fabric . . . These may be in the interests of the individuals concerned and society more generally, in terms of reductions in crime, but raise ethical issues about the appropriate limits of government intervention, the balance between potential crime-preventive benefits and other social goods, and the impact on those targeted who might never have developed into criminality.
>
> (Crawford 2007: 883)

Furthermore, he argues, some forms of intervention which aim, for example, to ameliorate adverse circumstances which are likely to lead to involvement in crime or anti-social behaviour could involve giving those 'at risk' more benefits than others.

Further criticisms of crime prevention and community safety policies relate to the relatively narrow range of crime which they encompass. The focus has largely tended to be on public, street crime, and more recently on a range of incivilities and disorderly behaviour – largely among working-class youth. Other forms of crime may be relatively neglected, such as the large amounts of violence in the more private areas of homes and workplaces, organised crime and white collar and corporate crime. The latter may have an impact on the safety of local communities by, for example, illegal pollution, unsafe building sites and many forms of crime against consumers (**Croall 2007**; **Tombs and Whyte 2006**). The term 'community safety' has become associated with a relatively restricted range of crimes whereas in theory the notion of community safety could embrace a wider range not only of crime but of other harms, such as pollution, transport and other threats to safety. Some have accordingly called for a broader, 'pan hazard' approach to community safety which deals with a wide range of harms (**Hughes 2002**).

Finally, crime prevention has been regarded in the past as a bolt-on to the mainstream activities of the criminal justice system. Two things have changed this: one is the New Labour strategy that insists that all criminal justice agencies work together to concentrate on the objective of reducing crime, and that it is not just the business of local communities or a matter of designing out crime; this new direction in crime prevention was also reinforced by a mood of optimism following the introduction of policies such as the zero tolerance policing described above. This was significant as the need to include community consultation was central to the project. The police alone are not able to control crime and (as will be seen in Chapter 6) they need the cooperation of the public, and to do this they had to show they were acting in the interest of the public. Community partnership was a crucial element of these policies and this had considerable influence. In particular it underlines the crucial role of the police working with groups seen to present a particular threat, such as gangs or knife carriers, along with a visible presence in an area, in enhancing public reassurance. It further indicates that criminal justice agencies such as the police can play a role in wider crime prevention, particularly in partnerships with a range of agencies.

Conclusion

Crime prevention has therefore become a crucial area for many criminal justice agencies, working in partnership with a wide range of other groups. This so-called preventive turn in criminal justice policy grew out of a recognition that the criminal justice system as it was had a limited capacity to reduce crime, but that more effective policing and more focused sentencing, along with partnerships with other agencies, could contribute to crime reduction.

From being restricted to schemes seeking to change the immediate situation in which crime is committed to make it more difficult for that crime to be committed, crime prevention has broadened to include a concern with community safety and more recently to what could be seen as a narrower conception of crime reduction. The reach of crime reduction policies has become more varied, from the growth of surveillance, through to schemes which aim to target 'at-risk' offenders at a very early age. While many policies undoubtedly have had considerable success and have reduced crime, and in some cases the fear of crime, issues around displacement and difficulties of evaluation mean that their net impact on crime levels is far less easy to establish. Furthermore, many community-based schemes have been slow to develop and hampered by the difficulties of different agencies working together. Nonetheless, many schemes do have considerable local impacts and far more evaluative work needs to be done.

Further developments are also possible in the design of housing and goods. It is important to bear in mind, however, that an overemphasis on crime prevention may be divisive in that some individuals, particularly those assumed to be likely to pose a risk, will face further exclusion from areas where they are seen not to belong, and that some people are more able to prevent victimisation than others. As Gilling points out, it is apposite to ask whose community is being privileged in relation to community safety (Gilling 2001).

Criminal justice agencies have many functions, other than crime reduction and, as seen above, tertiary crime prevention refers to work with offenders after conviction, which will be dealt with in subsequent chapters. Moreover, an essential part of crime reduction is the detection and prosecution of offenders; and the next chapter will look at the agency responsible for this – the police.

Review questions

1. Examine the following extract on the broken windows account of the causes of crime in a community. Answer the following questions:
   - What type of crime are the authors describing?
   - What is the sequence of causes that makes crime in the community more likely?
   - In terms of crime prevention how this type of crime could be prevented or reduced?

. . . at the community level, disorder and crime are usually inextricably linked, in a kind of developmental sequence. Social psychologists and police officers tend to agree that if a window in a building is broken and is left unrepaired, all the rest of the windows will soon be broken. This is as true in nice neighbourhoods as in rundown ones. Window-breaking does not necessarily occur on a large scale because some areas are inhabited by determined window-breakers whereas others are populated by window-lovers; rather, one unrepaired broken window is a signal that no one cares, and so breaking more windows costs nothing. (It has always been fun.)

Philip Zimbardo, a Stanford psychologist, reported in 1969 on some experiments testing the broken-window theory. He arranged to have an automobile without license plates parked with its hood up on a street in the Bronx and a comparable automobile on a street in Palo Alto, California. The car in the Bronx was attacked by 'vandals' within ten minutes of its 'abandonment'. The first to arrive were a family – father, mother, and young son – who removed the radiator and battery. Within twenty-four hours, virtually everything of value had been removed. Then random destruction began – windows were smashed, parts torn off, upholstery ripped. Children began to use the car as a playground. Most of the adult 'vandals' were well-dressed, apparently clean-cut whites. The car in Palo Alto sat untouched for more than a week. Then Zimbardo smashed part of it with a sledgehammer. Soon, passersby were joining in. Within a few hours, the car had been turned upside down and utterly destroyed. Again, the 'vandals' appeared to be primarily respectable whites.

Untended property becomes fair game for people out for fun or plunder and even for people who ordinarily would not dream of doing such things and who probably consider themselves law-abiding. Because of the nature of community life in the Bronx – its anonymity, the frequency with which cars are abandoned and things are stolen or broken, the past experience of 'no one caring' – vandalism begins much more quickly than it does in staid Palo Alto, where people have come to believe that private possessions are cared for, and that mischievous behaviour is costly. But vandalism can occur anywhere once communal barriers – the sense of mutual regard and the obligations of civility – are lowered by actions that seem to signal that 'no one cares'.

We suggest that 'untended' behaviour also leads to the breakdown of community controls. A stable neighbourhood of families who care for their homes, mind each other's children, and confidently frown on unwanted intruders can change, in a few years or even a few months, to an inhospitable and frightening jungle. A piece of property is abandoned, weeds grow up, a window is smashed. Adults stop scolding rowdy children; the children, emboldened, become more rowdy. Families move out, unattached adults move in. Teenagers gather in front of the corner store. The merchant asks them to move; they refuse. Fights occur. Litter accumulates. People start drinking in front of the grocery; in time, an inebriate slumps to the pavement and is allowed to sleep it off. Pedestrians are approached by panhandlers.

At this point it is not inevitable that serious crime will flourish or violent attacks on strangers will occur. But many residents will think that crime, especially violent crime, is on the rise, and they will modify their behaviour accordingly. They will use the streets less often, and when on the streets will stay apart from their fellows, moving with averted eyes, silent lips, and hurried steps. 'Don't get involved.' For some residents, this growing atomization will matter little, because the neighbourhood is not their 'home' but 'the place where they live'. Their interests are elsewhere; they are cosmopolitans. But it will matter greatly to other people, whose lives derive meaning and satisfaction from local attachments rather than worldly involvement; for them, the neighbourhood will cease to exist except for a few reliable friends whom they arrange to meet.

Such an area is vulnerable to criminal invasion. Though it is not inevitable, it is more likely that here, rather than in places where people are confident they can regulate public behaviour by informal controls, drugs will change hands, prostitutes will solicit, and cars will be stripped. That the drunks will be robbed by boys who do it as a lark, and the prostitutes' customers will be robbed by men who do it purposefully and perhaps violently. That muggings will occur.

(James Q Wilson and George L Kelling (1982) 'Broken Windows: The police and neighbourhood safety', *The Atlantic Monthly*, March, pp. 29–37)

2. Are the crime solutions discussed in the extract from Wilson and Kelling above?
   - primary, secondary or tertiary; and
   - focused on offender, situation or victims?

Discussion questions

1. The 'Not in my neighbourhood week' focuses on and publicises local initiatives to reduce crime. Use the Crime Reduction Partnership's website and/or local media reports to identify initiatives in your area, and examine the typology of the strategy involved.

2. On 4 November 2008, the Home Secretary and the Design and Technology Alliance announced a programme to 'develop new and innovative design solutions to help prevent robbery, to crime-proof hot new gadgets and to embed public safety in the design of new public spaces and housing'. Give some examples of design solutions which might be implemented. What approach to crime prevention are you adopting?

Further reading

Crawford A (2007) 'Crime prevention and community safety' in Maguire M, Morgan R and Reiner R (eds) *The Oxford Handbook of Criminology* (4th edn), Clarendon Press: Oxford

Hughes G (2007) *The Politics of Crime and Community Safety,* Palgrave Macmillan: Basingstoke

Tilley N (ed) (2005) *Handbook of Crime Prevention and Community Safety,* Willan Publishing: Cullompton

Weblinks

Crime reduction partnerships: **www.crimereduction.homeoffice.gov.uk/cpindex.htm**

British Security Industry Association (BSIA): **www.bsia.co.uk/cctv**

Anti-social Behaviour, Crime and Policing Act 2014: **www.legislation.gov.uk/ukpga/2014/12/contents/enacted**

CRIMINAL JUSTICE PROCESS: LAW ENFORCEMENT

The police

Key statistics

- The total police strength in September 2013 included 128,351 full-time police officers in England and Wales, 13,552 full-time police community support officers (PCSOs), and 18,068 special constables (volunteers who do a minimum of four hours a week)
- In 2013 there were 64,961 civilian support employees working for the police
- The eight largest metropolitan forces of Greater Manchester, City of London, Merseyside, The Metropolitan Police, Northumbria, South Yorkshire, West Midlands and West Yorkshire, account for 66 per cent of the total police strength
- In 2010/11, police carried out 1.27 million stop and searches in England and Wales, a decrease of 16 per cent from the peak of stop and searches conducted in 2008/09 (the highest in the last decade)

- In 2012, of those arrested in England and Wales by the police, 80% defined themselves as White, 8% Black and 6% Asian
- There were 249 persons arrested for terrorism-related offences in 2012/13. Of all persons stopped and searched in 2010/11 in England and Wales under section 44 of the Terrorism Act 2000, 47% were White, 15% were Asian and 8% were of Black ethnic origin
- Out of every 100 people arrested in England and Wales in 2011/12, 85 were male and 15 females

Introduction

Policing attracts much public interest. Police dramas and documentaries nightly fill up television schedules and detective fiction and crime stories regularly feature in publishers' bestseller lists. But these popular images are often very far from the reality of policing. Police dramas feature murder, violent and organised crime, and investigations involve following up clues, dramatic car chases and almost always the police catch the offender and bring him or her – or them – to justice. In reality, as we have seen, clear-up rates are more modest, murders are rare, many crimes are solved because the victim identifies the perpetrator, or they are discovered by chance, and in the life of an average police officer, car chases and violent encounters with suspects are, perhaps fortunately, rare. The routine work of policing is less dramatic than television portrays, but is no less important for everyday life in the community. In addition, the police perform a wide range of essential roles – they are at the forefront of the 'wars' against terrorism and serious crime and have to respond to major incidents and disasters as well as dealing with a host of non-criminal problems such as missing persons.

There are other, less positive, images of policing. In riots and demonstrations the police can be seen in pitched battles with demonstrators and there have been allegations of incompetence as well as improper behaviour: planting evidence, 'fitting up' suspects and violence by the police. These different images illustrate some of the problems in defining the role of the police. Are they better described as a force or a service? Is it possible to talk about consensus policing or are the police essentially a paramilitary force waging a war against crime and disorder?

The conflicting demands of due process, crime control, bureaucratic efficiency and offender management strongly affect how the police are organised and evaluated. They are expected to find and bring to court those suspected of having committed an offence, but while doing so must stay within the law, and the requirements of the adversarial system of justice. The police must have powers to investigate crime but the public must be able to proceed without undue interference. Policing must be cost-effective, but this is difficult to measure – how, for example, can the value of due process be measured? Having more police on the beat may make the public feel happier, but it might be costly and have little effect on crime. The police have also been affected by the managerialist policies affecting all parts of the criminal justice process, with an emphasis on national and local plans, targets for specific offences and 'intelligence-led' policing. While collecting evidence and bringing offenders to justice is often perceived as the major role of the police, they also play a major role in crime prevention **(as seen in Chapter 5)** and in managing offenders and suspects, such as in Community Safety Partnerships, and in diverting potential or actual young offenders from crime or the criminal justice system.

There have been major reforms to police work in the last three decades. A key piece of legislation affecting police powers was the Police and Criminal Evidence Act 1984 which brought together and rationalised many disparate rules, including providing a clearer set of procedures for stopping, searching and detaining and questioning suspects. Major changes to police organisation and management followed the Sheehy Report of 1993 (not all of the recommendations were taken up) and the subsequent reform enacted in the Police and Magistrates' Courts Act 1994. Responses to concerns raised about 'institutional racism' in the MacPherson Report of 1999 have driven further legislative and practice changes. The Police Reform Act of 2002 introduced new procedures regarding the supervision of police forces and a new independent system for handling complaints against the police. This broadened the circumstances in which senior officers can be removed, and made changes to police powers.

The police have not been immune to the cost reduction efforts of recent governments whereby all public services have had to become more cost-effective and one aspect of this was to identify policing priorities and use civilians, as they were less costly employees, to replace the more costly police officer, as the following extract indicates.

Priorities and the civilianisation of police work

Pressure on and managing of resources to fund the delivery of policing services has been on the political agenda since the 1980s. A Home Office Circular (114/83) placed limits on Chief Constables on the acquisition of additional resources and required them to consider greater cost efficiencies. Force strengths were reduced, forces re-structured and a 'civilianisation' programme accelerated whereby roles in research and development, personnel, finance and computing were reassigned to professional 'civilian' members of staff, ostensibly at lower cost, thereby encouraging the previous police officer incumbents to return to operational duties. In the1990s, in England and Wales the Posen review distinguished between core and ancillary tasks with a reduction in police undertaking the latter and private security taking on the escorting of wide loads, custody services and prisoner escorts. **Bayley and Shearing (1996: 585)** argue that this, in the North American context, could be seen as 'when one system of policing finished and another took its place'.

(Roycroft, M (2013) 'Private and Public Policing' in *The Future of Policing*, Swales Willis.)

Since the terrorist bombings in London in July 2005, the police have been at the centre of controversies as to the additional powers they should be allowed to use to stop future bombings. The conflict is because the ideals of due process and law enforcement, with rules as to how to bring an offender to justice following a crime, are very different from the task of stopping a crime before it happens.

This chapter will examine many of these issues and explore the current organisation of policing in England and Wales. It will start by looking at the role and development of the police. It will then examine how the police are organised and how accountable they are. Legislation regulating how the police exercise their powers will be considered, followed by an outline of different forms of police work and community policing. The police have considerable discretion, and how they exercise this will be explored along with issues identified in relation to the particular topics of policing of minority ethnic communities. Many discussions of the police automatically refer to the police in the public sector, but it is important to recognise that there is a vast and growing private security sector, its members carrying out an increasing number of police tasks. This chapter will look primarily at the work of the public police service.

6.1 The role and development of policing

Objective 1

Describe the roles and development of policing in England and Wales

Policing in its general sense is a part of social control and can be carried out in many different settings, only some of which involve the organisation known as 'the' police. To **Reiner (2010)** 'policing' is:

> an aspect of social control processes which occurs universally in all social situations in which there is at least the potential for conflict, deviance or disorder. It involves surveillance to discover actual or anticipated breaches and the threat or mobilisation of sanctions to ensure the security of the social order.

Policing may be carried out without involving any specialist organisation – it takes place, for example, in schools and workplaces. Surveillance may involve CCTV or can be incorporated into the design of city spaces and buildings (**as seen in Chapter 5**); thus, preventing crime need not involve 'the police'. In pre-industrial societies policing was carried out by an assortment of constables or watchmen, by gamekeepers or by individuals employed to protect property. In contemporary societies many organisations carry out policing functions – government departments such as the Revenue & Customs or the Department for Business, Innovation and Skills have investigatory agencies who may prosecute offenders; and the Health and Safety Executive, Trading Standards Officers and Environment Agency also 'police' compliance with health and safety legislation, consumer protection and pollution control. There are a large number of security firms, and many large companies have security departments. Citizens (**as seen in Chapter 5**) are involved in Neighbourhood Watch Schemes or may join the Special Constabulary and there are vigilante organisations. Indeed there has been an enormous growth in what are often described as private police organisations, such as G4S (Group 4). These are distinguished from the 'public police', most commonly described as 'the police', who are tasked with the investigation of crime, the **arrest** and detention of suspects and preparing cases to pass on to the CPS. 'The police' are distinct in that they can legitimately use coercive force; and organised state police forces emerged along with the modern state.

The police are responsible for law enforcement, for investigating crime, arresting suspects and deciding whether or not to pass the case on to the Crown Prosecution Service (CPS). This reflects their key role as enforcers of the criminal law. They are also the guardians of the Queen's Peace and preserving law and order in society. This involves a peace-keeping role characterised by patrolling the streets and dealing with local disputes and disorder along with a more 'militaristic' role in dealing with major disturbances and demonstrations. They are expected to play a role in reducing crime, and reassuring the public. In addition they perform roles which are less involved with crime but rather with what has been described as 'social' or emergency service, in which they trace missing persons, inform citizens about the death or injury of relatives, deal with accidents and a host of other non-criminal incidents. Some of the many different roles of the police (whose main functions are outlined in **Chapter 1**) are:

- *Crime control and investigation*: 'crime fighting' – detecting and identifying suspects and compiling a case against offenders.
- *Crime reduction*: patrolling and playing a role in crime and disorder partnerships; giving advice about crime prevention (**see Chapter 5**).
- *Order maintenance*: dealing with crowds at, for example, sporting events and demonstrations.
- *Peace-keeping*: maintaining the 'Queen's Peace' which involves dealing with neighbours' disputes and minor skirmishes.
- *Social service*: dealing with reports of missing persons and other non-criminal issues which are reported to them.
- *Emergency*: providing an emergency service and responding to disorder, accidents and other emergencies.
- *State security*: protecting public figures, state buildings and intelligence work in relation to terrorist and other perceived threats to the state.

In practice, these roles are interrelated and not all incidents the police are called to are immediately identifiable as either 'crime' or 'public order' – they are incidents requiring some form of action. Imagine, for example, a situation in which officers are called to investigate complaints about noise and disturbance in a street. In this situation, they will principally be concerned to calm the situation, which might be achieved by their very presence or might involve making arrests. If they behave too aggressively, however, they might exacerbate the situation. In other circumstances, they may proffer advice and help or refer parties to another agency. Thus in many 'potential crime' situations, roles are combined. In 2006, police forces in England and Wales dealt with around 33 million incidents. Of these, on average only 17 per cent were classified as emergencies requiring an 'immediate' response and another 20 per cent as requiring a 'priority' response

– i.e. within one hour. A further 31 per cent received a scheduled response – that is, where the police and the caller agree that the police will attend at a mutually agreeable time – some 25 per cent were resolved without deploying officers and 7 per cent were referred to other agencies (**HMIC 2007**). Much police work therefore does not involve dealing with serious crime and is much more mundane than the 'crime fighting' or 'detecting' images suggested in the media.

There can be conflicts between these different roles. **Bowling and Foster (2002)**, for example, discuss the potentially opposing 'liberal' and 'military' models of policing. The British Police have been noted for an emphasis on consensus policing, underlining their role as peace-keepers providing a *service*, who use minimum force and stress community safety. On the other hand, the police are expected to provide a rapid and efficient response to major disturbances, which may emphasise their military role, and describing them as a *force* emphasises 'harder' policing styles using vocabulary such as the 'war on crime'. The style adopted may affect other roles – if, for example, the police are seen as a 'force' from outside imposing order, people may be less likely to provide them with the information which is so vital for collecting evidence for prosecution.

The adversarial system of criminal justice may create further dilemmas. This system does not seek to establish the truth, but requires that a case is proved beyond reasonable doubt through the provision of legally admissible evidence (**as seen in Chapter 1**). Thus the test of success for the police becomes whether an investigation leads to a prosecution and finding of guilt. In some of the cases which have been labelled as **miscarriages of justice** it has been alleged that the police have tampered with evidence or improperly gained confessions in order to provide evidence to support their view of the defendants' guilt. If no other source of evidence is available they face the possibility that a guilty person will escape justice. In high-profile cases arousing public outrage, especially those involving terrorism, pressure to get a result may lead to the use of illegally obtained evidence. The Police and Criminal Evidence Act 1984 recognised these pressures by enacting a range of measures from disciplinary proceedings to the inadmissibility of evidence to make such temptations easier to resist.

Table 6.1 Persons arrested for notifiable offences 2002–2012 (numbers in thousands) by type of crime

	Total	Violence Against theperson	Sexual offences	Robbery	Burglary	Theft and handling Stolen goods	Fraud and Forgery	Drugs	Criminal damage
2002/03	1,313.1	284.0	28.9	35.8	108.9	419.9	38.6	134.1	131.1
2003/04	1,330.4	332.1	30.0	34.7	108.9	392.3	38.4	146.2	113.1
2004/05	1,353.4	395.2	30.4	32.8	97.7	367.2	37.8	160.8	84.8
2005/06	1,429.8	448.3	32.1	35.4	99.1	363.7	35.4	169.6	88.6
2006/07	1,482.2	487.6	32.0	40.9	100.8	343.8	29.5	167.8	89.4
2007/08	1,475.3	477.7	32.0	36.3	94.6	327.8	31.8	152.9	104.5
2008/09	1,462.1	464.1	33.7	34.7	96.4	327.4	34.5	140.3	115.3
2009/10	1,385.3	456.7	36.9	32.7	91.7	295.6	33.1	124.0	121.0
2010/11	1,362.0	431.6	37.5	34.0	93.5	291.3	31.0	113.1	124.9
2011/12	1,235.0	384.2	34.5	31.6	90.7	270.4	27.8	95.5	121.2

Source: Police powers and procedures England and Wales 2011/12, National Statistics, 18 April 2013

▶ Development of policing

Some of these issues can be seen in a brief account of the development of policing in England and Wales, particularly since the inception of the 'new police' in the nineteenth century, before which there was no one public organisation responsible for policing.

In 1829, the Metropolitan Police Improvement Act set up the Metropolitan Police Force. Initially this consisted of 1,000 officers controlled from No. 4 Whitehall Place – backing on to Scotland Yard. Similar forces were set up in municipal corporations and counties and, following the County and Borough Police Act 1856, there were 239 forces operating in England and Wales. These early police forces concentrated largely on patrolling the streets. In 1842, following two attempts on the life of Queen Victoria, a small detective branch was set up, consisting of two inspectors and six sergeants. By 1877 it had expanded to 250 men. A Fenian bombing campaign during the 1880s led to the formation of the Special Irish Branch, later to become the Special Branch, specialising in counteracting subversive political and industrial activity. As the police force grew and new technology became available, new specialist functions emerged. In 1901, the system of classifying fingerprints was introduced and in 1910, the Metropolitan Police first caught a criminal using radio telegraphy. In 1920, the police acquired two motor vans – the birth of the flying squad. Women officers were introduced in 1919, although women, often police constables' wives, had previously been employed as 'matrons' to deal with female convicts and matters involving children. Until 1973, women were organised in a separate department and paid less than male officers. After 1973, the women's organisation was abolished and the force was integrated.

The police have not always been popular with everyone. The working classes saw them as a potentially oppressive force, popularly described as a 'plague of blue locusts', 'blue devils', or 'crushers'. The middle and upper classes saw a threat to their liberty from so-called government spies. Gradually, however, opposition from both groups was overcome and the police gained legitimacy. This success, according to **Reiner (2000)**, was due to the policies adopted by early commissioners that created the distinctive style of English policing. Crucial to these policies, devised in an attempt to secure the support of the public at large, was the emphasis on the independence of the police from any particular class or political influence and a recruitment policy whereby the police were presented as 'citizens in uniform'.

Reiner identifies several key elements of these early strategies. In the first place, a quasi-military command structure incorporated elements of rank, authority and discipline. This bureaucratic organisation, which included training and a career structure to attract high-quality recruits, distinguished the 'new' police from their disorganised and often corrupt forerunners. In addition, the importance of upholding the rule of law was stressed, thus protecting citizens from any abuse of police powers. A policy of minimum force sought to allay fears of the working classes that the police would be unduly oppressive. This led to one of the most distinctive features of British policing – the absence of firearms in everyday duties and a reluctance to use paramilitary tactics more common in the United States and many European countries. In addition, the police were to be non-partisan and impartial in their enforcement of the law, favouring the interests of neither one class nor the other. This impartiality was underlined by denying police officers the vote until 1887, and they are still not allowed to affiliate to political parties or have a trade union. The Police Federation represents police officers of the rank of constable (up to chief inspector) but they are not allowed to take industrial action.

The reluctance to expand the detective branch arose out of a deep-rooted suspicion of the plain clothes officer. Hostility was reduced as the new police gained a reputation for being relatively effective in preventing and detecting crime. Finally, argues Reiner, their legitimacy increased as a result of changes in society itself. By the 1950s, there was less class conflict than before, the working classes had become more incorporated into society and were relatively homogeneous – thus the public as a whole tended to have a shared conception of what they expected from the police.

By that era, generally depicted as a golden age of consensus policing, the legitimacy of the police was established. This was symbolised by the popular *Dixon of Dock Green* television series which portrayed a friendly local bobby whose knowledge of his patch helped him to prevent crime, catch local villains, and help many members of the local community. Dixon was followed by very different TV heroes in such programmes as *The Sweeney* and *The Professionals* in the 1970s and 1980s, and the popular series of the early 1990s, *Between the Lines*, dealing with police discipline and complaints.

After the 1950s, the legitimacy which the police had established was challenged on several fronts. The urban disturbances of 1981, which led to the Scarman Report, were in part attributed to the frequent use in multi-racial areas of stop-and-search powers. Increasing evidence emerged of cases where the police were found to have tampered with evidence, secured false confessions and abused their powers. Other complaints concerned how suspects were dealt with in custody. This raised the issue of how accountable the police were – both in terms of individual complaints and police policy. What happened to change the image of the police, in Reiner's words, from 'plods to pigs' (ibid.: 59)?

The key factors which led to increased legitimacy, according to Reiner, can also account for its decline. Revelations about corruption on the part of police officers during the 1960s and allegations about improper behaviour severely dented the image of the police as a disciplined force, showing that they could readily break the law in order to enforce it. The 1970s and 1980s saw the increasing use of riot shields and other modern hardware in the control of industrial disputes and urban unrest, replacing the 'pushing and shoving' strategy used in demonstrations during the 1950s and 1960s. The accidental killing of innocent citizens by armed police officers attracted much criticism, especially from their traditional supporters, the middle classes. The traditional political impartiality of the police was also questioned during the general election of 1979, when they campaigned vigorously for stronger law and order policies. Finally, society itself had changed. Whereas during the so-called golden age, the working class was a more homogeneous community, by the 1980s it was increasingly fragmented and divided with the growth of unemployment, the increasingly multi-racial nature of urban communities, and the growth of what some describe as an underclass. This made it more difficult for the police to satisfy the now conflicting expectations about how areas should be policed.

Police relationships with the public were also affected by the consequences of changes in the nature and organisation of policing. Like any organisation the police face pressures for efficiency, and must respond to changes in crime which may lead to the use of more sophisticated technology. These pressures also produced specialisation. This necessitated organisational changes which vitally affected relationships between the police and local communities.

A simple example of this is the effect of expansion in cars, traffic and car ownership. The increasing volume of cars on the roads necessitated the development of techniques of traffic control and the enforcement of road traffic legislation. Specialist traffic control using increasingly sophisticated technology followed. As car ownership spread, many groups, particularly the middle classes, previously unlikely to encounter the police in their law enforcement role, became the subject of police attention. Cars also became an essential tool in law enforcement and patrolling, and had a fundamental impact on the job of the police constable. The car chase has become a symbolic feature of policing in both popular imagery and police folklore. And, of course, as well as increasing the mobility of criminals, cars have provided multiple opportunities for crime – from vandalism to serious car theft, ramraiding, joyriding and 'car-jacking': for some joyriders part of the thrill is the chase with the police. Violence resulting from motoring incidents has even led to the coining of a new term for such crimes: 'road rage'.

Similar points could be made about other technological developments – computers have radically changed the nature of policing, as have developments in communications. The beat officer of 50 years ago could not instantly call on the police computer, let alone the local station, to provide immediate back-up. Information had to be gathered directly from the public. While undoubtedly these developments have increased the ability of the police to respond quickly to emergencies, to call for help and to sift through large amounts of information, they have had important consequences for relations between the police and public, and for the basic role of the police officer.

This can be seen in contrasting the work of officers during the period of the so-called golden age of policing, when officers were allocated a beat and were responsible for patrolling it, often on foot. This meant that officers got to know the local community – they would make purchases from shopkeepers, visit local cafés and come into contact with many residents. The intelligence they gathered from these natural social contacts may have helped when they came to investigate a crime. Armed only with a truncheon and a whistle to call for help, the constable had to rely on his or her own wits to handle troublesome situations. Communication with the station was made through the police box and incidents had to be handled on the spot.

This form of policing could, however, be seen as inefficient. One officer could cover only a limited area, whereas two officers, in a car, receiving their information from a radio link with the station, could cover a much larger area and arrive at incidents much more quickly. The lone officer on patrol is also unlikely to catch many criminals – no self-respecting burglar is going to break in when they see a constable walking down the road. The growth of many specialised functions also fundamentally changed the job of the basic constable on the beat, who became less involved in detecting crime and proportionately more involved with the more mundane elements of police work such as dealing with drunks, vagrants or handling minor local incidents.

This affected relationships between the police and the public. Whereas the old-style beat officer encountered many members of the public while pounding the beat, officers in cars had less immediate contact. The public were less likely to know or have encountered these officers, and information tended to come from the police station rather than from the public. The ability to call instantly for back-up meant that officers were less reliant on their own personal skills to handle situations and the cars and radios in themselves became symbols of authority.

In addition, pressures for efficiency led to a stress on law enforcement as opposed to service or preventative roles – to the more readily measurable aspects of police work such as arrest rates, clear-up rates and response times, often described as fire brigade policing. This meant that other, less easily measurable, tasks became seen as less significant. The 1970s and 1980s also saw the rise of what is often called paramilitary policing. A spate of urban unrest and industrial disputes prompted the development of specialist squads trained to deal with riots and crowd control. These units, including the Special Patrol Group (the SPG were not used in disturbances after the Blair Peach incident in Southall in 1979), were increasingly armed with the hardware used for disturbances in Ulster and abroad, although water cannons were not used on the mainland. Some tactics – such as the National Reporting Centre that acted to coordinate the police response during the miners' strike of 1984–5 and was an early version of more centralised national policing – caused enormous controversy. Some were also used as a back-up for crime-fighting initiatives, which involved the intensive use of stop-and-search powers. These kinds of tactics were found by the Scarman Report to have been partly responsible for local resentments which contributed to the breakdown in relations between the police and public preceding the Brixton disturbances of 1981.

All of these factors illustrate the many tensions in the role of the police, and there are different views about which roles they should prioritise. An Audit Commission report, for example, recommended that the police should adopt a more **proactive**, 'intelligence-led' approach involving targeting the most prolific offenders and using intelligence gathered from informers and surveillance. This may conflict with public opinion, which consistently indicates a preference for more 'bobbies on the beat' and foot patrols (**Morgan and Newburn 1997**).

A report by the Institute for Public Policy Research (IPPR), *A New Beat: Options for more accountable policing* (2008) states that the proportion of people who say the police do a 'good or excellent job' fell from 64 per cent in 1996 to 48 per cent in 2005. The report claims public confidence in the police is low and that they are not felt by the public to be sufficiently responsive. People who have been victims of crime in the last year rate the police lower than those who have not been a victim of crime: 41 per cent of victims say the work the police do is 'good or excellent', compared to 52 per cent of non-victims. IPPR claims the decline in satisfaction with the police is related to a perceived decline in traditional community policing and the loss of 'bobbies on the beat'. When asked what the police should do more of, 59 per cent said more foot patrols, followed by 36 per cent saying community policing. This may, however, conflict with police officers' own preference for what to them is 'real police work' and is associated with action, arrests and catching serious offenders (ibid.).

6.2 Organisation and accountability

Objective 2

Outline the organisation and accountability of the police service

Policing in England and Wales is carried out primarily by 44 forces (43 regional forces and the British Transport Police) and in 2010–11, expenditure by central and local government on policing in England and Wales was £12.9 billion.

The total police strength in September 2013 included 128,351 full-time police officers in England and Wales, 13,552 full-time police community support officers (PCSOs), and 18,068 **special constables** (volunteers who do a minimum of four hours a week). Alongside the 43 regional forces, there are five others which have specific roles and responsibilities: British Transport Police, Port of Dover police force, Port of Liverpool police force, Ministry of Defence Police and the Civil Nuclear Constabulary.

There are large differences in the size of force, with the eight metropolitan forces of Greater Manchester, City of London, Merseyside, the Metropolitan Police, Northumbria, South Yorkshire, West Midlands and West Yorkshire accounting for 47 per cent of the total police strength. Scotland had eight regional police forces that were amalgamated in 2013 into Police Scotland, a jurisdiction within the UK but with a different legal tradition and accountability structure. The Police Service of Northern Ireland replaced the former Royal Ulster Constabulary in November 2001.

Police officers are distributed between various ranks, a feature introduced to maintain discipline. The rank structure was felt by the Sheehy Report to contain 'too many chiefs and not enough indians' and the number of ranks was reduced by the Police and Magistrates' Courts Act 1994.

The Current ranks are and their epaulette insignia are set out in Figure 6.1.

Each force is divided into geographical areas or divisions and, while there is considerable variation in organisation, there will typically be a force headquarters which houses strategic managers and support departments, and a number of **Basic Command Units** (BCUs), which deliver policing services within a geographical area.

Basic Command Units are seen as a central element of the police structure and, since April 2001, they have been subject to inspection by HMIC and to a range of performance indicators. The responsibility for working with the Community Safety Partnerships (**outlined in Chapter 5**) is placed with BCUs, although it is often passed to Local Policing Units or 'sectors' which have responsibility for local areas, with some officers being responsible for maintaining links with the local community on 'beats' and 'micro-beats' (**Mawby and Wright 2003**).

The Metropolitan Police have a number of specialist squads and departments dealing with forensic investigations, intelligence, serious crimes and terrorism. These squads can all call on specialist departments such as the Forensic Science Laboratories, the Fingerprint Branch, the Photographic Branch and the National Identification Bureau. There are also the traffic police, the Thames Division which patrols the River Thames 24 hours a day, a Mounted Branch and an Air Support Unit which assists with traffic and crowd control, along with the Royalty and Diplomatic Protection Department, the Special Escort Group and an art squad. Not all forces have such a large number of branches.

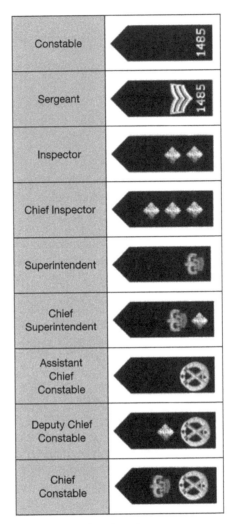

Constable	
Sergeant	
Inspector	
Chief Inspector	
Superintendent	
Chief Superintendent	
Assistant Chief Constable	
Deputy Chief Constable	
Chief Constable	

Figure 6.1 Police ranks in England and Wales

Source: http://policeuk.com/police_ranks.php

While the police in England and Wales are organised primarily on a local level, the increasingly international and organised nature of serious crime has led to the development of nationally and internationally organised policing (ibid.). These are particularly important as what is often called serious crime, which includes organised crime, operates across regional and national borders – often described as 'cross-border' or transnational crime. The drugs industry and serious crimes such as organised art theft, people trafficking, counterfeiting and money laundering are now global enterprises requiring much more cooperation between regional and national police organisations.

National Crime Agency

The first Director General of the National Crime Agency was appointed in 2013 (Keith Bristow). His tasks and responsibilities are defined in the Crime and Courts

Act 2013 and the Proceeds of Crime Act 2002. This new agency will lead on crime reduction with respect to organised crime and serious crime; and on criminal intelligence by gathering, storing, processing, analysing, and disseminating information on organised crime or serious crime; and in lead investigations under the Proceeds of Crime Act 2002. There are caveats with regard to its activities in Scotland and Northern Ireland. It will incorporate the activities of the Serious Organised Crime Agency.

Serious Organised Crime Agency

The demands of policing serious and organised crime has led to a gradual centralisation of these functions, initially through the emergence of Regional Crime Squads, and subsequently the National Crime Squad (NCS) and the National Criminal Intelligence Service (NCIS) (**Maguire 2003**). However, following the Serious Organised Crime and Police Act 2005 these were disbanded and merged into the Serious and Organised Crime Agency (SOCA). On 1 April 2008, SOCA also absorbed the Assets Recovery Agency (ARA) as provided for by the Serious Crime Act 2007. Initially with 4,200 staff, SOCA amalgamated the functions of each of these agencies together with the investigative branches from the Immigration Service and the Revenue and Customs Service to form a centralised intelligence-led law enforcement agency. SOCA was an Executive Non-Departmental Public Body sponsored by, but operationally independent from, the Home Office and was charged with reducing the harm caused by organised crime, including the illegal drugs trade, money laundering and people trafficking. In 2010, the Home Secretary announced the establishment of the broader-focused National Crime Agency, which came into being in 2013. The new agency absorbed SOCA's responsibilities as well as the Child Exploitation and Online Protection Centre and parts of the National Policing Improvement Agency (NPIA).

Interpol

Interpol is the world's largest international police organisation, with 190 member countries. Created in 1923, it facilitates cross-border police cooperation and supports and assists all organisations, authorities, and services whose mission is to prevent or combat international crime. In 2011, Interpol's budget was 60 million euros (*Interpol Annual Report* 2012).

Interpol has identified four core functions on which to concentrate its efforts and resources, including:

1. *Secure global police communication services* – Interpol manages a global police communications system known as I-24/7 which enables police in all of its member countries to request, submit and access police data and information in a secure environment.

2. *Operational data services and databases for police* – Interpol manages a range of databases with information on names and photographs of known criminals, wanted persons, fingerprints, DNA profiles, stolen or lost travel documents, stolen motor vehicles, child sex abuse images and stolen works of art. Interpol also disseminates critical crime-related data through its system of international

notices. There are seven kinds of notices, of which the most well known is the Red Notice, an international request for the provisional arrest of an individual.

3. *Operational police support services* – Interpol has six priority crime areas: corruption, drugs and organised crime, financial and high-tech crime, fugitives, public safety and terrorism, and trafficking in human beings. Interpol also operates a 24-hour Command and Coordination Centre to assist any member country faced with a crisis situation and coordinate the exchange of information, and assumes a crisis-management role during serious incidents.

4. *Police training and development* – Interpol provides focused police training initiatives for national police forces, and also offers on-demand advice, guidance and support in building dedicated crime-fighting components. The aim is to enhance the capacity of member countries to effectively combat serious transnational crime and terrorism. This includes sharing knowledge, skills and best practices in policing and the establishment of global standards for combating specific crimes (**Interpol 2008**).

Europe-wide police arrangements

Europol was set up following the Maastricht treaty in 1993 to develop information exchanges between law enforcement agencies in EU member states. In the last five years Europol's mandate has been extended to allow it to investigate murder, kidnapping, hostage-taking, racism, corruption, unlawful drug-trafficking, people smuggling and motor vehicle crime (**Lavranos 2003**). European Union sharing of information and intelligence with the United States has occurred primarily through Europol, but also through the establishment of Eurojust – the EU intergovernmental organisation responsible for judicial cooperation around crime (**Dubois 2002 cited in Newburn and Reiner 2007**).

The process of reform by 2013 has seen the police functions be restructured in a new formula with aspects of policing functions that are now divided between the National Crime Agency, Police and Crime Commissioners, the College of Policing and the Home Office.

▶ To whom are the police accountable?

A key issue in looking at police organisation is to whom they are answerable, or accountable. As we have seen, a major characteristic of the British police has been their independence from direct political control. The issue is the degree of autonomy that the police should have from political masters at local and national level, to allow them to act in a professional manner to reduce crime and enforce the law in a fair and transparent manner. Add to this the increasing global nature of crime (think of fraud or pornography via the internet) and you can see that the issue of accountability is about the balance between the different demands on police work. The Police Reform and Social Responsibility Act 2011 abolished police authorities (except in London) and replaced them with directly elected Police and Crime Commissioners (PCCs) with the objective to improve police accountability. PCCs will hold office for four years and will be mainly responsible for publishing a plan outlining the local police and crime objectives as well as setting the annual force budget. Following the first election of PCCs, the successful candidates for 41 of the 43 police forces in England and Wales, took office on 22 November 2012.

In London, the democratic accountability for the police is provided via the Mayor's Office for Policing and Crime (MOPAC). In the City of London, the Court of Common Council is responsible for the City of London force and also for the National Fraud Intelligence Bureau (NFIB).

Historical background – Local Police Authorities

Outside London, local police authorities (LPAs) were responsible for a variety of functions.

The Police Act 1964 set up a tripartite structure involving, outside London, chief constables, the Home Secretary and police authorities which were composed of two-thirds elected representatives from local councils and one-third justices of the peace. The Metropolitan Police area does not have a police authority and the Commissioner (the London equivalent of the Chief Constable elsewhere) formerly directly answerable to the Home Secretary, now reports directly to the Mayor of London. By the 1990s, the LPAs were subject to criticism that they were too large, some having as many as 46 members, and that their links with the local community and the extent of their powers were uncertain. While they were, for example, responsible, under section 5(1) of the Police Act 1964, for 'the maintenance of an adequate and efficient police force for the area', exactly how they should do this was ambiguous. Two key roles of the LPAs were the appointment of a chief constable and approving the budget. The Home Secretary, however, approved the appointment of chief constables and in practice police authorities had little control over how budgets were spent or over police policy. While they could ask for a report from the chief constable, this could be refused if it would contain operational matters which it would not be in the public interest to disclose. A study by the Policy Studies Institute found that policy developments such as crime prevention, crimes against women and children, and the diversion of administrative tasks from uniformed officers to civilian employees were increasingly determined by central government, and that local police authorities had little influence over these developments (**Jones and Newburn 1994**). This study also found that police authorities took too narrow a view of their role, lacked relevant information and expertise and were too large and cumbersome to carry out effective discussion.

The Police and Magistrates' Courts Act 1994 changed this structure. The government sought to make chief constables more responsible for budgets and to exert more control over their appointment. Many of the original proposals, which might have led to greater centralisation, were dropped, and the Act set up a new structure for LPAs (**Leishman *et al*. 1998; Mawby and Wright 2003**).

- The primary duty of the police authority was 'to secure the maintenance of an efficient and effective police force for its area'. Financial management was the responsibility of the chief constable, with the authorities having a monitoring role. It also stipulated that each authority would develop a local policing plan, drafted by the chief constable, who must be consulted about any changes which the police authority, who retain 'ownership' of the plan, wish to make. The Home Office determined the cash grant to police authorities, approved the appointment of Chief Constables, set national objectives for policing and empowered the Home Secretary to amalgamate forces.

- Changing policy views on the correct balance between local and national policing have been evident in legislation. Part of the intention of the Police and Magistrates' Courts Act 1994 was to strengthen the role of local police authorities. Despite this, considerable local variations have been found in local policing plans, and later legislation has moved more power to the centre with an apparent shift from political to managerial accountability and greater emphasis on national policing objectives and key performance targets (**Bowling and Foster 2002**). The Police Reform Act 2002 introduced the National Policing plans, which set out the government's strategic priorities for the police service.

Centralisation vs. Community empowerment

The question of how best to allow local communities to have a say in the policing of their area without neglecting national and international policing responsibilities is a long-running issue. One innovation to improve community relations was the establishment of Police Community Consultative Groups (PCCGs). Such groups consist of local members of the public, usually invited from a number of relevant organisations, and a number of local officers who meet to discuss local community issues. They hold regular meetings, some of which are usually open to the public. They have no formal power, and members tend to be drawn from a very small section of society, with few representatives from groups who are likely to suffer most from any abuse of police powers or from the adverse effects of policies (**Morgan 1989**), although the Crime and Disorder Act 1998 gave local authorities and the police a specific duty to consult with 'hard to reach groups'.

The problem for the Metropolitan Police Service is that it tries to respond to the diverse voices of pluralistic London and demands for more accountability, while also being a major player in the national and international business of dealing with the threat of terrorism and global crime. The system of accountability we inherited from the nineteenth and twentieth century's neither meets the needs of those who seek more transparent local public input into setting the policing agenda – as Sir Ian Blair, the former Metropolitan Police Chief, suggested in his Dimbleby Lecture in 2005 – nor allows enough room for the professional policing experts to get on with their job in this age of regulation, target-driven agendas, and litigious and media-conscious communities and individuals.

Police and Crime Commissioners

The Police and Social Responsibility Act 2011 introduced changes intended to make police more accountable to the local community as well as give police greater control over their budget and priorities. The most prominent was the plan to replace local police authorities with Police and Crime Commissioners, who campaign for office as would a mayor, and were directly elected by the public for the first time on 15 November 2012 in all areas outside London, and at four-year intervals thereafter. Within London, the Commissioner of the Metropolitan Police is already answerable to the Mayor's Office for Policing and Crime, run by the Mayor of London since January 2012. Anyone – as long as they are not a public servant and have never been convicted of an offence – may stand for election. The majority of candidates come from a background in politics and are affiliated to one or other political party.

To provide stronger and more transparent accountability of the police, PCCs will be elected by the public to hold Chief Constables and their forces to account; effectively making the police answerable to the communities they serve. PCCs will be responsible for setting the police force's strategic priorities, cutting crime, appointing and, if necessary, dismissing the Chief Constable, and ensuring that policing is efficient and effective . . . Being directly elected by the public means that you will be held to account on election day. Police and Crime Panels are being set up in each force area to help ensure that local authorities support you. They will also be scrutinising your work on behalf of the public on a regular basis. They will help to ensure transparency. You will need to discuss your plans with them and take their views into account.

Her Majesty's Inspectorate of Constabulary will also have the power to inspect forces and report back to the public with objective and robust information on which to make informed judgements about the effectiveness of the force and your work as the PCC.

(*Police and Crime Commissioners: Have you got what it takes?*, Home Office Information Booklet)

Dr Tim Brain, a former chief constable and a member of Lord Stevens's independent commission on the future of policing in England and Wales, wrote about the risk of 'politicised policing' in *The Guardian*:

'. . . Commissioners will most likely be elected on a party ticket – Conservative, Labour, maybe a few Lib Dems – with the party machine behind them. What's to say x, y, or z won't give them a ring and tell them how they should be thinking? Or to skew policing priorities to more attractive, popular measures that may give them an electoral advantage.

Chief constables have always faced political pressure from politicians, but the ultimate power in policing authorities was dispersed. Now, there will be a risk of more subtle influence: behind closed doors, a PCC may ask a chief constable to focus on a particular local area where the commissioner has a lot of support.

('The big debate: police and crime commissioners', *The Guardian*, 16 April 2012)

There is further concern about the power of PCCs to appoint or remove Chief Constables. The events in London in 2008, when the new Mayor, Boris Johnson, effectively sacked Sir Ian Blair – despite the support he had from the government – suggests that the 'mayor model' of police accountability might result in a system of governance in which it becomes normal for the mayor to intervene in operational policing matters. The fear is that this new democratic input will encourage the political parties to use policing issues as a political football.

It is vital for the rule of law that, as with the judiciary, political parties and governments both national and local should refrain from trying to intervene in the daily business of police work. Police work is difficult and demanding, and inevitably clashes at times with popular sentiment or the interests of the political elite. Police chiefs, on matters of operational direction and discretion should have autonomy, in the same way as judges do, once appointed they should be left to get on with a job until their contractually agreed term in office is over.

▶ Legal accountability

The police are not above the law. They must operate within the same laws as the public and within additional rules specific to the police. The rules both give power to the police and limit their actions. The Police and Criminal Evidence Act 1984 (PACE) and the codes made under its authority, outlined below, are there to protect the citizen from the abuse of police powers, and also to set out what is acceptable behaviour on the part of the police, and so protect them.

Under PACE, the police must publish annually details of their powers used under the Act. The following details are from the annual report, *Police Powers and Procedure 2011/12*, published in April 2013

- There were 1.2 million persons arrested by the police for recorded crimes in 2011/12, down 9% on 2010/11.
- The police stopped and searched 1.1 million persons and/or vehicles under section 1 of the Police and Criminal Evidence Act in 2011/12.
- Stop and searches on suspicion of drugs accounted for 50% of the overall total.
- They also made 46,961 stop and searches in anticipation of violence (under section 60 of the Criminal Justice and Public Order Act 1994).
- The police issued 1.5 million fixed penalty notices for motoring offences in 2011. Speed limit offences accounted for over half of them.
- The police carried out 685,992 screening breath tests during 2011. The number of positive or refused tests . . . accounted for 12% of the total.

In order to convict, a court must be sure that an offence has been committed and that the evidence to prove this is admissible in court. PACE affects what is admissible in court by giving the courts the power – in some cases the duty – to exclude evidence that has been obtained in contravention of some of its major provisions. Thus the courts and the judiciary play a role in police accountability. Abuse of powers in the early stages could ultimately prevent a conviction being obtained.

Evidence obtained that is not consistent with PACE Codes may be given, if the judge and jury are convinced that it is reliable and relevant evidence. In court, in some cases the reality often is that it is a police officer's word against a defendant's.

Given that the police are trained to present evidence in court they are likely to appear more credible witnesses, especially where they enjoy public confidence.

Aggrieved citizens can complain to the police force in question, and internal discipline within the police also protects the citizen (**see Chapter 4, section 4.7**). Prior to 2002, all complaints were recorded and, if not dealt with informally, were investigated under the auspices of the Police Complaints Authority (PCA). Complaints were investigated by an officer within the force but serious complaints, or those against a senior officer, involved the appointment of an officer from another force. This structure attracted criticism, particularly on the grounds that it was largely the police investigating themselves. This was justified on the basis that professionals such as the police, along with doctors and lawyers, are the only people with the necessary knowledge and expertise to investigate complaints. Many who complained expressed dissatisfaction with the process and there was considerable support for an independent system. The call for an independent body to oversee and investigate police complaints was debated for more than 20 years. Both Lord Scarman's inquiry into the Brixton riots in 1981 and the Stephen Lawrence Inquiry 1999 called for the establishment of an independent body. In April 2000 Liberty issued a study called 'An Independent Police Complaints Commission'. In May 2000, the government carried out consultation on a new complaints system and produced a briefing note called 'Feasibility of an independent system for investigating complaints against the police', with the document 'Complaints against the Police – Framework for a New System' setting out the emerging structure. These two documents culminated in provision of an Independent Police Complaints Commission (IPCC) in the Police Reform Act 2002.

The Police Reform Act 2002 set out the statutory powers and responsibilities of the IPCC, Chief Police Officers and Police Authorities for the new complaints system. This guaranteed the independence of the Commission, outlined its role as guardian of the police complaints system as a whole, and gave the IPCC a duty to raise public confidence. The Police Reform Act (2002) states (Schedule 3, paragraph 15(2)) that it is the duty of the Commission to determine the form which the investigation should take when a complaint or recordable conduct matter is referred to it. Paragraph 15(3) states that in making the determination the Commission shall have regard to (a) the seriousness of the case and (b) the public interest. The IPCC investigated the fatal shooting of a black male, Mark Duggan, in Tottenham, north London by a police officer on 4 August 2011. This shooting and the subsequent rumours set off the summer of mass rioting across several cities in England resulting in deaths, arson and thousands arrested for criminal damage, murder, looting and robbery and 1,292 offenders were sent to prison. The IPCC was criticised by the victim's family and the press for delaying the inquest into Duggan's death (*The Report*, BBC Radio 4, 26 April 2012).

However, some clarification of the incident was offered by the trial at the Old Bailey in January 2013, of Kevin Hutchinson-Foster who was convicted of illegally supplying a firearm to Mark Duggan. During the trial the jury heard from a witness, who was driving the taxi with Mark Duggan in it when it was stopped by police, who testified that Mr Duggan had collected a handgun in a shoebox just 15 minutes before the car was stopped by police. When Duggan was shot by the police, a gun was found nearby. It was wrapped in a sock and had not been fired during the incident.

Experience in other countries suggests that independent investigation of complaints is not a panacea for regulating police conduct (**Goldsmith and Lewis 2000**). High-profile cases involving the IPCC, such as the shooting of Jean Charles de Menezes at Stockwell tube station in July 2005, contribute to public awareness of the IPCC.

6.3 Police powers and the Police and Criminal Evidence Act 1984

Objective 3

Explain police powers and PACE

PACE reforms were introduced as a consequence of a number of proposed police and prosecution reforms that led not only to the introduction of the PACE codes but also the establishment of a separate and new prosecuting agency in England and Wales, the Crown Prosecution Service (CPS), by the Prosecution of Offences Act 1985.

The findings of the Royal Commission on Criminal Procedure (RCCP) 1979–81, which was chaired by Sir Cyril Philips, led to subsequent parliamentary debates and resulted in the enactment of the Police and Criminal Evidence Act 1984. The Royal commission highlighted the need for a separate agency from the police to prosecute crime and hence the origins of CPS to ensure a more professional and independent review at the case evidence. The RCCP highlighted the inefficiency and the cost of too many judge-directed **acquittals** because of inadequately prepared evidence. Finally, it argued there was a need to standardise the rules governing the encounters between the public and police on such matters as stop and search, conducting interview with suspects, and the conditions in police custody. At the time prior to 1984 each force had its own procedures, and practices varied considerably between police forces.

The history of PACE is sometimes mistakenly explained as a response to high-profile miscarriages of justice cases such as that of the Birmingham Six. It is unlikely that at the time of the debate on these police reforms in the early 1980s, that many parliamentarians and few in the public would have been concerned at this stage by the conviction of the Birmingham Six, who were not released until 1991. The Court of Appeal heard one appeal case in January 1988 and ruled the convictions to be safe and satisfactory. Their second full appeal, in 1991, was successful. There had been a widespread public campaign to overturn the **verdicts**, most notably the work of Chris Mullin and Granada TV's series called *World in Action*. In 1985, the first of several *World in Action* programmes casting doubt on the men's convictions was broadcast. In 1986, Mullin's book, *Error of Judgment* was published. But by then the PACE law had already been enacted in 1984.

There was a concern in the RCCP about police interviews and the potential for bullying suspects and one major miscarriage of justice case that preceded the RCCP and influenced the deliberations was the Maxwell Confait case. In 1972 a strangled transvestite prostitute led to the false conviction of three teenage boys who had been bullied by the interviewing CID officers into a confession. The boys were released following an appeal in 1975. The subsequent inquiry by Sir Henry Fisher focused on the Judges Rules and the clarification of the rules governing how police should treat suspects. This influenced the establishment of the RCCP in 1979, but the Birmingham Six was not part of the deliberations.

PACE provides for the creation of Codes of Practice to deal with the minutiae of implementation. While the Codes are not part of direct legislation and while breaches of a provision of a Code by the police does not of itself constitute an offence, they can be the basis of a complaint against the police which may lead to a disciplinary matter or, in appropriate cases, criminal proceedings or a civil claim. Additionally, and importantly, significant transgression of any Code provision may mean that evidence obtained as a result might be excluded in any subsequent trial (**see Chapter 10**).

Codes are regularly reviewed and can more easily be amended than Acts of Parliament. The Codes (now Codes A to H) themselves, which in their latest form emerged in May 2010 (Codes E and F), February 2011 (Codes A, B and D) and July 2012 (Codes C, G and H) are supplemented by Annexes and Notes for guidance to aid interpretation, and cover the following areas:

A. the exercise by police officers of statutory powers to search a person or a vehicle without first making an arrest. It also deals with the need for a police officer to make a record of a stop or encounter;

B. powers to search premises and to seize and retain property found on premises and persons;

C. requirements for the detention, treatment and questioning of people in police custody by police officers (not related to terrorism: see section H);

D. identification of people in connection with the investigation of offences, and the keeping of accurate and reliable criminal records;

E. audio-recording of interviews with suspects in the police station;

F. visual recording (with sound) of interviews with suspects. There is no statutory requirement on police officers to visually record interviews. However, the contents of this Code should be considered if an interviewing officer decides to make a visual recording (with sound) of an interview with a suspect;

G. powers of arrest under section 24, the Police and Criminal Evidence Act 1984 as amended by section 110 of the Serious Organised Crime and Police Act 2005;

H. matters relating to terrorism suspects.

Codes G and H are new additions and relate to the significant changes in arrest powers introduced by the Serious Organised Crime and Police Act and to the differing procedures and police powers in relation to those suspected of offences in connection with terrorism.

While the detail of the Codes are reviewed regularly, and amended in the light of developing practice and new technology. Likewise, the operation of PACE – the body of legislation itself – has been considered several times in the context of reviews of the criminal justice system, such as the Runciman Commission. Acts of Parliament will often include changes to legislation which affect PACE, which are not immediately amended within the PACE guidelines, but which are included in memos or Home Office Circulars. The provisions within these Acts will normally commence at a date later than the date of the Act, which allows time for the relevant agencies to acquaint themselves with new procedures and to make necessary changes within their organisations. Additionally, in May 2002 the Home Secretary announced a joint review, specifically of PACE, by the Home Office and the Cabinet Office. The purposes of that review were to focus on simplifying procedures, reducing administrative burdens on the police and speeding up justice. Some of the Review's recommendations were incorporated into the Criminal Justice Act 2003, the Serious Organised Crime and Police 2005 and the Police and Justice Act 2006 in relation to changes to police powers.

The PACE Act of 1984 sets out the powers of the police in various circumstances, and provides safeguards for suspects as to when the powers can be exercised. In some cases an officer can act only after authorisation from a senior officer (for example, in delaying access to legal advice). In certain situations, reasons for a procedure must be given to a suspect – for example, the reason why an officer wishes to stop and search a suspect. On other occasions, the police officer must formally explain the individual's rights – for example, when someone is arrested they must be informed of their right to remain silent and the consequences of so doing.

There is also a requirement for written records. Custody records must show all the details of a suspect's stay in police detention, and may be analysed by the defence. Any irregularities would support their argument for the exclusion of evidence. Two highly significant areas covered in detail by PACE are those setting out the powers of the police in relation to the searching of persons and property, and in the detention and questioning of suspects. While such powers are vital in the investigation and prevention of crime, they also provide opportunities for significant intrusions into individual freedoms. Finding the correct balance is not easy. The requirement to record police activities, such as stop and searches (this allows for monitoring of how, and against whom, the police use their powers), supports a due process model of policing, but has been the subject of recent criticism and suggested changes because of the time and bureaucracy involved. Two important areas where the balance between due process, crime control and efficiency can be examined are in respect of powers of stop and search, and powers of arrest and detention, which are the subject of the following sections.

▶ PACE Code A: Powers to stop and search

Stop and search powers allow an officer to stop and search a person or a vehicle in a public place without first making an arrest, where the officer reasonably suspects that the person stopped has with them stolen goods, weapons, drugs or articles for use in offences such as theft or burglary. Detention for a reasonable period is allowed to carry out the search, and the person searched must be told, and the information must be recorded, as to the reasons for the search, the identity of the police officer, the date, time and place of the search as well as the ethnicity of the individual.

Further powers to stop and search, when authorised in a particular area by a senior officer, exist without there being any need for reasonable suspicion of the individual, because there is a threat of public disorder (section 60 Criminal Justice and Public Order Act 1994). Stopping cars to check whether they are carrying offenders, or witnesses, is provided for in section 4 of PACE.

Reasonable grounds for suspicion may be based on information about a suspect or circumstances. It can also be based on the behaviour of a suspect, e.g. trying to conceal something, or where there is reliable information or intelligence about a gang whose members regularly carry knives weapons or controlled drugs, and may wear a distinctive clothing or style or insignia associated with the gang.

Police also previously had powers under sections 44–47 of the Terrorism Act 2000 to designate any area for a period of 28 days as an area of high alert. This would then entitle police to randomly stop and search any person or vehicle within that area for items that could be used in connection with terrorism, without any requirement for the officer to have any actual suspicion that such items would be found. The designation of an area as one of high alert could be made on a rolling basis, meaning that within some perpetually 'high alert' areas, police could indiscriminately stop and search anyone at anytime, regardless of reason.

These sections of the Terrorism Act 2000 came under public scrutiny when the case of *Gillan & Quinton* v. *UK* was brought before the European Court of Human Rights (ECHR). Kevin Gillan and Pennie Quinton had been attending a demonstration in 2003 against the annual arms fair in the Docklands when police detained and searched them under sections 44–47 of the Terrorism Act 2000. Gillan and Quinton felt that there had been little justification for the search and took their case to the ECHR. During the case it was revealed that the whole of Greater London had been designated as an area of high alert since 2001. The police powers were found to contravene Article 8 – the right to privacy – of the European Convention on Human Rights. These powers were replaced in the Protection of Freedoms Act 2012 with more limited powers to stop and search persons and vehicles reasonably suspected of being involved in terrorist activities as well as anyone within a specified area on terrorist alert.

▶ PACE Code B – Powers to search property

Code B sets out the powers covering the right of the police to enter property to conduct a search of premises and property, and the rights of the police to the seize property found by the police on persons or on searched premises. The latest Code B came into force in March 2011.

A police officer has power to enter property to carry out an arrest for indictable and certain other offences, or to prevent injury or damage. They can also enter and search the premises where the suspect was found, for evidence, or for things that might help them escape, or with which they might harm themselves.

An officer can obtain a search warrant from a magistrate when it is reasonable to believe that there would be evidence relating to an offence (e.g., drugs or stolen property) on the premises to be searched. With such a warrant, the officer may enter and search the specified premises, and remove any such evidence. Under the extended powers granted under the Serious Organised Crime and Police Act 2005, warrants can be issued for the search of multiple premises and repeat entry to premises.

Code B was amended in the light of the Crime and Security Act 2009 which inserted new powers into the Prevention of Terrorism Act 2005 giving police the power to search the premises of persons subject to control orders, and to seize and retain articles found.

▶ PACE Code C: Detention and interview

Code C deals with the detention, treatment and questioning of suspects and seeks to provide that all people should be dealt with quickly and not be detained any longer than necessary. It places the overall responsibility for the control, recording and supervision of the custody period with a custody officer: a police officer, usually with the rank of sergeant or above, who has overall responsibility for ensuring the correct treatment of those held at the police station.

The Police Custody Officer must keep a record of what happens to an offender during detention and provide information to suspects about their rights. Other provisions relate to the minimum level of comfort that should be provided to all suspects. Rules limit the time a suspect can be kept in police custody before being charged (known as the PACE Clock). The most important of these matters are described below.

- The custody record is made a fundamental part of the custody process, in which must be written everything that affects the suspect while in the police station, including time of release, comments made by the suspect at various stages, and a list of the suspect's property. The suspect's lawyer has the right to examine this record at the police station or during any subsequent court proceedings. An examination of the record may reveal that procedures were not correctly followed, or indeed establish that they were, as the suspect will be asked to sign the custody record, to indicate for example that legal advice has been offered. If the suspect refuses to sign when asked, that refusal must also be recorded. Any interview with the suspect must be recorded in full. This will usually be by means of tape recording (governed by Code E) which replaced the old system of 'contemporaneous notes' as they were more susceptible to fabrication by the police or unfounded challenge by those interviewed. Interviews should be carried out only at designated police stations, except when an interview is urgent – for example, to get information about an imminent attack on a person.
- When an interview forms part of the evidence against a defendant, he or she is entitled to a balanced summary (i.e. a shortened transcript of the recording, but which properly reflects its content), and can demand a copy of the full audio-recording. While the recording of interviews protects the accused, it may also prevent unfounded complaints against the police and allegations of false confessions.
- The Code states that suspects should be held usually in single cells, which should be adequately heated, cleaned, lit and ventilated, with adequate clean bedding and access to toilet and washing facilities. They should be offered two light meals and one main meal in a 24-hour period, and a reasonable number of drinks. Medical assistance should be called if necessary.

Perhaps the most significant provisions relate to the continuing assessment of whether an arrested person can be charged or released. Under the Criminal Justice Act 2003 a range of options is provided, depending on the state of the evidence and investigation:

- charge with an offence;
- release without charge and without bail, which concludes the case unless new evidence comes to light;

- release without charge on bail for further enquiries to be made;
- release without charge and on bail for the police to take legal advice from the Crown Prosecution Service. Where this course is taken, the suspect must be informed that this is the position.

Section 54 sets out the responsibilities and powers of the custody officer and other officers in relation to search of people in police detention. The police must make a record of the arrested person's possessions. They are entitled to search for, and remove, things that might allow the person to harm themselves or someone else, or for things that might be used to escape. They must explain why such items are being removed.

Section 55 limits the situations in which intimate searches can be carried out to searches for things that can harm the suspect, or injure other people, and drugs. The search can be carried out only by an officer of the same sex.

Thus, while it can be seen that the rules, outlined above, provide sensible and necessary powers for the police to carry out their functions, the detail of the limitations and the safeguards may make quick and effective implementation difficult. On the other hand, limitations are necessary to prevent arbitrary use of a very intrusive power.

Detention in a police station without charge usually arises to allow the person to be questioned to obtain evidence. Once sufficient evidence has been obtained, and the suspect has said what he or she wishes to say, the questioning must stop and the suspect must be charged. After charge, suspects may be released on bail either to attend court for the start of proceedings against them or to re-attend the police station at a specified date, or they may be kept in police custody and taken to the next sitting of the magistrates' court to seek further remand in custody.

Detainees should have access to a solicitor. If one is not available to attend a police station they will be offered the opportunity of contacting the new Defence Solicitors Call Centre. This is run by the Legal Services Commission (LSC) which provides legal advice by telephone for those detained in police custody for less serious crimes such as a non-imprisonable offence, or following arrest for a bench warrant for failing to appear, or arrested for driving with excess alcohol, or when detained for a breach of bail condition.

The need to detain the individual must be regularly reviewed to determine whether it is necessary to keep the suspect any longer, or indeed whether the police have enough evidence to charge him. The time limits for review (the PACE Clock) are: 6 hours after detention was first authorised, and then at not more than 9-hourly intervals from when the detention was first authorised, up to a total of 36 hours.

Further detention must be specifically authorised for a period longer than 24 hours, by an officer of the rank of superintendent or above. This further period can extend the detention to 36 hours, and then only if necessary for the effective investigation of an indictable offence. If the police want to interview the suspect further they must apply to a magistrates' court for permission to hold the person for any longer time. A court can authorise an extra 36 hours of detention, on two occasions. The overall maximum period of detention is 96 hours.

In 2011, a clarification was made to this rule via the Police (Detention and Bail) Act. This was prompted by the outcome of *R (on the application of the Chief Constable of Greater Manchester Police)* v. *Salford Magistrates' Court and Paul Hookway* (2011), a dispute over whether the police had legally detained Paul Hookway – a man arrested on suspicion of murder who was questioned, then released without charge on bail to re-attend the police station at a later date, but who was later recalled for further questioning (without new evidence coming to light) – or whether the permitted time for holding a suspect without charge had in fact expired by the time the police recalled him. This was due to Greater Manchester Police's and Salford Magistrates' Court's using different methods to calculate the PACE Clock. The police judged that only the time spent in police detention counted towards the PACE Clock. Salford Magistrates' Court, on the other hand, who had authorised the extended time for questioning, judged that the PACE Clock ticked in real time, i.e. that despite the suspect having been released before the PACE Clock expired, the remaining time duly expired while he was released, therefore the police could not legally recall the subject without re-arresting him (which they cannot do without further evidence coming to light). In *Hookway*, the judge ruled in favour of Greater Manchester Police. The ruling prompted the Police (Detention and Bail) Act 2011, which clarified that only time spent in police detention should count towards the maximum detention period, and therefore that, if at the point of releasing a suspect without charge there is unexpired detention time remaining, and if the police require more time to question him, they can legally recall and detain the suspect for further questioning until the total period of detention has expired.

Further changes to PACE Code C came into effect in July 2012 and these include:

- permission for the custody officer to explain the arrangements for free legal advice in cases where the 'voluntary' interview takes place outside of a police station;
- amended provisions regarding self-administration of controlled drugs and simplified process of the application of safeguards for detainees believed to be under the influence of alcohol or drugs, or both;
- clear guidance for the process to be used when searching transgendered suspects in custody;
- a revision to the notification required when a foreign national is detained.

Differing provisions relate to those suspected of terrorism offences, and these additional powers have themselves been subject and continue to be subject to controversy. The Protection of Freedoms Act 2012, reduced the period of detention for terrorism suspects to 14 days. Previously, with the Terrorism Act 2006, those suspected of terrorism could have been detained for a total of 28 days without charge. The period of detention was hotly debated in Parliament, with the original attempt to extend the period (then 14 days) to 90 days being defeated. The fact that different rules apply to terrorist suspects, and the difficulty in arriving at the appropriate balance, indicates an important area where due process and crime control or prevention are given differing importance from other offences. However, it should be remembered that the detention limits refer to detention prior to charge. Detention after charge is governed by other principles. The charge is significant, and signifies the point at which interviewing must cease. As part of the debate on the detention of suspected terrorists, it has been argued that this rule should be changed to allow interviews to continue after charge.

▶ PACE Code D: Identification

Code D deals with procedures to identify a criminal suspect. It explains police powers to use visual witness identification via video identification, identification parade or similar procedure. It also accounts for police powers to take fingerprints, DNA samples, footwear impressions and photographs, or to subject suspects to body searches when seeking identifying features such as tattoos or scars.

It also provides details as to how this information may be used, stored and ultimately destroyed. Code D has recently been subject to a number of legislative changes. The Crime and Security Act 2010 made provision for the following changes which came into effect with the issuing in March 2011 of the Police and Criminal Evidence Act 1984 (Codes of Practice):

- New powers for police to take fingerprints and samples from someone convicted outside of England and Wales of certain 'qualifying offences'.

- New police powers to call for a person to attend a police station to have their fingerprints and samples taken.

- Changes to the information to be given to an individual before fingerprints and samples are taken, and recorded after taking them.

- Commencement of the power to take fingerprints using mobile fingerprinting technology, originally inserted into PACE by section 117 of the Serious Organised Crime and Police Act 2005.

- New guidance to distinguish eye-witness identification procedures such as video identification from procedures for obtaining recognition evidence by viewing CCTV and similar images.

- Greater protection for witnesses attending a video identification by removing a suspect's entitlement to be informed of the date and time of the viewing and to have a representative other than a solicitor attend the viewing. This does not remove the requirement to record a viewing if no representative of the suspect attends, but aims to prevent associates of the suspect intimidating a witness before a viewing.

Under the Freedom of Information Act 2012 there were changes to PACE Code D regarding the retention of profiles and fingerprints:

- A standard three-year retention period for the profiles and fingerprints of all persons, adult or juvenile, arrested or charged with, but not convicted of, 'qualifying offences' (broadly, serious violent, sexual and terrorist offences). This can be extended for a further two years on application to District Judge. If the extension is refused the police may appeal to the Crown Court, and likewise an individual may appeal to the Crown Court against a decision to extend the retention period.

- The data of previously unconvicted individuals who are arrested for or charged with a 'non-qualifying' or minor offence must be destroyed immediately upon non-conviction.

209

- If convicted of a recordable offence (or 'qualifying' in the case of a juvenile), an individual's data can be retained indefinitely.
- New powers to take identifying data from people convicted of a qualifying offence outside the UK and to retain them indefinitely.
- New retention periods for the data of juveniles convicted of minor offences relative to their sentence: the data of those who receive five years of more in custody will be retained indefinitely; those of juveniles who receive custodial sentences of less than five years will be retained for the duration of their sentence and then for a further five years; the data of those who receive community sentences will be kept for five years; reconviction for the same offence will result in indefinite retention.
- The data of individuals given a penalty notice will be destroyed after two years.
- New measures, briefly mentioned above, in the interest of national security, to enable police to apply for repeat extensions of two years to the data-retention period.
- Material given voluntarily is to be destroyed as soon as it has served its purpose, unless the individual is subsequently convicted of a qualifying offence.
- Material may be retained with written consent of the individual.
- Actual samples must be destroyed once they have been profiled and loaded satisfactorily onto the national database within six months of their being taken or if they have been taken unlawfully. Exceptions to this rule may occur in circumstances where samples are required for evidential purposes in criminal cases.
- Footwear impressions must be destroyed except in certain circumstances.

▶ PACE Codes E and F: Recording of interviews with suspects

Code E concerns the audio recording of police interviews with suspects, while Code F concerns the visual recording of the same. The codes were updated in 2010 to reflect changes laid out in the Police and Criminal Evidence Act 1984 (Code of Practice) (Revisions to Codes E and F) Order 2010, which enable the police to record interviews in digital format.

▶ PACE Code G: Arrest

Perhaps even more difficult than the decision to stop and search an individual can be achieving the correct balance in identifying when a person should be able to be arrested, detained and questioned, and how such a person should be treated. Such powers are the ultimate interference with liberty.

Sections 24–33 of PACE deal with powers of arrest. The Act lays down the circumstances in which any individual, including a police officer, store detective or ordinary person carrying out a citizen's arrest, can arrest a person. They may arrest anyone who is, or whom they reasonably suspect to be, committing an offence, and anyone who has committed or who can reasonably be suspected of having committed an offence. Additionally, police officers have wider powers of arrest including the power to arrest someone when they believe that person is about to commit an offence. While police officers can arrest for any offence, they can only do so if they reasonably think it necessary to verify the name or address of the person, or to prevent them from causing injury or being injured, damaging property, committing an offence of obstruction or indecency, to protect a vulnerable person, or to help investigation of the suspected offence or prevent the suspect disappearing. This 'necessity' provision was introduced, along with a wider power of arrest, amidst some criticism, by the Serious Organised Crime and Police Act. Prior to the changes the police had a variety of different powers of arrest in different circumstances. The primary power was related to what were called arrestable offences (offences carrying at least five years' imprisonment). However, the police curiously had power to arrest for non-arrestable offences, either because arrest powers had been specifically given (e.g. driving with excess alcohol) or where it was necessary in circumstances similar to those set out above. Changes were introduced to make a single power of arrest available to the police, to avoid technical worries and legal arguments about the precise power being used (the bureaucratic efficiency model). Criticisms were focused on the widening of the power and the fear that the list of circumstances which may amount to a justification for the 'necessity' of arrest might become a 'catch-all justification' for arrest.

Although these provisions provide the police with wide powers, they are not limitless and any officer infringing them may be liable to civil or criminal proceedings or disciplinary action. Perhaps most importantly they risk losing an otherwise promising case, as evidence obtained after a wrongful arrest may be excluded by the court. Where an arrest is improperly made the police may also be liable for damages to the wrongfully arrested person.

Provisions about the suspect's rights on arrest and at the police station were also consolidated by PACE. On arrest, any person arrested on suspicion of committing a crime is entitled to be:

- told that he or she has been arrested and why;
- arrested without excessive use of force;
- cautioned;
- taken to a designated police station for interview and not interviewed before arrival at the police station except in urgent cases.

The Criminal Justice Act 2003 provides for an alternative procedure to what has become seen as an unwieldy process, taking up much police time: as of January 2004 police officers can also bail those they have arrested to attend a police station at a later date without first taking them to a designated police station (street bail). This procedure will be used for minor offences where the offender's identity is certain and the offender is not in a particularly vulnerable category.

At the police station, PACE and the Codes provide a comprehensive and detailed framework for the treatment of suspects and arrestees at the police station. Those in custody are the responsibility of the custody officer, a police officer not involved in the investigation. This officer is wholly responsible for all aspects of the period of custody, for any incidents which occur, and for the custody record. The Act provides a complex timetable for the review of detention before charge to ensure that arrested people are not kept in custody for long periods without charge.

On arrival at the police station, the custody officer must ensure that persons arrested are informed about their rights. These include, first, a right to inform someone that they have been arrested. Second, any persons arrested have the right to contact and consult a legal adviser in private. If they do not wish to or cannot contact a solicitor, or do not have one, free advice is available from a duty solicitor who can be contacted round the clock. And third, arrested persons have the right to have access to PACE and the Codes. This is to a certain extent window dressing, as few arrested persons are likely to pore over the minutiae of the Codes, but it is an important reminder to suspects and the police of their provisions.

Prior to 1995, throughout the period of arrest and interview suspects had the 'right to remain silent' and were reminded of this in a caution given on arrest, before any interview, and on charge. Thus, they should have been advised that:

> You do not have to say anything unless you wish to do so but what you say may be given in evidence.

The right to silence was redefined by the Criminal Justice and Public Order Act 1994. This, contrary to some assertions, does not remove the right, but affects the use that can be made of silence in the trial. Before 1995, in any trial juries were told that they should not assume a defendant was guilty because he or she failed to answer an accusation at the time of arrest or when interviewed at a police station. Under the 1994 Act, the jury is told that they can, in certain circumstances, make 'adverse inferences' from silence. For example, a jury might take the view that a defendant did not answer the questions asked of him about the allegation against him because he could not think of a plausible excuse for something he had done. Where appropriate the jury should, however, be reminded that there are other reasons why someone might not answer: fear, bewilderment or drunkenness, for example.

The words of the caution needed to reflect the change. The caution introduced in 1995 is as follows:

> You do not have to say anything. But it may harm your defence if you do not mention when questioned something which you later rely on in court. Anything you do say may be given in evidence.

Additionally, where a suspect is asked about his or her presence at or near the scene of a crime, or why he or she is in possession of an item, a warning must be given about the implications of failing to respond. Vulnerable groups are given extra protection by PACE in that young people should not be interviewed in the absence of an appropriate adult, usually a parent or social worker; and a similar provision protects the mentally ill. Those who do not speak English fluently, and the deaf, should have appropriate translators present at interview and foreign nationals must be told of their right to contact their embassy or High Commission.

The amendments to the latest version of the Code came into force in July 2012 and the revisions place additional emphasis on the requirement for an arresting officer to have reasonable grounds that an offence has been committed and that the person has committed it. The officer must believe that the arrest is necessary and cannot be made solely to obtain fingerprints and DNA. These changes brought Code G into line with the sections of the Legal Aid, Sentencing and Punishment of Offenders Act 2012 which clarify the legal position of house-holders who use force in self-defence against intruders. The amended Code G sets out that, if an offence involves the use of force and a person claims to have been acting in self-defence, an officer contemplating an arrest must take account of the circumstances under which the law allows the use of reasonable force.

▶ PACE Code H: Matters relating to terrorism suspects

This Code concerns the detention, treatment and questioning of terrorist suspects in police custody. It covers those who are arrested under the Terrorism Act 2000 or the Counter-Terrorism Act 2008.

It covers the post-charge questioning of terrorist suspects (s. 15) and provides powers for the police to apply to the Crown Court for authorisation to continue questioning a terrorism suspect who has already been charged. The Code also incorporates changes to the detention process of terrorist suspects (s. 14), which allow the police officer (superintendent rank or higher) or Crown Prosecutor to apply for a warrant of further extension in cases where the detention is necessary for longer than 48 hours.

Under review is the process involved in applying to the High Court to extend the detention of a person beyond 14 days from the time of their arrest, in the light of the changes to the detention period made by the Protection of Freedoms Act 2012. Also under consideration is the introduction of video-recording with sound in terrorism cases. The latest version of Code H came into force in July 2012.

Aspects of the use of police powers under PACE in England and Wales in 2010/11 (excluding British Transport Police figures)

- The police stopped and searched 1,284,025 persons and/or vehicles
- Of 1,205,495 stop and searches overall, 49% of searches were for drugs, 20% were for stolen property and 10% were for offensive weapons
- 9% of searches led to an arrest
- 66% of stop and searches were of people or vehicles carrying people who defined their ethnicity as 'White', 15% were of 'Black (or Black British)' ethnicity and 10% were of 'Asian (or Asian British)' ethnicity of stop and searches carried out on those described as 'White', 9% of those carried out on 'Black (or Black British)' and 7% of those described as 'Asian (or Asian British)' resulted in an arrest
- 3,997 persons were detained for more than 24 hours, 98% of which were subsequently released without charge
- A total of 94 intimate searches were carried out; mainly for drugs

Source: Compiled from 'Police Powers and Procedures England and Wales 2010/11', Home Office website, April 2012

6.4 Police work

It can be seen from the above that there are many different aspects of policing. The police have an increasing array of technological aids to assist investigation, and have to cope with organised and serious crime which operates at a national and global level. Government policies and national policing plans have to be complied with, managerialism has introduced targets and performance indicators, and the Audit Commission and others emphasise the importance of 'intelligence-led policing'. At the same time the police are expected to take into account the requirements of, and to involve, local communities. This section will explore some of the many dimensions of police work.

❱ Investigating crime and new technologies

The police have a unique role in investigating crime and, apart from a few specialist agencies, handle most crime investigation in this country. Thus most prosecutions depend on the routine information collected by uniformed officers and the detective work of their non-uniformed colleagues in the Criminal Investigation Departments, the CID.

Criminal investigations over the years have stimulated the development of technical and expert services such as forensic services. In 1995, the DNA database was run by the Forensic Science Service (FSS) as a national public service. The FSS was abolished in 2012 and since then forensic service have been delivered by an array of agencies and private companies. The Metropolitan Police Service has its own laboratory and forensic department.

Today's police have access to computer information systems such as those storing details of all car registrations, and more recently they have employed psychological profiling in murder cases. The most widely accepted form of forensic evidence is the fingerprint test. The idea was developed by Edward Henry, Inspector-General of the Nepal Police, who noticed its use in nineteenth-century India, and the Metropolitan Police introduced it in 1901. Its use led to the conviction of two brothers – the Strattons – for murder in 1905. The basic premise of the fingerprint is that no two sets are the same. Each fingerprint is based on the ridges made by the barely visible papillary lines on the skin's surface and each print can be classified in terms of the patterns of arches, whorls and loops that are displayed and the distinctive characteristics in a fingerprint – split, lake, island or end of ridge. Fingerprinting until recently was widely regarded as foolproof and conclusive of guilt by police and juries. But doubt was raised about the ability of fingerprints to determine individual identity, in the case of Neville Lee, who was arrested solely on the basis of a fingerprint left in blood in a lavatory cubicle after a brutal rape of an 11-year-old girl in Clumber Park near Worksop in August 1991. He was arrested by the Nottinghamshire police and detained in custody for six weeks before another sexual attack in the same park led to the arrest of a person who confessed to the rape of which Lee had been accused.

Computers are used in police investigations and prosecutions to search a national fingerprint database using the National Automated Fingerprint

Identification System (NAFIS). The widespread use of mobile phones has brought a bonus for police investigation in that users can be tracked by global positioning satellites. New digital technology allows for enhanced-quality face recognition such that suspects' details can be used to scan public spaces where there are CCTV cameras. The greater use of this technology has implications for its use as evidence and hence the development of the PACE Codes with respect to video and CCTV evidence. The development of specialist forensic science has given the police new techniques to analyse crime scenes, such as the use of blood pattern analysis, and forensic archaeologists and botanists to determine the timing of events – what pollen was on the tyre tread, which may show whether, and when, a car has visited a crime scene.

The use of DNA profiling is believed to be as reliable as fingerprinting to check the unique characteristics of an individual. Developed by Dr Alec Jeffries, the technique is now used in criminal and civil cases around the world. The DNA technique involves comparing a number of bands in the suspect's DNA with those of the DNA from body fluid or tissue involved in the crime. A calculation is then made on the probabilities of another person having a similar match. The Criminal Justice and Public Order Act 1994 amended the section in PACE 1984 to enable the police to take DNA samples, such as hair or mouth swabs, without consent of the accused, from offenders charged with, or convicted of, recordable offences – broadly those that are imprisonable. The Act ordered the creation of a national DNA database on which to store all the DNA profiles, duly started in 1995 and which in April 2012 held the profiles of 5.5 million people and 390,275 crime scenes. If an individual who had submitted a sample was later acquitted, the 1994 Act held that the profile should be destroyed.

Successive legislation subjected the DNA database to a number of changes regarding the taking and retention of DNA and fingerprints, as described above: the Criminal Justice and Police Act of 2001 removed the obligation to destroy a sample or profile in the event of no-charge or acquittal, and then, the Criminal Justice Act 2003 made it possible to take and retain indefinitely the DNA samples of anyone arrested for a recordable offence and detained in a police station, whether charged with an offence or not.

In 2008, a case brought before the European Court of Human Rights over-turned much of the UK legislation on DNA records. The case of *S and Marper* v. *United Kingdom* [2008] ECHR 1581 concerns two separate individuals: Mr S. aged 11 was arrested in 2001 for attempted robbery. His fingerprints and DNA samples were taken. He was later acquitted. Following a complaint from his partner, Michael Marper was arrested in 2001 and charged with harassment. His finger-prints and DNA samples were taken. Both claimants asked for samples of their DNA to be destroyed but they were not. The claimants appealed for a judicial review at the High Court of this decision, which was refused, and this refusal was in turn upheld by the Court of Appeal in 2003. The matter was put sent to the European Court of Human Rights, where it was ruled that the 'blanket and indiscriminate' retention of DNA from unconvicted individuals was a violation of the 'right to privacy' element of the European Convention on Human Rights.

Six months after this ruling, a consultation was proposed to establish how best to incorporate the ruling into UK law. This led to inclusion of relevant provisions in both the Crime and Security Act 2010 and in particular the Protection of

Freedoms Act 2012. The latest legislation seeks to protect the privacy of those who submit their data while maintaining some level of protection for the public against crime. The law today means that only the data of those convicted of very serious crimes are retained on the database indefinitely. There is concern from organisations such as Victim Support that this will limit the crime-solving capabilities of the database. Case studies published on the National Policing Improvement Agency (NPIA), which use to oversee the National DNA Database, (now the responsibility of the Home office) were testament to the unique value of the database as a resource for establishing links between crime scenes and offenders. It is estimated that 0.3% of crimes result in charges via the database, the cases solved are of the most serious nature such as murder and rape (*The National DNA Database Eighth Report of Session 2009–10, Volume I*, House of Commons Home Affairs Committee).

The Protection of Freedoms Act 2012 provided for the appointment of a Commissioner for the Retention and Use of Biometric Material who will be responsible for reviewing police decisions about the retention of fingerprints and DNA profiles for national security purposes, and the use to which the data are being put. On 4 March 2013 Mr Alastair MacGregor QC became the first Commissioner for the Retention and Use of Biometric Material ('Biometrics Commissioner').

The DNA database will remain an invaluable tool for matching current DNA taken for offences with DNA gathered from historical crime-scenes. Whether retained or destroyed, all profiles will initially be kept on the system for six months in order for police to check them against existing profiles and crime-scene data.

An example of DNA as an invaluable tool for police investigation is illustrated by the public disorders in England, otherwise known as riots, of August 2011. 'Following the public disorder, DNA profiling has contributed to an identification and arrest of 479 suspects out of 3,654 riot related offences recorded by the Metropolitan Police, majority of which were charged with burglary and theft offences.'

(National DNA Database Annual Report 2011–2012)

While fingerprints and DNA profiling are familiar, at least in concept, to most people, other identification evidence can be important, such as voice analysis or earprint identification as used in the conviction of Calvin Sewell for burglary in February 1998 (see Figure 6.2).

Forensic evidence, based on scientific procedure, provides valuable evidence for investigators and prosecutors, in contrast to the unpredictability of human witnesses. Scientific evidence can be used in all manner of circumstances, as in the case of Tracie Andrews. She was convicted of the murder of her boyfriend who, she claimed, was a victim of a road rage attack. Examination of a hat, which she said had nothing to do with her, showed hairs belonging to her mother's cat. But the faith in scientific evidence has been shown to be unjustified in dramatic cases such as the Birmingham Six, convicted in 1975 for the murder of 21 people in 1974 after a bomb was left in a public house in the central shopping district.

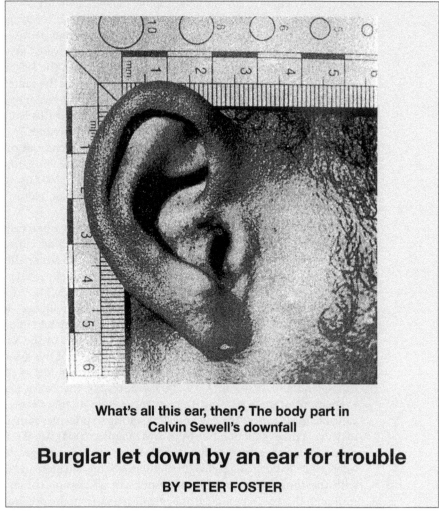

**What's all this ear, then? The body part in
Calvin Sewell's downfall**

Burglar let down by an ear for trouble

BY PETER FOSTER

Figure 6.2 Earprint identification

Source: The Times, 21 February 1998. © Times Newspapers Limited, 1998. Photo © Photonews Service, 1998

The conduct of the test to show that the suspects had been handling explosives was later proved unreliable.

An extension to the use of DNA techniques is a process called 'familial searching' which led to the conviction in April 2004 of Craig Harman for the manslaughter of Michael Little, a lorry driver. He died after a brick was thrown through his cab window. DNA evidence led to the identification of a close relative of the offender and thence to the defendant. Familial DNA-searching, along with several other sophisticated DNA-profiling techniques, was developed by the Forensic Science Service (FSS), a government-owned company.

DNA has played a pivotal role in 'cold-cases' where no progress on solving the crime has meant that there is no longer an active inquiry; and, has helped to solve some notorious criminals cases. One such cold case was 30 years old. In March

2012, DNA helped to convict a paedophile named David Bryant for four incidents of abduction and sexual assault on young children in the 1980s and 90s. The DNA gathered from the crime-scenes was submitted to familial DNA-searching and the database produced several dozen DNA profiles which were likely to be those of the attacker's family members. Going one step further, the FSS then used Y-STR-searching on those profiles in search for males carrying the same Y chromosome as those of the attacker – which would make them his father or brother. In this case, a relative's DNA was present on the database and this led police to David Bryant. When shown the DNA evidence, admitted the crimes.

Another innovation developed by the FSS was the technique of low copy number (LCN) profiling which enables a profile to be obtained from miniscule samples of DNA. The murderer, Ronald Castree was convicted in 2007 using the technique, for the killing of Lesley Molseed in 1975, after analysis of microscopic samples of his DNA found in the seams of her garments.

Information technology is also employed in what is often called intelligence-led policing, which relies on the use of information to develop and maintain a detailed and up-to-date picture of patterns of crime and criminality (**Tilley 2003**). It is almost impossible to discuss the concept of intelligence-led policing without making reference to the National Intelligence Model (NIM). While the National Intelligence Model is not entirely synonymous with intelligence-led policing, the NIM has been adopted as a business model through which to implement the conceptual framework of intelligence-led policing. Released by the National Criminal Intelligence Service in 2000 and becoming the policy of the Association of Chief Police Officers in the same year, the NIM became the model of all police services in England and Wales in April 2004, courtesy of the Police Reform Act 2002. Evaluations of the NIM have, to now, focused on its effectiveness to provide for valuable information sharing and clear setting of priorities rather than its ability to deliver crime reduction (see **John and Maguire 2004**). More recently, some UK police forces have tried to use the NIM as a way to manage and integrate the intelligence-led policing paradigm of information evaluation and decision-making with the community policing philosophy of addressing community concerns. Although this could be argued as being different from the original conceptualisation of intelligence-led policing, it is likely that the future success of such policing will be judged alongside the success of the National Intelligence Model.

With the rapid expansion of digital technologies, cyber crime and e-crimes have become in recent decades a global reality. Crimes such as fraud or stalking can be done on line from anywhere in the world. In 2010, the Office of Cyber Security and Information Assurance (OCSIA) was established. OCSIA works with government-led agencies, such as the Home Office. Cases of cyber fraud and intellectual property theft are thought to cost the UK £27 billion a year (*2011 report by industry and government on the cost of cybercrime. A report by information intelligence experts Detica, in partnership with the Office of Cyber Security & Information Assurance, Cabinet Office. Published by HM Government*).

▶ Community policing

An important source of 'intelligence' at the local level is the wealth of information provided by victims, witnesses and the general public, and it has long been recognised that the relationship between the police and the community is vital to enhance not only police–community relations but the effectiveness of the police. From the late 1970s, a growing number of initiatives emerged, described somewhat loosely as community policing, including the more familiar policing tasks of patrolling and investigating crime along with strategies aimed at crime prevention and reducing the fear of crime (**many of which were outlined in Chapter 5**). A pioneer of the concept of community policing was Chief Constable John Alderson of the Devon and Cornwall force, who argued:

> . . . community policing would exist in its purest form where all elements in the community, official and unofficial, would conceive of the common good and combine to produce a social climate and an environment conducive to good order and the happiness of all those living within it.
>
> (Alderson 1978)

In Alderson's version the community constable was seen as a 'social leader' working with the community and the emphasis is firmly placed on preventative rather than reactive policing. In theory, community policing is based on ideas that the police should consult and seek cooperation with the public and in 'general notions of creating a tranquil and safe environment' (**Bennett 1994a: 6**).

In practice, community policing encompasses a wide variety of different schemes and Bennett identifies five models or styles (**Bennett 1994b**). First, many schemes involve area-based policing, known variously as neighbourhood, zonal, team or sector policing, in which a small team of managers, supervisors and officers are allocated to a local area. As seen above, this is a major element in most forces. Bennett's second model of community policing refers to the multi-agency approach, in which the police work in partnership with local authorities and voluntary agencies – some examples of which were outlined in **Chapter 3** in respect of police working with victims, and **Chapter 5** in relation to Crime and Disorder Partnerships. Bennett's third theme, crime prevention, includes neighbourhood watch schemes (**also discussed in Chapter 5**). Bennett's fourth model identifies schemes which involve police contact with the public. This may be through foot patrols or setting up shops on estates and high streets away from the police station. It may also involve the police knocking on doors to contact the public directly. His fifth style of community policing refers to the consultation mechanisms outlined above and the introduction of lay visitors to police stations.

Despite the many potential benefits of community policing, it has not proved easy to implement. Full implementation would, argue many, involve a total reorganisation of police forces in which prevention and service roles take precedence over law enforcement and public order roles. Yet within the police, law enforcement and investigation are often seen as 'real' police work, with community policing being accorded lower status, community-based officers having been described derogatively as 'hobby bobbies'. Some have discerned a tendency for community police functions to be 'bolted on' to existing organisations and seen as an addition to, rather than the main purpose of, organisations (ibid.).

In addition, given the vast number of tasks which the police are expected to perform, there may simply not be enough officers to allocate to beats on a semi-permanent basis. In times of emergency they may be called off the beat to deal with football disturbances, public order incidents or other duties. This means that the community cannot rely on consistency of cover. In addition, community constables spend much time on administrative duties and in the police station, and relatively small amounts of time on 'community contacts' (**Bennett and Lupton 1992**). Moreover, in organisations where community policing has a low status, officers may be keen to move on from such roles, meaning that few gather sufficient experience. In general, community policing has been found to be more successful in smaller, suburban middle-class communities than in inner city areas where the greatest problems have occurred, and which arguably stand to benefit more from it (**Fielding** *et al.* **1989; Tilley 2003**). As **Tilley (2003: 331)** comments, 'communities most in need of community policing seem to have taken to it least enthusiastically'.

A recent variant of 'community policing' in England and Wales is called 'neighbourhood policing'. The basis of a neighbourhood policing model is to have dedicated police resources for local areas and for police and their partners to work together with the public to understand and tackle the problems that matter to them most. The implementation of neighbourhood policing has represented a significant undertaking for the government, Police Service and their partners.

Neighbourhood policing was initially piloted at a ward level as part of the National Reassurance Policing Programme (NRPP) between October 2003 and March 2005. Following the small-scale pilot, the three-year Neighbourhood Policing Programme (NPP) was officially launched in April 2005.

The national programme has sought to deliver on the government's commitment for every neighbourhood in England and Wales to have a neighbourhood policing team by 2008, and for the accelerated roll-out of 16,000 Police Community Support Officers (PCSOs) by the end of April 2007 (**Home Office 2004, 2005**). In 2007/08, the Home Office made available £315m to fund the growth in PCSO numbers and support the introduction of neighbourhood policing (**Home Office 2006**). Neighbourhood policing shares much with other community-orientated models of policing and has been referred to as the 'new' community policing (**Innes 2006**). Policymakers, however, deliberately adopted the term 'neighbourhood' to:

- reflect growing awareness among police officers about the complexity of the policing environment;
- distance the programme from earlier community policing efforts that were not sustained over time;
- bring together a range of national and force initiatives under a single banner (e.g. quality of life policing, micro-beats, and Policing Priority Areas); and
- highlight what were seen as neighbourhood policing's distinctive features. See **Tuffin 2007; Innes 2006**. (Quoted from Quinton P and Morris J (2008) *Neighbourhood Policing*. Home Office Online Report 01/08).

In contrast to earlier forms of community policing, neighbourhood policing has been managed by ACPO as central programmes that have tried to encourage and support local implementation, and to monitor its progress. Moreover, the NRPP and NPP both attempted to systematise the work of neighbourhood officers, integrate it with other policing functions rather than to treat it as a bolt-on, and link it to the 'neighbourhood' as a specific geographic entity. There has also been an increasingly explicit expectation that neighbourhood policing, perhaps unlike community policing, will involve law enforcement as well as order maintenance, and may reduce crime by addressing the concerns of local people, in addition to improving their confidence in the police (**Innes 2005**).

Most neighbourhoods in England and Wales now have their own or shared neighbourhood team made up of one sergeant, two constables and three PCSOs. They are often called 'safer neighbourhoods' teams. The teams are required to operate a highly visible service, often chatting to locals on an informal basis. They generally deal with low-level nuisance crime and what is broadly termed 'anti-social behaviour', which can cover anything from loitering in a threatening manner – blocking pavements and gesturing at passers-by – to setting off fireworks late at night, littering or owning a badly behaved pet. They often work in partnership by sharing funding, offices or meetings – with other local agencies such as housing associations and educations providers. Research shows that the strongest teams tend are those with good information-sharing relationships with other partners and which are overseen by a neighbourhood manager (**Turley et al. 2012**).

The neighbourhood policing teams take their cue from the Community Safety Partnership (CSP) operating in their area. Often they will be allocated some CSP funding and they consult with a local neighbourhood panel, made up of anyone who wants to be on the panel, which helps them identify priorities. For example, one team operating in Crouch End, North London identified its priorities in 2012 on their webpage as: anti-social behaviour by local youths, burglary and personal safety. In response to the anti-social behaviour concerns, the team conducted 'weapons sweeps' and took those found out of circulation, increased patrols around fast food outlets (which typically witness higher rates of anti-social behaviour), held meetings with staff from these venues and young peoples' representatives, and identified and targeted young people who were known to have caused anti-social problems. In response to the burglary concerns, the team visited every household in roads affected by burglary providing crime prevention advice and offering bespoke home security surveys to residents, carried out road checks in highlighted areas as a tactic to identify suspicious vehicles and occupants while acting as a high profile deterrent to offenders and reassurance to local communities, shared intelligence and conducted joint patrols with neighbouring wards to tackle cross border issues, which resulted in the setting up of a new Neighbourhood Watch covering the cross border area and improving information-sharing on local issues. With regard to personal safety, the team worked with local schools and policing units to target areas highlighted for robberies of young people, carried out increased patrols and youth surgeries advising on safety and crime prevention, and held a safety event on a local parkland route often associated with criminal activities to provide safety advice and reassurance to people they met along the route. The team also sends out regular newsletters to volunteer co-ordinators, who then disseminate the information to people they know in the community, including details of local crime-related activity and offering tips for personal safety and household security. Most recently, co-ordinators were warned of an increase in household burglary and given a list of helpful tips on how to secure their properties.

Community policing has been given a major boost by the introduction of elected police and crime commissioners, whose priority is to make sure that their police force is responding to the needs of the community they serve. 'Community' policing will no longer be the preserve of a single small team on foot patrol; rather, it will define the approach of everyone working for the local police force.

Another innovation which helps community policing is the introduction of street level crime maps. These allow anyone to see, online, a map of their local area detailing all the reported crimes and incidents of anti-social behaviour that occurred there each month. These were developed partly in response to the 'Policing in the 21st Century' consultation of 2010 and are part of the Coalition Government's plan to increase public access to crime and policing information in their areas. With more information about crime happening on and around their street, locals are better equipped to vote in the police and crime commissioner elections and to raise issues or take an active role in tackling crime and antisocial behaviour.

In the summer of 2011, a new 'non-emergency' national crime-reporting telephone number of just three digits, 101, went live as a means of encouraging people to report instances of low-level crime and anti-social behaviour. Eventually it will replace police forces' individual phone numbers as more people become aware of it. It is hoped that the easy-to-remember number will encourage people to report instances of criminal activity which previously might have gone un-reported due to the hassle of having to look up the relevant phone number, thus enhancing the police's awareness of crime problems in a particular area.

6.5 Front-line definers of crime: police discretion

Objective 5

Discuss and analysis the notion of the police as the front-line definers of crime.

Legislation such as PACE, local and national policing plans and emphases on community or intelligence-led policing all provide the context within which the police carry out their work at a day-to-day level. A major feature of this work is that the police have considerable discretion at all stages of the criminal justice process – quite simply, they cannot enforce all the laws all the time. To attempt anything approximating full law enforcement would result in extremely large numbers of police officers exercising surveillance over the population by means of video cameras and intensive patrolling. This would be extremely costly and could lead to what some would regard as a police state. The police however have neither the numbers, resources nor technological expertise to enforce all laws fully. How this discretion is exercised from chief constables to beat police officers is a major determinant of how well any policies or strategies will work. Many criticisms of the police involve the use of discretion and many laws and rules seek to limit its impact.

Although the use of discretionary powers is regarded by police critics as an example of potential unfairness when police powers are used selectively against some communities and individuals, it is regarded by others as a strengths of the British Police that the ordinary police constable has the constitutional right to decide how best to use their powers and under law are not bound by the orders of the Chief Constable.

Chief constables must determine the style of policing and priorities for their area within their given budget and national and local policing plans. Some may favour an emphasis on community policing, others may target particular offences. These general policies are implemented by areas and divisions who may also interpret policy in the light of what they see as the most pressing problems of their area. In the police station yet more discretionary decisions are involved. How suspects are dealt with, interrogated, and charged are all decisions made at this level, along with decisions about cautioning or proceeding with charges. Police officers on the streets have discretion in deciding where to patrol, what to investigate, whether and how to intervene in incidents, or whether to stop and search members of the public. Unlike many other organisations where those at the top exercise the greatest amounts of discretion, police officers on the street have to make difficult decisions on the spur of the moment. This is illustrated in comments made by the then Commissioner of the Metropolitan Police, Sir Paul Condon, who, in a speech in October 1993, said that many key decisions have to be taken by some of the most junior officers. He went on to say, 'they are expected to be counsellors, negotiators, mediators, managers, advisers, experts, parental figures, law enforcers and humble servants, ready to make contentious decisions, some involving life or death'.

There have been many studies of aspects of police discretion exploring how decisions are made and how tasks are prioritised. Clearly the law constrains the use of discretion, but a variety of non-legal or extra-legal factors are also important, and there may well be a gap between the law in action and the law as described in books.

In general, while legal factors form a backcloth against which decisions must be made, the law is often ambiguous and requires interpretation – what situations, for example, amount to 'reasonable suspicion'? As seen in previous chapters, the police must judge when actions are to be defined as criminal. The immediate situation affects the way an incident will be dealt with. Outcomes may be affected by apparently trivial circumstances such as the weather, the officer's mood, or the time of day. For example, at the end of a long shift, an officer may not want to be delayed by the amount of paperwork which could result from an arrest.

Alternatively, on a wet, cold night they might want to get back to the station and might even look out for people to arrest (**Cain 1973**). Many studies of police have found that a wide variety of factors affect how they react to specific incidents such as drunken brawls, disturbances by youths or disputes between neighbours. Particular offences, offenders, groups or neighbourhoods may be specific targets of special attention as a result of national priorities or local consultation (**see Chapter 5**).

Whether a person is likely to be seen as 'suspicious' depends also on cultural cues. The police have a set of expectations about what kinds of people belong in a certain area, and when and in what circumstances one would expect to find them. Behavioural cues like walking slowly or quickly may also affect judgments of 'suspiciousness' – and these are also culturally determined. The local knowledge and experience of the officer is likely to be important here, as is the local police culture which defines certain areas and groups as representing trouble, and which also provides guidelines for appropriate responses. This can be seen particularly in relation to the decision to stop and search.

Dilemma of policing – due process model (following the rules) versus the Justice model (criminals are punished for their criminal acts)

'The Law that lets off a self-confessed killer.'

The above headline from the *Sunday Times* referred to an article written by Zoe Brennan regarding Detective Superintendent Steve Fulcher who was suspended following the investigation of a murder in Wiltshire and the conviction of Christopher Halliwell. Halliwell led the police to the body of Sian O'Callahan, a 22 year old woman who had been abducted and killed by Halliwell.

At the scene where the first body was found Halliwell then said, 'Do you want another one' and took the police to the body of another murder victim Becky Godden-Edwards.

Because Detective Superintendent Steve Fulcher did not caution Halliwell at this time for the second murder a judge has ruled that Halliwell should not face trial for the second murder despite knowing where the body of the second murdered woman was hidden.

Mrs Justice Cox commented, 'There were serious and irretrievable breaches by the senior investigating officer of the mandatory rules governing the detention and interview of arrested suspects by the police.' Halliwell's barrister argued that 'the PACE rules were a fundamental right'.

(*Sunday Times*, 28 October 2012 in the News Review section, p. 6)

▶ The decision to stop and search

The significance of the words 'reasonable suspicion' in relation to stop-and-search powers has already been indicated. The PACE Codes state that this must not be based on someone's race or hairstyle (unless this is likely to signify gang membership), or on the fact that they are members of a group or community that have a higher than average record of committing that type of offence, nor on the fact that they are known to have previous convictions for possession of an unlawful article. These guidelines, however, like the law, are limited. Decisions to stop and search are made on the spot, and rely on the individual officer's judgment of the situation. In deciding who to stop, officers will be guided by a host of cues which relate to their conception of what is 'normal' and what is suspicious, taking account of their knowledge of the area, their knowledge of what the most common kinds of crime are and the circumstances in which they are committed, and their assumptions about which individuals and groups constitute the 'usual suspects'. They are encouraged to learn, as part of their training, to identify such situations, and indeed the public is reliant on them to prevent crime by apprehending suspects. No one factor, be it age, colour, style of dress or the circumstances in which they find someone, can be responsible for any one stop. The complexity of this situation is thus difficult to capture in guidelines, and informal considerations may take precedence over formal ones. This may not, however, emerge in subsequent written reports.

◗ Discretion in the police station

The Police and Criminal Evidence Act 1984 also deals with the exercise of police discretion in the police station, where individual suspects are interviewed and decisions are made about how to proceed with a case. As we have seen, it introduced requirements for the taping of interviews and custody records. Nevertheless, as in any job, ways are often found to circumvent formal rules, and informal practices may become the norm. The PACE Codes cannot, for example, control the informal interviews which police have with suspects outside the police station, in the car or in the cells (**Leng et al. 1992**). Such conversations are not officially defined as interviews. In addition, in recorded interviews, the fear of the suspect and the attitude of the officer cannot be fully reproduced on tape. Thus even although confessions which are involuntary, or produced in oppressive circumstances, are inadmissible, these factors may still mean that tactics used by skilled and experienced officers may 'put words into' a suspect's mouth.

These considerations do not imply that the police act illegally – many practices are essentially a way around the perceived constraints of law. To the police, obtaining evidence to secure a conviction of someone they have good reason to believe is guilty is part of their job. Nor does it mean that laws such as PACE are entirely without effect as they may curtail blatant abuses of police powers, as was indicated above (**Brown 1997**).

◗ Police culture

The exercise of discretion is strongly affected by what is often described as the occupational culture of the police. This includes the informal rules which affect how the police behave in any particular incident or situation. Many occupations have associated cultures, within which members use a special language, and share a similar view of the world and their occupation. Anyone starting a job very quickly learns the distinction between how things should be done and how they really are done. These informal rules are learnt during what sociologists call occupational socialisation where a recruit learns the norms and values associated with the occupation. The expectations associated with the job and what constitutes success are part of such a culture, as are attitudes about the role of the occupation. This is particularly the case where the occupation faces hostility or misunderstanding from the public – as may be the case with the police. In this case the culture may have a justifying role, justifying the job that members do.

In some occupations this culture is stronger than others – policing is not a 'nine to five' job from which officers can switch off when they leave the station. It makes heavy emotional demands on officers, involves high levels of stress, danger, and is a vocation as well as a job. Police work involves shift work, reducing the time officers spend with 'civilians'. This makes for closer relationships between officers and a stronger culture than in many jobs. The job may also affect how the police carry out their work – for example, the police must display authority in order to handle some situations, especially where large numbers of people are involved. Police can 'handle' situations only if the public respect the authority of the police. This may affect decisions about suspects to the extent that those who appear to challenge authority may be more likely to be stopped, arrested or charged. Authority is reinforced by the symbols of the job – cars, radios and uniforms all signify the authority vested in the role of police officer (**Holdaway 1983**).

All these factors give rise to a strong occupational culture within the police, described by many authors (**Reiner 2000; Holdaway 1983; Foster 2003**). While it is impossible to make sweeping generalisations, certain themes appear to characterise police culture in Anglo-American societies:

- *A sense of mission:* police officers feel that their job is important and they often see themselves as forming a 'thin blue line', protecting society from disorder. A key part of this mission is catching criminals.

- *'Real police work':* law enforcement is seen as 'real' work in contrast to much-hated desk or paperwork and also when compared with some community work.

- *Action:* this involves action seen most clearly in the imagery of the car chase. Car chases, according to Holdaway (ibid.), are often the subject of animated conversations in dull moments in the canteen and they form an important part of the police folklore.

- *Machismo:* there is a strong element of machismo within police culture which may affect attitudes to some kinds of work and to female officers who may be treated protectively and assumed not to be able to cope with elements of the job – not a 'suitable job for a woman' having been a pervasive attitude (**Heidensohn 1992**).

- *Racism:* as will be seen in the next section, many studies have found strong elements of racism within police culture, with derogative language being used to describe not only people of colour but also members of groups such as the Irish, Scots and inhabitants of areas associated with high crime rates.

These are some of the major characteristics of police culture, although it should also be recognised that there are in practice many variations (**Foster 2003**). Detectives may have a perspective and a culture very different from uniformed officers and may need to adopt very different styles to perform their job adequately (**Hobbs 1991**). Different stations within a particular area may have very different cultures, affected by the policy of the division (**Foster 1989**). Some officers may value their role within the community, whereas others may see themselves more as crime fighters. Rural policing may be very different from urban policing, with rural police being more involved in all the tasks of the police simply because of the time it may take to call in the specialists from the town (**Cain 1973**). Those involved in public order duties, especially those in special patrols, may also come to look forward to a 'piece of action' (**Jefferson 1990**). Whatever the variations, an understanding of police culture is important when policy reforms and new laws are considered. Cultures where 'real police work' is strongly related to law enforcement may resist efforts which may be perceived to curtail their powers and discretion or to foster more community-orientated schemes. This is not to say that attitudes cannot change and it is important not to paint too static or simple a picture.

▶ Police and ethnic minority communities

A major issue affecting policing and policing policy is the relationship between the police and ethnic minority communities, highlighted by, among other indicators, flashpoints of urban unrest. The exercise of discretion can, where insufficiently regulated, lead to discrimination, and there have been recurrent allegations that some ethnic minorities have been subjected to over-policing, evidenced by higher rates of stops, searches and arrests than would be expected, which has led to higher rates of dissatisfaction with the police among some communities. The victimisation of different ethnic groups (**outlined in Chapter 3**) raised concerns that the police were reluctant to acknowledge that some offences were racially motivated, and indeed might be more likely to suspect some groups of being perpetrators rather than victims. The numbers of ethnic minority officers within the police have also been perceived to be a problem. The extent to which this can be accounted for by racism within the police has been subjected to considerable investigation, culminating in the MacPherson Report in 1999 which found what it described as institutional racism and made several recommendations for reform.

Concerns about relationships between the police and minority communities date back to the 1960s; since then a wide range of reports have detailed what **Bowling and Phillips (2003)** describe as oppressive policing of minority communities. The declining relationship between police and black people was highlighted by the Scarman Report which followed the riots in Brixton and other English cities in 1981. The Brixton disturbances followed an aggressive street policing strategy described as Operation Swamp '81, when high numbers of black youths were stopped on suspicion. The Scarman Report of 1982 identified widespread resentment against the police among black youth and was critical of many aspects of policing. Its many recommendations included improvements in police community relations, such as the community policing strategies outlined above, employing more ethnic minority police officers, identifying racial prejudice among police recruits, and improvements in training and supervision. This report did produce many changes, and stimulated a large body of research. However, the 1980s saw further instances of urban unrest – in particular the riots on the Broadwater Farm estate in Tottenham in which PC Keith Blakelock was stabbed to death. While later urban disturbances were not specifically linked to the issue of race, disturbances in the summer of 2001 in the North of England, in Burnley, Bradford and Oldham, followed a series of attacks on Asian youths by white youths and, yet again, as Bowling and Phillips (ibid.) recount, subsequent reports called for more ethnic minority police officers and better communication between the police and the community. The riots of August 2011 were blamed by some commentators on poor race relations between the police and ethnic minorities, and the report that followed it in March 2012, 'After the Riots', made an explicit recommendation that that police forces should 'proactively engage with communities' to increase people's trust in the police and that police should seek to improve the quality of encounters with black and ethnic minority people, in order to make contact with police a better experience for them. All these instances draw attention to the factors which may be important in affecting police relationships with ethnic minority communities. *Four days in August* provides an insight into the events from the perspective of the Metropolitan Police (see Met Police website).

To Bowling and Phillips (ibid: 534) the 'use of stop and search powers by the police has been the most controversial issue in debates about policing ethnic minorities'. As seen above, while PACE Codes govern the use of stop and search powers the concept of 'reasonable suspicion' can be contested and can give rise to concerns about discrimination and the use of stereotypes in determining what circumstances might merit a stop. From the 1980s onwards, research has indicated that black people have a higher chance of being stopped than might be expected if criminal activity is assumed to be evenly distributed across the different communities.

There are ongoing concerns regarding disproportionate use of stop and search. A report published by the Equality and Human Rights Commission in 2010, examines official statistics from 2007–8 detailing stops and searches under section 1 of the Police and Criminal Evidence Act 1984 for disproportionality trends and found that the black population had the highest rate of stop and search at 129 incidents per 1,000 black people. The rate for Asian people was 40 per 1,000, and for white people it was 17 per 1,000. (*Stop and Think, A critical review of the use of stop and search powers in England and Wales*, EHRC, 2010). The latest report on stop and search powers was published in July 2013 by **Her Majesty's Inspectorate of Constabulary (HMCI)**. In 2012, John Winsor was appointed as the latest HMCI inspector – he was the first to be appointed without a policing background.

However, the notion of disproportionality has to be used with care because it assumes that the supposed excessive response by the police towards some groups is based on an assumption that everyone has an equal chance of being stopped and search on the streets, but clearly there are key factors that are likely to effect when the police make a decision to stop and search a suspect. Fundamentally, this will include the type of population on the street at a time when stop and searches are made, and the type or types of crime that are the focus of the police attention. Therefore, it is of little surprise to find that younger people are more likely to be stopped than older ones, and that more males are stopped than females. Similarly, the assumption that criminal activities that are the focus of police attention are spread evenly across all communities is an assumption open to criticism, because it would require that there are no differences in crime activities between communities. However, the awareness of criminal subcultures and counter cultures shows that there are some types of crimes that are more likely to be committed within a particular community in contrast to other communities or in the general population as a whole.

In the year 2010–11, police carried out more than 1,200,000 stop and searches on individuals and vehicles under section 1 of the PACE Act 1984, of which 15 per cent were black (approximately 180,000 stops) and 10 per cent were Asian. Ongoing criticism of the disproportionate use of stop and search under section 1 of the PACE Act 1984, sections 44–47 of the Terrorism Act 2000, and section 60 of the Criminal Justice and Public Order Act 1994, predominantly in the Greater London area, has led to some legislative changes: as described above, PACE Code

A was updated in 2011 in order to emphasise the need for caution against discrimination when exercising the right to stop and search anyone thought to pose a threat to public under section 60 of the Criminal Justice and Public Order Act 1994. Further care has been taken in the light of the changes included in the Crime and Security Act 2010 to ensure that the ethnicity of individuals stopped continues to be recorded, while other personal details of the individual are no longer required, as a precaution against abuse of police discretion.

It is very difficult to interpret these statistical indicators and to attribute them, as some critics do, to direct racism on the part of the police. It was seen above, for example, how many factors the police have to take into account when making a decision to stop, and the area, the circumstances of the stop and indicators of a variety of factors such as age, gender, income, employment are all important – for example, young people are more likely to be stopped than older people and males more than females. As some ethnic groups are more likely to be involved in certain types of street crime such as street robbery, violence and gun murders then it is also the case that suspect descriptions will not reflect the population as a whole and therefore it would be surprising if all groups were stopped in proportion to their numbers in the community. Age profile and crime profiles will mean that the police will be stopping proportionally more of some groups compared to others. A recent example that illustrates this is that police stops for terrorist activities have focused on younger male Muslims because in recent times it has been those with this profile who have planted bombs with the aim of killing as many people as possible. Following the bombing and attempted bombing on London Transport in 2005, there was an increase in stops of Asian youths.

The many factors involved in the decision to stop and search make it very difficult to establish statistically a 'race factor' (**Holdaway 1997**). If more black people live in and are more likely to be on the street in areas which attract heavier policing, they will be more likely to be stopped. Attempts to assess 'stop rates' controlling for the relative proportion of ethnic groups on the street indicate that black people's rate of being stopped is not necessarily higher than white, and rates vary across different areas. Consideration of these factors also suggests that it cannot be assumed that stop rates for different groups should be the same, making it difficult, therefore, to see these figures as indicating large amounts of racism on the part of individual officers.

Nevertheless, there are also indications that the attitudes of individual police officers and police culture mirror the racism prevalent in wider society and that decisions to stop may be affected by racist stereotypes. As the October 2003 BBC documentary, *The Secret Policemen* demonstrated only too clearly, some police officers display strongly racist attitudes. (The programme led to an inquiry, discussed below, by the Commission for Racial Equality (CRE)). This does not in itself mean they exercise discrimination on the street or that they are reflective of the majority of the police – the Policy Studies Institute (PSI) studies, for example, found little evidence that racist attitudes led to discrimination on the street. What is more likely is that there may be indirect discrimination, which exists where the policies or practices of an institution are applied evenly, but have an unequal impact on different groups. Thus when the police prioritise lower-class, high-crime areas containing a large proportion of ethnic minority residents, more lower-class and black people become subject to stops, searches or arrests and searches. Wider social inequalities such as unemployment, poor housing conditions and family breakdown further compound the disadvantages of black youths as they enter the criminal justice system – as they may then be less likely to be cautioned or warned and more likely to be taken to court.

Research conducted by the PSI found that police officers used derogatory language when describing black people, and that the 'canteen culture' contained many racist elements (**Smith and Grey 1985**). Reports from the Chief Inspector of Constabulary have cited unacceptable levels of prejudice and sexist and racist behaviour on the part of the police as a disincentive for both women and ethnic minority individuals to join the police (*The Guardian*, 14 June 1994). In a report in 2003 for the Commission for Racial Equality (CRE), Sir David Calvert-Smith (Director of Public Prosecutions of England and Wales from 1998 to 2003) commented:

> . . . There is no doubt that the Police Service has made significant progress in the area of race equality in recent years. However, there is still a long way to go before we have a service where every officer treats the public and their colleagues with fairness and respect, regardless of their ethnic origin. Willingness to change at the top is not translating into action lower down, particularly in middle management where you find ice in the heart of the Police Service.
>
> (Commission for Racial Equality, 2003)

In addition, there is now considerable evidence that being a member of a group associated with crime can become grounds for 'reasonable' suspicion. For example, research indicates that factors such as style of dress and types of car can all arouse suspicion – which can be negatively associated with African/Caribbeans (**Phillips and Bowling 2002**). One study reported officers who were said to 'subscribe to the philosophy that, if you see four black youths in a car, it's worth giving them a pull as at least one of them is going to be guilty of something or other' (**Cashmore 2001: 652, cited in Bowling and Phillips 2003: 537**).

Attitudes within the police may also lead to discrimination against and the alienation of ethnic minority recruits in the police. As seen above, the Scarman Report recommended the recruitment of more ethnic minority officers and efforts have been made to redress the low representation of such officers. In 2013, 5 per cent of police officers were classified as having a minority ethnic identity in the 43 forces of England and Wales, compared with 3.9 per cent in 2007.

Research has indicated that such officers experience a variety of problems fitting in with police culture, including coping with racist attitudes and developing social networks with other officers. They are more likely to leave the police and cite these experiences and dissatisfaction with how racism has been dealt with by senior officers as reasons for leaving (**Holdaway and Barron 1997**). They are also under-represented in senior ranks and take longer to be promoted. Recruitment targets were set in 1998, not only for the police but also for the Probation and Prison Services, which recommend positive action to achieve equality of representation including strategies to encourage local people within communities to join the police and conducting targeted recruitment campaigns. Potential recruits may, however, be put off by the experiences of existing ethnic minority officers.

Many of these issues were highlighted by the case of Stephen Lawrence, the black teenager who was stabbed to death in Eltham, south-east London on 22 April 1993 by what was widely accepted to be a group of hostile and abusive white youths (**Newburn 2003**). At the time, no one was successfully charged with murder, although there was an unsuccessful private prosecution against five suspects in 1996. Mainly due to public outrage about the failure to convict any-one for Lawrence's murder, the law of double jeopardy was amended by the Criminal Justice Act 2003 to allow for previously acquitted suspects to be re-tried in certain circumstances. Re-trial is only permitted in cases of very serious crimes such as murder, kidnapping and armed robbery, and the prosecution must be in possession of some new, viable evidence. Any retrial has to be approved by the Director of Public Prosecutions and the Court of Appeal has to formally quash the previous acquittal of the defendant, so that the trial is officially deemed to be that of a defendant who in law is presumed to be innocent.

This paved the way for two of the suspects, Gary Dobson and David Norris, to face a re-trial in 2011 following the a cold case review which resulted in the discovery of a tiny stain of Stephen Lawrence's blood on Dobson's jacket, and some of Lawrence's hairs on their clothing. This evidence was only made possible by advances in DNA-profiling which enables the analysis of microscopic DNA samples. The two men were convicted of Stephen Lawrence's murder in January 2012. They both received minimum sentences of 15 years.

The conduct of the original police investigation into Lawrence's murder was widely criticised by the victim's family and subsequently more widely by interest groups and the media. The claim was that the police had initially assumed that Lawrence and his friend Duwayne Brooks had initiated the violence, and failed to follow up leads to find the perpetrators. Following considerable representation, the New Labour Government in July 1997 set up the MacPherson Inquiry, whose terms of reference were 'to inquire into the matters arising from the death of Stephen Lawrence . . . and to identify the lessons to be learnt for the investigation and prosecution of racially motivated crimes' (cited in **Newburn 2003: 90**). The Inquiry reported in 1999 (**MacPherson 1999**) and, in addition to revealing deep-seated racism within the police, made a number of important recommendations.

The Inquiry documented the police denial of any racial motive for the murder, along with the racist stereotyping of Duwayne Brooks. There was, according to MacPherson (para. 2.10), 'no doubt whatsoever but that the first MPS investiga-tion was palpably flawed and deserves severe criticism'. The use of inappropriate and offensive language was criticised, along with the insensitive and patronising handling of Mr and Mrs Lawrence. It found that the 'investigation was marred by a combination of professional incompetence, institutional racism and a failure of leadership by senior officers' (para. 46.1). This incompetence, according to **Newburn (2003)**, included a 'lack of direction and organisation in the hours after the murder, little or no pursuit of the suspects, inadequate processing of intelligence, ill-thought-out surveillance and inadequate searches'. It defined institutional racism as follows:

> . . . The collective failure of an organisation to provide an appropriate and professional service to people because of their colour, culture or ethnic origin. It can be seen or detected in processes, attitudes and behaviour which amount to discrimination through unwitting prejudice, ignorance, thoughtlessness, and racist stereotyping which disadvantage minority ethnic people.
>
> (MacPherson 1999: 6.34)

It also commented on the absence of confidence and trust in the police among ethnic minority communities as a result of a failure to respond to racist violence, the use of stopandsearch powers, and the high numbers of deaths of black people in police custody; and the Inquiry concluded that the black community was 'over policed . . . and under protected' (ibid: 312).

The MacPherson Report made 70 recommendations, which included the following:

- making it a 'ministerial priority' to increase trust and confidence among ethnic minority communities;
- the application of freedom of information and anti-discrimination legislation to the police;
- the monitoring and assessment of police performance;
- improved reporting and recording of racist incidents and crimes;
- improvements in the investigation and prosecution of racist crime;
- improvements in arrangements for family liaison;
- improvements in the treatment of victims and witnesses;
- improved training and discipline;
- improvements in procedures for dealing with complaints;
- improvements in the use of stop-and-search powers;
- improvements in relation to the recruitment and retention of ethnic minority police officers.

The Report was not without criticism. The definition of institutionalised racism means that it is subjective and dependent on an interpretation and only requires an assertion to be made. MacPherson defines a racist incident as 'any incident which is perceived to be racist by the victim or any other person' (ibid: 328). This 'unwitting racism' means that members of the host culture, especially police officers, must not offend the cultural sensitivities of people from other backgrounds or they risk being labelled as racist. Furthermore the use of the term institutional could be taken to imply that it is an institutional goal, i.e. an aim of an institution; but nothing could be further from the truth given the unprecedented efforts of the police to combat racism in recent years.

Police interactions with ethnic minorities become difficult if encounters are interpreted from a racially sensitive perspective so that a discriminatory motive is imputed to comments made by police officers. Robert Skidelsky writes with reference to the MacPherson Report:

> Thus from the fact that Police Constable Joanne Smith described Duwayne Brooks, who had been with Stephen Lawrence when he was stabbed, as 'irate and aggressive' – he called her 'a f****** C***' – the Report deduces that: 'Mr Brooks was stereotyped as a young black man exhibiting unpleasant hostility and agitation.'
>
> (Skidelsky in David Green 2000: 3)

Skidelsky continues to make a point concerning the priorities that are being established by the MacPherson Report:

> When officers arrived on the scene of the crime to find Stephen Lawrence dying, none of them knew how to give him first aid. This, one would have thought, is a far more serious defect than their lack of training in race relations.
>
> (Skidelsky in Green 2000: 4)

Michael Ignatieff sees this as a tragedy which has reduced 'institutional incompetence' to an issue of police racism. He wrote:

> As with the Scarman report after Brixton, we seem unable to come to any awareness of these issues without a convulsion of guilt ridden confusion. What is most dismaying, looking back on Lawrence, is that it becomes a story about just one thing – race. But the central issue was not race, it was justice. Why were we talking about institutionalised racism, when the issue was institutionalised incompetence? Why were we talking about 'race awareness' when the issue was equal justice before the law?
>
> Everyone talked as if the Lawrence family and a larger fiction called the 'black community' had been 'let down'. The 'black community' is no more of a reality than the 'white community'. To suppose this is to believe that skin trumps all other identities, that we are only our surfaces. In reality the Lawrence family were denied justice, and because they were denied justice, all of us have good reason to feel anger and shame that we cared so little about institutions which operate in our name.
>
> (Ignatieff in Green 2000: 21)

Overall, the Report and its recommendations, a large number of which were accepted, is widely agreed to have made a significant difference to contemporary policing. **Newburn (2003: 91)**, for example, argues that the 'climate of policing has changed since Lawrence', and **Reiner (2000: 211)** that the MacPherson Report has 'transformed the debate about black people and criminal justice'. To **Bowling and Phillips (2002)**, its recommendations for a fully independent complaints system and bringing the police into the ambit of race relations law reflected its view that the failings of the police were systemic and resulted from insufficient accountability. It also recommended lay oversight into all areas of police work. They are optimistic in relation to the visible support on behalf of the police to improve policies in relation to racist violence and their response to ethnic minority crime victims, along with the acceptance of a commitment to recruit more ethnic minority officers.

Following the Macpherson report there have been some policy changes and **Bowling and Phillips (2003)**, for example, cited a 'MacPherson' effect in relation to the use of stop-and-search powers – as overall stops declined and there appears to be a decline in the significance of race as a factor affecting stops for all categories except stops of black people in cars.

A major issue is the extent to which concerns about race relations supersede other goals of policing, such as reducing crime. The warning from the Police Federation has been that the unintended consequence of MacPherson has been that police officers have become reluctant to use their powers of stop and search for fear of accusations of racism in some areas. This causes particular difficulties when police and community crime reduction programmes are trying to target young people carrying weapons in communities with a high proportion of ethnic minorities. This is a problem for policing crimes such as black on black murders associated with control of the illegal drug trade, and robbery to steal mobile phones. In 2000/1, data on phone robbery from London and Birmingham showed that 90 per cent were male, one-third of all offenders cautioned were aged 15 and 16, and that 71 per cent of suspects in the Metropolitan police area were black. In the West Midlands 54 per cent were black (**Harrington and Mayhew 2001**). In these areas a clamp-down on street robberies involving mobile phones is likely to lead to the problem of at least some community spokesperson claiming the police are picking on and stereotyping young black males as robbers.

The Home Office, in April 2000, produced a Code of Practice on Reporting and Recording Racist Incidents and ACPO produced guidance on Identifying and Combating Hate Crimes in 2000. Additionally, the Metropolitan Police has created a Racial and Violent Crimes Task Force and Community Safety Units in all London boroughs, whose officers are especially trained to investigate 'hate crimes'. While these policies have had some impact there remains a risk that this will be seen as a specialist area and as not applying to other areas of policing (**Bowling and Phillips 2003**).

Conclusion

The police are crucial to the criminal justice system as they are in effect the front-line definers of what comes to be regarded as crime and who are to be considered the criminals. This chapter has shown how the police are organised and has looked at different ways of assessing their role and function. It has also outlined the main laws governing police investigation, along with how the police are made accountable and discussed the new wave of Police and Crime Commissioners. The rules and guidelines, such as PACE, provide only a backcloth against which the police operate on a day-to-day level, which is inevitably affected by their own perception of their job, the crimes they have to deal with, their occupational culture and how they interpret the many rules and guidelines. Given the complexity of regulations and restraints on police work it becomes even more important to understand how the police decide upon their priorities. This is important for a number of reasons. Should the police, for example, perceive their main role as one of crime control, then they may be tempted to neglect due process in the interests of making sure that those guilty of crime are brought to court and found guilty. They may, as we have seen, downgrade the service or preventative aspects of their role. Discussions of police policy must therefore recognise the significance of discretion in police work and the role of the police culture and its influence on police work.

This chapter also raises questions about the role of the police, vital to our understanding of the criminal justice process as a whole. What is their main role? Should they be seen and assessed primarily as 'crime fighters' or as crime preventers and public protectors? Should they work more with local communities or spend more time in the war against serious, organised and transnational crime and terrorism? What might be the unintended effects on police community relations of moves towards the greater use of technology and intelligence-led policing? One of the functions of the police not yet explored is their role in determining whether a suspect is prosecuted or diverted out of the criminal justice system. This will be discussed in **Chapter 7**.

Review questions

1. Discuss what you think should be the main duties of a Police Service.

2. What are the main ways in which the police are rendered accountable? How and why have these arrangements recently been changed?

3. Identify the possible infringements of PACE and Code C in the following:

   At 10 p.m. Alan is seen at the scene of a suspected burglary with a video camera thought to come from the burgled house. PC Bob asks him where he got the camera. Alan does not reply, whereupon, without more ado, he is bundled into the police van and taken to the police station.

   At the police station, Alan is placed in a cell with three other people, and told he will be seen when the officer has time. The only light in the cell is broken. Four hours later Alan has not been interviewed. He wants to sleep but cannot as the only bed is occupied. Alan is very cold, and asks the custody officer for a cup of tea. He is told that there has been a problem in the canteen and he can have a glass of water. This arrives one hour later. At 6 a.m. Alan is interviewed about his possession of the camera and suspected involvement in the burglary. He asks to see a solicitor, but is told the duty solicitor has just left and is not likely to want to come back before morning. Alan states that he stole the camera. Alan is 16.

   Consider the following in framing your answer:

   - Was Alan arrested properly?
   - Should anything have been said when he was taken to the police station?
   - Should anything have been said to him when he got to the police station?
   - Were the conditions in his cell acceptable?

- Should he have been asked if he wanted to contact anyone?
- Should he have been given refreshments?
- Should he have been given anything else?
- Was the time during which he was kept at the police station acceptable under the Code?
- Should he have been allowed to speak with a duty solicitor?
- Should anyone else have been present during the interview?

4. Read the extract below and answer the following questions about the relevance of these nine principles, published in 1829, to policing in the twenty-first century.

The following set of principles, which lay out in the clearest and most succinct terms the philosophy of policing by consent, appeared as an appendix to *A New Study of Police History* by Charles Reith (London: Oliver and Boyd, 1956). Reith was a lifelong historian of the police force in Britain, and this book covers the early years of the Metropolitan Police following the passage of Sir Robert Peel's 'Bill for Improving the Police in and near the Metropolis' on 19 June 1829. Reith notes that there are particular problems involved in writing police history, owing to the loss or destruction of much early archive material, and, probably for this reason, the principles appear without details of author or date.

However, it seems most likely that they were composed by Charles Rowan and Richard Mayne, as the first and joint Commissioners of the Metropolitan Police. Rowan was a military man and Mayne, 14 years his junior, a barrister. Rowan retired in 1850 leaving Mayne as sole Commissioner until his death in 1868. The sentiments expressed in the 'Nine Principles' reflect those contained in the 'General Instructions', first published in 1829, which were issued to every member of the Metropolitan Police, especially the emphasis on prevention of crime as the most important duty of the police.

Reith notes that Rowan and Mayne's conception of a police force was 'unique in history and throughout the world because it derived not from fear but almost exclusively from public co-operation with the police, induced by them designedly by behaviour which secures and maintains for them the approval, respect and affection of the public' (p. 140).

The Nine Principles of Policing

1. To prevent crime and disorder, as an alternative to their repression by military force and severity of legal punishment.
2. To recognise always that the power of the police to fulfil their functions and duties is dependent on public approval of their existence, actions and behaviour and on their ability to secure and maintain public respect.
3. To recognise always that to secure and maintain the respect and approval of the public means also the securing of the willing cooperation of the public in the task of securing observance of laws.
4. To recognise always that the extent to which the cooperation of the public can be secured diminishes proportionately the necessity of the use of physical force – and compulsion for achieving police objectives.
5. To seek and preserve public favour, not by pandering to public opinion; but by constantly demonstrating absolutely impartial service to law, in complete

independence of policy, and without regard to the justice or injustice of the substance of individual laws, by ready offering of individual service and friend-ship to all members of the public without regard to their wealth or social standing, by ready exercise of courtesy and friendly good humour; and by ready offering of individual sacrifice in protecting and preserving life.

6. To use physical force only when the exercise of persuasion, advice and warning is found to be insufficient to obtain public co-operation to an extent necessary to secure observance of law or to restore order, and to use only the minimum degree of physical force which is necessary on any particular occasion for achieving a police objective.

7. To maintain at all times a relationship with the public that gives reality to the historic tradition that the police are the public and that the public are the police, the police being only members of the public who are paid to give full-time attention to duties which are incumbent on every citizen in the interests of community welfare and existence.

8. To recognise always the need for strict adherence to police-executive functions, and to refrain from even seeming to usurp the powers of the judiciary of avenging individuals or the State, and of authoritatively judging guilt and punishing the guilty.

9. To recognise always that the test of police efficiency is the absence of crime and disorder, and not the visible evidence of police action in dealing with them.

(*Source*: Civitas website: www.civitas.org.uk)

Answer the following points:

a. To what extent has the crime problem changed since that time? Identify new crimes not known to the police in 1829.

b. To what extent do you think the public's expectations about the police have changed since 1829?

c. What have been the main changes to the organisation and routines of police work since 1829?

d. Consider each of the nine principles in turn and state whether you think they are valid today.

Discussion questions

1. What are the arguments for and against the election of a Police and Crime Commissioner?

2. Look at the way in which the police are portrayed in the media through police dramas, documentaries or news stories. How does this reflect the different roles of the police?

3. Look at your police crime map of your district and identify the locations and types of crime that are most frequent recorded in your area. Street level crime maps: use the following link, www.police.uk/ and go to 'view crime maps for local crime statistics'.

Further reading

Newburn T (ed) (2008) *Handbook of Policing* (2nd edn), Willan Publishing: Cullompton

Newburn T and Reiner R (2007) 'Policing and the police', in Maguire M *et al.* *Oxford Handbook of Criminology*, Oxford University Press: Oxford

Phillips C and Bowling B (2012) in Maguire M, Morgan R and Reiner R (eds) *The Oxford Handbook of Criminology* (5th edn), Clarendon Press: Oxford

Reiner R (2010) *The Politics of the Police* (4th edn) Oxford University Press

Savage S (2007) *Police Reform*, Oxford University Press.

National Statistics: *Police powers and procedures England and Wales 2011/12*, Home Office, Published April 2013

Weblinks

www.actionfraud.police.uk

www.police.uk

www.data.police.uk – provides information about local forces and local crime with maps of street level crime and the outcomes.

www.statistics.gov.uk/hub/crime-justice – National Statistics on policing

www.archive.official-documents.co.uk/document/cm42/4262/4262.htm – report of the Stephen Lawrence Inquiry

www.met.police.uk/ – Metropolitan Police:

www.met.police.uk/about/charts/mps_org_chart_may_june_13.pdf – this shows the organisational structure of the Metropolitan Police in 2013

www.civitas.org.uk – Civitas

www.gov.uk/government/statistics/operation-of-police-powers-under-the-terrorism-act-2000-quarterly-update-to-june-2014 – MI5 – Counter terrorism statistics (gov.uk website)

Chapter 7

Prosecution, caution and diversion

Learning objectives

After reading the chapter you should be able to:

1. Explain the different types of fixed penalties used instead of prosecution
2. Outline the use of cautioning as a form of diversion
3. Describe the system of prosecution in England Wales and the role of the Crown Prosecution Service
4. Show the way that the Code for Crown Prosecutors is used in determining whether to prosecute an offender or not
5. Describe what is meant by private prosecutions and be able to name other prosecuting agencies
6. Explain the significance and outcomes for mentally disordered offenders

Key statistics

- There were 1,309,100 Fixed Penalty Notices (FPN's) for motoring offences issued in 2012
- There were 106,205 Penalty Notices for Disorder (PNDs) issued in 2012
- There were 168,260 cautions issued to adults in 2012
- There were 70,114 cannabis warnings issued in 2012
- Breach of an ASBO – in the 12-year period from June 2000 to December 2012, 58% of the ASBO's issued resulted in a breach of the order
- The CPS prosecuted 640,657 cases in the magistrates' courts in 2013/14 compared to 787,547 in 2011/12

Introduction

Once the police are reasonably sure they have identified a suspect, they have several options. They may decide to take no further action at all, or give an informal warning, or decide to issue a police caution, or refer the case to some form of mediation, and for young offenders there is a diversionary system of final warnings and reprimands. In some cases a fixed penalty notice, a cannabis warning or an Antisocial Behaviour Order (ASBO) can be issued. The police may instead decide to pass the papers to the Crown Prosecution Service. Many criminal cases are therefore diverted from the criminal justice process without any public trial or hearing or conviction. The decision whether to prosecute is a vital one and we will look at the rules and guidelines surrounding this decision, at the agencies responsible for it, and at the issues raised for criminal justice.

Prosecution and diversion raise many issues which can again be highlighted by looking at the different perspectives on criminal justice. Under a crime control approach, for example, it is clearly important that guilty offenders are convicted and punished and the system would be seen to lack any deterrent potential if this does not happen. Principles of due process also require that the defendant should have the opportunity to be publicly tried and enabled to refute any allegations of guilt. In addition, the notion that all are equal before the law underlies the principle that justice should be seen to be done. Diversion of some at the expense of others might produce a situation where critics from a class domination perspective could argue that some groups of offenders enjoy advantages. In addition, it is important to proponents of a denunciatory approach that offenders ought to be publicly tried and punished for the system to perform its function of expressing society's disapproval of particular behaviour. Victims also may feel aggrieved if they do not see those who have harmed them publicly held to account.

There are strong arguments that all suspects should be prosecuted (**Gross 1979**). Such an approach, however, would pose considerable problems. The process of prosecution and trial is costly. Police officers, prosecutors and the legal profession must collect evidence and produce and contest it in court, which also occupies the time and resources of court personnel. Diverting offenders from the formal process can therefore produce considerable savings and reduce delays.

The principles of adversarial justice requiring the law enforcement agencies to collect and identify admissible evidence are not only expensive and time consuming but dependent on witnesses being willing to give evidence. This does encourage both victims and law enforcement officials to adopt a view that has been known to criminologists for many years, that most crime goes unrecorded and unpunished as it is of a minor nature and not a priority to victim or police officers. Hence, often nothing is done by a shopkeeper about shoplifting or in response to minor criminal damage, even when the offender is known. This might be a sensible policy in terms of victim, witness or police time and resources but it helps to encourage a culture that crime is tolerated and sends out a message, particularly to younger offenders, that people can get away with crime. So measures such as fixed penalty notices, cannabis warnings and ASBOs were an attempt to send out a message that minor crime is not ignored and there are consequences of breaking the law, while not overburdening the enforcement agencies.

There may be circumstances in which diversion is desirable. It is argued that the stigmatising effects of public trial and punishment could propel some offenders into more crime. For young offenders particularly it may be desirable in the interests of rehabilitation to avoid prosecution and eventual punishment. Some offenders, such as the very young or the mentally disordered, may be considered to be not fully responsible for their own actions, making trial and punishment inappropriate.

In recent years a number of policies have encouraged diversion, although not, as we shall see, without some criticism. This chapter will focus on six main aspects of prosecution and diversion. It will first look at widening the use of the fixed penalty procedure and go on to examine the considerations surrounding the cautioning of offenders. It will then explore the decision to prosecute, and describe the agency responsible for the majority of prosecutions, the Crown Prosecution Service (CPS), and will outline the Code for Crown Prosecutors. It will go on to look at other agencies involved in prosecution and then at the treatment of one group for whom diversion is often seen as particularly appropriate: the mentally ill. The arrangements for these offenders are clearly distinguishable from others and we will outline the options available to the court and in the pre-trial stage to divert these offenders from being prosecuted.

7.1 Fixed penalties (FPN and PND)

Objective 1

Explain the different types of fixed penalties used instead of prosecution

The issuing of fixed penalty notices for low-level driving offences, primarily speeding, has been in place since the 1950s and is familiar to most people. Under this procedure, on detection of an offence, a fixed penalty notice (FPN) is issued to the suspect, who can either accept that they committed the offence and pay a fixed fine (together with the endorsement of penalty points on their licence) or can choose to go to court to dispute the case. The use of this procedure has been extended to a variety of broadly anti-social environmental offences such as littering, minor graffiti, minor pollution and noise disturbance, where notices can be issued by Police Community Support Officers (PCSOs) and local authorised agencies. The penalties can be imposed upon anyone over 10 years old. Abandoning a vehicle, contrary to the Refuse Disposal (Amenity) Act 1978, for example, now carries a penalty of £200. For some offences the amount can be fixed (within parameters set nationally) by local authorities. A fixed penalty is not a conviction, but unpaid sums can be pursued through the courts.

For more serious offences, the Penalty Notice for Disorder (PND) was introduced by the Criminal Justice and Police Act 2001 and can be issued, normally by the police to anyone over 18 years, but in some cases by PCSOs and other authorised agencies, for a variety of offences, including:

- theft from a shop of under £200;
- being drunk and disorderly in public;
- criminal damage up to £500;
- selling alcohol to under-age customers or to someone who is drunk;

- fireworks offences;
- some public order offences such as using threatening words or behaviour.

The penalty in July 2013 was either £60 or £90 depending on the offence. Under both the FPN and PND procedure, the recipient has the opportunity to accept liability and pay the fixed amount or request a court hearing. Failure to pay or to pay in time may result in a higher penalty or even imprisonment.

The mechanics of these two linked procedures demonstrate quite starkly the conflict between the models of criminal justice inherent in all diversionary procedures: the due process model with evidence being tested in judicial settings and the model based on bureaucratic efficiency. The formal, costly due process model has the risk that much crime is ignored because of the costs and time involved with adversarial justice, and this stands in contrast to a more pragmatic approach in which some action is taken without involving the courts and the full cost of adversarial justice. An argument could be made for a twin-track approach with adversarial process for the more serious crimes in contrast to immediate or instant administrative-style justice or diversion for lower-level crime.

The expansion of the fixed penalty procedure into what has hitherto been regarded as 'real crime' such as theft and criminal damage takes us to the examination of what had historically been the major focus of diversion from prosecution: the caution.

7.2 Cautioning

Objective 2

Outline the use cautioning as a form of diversion

Before looking at formal **cautions** given in lieu of trial and sentence, it is important to recognise that some cases are diverted from the system with no formal action being taken. Whereas an official caution is recorded and can be referred to on subsequent court appearances, cases which result in no further action (NFA), detected but not proceeded with (DNP) or an informal warning are not recorded. While precise numbers are not officially recorded, on the basis of research it has been estimated that as many as 25 per cent of known offenders are so dealt with (**Sanders 2002**).

No further action may be taken in a variety of situations. An individual officer may do nothing because the matter is too trivial and making an 'issue' of it could create further problems out of proportion to the incident. In other cases there may be a formal reason why the police cannot proceed with a prosecution: for example, where they cannot provide sufficient evidence for the court, or where the offender is too young. In other situations they may feel that no useful purpose will be served by taking matters any further, particularly where offenders are elderly or mentally ill.

No further action may also reflect the use by the police of what Sanders describes as speculative arrests, which might occur where the police arrest people to encourage them to give information (ibid.). Arrest may in effect be a strategy to assist further investigation and may not be intended to lead to prosecution.

The officer may, instead of doing nothing, give an immediate informal caution or warning. This might happen with trivial offences, such as where an officer observes young people riding bicycles on the pavement, and issues a few words of warning (**Evans and Wilkinson 1990**). This is only appropriate in less serious matters and is completely within the discretion of the officer. In some offences involving the maintenance of vehicles, an officer can issue a Notice to Rectify advising the motorist to correct the defect within a number of days, to avoid prosecution. Only if this is not done will prosecution result. A further option is the formal warning, a system which operates in some areas where a written warning is given in lieu of prosecution after the suspect has been reported for a possible offence. These alternatives are used for a variety of minor infringements – road traffic matters and very minor public order matters being the most common. Formal warnings for cannabis possession were introduced on a non-statutory basis in 2004.

The most significant alternative to prosecution is the simple (previously called 'formal') caution, which is used primarily for low-level first time offences, though more serious – even indictable – offences can be dealt with by a caution. The issue of a police caution is a regulated and recorded procedure whereby a potential defendant admits guilt and is formally warned by a senior police officer 'not to do it again'. Cautions are recorded at the local **Criminal Record Office**, and may be quoted in court in subsequent proceedings. They must also be disclosed to employers who ask about cautions. Originally cautions were especially used with young offenders, a process which was given statutory authority in the Children and Young Persons Act 1969. Further changes were made by the Crime and Disorder Act 1998 which introduced reprimands and warnings as the special form of cautioning for those under 18. This system was repealed by the Legal Aid, Sentencing and Punishment of Offenders (LASPO) Act in 2012 and replaced with a new youth caution which will be given in the same circumstances – i.e. to youths aged 17 and under who have committed a first-time minor offence and whom to take to court would not be in the public interest. Sections of the Act also provide that anyone given a youth caution must automatically be referred to an appropriate youth offending team, and places a duty on that youth offending team to consider whether the individual should be recommended for a rehabilitation programme. Since 2003, adult cautions can be accompanied by conditions with which the offender must comply, and these are further discussed below.

Cautions can be referred to in court, and, as they constitute a significant diversion from prosecution, the system is regulated. A number of guidelines have been issued, including the Attorney General's guidelines entitled *Criteria for Prosecution* issued in 1984, and Home Office Circular 14 in February 1985 which encouraged the greater use of cautioning. In 1990, Home Office Circular 59 was issued to promote national standards for cautioning. Home Office Circular 30 of 2005 refined the guidance given as a result of the introduction of the conditional caution, and sets out the process, criteria and consequences of the two types of caution. The Code for Crown Prosecutors also gives guidance on the use of cautioning. In some circumstances chief constables issue internal guidelines indicating which offences are appropriate for a caution. The most important prerequisite for a caution is that the offender accepts guilt. In order for a simple caution to be administered, the following conditions must be fulfilled:

- the offender must be 18 or over;
- there must be sufficient evidence to warrant a prosecution;

- the offender must 'clearly and reliably' admit guilt;
- the person being cautioned must consent to being cautioned after being warned that the caution may be cited in future court appearances, and should be given an opportunity to consider whether to accept one.

A number of criteria guide the decision of whether it is in the public interest to initiate a prosecution or to deal with the matter by caution, including the following:

- the nature and seriousness of the offence;
- the likely penalty if the offender was convicted by the court;
- the offender's age, personal circumstances and state of health;
- the offender's character and previous criminal history;
- the offender's attitude to the offence, including practical expressions of regret;
- the view of the victim.

The 2005 Circular refers to some of the benefits of a simple caution, in terms of benefit to the victim of having a recorded outcome, and to the police in increasing detection statistics as well as the fact that it can be cited in court appearances if the offender reoffends.

The cautioning rate is the number of cautions as a percentage of the totals of all those found guilty by the courts. Cautioning grew in use throughout the 1980s to over 300,000 offenders cautioned annually, with an average increase of 6 per cent per year from 1985 to 1992. After that the number fell and in 2002 a total of 225,400 offenders were cautioned but this had increased to 367,300 in 2007. Since then the use of cautioning has dropped quite dramatically, with a total of 337,600 offenders receiving a caution in 2008 followed by a fall with 100,000 fewer receiving a caution three years on in 2011 (see Figure 7.1). In particular the

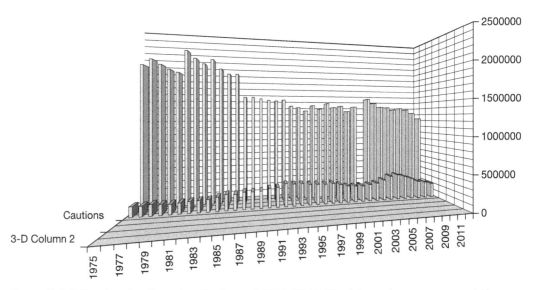

Figure 7.1 Offenders Cautioned or Sentenced 1975–2012. The blue columns represent those sentenced and the grey columns represent those cautioned.

Source: Criminal Statistics England and Wales

Table 7.1 Cautioning data 2002–2012 England and Wales

Type of offence	2002	2003	2004	2005	2006	2007
Violence against the person	21,900	27,600	34,400	46,800	57,200	54,400
Burglary	5,800	5,600	5,500	6,300	7,400	7,400
Theft and handling stolen goods	56,500	53,100	59,900	66,000	71,000	75,500
All offences (excluding motoring offences)	225,000	234,700	254,300	284,300	339,400	367,300

Type of offence	2008	2009	2010	2011	2012
Violence against the person	42,700	28,700	22,600	17,800	13,500
Burglary	5,800	4,600	3,600	3,400	2,700
Theft and handling stolen goods	65,000	63,000	50,000	44,300	36,200
All offences (excluding motoring offences)	337,600	301,700	250,600	235,000	205,700

Source: https://www.gov.uk/government/uploads/system/uploads/attachment_data/file/220090/criminal-justice-stats-sept-2012.pdf (Table Q2.3 on p. 25)

use of cautions for more serious offences such as violence against the person has become much less frequent, dropping from a high of 57,300 in 2006 to just 16,100 in 2011, while cautions for drug offences have gone up in the same period from 37,400 in 2008 to 42,700 in 2011. Younger offenders are more likely to be cautioned than older, with 80.9 per cent of first time juvenile entrants into the criminal justice system receiving a caution in 2011 whereas only 51.2 per cent of first time adult entrants to the criminal justice system receiving the same (*Criminal Justice Statistics Quarterly Update to December 2011*).

The 1990 standards were in part a response to the diversity in cautioning rates (see, for example, **Evans and Wilkinson 1990; Ashworth 1994a**). In 2011, most police forces had similar cautioning rates for indictable offences of between 23 and 35 per cent, with only a couple of outlying figures: Greater Manchester had the lowest rate at 19 per cent, and Warwickshire had the highest at 39 per cent (not including the British Transport Police rate of 99 per cent (*Criminal Statistics England and Wales 2011*).

This illustrates an element of discretion underlying these decisions: the Home Office Circulars referred to above are intended to increase consistency across police areas. For example, guidelines do not specify precisely what account needs to be taken of particular factors and the police may use the decision to caution or prosecute in a way that accords with their working rules. Thus officers may simply feel that some offenders deserve prosecution, and cautions may avoid unnecessary paperwork. Indeed, while cautions should only be given where there *is* sufficient evidence to prosecute, Sanders points to research indicating that some suspects were cautioned *because* there was insufficient evidence to prosecute – thus a caution can be used to clear up a case which might otherwise not have been prosecuted (**Sanders 2002**).

The exercise of discretion also raises issues of possible bias. Girls are more likely to be cautioned than boys. Ethnic minorities have been found to be cautioned less, which may reflect findings that ethnic minority suspects are more likely to contest a case – as seen above, a caution can be given only if guilt is admitted. In addition, there have been some indications that black juveniles are less likely to have cases referred to the multi-agency panels which exist for juveniles, a difference which remained even after admission of guilt was taken into account. This, speculate **Phillips and Bowling (2002)**, might reflect the more hostile attitudes pertaining between black youth and the police.

There is also some concern that cautioning may have a built-in class bias. Many of the criteria relating to offenders' circumstances may unintentionally advantage more socially skilled or better-off offenders or young people from middle-class homes. Ashworth indicates how the criterion concerning attitude to the offence may work in this way. This criterion includes consideration of whether the offender has made some practical demonstration of regret, such as an apology to a victim, or an offer to put matters right, for example by voluntary compensation (**Ashworth 1994a: 134–9**).

In addition, the regulatory agencies, such as HM Revenue and Customs or local authority consumer protection departments, which are responsible for the prosecution of offences involving white collar or business offenders, often, as will be seen in a later section, follow a policy of not prosecuting offenders and extensively use both informal and written cautions. Indeed these agencies regularly caution offenders on many occasions before a prosecution is considered, and the extent to which offenders have sought to rectify matters is part of this decision (see, for example, **Croall 2001; Ashworth 1994a**).

The LASPO Act 2012 gave authority to police officers to issue all cautions, both simple and conditional, rather than having to apply to the CPS for the latter type as was formerly the case. Cautions for juveniles must be given in the presence of an appropriate adult. Once a caution is given, that is usually the end of that matter.

However, it is possible for a private prosecution to be taken out against an offender who has been cautioned by the police. Thus, Mr Hayter instituted a private prosecution in Basildon against two youths who had assaulted his son. The police were of the view that a caution was the appropriate means of dealing with the matter, and both boys agreed after having legal advice. In the cautioning process, both were told that it did not prevent an aggrieved person bringing proceedings, and that is what Mr Hayter duly did. Although it was argued that the prosecution should not continue, the Queen's Bench Division of the High Court (QBD) decided that the case could continue (*Hayter* v. *L and Another*, 1998).

Conditional cautioning was introduced by the Criminal Justice Act 2003. This was recommended by both the Runciman Commission in 1993 and the Auld Review in 2001.

Conditional cautions were issued until 2014 by the CPS (LASPO 2012 allows the police to now issue conditional cautions)and were originally for adults aged 18 years or older. For those 10 to 17 years old a youth conditional caution became law in 2008. The conditional caution complements the simple or formal caution, which continues to be available as an alternative to prosecution. The purposes of the conditions are either rehabilitative or **reparative**, i.e. paying back for the harm done either to an individual victim or the community. For example, a drunk who steals a bottle of alcohol might be given a conditional caution requiring him to pay back the cost of the alcohol to the shop owner (reparative) and attend an alcohol dependency programme (rehabilitative). In some cases a restrictive condition might also be applied in addition to either a rehabilitative or reparative condition. Since the passing of the LASPO Act in 2012 conditional cautions given to foreign nationals without legal right to remain may also include a condition that they return to their home country and do not re-enter the UK for a specified period.

To give a conditional caution the same principles apply as with a regular caution although a prosecutor will make the decision, and must be satisfied that the public interest justifies a prosecution, that there is sufficient evidence on which to prosecute, and that the wider interest of suspect, victim or community is better served by a conditional caution.

If the offender accepts the conditional caution conditions but subsequently fails to meet the conditions, then they may be prosecuted for the original offence. If failure to comply means the offender is sent to court and convicted, the court will be informed at the time of sentencing that the offender had previously agreed to a conditional caution for this offence but had subsequently failed to meet the conditions.

Conditional cautions provide an opportunity for both a warning to be given and the offender to actually do something to show a change of heart, and for restrictions to be placed on the offender. The conditions will usually involve those cautioned making financial or other recompense to the victim or undertaking activities designed to help the offender change his offending behaviour.

The following requirements must be met before a conditional caution can be issued:

- the police or investigating officer must have evidence that the offender has committed an offence;
- there must be sufficient evidence to charge, and the prosecutor (not the police) must decide it is appropriate to caution;
- the offender must admit the offence (as with unconditional cautions);
- the offender must have the effect of the caution explained and, in particular, that failure to comply with the conditions may result in prosecution; and
- the offender must sign a document setting out the terms of the caution.

Thus the conditional caution is intended to be more proactive (by imposing restrictions) than the unconditional caution, while still removing many – usually first-time – offenders from the court process.

▶ Cautioning and young offenders

Cautioning was originally predominantly used in relation to young people as a means of diverting young offenders from the court system in the hope that they would behave better without the stigma of being labelled a criminal. Arguments critical of its use focused upon the problem of net widening, suggesting that the apparently more benign approach might be responsible for increasing the number of youngsters caught in the net of the criminal justice system. Other critics looked at the high proportion of crime committed by young offenders (**see Chapter 8**) to suggest that it was not an effective means to control delinquency.

These arguments about the use of cautioning with young offenders came under fire in 1996 in the Home Office document *Misspent Youth*, which provided evidence that pointed to the limited effectiveness of repeat cautioning, the problems of inconsistent usage and the fact that cautioning does not 'nip offending in the bud' (**Home Office 1997b, para 5.10**). The Crime and Disorder Act 1998 replaced the system of cautioning for young offenders from 1 June 2000 with 'reprimands' and '**final warnings**'. Under the Act, when an offence is committed by a young person, the police can take no action at all, or give a police reprimand, or give a final warning, or start a prosecution. Normally, for a first offence the police would decide upon one of the following:

- a reprimand if the offence was not very serious;
- a final warning if it was more serious;
- a decision to prosecute.

For a further offence, if a reprimand had already been given, a further reprimand could not be given and the young person would be given a final warning, or prosecuted. After any final warning the commission of a further offence was intended to automatically result in criminal proceedings unless two years had elapsed from the warning and the new offence was minor. However, this system was felt not to have enough impact on offending rates and too often further offences following a final warning were *not* resulting in criminal proceedings, hence this system being abolished by LASPO 2012.

As noted above, in the Criminal Justice and Immigration Act 2008 a conditional caution was introduced for children and young offenders aged 10 to 17. This is still effective but the LASPO Act made some amendments to the eligibility criteria for youth conditional cautions so that youths who have been previously convicted for other offences may still receive a conditional caution.

The rights of both defendants and victims are affected by cautions. As already noted, a caution can be given only following an admission of guilt. This raises the question of the extent to which defendants may be under pressure to admit guilt which they otherwise deny in order to avoid the stress of a court appearance. The low visibility of cautions raises concerns about how far defendants' rights are observed at this stage, especially since a caution may have a bearing on subsequent sentence.

There may also be a conflict between the benefits of diversion and the interest of victims. When offenders are cautioned, victims are deprived of the opportunity to obtain compensation (**Ashworth 1994a**). While some areas have provisions for offering mediation between offenders and victims as a form of diversion, this practice is by no means widespread (**see Chapter 14 for fuller discussion**).

Once the police have decided that a prosecution rather than any other form of action is appropriate, the papers are referred to the CPS for consideration.

7.3 Prosecution

Objective 3

Describe the system of prosecution in England Wales and the role of the Crown Prosecution Service

The vast majority of prosecutions are undertaken by the CPS, but a number of other agencies also have responsibility for undertaking criminal prosecutions. These include the agencies responsible for enforcing laws regulating many aspects of business, trade and commerce. Their work will be outlined following an examination of the CPS. Private bodies and individuals may also prosecute, but this accounts for only a very small number of prosecutions.

The process of prosecutions is formally started either following the arrest and charge of a suspect, or after a summons has been issued by a magistrates' court. The court issues a summons after receiving information from the police or other prosecuting bodies or from individuals about an alleged offence; this is referred to as 'laying an information' and is specific to procedure of prosecuting via the magistrates' court. This was replaced in 2011 by **requisitions** and written charges under the Criminal Justice Act 2003, under which system a public prosecutor may institute criminal proceedings by issuing a written postal charge and requisition. There are many more summonses issued than people arrested and charged (**see Table 9.5**). A large number of prosecutions for 'summary only' offences such as motoring offences are started this way.

The CJA 2003 introduced a new procedure requiring custody officers in police stations to seek advice from the CPS on the charge to be made. The charging decision on all but the most minor offences now rests with the prosecutor, and prosecutors therefore 'moved into police stations' to be able to give advice.

The following options are available when dealing with an arrested person:

- to charge and bail;
- to charge and keep in custody until the next court sitting;
- to release without charge or bail, bringing the proceedings to an end unless new evidence comes to light;
- to release without charge on bail pending further investigations.

▶ The Crown Prosecution Service

Before the creation of the CPS in 1985, the police and the Director of Public Prosecutions (DPP) were responsible for prosecution. The office of the DPP was set up by the Prosecution of Offences Act 1879, and its task was to institute, undertake or carry on criminal proceedings, and to give advice and assistance to chief officers of police and other persons responsible for the prosecution of offences. The DPP was responsible for prosecuting cases of murder, along with those involving national security, public figures and police officers.

The police were responsible for the prosecution of routine offences in magistrates' courts, and there were 43 prosecution authorities in England and Wales. They were advised by solicitors, who were either employed or consulted by them, and who conducted more complex cases in the magistrates' courts. Cases in Crown Courts were conducted by barristers on behalf of the police.

The police were therefore both investigators and prosecutors, a dual role which caused considerable concern. It was argued, for example, that the crime control function of investigation could clash with the interests of due process in ensuring that prosecutions be undertaken only on the basis of sufficient evidence. The potential conflict was noted by Royal Commissions in 1929 and 1962 and the Royal Commission on Criminal Procedure, known as the Phillips Commission, which was set up in 1978 and reported in 1981.

It pointed out that there was no uniform system of prosecution in England and Wales. It argued that a new prosecuting agency would encourage greater consistency in approach to prosecution. It stressed that the roles of investigating crime, collecting evidence and arresting suspects were likely to interfere with the impartial review of a case and decisions about whether prosecution was necessary or likely to be successful. The dual responsibility for policing and prosecution could lead to the abuse of the rights of the arrested person by the police, born out of an anxiety to convict those whom the police believed were guilty.

There were also concerns from an efficiency viewpoint about the number of weak cases, where the evidence was insufficient to lead to a conviction, being taken to court and then thrown out as a result of a judge-directed acquittal, which was both costly and time consuming.

Following a debate in the House of Commons and the Bonan Working Party whose report was published in August 1983, a White Paper proposed the setting up of a Crown Prosecution Service. The Prosecution of Offences Act 1985 established the CPS and specified its functions, which included taking over the conduct of all criminal proceedings instituted by the police. The introduction of the CPS was closely linked with the Police and Criminal Evidence Act 1984 (PACE) (**as seen in Chapter 6**).

There was much debate over whether the service should be a centralised national service or a local one, or combine elements of both. In the end a national service was created: the CPS therefore represents a single independent and nationwide authority for England and Wales. It is independent of the police and has the power to discontinue prosecutions. Unlike prosecution agencies in other jurisdictions it has no powers to institute proceedings or to direct the police to carry out any further investigations. Its introduction had substantial constitutional significance for a number of reasons. For the first time there was a single state prosecuting authority charged with making decisions of a quasi-judicial nature which could ultimately affect the rights and liberties of the individual. It also created a new legal interest group directly linked to government. These lawyers, although civil servants, were expected to be independent of government control, although little was put in place to guarantee this, save the *Code for Crown Prosecutors* and the existing *Codes of Professional Conduct for the Legal Professions*.

The introduction of the CPS as a body with a duty to review cases at every stage of a prosecution inevitably caused problems. Some of these sprang from initial rivalry between the police and the CPS and misunderstandings about their respective roles. The necessary bureaucratic changes also produced problems – major delays followed changes in the system for transmitting files to court and prioritising cases. The Royal Commission on Criminal Justice in 1993 commented that the service was hastily conceived and inadequately resourced. A report in 1990 by the Public Accounts Committee on a Review of the Crown Prosecution Service

(**House of Commons 1990**) found that estimates of how much the system would cost were initially too low and that many problems were caused by understaffing and inadequate resources.

The powers of the CPS to discontinue cases also caused friction with the police and frustration on the part of victims and courts. As we shall see below, the rate of cases discontinued remains a cause for concern (even within the CPS itself), although one of the roles of the CPS was to reduce the number of trials aborted on evidential grounds. The recent closer working of the CPS and police in relation to the transfer of the charging function to the CPS has resulted in a concern that to erode the distinction between the arrest and prosecution decision might lessen the independent review function of the CPS; but on the other hand it is argued that the CPS should be seen as a 'legal resource that investigators need' for more effective decision making on charging offenders (**Starmer 2009**).

▶ The organisation and functions of the Crown Prosecution Service

In England and Wales the CPS, with total expenditure in the year 2013/4 of £559 million, has become the main agency responsible for the prosecution of offenders. It started in 1986 as a result of the Prosecution of Offences Act 1985, and its establishment was part of a complete reform of the laws governing police investigation (PACE 1984) and the prosecution of offences (**see Chapter 6**).

Between 2010 and 2014 it reduced its full-time equivalent staffing numbers from 8,304 to 6,204. The newly reduced number includes 2,209 prosecutors and 3,614 paralegals and administrators. In 2013/14 they made 304,982 pre-charge decisions, 3,727 out of court disposals and prosecuted 640,657 cases in the magistrates' courts and in the Crown Court. They are responsible for carrying out the major tasks of the CPS, which are as follows:

- to review cases to determine whether they should continue or be discontinued;
- to determine who is eligible for conditional cautions and to set the conditions;
- to determine the criminal charge in individual cases;
- to advise the police on evidence;
- to establish charging standards;
- to liaise with barristers who represent the prosecution in the Crown Court;
- to present cases in the magistrates' courts at all pre-trial and trial stages;
- to provide information for witnesses and victims.

The CPS's role as civil servants and Crown employees is tempered by the *Code for Crown Prosecutors* and by their professional ethics as lawyers, with a primary duty to the court. The head of the CPS is the Director of Public Prosecutions (DPP). Sir Ken Macdonald QC was appointed DPP in November 2003 and was succeeded by Keir Starmer QC in 2008. In 2013 Alison Saunders became the DPP.

The work of the CPS is divided into 13 different geographical areas. Between 1986 and 1998 there have been three reorganisations of the CPS. These have sought to create a balance between areas so that they have similar case loads while, where possible, having boundaries that are coterminous with other agencies, especially the police.

The Phillips Commission (1978–81) originally conceived the CPS as a locally accountable organisation and recommended dividing the country into 43 areas reflecting the 43 police force areas. However, when introduced in 1986, the CPS was organised into 31 areas, in an attempt to equalise workloads. In 1992, reorganisation to achieve a more cohesive national structure led to these being re-divided into 13 areas.

In April 1997, the Labour Party produced a policy document, *The Case for the Prosecution*, suggesting another reorganisation into 42 areas, each with a Chief Crown Prosecutor, with one to cover the entire area of the Metropolitan and City of London forces. Outside of London the boundaries are the same as for the police. The document underlined the need for an independent service but with opportunity for closer liaison with the police. After the Labour Party was elected, the new Attorney General announced that this policy statement would be put in force. However in June 1997, the Glidewell Review of the CPS was initiated with wide-ranging terms of reference covering the organisation and structure of the CPS, with a view to enhancing the efficient prosecution of crime within existing resources. Specific questions were re-examined in connection with falling conviction rates, downgrading of charges and CPS relations with the police. The report, in 1998, recommended the boundary and administrative reforms outlined above.

Once an accused person has been charged, summoned or a requisition issued the files are forwarded to the appropriate branch of the CPS which deals with cases from the police station where the offence originates. On receipt of these files, the CPS is under a duty to review the case in accordance with two criteria involved in the decision to prosecute. These two criteria, which will be discussed in detail below, are (a) that there is sufficient evidence to continue the case, and (b) that it is in the public interest to continue.

When the accused is first brought to the magistrates' court in custody, the CPS normally receive the files on the morning of the first hearing and are expected to represent the prosecution on adjournments and applications for bail. Once files are received, the CPS is entirely responsible for the conduct of the case. This includes deciding which charges should be proceeded with, what evidence is relevant and admissible and whether or not it is sufficient – in effect, whether there is a reasonable prospect of success. It also includes assessing whether or not it is in the public interest to continue with the prosecution and, if so, ensuring that the case is prepared and ready for trial.

By 1998, as mentioned above, the CPS was waiting to implement the range of reform proposals emanating from the New Labour Government, incorporating the ideas from the Glidewell Review (1997/8) and the Narey Report on the *Review of Delay in the Criminal Justice System* (**Home Office 1997c**). The Narey report made sweeping recommendations for all stages of the criminal justice system and may reflect a more systems-based approach to criminal justice involving greater cooperation and liaison between agencies. The recommendations affecting the CPS included the following:

- an enhanced role for CPS staff without legal qualifications to review files and to present non-contested cases in the magistrates' courts;

- an end to the discontinuance of cases on the public interest ground that it considers the case as not serious;
- greater local autonomy;
- closer cooperation with the police on the preparation of prosecution files to reduce delay – this includes a permanent CPS presence in police administrative support units with the aim of prosecuting, as soon as possible after the charge, those cases where a guilty plea is likely;
- closer liaison with the courts and improved communications between the CPS and the magistrates' courts through daily telephone contacts on hearings listed for the next day.

The use of non-legally qualified staff (**Designated Case Workers** renamed **Associate Prosecutors** in 2008) to take over some of the duties of legally qualified staff was made possible by the Crime and Disorder Act 1998. It allowed non-lawyers to review cases with regard to decisions whether to continue prosecution and also allowed a right of audience to present criminal proceedings in magistrates' courts, although they are not allowed to represent the prosecution at the trial stage. They now therefore have the right to conduct much more of the pre-trial stages in the magistrates' court such as hearings regarding bail, including since 2006 contested bail hearings, and some work in the Youth Court. In 2006–7, Designated Case Workers conducted 14.7 per cent of magistrates' courts sessions. Associate Prosecutors may only deal with contested trials for summary and non-imprisonable offences.

7.4 The Code for Crown Prosecutors

Objective 4

Show the way that the Code for Crown Prosecutors is used in determining whether to prosecute an offender or not

The Code for Crown Prosecutors is a public statement of the guidelines to be applied to the decision on whether to prosecute an offender. In June 1994, the Code was revised to clarify it. The fourth edition of the Code, taking account of the Human Rights Act 1998, was issued in 2000 and the fifth in November 2004, dealing with the CJA 2003. In January 2009, a public consultation on the proposed sixth edition was launched. The current seventh edition was issued in 2013.

Two statements explain the CPS approach.

> . . . One of the most important tasks of the CPS is its review function. This means that we consider the evidence supplied by the police, and any other relevant information, and make a decision . . . in accordance with . . . the Code . . . At all times, we exercise an independent judgement about the case presented, on the basis of the tests set out in the Code . . .

> The decision to prosecute . . . is a serious step. Fair and effective prosecution is essential to the maintenance of law and order . . . a prosecution has serious implications for all involved – the victim, a witness and a defendant. The Crown Prosecution Service applies the Code . . . so that it can make fair and consistent decisions about prosecutions.
>
> (CPS Annual Report 1993/4: 6)

The Code is the cornerstone of the CPS's review and decision-making role and embodies the values and principles of the CPS. First issued under s 10 of the Prosecution of Offences Act 1985, it restates principles concerning the fairness, objectivity and independence of the CPS, and gives guidance about cautions, charges, mode of trial, acceptance of guilty pleas and restarting prosecutions which have been abandoned. The 2004 Code recognises the role of the CPS in post-conviction matters and in conditional cautions. The bulk of the Code is concerned with the two tests involved in the decision to prosecute: **evidential sufficiency**; and **public interest**.

There is however, a third, interim test called the *threshold test*, which is used when prosecutors are making a decision to charge pending obtaining of evidence upon which the Full Code Test is applied. The threshold test means that the prosecutor has to decide whether there is at least a reasonable suspicion that the suspect has committed a crime and that it is in the public interest to charge them. This test is a response to the limitations on the length of time that an individual may be detained pending charge. The Full Code Test must still be applied as soon as practicable thereafter.

The evidential sufficiency test is applied first; if the case does not pass this test, no matter how serious, important, or publicly notorious, it will not go ahead. Only if the case passes the evidence test will the second test, public interest, be applied.

The purpose of the evidential test is twofold. First, on a financial and practical basis, there is no point in proceeding with a case which will inevitably be thrown out by the court because there is not enough evidence. To proceed in such cases would be very wasteful of limited resources. Second, it follows the general principle underpinning the adversarial justice system, that convictions should only be based on a high level of proof based on evidence (standard of proof), and that the duty of providing sufficient evidence is always on the prosecution (burden of proof). Some have argued that in certain cases it is important to air the matter in the public domain – even if it is doomed to failure through lack of admissible evidence, because of public interest in the case and speculation about the effectiveness of the investigation and rumours of a cover-up or police collusion, such as in the Stephen Lawrence murder case.

▶ Evidential test

The CPS must be satisfied that there is a 'realistic prospect of conviction' on the available evidence. The test must be applied in respect of each defendant and each charge. A realistic prospect of conviction means that – in the view of the CPS – the magistrates or a jury, properly advised on the law, are more likely than not to convict. This involves considering the availability, admissibility and reliability of evidence. In reaching a view, the CPS must consider whether any of the available evidence is admissible and reliable.

In considering admissibility the CPS will consider whether the evidence:

- is likely to be excluded by the judge because it has been illegally obtained – for example, by breaches of PACE and its Codes;
- is confession evidence likely to be excluded because of a breach of PACE (s 76) where the confession has been obtained by improper means;
- emanates from witnesses who are legally incompetent (cannot give evidence); who are unwilling and cannot be compelled to give evidence; or who are children, to whom special rules and considerations apply.

With regard to reliability, the CPS will consider the following:

- the defendant's age, understanding and intelligence in considering any confession;
- whether a defendant's explanation is credible as a whole;
- whether the witness's credibility is affected by background matters;
- if identification evidence is involved, whether the evidence is strong enough, bearing in mind the special difficulties with identification evidence.

▶ Public interest test

This refers to criteria by which the CPS may, even after satisfying the evidential sufficiency criteria, decide not to proceed with a case. The use of the phrase 'public interest' is somewhat misleading as what is deemed to be in the public interest involves no consultation with the public, but relates to a list of questions set out in the Code. Why this was called the public interest criterion is difficult to discern. Until the revision of the Code for Crown Prosecutors (CCP) was published in June 1994, the criteria indicated a series of points which favoured dropping the case against a defendant; the public benefit being to save money. It assumed that only certain cases needed to go forward for the public interest to be served. This assumption generated concern from victims and the public. Lord Shawcross, a former Attorney General, is quoted to justify this criterion, although it must be queried, if for no other reason than consistency, why Shawcross's view should still be regarded as relevant today:

> ... It has never been the rule in this Country – I hope it never will be – that suspected criminal offences must automatically be the subject of prosecution. Indeed the very first Regulations under which the Director of Public Prosecutions worked provided that he should ... prosecute 'wherever it appears that the offence or the circumstances of its commission is or are of such a character that a prosecution in respect thereof is required in the public interest'. That is still the dominant consideration.
>
> (Shawcross 1951)

Prosecutor Code: 7th edition published in 2013

Public interest: questions asked by the CPS

Section 4.12 Prosecutors should consider each of the following questions:

1. **How serious is the offence committed?**

   The more serious the offence, the more likely it is that a prosecution is required.

   When deciding the level of seriousness of the offence committed, prosecutors should include among the factors for consideration the suspect's culpability and the harm to the victim.

2. **What is the level of culpability of the suspect?**

   Culpability is likely to be determined by the suspect's level of involvement; the extent to which the offending was premeditated and/or planned; whether they have previous criminal convictions and/or out-of-court disposals and any offending while on bail; or while subject to a court order; whether the offending was or is likely to be continued, repeated or escalated; and the suspect's age or maturity.

   Prosecutors should also have regard when considering culpability as to whether the suspect is, or was at the time of the offence, suffering from any significant mental or physical ill health as in some circumstances this may mean that it is less likely that a prosecution is required. However, prosecutors will also need to consider how serious the offence was, whether it is likely to be repeated and the need to safeguard the public or those providing care to such persons.

3. **What are the circumstances of and the harm caused to the victim?**

   The circumstances of the victim are highly relevant. The greater the vulnerability of the victim, the more likely it is that a prosecution is required. This includes where a position of trust or authority exists between the suspect and victim.

   A prosecution is also more likely if the offence has been committed against a victim who was at the time a person serving the public.

Prosecutors must also have regard to whether the offence was motivated by any form of discrimination against the victim's ethnic or national origin, gender, disability, age, religion or belief, sexual orientation or gender identity; or the suspect demonstrated hostility towards the victim based on any of those characteristics. The presence of any such motivation or hostility will mean that it is more likely that prosecution is required.

In deciding whether a prosecution is required in the public interest, prosecutors should take into account the views expressed by the victim about the impact that the offence has had. In appropriate cases, this may also include the views of the victim's family.

Prosecutors also need to consider if a prosecution is likely to have an adverse effect on the victim's physical or mental health, always bearing in mind the seriousness of the offence. If there is evidence that prosecution is likely to have an adverse impact on the victim's health it may make a prosecution less likely, taking into account the victim's views.

However, the CPS does not act for victims or their families in the same way as solicitors act for their clients, and prosecutors must form an overall view of the public interest.

4. **Was the suspect under the age of 18 at the time of the offence?**

   The criminal justice system treats children and young people differently from adults and significant weight must be attached to the age of the suspect if they are a child or young person under 18. The best interests and welfare of the child or young person must be considered including whether a prosecution is likely to have an adverse impact on his or her future prospects that is disproportionate to the seriousness of the offending. Prosecutors must have regard to the principal aim of the youth justice system which is to prevent offending by children and young people. Prosecutors must also have regard to the obligations arising under the United Nations 1989 Convention on the Rights of the Child.

As a starting point, the younger the suspect, the less likely it is that a prosecution is required.

However, there may be circumstances which mean that notwithstanding the fact that the suspect is under 18, a prosecution is in the public interest. These include where the offence committed is serious, where the suspect's past record suggests that there are no suitable alternatives to prosecution, or where the absence of an admission means that out-of-court disposals which might have addressed the offending behaviour are not available.

5. **What is the impact on the community?**

The greater the impact of the offending on the community, the more likely it is that a prosecution is required. In considering this question, prosecutors should have regard to how community is an inclusive term and is not restricted to communities defined by location.

6. **Is prosecution a proportionate response?**

Prosecutors should also consider whether prosecution is proportionate to the likely outcome, and in so doing the following may be relevant to the case under consideration:

- The cost to the CPS prosecution service and the wider criminal justice system, especially where it could be regarded as excessive when weighed against any likely penalty (Prosecutors should not decide the public interest on the basis of this factor alone. It is essential that regard is also given to the public interest factors identified when considering the other questions, but cost is a relevant factor when making an overall assessment of the public interest).

- Cases should be capable of being prosecuted in a way that is consistent with principles of effective case management. For example, in a case involving multiple suspects, prosecution might be reserved for the key main participants in order to avoid excessively long and complex proceedings.

7. **Do sources of information require protecting?**

In cases where public interest immunity does not apply, special care should be taken when proceeding with a prosecution where details may need to be made public that could harm sources of information, international relations or national security. It is essential that such cases are kept under continuing review.

Since the publication of the 1994 edition, the CPS Code provides for a more balanced public interest test based on a series of questions. As a general rule more serious cases are less likely to be discontinued but the criteria must be applied in each case. The factors for and against prosecution must be weighed carefully. It is in this context that the greatest discretion lies, and where most concern or confusion is caused. Thus, it is stated that the factors for and against prosecution are not exhaustive, must be considered where appropriate, and that all factors do not apply in all cases. Prosecutors are specifically expected to consider the interests of the victim, of young offenders, the possibility of a police caution, and guidelines for dealing with mentally disordered offenders.

Particular reference is made in the Code to young offenders. While the CPS must consider the interests of the youth when deciding whether to prosecute, the Code takes account of the fact that cases involving young offenders will usually be referred to the CPS only after out-of-court disposals have been given, unless the case is serious. Thus the public interest test is already usually met in youth cases.

The criteria used by the CPS are broadly similar to those used in sentencing. In other words, the offences which will be perceived as less serious by a court, thus attracting the lowest sentence, are unlikely to be prosecuted at all. This may have a number of implications for the criminal justice system. First, the 'bottom layer' of offences will be removed, with the possible consequent downgrading of remaining incidents. Second, the CPS is applying a quasi-judicial function, 'second-guessing' possible sentences. Third, the public interest in the denunciatory effect of bringing a range of offences to court is weakened. Fourth, the danger of ignoring minor breaches of societal rules is that it might have an impact on the level of civic awareness of appropriate civic conduct in general, and might weaken the wisdom of the rule that if you take care of the moral pennies the moral pounds take care of themselves.

The Code also sets out guidelines in relation to what charges should be made – for example, which offences a defendant should be charged with. This can on occasion cause disquiet, where, for instance, it appears that a defendant is being charged with a lesser offence than that merited by the facts of the incident. Charges should therefore be chosen, according to the Code, to reflect the seriousness of the offence, and to enable the case to be presented in a straightforward way.

In August 1994, the first charging standards were published, resulting from cooperation between the CPS and police to encourage consistency and understanding between the two agencies and those dealing with the courts. The first standards related to an area where most confusion and inconsistency is likely – that of assaults:

- Common assault will be the appropriate charge where the injuries include no more than grazes, scratches, abrasions, bruises, swellings, black eye, or superficial cuts.

- Assault occasioning actual bodily harm (ABH) will be appropriate where there is loss of, or a broken tooth, temporary loss of sensory functions, extensive bruising, displaced broken nose, minor fractures, minor cuts, or psychiatric injury more than fear.

- Examples of grievous bodily harm (GBH) are injury resulting in broken limbs, permanent disability, or more than minor, permanent visible disfigurement.

It should be emphasised that these charging standards are statements of prosecution practice, not of legal definition, and the aim of publishing them has been to foster a greater consistency of approach between agencies and areas. By 1998, further charging standards had been issued in relation to driving and public order offences (including football offences and drunk and disorderly behaviour). The process has been further enhanced since 2006 as the CPS became responsible for deciding the charge in most cases under a process referred to as statutory charging. This has been associated with greater detail being provided by means of what is called Director's (i.e. DPP's) Guidance to the 42 police and CPS areas to ensure consistency. Additionally an out-of-hours telephone service (CPS Direct: presumably modelled on the former NHS Direct) has been made available to the police to support evening and weekend decision making on charges.

General practice guidance from the CPS on charging advises that charges should:

- accurately reflect the involvement and responsibility of the accused;
- enable clear and simple presentation of cases with several accused;

- not be overloaded (prosecutors should not make large numbers of charges in order to encourage a guilty plea to some) nor be set 'too high' in order to encourage a guilty plea to a lesser offence.

Specific and detailed guidance on charging now covers theft, fraud, sexual and firearms offences among others, and incorporates a full range of considerations to be taken account of, including advice, for example, as to when theft or robbery should be charged.

▶ The work of the Crown Prosecution Service

The following data gives a summary of key facts about the workload of the CPS in 2013/14 in the magistrates' courts and the Crown Court:

CPS workload

CPS workload in the magistrates' courts 2013/14

- 304,982 pre-charge decisions
- 640,657 prosecutions by CPS completed in the magistrates' court

The following cases did not result in conviction:

- 62,200 (9.7%) were discontinued (continuing an overall declining trend of discontinuances)
- 9,698 (1.5%) could not proceed and resulted in the issue of a bench warrant for the arrest of the defendant, or were closed where the defendant had died, or adjourned indefinitely
- 313 (0.05%) defendants discharged at committals (i.e. in indictable cases needing committal to the Crown Court, the committal was not 'successful')
- 1,450 (0.2%) resulted in a discharge because there was no case to answer (i.e. the magistrates held there was insufficient evidence and thus the defendant was found not guilty)
- 17,975 (2.8%) of the cases resulted in a not guilty verdict after all the evidence had been heard

The following cases resulted in convictions:

- 58,169 (9.1%) cases were proved in the absence of the defendant (this procedure is only available for minor, mostly motoring offences and involves the prosecution proving their case, but the defendant choosing not to or failing to defend the case)
- 462,733 (72.2%) resulted in guilty pleas by the defendant
- 28,119 (4.4%) resulted in conviction after trial

CPS workload: cases completed in the Crown Court in 2013/14

- 94,617 prosecuted by CPS of which:
  - 76,685 defendants were convicted
  - 68,937 (72.9%) after pleading guilty
  - 7,748 (8.2%) being found guilty by a jury after a trial

17,042 were acquitted

- 5,599 after a trial
- 627 on the direction of the judge, without the jury being involved, usually because of a problem during a trial with the evidence
- 10,816 (11.4%) were judge ordered acquittals after the prosecution offered no evidence
- CPS dealt with 10,358 appeals to the Crown Court after hearing in the magistrates' courts
- There were 19,894 committals by the magistrates of triable either way offences to the Crown Court for sentence for greater punishment than the magistrates' court could impose

(CPS *Annual Report 2013/14*)

In assessing the effectiveness or otherwise of the CPS, we need to consider its working relationship with the police. As we have seen, the police also consider the sufficiency of evidence and make decisions on whether to take any further action or to caution. In theory, therefore, the police should initially have sifted out cases which do not merit prosecution. Therefore, as Ashworth points out in relation to discontinuances on public interest grounds, these could either be interpreted as 'police failures' or 'CPS successes' (**Ashworth 1994a: 182**). It could also reflect changes in circumstances and availability of witnesses and evidence.

Thus to understand the developing relationship between the police, CPS and the courts we must recognise that:

> . . . prosecution decisions are taken not in a laboratory atmosphere but in a working context that brings the CPS into contact with the police, with victims, and with magistrates . . . any attempt to explain practical decision making must take account of the organisational and operational contexts in which the decisions tend to be made.
>
> (Ashworth 1994a: 193)

The evidential sufficiency criteria essentially ask the CPS to predict the likely outcome of a case. This may change, however, as a case proceeds because vital witnesses may refuse to give evidence, or new evidence may come to light. The CPS will not always know in advance what the defence is likely to be except in the Crown Court, where **disclosure** is required. Weak evidence may not, however, lead to a case being dropped, especially where defendants indicate at an early stage that they intend to plead guilty. Factors such as the attitude of local courts may also affect prosecution decisions in that prosecutors may second-guess the likely attitude of the courts. This can produce local variations. The local CPS builds up a working relationship with the local police, who in turn may come to anticipate the decision of the prosecutor. Figures on discontinuances, therefore, may reflect the operation of these informal factors. The statistics on the number of cases that are dropped or subsequently acquitted could be taken to indicate a failure of the review process. But the reasons why cases are dropped may not, as seen above, be evident at the start of a case, and may emerge only during the trial.

Rising numbers of cases discontinued in the early 1990s raised questions about the benefits of prosecution and diversion. In 1993, for example, a total of 193,000 cases were discontinued. If these figures are taken alongside the large numbers of cautions and the under-reporting of crime it means that fewer and fewer cases are being taken to court. This could be seen as reducing any deterrent, denunciatory or crime control potential of the criminal justice system. In addition, defendants who are repeatedly asked to attend court and then told that the case has been dropped may have a valid grievance: not least those who wished to clear their name positively in court. Such defendants do have the right to seek repayment of costs incurred by them – for many, this, combined with the relief of having the case dropped, is sufficient. Studies show that the CPS discontinues cases on public interest grounds as well as on the grounds of evidential insufficiency. This was seen in a survey of discontinued cases carried out by the CPS (CPS Survey, January 1994) of 11,000 cases in November 1993. Prosecutors across the country were asked to record the reasons for discontinuance under four main headings: insufficient evidence, public interest, prosecution unable to proceed, and defendant producing documents in court for the first time. Forty-three per cent of cases dropped or discontinued were through the application of the 'insufficient evidence' criteria and 31 per cent through the application of the 'public interest' criteria. Forty-one per cent of all cases discontinued during the month of the survey were minor motoring offences. The following box summarises the main reasons why cases were discontinued.

Results of CPS Discontinuance Survey (1993)

Insufficient evidence (43%)

- 11% of the cases discontinued related to insufficient evidence about the identity of the accused – for example, a witness identified a man she said she had seen committing a burglary, but she had seen him in poor lighting and had not had a good view of him (there was no other evidence to link the man with the offence)
- 13% of the cases dropped due to insufficient evidence were dropped because there was a legal element missing – for example, a defendant was charged with theft of a car radio cassette even though there was no evidence that it was stolen property
- 19% of the cases had an essential legal element missing

Prosecution unable to proceed (17%)

- 13% were because of a missing witness
- 2% related to offences already taken into consideration
- 2% case not ready and adjournments refused

Defendants produced driving documents in court for the first time (9%)

Public interest (31%)

- 9% were convicted or sentenced on other matters
- 6% a nominal penalty was anticipated
- 4% staleness
- 3% complainants' attitude
- 2% defendant's age
- 1% defendant mentally ill
- 6% other

(Compiled from *CPS Annual Report 1993/4*: 15–16)

The most common single factor leading to discontinuance on public interest grounds was that the defendant had been convicted or sentenced for other offences, and in a further 6 per cent the court was expected to impose only a nominal penalty, such as an absolute discharge. An example of staleness was a case where a defendant was summoned for having no driving licence, test certificate or insurance. The CPS did not receive the papers until almost 33 months after the offences were committed. Examples of discontinuance using other criteria include that of a woman charged with being drunk and disorderly and subsequently admitted to a psychiatric hospital. Consistent with the spirit of the Home

Table 7.2 Rate of discontinuances

Year	Number of discontinuances	As percentage of magistrates' courts case outcomes (%)
2003–4	175,779	13.8
2004–5	146,261	12.5
2005–6	126,047	11.8
2006–7	107,651	10.9
2007–8	95,513	9.9
2008–9	80,661	8.7
2009–10	78,901	9.0
2010–11	80,911	9.6
2011–12	75,579	9.6
2012–13	68,092	9.6
2013–14	62,200	9.7

Source: Compiled from Crown Prosecution Service, *Annual Report and Accounts* (for the period April 2003–March 2014)

Office Circular on Provision for Mentally Disordered Offenders the CPS decided that the wider public interest did not demand a prosecution. In another case, an 82-year-old motorist collided with a parked car without causing injury. The motorist surrendered his licence to the Driver and Vehicle Licensing Agency so the CPS decided that it was no longer necessary to prosecute. The CPS's responsibility for charging since the CJA 2003 has further reduced the discontinuance rates, and the CPS now sets an annual target to reduce the rate. The rate of discontinuances over the last few years has been in the 9.6 to 9.7% range (see Table 7.2).

Other cases are not proceeded with or fail because of the non-attendance of witnesses. William and Valerie Wicks were jailed in November 1994 for four weeks for contempt of court after refusing to give evidence against a person charged with causing grievous bodily harm to Mr Wicks. The attack on Mr Wicks was witnessed by his wife (*Daily Telegraph*, 19 November 1994). In another case an expert witness went on holiday instead of giving evidence at a rape trial. The defendant was acquitted, and Dr Kusum Agrawal (the police doctor involved) was fined £3,000 by an Old Bailey judge (*The Times*, 21 January 1995).

A final issue to be raised is what role victims can or should play in the prosecution process. Recent attention to the victim in the criminal justice process lay behind the criterion that victims' interests should play a part and that victims' views are considered at varying stages of the process (**see Chapter 3**). But to what extent does this conflict with other criteria? What, if any, role should victims play? If the victim does not wish to proceed with a case, and is unwilling to give evidence, then the prosecution may be unsuccessful. Thus, the victim's role in the provision of evidence may be crucial, as in the Wicks case referred to above. In addition, as with cautions, a failure to prosecute may deprive the victim of compensation, although some diversionary schemes provide for mediation between victim and offender (**see Chapter 14**). Any further role for the victim is problematic as it could be argued that to take the victim's attitude into account might conflict with any public interest there may be in prosecuting the offender to ensure that they are duly punished.

7.5 Private prosecutions and other prosecuting agencies

Objective 5

Describe what is meant by private prosecutions and be able to name other prosecuting agencies

Private prosecutions may be started by, for example, department stores to deal with shoplifting on their premises, or individuals who feel that an issue should be dealt with by the courts, as when, in January 1998, 72-year-old Roy Edney of Harrow started proceedings against Bath rugby player Kevin Yates, alleging that he had bitten off a lump of skin from another player's ear during a match. Sometimes aggrieved victims and their families take up a prosecution, as with the Hayter case cited above and with the murder of Steven Lawrence, because they feel that the police or the CPS have taken insufficient action. The right to start a private prosecution is subject to limitations:

- the magistrates may refuse to issue proceedings;
- the Attorney General can stop what are called 'vexatious litigants' from bringing cases;
- the DPP has a power to take over prosecutions and end them.

▶ Prosecution by regulatory agencies

While the CPS is responsible for the majority of prosecutions (75 per cent in the magistrates' court and 95 per cent in the Crown Court), many other agencies also undertake criminal prosecutions. These include: local authority departments responsible for consumer protection and environmental health; the Health and Safety Executive; agencies responsible for pollution control; Driver and Vehicle Licensing Authority (DVLA) for the non-payment of motor vehicle tax; and the TV Licensing Records Office for non-payment of a TV licence. The RSPCA may prosecute those accused of neglecting or mistreating animals; and the National Society for the Prevention of Cruelty to Children may do the same with regard to the maltreatment of children. The Department for Work and Pensions (DWP) also prosecutes in relation to social security frauds. General taxation matters are the responsibility of the Revenue and Customs department, and many more government departments are responsible for investigating frauds and other offences involving business, trade and financial services. These include the Serious Fraud Office and the Department for Business, Innovation and Skills (BIS). Many of these offences are not included in the criminal statistics, and statistics on how many offences are prosecuted in relation to known offences are not generally available, although some can be found on the websites of the agencies concerned along with details of prosecutions (**see Chapter 2**). Research into these agencies indicates that they prosecute only a very small proportion of known offenders. It has already been seen that they use the caution extensively and prosecution is often seen as a last resort (see, e.g., **Croall 2001**).

It is interesting to examine briefly how these agencies proceed, as their attitude to prosecution is very different. In his study of the origins of the Factory Inspectorate, established by the Factory Act 1833, which regulated the labour of children and young persons in mills and factories, W G Carson made the following observation:

> ...We...need to understand the social origins of an enforcement agency which, from its very inception, has not seen itself as being busy about the business of catching criminals. In adopting this historically explicable stance, the Factory Inspectorate has played its own inadvertent part in perpetuating a collective representation which portrays crime as being concentrated in circumscribed and morally peripheral segments of the community.
>
> (Carson 1974: 138)

Different attitudes to prosecution are strongly related to the perceived role and function of these agencies. Many see themselves not as industrial police officers with a primary duty to prosecute the guilty, but as agencies responsible for improving standards of business, trade or commerce by ensuring that businesses comply with regulations. Securing compliance is therefore seen as their primary aim, and prosecution is only one of many tools to achieve this. Therefore, they tend to pursue what are often described as compliance strategies, which can be compared with a prosecution strategy (see, e.g., **Croall 2001, 2003**). Under a compliance strategy, the prevention of offences is seen as paramount, with education, advice and persuasion being seen as preferable to prosecution. Prosecution is likely to be seen by many agencies as costly and counter-productive, as it may lead to poor relationships between agencies and businesses.

Cost-effectiveness underlies many of these strategies. In many areas prosecution involves high costs. Many offences in the world of business and finance are very complex, and investigation may involve gathering enormous amounts of evidence and interviewing many witnesses. Fraud trials, for example, can be lengthy and involve extremely complex evidence. Fraud trials are also seen as risky – the chances of conviction may be lessened by the complexity of the case and the ability of defendants to contest it. If there is a chance for the matter to be resolved without trial an out-of-court settlement becomes an attractive prospect. For local authority departments, if a prosecution is unsuccessful, they may have to bear the costs of prosecution themselves, thus reducing the resources they have for investigation.

In addition, many agencies have options other than doing nothing, cautioning or prosecuting. Some, such as environmental health departments, may be able to grant or withhold licences from offending businesses, thus effectively threatening their viability. Others, such as the Revenue and Customs, can impose sanctions or fines without taking offenders to court. Yet others can disqualify those who need licences to operate, such as financial service employees. Many would argue that these powers constitute a greater deterrent than prosecution, which may be followed by only a small fine.

Prosecution may only result if compliance is not forthcoming after a series of other measures. A prosecution may therefore reflect enforcers' attitudes that defendants are more blameworthy and deserve prosecution. In addition, the threat of prosecution may be used as a bargaining counter in persuading offenders to comply (**Hawkins 1984**). In some cases, however, these considerations can be overridden where, for example, there has been considerable public interest in a case and where prosecution may be considered necessary given the seriousness of the case. This may happen following major incidents in which there has been large-scale pollution or where members of the public have been killed or injured.

The former Head of the Serious Fraud Office (SFO), Rosalind Wright, lists a number of situations in which criminal proceedings are more appropriate. These include situations in which there is evidence of serious dishonesty; there is a high level of public concern and a need for urgent action; the nature of the offence requires strong deterrence and there is little cooperation. Regulatory action, action short of prosecution, is more appropriate in situations where the offence is seen as 'technical' or lies in a 'grey area'; regulatory penalties seem sufficiently severe and are publicly known; regulators can take urgent action; there is no motive of personal gain; regulation is more likely to succeed and the main issue relates to the protection of markets rather than serious dishonesty. She argues:

> . . . the very public nature of many of our prosecutions and the press attention paid to them can provoke fundamental changes in attitudes and practices among businessmen . . . The mere fact that a solicitor or accountant has been investigated or charged with a criminal offence . . . can send shock waves through the profession.
>
> (Wright 2000)

Regulatory agencies play a major diversionary role, and in addition some may have powers to sanction offenders. Some argue that this means that justice is being done in private rather than in a public hearing. To others, these powers represent an important and cost-effective means of diverting offenders from the full process of trial and conviction and there have been suggestions that prosecution agencies such as the CPS should have similar powers. In Scotland, for example, there is a system known as the Fiscal Fine, which the Royal Commission on Criminal Justice 1993 has recommended should be considered in England and Wales.

The Regulatory Enforcement and Sanctions Act 2008, which reflects government policy in relation to reducing the burdens of business regulation, and which sets up Local Better Regulation Offices, will provide for less use of the criminal sanction and more use of administrative sanctions such as Fixed and Variable Monetary Penalties which will be implemented by enforcement agencies as alternatives to prosecution.

7.6 Mentally disordered offenders

Objective 6

Explain the significance and outcomes for mentally disordered offenders

There are strong arguments for diverting mentally disordered offenders from the criminal justice system before trial and before punishment. At the same time, however, mentally disordered offenders may constitute a danger to themselves and others and may arouse fears on the part of the public. The Code for Crown Prosecutors explicitly seeks to balance these matters. In addition, Home Office

Circular 66/90 highlights factors such as the availability of mechanisms for care and treatments from health and social services, as matters to bear in mind when the CPS decides upon whether the public interest criterion is satisfied. While both the Code and the circular encourage the use of diversion from prosecution in the case of mentally disordered offenders, it is accepted that in order to protect the public, it may be necessary to commit the offenders to hospital, or, if this is not possible, to some form of containment or supervision, even where their offences are not so serious as to merit a prison sentence. Thus, due process may conflict with a protectionist stance which raises issues concerning the rights of mentally disordered offenders.

The approach to the mentally disordered offender, as with the younger offender, is affected by notions of responsibility and liability. The criminal law, as we have seen, depends by and large on the concept of a 'guilty mind' and harm to create criminal liability, which provides the justification for intervention and punishment. It is important to recognise that the mental state of the defendant is formally considered at three stages in the criminal justice process. In the first place, there is the issue of whether someone is culpable for an act committed while they were suffering from some kind of mental disorder. A second question arises in establishing whether a person is mentally fit and able to undergo a trial. Finally, there is an issue as to whether someone who was mentally disordered at the time of the offence, or has subsequently become mentally disordered, can or should be punished.

▶ Responsibility for the offence

The criminal courts do not regard as culpable or blameworthy for an offence a person who is deemed 'not guilty by reason of insanity', or where the court accepts the statutory defence of diminished responsibility, or where the state known as automatism is established, as described below.

Insanity is governed by the M'Naghten Rules, formulated after the trial in 1843 of Daniel M'Naghten who, suffering from a delusion that he should kill the then Prime Minister, Sir Robert Peel, killed his secretary by mistake. The rules provide that a defendant is not guilty by reason of insanity if 'he was labouring under a defect of reason because of a disease of the mind so that he did not know the nature and quality of his act, or if he did know it, did not know it was wrong'. If the defendant is found not guilty by reason of insanity, the court may make a hospital order, a guardianship order, a supervision and treatment order or an absolute discharge. There is a right of appeal against such a verdict.

This definition has caused many difficulties, principally surrounding what is to be counted as a disease of the mind. For example, in the case of *Sullivan* in 1984, it was held that a minor epileptic seizure fell within the definition of insanity. In addition, courts have distinguished between defects of reason caused by internal factors, such as medical conditions, which can give rise only to an insanity defence or verdict and external factors, such as a blow to the head or medication, which can give rise to a non-insane automatism defence.

Automatism describes a condition where a person is not strictly in control of his or her actions. If a criminal act is not voluntary the defendant is not responsible for the *actus reus*. Where automatism is caused by something deemed to be a disease of the mind the verdict should be not guilty by reason of insanity. If the automatism is caused by any other reason – for example, an injury – the defendant should be acquitted. As described above, there has been much unease about the line between non-insane and insane automatism, first because of the possible stigma attached and, second, because of the consequent disposal.

Diminished responsibility is a special defence only to murder and is defined in section 2 of the Homicide Act 1957, under which a person who kills, or is a party to the killing of another, cannot be convicted of murder if found to be 'suffering from such an abnormality of mind as substantially impaired his mental responsibility for his acts or omissions'. The abnormality in question may arise from arrested or retarded development, an inherent cause or disease or injury. The onus of proving such an abnormality is expressly placed on the defence. As diminished responsibility is only a defence to murder, if the *actus reus* is established the accused using such a defence will be found guilty of manslaughter instead. Diminished responsibility is therefore a partial defence, which reduces the level of culpability of the defendant and avoids the mandatory life sentence. The Coroners and Justice Act 2009 modified the defence of diminished responsibility.

Before reaching a trial, defendants may be found unfit to plead. It is inherent in a criminal trial that a defendant must be 'fit to plead' – that a defendant knows and understands any charges and is able to instruct a lawyer. A defendant is held to be unfit to plead if he or she is either physically or mentally incapable of instructing legal advisers, following the proceedings or objecting to jurors.

The procedure of establishing fitness to plead is governed by the Criminal Procedure (Insanity) Act 1964, as amended by the Criminal Procedure (Insanity and Unfitness to Plead) Act 1991, and the Domestic Violence, Crime and Victims Act 2004 which provides that the issue can be addressed by the court at any time up to the beginning of the defence case. Unfitness must be determined by the judge on the evidence of two or more doctors. If the defendant is found unfit, the trial proceeds to establish whether or not the jury finds that the defendant has committed the *actus reus* – this is to avoid a mentally ill person being sentenced without proof of an offence. If the defendant is found fit to plead, the trial is carried on in the normal way, and any issues of mental disorder are raised in defence or mitigation. In cases where defendants are found to be both unfit to plead and have committed the *actus reus*, the court may make a hospital order, a supervision order or impose an absolute discharge.

▶ Police and the mentally disordered

In responding to a breach of public order or breach of the peace the police may find they have arrested a mentally disordered person. On other occasions a theft or violent crime may result in the police arresting and detaining someone who is mentally disturbed. In the main they will be taken to the police station. A Home Office Research Study in 1997 commented, 'Up to two per cent of detainees are treated by the police as mentally disordered or mentally handicapped. In London, the figure may be nearer four per cent. Up to one-third are brought to the police station as a place of safety, rather than on suspicion of committing an offence' (**Brown 1997: 213**).

If the police know or suspect that they have a person with a mental disorder or a mental disability they must, under PACE, get an appropriate adult to attend the police station to be present at the interview. The arrested person may be regarded as unfit for interview. Often there is no interview. 'Custody officers often summon the police surgeon in the first instance and, acting on the doctor's advice, do not then call for an appropriate adult in many cases' (ibid.). Mental health and social work specialists are also called in as an appropriate adult as they are able to respond quickly to calls from the police.

The police are unlikely to take further criminal proceedings with those they arrest that are **certified as mentally ill**. Usually no criminal charges are involved and the local health authorities are informed. In one Home Office study of 2,739 people arrested by the police, 18 were considered mentally ill and in need of care and control in a 'place of safety' (Mental Health Act 1983, s 136). Of the remaining 2,721, the researchers estimated that a further 37 showed signs of serious mental illness. Of these, 52 per cent were arrested for breach of the peace or public order offences and they were much more likely to be released without further action (46 per cent) than detainees arrested for similar offences who were not considered mentally ill (11 per cent) (**Robertson *et al*. 1995**).

▶ Orders available to the courts for mentally disordered offenders

The courts have a number of options in dealing with mentally disordered offenders. These raise the issue of the rights of mentally disordered offenders, who may find themselves being deprived of their liberty for longer periods of time than if they were not mentally disordered, arising from the inevitable tension between the desire of the court to protect the public and the rights of offenders. In addition, diagnosing what form of mental disorder an offender is suffering from is not always straightforward, as is assessing how amenable the condition is to treatment. There were four types of mental incapacity defined in section 1 of the Mental Health Act 1983.

Mental disorder was defined as 'mental illness, arrested or incomplete development of mind, psychopathic disorder and any other disorder or disability of mind'. More specifically, *mental impairment* is defined as 'a state of arrested or incomplete development of mind (not amounting to severe mental impairment) which includes significant impairment of intelligence and social functioning and is associated with abnormally aggressive or seriously irresponsible conduct on the part of the person concerned'. *Severe mental impairment* was defined as 'a state of arrested or incomplete development of the mind which includes severe impairment of intelligence and social functioning and is associated with abnormally aggressive or seriously irresponsible conduct on the part of the person concerned'. A *psychopathic disorder* was defined as 'a persistent disorder or disability of mind (whether or not including significant impairment of intelligence) which results in abnormally aggressive or seriously irresponsible conduct on the part of the person concerned'.

In November 2008, the Mental Health Act 2007 replaced these four with one general category of 'mental disorder' encompassing any disorder or disability of the mind. The change means that personality disorders are included. The new definition however will exclude those suffering from learning disabilities unless the learning disability is associated with 'abnormally aggressive or seriously irresponsible conduct'.

The test for detaining such patients is also modified under the MHA 2007. A new 'appropriate medical treatment' test is introduced which will apply to all the longer-term powers of detention. This means that patients can only be compulsorily detained if medical treatment which is appropriate to the nature and degree of mental disorder and all other circumstances is actually, not merely theoretically, available. Treatment means both treatment to improve and treatment to prevent the worsening of symptoms: the impact of this change (the extension of the meaning of treatability) is described below.

The main options for the criminal courts after the implementation of the new Act when dealing with a mentally disordered offender are as follows (section numbers refer to the MHA 1983 as amended by the MHA 2007):

- Remand to a hospital for a report (s 35) or for treatment (s 36).
- Hospital order (ss 37 and 51) for up to six months, but renewable. Section 51 allows a magistrates' court to make such an order without there being a conviction where a person has been charged and the court would have power on conviction to make a hospital order. The court may, if satisfied that the accused did the act, make a hospital order without a conviction. This section means that a court can deal with an act (finding that the *actus reus* was carried out) but without having to determine that it was accompanied by the requisite *mens rea*.
- Interim hospital order (s 38) for a 12-week period, and renewable.
- Hospital and limitations direction (s 45): a court can impose a sentence of imprisonment and direct that the person be sent to a hospital.

In December 2005, there were 3,395 restricted patients detained in hospitals and some were admitted to high security hospitals (112 in 2005). Restricted patients admitted in 2005 were admitted in relation to the following types of mental disorder: 1,133 for mental illness; 53 for mental illness with other disorders; 99 for psychopathic disorder; 25 with mental impairment; 5 had mental impairment with psychopathic disorder; and 3 for severe mental impairment (*Home Office Statistical Bulletin* 05/07: 8). In 2010 the numbers detained in hospital under the MHA was 4,404 (*Ministry of Justice Offender Management Caseload Statistics 2010*).

The Mental Health Act 2007 also made provisions for clinicians to discharge detained patients into the community under a community treatment order (CTO), subject to recall to hospital. A supervised treatment order (SCT), previously known as a community order, will oblige people to have treatment outside of hospital. This provision is introduced to try to remedy the problem of those discharged from detention subsequently stopping taking medication resulting in readmission for further treatment: often referred to as the 'revolving door' syndrome.

A major conceptual change broadens the definition of 'treatability'. Under the MHA 1983 if a person had a personality disorder (such as Michael Stone who was convicted in 1996 for the murder of Lin Russell, aged 45, and her daughter) which was defined as untreatable, then the MHA could not apply to them as they could not be deemed a patient who would benefit from treatment. The MHA 2007 extends the notion of medical treatment, in relation to mental disorder, and states 'a reference to medical treatment the purpose of which is to alleviate, or prevent a worsening of, the disorder or one or more of its symptoms or manifestations.' The Zito Trust commented in 2007 in a Memorandum submitted to the Mental Health Bill Committee:

> 1.1 We welcome the broader definition of mental disorder as this will enable mainstream services to provide appropriate treatment to a group of people who have been consistently labelled as 'untreatable'. It has become clear to the Trust that the medical model which is now the basis of modern psychiatry has created an underclass of potential service users who have complex health and social needs and who have as much right to treatment as anyone else. It is no longer justifiable to write these people off as untreatable.
>
> 1.2 The legal 'treatability' loophole in the Mental Health Act 1983 is an unnecessary (and sometimes dangerous) obstacle to services for people with complex needs. In May 2000, 12-year-old Diego Pineiro Villar was stabbed 30 times and killed in Covent Garden by Alexander Crowley. At an earlier court hearing, before the homicide, the judge expressed his frustration that he could not give the defendant a hospital order because he found himself legally unable to do so. He was therefore given bail, during which period he killed Diego Pineiro Villar.
>
> (Memorandum submitted by The Zito Trust (MH 45))

The MHA 2007 also makes some key changes in relation to rights of both victims and patients. It gives for the first time the right to victims to get information about mentally disordered offenders. It also enhances the rights of the patient with new safeguards so that patients will be able refuse electro-convulsive shock therapy treatment; and introduces a new agency providing statutory advocacy services for all those in detention. The 'Independent Mental Health Advocates' will be available for all patients liable to be detained or on a Community Treatment Order.

▶ De-institutionalisation and care in the community

The Mental Health Act 1959 brought about a major revision in the treatment of the mentally ill. The policy of placing psychiatric patients into mental hospitals had its origins in the county asylums of the late eighteenth and early nineteenth century. The new approach was called 'community care' and was based on a new respect for the rights of the mental patient and a wish to avoid the use of the gloomy institutions that, in some places, held regimes that were brutal and uncaring. It was also believed that rehabilitation was more likely to take place in the more normal world of the community rather than the closed worlds of total institutions (**Goffman 1961**). Advancement in pharmaceutical drugs meant that new methods of treatment were available for the control of behaviour and the cure of patients. It was a policy that was also cheaper if measured in monetary terms. The number of beds available for psychiatric patients fell from 140,000 in 1959 to 37,000 in 1998.

While few would dispute that it is desirable to divert mentally disordered offenders from the criminal justice process or refer them for treatment rather than punishment, there are some concerns about the orders outlined above. Particularly problematic was the definition of different kinds of mental disorder. These definitions were somewhat narrow and might not accord with psychiatric diagnoses. The definition of psychopathy has raised special problems, as there was little agreement over what kind of underlying condition produces the behaviour which amounts to its definition. In essence, argues Peay, it was 'a legal category defined by persistently violent behaviour', rather than being a clearly defined mental disorder (**Peay 2002: 1146**). This problem is addressed by the change in the Mental Health Act 2007 to a generic definition of mental disorder.

A person's mental condition may change and indeed be affected by the process of being arrested or institutionalised, making predictions of whether and how the condition will respond to treatment extremely problematic. It is difficult, therefore, to state with any certainty how long a mentally disordered offender should be held in hospital. Given the fear that released offenders may re-offend, this may lead to longer periods of hospitalisation than would be merited either by considerations of the offence or the needs of the offender for treatment.

However, tragedies have shown that these fears are not imagined; fears which have been exacerbated by the policy of treating mentally disordered offenders in the community. One of the first cases to come to prominent public attention was that involving Jonathon Zito. In December 1992, Zito, a musician aged 27, was waiting for an Underground train at Finsbury Park Station in London when he was stabbed in the face and killed by Christopher Clunis, a diagnosed schizophrenic. Clunis had a long history of violence which included stabbing a person in the neck. He had been released from prison to a mental hospital, from which he had been discharged in 1992. As a result of this tragedy, his widow, Jayne Zito, set up the Zito Trust which has been instrumental in highlighting other cases and campaigning for changes in procedures and in the law. Hers was not the last such case.

The danger to the public was highlighted by two cases in 2005, of John Barrett and Peter Bryan: both were diagnosed as paranoid schizophrenics.

Case 1

John Barrett stabbed and seriously injured two patients and a nurse in St George's Hospital in Tooting in London. He was sent to a Secure Unit in 2002 as a 'restricted' mental health patient. An Independent Mental Health Review Tribunal ruled that he should be released on conditional discharge in October 2003. This release was opposed by the Home Office but the tribunal has to take into account the medical progress and the human rights of the patient. As a conditionally discharged patient Barrett should have been seen once every four weeks by a psychiatrist but was seen only once by a social worker.

On 1 September 2004, a friend informed the hospital of their growing anxiety about his condition. Barrett attended that day as a voluntary patient and was assessed by a psychiatrist. The doctors did not detain him and Barrett discharged himself that evening and bought a set of kitchen knives. Next morning he went to Richmond Park and at 10 a.m. he saw a 50-year-old male, Denis Finnegan, riding his bike through the park. He stabbed him through the heart several times and then ran off but was detained within minutes by police called to the crime. Finnegan died on the way to hospital.

Case 2

In March 1993, Peter Bryan killed Nisha Sheth (20) in the family's clothes shop in Chelsea, following a dispute with her parents who were his former employers. He also attacked and beat her brother aged 12 with a hammer. Following a trial at the Old Bailey in 1994, Bryan was sent to Rampton Mental Hospital on an indefinite hospital order under the Mental Health Act. He was diagnosed as schizophrenic and as a danger to the public.

In 2002, a Mental Health Review Panel discharged him from the hospital order. He moved to the Riverside Hostel in North London. In February 2004, he was sent to an open psychiatric ward at Newham General Hospital, London. There were no restrictions on his liberty.

Later that month he bought a hammer and a screwdriver and visited an acquaintance, Brian Cherry, and battered him with 24 hammer blows to his head. He cut off his victim's arms and a leg and cooked his brain in butter and ate them. Arrested and charged with murder, he was detained in HMP Pentonville and then moved to HMP Belmarsh where he assaulted two prison staff.

On 15 April 2004 he was admitted to the medium secure unit in Broadmoor, where on 25 April he attacked fellow inmate Richard Laudwell, aged 59, by repeatedly banging his head against the floor and strangling him with his pyjama cord. Laudwell did not recover consciousness and died on 8 June.

On 15 March 2005, he was once again convicted of manslaughter on the grounds of diminished responsibility. Judge Giles Forrester stated that he should never be released because he was too dangerous and sentenced Bryan at the Old Bailey to two life sentences.

A report from the Royal College of Psychiatrists (17 August 1994) revealed, in a survey of an 18-month period from July 1992 to December 1993, that 34 people were killed by newly released mental patients. William Boyd of the Royal Edinburgh Hospital investigated 22 of the 34 killings and discovered that all the perpetrators had been in the care of psychiatric services in the 12 months preceding the killings. Of the 22, 17 had histories of violence. Fifteen of the killings were committed by men, most of whom had been diagnosed as schizophrenic or paranoid psychotic. Nine of the 15 men had convictions for violent behaviour. The seven women in the study were mostly suffering from depression and six of them killed their own children.

❯ Community care and public safety

Since the Clunis incident a number of changes of practice have been introduced to avoid the problem of dangerous mentally ill people being left unsupervised in the community. The Mental Health (Patients in the Community) Act 1995 introduced provisions that make it easier to return a mental patient to hospital. The Act gives the supervisor the power to take and convey the patient to any place where the patient is required to reside or to attend for the purpose of medical treatment. There is a new system in which each patient has a 'responsible medical officer' (a doctor), a 'key worker' (care/social worker), a 'key plan' and should be put onto a 'supervision register'.

While it is recognised that only a small proportion of offenders are considered to be mentally ill and that the vast majority of mentally disordered people do not commit crime, the view that mentally ill people are neither more nor less dangerous than other offenders has also been challenged by recent reports. In October 1997, the Zito Trust published the results of its survey on homicides by people released from institutions and who were being supervised in the community. Between 1990 and 1997 there were 141 homicides, that is two a month on average, resulting in the deaths of 44 strangers, 23 acquaintances, 3 health professionals, 13 co-residents, 34 family members and 33 children under the age of 16 (Zito Trust 1997). Research by the Zito Trust continues to highlight the problem:

> The *National Confidential Inquiry Report* into suicide and homicide was published on Monday 4 December 2006. It is called 'Avoidable Deaths' and states that 400 homicides have been committed in the past eight years by people in contact with mental health services: one every week.
>
> (Zito Trust website July 2008: www.zitotrust.co.uk/)

There is a problem of balance between patients' rights and the public's right to be protected from dangerous people. Doctors take as their priority the care and treatment of their patients. Community control by medically trained staff is a problem as they are likely to put patients' rights before the needs of the criminal justice system. When they wish to take action there is often a problem of lack of beds in the medium security wards available to the local health authority. There is also the problem of monitoring mentally ill patients released from secure accommodation. Lack of contact with their case workers and failure to take medication have been cited in inquiries into deaths caused by psychiatric patients. One relatively recent case illustrates how easy it is for dangerous patients in the community to slip through the net: Tennyson Obih, a Nigerian-born immigrant who was diagnosed with paranoid schizophrenia in 2005 and twice admitted to a psychiatric unit, was allowed to return to the community under the care of a mental health nursing team. He was known to have stopped taking his medication in December 2006, but nothing was done about this. In June 2007 he armed himself with a five-inch knife and brutally stabbed a police constable called Jon Henry to death in Luton town centre. Under the conditions of Obih's release into the community, nurses had been required to visit him at his home on a regular basis, which should have allowed the nursing team to act upon any serious deterioration of his mental health, but it was noted during the trial that Obih was often not at home when they called, and that the last scheduled appointment was not carried out. This caused many commentators to speculate on whether the conditions under which mentally disordered patients are allowed to live in the community are stringent enough, and what backstops are in place to ensure that the alarm is raised well before such cases reach their tragic denouement.

Coordination of services and sharing of information were identified as problems in the inquiry led by Louis Blom-Cooper, a former chairman of the Mental Health Tribunal, into the case of Jason Mitchell. In December 1994 Mitchell was released into the community from St Clements Hospital in Ipswich on the advice of the consultant psychiatrist. He was staying in a halfway house when he broke into the home of a couple, both aged 65, and killed them before going to his father's home nearby in Bramford in Suffolk where he beheaded and dismembered him. The inquiry found that records from his time in a **young offender institution**, identifying him as a potential killer, had been lost and a later report on his attitudes revealing a violent disposition was ignored by doctors. In July 1995 he was given three life sentences and sent to Rampton Hospital.

The balance between patients' rights and public safety has been the focus of much concern. The then Health Secretary, Frank Dobson, announced in 1998 that the policy of 'care in the community' had not been a success and a review was in progress, and added that 'Care in the community has become a discredited policy'. Paul Boateng, then a Health Minister, stated: 'There will be no return to grim Victorian asylums. But the old mantra, "community good, hospitals bad" is dead' (BBC, 17 January 1998).

As a result of concerns about the way in which people with mental health problems are treated – not only those whose problems led to or contributed to offending – an expert committee was set up by the government to review the Mental Health Act 1983 and reported in 1999. At the same time as the committee reported, the government issued proposals for consultation. This was followed by a White Paper, *Reforming the Mental Health Act*, and a draft bill. In November 2003, the Health Secretary, John Reid, stated:

> The government is fully committed to reforming mental health legislation. We must make significant improvements to patient safeguards, provide a modern framework of legislation in line with modern patterns of care and treatment and human rights law, and protect public safety by enabling patients to get the right treatment at the right time.
>
> (Department of Health Press Release, 26 November 2003, 2003/0481)

The subsequent Mental Health Act 2007 contains a single definition of mental disorder and provides a framework for the consideration of the needs of individuals including those whose condition makes them a danger to others. It also 'breaks the automatic link between formal treatment and detention in hospital'. While trying to provide for the most appropriate form of treatment, whether in hospital or in the community, one object of the legislation is also to safeguard patients' rights.

Thus it can be seen that, in considering the issues involved in offending by those who are mentally ill, the various approaches to criminal justice can be seen in tension with each other – due process and the rights of individuals, in contrast to crime control and crime prevention – which may mean intervention in anticipation of offending for those perceived as dangerous to others.

Conclusion

We have come to understand by now that not all criminals are prosecuted, in the main because most crime is not reported by victims, and when they are reported, the majority of recorded crimes are not successfully cleared up (see Chapter 2.3). Even when a crime is reported and solved, it is not necessary that a formal prosecution will take place and this is evident from the work of the CPS in which on average 12 per cent of cases a year are discontinued. Others are discontinued not because there is no record or a lack of evidence but for purposeful policy reasons, and in this chapter we have examined the pre-trial decisions by which some offenders are diverted away from formal prosecution and trial. This might be because they are dealt with by a type of fine, as with the fixed penalty notice, or because of their status either as young offenders or because they are mentally disordered; others are diverted because of decisions made by the police and the CPS through conditional or simple cautions. Many of the issues involved in these decisions and the policy that drives them have their roots in our concepts of criminal responsibility (see Chapter 2.1). Diversion also demonstrates the conflict in goals of the criminal justice system: to treat all equally before the law, to provide a cost-effective system, and to ensure judicial decisions are made openly, fairly and even-handedly.

It is, for example, clearly cheaper and less wasteful of resources to divert offenders who for various reasons might not be convicted, or if convicted would receive only a nominal penalty or would receive some form of treatment rather than punishment. It may even be seen as desirable in the interests of equity and efficiency to allow prosecutors greater powers to impose sanctions for some offences without taking offenders to court. To prosecute all offenders uses valuable resources so there is always an issue of cost effectiveness and priorities (see bureaucratic or management model) as prosecution is a very costly and time-consuming process.

At the same time, however, this means that justice is being done in private rather than in public, which in turn means that it is less publicly accountable and that equal treatment cannot be guaranteed. Diverted defendants have less chance to dispute allegations, and treatment programmes which may seem more desirable than punishment may involve more control than punishment. In addition, as we have seen, it may be in the public interest to see offenders publicly tried and punished, as well as giving victims the chance to obtain compensation and the satisfaction of seeing justice being done. Another consideration from a crime control perspective is the potential threat to the public of dangerous offenders, be they young or mentally ill, being released back into the community. Many of these considerations also affect pre-trial processes. Chapter 9 describes the procedures they will go through before they reach the trial stage.

Review questions

1. What are the arguments in favour of, and against, the issuing of fixed penalty notices instead of prosecution or taking no further action? What models of criminal justice are involved?

2. Identify the main considerations underlying the decision to give a caution (whether a simple or a conditional caution) or prosecute, and relate these to the models of criminal justice.

3. At what stages are those suffering from mental incapacity dealt with differently from others?

4. Identify the dual test used by the Crown Prosecution Service in deciding whether to continue with a prosecution, and list the criteria used in these tests.

Discussion questions

1. What are the main arguments in favour of a 'compliance' as opposed to a 'criminal' approach to law enforcement for business offenders?

2. Should the mentally ill be treated differently in the criminal justice system? What models of criminal justice are involved in assessing this question?

3. Consider Table 7.3 and explain why a defendant might be acquitted, and why it would appear that the success varies by types of offence.

Table 7.3 Convictions in January 2007

	Defendants convicted		Defendants not convicted	
	Number	%	Number	%
Homicide	77	81.9	17	18.1
Offences against the person	9,462	73.1	3,480	26.9
Sexual offences	587	66.2	300	33.8
Burglary	2,052	83.1	418	16.9
Robbery	856	77.7	245	22.3
Theft and handling stolen goods	11,354	91.0	1,128	9.0
Fraud and forgery	605	86.3	96	13.7
Criminal damage	3,956	84.9	703	15.1
Drug offences	3,730	94.1	234	5.9
Public order offences	7,137	83.3	1,434	16.7
All other offences (excluding motoring)	4,032	83.3	808	16.7
Motoring offences	32,487	90.8	3,301	9.2
Other	0	0	2,010	100
Total	**76,335**	**84.3**	**14,174**	**15.7**

Source: Defendant Outcomes Universe, CPS Management Information System: www.cps.gov.uk/publications/performance/case_outcomes/2007_01/index.html

Table 7.3 is based on the Crown Prosecution Service data showing the number and percentages of successful and unsuccessful prosecution outcomes in the criminal courts in January 2007.This information gives a picture in one month of the number of offences prosecuted in court by the CPS, and shows the outcome when a final decision was made in court either to convict or acquit a defendant: resulting in 76,335 convicted defendants and 14,174 acquitted. Differences in success rates can be noted between types of offence, with 94.1% of drug cases resulting in a conviction compared to 66.2% of sexual offences.

Further reading

Ashworth A *et al.* (2005) *The Criminal Process* (3rd revised edn), Oxford University Press: Oxford

Kaye C and Howlett M (eds) (2008) *Mental Health Services Today and Tomorrow*, Radcliffe Publishing: Oxford

Peay J (2002) 'Mentally Disordered Offenders', in Maguire M, Morgan R and Reiner R (eds) *The Oxford Handbook of Criminology* (3rd edn), Clarendon Press: Oxford

Weblinks

Crown Prosecution Service: **www.cps.gov.uk/**

Conditional Cautioning Code of Practice: **www.homeoffice.gov.uk/documents/cond-caution-cop?version=1**

Mind (mental health charity): **www.mind.org.uk/**

Chapter 8

Youth justice

Learning objectives

After reading the chapter you should be able to:

1. Describe the pattern of youthful criminality
2. Outline and explain the youth justice system
3. Describe the processes and agencies involved when young offenders are sent to Youth Court
4. Explain the differences in sentencing aims and court disposals for young offenders

Key statistics

- In 2010/11 there were 1,360,451 arrests in England and Wales, of which 210,660 were of young people aged 10–17. The 10–17 age group accounted for 15.5% of all arrests but were 10.7% of the population of England and Wales of offending age

- There were 40,757 reprimands, final warnings and conditional cautions given to young people in 2011/12 in England and Wales. This is a decrease of 57% on the 94,836 given in 2001/02

- Overall, there were 137,335 proven offences by young people in 2011/12, down 22% from 2010/11 and 47% since 2001/02

- There were 59,335 sentences given for all offences to young people in 2011/12 in England and Wales. The number of custodial sentences (3,925), accounting for 6.6% of all sentences given, has fallen 48% since 2001/02

- In 2010/11, the overall reoffending rate for young people aged 10–17 was 35.8%, with an average of 2.87 reoffences per reoffender. The rate of re-offending has risen from 32.8% in 2008/09 and 33.3% in 2009/10

- A total of 210,660 of persons aged 10–17 were arrested for notifiable offences in 2010/11 in England and Wales

Table 8.1 Persons aged 10–17 arrested for notifiable offences by offence group, 2010/11 in England and Wales

TOTAL	Violence against the person	Sexual offences	Robbery	Burglary	Theft and handling stolen goods	Fraud and forgery	Criminal damage	Drug offences	Other offences
210,660	53,983	4,564	14,087	22,608	49,431	1,258	27,011	14,632	23,086
%	26	2	7	11	23	1	13	7	11

Source: https://www.gov.uk/government/uploads/system/uploads/attachment_data/file/186815/ppp-arrests-1112-tabs.xls

- A total of 198,960 of individuals aged 18–20 were arrested for notifiable offences in 2010/11 in England and Wales

Table 8.2 Persons aged 18–20 arrested for notifiable offences by offence group, 2010/11 in England and Wales

TOTAL	Violence against the person	Sexual offences	Robbery	Burglary	Theft and handling stolen goods	Fraud and forgery	Criminal damage	Drug offences	Other offences
198,960	57,660	3,928	7,351	17,696	39,236	3,176	20,067	20,431	29,415
%	29	2	4	9	20	1.5	10	10	14.5

Source: https://www.gov.uk/government/uploads/system/uploads/attachment_data/file/186815/ppp-arrests-1112-tabs.xls

Introduction

In 2010/11 there were 1,386,030 arrests in England and Wales of which 241,737 were of people aged 10 to 17. Thus, 10–17-year-olds accounted for 17 per cent of all arrests but were 11 per cent of the population of England and Wales of offending age (i.e. 10–17). While this age group is over-represented in arrests, the figures do not suggest that youths are the overwhelming problem as might be suggested (Youth Justice Board [YJB]/Ministry of Justice [MOJ] Statistics, January 2012). Whatever the spin the YJB would want to put on the figures, they do show that 30% of all arrests in 2010/11 were of people below the age of 21.

It is important to look at the different ways in which young people are involved in crime. Most jurisdictions have different systems for dealing with young offenders, to attempt to divert them from the more formalised systems of courts and to develop criminal justice policies that seek to prevent further offending. Systems of youth justice have been based on a balance between the need to punish or control young offenders and to encourage them to take responsibility for their actions, and the need for strategies which take account of the many problems which may have led to an involvement in crime and to intervene so as to rehabilitate where possible, and control the threat posed by the young offender, i.e. a management of offender behaviour approach. The Crime and Disorder Act 1998 made radical changes to the system, some of which have already been referred to, and 'youth justice', according to some commentators, provided a very clear example of the Labour Government's approach of being 'tough on crime, tough on the causes of crime' **(Newburn 2012)**. The approach illustrates our eighth and new model of criminal justice **(see Chapter 1)** whereby the offender becomes the focus of a wide range of intervention strategies that combine rehabilitative and punishment aspects with intensive monitoring in an effort to control and limit the opportunities for criminal activity. An example of this is the **intensive supervision and surveillance programme** (ISSP) aimed at the persistent young offender – estimated to be responsible for 25 per cent of all youth crime – and combines supervision for at least 25 hours a week with specified activities, curfews and electronic monitoring as part of a Youth Rehabilitation Order.

Many further policy initiatives and legislation have followed. In November 2005, the Youth Justice Board published a strategy for dealing with young offenders in custody, entitled *Strategy for the Secure Estate for Children and Young People*. In January 2006, the government published its *Respect Action Plan*, in which the government proposed addressing anti-social behaviour through:

- supporting and working with families;
- improving school behaviour and attendance;
- involving children and young people in positive activities;
- strengthening communities;
- providing effective enforcement of laws and community justice.

Much of the concern over youth offending and the response to it reflects the offender management model, which is applied to the management of potential offenders as well as to those who have actually committed and been convicted of crimes **(see Chapter 1)**.

Increasingly, a twin-track governmental strategy is perceived with diversion aimed at the lower-end offender as well as punishment and reform for the more serious. The Criminal Justice and Immigration Act 2008, which received Royal Assent in May 2008, focused again on reform and diversion with the introduction of the Youth Rehabilitation Order and the Youth Conditional Caution. In June 2008 an inter-departmental Youth Crime Action Plan was published. These two developments, reflecting prevention, diversion and reform objectives, are discussed in detail below.

The different approaches to youth crime reflect the complex approaches to youth offending. This focuses upon the issue of culpability, i.e. the responsibility of young offenders for the crimes they have committed, and on questions of whether children are to blame for their behaviour.

Children may not be considered responsible for their actions as are adults or older children. They may not appreciate that something is wrong, or understand the consequences of their actions; children who act badly my do so as a consequence of poor parenting or difficult material circumstances; and offending can be a phase that could be 'grown out of' given the right opportunities and guidance. There is a concern that some responses to crime may make young offenders worse; and there is also an awareness that some children are out of control and exploit the above attitudes to their advantage.

The Institute for Public Policy Research report (November 2006), *Freedom's Orphans: Raising Youth in a Changing World*, compared the lives of thousands of children and discovered that young people who participated in structured after-school activities, such as sport, drama or outdoor groups, were less likely to become involved in anti-social behaviour and crime. The key to reducing such behaviour was adult supervision and after-school activities.

The report also shows that more than 1.5 million Britons thought about moving house and 1.7 million avoided going out after dark because of loitering young people, and were three times more likely to cite young people on the streets as a problem than they were to complain about noisy neighbours. The report compared views of adults in a number of European countries: 79 per cent of Britons thought poor parenting was responsible for anti-social behaviour, compared to 69 per cent of Spaniards, 62 per cent of Italians and 58 per cent of French people.

Adults in the UK would be the least likely to intervene if they saw a group of 14-year-old boys vandalising a bus shelter: 34 per cent said they would intervene, compared with 65 per cent of Germans, 52 per cent of Spanish people and 50 per cent of Italians. Thirty-nine per cent of those who would refuse to intervene feared they would be physically attacked, 14 per cent thought they might be targeted for reprisals and 12 per cent feared being verbally abused.

Public perceptions in relation to youth crime are complex and sometimes difficult to analyse. The Crime Survey in England and Wales 2010/11 (formerly British Crime Survey) suggested that 64% of respondents thought that young offenders were dealt with too leniently by the police and courts and yet, the same survey suggested that 45% believed rehabilitation should be the main aim of the Youth Justice System. Rehabilitation will often have the 'smell of leniency' and yet, was the most popular response as to what ought to be done with young offenders.

The complexities of responding to these views will form the content of this chapter. We will start by looking at the problem of youth crime and the different ways in which young people are involved in crime. We will go on to look at how the welfare and justice approaches have affected policies towards young offenders and at the way in which youth justice systems attempt both to control offenders and respond to their welfare. It will outline the main changes made to the system and look at the structure of Youth Courts and at the sentencing of young offenders.

8.1 Youth and crime

Objective 1

Describe the pattern of youthful criminality

It is interesting to place contemporary concerns about youth crime in a historical context. While it is common to hear politicians and the media commenting adversely on the 'state of youth today' and the need to take action against unruly, disorderly and criminal youth, concerns about such activities have been prominent throughout the centuries. A newspaper editorial in 1843, for example, contained the following statement: 'morals are getting much worse. When I was young my mother would have knocked me down for speaking improperly to her'. Similarly, the Howard Association in 1898 commented that 'the manners of children are deteriorating . . . the child of today is coarser, more vulgar, less refined than his parents were' (both examples from **Muncie 1999: 50**).

Social change, the effects of alcohol and the adverse influence of popular entertainment such as 'penny dreadfuls', football and music halls were all held to be responsible for hooliganism during the nineteenth century. A social commentator and advocate of boys' clubs commented in 1917, 'their vulgarity and silliness and the distorted, unreal Americanised view of life must have a deteriorating effect and lead to the formation of false ideals' (cited in ibid.).

Today, violent computer games and the apparent celebration of violence in films and on television are criticised. The twentieth century saw recurrent moral panics about young people, their expressive subcultures and involvement in illegal leisure pursuits, such as the consumption of illegal drugs, involvement in petty crime and in subcultures which were associated with fighting and violence. The term 'moral panic' was used in relation to highly publicised confrontations between the Mods and Rockers of the 1960s. Research indicated, however, that many self-styled mods and rockers were not involved in these activities (**Cohen 1980**). Throughout the latter part of the twentieth century there were panics about skinheads, lager louts, yob culture, football hooligans, and rave culture; and, more recently, about persistent young offenders, binge drinking, gangs, use of knives, use of guns and anti-social behaviour.

Young people in recent years have been seen as 'out of control' or lacking in self-discipline or respect for authority. This reflects in part the many changes in the dominant culture such that a clear civic culture and moral consensus is less obvious in the early twenty-first century. It is also, in part, related to the nature of youth and its associated lifestyle, especially as it developed in the latter part of the twentieth century. Young people are more likely to spend their leisure time in public; 'hanging about' and looking for diversion, fun and excitement is normal for most young people. This may lead to their being victims of crime as well as perpetrators that young people are often victims as well as villains (**as seen in Chapter 3**). Young people are also far more likely to the victims. British Crime Survey estimates suggest that young men aged 16 to 24, are, for example, more than four times more likely to become the victim of violent crime than the general population and there were over 500,000 violent incidents against 10–15-year-olds in 2010/11(*Crime in England and Wales 2010/11*, Home Office 2011).

Changes in lifestyle and youth culture since the end of the Second World War have meant that young people are drawn to expressive subcultures, encouraged by the commercialisation of style for teenagers; and this search for novelty and the public nature of young people's leisure can be seen by older people as a threat. The sight of large groups of young people hanging about can be seen as intimidating and lead to complaints to the police. Young people are more likely to come into contact with the police on the streets than other groups.

Nevertheless, concerns about youth crime cannot be dismissed solely as a moral panic and, as **Newburn (2007)** points out, young people aged between 10 and 17 constitute around one-fifth of those cautioned or convicted annually, and self-report studies have found that around one-third of young males and just under one-fifth of young females aged between 10 and 25 reported at least one offence in the last year. The citizens of many neighbourhoods have real concerns about the effects of unruly behaviour on their quality of life and make frequent complaints to the police and to community representatives. The following section will explore aspects of young people's involvement in crime.

▶ Young people's involvement in crime

Young people predominate among offenders (**as seen in Chapter** 2). Statistics for 2006 show that males aged 17 have the highest rate of known offending for indictable offences at 6,116 per 100,000 population, and the highest rate for female offending is among 15-year-olds at 2,168 per 100,000. For male offenders, more cautions (or their youth equivalent, reprimands and warnings) were given to 15-year-olds than to any other age. Nineteen is the age at which most are convicted. Among female offenders the most common ages to be reprimanded in 2006 were 14 and 15, with 16 being the most common age for a female to be convicted. Table 8.3 shows the number of juveniles (aged 10–17) involved in various criminal justice processes from 2005–2010.

It is important to recognise that perceptions of the relationship between age and crime are affected by the different types of crime associated with different age groups. Young people's offending is often more public and visible, whereas older people have more opportunity to commit crimes at work or in the home, which may have a lower chance of detection. Some indication of this is provided by self-report studies, which indicate that 14–15-year-olds tend to be involved in fights, buying stolen goods, theft and criminal damage, 16–17-year-olds are less involved in criminal damage, theft and buying and selling stolen goods, whereas 18–21-year-olds show a declining involvement in shoplifting and criminal damage and an increasing involvement in fraud and workplace theft as they move towards offences which have a lower chance of being caught (**Flood-Page** *et al.* **2000**).

Young people show different patterns of involvement in crime. Self-report studies indicate, for example, that high numbers of young people report committing offences but for many this is only a transitory involvement in less serious forms of crime (**Anderson** *et al.* **1994**). Many young people engage in vandalism, petty theft or get involved in fights but this may be seen as a relatively normal part of growing up and does not lead to a criminal career. Some activities, which to the observer may be criminal, may be perceived by a young person as fun or exciting, as he/she may experimenting with some forms of drugs and alcohol. Thus, while many report having used an illegal drug in their lives, far fewer report doing so regularly and persistently. It has also been recognised that many young people grow out of crime as they mature, find legitimate work and get married. Indeed, the delayed entry of some young men into employment, with high rates of youth unemployment and the consequent decline in numbers getting married, could in itself contribute to the higher peak age of crime and to the rates of 18–30-year-olds committing crime.

A minority, however, may be involved in more serious offending – committing more offences and more serious offences – being what is often described as persistent

Table 8.3 Youths (10–17) involved in criminal justice system 2002–2012

	2002	2003	2004	2005	2006	2007	2008	2009	2010	2011	2012
Appearing in Crown Court for trial	5,100	4,100	4,200	3,600	3,500	3,600	3,700	3,400	3,100	2,900	2,400
Reprimands/final warnings for all offences	86,589	91,933	95,251	118,875	119,928	127,326	98,175	78,679	52,989	44,232	32,673
Offenders found guilty (indictable offences)	49,100	46,100	46,900	47,700	47,500	50,700	46,000	43,700	41,300	36,600	27,900
All Disposals (in and out of court)	268,480	287,883	287,013	301,860	295,129	277,986	244,583	198,449	176,511	137,335	98,837
Court Disposals (all offences)	**94,548**	**92,531**	**96,188**	**96,104**	**93,806**	**97,387**	**88,375**	**81,544**	**73,866**	**63,424**	**47,515**
Penalty Notices for Disorder (16–17 only)	–	–	–	12,454	19,598	19,246	14,497	11,737	8,192	6,229	3,467

Source: Criminal Justice Statistics 2006, 2008 & 2012: Ministry of Justice

offenders. A high proportion of all youth crime may be attributable to a small group, and the factors associated with their offending may be very different. 'We estimate that 5% of young people are responsible for over half of youth crime' (Youth Crime Action Plan, July 2008).

Whereas young people across the social spectrum report being involved in some forms of crime, those reporting more serious involvement tend to be more concentrated in lower-class areas and have also been found to have more chaotic lifestyles involving family, school or housing problems (**Hagell and Newburn 1994**).

Violent crimes have risen steadily among the young and we are aware of the high-profile gratuitous acts of violence leading to murder, for example:

> Garry Newlove was murdered in August 2007 by being beaten to death outside his home for complaining to a group of youths who had damaged his wife's car. One of those convicted of his murder, Adam Swellings, had been involved in four previous violent incidents but was considered low-risk by the Local Authority Youth Offending Team.

Ernest Norton, aged 67, was the victim of a hail of stones and bricks thrown by a group of youths while playing cricket with his son in February 2006. He suffered a fractured cheekbone before collapsing and dying of a heart attack. The five youths, convicted initially for manslaughter, had their conviction and sentence reduced on appeal to the lesser offence of 'violent disorder' and were sentenced to 12-month supervision orders.

Along with these high-profile cases, statistics suggest there has been a growth in serious and violent crimes in recent years among younger offenders. For those aged 10 to 18 the number who were convicted or cautioned for violent offences rose from 17,590 in 2003 to 24,102 in 2006. For all crimes resulting in a conviction or caution for this age group, figures rose from 222,750 in 2006 to 277,986 in 2007/8 (*Youth Crime in England and Wales*, Civitas, 2010).

Growth in gangs and gun and knife crimes between young people has also been confirmed by recent data. Almost 50% of shootings and 22% of serious violence in London is thought to be committed by known gang members (Metropolitan Police Intelligence Bureau research, October 2011). In 2011, the government published its *Ending Gang and Youth Violence* report. Its proposals focused on five areas:

1. prevention: early intervention at home including domestic violence, through schools and education;

2. pathways out: focus on education within the secure estate, support for behavioural issues and programmes for mental health and substance misuse problems and re-housing for gang members;

3. punishment: consideration of new curfew powers for police, introduction of new gang injunctions and mandatory sentencing for certain knife crime offences;

4. partnership working including enhanced multi-agency working and sharing of data;

5. providing support.

That criminal behaviour is relatively common among some young people is also confirmed by non-police data. Some indication of this can be found from studies of young people, which include self-report material, such as the Youth Lifestyle Survey (YLS), first carried out in 1992/3 (**Graham and Bowling 1995**) and again in 1998/9 (**Flood-Page** *et al.* **2000**). This survey interviewed 4,848 people aged between 12 and 30 in England and Wales and asked them about their involvement in 27 different offences. The report's findings included:

- Offending was found to be common – 57 per cent of men reported committing at least one offence during their lives and 26 per cent in the last year. Figures for women were lower, with 37 per cent reporting having committed an offence in their lives, and 11 per cent in the last year.

- Those aged between 14 and 21 committed most offences.

- A small number (8 per cent in total: of which 12 per cent were men and 4 per cent women) were counted as 'serious' or 'persistent' offenders because they had either committed three or more offences in the last year of one of a group of more serious offences such as violence, burglary, car theft or robbery. Ten per cent of offenders were responsible for nearly one-half of all the crimes reported by the sample.

A variety of factors have been associated with crime, particularly youth crime (**as seen in Chapter 5**), and criminologists have studied the association between involvement in offending and a host of factors including individual characteristics, family factors and wider social factors. Given the importance of the family in young people's early lives, particular attention has been paid to a range of circumstances within families. As they grow up, however, young people spend more time out of the home, at school and with their friends; and performance and attendance at school are also associated with offending, as is the presence of friends who are also involved in crime. Social structural factors may affect employment and leisure opportunities – with those who cannot participate in employment and desired leisure facing temptations to engage in crime. A wide range of factors, therefore, affect young people's participation in crime – and many have looked at what are now described as 'risk factors'.

Again the YLS provides a good illustration of a combination of factors. The study identified a group classified as 'offenders' which excluded those who had committed one or two minor crimes, and a group of serious or persistent offenders, and explored which factors were most strongly associated with offending. While these were present for both male and female offenders, because of the smaller number of female offenders the figures are most reliable for boys. For 12–17-year-old boys the 'risk factors', in order of importance, were:

1. having used drugs in the last year;

2. being disaffected from school;

3. hanging around in public places;

4. having **delinquent** friends or acquaintances;

5. poor parental supervision;

6. persistent truancy.

A broadly similar picture emerged for those aged 18 and over, with heavy drinking emerging as a strong factor and not having any educational qualifications being the second most important predictor. Family influences, on the other hand, appeared to be less important.

These factors cannot be said directly to lead to participation in crime. Those already likely to be involved in crime could, for example, also start truanting and seek out the company of like-minded youth – thus leading to a mutually reinforcing situation. Thus crime may lead to truanting rather than the other way round. Nevertheless, the strength of these associations demonstrates, as the authors argue, the importance of directing policies towards families and looking closely at how to prevent young people becoming disengaged and excluded from school. The report by **HM Inspectorate of Prisons** on *Children and Young People in Custody 2010/11*, showed that 86 per cent of young men and 82 per cent of young women in custody said they had been excluded from school (rather than truancy).

In the consultation (*Developing the Secure Estate for Children and Young People in England and Wales, Government Response to the Consultation*, YJB, March 2012), young offenders effectively 'self-analysed' factors that would reduce their risk of re-offending. They overwhelmingly suggested having more money, avoiding negative peer influences (perhaps, compounded by truancy and exclusion), avoiding drugs and alcohol and gaining employment but less than a quarter (23%) felt that they currently received enough help with these issues.

The major public disorder in August 2011 has focused thoughts on why such large numbers of young people became involved. In relation to the riots, 26 per cent of those who appeared before the courts across the country (of 1,984 appearing) were aged 10 to 17 and a further 27 per cent were aged 18 to 20 (**MOJ 2012**). The majority had been in trouble before; figures suggesting that some 62 per cent of the youths having a previous caution or conviction. The riots occurred primarily in areas of social deprivation where there are higher rates of offending among the local population. (*Statistical Bulletin on the Public Disorder of 6th to 9th August 2011*, MOJ 2012). The same paper suggested a direct link with social deprivation in that 64% of the 10–17-year-olds appearing lived in the 20% most deprived areas while only 3% lived in the 20% least deprived areas. However, the majority of young people living in these areas did not take part in the riots, and those who did were distinguished by their criminal lifestyles as defined in terms of the high number of previous cautions and convictions.

Whatever the reason, the number of convictions of young people involved in grave crimes (crimes that could attract 14 years in prison if committed by an adult, such as murder, manslaughter, wounding with intent, rape, robbery and burglary) had increased from 6 in 1970 to 561 in 2000. This inevitably brings them into contact with the youth justice system and leaves open the question of whether there is a moral panic about youth crime – moral panic is defined as an over-exaggerated response to a problem – or whether the response, panic or not, is justified.

However, against this backdrop of a general fall in crime, there has been a steady rise in recorded violent crime since 1991. The number of youths cautioned or convicted for violence, drug offences and robbery has also risen, although this accounts for only around one-third of indictable youth crime. Robbery offences committed, for example between 2009/10 and 2010/11, were up by 11%. That said, 4,657 young people were given a custodial disposal in 2010/11, some 10% less than a year earlier and only half as many as there were ten years ago. There is, therefore, a clear downward trend in sending young people into detention.

Only 21 per cent of the public are 'very' or 'fairly' confident that the criminal justice system is effective in dealing with young people accused of crime (**Audit Commission 2004**).

8.2 Youth justice system

Objective 2

Outline and explain the youth justice system

The law distinguishes between different age groups in an effort to recognise differences in maturity and understanding. Section 107 of the Children and Young Persons Act 1933 (CYPA 1933) defined:

- a child as a person under the age of 14;
- a young person as someone who has attained the age of 14 and is under 18.

The term 'young adult', not defined by statute, is used to describe those aged 18 to 20.

Children under 10 years of age are deemed by the law to be incapable of telling right from wrong and therefore incapable of doing wrong – in legal terms **doli incapax**. As they are not regarded as responsible they cannot be put on trial, punished or regarded in law as blameworthy. In a trial at the Old Bailey in January

Table 8.4 Minimum Age of Criminal Responsibility

Jurisdiction	Age
South Africa	7 (but has *doli incapax* provision to age 14 i.e. there is a presumption in law that children under 14 are incapable of forming the intent to commit a crime and therefore cannot be prosecuted unless proved otherwise
Belgium	18
Spain	16
United States	6 to 12
Australia	10
England and Wales	10
New Zealand	10 (but addresses offending of most children through, restorative justice)
Netherlands and Scotland	12
Germany and Italy	14
Sweden, Finland, Denmark, and Norway	15

1998 (**described later in this chapter**) two 10-year-old boys were accused of rape in a West London school. A third boy was not prosecuted because he was 9 years old at the time of the offence.

The age at which children are regarded as responsible for their actions in law varies across Europe.

In the case of *T* v. *United Kingdom*, it was argued that the age of criminal responsibility as low as 10 breached the Human Rights Act 1998. The European Court of Human Rights said that, although there was no common standard among the member states as to the age of criminal responsibility and even though England and Wales had a low age, the age of 10 was not so young 'as to differ disproportionately from the age-limit followed by other European States'. This issue will not go away though there appears to be no political appetite to change things. The Centre for Social Justice (CSJ) is among a number of groups campaigning for the age of criminal responsibility to be raised and in January 2012, in a report entitled *Rules Of Engagement, Changing the heart of youth justice*, the CSJ again called for the age to be raised to 12 for all but the most grave offences (murder, attempted murder, rape, manslaughter and aggravated sexual assault).

Apart from legal liability for a crime, the age of an offender will also affect where and how the young person is dealt with in the criminal justice system.

It has been accepted for many years that special procedures are needed to deal with young offenders, and a series of different arrangements have developed. These arrangements reflect conflicting views over how such offenders should be dealt with. In general, two broad approaches can be contrasted. On the one hand, what is often described as a welfare approach seeks to protect children and young persons from the potential stigma of a criminal prosecution and encourages courts to take the welfare of the child or young person into account at all stages. Under this approach, diversion is encouraged and prosecution should be a last resort; and when taken to court, special procedures should protect young people from the harshness of a criminal trial and ensuing punishment. The rehabilitative approach was of particular relevance for young offenders, who were seen to be potentially more likely to respond to measures involving help, treatment, discipline and education. On the other hand, many of these measures have been criticised as not working to change criminal behaviour, as ineffective, too soft, or as insufficiently **deterrent** or punitive, and have attracted recurrent calls for tougher or more effective measures. A Royal Society paper on advances in neuroscience has supported quotes some experts as stating that the age of criminal responsibility is 'unreasonably low' suggesting that some parts of the brain are not fully mature until at least the age of 20 and this affects judgement and decision making by young people. But some care must be taken with direct comparisons with other jurisdictions – while some have much higher ages of criminal responsibility and focus on welfare, support and rehabilitation for deviant behaviour, they also still retain *removal* of youths into residential care, special psychiatric and detoxification units rather than our formal detention as part of a criminal process.

The range of measures, therefore, has tended to reflect a mixture of approaches, and very serious incidents involving young offenders renewed these conflicts. When the toddler James Bulger was abducted and murdered in Liverpool by two children in 1993, a shocked public was exposed to the views of the experts, whose opinions ranged from the call for more treatment to the demand for the punishment of the offenders. In January 1998 an Old Bailey rape trial involved two 10-year-old defendants who were eventually acquitted of raping a 9-year-old victim. The prosecution and trial of these boys highlighted concern and horror at the serious allegations, together with concerns over the way that such young defendants should be tried. Great efforts were made to make the courtroom less intimidating. A report in *The Times* described the scene:

> Court 12 at the Old Bailey has been transformed like a stage set into a modern primary school classroom. The only thing missing is a sandpit, a lump of Play-doh or a large frieze showing the letters of the alphabet . . . Four square tables have been arranged in the middle of the room . . . just as at school. The four barristers have dispensed with their wigs.
>
> (*The Times*, 16 January 1998)

The Criminal Justice and Public Order Act 1994 was enacted amid concerns about increasing rates of offending by the young, and introduced a number of tougher measures. Publicity given to cases where young offenders were sent to holiday camps or abroad as part of their sentences attracted criticism that offending youngsters should not be given advantages not enjoyed by their law-abiding counterparts. This reveals the conflicting pressures on youth justice policy – on the one hand, to punish young offenders and ensure that they are made to recognise the seriousness of their offences and, on the other, to take action against what are often seen to be the causes of their behaviour – adverse family or social circumstances. In addition, the youth justice system has been subject to considerable criticism as being too disparate and lacking coherent policies and has, like many other areas of criminal justice policy described in this book, been subject to auditing processes and the increased effect of managerialism, seen particularly in the reforms introduced in the Crime and Disorder Act 1998, described below, which focus more specifically on identifying risk factors and developing policies which more clearly target these risks.

▶ Special provision for youths

Before the nineteenth century, juvenile offenders were treated in a similar way to adults and could be sent to adult prisons, hanged or transported. Throughout the nineteenth century, however, there was a gradual development of measures specifically directed at young offenders, influenced by arguments that juveniles could be 'saved' and rehabilitated. This led to the development of special institutions such as **reformatories**, whose very name indicated an emphasis on reform through education and training. Reformatories catered for those with criminal convictions, and the industrial schools for children in need of care as manifested by truancy, vagrancy or who were in the care of adults with criminal or drunken habits. They were established by the Reformatory Schools Act 1854. At this time, a separate prison for boys was opened at Parkhurst on the Isle of Wight.

The Children Act 1908 established the **juvenile court** and formally separated cases involving juveniles from adult courts. It also abolished the use of imprisonment for juveniles. A mixture of welfare and punitive philosophies can be seen in the comment of the minister responsible for introducing this Act, Herbert Samuel, who stated that the 'courts should be the agencies for the rescue as well as the punishment of juveniles' (cited in **Gelsthorpe and Morris 1994: 951**). Other institutions for juveniles also reflected a welfare and punishment approach – special institutions were set up as part of the prison system, the first being in Borstal in Kent. The **Borstal** system, as it came to be known, emphasised a mixture of discipline and training. Some Borstals stressed education, being strongly imbued with the values and traditions of English public school education, and later some adopted a therapeutic approach (see, for example, **Hood 1965**).

Further moves towards a more welfare-based approach included the Children and Young Persons Act 1933 which established a special panel of magistrates to deal with juvenile offenders and stipulated that the court should have regard to the welfare of the child. In addition, the court could act in the place of parents, **in loco parentis**, and take such steps as necessary to ensure that the welfare of the child was being met. Approved schools, established in 1933, were residential schools for primarily **delinquent** boys and girls. They included naval and agricultural colleges and were mainly run by charitable groups or local authorities. They had to be approved by the Home Office. They were later abolished by the Children and Young Persons Act 1969. In 1948 local authorities were enabled to take into care those children considered to be 'in need of care and protection'. The same year, however, saw the introduction of detention centres and attendance centres which reflected a more disciplined approach. Detention centres were institutions in which young offenders could be sentenced to a short period of custody, in a regime intended to be tough and disciplinarian. Much emphasis was laid on physical education, although there were also elements of education and training. Attendance centre orders required juveniles to attend a centre, run mainly by the police, for a number of hours per week, often on a Saturday afternoon. They aimed to deprive delinquents of their leisure time and were often used in an attempt to take football hooligans off the terraces. Discipline was a key feature of early attendance centres, which mixed elements of physical education with more practical pursuits.

▶ Diversion

The argument that there is little point in punishing juveniles whose delinquency may be related to family or other problems continued to influence policy. Some went so far as to suggest that juveniles should be removed from the criminal justice system entirely. This approach forms the basis of the Scottish Children's Hearings system in which children who offend are referred to a Children's Panel which is not a court of law and deals with offending and non-offending young people. These ideas strongly affected the next important piece of legislation dealing with young offenders, the Children and Young Persons Act 1969 (CYPA 1969). This Act, often seen as representing the peak of the welfare approach, was based on a mixture of welfare and **diversionary** policies and made several radical and controversial changes (**Morris and Giller 1987**).

The benefits of diversionary policies were stressed and it was proposed that all offenders under 14 should be dealt with by care and protection rather than by criminal proceedings. The police were encouraged to use cautions for juvenile offenders and only refer them to court following consultation with the social services. The expanding role of the social worker was also reflected in provisions for care orders, which, after being given by magistrates, were to be implemented by social workers. Social workers rather than magistrates, therefore, would make the key decision as to whether the young person would be sent to a residential institution or left at home. Community homes, which were to house all children in care whether or not they had committed an offence, replaced the approved schools which dealt only with delinquents. It was also intended to phase out Borstals and detention centres and to replace them with a sentence of intermediate treatment – again run by social services.

In the event, many sections of the CYPA 1969 were never implemented and it attracted considerable controversy and opposition among observers of and practitioners involved in the system. Magistrates, for example, felt that too much power had been lost to social workers and that they were powerless to determine what might happen to an offender. Rising rates of juvenile crime attracted criticisms that the system was too soft and was unable to cope with serious juvenile offenders.

Diversion increased in the years following the CYPA 1969 with an enormous rise in numbers cautioned by the Juvenile Liaison Bureaux set up by the police. In the 1980s there was a growing recognition of the limitations of custodial or institutional treatment. Not only was such treatment costly – with detention in some institutions costing more than boarding schools – but the vast majority of juveniles coming out of such institutions went on to reoffend. **Recidivism** rates for detention centres, for example, were as high as 80 per cent. Many also argued that institutions for juveniles acted like schools of crime where offenders perpetuated a delinquent or criminal subculture. Concern was also aroused by evidence of violence and bullying within institutions. Treatment in the community, therefore, was seen as being preferable and as no less effective in terms of reconviction rates.

The Criminal Justice Act 1982 introduced criteria to restrict the use of care and custodial orders and requirements for juveniles to be legally represented. Custodial orders were only to be made in cases where it could be established that the offender had failed to respond to non-custodial measures, where a custodial sentence was seen as necessary for the protection of the public or where the offence was serious. Borstals were abolished, removing any element of indeterminacy from the system. Until then offenders had been sentenced to a period of Borstal training, with the date of release of up to three years to be decided by those running the system. Borstal was replaced by a fixed-term youth custody order and the Act also abolished the use of imprisonment for offenders under the age of 21. New sentences were then introduced and abolished with bewildering speed. From 1983 a determinate sentence of youth custody was introduced for offenders between 15 and 21, with a maximum sentence for those aged under 17 of 12 months (raised to 2 years in 1994). A sentence of custody for life was introduced as the equivalent to life imprisonment when the offender was aged 17 and under 21. Detention sentence orders for males were changed so that the usual sentence ranged from 21 days to 4 months instead of 3 to 6 months. The Criminal Justice Act 1988 abolished the detention sentence order and youth custody. The new term for youth custody was to be detention in a young offender institution.

Diversionary policies continued throughout the 1980s, with a series of Home Office circulars stressing that prosecution should be used as a last resort for young offenders. There was also encouragement for the greater use of informal warnings instead of cautioning to avoid net widening. The use of cautions for second and third offences was encouraged, along with the development in some areas of **caution-plus** schemes, which incorporate a caution with some form of super-vised activity in the community. The open-handed use of cautioning was to come in for criticism as to its effectiveness. Cautioning for younger offenders was revised by the Criminal Justice Act 1998 into a more restricted use of reprimands and warnings. Since then, there has again been a reverse in policy, with the abolition of reprimands and warnings and their replacement with cautions and conditional cautions by the Legal Aid Sentencing and Punishment of Offenders Act 2012. There is now, again, no limit to the number of occasions a young offender can be diverted away from the courts. It is worth noting that intervention through cautions or conditional cautions effectively allows punitive, rehabilitative and restorative activities in the community without conviction. Now, a young offender can receive a caution or conditional caution even with previous convic-tions. The new scheme therefore allows a far wider discretion pre-charge to decide whether offending justifies formal court proceedings. It will be interesting to see whether this move to allow far more flexibility in disposing cases without court process and conviction raises the same concerns previously raised.

From the 1970s until the 1990s, diversion policies were seen to work (in diver-sionary terms) in that they kept children (10–13), young people (14–17) and young adults (18–20) out of the courts and out of custodial institutions during a period when crime was rising steadily.

From the mid-1990s the main trend in sentencing has been the greater use of community penalties (64 per cent in 2002) with males aged 15 to 17. The use of immediate custody for this age group remained relatively stable (15 per cent in 2001 and in 2002); for offenders aged 12 to 14 the custody rate was 7 per cent, the same in 2001 and 2002. In the 10 to 17 age range 500 females were given custody in 2002 in contrast to 5,700 males (*Criminal Statistics in England and Wales 2002*: 89–90).

By 1990, a new mood had set in and there was a growing disillusionment with diversionary and welfare approaches to young offenders. This reflected a growing concern about a number of related issues; and criticisms involved a perceived reluctance of the system to respond to younger offenders, the type of sentences given by the courts, the lack of control and the leniency of the treatment of delin-quents. There was a view that the system had moved too far in the direction of concern for the welfare of the young offender. It was felt that the wish to avoid **labelling** young offenders had resulted in a diversionary approach where young-sters felt they could get away with most things, and that the public was not being protected from dangerous or persistent young criminals. There were concerns, for example, about persistent young offenders who committed further offences while on bail, about the lack of secure facilities to hold such offenders, and about the absence of public protection provided by the system.

In the 1990s, the then Conservative Government introduced a number of measures to deal with these concerns. The Criminal Justice and Public Order Act 1994 introduced a secure training order for persistent offenders aged from 12 to 14. The Crime (Sentences) Act 1997 extended the use of community sentences for younger offenders and allowed for electronic tagging of 10–15-year-old offenders.

▶ The Crime and Disorder Act 1998

In 1996, a highly influential Audit Commission Report, *Misspent Youth*, was very critical of the youth justice system as being expensive and inefficient. It stressed the need for some consistency in the aims of the system, for greater inter-agency cooperation and for appropriate performance indicators for all agencies and better monitoring of performance. This had a considerable influence on the new government and in November 1997 the Home Office published a White Paper, *No More Excuses*, and a number of consultation papers which promised a radical overhaul of the youth justice system. The government (**as seen in Chapter 5**) was also influenced by the Wilson and Kelling 'broken windows' argument which proposed early action against disorderly behaviour. The resulting Crime and Disorder Act 1998 included the introduction of the following:

- Youth Justice Board for England and Wales: to monitor the performance and operation of the youth justice system, by preventing crime and the fear of crime, identifying and dealing with young offenders and reducing reoffending. Youth Justice Service: local authorities, police and probation to combine to tackle crime by younger offenders.

- Multi-disciplinary Youth Offending Teams (YOTs) in every local authority area including representatives from probation, social services, police, health authority, local authority education department, drugs and alcohol misuse teams and housing departments.

- A system of pre-court reprimands and final warnings replaced the more informal process of police cautioning of younger offenders for the purpose of diversion.

- **Disposals** based on supporting parents in their control of their children (**Parenting Orders**). Parents can be required to attend counselling and guidance sessions once a week for a period up to three months.

- Anti-Social Behaviour Orders (ASBOs) for up to two years to deal with bad behaviour, criminal or otherwise. These orders, primarily though not exclusively aimed at young people, were seen as an important plank in controlling the behaviour of troublesome teenagers who caused fear and annoyance in housing or shopping neighbourhoods, especially late at night. ASBOs were intended to deal with those offenders whose behaviour or age did not warrant or allow for other forms of intervention.

- A disposal to control behaviour in local areas, the local child curfew: this gives power to the local authority and the police to set up curfew schemes, after application to the Home Secretary, for children under 10. This means that in specified curfew areas children under 10 should not be out without supervision late at night. If the order is breached a 'child safety order' can be made.

New kinds of community orders were introduced:

- *Action plan orders:* for those aged 10 to 17, for a three-month period, combining elements of punishment, rehabilitation and reparation.

- *Reparation orders:* available for 10–17-year-olds, which the courts have to consider when a compensation order is not imposed. This order can require the offender to make direct recompense (or reparation) to the victim and may include mediation or apologising.

- The **Detention and Training Order (DTO)** for those aged 10 to 17 years of age. This replaced the sentence of detention in a young offender institution and the secure training order. It is intended for serious offences where custody is justified and, for the younger age groups, additional criteria are met. In relation to 10- and 11-year-olds the criterion is 'for the purpose of protecting the public', although this disposal has not yet been made available for this age group; for 12–14-year-olds the DTO can only be used with respect to persistent offenders. One-half of the term of a DTO is spent in custody and the other half under community supervision. Offenders can be detained in a young offender institution, secure training centre, youth treatment centre or local authority secure unit supervised by the Youth Justice Board.

These provisions, and the discussions surrounding them, display elements of control and elements of requirements to deal with bad behaviour.

ASBOs were orders to tackle disorderly and anti-social behaviour. They are civil orders which can, however, involve criminal enforcement following non-compliance. The orders were frequently not complied with. A report by the National Audit Office published in December 2006 suggests that more than 55 per cent of those given ASBOs did not comply and that approximately one-fifth of the cases examined in the report found defendants who persistently breached their orders. The report suggested wide geographical variations in the predominance of anti-social behaviour. It also pointed to an increased success rate in 'pre ASBO action' by use of warning letters and acceptable behaviour contracts. The Youth Justice Board also conducted research into the effectiveness of ASBOs and were similarly concerned about the levels of breach. They also raised the concern that ASBOs might be seen as a 'badge of honour' which increased a young person's 'street credibility' among his or her peers. Of course the other options – either to do nothing (justified by the non-interventionist labelling approach) or to use the police and courts to prosecute criminal behaviour – also have their critics.

Whether the criminal justice system is really geared to promote 'good' behaviour is the fundamental criticism of the welfare approach to crime, in contrast to those who think that the main concern of the system is to respond to bad behaviour by attempting to control it and protect the public. The use of ASBOs as a standalone civil order has, in fact, more than halved since 2005 and is now predominantly attached to criminal convictions.

In May 2011, the Coalition Government published a consultation 'More effective responses to anti-social behaviour' in which it was proposed that ASBO's be reviewed. The Anti-social Behaviour, Crime and Policing Act 2014 replaced ASBO's with an 'injunction to prevent nuisance and annoyance' (IPNAs) and 'Criminal Behaviour Orders' when imposed upon conviction. The injunction is a civil order, attracts a civil burden of proof to tackle behaviour which in itself might be criminal or non-criminal. Under the Act, the Youth Court now hears applications for injunctions for those under 18, rather than the County Court or High Court which deal with adults. It continues the trend of trying to control youth behaviour by the use of civil court orders rather than the criminal process, albeit providing for specialists in the Youth Court to deal with applications rather than judges in civil courts (unlike, for example, gang injunctions introduced by the Policing and Crime Act 2009).

Recent initiatives retain strong elements of welfare philosophies. The emphasis, for example, on early intervention in the 2003 Green Paper *Youth Justice – the next steps*, on addressing the 'causes' of youth crime, on looking at families and, in particular, the emphasis on restorative justice, illustrates the persistence of welfare principles; and the Act has led to greater funding for the youth justice system. Youth justice policy continues, therefore, to contain an at times uneasy balance between welfare and punishment (**Newburn 2003**).

The Criminal Justice and Immigration Act 2008 (CJIA) implemented the changes suggested in the 2003 Green Paper. In April 2009, it brought in important changes to cautioning of, and community sentences for young people. It also removed some pre-existing orders such as the action plan order. These provisions are, in some respects, a departure from previous initiatives in that the youth provisions are now similar to those applicable to adults, with necessary modification.

There is also a clarification of the purpose of sentencing and indeed of the youth justice system. The principal aim of the youth justice system is stated as being: to prevent offending (or reoffending) by persons aged under 18, as well as the welfare of the offender. The purposes of sentencing young offenders are stated as:

a. the punishment of offenders;

b. the reform and rehabilitation of offenders;

c. the protection of the public;

d. the making of reparation by offenders to persons affected by their offences.

Deterrence as a purpose of sentence was not adopted (see purpose of sentencing adults in s 142 CJA 2003) as presumably, it is not consistent with the welfare of the offender.

The Act introduced the Youth Conditional Caution (YCC), available in the first instance for those aged 16 and 17 but is now for all young offenders aged 10 to 17. As a result of more recent amendments brought in by LASPO 2012, they are now available for repeat offenders and even those with previous convictions.

The criteria for imposing a YCC are that it is explained (in the presence of an appropriate adult if the young person is under 16):

• there is evidence that the offender has committed an offence;

• there is sufficient evidence to charge;

• the young offender admits the offence.

In receiving a caution the young person will sign a document containing:

a. details of the offence;

b. an admission by them that they committed the offence;

c. their consent to being given the youth conditional caution;

d. the conditions attached to the caution.

In the case of indictable only offences, a conditional caution, (breach of which may result in prosecution), must be authorised by the CPS and can include a fine (up to £100), compensation, attendance at specified places, for instance for courses or programmes, and any conditions must be designed for rehabilitation, reparation or punishment.

In recent years there has been a significant drop in the number of cases heard in the Youth Court. The reasons for this are complex but must, to some extent, be due to the use of diversionary policies by the police. Rather than charging and bailing the offender to court, they refer cases to Youth Offending Teams who will devise the programmes which form the conditions. This power to impose programmes upon those who admit offences is significant, in that they effectively replace the court in imposing non-custodial disposals. While the debate continues on the merits of an adversarial criminal process to deal with deviant behaviour by youths, it could be said that the court process is already being replaced 'through the back door' with more and more out-of-court disposals by the police. On current policy, it seems clear that the function of the court will be increasingly restricted to very serious offences and where other disposals fail to prevent serious reoffending. It raises the question whether such issues are better dealt with by 'professionals' on youth panels rather than by magistrates and judges in court. That will ultimately depend on whether overall offending is reduced by such measures.

The pre-court stages were considered further in **Chapter 7**. In this chapter we now consider the court and sentencing stages.

▶ Youth Courts

Objective 3

Describe the processes and agencies involved when young offenders are sent to youth court

Youth Courts were set up by the Criminal Justice Act 1991 and replaced and extended the jurisdiction of the juvenile courts in 1908. They now deal with the majority of offenders aged 10 to 17, although some in this age group may be dealt with in the adult Magistrates' Court or in the Crown Court for the following crimes: where defendants are charged with homicide (murder or manslaughter) or where a 16–17-year-old is charged with certain firearms offences they must be sent to the Crown Court for trial (Magistrates' Court Act [MCA] 1980, s 24A).

Defendants when charged with other grave crimes – defined as any offence which carries a maximum term of imprisonment of 14 or more years, plus indecent assault on women, causing death by dangerous driving and causing death by careless driving while under the influence of drink or drugs – must be sent to the Crown Court for trial if the Youth Court's powers of punishment, i.e. two-year Detention and Training Order do not seem sufficient (MCA 1980, s 24A and Powers of Criminal Courts (Sentencing) Act 2000, s 91).

Young people classified as dangerous offenders under the Criminal Justice Act 2003 must be sent for trial in the Crown Court or committed for sentence where there is significant risk of public harm from further offences. This applies to specified very serious violence and sexual offences.

Young defendants may be tried in the Crown Court if charged in association with another defendant, aged over 18.

Guidelines indicate that a youth aged 12 to 15 should be sent to the Crown Court where he is charged with an offence of such gravity that a sentence *substantially beyond* the two-year maximum for a detention and training order is a realistic possibility (para 12.11 *Overarching Principles – Sentencing Youths, Definitive Guideline*).

The procedures in the Youth Court are more informal than in adult courts, and special rules protect young people from publicity and contact with older defendants. Members of the public other than those directly concerned are not allowed to be present at a Youth Court hearing, and although members of the press are allowed to attend, they may not publish any information which can identify a young defendant. The CYPA 1933 empowers the court to restrict any reporting of cases revealing the name, home or school address of a defendant or containing any particulars which could lead to the identification of any child or young person concerned in proceedings. This provision applies to witnesses as well as defendants, and may be applied in the adult court. Most magistrates' courts have a separate courtroom set out appropriately for Youth Courts, so the young person is seated on the same level as the magistrates, rather than in the dock, and make arrangements to minimise the chances of young defendants being in contact with adult offenders. Defendants are addressed by their first names, and although they plead guilty or not guilty a finding of guilt rather than a conviction is recorded. For defendants under 16 the court must require a parent or guardian to attend also. For those over 16 the court may require the parent or guardian to attend. Where a child or young person is in the care of the local authority, a local authority representative can be required to attend.

A Practice Direction (Crown Court: Trial of Children and Young Persons (2000)) set out the arrangements for trial of young offenders in the Crown Court, after concern was raised about the effect of the Crown Court trial process on young defendants in the case of *T and V* v. *United Kingdom* 1999. The Practice Direction (guidance from the Lord Chief Justice) advises that the defendant should be able to visit the court in advance, should be able to sit with parents or other supporters, that robes and wigs should not normally be worn and that care should be taken to ensure that they understand what is going on. In 2010, however, the very decision to have a Crown Court trial for a 10-year-old and an 11-year-old for rape was criticised by the Court of Appeal. Lord Justice Hughes expressed dismay at the trial taking place at the Old Bailey and that 'it had become necessary for two ten-year-olds and an eight-year-old, all with impeccable upbringings, to be the key participants in a trial before the Crown Court'. The case re-iterated that those who are under 18 and particularly children under 15, should, wherever possible, be tried in the Youth Court.

Each Local Justice Area has a Youth Court Panel made up of magistrates especially chosen from the bench because of their special knowledge of, or interest in, young people. As a result of this interest many magistrates sit in both the Youth Court and the Family Proceedings Court which deals with care proceedings. The bench dealing with a Youth Court hearing will be composed of two or more (usually three) members of the Youth Court panel. A lay bench should contain at least one male and one female magistrate. The court has a wide discretion but is guided by CYPA 1933 section 44, which states that every court shall have regard for the welfare of the child or young person and, where proper, take steps to remove him or her from undesirable surroundings and ensure that adequate provision is made for training and education. However, the aims of sentencing are now clarified in the CJIA 2008 and the aims are now not exclusively focused on the welfare of the child (**see section above**). Some **district judges** who have specialist training in youth work additionally sit alone in the Youth Court and a few are specifically authorised to deal with rape and serious sex offences in an attempt to deal with the critique mentioned earlier.

▶ Sentencing young offenders

Objective 4

Explain the differences in sentencing aims and court disposals for young offenders

Before sentence is passed, the offender, either personally or through a lawyer, parent or guardian, must be allowed to make representations and the court has to consider all available material concerning the offender, his or her background, education and medical history. It is usual to have reports from the local Youth Offending Team and to be sentenced locally where the offender resides, irrespective of where the offence is committed and tried.

The sentences applicable to a young offender vary according to the court in which they are being sentenced. Normally, where a conviction is recorded in an adult court, a young offender will be remitted to the Youth Court for sentence. Young offenders can be given an absolute or conditional discharge, referral order, a fine or a youth rehabilitation order. Some special provisions relating to the sentencing of young offenders are set out below.

Referral Order

Where a youth appears before a court for sentence on an imprisonable offence and pleads guilty but has no previous findings of guilt, the Court must impose a **referral order** for a period between 3 months and 12 months unless the court imposes an absolute discharge, conditional discharge, custodial sentence or hospital order or the offence is so serious that it imposes a Detention and Training Order. The components of the order are decided by a youth offending panel and, significantly, the finding of guilt (conviction) is immediately 'spent' on completion of the order and generally, need not be disclosed. If a further offence is committed during the order or there is non-compliance with its requirements, the court can look at the order again. It was introduced as 'a last chance' for first time offenders at court. The Legal Aid, Sentencing and Punishment of Offenders Act 2012 (LASPO), now permits the court to impose a referral order on unlimited occasions where the offender pleads guilty. In theory, at least, an offender can now receive a referral order again and again for low level offending where greater intervention or punishment is not warranted.

Absolute and conditional discharge

An **absolute discharge** can be imposed when the court feels it is inappropriate to inflict punishment because the offender is morally blameless. A young person receiving a **conditional discharge** receives no immediate punishment because the court feels it is 'inexpedient to inflict punishment'. A period of up to three years is set and, as long as the young person does not commit a further offence during this period, no punishment will be imposed. If the young person re-offends during this period, they can be brought back to court and re-sentenced.

Fine

The maximum fine payable by an offender under the age of 14 is £250, and for an offender aged 14 to 17 is £1,000. Where the offender is under 16, the court is under a duty to order that payments are made by the parent or guardian, unless they cannot be found and it would be unreasonable for them to be ordered to pay. For offenders over 16, magistrates have discretion to make such an order.

Reparation Order

Beyond a fine, but for less serious offences the reparation order survived and can be imposed for up to 24 hours over a maximum period of three months. The victim's views are sought as to whether he feels the offence can be dealt with by reparation, either directly or to the community at large. Examples of reparation, might be a letter of apology to the victim or meeting with face to face to apologise, or, perhaps, the cleaning walls of graffiti in a case of criminal damage. The aim is to confront the offender with the consequences of his or her behaviour.

Youth Rehabilitation Order

As far as sentencing is concerned, the most important change in the Criminal Justice and Immigration Act 2008 was the introduction of the generic community order for young offenders, the Youth Rehabilitation Order (YRO). This replicated in large part the generic community order for adults and abolished many of the separate orders that previously existed: curfew orders, exclusion orders, attendance centre orders, supervision orders and action plan orders.

The YRO can run for up to three years with a range of attached requirements:

a. an activity requirement;

b. a supervision requirement;

c. an unpaid work requirement (16s and 17s only);

d. a programme requirement;

e. an attendance centre requirement;

f. a prohibited activity requirement;

g. a curfew requirement;

h. an exclusion requirement;

i. a residence requirement (see paragraph 16 of that Schedule);

j. a local authority residence requirement;

k. a mental health treatment requirement;

l. a drug treatment requirement;

m. a drug testing requirement;

n. an intoxicating substance treatment requirement;

o. an education requirement;

p. an electronic monitoring requirement.

The YROs can be extended by up to six months (only once) to allow for completion of requirements. Where the offence is imprisonable, intensive supervision and surveillance (ISS) or fostering must be considered first as part of a YRO if the court is of the view that the offence(s) are so serious that custody is appropriate. Non-custodial options must be rejected before a Detention and Training Order (DTO) is imposed.

Breaches of the YRO are governed by a statutory scheme setting out a warning procedure before an offender is returned to court and the options (e.g. fine, reviewing of the order, ordering unpaid work) available to the court.

When a young person or child is before the court for sentence, a parenting order must also be considered for all offenders under the age of 16. These can be given to the parents or carers of young people who offend, truant or who have received a child safety order or anti-social behaviour order or **sex offender order**. It lasts for three months, but can be extended to 12 months. It requires a parent or carer to attend counselling or guidance sessions. The parent or carer may also have conditions imposed on them such as attending their child's school, ensuring their child does not visit a particular place unsupervised or ensuring their child is at home at particular times. A failure to fulfil the conditions can be treated as a criminal offence and the parent or carer can be prosecuted.

The boxed text below shows a consistent trend in a reduction of disposals in the youth justice system, seemingly reflecting a reduction in first time entrants into the system. There is no single identifiable cause for this but police targets on disposals have been removed and it may be that more intervention has resulted in less young people being arrested as first time offenders. The actual numbers in custody have been greatly reduced.

Custody

When young offenders under the age of 21 are sentenced to a custodial sentence they may be sent to one of the following, depending on their age:

- *Secure Training Centres (STCs)* – privately run, education-focused centres for offenders up to the age of 17.

- *Local Authority Secure Children's Homes (LASCHs)* – run by social services and focused on attending to the physical, emotional and behavioural needs of vulnerable young people. For children there are secure units run by local authorities. They have high staff to student ratios: some have 30 adults looking after 8 children.

- *Young Offenders Institution (YOIs)* – run by the Prison Service, these institutions are for 15–21-year-olds.

- *Detention and Training Order (DTO)*. This is the most used custodial sentence for young offenders, introduced as a generic custodial sentence for 12–17-year-olds by the Crime and Disorder Act 1998, although powers exist (still not yet implemented) to extend this to 10–12-year-olds.

Extracts on sentencing and custody for young people

Youth Justice Statistics 2012/13
England and Wales

Published by Youth Justice Board / Ministry of Justice
Statistics Bulletin (30th January 2014)

Sentences given to young people in 2012/13

There were 25,577 young people sentenced for indictable offences 38 and found guilty of an offence in court in 2012/13. In 2012/13, there was a total of 43,601 young people sentenced for all types of offences. When examined by type of sentence:

2,780 young people were sentenced to immediate custodial sentences, with most (89 per cent) of these being Detention and Training Orders (DTOs);

29,343 young people were sentenced to community sentences, including 13,527 YROs;

11,478 young people were sentenced to first-tier sentences (these include discharges, fines and otherwise dealt with disposals).

Trends in the number of young people sentenced, 2002/03 to 2012/13

The total number of young people sentenced at all courts has fallen by 28 per cent from 60,258 in 2011/12 to 43,601 in 2012/13.

Custody

The average population in custody (under 18) in 2012/13 was 1,544. The average population in custody (under 18) has fallen by 49 per cent from 3,029 in 2002/03.

Detention for young people in custody 2012/13

Over half (58 per cent) of the average population of young people (under 18) in custody in 2012/13 were serving a Detention and Training Order (DTO). A further 22 per cent were held on remand. The remaining 21 per cent were serving long-term sentences for the most serious offences.

Offences resulting in young people going into custody, 2012/13

Most young people held in custody in 2012/13 were there for serious offences, including;

31 per cent for robbery offences;

23 per cent for violence against the person offences;

17 per cent for burglary (domestic and non-domestic) offences;

7 per cent were in custody for breach offences.

For 15–17-year-olds, the DTO test is simply that the offence is so serious that only custody is justified. For 12–14-year-olds, in addition the young person must be a persistent offender. The length of the sentence can only be specified periods of 4, 6, 8, 10, 12, 18 or 24 months. Before the imposition of a DTO, the court must first consider a YRO with intensive fostering or ISSP as an alternative. An ISSP adds 6 months high-intensity education, activities, reparation backed up by tracking and tagging with 25 hours a week contact time for first three months. It allows for strict and close monitoring of serious and high risk offenders. Intensive fostering is rarely proposed by the Youth Offending Teams in pre-sentence reports but involves removal of the offender from his immediate environment and imposition of appropriate behavioural boundaries in the care of foster carers in an attempt to prevent further offending.

The first half of a DTO is spent in custody while the second half is spent in the community under the supervision of the Youth Offending Team. The Youth Offending Team can also require the young person to be on an intensive supervision and surveillance programme (ISSP), which is discussed above, upon release on a DTO as a condition of the community period of the sentence.

The Legal Aid Sentencing and Punishment of Offenders Act 2012 (LASPO) has introduced minimum **mandatory** sentences of detention for two new knife offences even for a first-time offender. An offender aged 16 or 17 year must receive a sentence of at least four months' detention unless it would be unjust in all the circumstances. This sits uneasily with the individualistic welfare approach to sentencing for youths but is an attempt to send a strong message in relation to the most serious knife crime offences.

Dangerous and serious offenders might be sentenced under section 90 or 91, applying only to offences such as murder or rape or those offences for which an adult would receive a sentence of 14 years imprisonment or more. This sentence can be given by a Crown Court only, and the entire sentence is completed in custody. The release date for a young person sentenced under section 90 is decided by the Home Secretary. The release date for section 91 sentences is set automatically.

For dangerous young offenders, LASPO 2012 introduced the new '*extended determinate sentence of detention*' replacing '*detention for public protection*' and '*extended detention*'. This is for young people convicted of specified sexual or violent offences. It has a custody period and an extended licence period. People on this sentence must serve a minimum of two-thirds of the custody period (of up to five years for violent offences and eight years for sexual offences).

Detention for life is retained and can be imposed where a child or young person is convicted of an offence where the statutory maximum is life and is of the utmost gravity and the court is of the opinion that there is significant risk to members of the public of serious harm by the commission of further specified offences. An indeterminate sentence, release from detention for life is dependent on the recommendations of the Parole Board but the offender remains on licence for life.

In November 2011 there were 2,200 under 18s in custody of which 456 were on remand (Youth Justice Board and Chief Inspector of Prisons Report). There were 174 in Secure Children's Homes, 283 in Secure Training Centres and 1,579 in Young Offender Institutions. Those serving DTOs totalled 1,250, while 28 were serving indeterminate sentences for public protection and 25 were serving extended sentences. United Nations figures in 2005 suggest that England and Wales has the highest incarceration rate in Europe for those aged below 18 years and, of those jurisdictions providing data, it was the fifth highest in the world behind the United States, South Africa, Belize and Swaziland (**Muncie 2005**). That said, figures have come down every year since then. In 2002, England and Wales had 2,869 convicted persons under the age of 18 in a custodial establishment; this was 3.8% of the total prison population and 46.8 per 100,000 of the eligible population.

By 2010, that figure was 2,026, a figure close to 3% as successive policies have reduced the use of custody as a sentence. By 2013/14 the average population was below 2,000 (see latest numbers in the Box with data on sentencing and custody from the Youth Justice Board). In 2010/11, young people from a Black ethnic background accounted for 17% of young people in custody – an increase of 4% from 2007/08 (*Youth Justice Statistics 2010/11 England and Wales*, Ministry of Justice 2011). In comparison, young people from a Black ethnic background made up 3% of the general 10 to 17-year-old population (*Developing the Secure Estate for Children and Young People in England and Wales*, MOJ/YSB March 2012). The reasons for this are complex and cannot be dealt with simplistically in this chapter.

Local authorities are operationally responsible for youth offending services in relation to those resident in their area. In the courtroom, their youth offending teams prepare the **pre-sentence reports**, making suggestions as to sentencing options and carry out assessments including information on bail support.

Critics say the system has failed. For example, just under 40 per cent of young offenders are reconvicted within a year; this increases to 75 per cent for those completing custodial sentences (*Time for a Fresh Start*, Independent Commission on Youth Crime Anti-Social Behaviour 2010).

Several of the proposals of the Green Paper entitled *Breaking the Cycle: Effective Punishment, Rehabilitation and Sentencing of Offenders* and published in December 2010 have been implemented in the Legal Aid, Sentencing and Punishment of Offenders Act 2012. The paper suggested that 'the fundamental failing of policy has been the lack of a firm focus on reform and rehabilitation.' It highlighted the fact that 74% of offenders sentenced to youth custody and 68% of young people on community sentences re-offend within a year. To prevent young people committing crime and beginning a pattern of criminal behaviour that could last into adulthood, it said the government would:

- prevent more young people from offending and divert them from entering into a life of crime, including, by intervening early in the lives of children at risk and their families, simplifying out-of-court disposals and allowing police and prosecutors greater discretion in dealing with youth crime before it reaches court;
- protect the public and ensure that more is done to make young offenders pay back to their victims and communities and increasing the use of restorative justice;
- ensure the effective use of sentencing for young offenders. This includes introducing a single remand order for all under 18s, making local authorities gradually responsible for the full cost of court ordered secure remand and amending the Bail Act 1976 to remove the option of remand for young people who would be unlikely to receive a custodial sentence;
- incentivising local partners to reduce youth offending and reoffending using payment by results models;
- develop more effective governance by abolishing the Youth Justice Board;
- increasing freedoms and flexibilities for local areas including appointment of elected local Commissioners for Police.

Thus, thinking continued with emphasis on welfare and early intervention but controversially, also proposed 'payment by results' for programmed providers. In one 'payment for results' proposal, the government proposed sums of £3,900 to local authorities if they can reduce their local youth offending rates by a third and get 85% of children from 'troubled families' into education. Another suggested linking revenue of a private prison provider to reoffending rates of offenders on release.

It also proposed a further shift of responsibility for local youths to their local authorities by making the authority themselves financially responsible for the higher costs of a 'custodial' sentence. In doing so, it was a clear attempt to incentivise local authorities to do more in relation to local services in an attempt to stop escalation of any offending to the custodial bracket of sentencing.

Part 3 of the Legal Aid, Sentencing and Punishment of Offenders Act 2012 implemented the following changes some of which have been described above:

(i)   Promoting the use of informal restorative disposals by the police;

(ii) The repeal of penalty notices for disorder for 16 and 17 year-old (these are fixed penalties issued by the police for minor disorder offences); and

(iii) Replacing the reprimand and final warning with a system of youth cautions and youth conditional cautions.

Restorative Justice is a process whereby parties with a stake in a specific offence collectively resolve how to deal with the aftermath of the offence and its implications for the future. It involves bringing victims of crime together with their perpetrators in an attempt to repair the harm done, holding offenders to account and making amends. It attempts to make offenders think about the harm and impact of their offending and for victims to get answers to their questions. While, in theory, not restricted to just minor offences, some may have real concerns if serious offending was in the future, dealt with outside the courtroom with no judicial oversight. That of course, makes an assumption, that all youth offending is best dealt with in a criminal courtroom. That debate will be left for elsewhere.

The provisions now allow for youth cautions to be issued for minor offences committed by young offenders who have previously been convicted by a court. This means further offending, even where a youth has already been before a court need not come for another prosecution.

The next area of change was in relation to bail. Previously, if the court placed a child into detention upon refusal of bail (whether in a young offenders' institution or a secure remand, secure training centre or secure children's home), central government picked up two-thirds of the cost, the balance being met by the local authority. If, on the other hand, refusal of bail resulted in a remand to local authority accommodation (whereby the defendant lived somewhere directed by them), or the youth was granted bail with, say, electronic tagging or intensive supervision and surveillance conditions, the local authority met the entire bill. It was suggested that local authorities had not been incentivised sufficiently to promote alternatives to detention. The government, therefore, seeks through the changes to make local authorities financially responsible for all types of remands to youth detention thus encouraging them to develop alternatives to detention.

Secondly, a significant change in relation to bail for youths now only allows for detention in 'youth detention accommodation' where the court is of the view that there is a real prospect of a custodial sentence. This seeks to deal with the concern that around 75 per cent of youth defendants who were in detention upon being refused bail, would subsequently be either acquitted or given a community sentence. Critics might say that courts already take likely disposal into account when deciding whether to deprive liberty and some community sentences result exactly because it is felt that the spell already served in detention suffices in the circumstances.

Finally, 17-year-olds are no longer treated as adults for the purposes of bail. Previously, for the purposes of bail only, the criteria for them to be refused bail were the same as for adults even though for other purposes they were subject to the same regime as those aged 16 and under. Seventeen-year-olds will now fall within the same regime as other youths and bring our treatment of 17-year-olds in line with the United Nations Convention on the Rights of the Child that defines a child as those under the age of 18.

The cost of youth detention is between £69,600 and £193,600 per place per annum (Figures calculated from the Youth Justice Board's *Annual Report and Accounts for 2008/09* and its *2008/09 Corporate Business Plan*; as cited in The Independent Commission on Youth Crime and Antisocial Behaviour, *Time for a fresh start: The report of the Independent Commission on Youth Crime and Antisocial Behaviour*, London: The Police Foundation, 2010: 76).

Conclusion

Youth crime is widely perceived to be a major issue, although, as we have seen, much of it may be transitory and trivial. Nevertheless, a minority of young people are responsible for a large amount of recorded crime (23 per cent of police recorded crime was attributable to 10–17-year-olds according to *An estimate of youth crime in England and Wales*, Home Office Research Paper 64), and citizens can feel considerably threatened by youth crime. Measures to deal with youth crime have, over the years, developed a sometimes uneasy balance between the perceived need to control and punish young offenders, and not to be seen as 'soft' on youth offending, and the recognition that involvement in the formal systems of courts and prisons can have a damaging effect on young offenders and possibly exacerbate not only their involvement in crime but the problems which may have contributed to that in the first place. How much to control, punish, divert and how much to intervene in young people's lives are, therefore, major issues which youth justice systems must tackle. Future reforms continue in attempts to reduce the use of detention in relation to youths. Many will argue that the last few years have seen much success in an overall reduction in youth crime but all will agree that there is much more to do.

Review questions

1. In what ways and at what stages are young offenders treated differently in the criminal justice system?

2. Outline the main features of the welfare and punishment approaches to dealing with young offenders and illustrate them with some examples from the history of juvenile justice.

3. Identify the various orders available for young offenders and consider whether they represent a punishment or welfare approach.

4. Look at the different levels of crime prevention set out in **Chapter 5** (see Table 5.1).
   a. Have recent orders, such as parenting orders, neighbourhood curfews, and anti-social behaviour orders been aimed at the primary, secondary or tertiary level of crime prevention?
   b. In terms of the three levels of crime prevention, how does or might the family and parenting play a part in reducing crime among younger people?

Discussion questions

1. Why have separate systems of justice for young people been seen as desirable? Should young persons be dealt with in the criminal courts and to what degree do you think it desirable that they be diverted though alternative disposals?

2. Do you think that popular perceptions of youth crime reflect a moral panic and exaggerated responses based on media presentation of news stories about youth? In answering this question, consider: newspaper coverage of crime stories, crime statistics since 1950 (**see Chapter 2**), and other sources.

Further reading

Cooper C and Roe S (2012) *An estimate of youth crime in England and Wales*, London: Home Office Research Paper 64

Flood-Page C, Campbell S, Harrington V and Miller J (2000) *Youth Crime: Findings from the 1998/99 Youth Lifestyles Survey*, Home Office Research Study 209, London: HMSO.

Goldson B and Muncie J (eds) (2006) *Youth Justice*. London: Sage

Morgan R and Newburn T (2012) 'Youth Crime and Justice' in Maguire M, Morgan R and Reiner R (eds), *The Oxford Handbook of Criminology* (5th edn), Oxford: Oxford University Press

Muncie J (2003) *Youth and Crime* (2nd edn). London: Sage

Smith R (2007) *Youth and Crime* (2nd edn) Cullompton: Willan

Weblinks

Youth Justice Board: **www.yjb.gov.uk/en-gb/**

Every Child Matters: **www.everychildmatters.gov.uk/youthjustice/**

Youth Crime Action Plan: **www.dfes.gov.uk/publications/youthcrimeactionplan/**

Visit **www.pearsoned.co.uk/daviescrim** to access interactive self-assessment quizzes and activities, flashcards, and online glossary to test yourself on this chapter.

CRIMINAL JUSTICE PROCESS: CRIMINAL COURTS

Chapter 9

Criminal courts, judiciary and pre-trial procedure

Learning objectives

After reading the chapter you should be able to:

1. Outline the role of magistrates' courts
2. Outline the role of the Crown Court
3. Describe the membership and role of the judiciary
4. Explain the differences in procedure involved in a summons, bail and remands in custody
5. Explain the mode of trial decisions
6. Outline the stages and issues in trial case management

Key statistics

- In the 12 months to September 2013 a total of 1,431,848 defendants were proceeded against in the magistrates' courts in England and Wales for criminal cases – in 2009 the total number was 1,681,906
- In the 12 months to September 2013 the courts dealt with 355,456 indictable cases (this includes indictable only and triable either way cases) and 1,076,392 summary offences
- In 2011, there were a total of 166,808 trials at magistrates' courts in England and Wales – a decrease of 12% from 2007. Out of 166,808 trials, 72,058 (43%) were effective, 29,291 (18%) were ineffective and 65,459 (39%) were **cracked trials**

- Out of 13,479 appeals against decisions of Magistrates' Courts in 2011, 6,581 (49%) were against magistrates' verdict and 6,186 (46%) were against magistrates' sentence. Out of all appeals against verdict, 2,803 (43%) were allowed, and 2,202 (33%) were dismissed. Out of all appeals against sentence, 2,828 (46%) were allowed, and 1,792 (29%) were dismissed

- In 2012, there were 24,267 Justices of the Peace – a decline of 19% when compared to a peak in number of JPs in year 2007 – 12,445 (51%) were women and 11,822 (49%) were men

- In 2011, a total of 150,268 cases in England and Wales were dealt with in Crown Courts: 93,960 (62%) of cases were sent for trial; 42,829 (28%) have been committed for sentence; and, there were 13,479(9%) appeals against magistrates' decisions

- In the Crown Court in 2011, of 106,343 defendants sent for trial: 72,225 (68%) pleaded 'guilty' (to all counts), 31,574 (30%) pleaded 'not guilty' (to some or all counts) and 2,544 (2.4%) did not enter plea (see Figure 9.1)

- Out of 31,574 of defendants that pleaded 'not guilty', 19,422 (62%) were acquitted and 12,152 (38%) were convicted (Figure 9.2 shows who decided the 'not guilty' verdict)

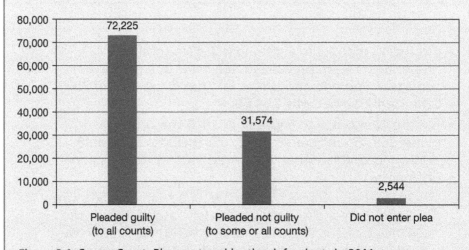

Figure 9.1 Crown Court: Pleas entered by the defendants in 2011

Source: https://www.cps.gov.uk/publications/docs/cps_annual_report_and_accounts_2012.pdf

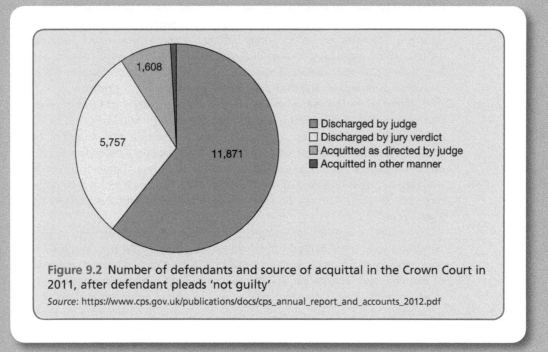

Figure 9.2 Number of defendants and source of acquittal in the Crown Court in 2011, after defendant pleads 'not guilty'

Source: https://www.cps.gov.uk/publications/docs/cps_annual_report_and_accounts_2012.pdf

Introduction

Following a decision to prosecute there are various stages to be undergone before an eventual conviction or acquittal can be arrived at. These stages are in part administrative: to ensure resources and paperwork are available at the right time in the right place; and part judicial: to ensure that the interests of justice, including those of the defendant, are met. Criminal cases are dealt with in either magistrates' courts or the Crown Court. Nearly all start in the magistrates' court, and before a full trial or hearing the magistrates may have to decide whether or not the **accused** is to be held in custody while awaiting trial. In some cases the accused has to decide whether to have the case heard by magistrates or before a judge and jury. As with the decision to prosecute or caution, many issues are involved with conflicting pressures between the goals of due process, crime control and cost efficiency.

In a trial the defendant, according to the principles of due process, is **presumed innocent** until proven guilty. But before the trial stage, defendants may be placed in custody, to ensure that they are present to answer the case against them, or to ensure that they do not interfere with evidence or with witnesses, or to protect the public. Crime control interests, therefore, may require that defendants' liberty be restricted before they have been convicted. Other procedures seek to ensure that defendants' interests are protected, particularly in respect of their rights to legal representation, to know the case against them, to have jury trial where appropriate and not to be tried on insufficient evidence. In addition, the organisation of criminal proceedings seeks, by including lay persons in both the magistracy and the jury, to involve representatives of the community as well as professionals and experts. As we have seen, however, due process may be lengthy and expensive and pressures for efficiency have resulted in changes in these procedures. This has led to fears, particularly from a class domination perspective, that too much power lies with the police and other professionals and that defendants' rights are being eroded.

Different courts in the English legal system deal with different kinds of cases and proceedings. The criminal justice system is concerned with criminal cases, which can be contrasted with civil cases. In criminal cases, a prosecution is conducted on behalf of the state or the Crown (or, occasionally, privately) against a defendant in order to establish whether or not that defendant is guilty of a crime. Guilt may be proved by evidence in a trial or accepted after a guilty **plea**, following which a conviction is recorded. This will normally be followed by a form of punishment referred to as a sentence.

Civil cases, in contrast, are mainly concerned with the settlement of disputes between two or more parties, often involving arguments over such matters as rent, boundaries, contracts, negligence, commercial disputes, family disputes on the break-up of marriage and inheritance. In civil cases a claimant sues another person – called the defendant – with a view to obtaining a judgment. A judgment may result in the court ordering the defendant to pay money as damages to compensate the claimant. Alternatively the court may issue an order or injunction requiring the defendant to do or to refrain from doing something. In other cases the court may make a declaration, or change the status of an individual – for example, by granting a divorce. The typical explanation of the difference between criminal and civil proceedings is that a criminal case is concerned with the relationship between the state and the individual, and a civil case is involved with regulating relationships between individuals.

Different courts deal with different types of cases: the county court can deal only with civil cases – it has only civil jurisdiction. Other courts – for example, the High Court and magistrates' courts – have jurisdiction in both civil and criminal matters. Magistrates' jurisdiction over civil law cases is limited to licensing matters and family proceedings.

A case may be transferred from one court to another. Nearly all criminal cases start in the magistrates' court and some are then passed to the Crown Court. Other cases may be heard by different courts because one or other party has appealed against the decision of the first court. Courts are therefore classified not only on the basis of the type of matter they deal with, but also in accordance with their jurisdiction to hear cases 'at first instance' or on appeal. Two criminal courts – the magistrates' courts and the Crown Court – deal with trials; they therefore have first instance criminal jurisdiction. The administration and organisation of the criminal courts, including how the work is allocated between these two tiers, has been criticised on many occasions and the most recent proposals for change were made in the Auld Review of the Criminal Courts (**Auld 2001**). This report proposed fundamental changes to the structure of the criminal courts, including the creation of a unified criminal court, divided into three divisions, to deal with serious, minor and mid-range offences. While the three-tier recommendation was not accepted, a Unified Courts Administration was provided for in the Courts Act 2003, and came into effect in April 2005. HM Courts and Tribunals Service was set up in 2011 to remove some of the administrative anomalies and delays.

The two levels of criminal courts will now be explored in more detail, starting with the magistrates, those voluntary workhorses of the system, along with their professional colleagues, the 'District Judges' who were known as **stipendiary magistrates** until August 2000, and then going on to examine proceedings in the Crown Court, before the thoroughbreds of the process, the judges. This chapter will then go on to consider crucial pre-trial decisions such as whether to **remand on bail** or in custody and the mode of trial decision, before going on to examine the process of establishing guilt in **Chapter 10**.

9.1 Magistrates' courts

Objective 1

Outline the role of magistrates' courts

Upon visiting a magistrates' court – all of which are open to the public, except when dealing with family matters or young people – it will be found that between 9.45 a.m. and 10.00 a.m., when business normally starts, the lobby of a typical urban court resembles a station ticket office during the rush hour. Defendants are looking for their names on lists pinned to the wall and lawyers and probation officers are seeking out their clients. Ushers and clerks are attempting to impose order by checking lists to see which defendants have arrived. Victims, witnesses, reporters and the interested public are also attempting to find out what is happening, which is not always immediately evident. To the uninitiated the high turnover of defendants making short appearances may give an impression of confusion with little being achieved.

Although there have been recent changes to remove delay and increase the throughput of cases – for example, by 'fast track' procedures and 'early administrative' and 'early first hearings' – only very trivial or straightforward cases can be dealt with on the defendant's first appearance. Most defendants are making their second or third trip to the court after an adjournment. They are therefore appearing at different stages of the **pre-trial** and trial process; some for remand or bail hearings, others to enter a plea or decide whether a case is to be heard in the magistrates' court or in the Crown Court. Other defendants will be returning for a summary trial to take place. Even that may not be the end of the matter as proceedings may be adjourned again to await a pre-sentence report before a sentencing decision. A magistrates' court is presided over either by lay magistrates, who are also known as justices of the peace (hence JP), who usually sit as a bench of three, or by a District Judge (magistrates' courts) sitting alone. Lay magistrates are advised on matters of law by a legally qualified clerk. A senior magistrate chairs the bench and speaks on its behalf, but all three magistrates have equal power. A specially trained panel of magistrates sits in the youth court.

In a summary trial (i.e. trial in the magistrates' court), magistrates decide on guilt in cases where the defendant contests guilt, that is, pleads not guilty. A contested case will involve a trial, which in a magistrates' court is known as a summary trial. Most defendants plead guilty and are sentenced by the magistrates, as are those who have been found guilty following a trial. Nearly all criminal cases start in the magistrates' court and most, over 90 per cent, end there.

All magistrates' courts are advised by a team of legal advisers (court clerks) who, since 1 January 1999, must be professionally legally qualified as a barrister or solicitor. These include the Clerk to the Justices who has overall responsibility for the administration of and legal advice to the court or group of courts. The court clerks are responsible for advising the bench on matters that arise during the day's proceedings and for ensuring the smooth running of the work of the court. The role of the legal advisers is seen as very important, in that they should be able to provide independent advice to the magistrates. The legal adviser should advise magistrates on legal matters including the development of human rights jurisprudence, matters of mixed law and fact, which includes guidance on their powers of sentence, the application of decision-making structure and the formulation and recording of reasons for decision making. Advisers, while being able to assist the bench by reminding them of evidence given to the court, should not take any part on questions of fact, such as whether the court believes a witness, whether to find a defendant guilty or not guilty; nor advise on the actual sentence to impose. Legal advice given to magistrates should be given or repeated in open court, so that both prosecution and defence know the legal advice on which the magistrates made their decision.

Decision making by magistrates

During the course of a case, the magistrates may make decisions about:

- in Triable Either Way cases, where the case should be tried;

- sending cases to other courts, for example, to another magistrates' court so that a number of matters can be dealt with together, or to the Youth Court if a young person has been charged with an adult;

- sending cases to the Crown Court for sentence or for trial;

- granting a **warrant to arrest** the defendant;

- whether to issue a search warrant;

- whether to hear a case in the absence of the defendant;

- asking for reports on a convicted defendant;

- remanding the accused in custody;

- remanding the accused on bail with or without conditions;

- whether to adjourn a case to another day, and how long the adjournment should be;

- whether someone is guilty or not, in a trial;

- the sentence to impose if someone is found guilty, including imposing disqualifications, for example, from driving or from owning an animal;

- whether to impose a different or further sentence if someone breaks an order of the court;

- enforcement of fines.

District Judges in the magistrates' courts (formerly stipendiary magistrates) sit in larger urban courts, or are appointed to a group of courts (such as in the Thames Valley), and have exactly the same sentencing and decision-making powers as lay magistrates. However, they sit alone and can exercise their powers alone. They assist with the workload in busy courts and also deal with more complex or sensitive cases, e.g. cases arising from the Extradition Act, Fugitive Offenders Act and serious fraud.

They are paid, and are professional lawyers with at least seven years' experience as a barrister or solicitor. In 2014 there were 140 such District Judges and 167 Deputy District Judges in the magistrates' courts. (Lay magistrates are unpaid, sit part time, and are not required to be legally qualified, although they undergo training and appraisal.)

In 2014 there were 21,500 lay magistrates in England and Wales. Magistrates are appointed by local panels, which include experienced magistrates, under the jurisdiction and direction of the Lord Chancellor (who is also Minister for Justice). Individuals may put their own name forward for appointment; others are nominated by existing magistrates, charitable bodies, political parties, trade unions or other organisations. The appointment panels, who as far as possible represent a cross-section of the community, then interview suitable candidates. They therefore attempt to balance the bench in terms of sex, age, political affiliation, ethnic origin and background.

The overriding consideration for appointment is that the candidate is suitable in terms of integrity and local standing. Thus, anyone who is an undischarged bankrupt or has a conviction for a serious offence or a number of minor offences is unlikely to be appointed. Certain categories of people employed in enforcing the law are ineligible to apply, even when retired. This includes police officers, members of the special constabulary, traffic wardens, civilians working for the police, and members of the armed forces.

An applicant will not be appointed to a district if he or she has a mother, father, son, daughter, brother or sister who is a police officer, special constable or traffic warden in that district. No one may be appointed with a close relative who works for the Crown Prosecution Service or the magistrates' courts in that district, or is a retired police officer, traffic warden or special constable. Members of Parliament, those adopted as political candidates, and full-time political agents in that district cannot apply to be JPs.

These restrictions are based on the need to keep those who adjudicate on the law separate from those who make or investigate it. A key feature of criminal justice in England and Wales is that all magistrates are lay people, as opposed to professional. They are therefore clearly distinct from other participants in the adversarial system such as the police, prosecution or defence and from other professionals such as probation officers. The magistracy is therefore independent of any other interest, and its members are there to represent the wider community. Magistrates are expected to have six key qualities:

- good character and personal integrity;
- ability to understand and communicate effectively;
- social awareness and an understanding of the rule of law and of local communities, and respect for and experience of those of different backgrounds;
- maturity and sound temperament, including confidence, courtesy and decisiveness;
- sound judgement: using objectivity;
- commitment and reliability: including a willingness to undertake training and between 26 and 35 sittings per year.

While few would doubt that these are the desired attributes of magistrates, the constitution of the magistracy has occasioned some criticism. It has been argued, for example, that it makes little sense for such vital roles as the adjudication of guilt and the sentencing of the offender to be carried out by amateurs, who cannot be expected to appreciate the finer points of criminal liability, let alone the complexities involved in making sentencing decisions. It could therefore be argued that criminal justice should be in the hands of full-time professionals.

On the other hand, leaving these decisions in the hands of professionals and experts could be seen as leaving too much power in the hands of experts, power which the involvement of lay persons in the system can check. Magistrates themselves clearly value their independence and argue that their experience and common sense are valuable assets in making the system work (see, for example, **Parker** *et al.* **1989**). Others are critical of the composition of the magistracy on the grounds that they are not elected and are not representative of the general population. The magistracy is often perceived to be dominated by middle-class, middle-aged white professional groups.

Women are well represented, and the magistracy is 'approaching ethnic representativeness of the population at a national level but with substantial local variations, so that, in areas where there are large minority ethnic communities, such as in London, the local bench may not reflect that' (**Auld 2001: 119**). A high proportion is retired from full-time employment and such people tend to sit more frequently because of this than their working colleagues. To attempt to combat some of these concerns, in October 2003 the then Department for Constitutional Affairs, following a recommendation in the Auld Review of the Criminal Courts, instituted a strategy for recruitment to increase diversity in appointments to the magistracy. In May 2008, the Ministry of Justice published its *Race Equality Scheme 2008–11*, which stated:

Ethnic minority communities and the magistracy

It is important that the application processes and materials make clear that candidates from all communities are welcome to apply to the magistracy. Advisory committees also monitor on a yearly basis the balance of gender, ethnic origin, location, occupation, industry, age, disability and social background on their benches.

In recent years there have been ongoing increases in the overall number of magistrates from black or minority ethnic (BME) backgrounds, with magistrates from BME backgrounds rising slightly to 6.9% at 1 April 2007. Although progress is limited, the trend is in the right direction. Appointment figures are particularly encouraging, with BME appointees accounting for 8.7% of magistrates appointed since 1 April 2007.

Source: Ministry of Justice (2008), *Race Equality Scheme*, paragraph 5.5

Critics have also focused on the social class profile of magistrates. Figures on the class composition of magistrates are difficult to obtain (see **Dignan and Wynne 1997**), but it is felt to be 'disproportionately middle class and almost certainly financially well-off compared to the population at large' (**Auld 2001: 119**, quoting Morgan and Russell).

Being a magistrate takes up a considerable amount of time. Many people are not able to leave young children, the office, the schoolroom or the factory floor for extended periods. This inevitably means that some groups, such as middle-class housewives or the relatively affluent self-employed, are over-represented and others, such as manual workers or homeless people, are under-represented. Furthermore, the latter are less likely to be proposed, or to be seen as having 'local standing' – a point which also militates against the appointment of the unemployed, the young and recently settled members of ethnic minorities. Magistrates can be between 18 and 70. In 2006, Lucy Tate, a 19-year-old law student, became Britain's youngest magistrate in the Yorkshire town of Pontefract.

The issue of representativeness is not, however, easy to resolve. What would a more representative magistracy achieve and just what, or who, should it represent? A representative magistracy on the grounds of demographic characteristics alone may not make different decisions in relation to either guilt or sentencing from the current magistracy. Women magistrates appear no more sympathetic, for example, to female offenders, who often come from very different socio-economic backgrounds (see, for example, **Eaton 1986**), and there is also little evidence of any direct bias on the grounds of social status in respect of business offenders (see, for example, **Croall 2001**).

Should magistrates in some way represent the views of the community? Should they be elected? In California, judges have to go through an election or re-confirmation process. This means that they must campaign for office as if politicians. This could itself be seen as undesirable as the magistracy should be free from political commitments – they are supposed to make decisions on behalf of the whole community, not just those who vote for them. Should the magistracy be selected on the basis that they represent the views of the population on punishment?

Representativeness in terms of community values could, for example, see a magistracy in which a large proportion would welcome the restoration of capital punishment. A 1993 survey of social attitudes confirms previous findings from opinion polls in that 74 per cent of respondents thought that, for some crimes, the death penalty was appropriate (**Jowell *et al.* 1994: 78**).

The magistracy represents a lay element in the system, which means that the public, albeit a somewhat selected group, play a part in the administration of justice and sentencing. A professional magistracy, which, as we have seen, would place more power in the hands of professionals, would also be less representative in terms of social class.

Other criticisms of the magistracy have focused on their lack of formal training, and lack of transparency in decision making. Although magistrates have for many years undergone initial and refresher training, the 1990s saw the introduction of a new form of training – the Magistrates' New Training Initiative (MNTI and from April 2005, MNTI2) – to meet specified competences. As a result of MNTI, for the first time magistrates had to be appraised by their peers. For those who sat as chairmen, special emphasis was placed on competences in structured decision making and the giving of reasons. The introduction of the Human Rights Act 1998 in October 2000 saw an increased need for all decisions in the magistrates' courts to be accompanied by full and public reason giving. Frequent changes in procedures, the sentencing structure and available disposals have led to increased training for magistrates.

9.2 Crown Court

Objective 2

Outline the role of the Crown Court

The Crown Court is presided over by a judge. Usually this will be a circuit judge, a full-time judge appointed by the Lord Chancellor from the ranks of barristers and solicitors to the circuit bench. (The Lord Chancellor no longer has the sole power to select which judge to appoint, but he can reject a recommendation by the **Judicial Appointments Commission**.) As of 2012, sitting in 97 Crown Court Centres there were:

- 660 circuit judges and
- 1,344 recorders.

Recorders are part-time judges drawn from the ranks of barristers and solicitors of a number of years' standing. A High Court judge presides over the most serious criminal cases.

The Crown Court system was introduced by legislation in 1971 and replaced the older system of assizes and petty sessions. Technically there is one Crown Court in England and Wales sitting at a number of locations or Crown Court Centres. Although the Crown Court has a limited civil jurisdiction on appeals, the vast majority of its work is on criminal matters. It is a first instance court which deals with more serious matters than the magistrates' court and also hears appeals against conviction or sentence from the magistrates' court.

Criminal cases come to the Crown Court in three main ways. Some have been previously sent or committed to the Crown Court for trial from a magistrates' court. These may not always lead to trials, as defendants may change their mind at the last minute and plead guilty. Other cases have been sent on from a magistrates' court for sentence.

The Crown Court, High Court and Court of Appeal all have appellate jurisdiction, which means the right to hear an appeal. Most appeals against conviction and sentence from the Crown Court go to the Court of Appeal, Criminal Division. A few appeals on points of law will go to the High Court, which is divided into Divisions; the Queen's Bench Division deals with appeals on criminal matters. The Court of Appeal has a wider appellate jurisdiction, hearing both criminal and civil matters, and the Criminal Division of the Court of Appeal is the usual venue for appeals from the Crown Court. An appeal from the Court of Appeal goes to the House of Lords, which is the highest domestic appeal court. In October 2009 this jurisdiction was transferred to the new Supreme Court under the Constitutional Reform Act of 2005. In certain cases there is an appeal to the European Court of Justice.

The number of cases dealt with in the magistrates' courts and the Crown Court is given in Tables 9.1 and 9.2. Table 9.1 shows the total number of cases; the cases not continued by the CPS; and the outcomes in the magistrates' court. It shows the high proportion of guilty pleas and the small percentage of cases determined by trials. Table 9.2 shows the Crown Court caseload in recent years and indicates the number of cases committed for trial from the magistrates' courts. It also gives the number of appeals that were sent to the Crown Court, either against

Table 9.1 Magistrates' courts: numbers of cases and outcomes

	2006/7	2007/8	2008/9	2009/10	2010/11
Total cases brought	1,067,361	987,981	966,626	928,708	872,585	840,983
Discontinuances (inc. bind overs)	126,047	107,651	95,513	80,661	78,901	80,911
as %	11.8	10.9	9.9	8.7	9.0	9.6
Arrest warrants, etc.	36,191	26,013	19,690	15,069	12,156	9,849
as %	3.4	2.6	2.0	1.6	1.4	1.2
Discharges	2,420	2,325	2,230		2,252	1,690
as %	0.2	0.2	0.2	0.2	0.3	0.2
Dismissals finding no case to answer	2,841	2,193	1,800	1,707	1,605	1,525
as %	0.3	0.2	0.2	0.2	0.2	0.2
Dismissals after trial	18,025	17,898	18,858	18,682	20,322	19,517
as %	1.7	1.8	2.0	2.0	2.3	2.3
Proofs (of guilt) in absence	168,874	150,741	139,618		150,741	124,573
					133,844	
as %	15.8	15.3	14.4	15.1	15.3	14.8
Guilty pleas	674,925	646,181	652,018	636,887	589,789	570,073
as %	63.2	65.4	67.5	68.6	67.6	67.8
Convictions after trial	38,038	34,979	36,899	33,390	33,716	32,845
as %	3.6	3.5	3.8	3.6	3.9	3.9

Source: Compiled from *CPS Annual Reports 2003/4 and 2007/8*

Table 9.2 Crown Court caseloads

Category	2005/06	2006/07	2007/08	2008/09	2009/10	2010/11
Committed or sent for trial	89,981	89,417	96,999	103,422	109,548	116,217
Appeals	12,741	13,364	13,823	13,989	14,221	13,961
Committed for sentence	21,918	20,695	20,656	21,509	18,920	19,857
Total	124,640	123,476	130,478	138,920	142,689	150,035

Source: Compiled from *CPS Annual Reports 2007/8 and 2010/11*

conviction or sentence, and the number of cases sent to the Crown Court from the magistrates' court for sentencing.

▶ The jurisdiction of magistrates' courts and the Crown Court

Jurisdiction for criminal cases – that is, where cases can be tried – is determined by a number of factors. The first is the type of offence. Criminal offences are divided into three categories as follows:

- summary offences;
- offences triable on indictment only;
- offences triable either way (TEW), i.e. summarily or on indictment.

The latter two categories are referred to as indictable offences. Cases triable only on indictment must be tried at the Crown Court. An indictment is the formal document used in a Crown Court trial setting out the charges against the defendant. The magistrates' court has power to hear summary offences and offences that are triable either way where a decision has been made to try them summarily, that is in the magistrates' court. In the twelve months leading up to June 2011, 1.61 million defendants were proceeded against, of which:

- 429,300 were indictable;
- 601,500 were summary non-motoring;
- 577,100 were summary motoring.

The time and place at which the alleged offence was committed can also affect where it is heard. Magistrates' courts can only try offences committed in their area, and normally proceedings for summary offences must be started within six months of the commission of the offence. Indictable offences may be tried in any Crown Court, and there is generally no time limit for the commencement of proceedings except in a few cases such as some Customs and Excise offences where there is a 20-year time limit.

▶ Classification of offences: summary and indictable

Summary offences are comparatively less serious crimes. Most motoring offences are summary, including driving with excess alcohol, but there is a wide variety of other summary offences, including common assault, assaulting a police officer, and taking a motor vehicle without the owner's consent. All summary offences are made so by statute.

The maximum penalty for a summary offence is six months' imprisonment or a £5,000 fine or both, but many summary offences carry much lower maximum penalties, and many are not imprisonable at all. The maximum financial penalties are determined in accordance with a range of levels established by Parliament. Level 1 offences currently carry a maximum fine of £200 and level 5 offences carry a maximum fine of £5,000. The offence of being drunk and disorderly, for example, is a level 3 offence with a maximum fine of £1,000. These five levels were introduced by the Criminal Justice Act 1982 and they mean that, as inflation erodes the value of money, fine maxima can be simply adjusted by legislation altering the value of the levels: the CJA 1991 raised the maximum to £5,000. A few summary offences, such as some pollution offences, carry much higher penalties. The Legal Aid, Sentencing and Punishment Act 2012 removed the £5,000 limit on fines in the magistrates' courts although the new limits – as of January 2015 – have not been determined.

Offences that are triable only on indictment are very serious matters, including murder, rape, blackmail, robbery, and wounding with intent. For those convicted of murder, the only sentence available to the court is life imprisonment. Maximum penalties for other offences are laid down by statute and may include a discretionary life sentence or a simple term of years. For example, 14 years is the maximum custodial penalty for blackmail and burglary of a dwelling, while

10 years is the maximum for burglary of a non-dwelling. Financial penalties for offences tried on indictment have no limit but fines are rarely imposed for such serious offences.

Triable either way (TEW) offences include theft, burglary, assault occasioning actual bodily harm, and unlawful wounding. This category covers many offences where the offence's relative seriousness can vary tremendously depending on the facts. Theft, for example, includes stealing a bottle of milk from a doorstep, shop-lifting and stealing from an employer. The seriousness of these matters is affected by the value of the theft and all the circumstances surrounding it, including the relationship between thief and victim.

Criminal damage is another offence where the circumstances can vary tremen-dously. The offence is committed when someone knowingly or recklessly inflicts damage on the property of another person, and it is generally a TEW offence. However, in criminal damage cases not involving threat to life or arson, and where the value of the damage inflicted is £5,000 or less, the charge is regarded as summary with a maximum penalty of three months' custody or a £2,500 fine. When the value of the damage is over £5,000 the offence remains triable either way. Where the offence is racially or religiously aggravated the offence is again made more serious.

Successive Acts have attempted to reduce the numbers of TEW offences, in part to reduce costs and to spread the work more efficiently between the courts. During the discussion of the Criminal Law Bill 1977, proposals were made to change the classification of some offences including criminal damage and theft. These changes were criticised on the grounds that they reduced the defendant's right to a trial by jury. In respect of theft, it was felt that anyone threatened with a conviction for dishonesty must retain this right, however trivial the offence. An offence which was reclassified in response to changing legislative and public perceptions of seriousness was taking a vehicle without the owner's consent, an offence under section 12 of the Theft Act 1968. This, in its original form, was a TEW offence. In the Criminal Justice Act 1988 it, along with common assault and driving while disqualified, became triable in summary proceedings only. The early 1990s saw an increase in public concern about offences involving a number of widely reported incidents where such cars were used to commit robberies, or resulted in the deaths of the drivers or bystanders. Vivid newspaper reports about ram raiders fuelled political disquiet. In response Parliament created a new indictable offence, 'Aggravated Vehicle-Taking', to cover the situation in which a car, taken without the owner's consent, was involved in an accident or crime.

In 2012, the Coalition Government started consulting on how to ensure that magistrates send fewer TEW cases for trial at the Crown Court. Concerned to retain the right of defendants to elect for trial by jury, yet determined at the same time to reduce the cost and delays caused by sending so many cases to the Crown Court, the Ministry of Justice published the White Paper *Swift and Sure Justice*. In 2014 committal proceedings whereby cases were first heard in the magistrates' court were abolished for the more serious TEW cases, which as with indictable only cases since 2001, will go automatically to the Crown Court.

▶ The Coroners' Court

A coroner is a legal officer with a 1,000-year history in England but is today responsible for investigating sudden, unpredicted or suspicious deaths. The Coroner's court has the power to call witnesses and a jury to investigate the cause of death. Coroners' courts carry out inquests into any deaths which have occurred in unexplained circumstances, namely those which are violent or deaths in unusual or unpredicted circumstances and those which have taken place in prison or police custody, and also deaths where there is uncertainty following a **post-mortem**.

The aim of an inquest is to establish the identity of the deceased, how, when and where the death occurred, and the details required by the Births and Deaths Registration Act1953.The Coroners and Justice Act 2009 made a number of changes to the coroner system, after a review prompted in part by the case of Britain's worst serial killer, Dr Harold Shipman in 2000.

When deaths occur in predicted environments such as in hospital or following a prolonged diagnosed illness with medical supervision there is no need for an inquest. Most routine deaths result in causes of death being recorded by doctors. When there is a sudden or unusual death then an inquest is required. However, most inquests are held without a jury but there are circumstances when a jury is required by law, as when a death occurred in prison or resulted from an injury caused by a police officer, or of a death at a workplace.

Unexpected deaths are normally referred to a coroner by the police or a doctor, and the coroner is then responsible for deciding whether or not to hold an inquest into the death. The coroner is normally a lawyer or a doctor, who works independently within his regional district, although recent legislation contained within the Coroners and Justice Act 2009 proposed the introduction of a dedicated Chief Coroner who would oversee a nationally service, and who would have powers to delegate investigations to other coroners outside the district in which the death was recorded.

At an inquest, witnesses may be called and the coroner may need to order a post-mortem if this has not already been carried out. Once a decision has been reached, a death certificate can be issued. If the coroner decides that a death has occurred as a result of homicide, investigations may then begin to discover by whose hand the deceased was killed, or, should somebody already be suspected of the homicide, legal proceedings may be set in motion against the suspect.

9.3 Judiciary

Objective 3

Describe the membership and role of the Judiciary

The role of magistrates is to decide on the guilt or not of a defendant and then, if guilty, to decide on the sentence. In Crown Court procedure, the content and style of a trial are different, to take account of the split in functions between those who decide on the guilt of the offender – the jury – and the person who decides on the sentence – the judge. In the Crown Court the presence of, and separation of, functions between judge and jury creates the need for special procedures and rules. Before these are considered in relation to the trial, we should put the trial process into the context of the judge's overall work, described below by the then Lord Chief Justice:

What do judges do?

Many people believe that when judges sit in the morning from 10.30 to 1 p.m. and in the afternoon from 2 to 4.30 p.m., they have a very cushy life. First of all, as any juror would confirm, sitting in court for 5 hours in the day is very exhausting in itself. It cannot be compared to attending an office or other workplace for 5 hours. Time in court requires concentrated attention on the evidence and the submissions. There is no scope for day-dreaming, telephone calls, cups of coffee, badinage with a fellow employee or even visits to the lavatory. But on top of that, what the public see of a judge's work between 10.30 and 4.30 is only the tip of the iceberg. He has to read all the papers and consult any legal authorities before coming into court. He also has to deal with paper applications, and find time to write reserved judgments. Most judges have in addition a number of extra-mural commitments, for example, Presiding Judges on the Circuits have much administrative work to do, others as members of the Parole Board, the Judicial Studies Board, Area Committees of Court Users, and there are many other commitments.

(Lord Taylor 1993)

Court proceedings are the most visible part of judges' duties. In a trial, the role of the judge is to direct the jury on the law, determine questions of the admissibility of evidence, determine sentence if the defendant is found guilty and generally to be 'in charge' of the proceedings. The overriding duty of the judge is to maintain the fairness of the proceedings. For trials to be regarded as fair it is important that judges are regarded as independent and not subservient to political or other interests. Lord Taylor also explains the importance of the independence of the judiciary.

To maintain not only the fact of judicial independence but its appearance, judges have to be cautious in their social activities and must avoid politics. The result of all this care to guard judicial independence is that litigants can be confident the judge will try their case on its merit and as the judicial oath requires: Without fear of favour, affection or ill-will.

(Lord Taylor 1993)

During the trial, the judge's function is to direct the jury on the law. The jury must accept these directions, but any views the judge has or expresses on the facts can be disregarded by the jury. The judge is entitled to comment on the facts, and a very important part of the judge's role is to help the jury assess the relevance of evidence, and to marshal what is often a large body of material into some order. It is often very difficult, therefore, to gauge when the judge oversteps the line and begins to usurp the jury's function by determining or appearing to determine issues of fact. If, however, the judge does exceed his or her function, convicted defendants may use this as a ground for appeal.

The judge's influence is paramount where it is argued that evidence (usually but not always prosecution evidence) should not be admitted in the trial. This could be an argument that the evidence fell within a category which is not admitted, or an argument asking the judge to exercise his discretion to make a judgment to exclude certain evidence. For example, the judge in a criminal trial has the power to exclude (that is, prevent) evidence being put before the jury where its prejudicial effect outweighs its value as evidence. In addition to this general discretion the judge has discretion under section 78 of the Police and Criminal Evidence Act 1984 (PACE) to exclude evidence whose admission would be unfair in all the circumstances, including the manner in which the evidence was obtained. This section is often relied upon in cases involving breaches of the Codes of Practice under PACE (**see Chapter 6**).

Judges have often been criticised as being out of touch, an impression fostered by media reports of judges who are unaware of current popular music or sporting icons. In recent years, attempts have been made to address this impression, partly by the appointment of some younger judges. Criticism of the racial composition of the judiciary was addressed by the then Lord Chancellor, Lord Irvine, in a speech to a Minority Lawyers Conference in London in November 1997. He said he wished to encourage ethnic minority applicants for appointment, and also made the point that he would like to remove some of the perceived secrecy about judicial appointments.

In April 2006, the Judicial Appointments Commission (JAC), created by the Constitutional Reform Act, took over responsibility for judicial appointments formerly made by the Lord Chancellor. Baroness Usha Prashar was the first chair; Christopher Stevens took over from her in 2011. The creation of the Judicial Appointments Commission has done much to dispel claims of secrecy in the judicial appointments procedure. The JAC has identified the following qualities required of appointees:

Judicial appointments: qualities required

1. *Intellectual capacity*

   High level of expertise in your chosen area or profession; ability quickly to absorb and analyse information; appropriate knowledge of the law and its underlying principles, or the ability to acquire this knowledge where necessary.

2. *Personal qualities*

   Integrity and independence of mind; sound judgement; decisiveness; objectivity and ability and willingness to learn and develop professionally.

3. *An ability to understand and deal fairly*

   Ability to treat everyone with respect and sensitivity whatever their background, and willingness to listen with patience and courtesy.

4. *Authority and communication skills*

Ability to explain the procedure and any decisions reached clearly and succinctly to all those involved; ability to inspire respect and confidence; and ability to maintain authority when challenged.

5. *Efficiency*

Ability to work at speed and under pressure; ability to organise time effectively and produce clear, reasoned judgments expeditiously; and ability to work constructively with others (including leadership and managerial skills where appropriate).

The JAC has also set up a more transparent process of selection, comprising four stages:

- advertising;
- application forms and eligibility checks;
- interviews and/or selections days;
- transparent decisions on the assessment process and recommendation for appointment against clear criteria.

In its report of its first full year of operation in April 2008, the JAC provided data on 27 judicial selection exercises completed up to March 2008. For 'fee paid positions' which relate to the 'first step on the judicial career ladder', 115 selections for appointment were made of which 62 were male and 53 female. Ten were from a black or minority ethnic background. Table 9.3 shows the numbers of judges in post in 2013 and their gender and ethnic profile.

The Constitutional Reform Act 2005 also removed what some have seen as constitutional anomalies in the relationship between the executive and the judiciary. The Lord Chancellor ceased to have a judicial role, and his role as head of the judiciary passed to the Lord Chief Justice.

Historically, the Lord Chancellor has had a role in the judiciary as career head of all the judges, and as taking an active role in hearing appeal cases; a role in the executive as a Minister and member of the Cabinet; and a role in the legislature, sitting as speaker in the House of Lords. The multiple roles did not sit comfortably with notions of the separation of powers, thought by many to be the mark of proper constitutional government. The Act specifically reinforces the Lord Chancellor's duty to uphold the rule of law: that is, the principle that the courts must uphold the law of the land and that all should be treated equally under the law.

Table 9.3 Profile of judges in post 2013

| Appointment name | Total in post | Gender | | | Ethnicity | | | | | | | | |
		Male	Female	% Female	White	Asian or Asian British	Black or Black British	Mixed	Any other background	Total BME	Unknown	% BME	Total in post
Heads of Division	5	5	0	0.0%	2	0	0	0	0	0	3	0.0%	5
Lords Justices of Appeal	35	31	4	11.4%	24	0	0	0	0	0	11	0.0%	35
High Court Judges	108	90	18	16.7%	86	1	0	1	3	5	17	4.6%	108
Judge Advocates	8	7	1	12.5%	8	0	0	0	0	0	0	0.0%	8
Deputy Judge Advocates	5	4	1	20.0%	3	0	0	0	0	0	2	0.0%	5
Masters, Registrars, Costs Judges and District Judges	45	32	13	28.9%	32	0	0	0	0	0	13	0.0%	45
Deputy Masters, Deputy Registrars, Deputy Costs Judges and Deputy District Judges	68	41	27	39.7%	35	0	1	1	1	3	30	4.4%	68
Circuit Judges	654	533	121	18.5%	571	4	1	3	7	15	68	2.3%	654
Recorders	1196	988	208	17.4%	869	25	16	17	10	68	259	5.7%	1196
District Judges (County Courts)	446	324	122	27.4%	393	15	3	5	4	27	26	6.1%	446
Deputy District Judges (County Courts)	764	488	276	36.1%	590	18	8	6	7	39	135	5.1%	764
District Judges (Magistrates' Courts)	142	101	41	28.9%	106	4	0	0	0	4	32	2.8%	142
Deputy District Judges (Magistrates' Courts)	145	98	47	32.4%	94	6	1	3	1	11	40	7.6%	145
Grand Total	**3,621**	**2,742**	**879**	**24.3%**	**2,813**	**73**	**30**	**36**	**33**	**172**	**636**	**4.8%**	**3,621**

Source: www.judiciary.gov.uk/publications/diversity-statistics-and-general-overview-2013/

9.4 Summons, bail and remands in custody

Objective 4

Explain the differences in procedure involved in a summons, bail and remands in custody

The court process starts with the attendance of the defendant. Most will have been summonsed, normally by post, as is the case, for example, with minor motoring offences. Some will have been arrested and may have been held overnight in police custody, or released on police bail to attend court. Yet others may have been remanded in custody and arrive from a prison. Cases are not normally completed on their first appearance and most are adjourned. This is necessary to allow both the prosecution and the defendant time to prepare their case, to seek legal or other expert advice or to contact witnesses. When sections 29–30 of the Criminal Justice Act 2003 are brought into force, a system of requisitions and charges (currently being piloted in 19 magistrates' courts) will replace the summons as a method for starting proceedings.

Both the police and the courts can make decisions about holding an accused person in custody prior to conviction. The police must decide whether to release arrested persons with or without bail, or to detain them in police custody. Following their first appearance in the magistrates' court, defendants may be released to await trial or may be remanded on bail or in custody by the magistrates. Similar decisions have to be made by the judge if the case goes to trial in the Crown Court. In 2006, 57 per cent of people appearing at magistrates' courts were summonsed and 43 per cent arrested and charged. About 15 per cent of those arrested and charged were held in custody by the police before their first appearance at court. About 55,000 defendants were remanded in custody by magistrates (*Criminal Statistics 2006*: 82).

Less serious cases will simply be adjourned and defendants will be notified of the date of the next hearing. In more serious cases, however, defendants will be remanded either on bail or in custody. Remands can only be for a fixed period of time, and remand length varies in relation to whether or not the accused is held in custody. There are fixed limits to the length of time that a person can be detained by the police at a police station and by the magistrates when remanding an alleged offender in custody.

PACE governs police powers in relation to detention without charge (**as seen in Chapter 6**). Under a strict timetable, a suspect may only be held for questioning for a limited time before being charged. If the time limit is reached the suspect must be charged or released. PACE also provides that once a suspect has been charged they may be released by the police on bail to attend the magistrates' court at a specified time. The time limits are extended in the case of those suspected of terrorist offences. The period for those suspected of terrorist offences has been the subject of much controversy (**see Chapter 6**). Under the Criminal Justice and Public Order Act 1994, for the first time, the police could impose conditions of bail generally in the same terms as a court. In January 2004, section 4 of the Criminal Justice Act 2003 was implemented, allowing police officers, as an efficiency measure, to admit suspects to bail (street bail) without first taking them to the police station. This provision was further amended in 2007 to allow conditions to be attached to street bail in the same way as to other bail decisions.

Table 9.4 Arrest or summons: offenders in the magistrates' court

	Number of persons proceeded against (in thousands)								
	2002		2004		2006		2008		2010
Indictable offences									
Summoned	51	[8%]	56	[10%]	48	[10%]	43	[9%]	40 [8%]
Arrested and bailed	462	[76%]	395	[73%]	343	[72%]	322	[70%]	308 [64%]
Arrested and held in custody	99	[16%]	93	[17%]	84	[18%]	92	[20%]	136 [28%]
Total	612	[100%]	544	[100%]	475	[100%]	458	[100%]	484 [100%]
Summary non-motoring offences									
Summoned	408	[61%]	459	[66%]	407	[64%]	386	[63%]	386 [62%]
Arrested and bailed	233	[35%]	212	[30%]	207	[32%]	201	[33%]	190 [30%]
Arrested and held in custody	24	[4%]	25	[4%]	27	[4%]	30	[5%]	48 [8%]
Total	665	[100%]	695	[100%]	641	[100%]	617	[100%]	624 [100%]
Summary motoring offences									
Summoned	695	[80%]	798	[82%]	647	[80%]	542	[82%]	536 [86%]
Arrested and bailed	152	[18%]	161	[16%]	148	[18%]	110	[17%]	81 [13%]
Arrested and held in custody	18	[2%]	16	[2%]	12	[1%]	9	[1%]	9 [1%]
Total	865	[100%]	976	[100%]	807	[100%]	661	[100%]	626 [100%]
All offences									
Summoned	1,154	[54%]	1,313	[59%]	1,102	[57%]	971	[56%]	961 [55%]
Arrested and bailed	846	[40%]	768	[35%]	698	[36%]	633	[36%]	579 [33%]
Arrested and held in custody	141	[7%]	135	[6%]	123	[6%]	131	[8%]	194 [11%]
Total	2,141	[100%]	2,215	[100%]	1,923	[100%]	1,736	[100%]	1,734 [100%]

Note: Rounding process affects detail of figures
Source: Compiled from Ministry of Justice Court Proceedings Statistics 2010

Defendants may be detained by the police without charge initially for 24 hours. If the offence is indictable, then the period of detention by the police may be extended for a further 12 hours on the authorisation of a senior officer of superintendent rank or above. After 36 hours, accused persons must be presented at a magistrates' court, who may return them to police custody for a further 36 hours. After this time they must again be returned to the court, when the magistrates may decide on a further period of remand. The maximum total period of remand without charge (for offences other than terrorism) in police custody is 96 hours. Thereafter the suspect must be charged or released. After charge, further decisions on **remand in custody** or bail are made and, if remanded in custody, the accused will be held in a remand wing or centre in a Prison Service establishment.

Unconvicted defendants may not be initially remanded in custody by magistrates for more than eight days at a time. They may be remanded for up to 28 days, however, if they have been previously remanded in custody for the same offence and are present in court. A convicted defendant can be remanded in custody for up to three weeks for reports. In order to prevent repeated custodial remands, custody time limits were introduced following the creation of the Crown Prosecution Service. These provide a maximum time limit for proceedings where the defendant is in custody. When the limit is reached, leave to extend the period must be applied for or the defendant must be given bail. Under the Prosecution of Offences (Custody Time Limits) Regulations 1987, the limits are 70 days between first appearance and summary trial or committal proceedings, unless the decision to have summary trial is reached earlier than 56 days, in which case the limit is 56 days. The maximum period for holding a defendant in custody between committal to the Crown Court and trial is 112 days.

▶ Bail

The operation of the bail system in England and Wales is governed by legislation: the Bail Act 1976, the Bail Amendment Act 1993, CJPOA 1994, CJA 2003 and by the Criminal Procedure Rules 2005. If a person accused, convicted or under arrest for an offence is granted bail, he or she is released under a duty to attend court or the police station at a given time. 'Street bail' was introduced by the CJA 2003 which allowed police to arrest at the scene of a suspected crime, but to release the suspect to attend later at the police station. Naturally, this power is used for less serious matters, where there is no danger to others, or fear that subsequent prosecution will be undermined.

Bail may be granted subject to certain conditions, which aim to ensure that the defendant appears for the next hearing. The court may ask for a *surety* (someone who will pledge to pay an amount of money set by the court should the defendant not turn up) or may require a *security* (the deposit of a sum of money). In other circumstances, the court may require that the accused lodge their passports with the police to ensure that they do not flee the country, or the court may decide to restrict defendants' movements by imposing a curfew, or insisting they report daily to a police station, or ban them from making contact with witnesses or victims.

Those who are granted bail must appear at the time and place specified, which they will be given in written details. If they do not surrender to custody, they are guilty of an offence, except when they are prevented from so doing because of, for example, an accident. A warrant may be issued for their arrest and if found guilty of the offence of failing to attend, they risk a fine of up to £5,000 from the magistrates' court or up to three months' imprisonment. The police may also arrest someone on bail if they have reasonable grounds for believing that any conditions are not being met or that the accused is unlikely to surrender.

Criteria for bail

The criteria for granting and refusing bail are also dealt with by the Bail Act 1976. In general there is a presumption in favour of bail for unconvicted defendants but there are some important exceptions. Bail need not be granted to defendants charged with imprisonable offences, if:

- the court or the police (for police bail) think there are substantial grounds for believing that, if released, the defendant:
  - will fail to return to court
  - will commit an offence
  - will interfere with witnesses, for example by contacting them about the court proceedings, or otherwise obstruct the course of justice;
- the defendant is already on bail at the time and is charged with a new indictable offence;
- it is necessary for the defendant's own protection or, if a young person, for his or her welfare;
- the defendant is already in custody on other matters;
- the defendant has already absconded in the present proceedings;
- it has been impracticable to obtain information in order to make a bail decision;
- in certain circumstances where the defendant is over 18 and has tested positive for a Class A drug and is charged with an offence in which Class A drugs were involved (added by s 19 CJA 2003).

In deciding whether grounds exist for refusing bail and in deciding whether to impose any conditions on the bail, the court or police will consider:

- the nature and seriousness of the matter and the probable sentence;
- the character and previous convictions of the defendant;
- neighbourhood ties such as family, job, property;
- any previous bail record (has the accused always attended court when asked?);
- strength of the evidence against him or her;
- any other relevant information.

For convicted offenders bail can be withheld if it is necessary to hold the person in custody to allow a report to be compiled.

Concerns about bail

Bail decisions have been criticised from a number of viewpoints: first, that defendants are unnecessarily and inappropriately remanded in custody; and second, that too many defendants are given bail and thus are free to reoffend. The fears of excessive numbers of offences committed by those on bail led to the provisions in the Criminal Justice and Public Order Act 1994 to remove the right to bail for a person charged with committing a further indictable offence while on bail. Re-offending fears have caused particular concerns in relation to those charged with very serious crimes such as murder. Finally concerns have been raised about breaches of bail and the potential for those who breach their bail conditions or abscond, still to be given bail on subsequent occasions: as far as responses to breaches of bail are concerned the Public Accounts Committee (PAC) reported in June 2005 that action over failure of defendants to attend court was slow and unreliable. For those who do not attend court following the granting of bail (i.e. they abscond), a **warrant to arrest** the person is often issued. Of

118,500 such warrants issued in 2002, only 45 per cent were served on the absconder by the police within three months after issue. Edward Leigh, MP, the PAC chairman, said: 'Public confidence in the criminal justice system is weakened if defendants skip their court hearings, leading to failed trials. Many defendants believe they can get away with snubbing the legal process and, disgracefully, there is some justification for that belief.'

The first issue has been addressed by the Criminal Justice and Immigration Act 2008 which includes provisions that when implemented will limit the situations when a court can withhold bail in minor cases to those where the suspect is likely to cause injury or the fear of injury.

As a result of increasing concern about the possibility of dangerous offenders being released on bail, the Bail (Amendment) Act 1993 gave the Crown Prosecution Service limited rights to appeal (in cases such as offences carrying a sentence of five years or more) against a bail decision made in a magistrates' court; this right was extended to all imprisonable offences by the CJA 2003 from April 2005.

Where someone is accused of offences involving rape, murder or manslaughter and has already been convicted previously for such an offence, there is now no right to bail and it will only be given in exceptional circumstances. The detail of the law has been changed on a number of occasions, to comply with the provisions of the Human Rights Act.

Jeremy Wright, a Minister from the Department of Justice, told the House of Commons on 16 October 2013 that in 2012 'around 132,000 offences' had been committed by those on bail. (Hansard) A previous answer of 6 February 2013 had shown that in 2011/12, 66,820 offenders had been convicted of offences while on bail. In 2012 one in seven murders, i.e. 56, had been committed by those granted bail.

Controversial bail decisions

1. In 2010, 26-year-old Jane Clough was stabbed 71 times by her former partner Jonathan Vass while he was on bail accused of raping her. Vass admitted her murder and was jailed for life in October 2010 with a minimum term of 30 years. Following her murder, Clough's family campaigned ceaselessly for a change in the law which would allow prosecutors to challenge bail decisions, meaning that dangerous offenders would be less likely to be granted bail. Their campaign was successful, and in 2012 the new law received Royal Assent as part of the LASPO Act.

2. James Allen was a violent offender with previous convictions for burglary and wounding with intent to cause grievous bodily harm. He was arrested in April 2012 for an offence involving assault and possession of drugs. While out on bail, he committed a brutal double murder: Colin Dunford, 81 and Julie Davison, 50, were battered to death in their homes on two consecutive days. Allen was later caught and charged in May 2012 with two counts of murder, rape, false imprisonment, assault and witness intimidation. The suspect reportedly smiled throughout the proceedings and raised his middle finger to the magistrates as he was led away by two security guards.

3. In July 2005, Anthony Peart stabbed to death Richard Whelan on a bus. Whelan had complained that Peart had thrown chips at other passengers. Peart had been involved in several other sets of criminal proceedings and had breached bail conditions.

On 31 January 2008, a snapshot count showed that 60 (13 per cent) of the 455 defendants awaiting murder proceedings had been given bail in those proceedings, along with 35 (85 per cent) of those charged with manslaughter.

The Ministry of Justice review did not recommend that bail be automatically banned in murder cases, not least because of the impact of the HRA. However, public concern over the freedom of dangerous offenders to commit murder has led to a change in the law: in 2012, the Legal Aid, Sentencing and Punishment of Offenders Act included a provision which enables prosecutors who are concerned for the safety of their clients and others may challenge a court decision to grant bail to the offender. This came about after a successful campaign by the family of Jane Clough, who was murdered in 2010 by her ex-boyfriend when he was out on bail.

A further concern: that of the link between drug use and offending on bail is reflected in a provision introduced under the CJA 2003: section 19 provides that where a person is shown to have Class A drugs in his body, the court believes that the drug caused or contributed to the offence and the suspect has refused to undergo drug assessment or has failed to take follow-up steps, then bail may be withheld unless the court is satisfied that there is no real risk of offending.

When bail is refused the court must consider whether it ought to be granted on subsequent occasions. This does not mean that the accused can make repeated applications on the same grounds. After bail has been refused for any of the stated reasons, other than insufficient information, only one further bail application is usually allowed and the court does not have to hear further applications unless there has been a change in circumstances. A remand in custody on the basis that there is insufficient information is not a refusal of bail as such and does not count as a bail application, so the accused may still make two applications.

Some concern has been expressed about the length of adjournments, especially where defendants are remanded in custody. This clearly causes immense stress to defendants, let alone the cost to the taxpayer. In addition, those remanded in custody and subsequently acquitted are not entitled to any compensation. In 2011, the average waiting time until trial for defendants committed for trial to the Crown Court who pleaded guilty was weeks, and for those who pleaded not guilty, 21.8 weeks. Those committed for trial on bail had to wait an average of 15.3 weeks and those in custody 8.6 weeks. (*Judicial and Court Statistics 2011*). In July 2012, the Coalition Government proposed a strategy to reduce the average waiting times in straightforward trials: following the exemplary period of rapidly deployed business by criminal justice practitioners in the aftermath of the riots of August 2011, Home Office Minister Nick Herbert launched a White Paper entitled *Swift and Sure Justice: The Government's Plans for Reform of the Criminal Justice System*. In the White Paper, the minister claims that the criminal justice system has developed a culture which is 'tolerant of delays'. Proposals for the administration of 'swift' justice encompass a new digitised and more efficient approach, making greater use of live video links and keeping courts open at weekends and on bank holidays. In his launch speech, using the example of a Lithuanian lorry driver who was apprehended for drink-driving in Kent the month before, and sentenced by a court two hours later, Nick Herbert described what he meant by 'swift' justice:

Normally, having failed a breathalyser test, the driver would have been charged and bailed to appear before magistrates at a future date, perhaps a couple of weeks later. During that period, the driver would be free to continue driving, and there is, of course, the very real risk that he wouldn't turn up in court. But in this case, the driver appeared at court from the police station via the virtual [live video link] court system. He was charged with the offence at 9.21 a.m., pleaded guilty, and by 11.35 a.m., he was disqualified from driving for 36 months, fined £1,500 and ordered to pay costs.

The issues underlying the granting of bail again illustrate the conflicting models of, and pressures on, the criminal justice system. As we have seen, there is an assumption that a defendant, who has not yet been proved guilty or sentenced by the court, should have a right to bail. Placing defendants, who may yet be found not guilty, in custody involves depriving possibly innocent persons of their liberty, disrupting their lives and possibly endangering their employment opportunities. The high cost of custodial remands also causes concern: the population in custody in March 2012 was 87,531 and included 7,890 untried and 4,017 unsentenced prisoners (Ministry of Justice, *Offender Management Statistics Quarterly*).

On the other hand, it is important from the point of view of due process, just deserts, crime control and denunciation that those who are suspected of a crime appear in court to be tried and sentenced. In 2011, 69,300 (12 per cent) defendants bailed by the magistrates subsequently failed to appear. In the Crown Court 3,100 (4 per cent) of those granted bail by judges failed to appear (*Criminal Statistics England and Wales 2011*). Remands in custody are also necessary from a crime control perspective as the public require protection from offenders who may commit further offences while awaiting trial.

▶ Remands in custody

Remanding defendants in custody raises important issues concerning civil liberties as some will not be found guilty and others will not receive a custodial sentence. This may suggest that some defendants are being unfairly dealt with – especially those who are eventually acquitted. It could be argued that depriving a person of their liberty before trial amounts to the police or the courts pre-judging guilt. On the other hand, however, as we have seen, conflicting arguments surround the granting of bail. If a person has been accused of a very serious offence, the interests of public protection require that they should be prevented from committing a 'further' offence. If they should subsequently commit a further offence, the public might well query why they were released back into the community. Also, as argued above, due process is not well served if defendants abscond and do not appear to answer any charges.

The other part of the argument concerns those who, having been remanded in custody, are subsequently given non-custodial sentences. Yet the principles underlying bail or custody decisions are different from factors shaping sentencing decisions. Remand in custody is not a punishment for an offence not yet proved;

it is a preventative measure, to prevent further offending, interfering with witnesses or evidence or absconding. In the case of remand, as we have seen, public protection may be a paramount interest, and full information about the risk posed to the public by a defendant may not be available. Defendants may, before sentencing, provide sufficient mitigation to limit their culpability by giving information which may not be available at the time of the decision on remand.

Time spent in prison on remand is also deducted from any eventual sentence. Furthermore, the fact that a defendant has had a 'taste of prison' may be a factor militating against an eventual custodial sentence. This is certainly an argument much used by defence counsel. On the other hand, it would not justify the use of such a 'taste of prison' as a tactic by magistrates to deter the offender before guilt has been proved. This again illustrates how difficult it is to examine any one stage of the criminal justice process in isolation from other stages. While theoretically separate, decisions on remands in custody and sentencing are necessarily interrelated.

While remand prisoners enjoy certain privileges compared to sentenced prisoners, there is considerable evidence that conditions in remand prisons can be severe – thus adding to the stress and frustration of those awaiting trial and sentence (**Morgan and Jones 1992**). However, although remand prisons and centres are among the most overcrowded, they do allow more freedom and they are usually nearer the defendants' home as they are often in urban areas. This may explain the finding of a survey asking defendants why they opted for trial at a Crown Court, in which 24 per cent responded that they wished to serve part of an expected sentence on remand. So, despite the poorer conditions found in many remand wings, the extra privileges of being on remand and the proximity to where they lived were an inducement for those who expected to be found guilty. Yet again we see how decisions which are theoretically separate are interdependent, and how informal considerations influence these decisions.

Whether or not it is felt that too many, or too few, defendants are granted bail, it is clear that the decision whether to remand on bail or in custody is a crucial one both for individual defendants and for the system as a whole. Accordingly, a number of initiatives have been suggested to assist magistrates in their assessment of which offenders are most suitable for bail. These include the use of information schemes which aim to provide more information about defendants on their first appearance. Bail can be denied if, at an early stage of the proceedings, there is insufficient information to make a decision. This may happen when the individual refuses to give a name and address, or where the court doubts the reliability of the information given. In these cases, **bail information schemes have** proved successful in enabling the courts to make decisions based on reliable and accurate information. Bail support schemes, involving a mixture of advice, counselling and surveillance, have also been suggested to cut down the numbers remanded in custody awaiting trial.

Bail hostels, run by the Probation Service, are available in many areas, providing accommodation for defendants awaiting trial. This provides a fixed address suitable for those of no fixed abode or where 'home' accommodation is considered to be related to the offending. Hostels provide a measure of freedom mixed with some supervision and enable those remanded to attend work. In recent years, the use of bail hostels as accommodation for those awaiting trial has become less common while their use as 'approved premises' for offenders leaving custody has increased, so much so that those leaving custody now represent the majority of residents (*Probation Hostels and High Risk Offenders*, NAPO, February 2011). This has raised questions by the probation service, the media and public about the levels of supervision bail hostels can really provide when handling higher-risk offenders.

We can see from this discussion of remand that not only do the conflicting pressures on criminal justice operate on pre-trial proceedings, but also that one stage cannot be treated in isolation from others. Whether or not the accused is remanded in custody or on bail is only one of many decisions taken before trial and magistrates also deal with cases that have moved further on in the process. One crucial decision with triable either way offences is the mode of trial decision.

9.5 Indications of plea and allocation decisions

Objective 5

Explain the mode of trial decisions

In summary cases and those that can be tried on indictment only, there is no choice as to where the case will be dealt with.

For triable either way (TEW) cases a decision has to be made about which court will hear the case. This is called the allocation decision (formerly called the mode of trial decision). Decisions over where these midway offences are tried, and who makes that decision, have been the subject of controversial reform or attempted reforms for many years. The issues demonstrate the tensions between bureaucratic efficiency, due process and increasingly the management approach to criminal justice. A cost-effectiveness model suggests that as many defendants as possible should be tried in the cheaper and quicker venue of the magistrates' court, and that defendants should not have the choice of going to the Crown Court when the case is trivial or where their choice is made for tactical reasons. Due process suggests, at least to some people, that everyone at risk of conviction of a serious category of crime, including offences that might damage their reputation, should have the option of trial by jury. This argument assumes that jury trial is better or safer than trial by magistrates. Thus the allocation or venue decision has important consequences in terms of the courts' cost-effectiveness and in terms of perceptions of justice.

Prior to the implementation of the Criminal Procedure and Investigations Act 1996 (CPIA 1996) the mode of trial decision was made before any plea was entered and without regard to any subsequent plea, but, since section 49 of the Act came into force in October 1997, the situation is reversed and the defendant is asked to indicate a plea of 'guilty' or 'not guilty' in advance of a decision on venue.

Before a decision on plea can be made, the defendant needs to have some knowledge of the case against him. The Magistrates' Court (Advance Information) Rules 1985 provide that for any TEW offence, if asked, the prosecution must give the defendant a copy of, or summary of, the statements or other evidence on which they intend to rely. This rule does not apply to summary offences, although often the CPS will voluntarily provide information in those cases. When the advance disclosure is provided, accused persons and their solicitors may well wish to have time to consider it, in order to make decisions about whether they wish to plead guilty or not. In those circumstances, the defendant may ask for an adjournment for that to take place. In other cases, defendants will be clear about which course they wish to take, and may not even wish to see the papers before pleading guilty immediately.

Once the court is satisfied that the defendant has had an opportunity to consider the evidence, or does not wish to take advantage of this process, the defendant will be asked to indicate a plea of guilty or not guilty. (The process is thus referred to as **plea before venue**.) The defendant will be told, in the event of a guilty plea, that the magistrates will deal with the case, but that they nevertheless may come to the conclusion that their sentencing powers are insufficient and may send the case for sentence to the Crown Court. If a defendant indicates a guilty plea, then the magistrates move immediately to the sentencing stage. If the defendant pleads not guilty or is unwilling to indicate a plea, then an allocation decision is required. This takes the following form:

- The prosecution outlines the basic allegations, highlighting points relevant to its seriousness.

- The prosecutor provides information about the offence and from 2014 this includes the defendant's previous convictions.

- The defendant, or their representative, may make their view clear as to the choice of venue, although that will probably not be necessary if the intention is to elect trial by jury in any event.

- The magistrates make their decision on whether they will accept jurisdiction, on the basis that, if the defendant were to be convicted, the case is within their powers of sentencing.

- If it is decided that the case can be heard in the magistrates' court, the clerk will tell the defendant that the magistrates are willing to deal with the case, but that the defendant has a choice whether to *consent to summary trial* or to *elect trial by jury*. At this stage, defendants are warned that if they are tried in the magistrates' court and found guilty, the magistrates might send them to the Crown Court if they feel that their powers of punishment are insufficient.

- If the defendant consents to a summary trial they will then be formally asked to plead not guilty. If they elect jury trial, then the case will be adjourned and sent to the Crown Court.

- If the magistrates decide that their powers of punishment are insufficient or that the Crown Court is a more appropriate venue for other reasons, they will *direct* that it is sent to the Crown Court. The case will then be adjourned. No formal plea will be taken, and the defendant will not be given a choice as to venue.

For the purpose of the allocation decision, the court assumes that the prosecution allegations are correct. In 2014 the provisions of the CJA 2003 were implemented, the court will, henceforth, be aware of previous convictions.) The decision is based, in part, on whether the sentencing powers of the magistrates would be adequate. The normal maximum powers of the magistrates' court in sentencing is six months in custody with an overall maximum of 12 months' custody for two or more TEW offences tried together.

When magistrates make their decision on allocation to the appropriate court they must consider, by virtue of section 19 of the Magistrates' Courts Act 1980:

- the nature of the case;
- the seriousness of the offence;
- the magistrates' powers of punishment (including compensation);
- other circumstances making one venue more suitable than the other;
- the representations of prosecution and defendant.

National Mode of Trial Guidelines were issued in October 1990 by the Lord Chief Justice, and amended in January 1995 by the Criminal Justice Consultative Committee to give guidance to magistrates on the mode of trial decision and to encourage them to commit fewer cases to the Crown Court for trial. These list the factors that should be considered in mode of trial decisions in general and give particular guidance in respect of the most common offences. General guidance includes the following:

- the decision should never be on grounds of convenience or expediency;
- a difficult question of law or fact should be dealt with on indictment;
- subject to the defendant's consent, the presumption is in favour of summary trial.

The guidance also lists specific factors that may make a case not suitable for summary trial, the overriding factor being the magistrates' powers of punishment. For example, for offences of violence that are TEW (sections 20 and 47 of the Offences Against the Person Act 1861), the guidance states that summary trial should take place unless one or more of the following features are present:

- use of a weapon of a kind likely to cause serious injury;
- a weapon is used and serious injury is caused;
- more than minor injury is caused by head butting, kicking, or similar forms of assault;
- serious violence is caused to someone working with the public, for example a taxi driver, publican, or police officer;
- a particularly vulnerable victim, for example very young or elderly;
- the offence has a clear racial motivation.

Appropriate guidelines are given for other offences. As jury trial is seen as a cornerstone of the criminal justice system, it is important that defendants are aware of their rights and can make an informed choice. The mode of trial procedure is therefore mandatory for a TEW offence unless the defendant indicates a guilty plea. Table 9.5 shows the number of cases between 2009/10 and 2011/12 committed to the Crown Court either as a result of the magistrates' direction or because the defendant chose or elected to have the case dealt with there. It also shows cases that could only be tried at the Crown Court.

A defendant's choice may be influenced by a number of factors, and research published in 1992 indicated that 70 per cent of defendants who opted for jury

Table 9.5 Allocation or mode of trial decisions 2009/10–2011/12

	Crown Court: source of committals for trial					
	2009/10	%	2010/11	%	2011/12	%
Magistrates' direction	59,624	54.4	63,771	54.9	59,703	56.0
Defendants' elections	9,170	8.4	10,427	9.0	7,777	7.3
Indictable only	40,754	37.2	42,019	36.2	39,209	36.8
Total	**109,548**		**116,217**		**106,689**	

Source: Compiled from CPS Annual Reports

trial did so on the advice of their lawyer (**Hedderman and Moxon 1992**). Almost one-third of defendants thought opting for Crown Court would delay the trial, while just over one-third thought it would be quicker. Rather unusually, 59 per cent of respondents in the survey thought that they would receive a lower sentence in the Crown Court, a perception which does not reflect the sentencing powers of the two courts. It may reflect a tendency for the Crown Court to give sentences at the lower end of their spectrum for TEW offences; and, as seen above, almost one-quarter of defendants were influenced by the consideration that they would, by delaying the trial, spend longer in remand prisons.

The most common reason given was the increased chance of acquittal (see Table 9.6). It is generally believed that juries are more likely to acquit than magistrates, and there is some justification for this view as the acquittal rates in the Crown Court have been found to be higher than in magistrates' courts (**Vennard 1985**). It is also generally believed that magistrates' courts tend to accept police evidence more readily (**Ashworth 1994a**). It may be, therefore, that defendants are encouraged to elect jury trial whenever the case against them is not very strong. However, the study also found that 70 per cent of those defendants who elected trial at the Crown Court pleaded guilty to all charges on the day of the trial. While numbers of committals by defendants' elections have declined substantially (in 2003/4 by contrast there were 13,037 defendant elections for jury trial) it is probable that those who elect are influenced by much the same factors as revealed in the research.

Table 9.6 Reasons defendants and solicitors gave for preferring Crown Court trial

Reason	Defendants (%)	Solicitors (%)
Better chance of acquittal	69	81
Magistrates on the side of the police	62	70
Lighter sentence	59	38
To get more information about the prosecution case	48	45
Would be sent to Crown Court for sentence	42	40
More likely to get bail	36	11
Crown Court quicker	34	6
Delay start of trial	28	19
Co-defendant wanted Crown Court	26	19
To serve part of sentence on remand	24	Not asked
Easier to get legal aid	19	4

Source: Hedderman and Moxon (1992: 20)

Since this research was carried out, as mentioned above, important changes in the law have been introduced that have affected the numbers of defendants committed to the Crown Court for trial. These are, first, the change described above so that defendants who plead guilty are dealt with in the magistrates' court, and, secondly, the so-called discount for a guilty plea set out in section 48 of the Criminal Justice and Public Order Act 1994. This provides that courts in sentencing must take account of the fact that the defendant pleaded guilty, and consider reducing the sentence, but in particular will take account of the stage of proceedings at which the guilty plea was entered. This means that defendants' sentences will often be significantly reduced if they plead guilty at an early stage.

One of the reasons behind the series of reforms that now encourage defendants to indicate their intention to plead guilty at an earlier stage of proceedings than was the case before October 1997, was the aim to reduce the number of 'cracked cases'. These are cases in which preparations for a contested trial at the Crown Court have been made with witnesses, and evidence assembled and barristers **briefed**; and, at the start or during the trial, defendants change their plea to guilty. Then an enormous amount of effort, time and money is wasted. In 2011, of the 41,402 cases listed for trial, 10,458 'cracked' because of a late guilty plea and another 5,923 were ineffective (compared with 12,407 of 51,209 trials in 2000). Of those ineffective total, 983 were because the prosecution was not ready, 1,047 because the defence was not ready, 1,343 because a witness was absent, 1,177 because the defendant was absent or declared unfit to stand, and 1,356 because of court administrative problems (*Judicial and Court Statistics 2011*).

The cost of a Crown Court trial far exceeds that of a summary trial. It is perhaps unsurprising, therefore, that on the grounds of cost-effectiveness there have been successive attempts to reduce the number of TEW cases. As has been referred to above, these attempts include the following:

- reclassification of offences as summary only;
- plea before venue procedure;
- 'discount' for early guilty plea;
- proposals to increase the sentencing powers of magistrates;
- indication of sentence procedures (so that defendants can gauge the risk of pleading guilty).

Case management generally has become an important issue for the courts and is discussed below. Cases that can be tried only at the Crown Court are 'sent' for trial under section 51 of the Crime and Disorder Act 1998, which provides a rapid procedure with the minimum of bureaucracy so that cases are moved to the Crown Court where all the preparation for trial or guilty pleas can take place.

Where a case is TEW the procedure for transferring it from the magistrates' court to the Crown Court is known as committal proceedings. These are held for TEW cases where a decision has been made to send them to the Crown Court. Committal proceedings were originally intended to allow the lower court to examine cases and sift out those that had insufficient evidence. Committals eventually took two forms: one without considering the evidence, and the other which provided for the calling of witnesses and their cross-examination. The procedure was criticised in the Runciman Royal Commission, which stated:

> We accordingly recommend that, where the defendant makes a submission of no case to answer, it be considered on the papers, although the defence should be able to advance oral argument in support of the submission and the prosecution should be able to reply. Witnesses should not be called: the right place to test their evidence is the trial itself. We do not accept that they should be required in effect to give their evidence twice over. Quite apart from the time and trouble wasted by unnecessary duplication, we agree that there is a significant risk that some of them will feel so intimidated on the first occasion that they will be unable to give their evidence at the trial satisfactorily or perhaps at all. We believe that a hearing on the papers would be sufficient to enable the court to prevent from proceeding to trial cases too weak to deserve it.
>
> (Lord Runciman 1993: 90)

Since October 1997, committal evidence has been tested by an examination of the documents only. The requirement for witnesses to be called to give oral evidence was removed. To that extent the recommendations of the Royal Commission of 1993 were accepted. Committal proceedings for indictable only offences were abolished by the Crime and Disorder Act 1998.

Implementation of the proposals in the Criminal Justice Act 2003 will have further impact on pre-trial procedures: for instance, committal proceedings were abolished in 2014, but committal for sentence remains. Before the magistrates' court decides whether its powers of punishment are sufficient, the court is now informed about the defendant's previous convictions. This will enable the court to make a full judgment about whether its powers of punishment are sufficient both on the facts of the case and on the basis of the defendant's record. This means that if the court accepts jurisdiction there will be only a limited power to commit for sentence.

The most important change to be introduced eventually is the right of defendants to ask for an indication of the sentence they would receive in the magistrates' court. Although the magistrates do not have to comply with the request, if they do, and as a result (because a non-custodial penalty is indicated) the defendant then changes the plea, the court is bound by that indication. This change in procedure offers inducements for the defendant both to plead guilty and to accept the magistrates' jurisdiction. A similar process has been available in the Crown Court for many years, in various formats, most recently by means of what is known as a *Goodyear* direction (Goodyear [2005] 1 WLR 2532).

9.6 Plea and case management hearings

Objective 6

Outline the stages and issues in trial case management.

There are significant issues for and criticism of the criminal justice system in relation to efficiency: see the Auld Report. Much has been made of the possible conflicts between the due process and the cost-effectiveness models. If a defendant is rushed through proceedings without having opportunity properly to address issues, this poses significant questions of principle and due process. However, delay and cost from courts being idle or being unable to progress cases because of faulty communications, missing or incomplete papers, defendants who have failed to attend without good reason or are not produced by the Prison Service, reports that are not prepared in time for the court hearing, or cases that take much longer or indeed a much shorter time than expected, are all matters that should in part be able to be solved by better organisation.

In October 1996, the Home Office set up a review of delay in the system, which reported in February 1997: *Review of Delay in the Criminal Justice System* (**Home Office 1997c**). Its terms of reference were wide-ranging over all aspects of the system and not limited by existing legislation. Fundamental changes about case management in the magistrates' court were introduced, including: giving justices' clerks wider powers, and early listing of likely guilty pleas. These fast-track 'Narey hearings', named after the report's author, take place soon after arrest in cases that are likely to be guilty pleas in the magistrates' court: notably for driving with excess alcohol. New (faster) committal procedures were introduced under the Crime and Disorder Act 1998. Administrative steps are used increasingly in the court to identify issues and ensure that only issues that are actually contested will be challenged. In magistrates' courts, pre-trial reviews are automatically arranged a number of weeks before trial to verify that the case will proceed to a trial, and that all sides are prepared for the trial date. In the Crown Court, a procedure called the 'plea and case management hearing' (PCMH) is held at the first stage after a case has been sent or committed. This is administered by a judge, often at the time when the defendant is arraigned (i.e. the plea is formally taken) so that it can be seen whether a guilty plea is expected at this stage, and administrative and legal matters are canvassed which will affect the time the trial will take and the state of readiness of the parties. The purpose of many of the questions on the PCMH questionnaire is to avoid matters suddenly arising at trial and causing delay. These hearings are now conducted in some courts by electronic means; and, increasingly, electronic mechanisms such as electronic presentation of evidence and digital audio recording are used.

In long or complex cases the CPIA 1996 made provision for **preparatory hearings**, as has occurred in serious fraud cases, which allows the trial judge to make decisions on the case without the jury needing to attend, thus limiting sometimes lengthy debate in the absence of the jury in such cases, with consequent waste of court and juror time. There are rights of appeal from rulings made in these hearings and limits on what can be reported in the press, so the eventual jury in the cases will not be affected by media reports.

In 2003, 42 **Local Criminal Justice Boards** were set up to improve communications and effectiveness within the criminal justice system. One measure they introduced was the setting of a number of local timeliness targets which supported national public service agreements. The targets in the Crown Court relate to committals for sentence, committals for trial, trials and appeals and in the magistrates' courts covering separately youth and adult cases, divided between initial guilty pleas, trials and committals. A survey on the effectiveness of Local Criminal Justice Boards reported in February 2008 that:

> ... A proven performance management model, conceived by Jack Maple and applied to police organisations and non-crime public services across North America, can be applied to the LCJB context.
>
> The key features of the model are:
>
> - accurate and timely information;
> - effective tactics;
> - rapid deployment of personnel and resources; relentless follow-up and assessment.
>
> Source: *A survey on Local Criminal Justice Boards Effectiveness*,
> Ministry of Justice Research Series 3/08

Thus concerns for efficiency have resulted in changes not only to court procedures, and in the allocation of work, but also in internal restructuring and in performance targets as in any other industry. The inherent tension is that for one of the end users at least – the defendant – this is not a 'service' that he or she wishes to be involved in, and for other end users such as the victim or public the concern is much more to do with ideas of justice and appropriate punishment than efficiency.

Conclusion

This chapter has explored the many important processes that precede a full trial or hearing, and shown that complex issues are involved in pre-trial procedures. We have also seen the interdependency between different stages of the process. Although very different considerations and rules surround decisions to grant bail and the sentencing decision, in practice what happens at one stage affects the later stage. A remand in custody may affect the eventual sentence and become part of defendants' calculations on mode of trial or plea decisions.

The pre-trial processes show the conflict between the different goals and models of criminal justice, and further illustrate how difficult it is in practice to balance these competing pressures, which are even more vividly illustrated by the problem of how to deal at the pre-trial stage with terrorist suspects (**see Chapter 4**). The due process model stresses the rights of the defendant throughout the process. Yet the crime control model requires that those who are guilty of crime be brought to court, convicted and punished. Due process requires procedures to assure that defendants are able to take advantage of their rights. As seen above, the issues raised by bail or custodial remands are particularly difficult to resolve. It is clearly in the interests of due process that citizens are not deprived of their liberty until proved guilty. On the other hand, there is understandable concern that dangerous or persistent offenders may be allowed to return to the community and that many offences may be committed while offenders are on bail. Crime control and prevention aims may conflict with due process.

The cost of keeping offenders in custody is high, and bureaucratic and financial pressures also indicate that remands in custody should be kept to a minimum and that court adjournment periods should be kept as short as possible. Many of these issues are also seen in **Chapter 10**, which deals with the processes by which guilt or not is established.

The bureaucratic efficiency model of criminal justice underlines the need for speed, efficiency and cost-effectiveness. The cost and speed of justice has become an increasingly important issue.

Despite the changes outlined above, a visitor to any magistrates' court would see many cases adjourned, almost without consideration because they are 'first time in', where a culture still exists that no progress is expected. Others will not be able to progress as expected because 'the defendant needs legal advice', or the prosecution papers are not ready, or available, or have not been shown to the defence in sufficient time for them to be considered. Current pressures to remove delay and reduce cost are beginning to take effect but dangers exist when pressures conflict with the due process issues which are fundamental to a fair criminal justice system.

Review questions

1. What are the three categories of criminal offences dealt with by the courts; how are they allocated between courts?

2. Describe the circumstances in which an allocation and plea and venue decision is made and outline its stages.

3. What changes have been made to the judicial appointments system?

4. Gary Fowles appears at the magistrates' court after being arrested the previous night and held in police custody for burglary. He is 25 years old and lives with his girlfriend and their 6-month-old child. They have lived together in their council flat since the birth of their child. He works on a market stall selling CDs. He takes home approximately £150 per week. His girlfriend does not work.

   He has previous convictions (as shown in the table) and is currently undertaking a 150-hour community order with an unpaid work requirement for a previous conviction of burglary. He has an absconding conviction.

   Gary was arrested coming out of a house last night carrying computer equipment worth £500. He had entered through an unlocked door. He made a full confession to the police and is anxious to be released on bail to return to his girlfriend. He is willing to comply with any conditions the magistrates may impose, but cannot offer any surety.

   He has the following previous convictions:

Date:	Conviction for:	Sentence:
2 years ago	Common assault	Fine of £150
1 year ago	Taking vehicle without consent	Fine of £200
6 months ago	Burglary	Community Order (unpaid work) for 150 hours
6 months ago	Absconding (missed court appearance)	Fine of £20

Questions:

a. Might the police or CPS object to bail?

b. On what grounds might they object?

c. If bail were granted, what conditions might be appropriate?

d. What do you think the magistrates should do?

Discussion questions

1. What are the advantages and disadvantages of having lay people make the decision on the guilt of the defendant?

2. Discuss the conflicting principles, as indicated by different models of criminal justice, underlying the use of remands on bail and in custody.

Further reading

Ashworth A and Redmayne M (2005) *The Criminal Process* (3rd edn), Oxford University Press: Oxford

Auld Report (2001) *Review into the Workings of the Criminal Courts in England and Wales*, Home Office: London

Sprack J (2008) *A Practical Approach to Criminal Procedure* (12th edn), Blackstone Press: London

Weblinks

Criminal Defence Service: **www.legalservices.gov.uk/criminal/**

Criminal Statistics Annual report: **www.justice.gov.uk/publications/criminalannual.htm**

Form for plea and case management hearings can be viewed at: **www.dca.gov.uk/ criminal/procrules_fin/contents/practice_direction/pd_consolidated.htm#6197710**

Judicial Appointments Commission: **www.judicialappointments.gov.uk/news/qualities.htm**

Judiciary and Courts Statistics: **www.justice.gov.uk/publications/ judicialandcourtstatistics.htm**

Chapter 10

The trial and establishing guilt

Learning objectives

After reading the chapter you should be able to:

1. Understand adversarial justice, the burden of proof and the standard of proof
2. Explain the significance and role of the trial
3. Describe the composition and role of the jury
4. Outline the rights of the defendant in court
5. Explain how to protect witness identity
6. Discuss the different types of evidence used in court and its role in the trial
7. Outline the appeals system
8. Describe the history and role of the Criminal Cases Review Commission

Key statistics

- In total 97,182 cases in were heard in the Crown Court in 2012/13. Of this total figure the number found not guilty following a trial was 6,030 (6.2%). The number of judge-directed or judge-ordered acquittals was 11,992 (12.3%). The number found guilty following a jury trial was 8,416 (8.7%). The numbers found guilty following a guilty plea by the defendant was 69,971 (72%). Of the total figure above, 773 (0.8%) did not appear for trial or had died. (*Source*: CPS Annual Report 2012/13)
- The role of Her Majesty's Inspectorate of Courts Administration (HMICA) was abolished in 2012
- 81,800 defendants were tried at the Crown Court in the 12 months ending in June 2012compared with 105,100 in the 12 months ending June 2011 (*Source*: *Criminal Justice statistics update to June 2013*, Ministry of Justice, Nov 2013)

Introduction

The criminal trial is usually seen as the focal event in the criminal justice process. It demonstrates the key principles underpinning the way the system of justice operates in England and Wales: the principles of adversarial justice, the burden and standard of proof, the right to silence, and limitations on what evidence can be heard. It is also the focus of much criticism from a variety of different viewpoints: the over-protection of the accused on the one hand, the sacrificing of the principle to expediency on the other, and above all the artificiality of the application of legal rules, rather than seeking the truth by hearing all the available evidence about the crime and the defendant. Such criticisms have led in the last part of the twentieth and the early twenty-first centuries to significant changes, attempting to achieve a 're-balancing of the criminal justice system in favour of the victim'. These changes, which effectively reflect shifting views of the appropriateness of differing models of criminal justice, are discussed below.

The most comprehensive recent review of the trial process was the Auld Review of the Criminal Courts which reported in 2001 (**Auld 2001**). Many of the report's recommendations were incorporated into the reforms in the Criminal Justice Act 2003, which has an impact on the role of judges and the laws of evidence – and involves in some areas a culture shift for criminal justice in England and Wales. His report was detailed, comprehensive and is a compelling commentary on the issues facing the adversarial system at the beginning of the twenty-first century.

The criminal court was the primary focus of the Auld Review and is the focus of this chapter. Court proceedings are the most public manifestation of the criminal justice process, the arena in which justice is very literally 'seen to be done'. This is especially true of the trial, generally assumed to be the stage in the process where the defendant has his or her day in court and the opportunity to assert innocence. The trial is a vital part of the adversarial system and, as we have seen, the right to trial by one's peers, represented by the jury system, is seen as a fundamental protection for the defendant against the power of the state. In the trial the defendant is presumed innocent until proved guilty beyond reasonable doubt. Rules of evidence, which may seem technical and abstract, embody the principles of due process, and are there to protect the defendant from unfair or unsuitable allegations. In addition, the trial plays a key role in denunciation and just deserts – it is the arena in which society expresses its moral disapproval of wrongdoing and it is important in the interests of justice that accused persons who say they are innocent are tried in public.

As we have seen, however, only a minority of defendants exercise the right to a full trial, with many being diverted before prosecution and yet more pleading guilty. Only a minority of defendants contest their guilt. Nevertheless, the court system is still subject to delays in dealing with those who do, and is very costly. The system operates with only a small number of defendants pleading not guilty and going to a full trial. Is there a pressure on defendants and officials in the system to speed up the process? Are defendants pressured into pleading guilty? Are defendants aware of their rights and of the protection offered to them by rules of evidence? One commentator from the United

States of America has argued that the pressures of crime control and cost-effectiveness may lead to what is in essence a presumption of guilt, whereby defendants are processed through the system like cars on an assembly line (**Blumberg 1967**).

It is sometimes suggested that the adversarial system is not sufficiently concerned with truth and justice but in winning the 'game'. These metaphors of 'adversarial dialectics' are most pronounced as the protagonists manoeuvre to gain advantage over their opponents in terms of facts that they want the jury not to hear, and through the tactical deployment of the procedural rules of evidence. In the meantime victims, witnesses, jurors and the public look on with astonishment as natural justice and common sense are apparently excluded as the game rules are manipulated. This criticism was taken seriously in Lord Justice Auld's *Review of the Criminal Courts in England and Wales* (2001), and his recommendations sought ways to restore public confidence in the trial process.

Although so few defendants exercise their right to a trial, whether in the magistrates' court or the Crown Court, it is nonetheless regarded as the epitome of the adversarial process. This chapter will begin by looking in more depth at the role and function of the trial and at its participants. In criminal courts in England and Wales the guilt of the defendant is in most cases determined by representatives of the public: lay magistrates or the jury. We have looked at the role and function of magistrates in summary trials and that of judges in the Crown Court (**see Chapter 9**). In this chapter we will look at the role of prosecution and defence in the trial, and we will outline the various arguments for and against the retention of the jury in the Crown Court. We will then examine the rules of evidence and procedure, which aim to ensure that defendants are dealt with fairly. As we have seen in previous chapters, however, the practical impact of all rules and procedures is affected by informal processes and working cultures. These will be explored before finally considering the implication for concepts of justice of the idea of plea and sentence negotiation – another topic which clearly illustrates the problems of balancing the *due process* and *just deserts* models of criminal justice with those of *bureaucratic efficiency* and *crime control* (**four of the eight models of criminal justice introduced in Chapter 1**).

10.1 Adversarial justice: the burden and standard of proof

Objective 1

Understand adversarial justice, the burden of proof and the standard of proof

In England and Wales, the trial, indeed the criminal justice system as a whole, is based on what is called an adversarial approach. This describes not only the format and structure of a trial, but the role of the trial itself. The adversarial approach can be contrasted with legal systems in most European jurisdictions which have a more inquisitorial approach. In the latter the court enquires into the circumstances of an allegation in order to find the truth of what happened. An adversarial (or accusatorial) approach is based on accusation and challenge. Someone – the prosecutor in a criminal case, the claimant in a civil – makes a claim or accusation which they then have to try to prove within the rules and procedures of the particular court. The opponent can deny or challenge the claim or can wait to see if the claim is sufficiently established. In an adversarial system, the court does not enquire into the truth of what happened but asks whether the prosecution has proved the allegation. This itself raises the following questions:

- What exactly has to be proved?
- Who has to prove it?
- To what extent must the allegation be proved?
- Who decides whether proof has been achieved: in other words who needs to be persuaded?
- What information can be placed before a court to prove the case?
- Who should make decisions and/or give guidance on the above?

These questions raise fundamental issues about the conduct and purpose of the criminal trial, but none is more fundamental to the concept of the adversarial procedure than the questions relating to the burden and standard of proof. The burden of proof is concerned with answering who has to prove the case, and the standard with answering 'to what extent?'. In England and Wales, the burden of proof lies with the prosecution and the standard of proof required is that the case must be proved beyond reasonable doubt. This means that the triers of fact – magistrates in the magistrates' court, the jury in the Crown Court – must be satisfied of the guilt of the defendant to that standard. Although the precise formulation of the standard may be varied by, for instance, the use of the phrase 'satisfied so you are sure', the famous time-honoured formulation 'proof beyond reasonable doubt' is still that most recognised. The rules concerning the burden and standard of proof are the most significant of all rules of evidence.

These two concepts must be examined closely as they underpin any criminal trial and set the parameters for determination of guilt. The phrase 'burden of proof' indicates where the onus of proving a case lies. In a criminal case, this burden lies with the prosecution. This means that the prosecution has the task of producing and explaining evidence to the court, on all the matters necessary to establish a conviction. The defendant need do nothing. The only exceptions are where the defendant is seeking to rely on insanity as a defence, or where an Act of Parliament states or implies that the burden is on the defendant. In these limited cases, it is the defendant who has to actively persuade the court (whether jury or magistrates) of that matter: the burden of proof lies on the defendant. Certain statutes explicitly place the burden of proof on the defendant. Perhaps the clearest example of this is where someone is charged with not having a licence – for example, a driving or shotgun licence. The relevant statutes place the burden of proof to disprove the allegation on the defendant, who must show the court that he or she did indeed have a licence. The rationale for this is that it is a matter specifically within the defendant's own knowledge, and easier to prove than disprove a situation.

The fact that the prosecution has to prove its case – and every element of it – is reflected throughout the trial process. The defendant is 'innocent until proved guilty' is the popular statement of the rule, and the defendant's right to remain silent during and before the trial is a natural concomitant of it. The defendant need, in principle, do nothing and wait to see if the case is made out against him or her. The role of the trial is to establish whether the case has been successfully proved.

Standard and burden of proof

Woolmington was a case heard in the House of Lords as the final Court of Appeal in 1935. The case helped to clarify the standard of proof in English law. The issue was not so much the facts of the case and the guilt of the defendant as the judge's statement about the burden of proof.

Reginald Woolmington, aged 21, was charged with murdering his 17-year-old wife, Violet, by shooting her with a rifle used for shooting rooks. Following domestic rows she had gone back to live with her mother. He went to her mother's house. A shout, 'Are you coming back home?' was heard by a neighbour, and then a shot.

When charged, he said: 'I want to say nothing, except I done it, and they can do what they like with me. It was jealousy I suppose. Her mother enticed her away from me. I done all I could to get her back. That's all.' Later in court, Woolmington admitted killing his wife but claimed it was an accident and that he unintentionally squeezed the trigger when he was threatening to shoot himself.

He was found guilty and the Court of Appeal upheld his conviction, but he was allowed to appeal to the House of Lords on a legal issue concerned with the way the jury had been directed on the burden and standard of proof.

At issue was the following statement by the trial judge:

'The Crown has got to satisfy you that this woman, Violet Woolmington, died at the prisoner's hands. They must satisfy you of that beyond any reasonable doubt. If they satisfy you of that, then he has to show that there are circumstances to be found in the evidence which has been given from the witness box in this case, which alleviate the crime so that it is only manslaughter, or which excuse the homicide altogether by showing that it was a pure accident.'

Viscount Sankey LC expressed the judgment:

'Juries are always told that, if conviction there is to be, the prosecution must prove the case beyond reasonable doubt. This statement cannot mean that in order to be acquitted the prisoner must "satisfy" the jury. This is the law as laid down in the Court of Criminal Appeal in *Rex* v. *Davies* 29 Times L R 350; 8 Cr App R 211, the headnote of which correctly states that where intent is an ingredient of a crime there is no onus on the defendant to prove that the act alleged was accidental. Throughout the web of the English Criminal Law one golden thread is always to be seen, that it is the duty of the prosecution to prove the prisoner's guilt subject to what I have already said as to the defence of insanity and subject also to any statutory exception.'

10.2 Role of the trial

Objective 2

Explain the significance and role of the trial

A Crown Court trial has some of the appearance of a theatrical performance with costumes, ceremony, dramatic setting and seating for an audience. These dramatic qualities are also evident in the cross-examination of witnesses to see who will play their part well, and the speeches of counsel to win the sympathy of the jury. They play out their roles in line with the adversarial principles of the trial. In the Crown Court, the prosecution and defence counsel present their arguments before a judge whose role is to ensure a fair trial, and the jury, who must decide on the guilt, or not, of the defendant. The real life drama of the trial lies in its public examination of and formal adjudication upon matters of human weakness and wickedness.

At a more prosaic level, the trial seeks to establish the guilt, or otherwise, of the accused. Whether a trial takes place in the magistrates' court or the Crown Court, the key issues are the same and relate to the principle of the presumption of innocence and the application of the adversarial approach to justice. The rules are largely the same, although differences do arise to take account of the different participants. In a summary trial, the magistrates determine the facts, including guilt or innocence, apply the law and in most cases will determine sentence. In a Crown Court the jury determines the facts while the judge alone is concerned with sentence.

At the trial stage a presumption is made that the defendant is innocent, and it is the duty of the prosecution to try to establish guilt: the trial is based on the principle that the burden of proof is on the prosecution. The prosecution must provide evidence to establish the defendant's guilt 'beyond reasonable doubt'. If the jury or magistrates suspect a person has committed a crime, they should not convict unless convinced that the evidence clearly demonstrates guilt beyond reasonable doubt. It was seen earlier that in an adversarial system a trial does not set out to establish directly the truth of what took place or enquire into its causes but rather whether there is sufficient evidence to establish whether a person (the accused) is guilty of the offence. Hence, the trial is the quality control mechanism to try to ensure that only the demonstrably guilty are convicted and punished. Of course, in the end this is a matter of human judgement and it does not guarantee that the jury or magistrates will not make mistakes, but the legal principle influencing the procedure of the trial is that a person is innocent unless and until proved guilty by a verdict of the court. If acquitted, does that mean the defendant is – in reality – innocent?

As pointed out by Lord Donaldson, Master of the Rolls from 1982 to 1992, this does not follow. In a letter to *The Times* he wrote:

> . . . A 'guilty' verdict means that in the view of the jury the accused undoubtedly committed the offence. It is not only the innocent who are entitled to a 'not guilty' verdict. They are joined and, in my experience, are heavily outnumbered by the almost certainly guilty. This is as it should be because, as every law student is taught, it is far better that ten guilty men go free than that one innocent man be convicted.
>
> (*The Times*, 19 August 1994)

Thus, jury members might well suspect from what they have heard that the person has committed a crime but they cannot be certain beyond reasonable doubt. They must, therefore, find the accused not guilty. Everyone is innocent until proved guilty in legal doctrine but this does not always reflect common-sense notions of responsibility for a crime. In Scotland, besides guilty and not guilty there is a third possible verdict of 'not proven'. A 'not proven' decision by a jury does not result in any punishment and means the prosecution may not reopen the case, but it might more accurately reflect the opinion of the jury on the evidence.

Rules of procedure and evidence have developed to try to ensure that only the guilty are convicted, and they take account of and reflect our adversarial system. Some rules seek to prevent the jury being misled or unfairly prejudiced by information which is not strictly relevant to the question of whether the defendant committed the offence in question. Thus rumour or gossip about the defendant or facts about the defendant's previous criminal behaviour are not routinely allowed as evidence. Anyone who has been involved in the case or who knows witnesses or the defendant can therefore not sit on a jury. Other rules reflect our increasing understanding about human memory and observation and, therefore, limit or prevent the admission of certain types of evidence. In criminal cases it has for long been recognised that there is a need to limit the extent to which defendants' confessions can be used in evidence against them. Out-of-court confessions are in principle admissible – why would defendants say something implicating themselves unless it were true? Rules are necessary, however, to protect those who might have been induced or pressured by the police into making confessions or those who admit liability through a misplaced sense of guilt or responsibility for others. Section 76 of PACE provides criteria which must be met before a confession can be adduced in evidence. Confessions obtained as a result of pressure by the police will be ruled as inadmissible.

Strict rules of procedure also determine the order the proceedings should follow and determine how and when evidence can be presented and challenged. This means that trials are formal proceedings which use legal rather than everyday language where lawyers are at home and familiar with the routine, but which can often be confusing for the lay participant or observer. This, however, ensures that the proceedings are regulated and that only appropriate and useful evidence is brought to the court. It also ensures that the defence has the opportunity to challenge evidence and witnesses in a systematic way.

Table 10.1 shows the number of cases resolved by the Crown Court (**see Section 10.3**). Most defendants, having reached Crown Court, enter a plea of guilty (**as seen in Chapter 9**). Cases not proceeded with account for some 7 per cent of the total. The Crown Prosecution Service (CPS) has a continuing duty to review the case (**see Chapter 6**). Cases are not proceeded with for a variety of reasons: a defendant may already have been dealt with by the Crown Court for other offences, or it may be found that the defendant has a serious medical condition. In other cases, witnesses may fail to attend to give evidence, or the CPS may feel that the evidence is not sufficient to proceed. In these latter cases, no evidence is offered by the CPS and the judge will order a formal verdict of not guilty. The amount of cases not proceeded with increased as a result of the 'sending' procedure introduced by the Crime and Disorder Act 1998 – committal proceedings are no longer used for indictable-only offences. Under this procedure cases which can be tried only at the Crown Court are sent immediately from the magistrates' court: the first opportunity for review is therefore after the case has already arrived at the Crown Court. Thus it can be seen that changes in one part of the criminal justice system, introduced to streamline the magistrates' court process, have impact in other areas. The plea-before-venue process reduced the number of trials sent to the Crown Court but doubled the number of committals for sentence.

Not all cases that go to the Crown Court. In addition to 'cracked trials' whereby the defendant enters a guilty plea after initially entering a not guilty plea at the start of the trial, there are trials that are scheduled but do not get started and these are referred to, by the Ministry of Justice, as 'ineffective trials'. In 2012, 14% of trials scheduled for the Crown Court were ineffective for the following reasons: the defendant was absent, the defendant was unfit to plea, witnesses are absent, prosecutors are not ready or available, defence counsel are not ready or available, Crown Court administration were not ready to proceed, interpreters were not available (https://www.gov.uk/government/ . . . /court-statistics-quarterly).

A prosecutor in a magistrates' court will usually be employed by the CPS, or other prosecuting authority. In trials this will be a legally qualified employee, although 'lay presenters' or 'associate prosecutors' (previously called 'designated case workers' (DCWs)), employed by the CPS may appear in less complex matters. The introduction of non-professional presenters was made possible by the Courts and Legal Services Act 1990 and their powers were extended by the Criminal Justice and Immigration Act 2008, so that they can deal with summary non-imprisonable trials, bail applications and non-contested matters in the Youth Court. In 2006–7, before the extension of these powers and the change of name, DCWs dealt with 14.7 per cent of magistrates' courts sessions.

In a Crown Court trial, the CPS will usually be represented by a barrister it has instructed. The duty of prosecutors is to present the evidence fairly, and to seek a conviction on the most serious offence warranted by the evidence. Their role is not to seek a conviction at all costs: they should prosecute, not persecute.

The Code for Crown Prosecutors also indicates that the prosecution must assess and balance all the arguments for and against prosecution in the particular case in accordance with the Code for Crown Prosecutors (as seen in **Chapter 7**). Lawyers are bound by codes of conduct, which provide that they must never knowingly mislead the courts. Barristers and solicitors are deemed to be officers of the court, and must assist the court in the administration of justice. The Criminal Procedure Rules 2005 introduced a specific additional duty on all members of the court process to comply with the 'overriding objective' of the criminal justice process; that cases should be dealt with justly. This includes: respecting the interests of witnesses, victims and jurors and keeping them informed of the progress of the case; dealing with the case efficiently and expeditiously; and ensuring that appropriate information is available to the court when bail and sentence are considered.

The prosecution is charged, in furtherance of the concept of fairness, to disclose information that might be of assistance to the defence. This includes details of previous convictions of prosecution witnesses, and unused witness statements. Sam Hallam, jailed for murder in 2004, was freed in May 2012 after the Court of Appeal ruled that Hallam's case had been undermined by the failure of the prosecution team to disclose evidence – in the form of photos taken on his mobile phone – that could have supported his case. The Court of Appeal strongly underlined the principle that the defence is entitled not only to information that the prosecution intends to use in the trial but also to any information collected by the police in the process of investigating a case which may assist the defence. The principle of prosecution disclosure was criticised in some quarters as giving the defence undue advantage. The Criminal Procedure and Investigations Act 1996 (as amended by the CJA 2003) introduced a comprehensive regime of disclosure of evidence for both the prosecution and, in the Crown Court, the defence, so that defendants are properly able to meet the case against them, and the prosecution is not taken by surprise by an 'ambush' defence in the midst of a trial (i.e. those entered at the last minute, which make it difficult for the prosecution to check or investigate).

The lawyers dealing with the defence case will include a solicitor who is instructed directly by the defendant, will take initial instructions, and may represent the defendant in the magistrates' court. If the trial takes place in the Crown Court, the lawyer appearing there will usually be a barrister, although increasingly solicitors have 'higher rights of audience' which means they can present cases in the Crown Court and the appeal courts. The role of the defence lawyer is influenced by the fact that the prosecution must prove the case, and that – strictly – the defence need do nothing. However, as a result of changes to the law introduced by the Criminal Justice and Public Order Act 1994 and the Criminal Procedure and Investigations Act 1996, there are grave dangers for defendants who do not state their account or give an explanation. This is because the court may be able to draw an 'adverse inference' from the fact that a defendant does not give evidence – that is, make assumptions about the reasons why the defendant has not given an explanation.

Defence counsel must represent the defendant fearlessly, without regard to his or her own view of the case or his or her own interests. This latter point is reflected in the so-called cab-rank rule, which demands that a barrister must always represent a client when asked, provided the barrister is not otherwise engaged, practises in the relevant court and is offered a suitable fee. This means that defendants with unpopular beliefs and those accused of even the most unpleasant crimes will be represented.

Is the cab-rank rule worth saving?

The Bar Standards Board, the body that regulates barristers in England and Wales, has just published a consultation paper, launching debate on when barristers can decline to be instructed on a case or withdraw from it.

Ruth Evans, chairman of the board, said: 'It is in the public interest to ensure that cases are able to proceed with certainty; the changes are designed to clarify the circumstances in which a barrister may withdraw from a case and where a barrister is obliged to provide representation.'

Changes in the way barristers may practice – with more in the pipeline under the Legal Services Act – make the time ripe to review the rule again. The argument about access to counsel of choice has been gradually weakened – by increasing numbers of solicitor-advocates and in-house barristers being able to appear in the higher courts for their employers. Partnership between barristers and solicitors looms – and with it issues of conflicts of interest.

('Is the cab-rank rule worth saving?', *The Times*, 1 May 2008 (Gibb, F.), Times Newspapers Ltd., © F. Gibb, NI Syndication Limited, 2008)

10.3 Juries

In the Crown Court, the body charged with determining guilt or not is the jury. Defended by some as the bastion of democracy, castigated by others as an unwieldy anachronism that allows miscarriages of justice to take place, the jury has been part of the criminal justice system in one form or another since the twelfth century. Juries are currently composed of 12 men and women drawn from the register of electors for the area in which the trial is to take place. The qualification for jury service is now laid down in the Juries Act 1974 as amended by the Criminal Justice Act 2003. This means that anyone who is:

- between the ages of 18 and 70;

- ordinarily resident in the United Kingdom for at least five years since the age of 13;

- not mentally disordered; and

- not disqualified;

is eligible to serve on a jury. Disqualified categories of persons include anyone who has received a custodial sentence of more than five years or a life sentence, or a community order or imprisonment within the last 10 years, or is currently on bail. Prior to the Criminal Justice Act 2003, members of the legal profession were ineligible for jury service, on the basis that they had specialist knowledge which might affect or overly influence other jury members. This ineligibility (together with that of certain other groups) has now been removed to make juries more representative of the population. The principle suggested by the Auld Review (**Auld 2001**) was that although certain disqualifications on the basis of criminal convictions or mental incapacity should continue, no one should be ineligible or excusable as of right. It is possible to seek excusal or deferral of jury service at the discretion of the Jury Summoning Bureau to take account of people's individual commitments.

The **Jury Central Summoning Bureau** was established in 2001 to coordinate and improve efficiency in calling jurors for jury service. About 344,000 people are called annually for jury service. The Bureau randomly selects jurors electronically from the electoral roll, and also checks that the individual does not have a criminal record. The group summoned form the jury panel, from which 12 are selected. Selection is done in the court of trial by the random selection of names. The 12 selected will then try the case unless any of them are challenged by the prosecution or defence or asked to 'stand by' for the prosecution. This may be done, if a juror is known to someone involved in the case or appears unable to understand the proceedings, by virtue of mental disability or language difficulties. Jurors who may be biased can be challenged also, but, as there is no normal power of **jury vetting**, by either side, it is unlikely that prejudices would be known. There is no power to create specifically a racial or gender balance, or indeed imbalance, on a jury, other than by the random selection process itself. There is a limited power of jury checking in cases involving national security, terrorism, or where there is reason to believe that disqualified persons are present on the panel.

Once jurors have been called and not challenged, they take the jury oath and a place in the jury box. The complete jury is then charged with returning a verdict on the charge or charges in the indictment. A jury is of course only required when the defendant pleads not guilty, so a plea is taken before the empanelling of the jury. Once the jury is sworn in, the trial can begin. The randomness of the jury selection process is often fiercely defended as its greatest strength. In principle, this ensures that no one grouping of opinion can dominate the outcome, and thus limits the ability of outside individuals or bodies to affect decisions. However, by definition this means that a randomly selected jury could all belong to one sex, one political party, one religion or one race.

In a criminal trial, the function of the jury is to determine the facts of the case, including the most significant fact – whether the defendant is guilty of the charge on the basis of the evidence. The jury members will be told by the judge that it is their duty to seek to arrive at a unanimous verdict. Majority verdicts have been possible since 1967, but are acceptable only when the jury has been deliberating for a long period (at least two hours in straightforward cases; longer if the issues are complex) and has been directed by the judge that a majority verdict (a verdict of at least 10) is acceptable. The judge will stress, however, that although he or she is prepared to accept a majority view, the jurors should still strive to achieve unanimity. When a majority verdict of guilty is accepted, the foreman is asked to announce the number comprising the majority and minority (10:2 or 11:1). When the verdict is not guilty, no information is sought about the distribution of views among the jury. In Scotland, the jury consists of 15 people and a simple majority verdict is acceptable.

In England and Wales, if at least 10 of the jury members are unable to agree and there seems no prospect of agreement, the judge will discharge the jury from giving a verdict. If the defendant has been convicted on other matters, the charge may be allowed to lie on the file (meaning it can be taken up again later, if in the public interest) or the prosecution may decide not to proceed. Normally, however, the defendant will be retried at a later date by a different jury. The judge may or may not be the same.

Proceedings within the jury room are entirely privileged, which means that conduct in the jury room cannot be investigated nor should it be revealed to others (Contempt of Court Act 1981). Jurors are forbidden to discuss the case or their deliberations with anyone else, for fear of distorting the trial process. If they do, they may be charged as being in contempt of court. The Royal Commission on Criminal Justice 1993, however, recommended that the Contempt of Court Act 1981 be amended so that properly authorised research can be carried out into the way juries reach their verdicts. This suggestion was repeated in the Auld Review of the Criminal Courts (**Auld 2001**) and subsequent changes have been noted in CJA 2003. The secrecy of jury deliberations also has the result that alleged irregularities in the jury's discussions cannot be a ground for appeal. This principle was reaffirmed in the case of *R* v. *Connor and Mirza* in 2004 in which a juror complained that a verdict had been influenced by racism. The House of Lords reaffirmed that it was not possible to look at what goes on in a jury room unless all jurors agreed they had abrogated their functions by, for example, deciding their verdict on the toss of a coin. The reason for secrecy is to protect the jurors from retaliation and from interference. The British tradition of juries not giving

Table 10.1 Crown Court outcomes 2009–2013

Outcome	2009/10	%	2010/11	%	2011/12	%	2012/13	%
Judge-ordered acquittals (including bind-overs)	12,930	11.7	14,958	12.8	12,527	11.7	11,209	11.5
Warrants, etc.	980	0.9	923	0.8	841	0.8	773	0.8
Judge-directed acquittals	1,048	1.0	1,101	0.9	857	0.8	783	0.8
Acquittals after trial	6,316	5.7	6,810	5.8	6,290	5.9	6,030	6.2
Guilty pleas	81,000	73.5	84,742	72.5	78,106	72.8	69,971	72
Convictions after trial	7,872	7.2	8,364	7.2	8,623	8.0	8,416	8.7
Total	110,146		116,898		107,244		97,182	

Source: Compiled from *CPS Annual Report 2012/13*

reasoned answers as to why they convicted or acquitted an accused stands in contrast to the Human Rights Act 1998, which has made transparency and reasoned decisions an aspect of a fair trial.

Misconduct by the jury or a jury member outside the confines of the jury room can, however, be a ground for appeal. If the problem is discovered during the trial, it can be a reason for the judge to discharge the juror, or the whole jury. An example of where this might happen is when information inadvertently falls into the jury's hands about previous convictions of the defendant, where such matters were not admissible in the trial. In some cases, individual misconduct by jurors in court has come to light. In June 2008, an Australian jury dealing with drugs and firearms charges was discharged after it was noticed that half the jury were playing the popular logic game *Sudoku*. In July 2007, in England, a juror was discharged and arrested for contempt of court for listening to an MP3 player under her hijab headscarf while supposedly listening to evidence in a homicide case. In May 2012, the judge sitting on the trial of seven men from Rochdale accused of grooming young girls for sex was pressured by the defence counsel to order that the jury – who had retired to the deliberating room to decide on their verdict – be discharged due to the alleged leak by a member of the jury describing the status of deliberations to the far-right BNP party leader Nick Griffin, who announced a 'guilty' verdict on his Twitter account before the verdict had been officially returned in court. The judge, however, was satisfied that no breach of law had occurred and allowed the jury to deliver its verdicts.

Table 10.1 shows the outcome of cases heard in the Crown Court, between 2009 and 2013, in terms of the number of guilty pleas, convictions after trial, acquittals and cases dealt with by the defendant being bound over to keep the peace. Table 10.2 presents the source of allocation for trial, that is, whether the proceedings were

Table 10.2 Source of allocation of trials in Crown Court

	2010/11	%	2011/12	%	2012/13	%
Magistrates' directions	63,771	54.9	59,703	56.0	54,918	56.8
Defendants' elections	10,427	9.0	7,777	7.3	3,958	4.1
Indictable only	42,019	36.2	39,209	36.8	37,849	39.1
Total	116,217		106,689		96,725	

Source: Compiled from *CPS Annual Report 2012/13*

serious enough to be sent for trial in Crown Court, or whether it was the defendant's decision, as well as the number of cases tried in Crown Court for the most serious, indictable offences only. About 70 per cent of all cases in the Crown Court result in a conviction. Table 10.1 also shows the number of defendants acquitted by the jury after full trial, and the number by the action of the judge.

Judge-ordered and judge-directed acquittals refer to cases that were discharged at different stages of the proceedings (respectively before or after the jury was involved) because of lack of evidence or some other cause which meant that the case could not continue. These account for around 12 per cent of cases. After nearly a decade of year-on-year increases in the number of cases resulting in guilty pleas, the proportion of around 73 per cent in 2011/12 appears to have stabilised, but there has been a corresponding decline in the rate of convictions after trial.

The use of juries has been the subject of conflicting views among lawyers, politicians and the public at large. Some of the arguments advanced in favour of and against juries are set out in the box.

Debate on the jury

Arguments for retaining the jury

- Juries represent a cross-section of the population so the accused is tried by his or her peers.
- Juries enable the public's view of the criminal justice system to be reflected.
- Juries ensure that unpopular or 'unjust' laws cannot be enforced.
- There is no acceptable alternative.
- Jury members are not 'case-hardened' and are more likely to have an open mind.
- The jury system is the cornerstone of our criminal trial process.
- Fact assessment is a commonsense matter best left to lay people.

Arguments against retaining the jury

- Juries are not representative of society as a whole.
- Juries are not able to handle complex issues.
- Juries are subject to prejudice and irrationality.
- Jurors are not treated with consideration, and are expected to perform a difficult, important function in uncomfortable surroundings and without preparation.
- Juries who are unwilling participants are thus unlikely to fulfil their obligations properly.
- Juries prolong the length and therefore the cost of trials.
- Juries acquit the guilty.
- Juries convict the innocent.
- Juries are too ready to believe the prosecution evidence.
- Juries are reluctant to believe the police.
- Juries are naïve and unaware of courtroom tactics to manipulate information.
- Jurors do not treat the task seriously.
- Jurors are overwhelmed by the significance of their task.

The arguments in favour of the jury involve fundamental principles developed over the centuries. The right to a trial by jury involves the concept of being tried by one's peers. It is therefore essential to this principle that jury members be chosen from a random selection of the population. In this way lay members of the public are involved in justice. Fears of oppressive laws and governments also underlie the argument that juries can affect the law itself. In so-called 'equity' verdicts, juries have acquitted on the grounds that they do not think that the law is right, even where the accused has quite clearly committed the act. This was apparently the situation in 1986 when Clive Ponting was prosecuted under the Official Secrets Act and acquitted by the jury despite a clear directive by the judge that he had no defence. Jurors may not wish to see the defendant receive a harsher punishment than they feel is deserved – juries during the 1950s, for example, often acquitted drivers accused of manslaughter. As a result of this, a new offence of causing death by reckless or dangerous driving was introduced in 1956. On the other hand, juries are costly largely because they slow down the process of justice.

In a complex society, ensuring trial by a random sample of one's peers can also raise difficult issues. Should minority groups, for example, be able to ensure that a sample of their group is on the jury? Seeking, as some have argued, a racially balanced jury necessarily militates against randomness. It is often suggested that juries, especially in cases involving a racial incident, should be racially balanced, or that trials of rape or other sexual offences should be equally composed of men and women, or even have a predominance of women. It is difficult to reconcile these views with the principles of due process – that all defendants should be tried in the same way – or with the existence of the jury at all. To seek a specially composed jury for certain cases suggests that the ordinary random jury is not able to perform its task in the required way. If that is the case, then surely the whole jury system should be reformed, and not merely in certain cases. Another problem is that some crimes have become more complex – especially frauds, where trials are lengthy and the ability of the jury to follow often complex financial evidence has been questioned. Yet frauds inevitably involve complex issues and judges themselves are not necessarily qualified in finance. There is a danger that the jury has become a scapegoat for other failings in the prosecution of serious frauds (see, e.g., **Levi 1987**). After much pressure to reduce reliance on juries, the Criminal Justice Act 2003 made provision for trial without juries where there was a fear of jury intimidation, to deal with concerns that juries or individual members of the jury might be threatened or pressured into verdicts. This came into effect in 2006. It also made provision for measures to introduce non-jury trial in serious and complex fraud cases. This was the latest attempt to allow for non-jury trial in fraud cases, partly because of the cost and time taken (between 2002 and 2005, 26 such trials lasted over six months) and arguably because some serious and complex fraud prosecutions have been unsuccessful. In November 2006 an attempt was made to implement this provision with the introduction of the Fraud (Trials without a Jury) Bill. However, parliamentary opposition prevented the bill passing into statute.

There is a concern over whether or not juries are likely to be swayed by eloquent arguments so as to produce 'perverse' verdicts. The research has been with either mock or shadow juries. The former consisted of a jury randomly chosen from the public who watched films of trials. Shadow juries watch the trial as a real jury and proceed to act as a jury. In general these studies found that juries did proceed in a rational manner, rarely disagreed over verdicts and that shadow juries tended to agree with the real jury (**McCabe 1988**). It can readily be objected that these juries were not dealing with real-life cases and were knowingly participating in a research activity – both of which might affect their discussions.

Another method is to question participants in the trial about how they viewed the verdict. Here, a slightly different picture emerges. **Baldwin and McConville**

(1979) found that out of 114 acquittals, judges expressed satisfaction in 70 and dissatisfaction in 41 cases. In many of the latter there appeared to be some reasonable explanation of the result, such as a weakness in the prosecution case. It is normally the trial judge who criticises the jury for being perverse, and yet one of the main arguments for the jury is that they are there to counterbalance the judge. Thus can there ever be a perverse acquittal? Lord Devlin argued, 'perversity is just a lawyer's word for a jury which applies its own standards instead of those recommended by lawyers' (Blackstone Lecture 1978, cited in **Harman and Griffith 1979**).

The approach to jury composition in England and Wales is in stark contrast with that in the United States of America, where jury selection and challenging potential jurors is a recognised and extensive part of the pre-trial process, especially in cases with emotive issues, as was seen at the jury selection in the trials of O J Simpson and Louise Woodward, and more recently in the trial of millionaire and former British newspaper magnate, Conrad Black. In such cases in the United States, shadow or test juries and jury consultants were used extensively to assess not only which jurors would be more likely to be amenable to one side or the other, but also what arguments would be likely to find favour with them.

The trial of nanny Louise Woodward in 1997 in Massachusetts for the murder of Matthew Eappen, a baby in her care, occasioned much debate about the value of juries. The US system has significant differences in such matters as jury selection, access to jurors, the roles of participants and culture of the courts, which is illustrated by the amount of access to the courtroom by the media during a trial. Nevertheless, much of the press discussion focused on factors that, although possibly extraneous to the court decision, might have affected the jurors' minds, and are equally applicable in British courts. Similarly, when local or national concern about a case is intense, it is sometimes difficult for members of juries to put out of their minds impressions of the case or the defendants gained from the press. Some have advocated the abolition of the jury, replacing the jury with lay assessors, or allowing the judge to decide not only on the law, but also on guilt and innocence. Others fear the power which would be placed in the hands of legal 'experts', were the jury to be substantially altered.

Furthermore, research into the perceptions of 361 jurors in six English courts as to their understanding, confidence and satisfaction of the system they participated in showed that they had a generally positive attitude to the experience and to the role of juries in the criminal justice system (**Mathews et al. 2004**). Jurors also were favourably impressed by the professionalism and courtesy of court personnel and the concern they saw demonstrated for due process. Main criticisms centred on the use of legal terminology and some lack of clarity in the presentation of evidence. Interestingly, while the majority (57 per cent) of those questioned recorded that a positive aspect of jury service was the greater understanding of the criminal justice system, a large proportion of those questioned listed purely personal aspects as some of the positive aspects of jury service (meeting new people 40 per cent; personal fulfilment 22 per cent; and enhancement of self-confidence 8 per cent) (ibid.: 3). Efforts have been made in recent years, for example by the production of online orientation videos and information, to make jurors feel better informed and more at ease.

The Criminal Justice Act 2003 removed ineligibility and the right of excusal from jury service for a number of groups (those aged 65 to 69, MPs, clergy, medical professionals and those involved in the administration of justice). But summoned jurors may still be disqualified or excused from jury service (due to age, residency, mental disability, criminal charges, language, medical or other reasons). In 2004, new juror eligibility rules came into effect. Surveys conducted both before and after these changes showed that the new rules increased the proportion of those summoned that served from 54 per cent to 64 per cent. Those serving on the date summoned increased by a third, disqualifications fell by a third and excusals fell by a quarter. The changes did not affect any single socio-economic group, with one exception. The proportion of serving jurors that were 65 to 69 years of age doubled from 3 per cent in 2003 to 6 per cent in 2005, after their right of excusal was removed (Jury Diversity Project, **Thomas and Balmer 2007**). In 2011, 343,949 juror summons were issued resulting in 170,421 jurors being presented at court.

Extracts from the Jury Diversity Project

This report examines whether the juror summoning process discriminates against black and minority ethnic (BME) groups, whether jurors serving at Crown Courts are representative of the local population in terms of ethnicity, age, gender, employment, income and religion, and whether a defendant's ethnicity affects the decision-making of racially-mixed juries.

The Jury Diversity Project found that the juror summoning process does not discriminate, directly or indirectly, against BME groups: a representative section of the local BME community are summoned and serve as jurors in virtually all Crown Courts in England and Wales. It also exposed a number of widespread myths about jury service, which have clouded both public perceptions and policy discussions about the jury system for many years. There is no mass avoidance of jury service among the British public, and juries are also not made up of people who are not important or clever enough to get out of jury service. There is no evidence of any unwillingness to do jury service or any particular lack of trust in the fairness of the jury system among the BME community or the British public in general. This was the reality of jury service in England and Wales even before the introduction of new juror eligibility rules in 2004, which have nonetheless increased participation in the jury system. On the fundamental question of whether juries discriminate against defendants based on race, the case simulation research with real jurors showed that racially mixed juries in highly diverse communities did not discriminate against defendants based on the race of the defendant.

Myths of jury service

A key finding of the Jury Diversity Project is that most current thinking about jury service in this country is based on myth, not reality.

In 2005, of all those who replied to their summonses, 64% of jurors served, 9% were disqualified or ineligible, 27% were excused. Of those excused, most were for medical reasons that prevented serving (34%), or child care (15%) and work reasons (12%). Fifteen per cent of all the summonses in the survey were either returned to the JCSB as undeliverable (5%) or not responded to (10%), which occurred most often in areas of high residential mobility.

The report reveals that there is no mass avoidance of jury service by the British public: 85% of those summoned replied to their summonses and the vast majority served.

The report found that there was no significant under-representation of British minority or ethnic groups (BME) among those summoned for jury service at virtually all Crown Courts in England and Wales.

Jury service myth – avoidance of jury service
There is widespread avoidance of jury service by the British public in general, and Londoners (and by implication, the BME community) in particular.

Reality: There is no mass avoidance of jury service by the British public. The vast majority of Londoners return their summonses and serve. Where ethnic minorities do not serve this is largely due to ineligibility and disqualification (language and residency).

Jury service myth – avoidance of jury service by class
The middle classes and the important and clever avoid jury service. Juries are mostly made up of the retired and unemployed.

Reality: The middle class and the important and clever do not avoid jury service, and the retired and unemployed are in fact under-represented among serving jurors.

Jury service myth – women and young people are under-represented
Women, young people and the self-employed are under-represented among serving jurors, and the unemployed are virtually exempt from jury service.

Reality: Jury pools closely reflect the local population in terms of gender, age and the self-employed.

(Thomas C with Balmer N (2007) *Diversity and Fairness in the Jury System*, Ministry of Justice Research Series 2/07, June 2007)

Having identified some of the participants, we will now examine the principles and procedures to be followed in the trial, which, as we have seen, are guided by the due process model, and affected by – or created for – the adversarial system in England and Wales.

10.4 Rights of the defendant in court

Objective 4
Outline the rights of the defendant in court

A person suspected, arrested, prosecuted or convicted of an offence has rights under the law at each stage of the criminal justice system. These laws, whether deriving from common law or statute, including the overarching protection of the Human Rights Act, are there to protect the suspect or defendant against the greater power of the state as embodied by the police, the courts and the prison system, and are a key feature of the due process model. The most important protection for the citizen is that no official is above the law and that all officials are accountable for their actions regardless of their rank (**as seen in Chapter 1**). We have also seen how laws relating to police powers seek to balance the interests of the citizen with those of efficient law enforcement (**see Chapter 6**).

Along with this general principle established by the rule of law, the citizen has specifically defined rights at each stage of the system. Many of these arise from the key principle that the prosecution must prove beyond reasonable doubt that the accused person is guilty of a crime and that it is not the duty of the suspect to help them to prove guilt. Prosecutions can be started by the accused being arrested and charged or by the laying of an information and the issue (by the court) of a summons or arrest warrant. Many minor offences, particularly road traffic offences, are started by the summons procedure. After the police or other prosecuting authority form a provisional view that an offence has been committed they will usually (and in the case of some driving offences, must) warn the person that they may be prosecuted. A decision will then be made whether to commence proceedings or to caution the suspect informally. If the decision is made to proceed to prosecution, a document is prepared called an 'information'. This informs the relevant magistrates' court of the details of the alleged offence, the name and address of the accused and the informing officer. Provided it appears in order, the court will then issue a summons based on the allegation, and it will be served on the defendant by post. The summons, as its name suggests, summons the defendant to court at a specified date and time to answer the charge. This procedure was replaced by the 'written charge' and 'requisition' under the Criminal Justice Act 2003. The requisition requires the attendance of the defendant at a magistrates' court, much as a summons does currently. Both documents are served on the defendant and the court. The changes in procedure are intended eventually to streamline the process by removing repeated wasted appearances in minor magistrates' matters. Having been charged by the police, the suspect now becomes a defendant and is entitled to certain rights even before the case is heard. These include the following rights:

- To know the nature and details of any charges against them.
- The opportunity to be legally represented by a solicitor or barrister.
- An entitlement to unconditional bail except where there are legally acceptable reasons for not granting bail.
- If remanded in custody defendants are entitled to apply again for bail on their next appearance if their circumstances have changed.
- To jury trial in TEW cases.
- To advance disclosure of the evidence in any TEW offence.
- To see unused prosecution evidence before Crown Court trial and be notified of witnesses interviewed by the prosecution but not called. The prosecution has a general duty to give the defence information of use to them, under the Criminal Procedure and Investigations Act 1996.

Defendants have the right to a fair trial in which they are entitled to challenge any evidence or witness used in the case against them. They are also entitled to call witnesses and evidence on their own behalf to counter the accusations of the prosecution. The defendant should expect to be found not guilty unless the case has been proved beyond reasonable doubt. The defendant should be assured that the usual established procedure for trial applies to him or her. In particular, defendants have the following rights:

- To seek legal representation, and to have legal aid if the interests of justice require (subject to a means test).
- To have the assistance of a Mackenzie friend (someone to assist them if they are unrepresented).
- To challenge jurors, if they have a good reason (i.e. 'cause').
- Not to give evidence.
- To call evidence on their own behalf.
- To cross-examine (i.e. question) witnesses against them.
- To face their accusers in most cases.
- Not to have previous convictions mentioned during the trial stage except in limited and well-defined circumstances.
- To argue that the prosecution has not made out a case to answer.

10.5 Protecting witness identity

Objective 5

Explain how to protect witness identity

As already mentioned, witnesses normally give evidence in open court and for all to see, and in particular for the defendant to confront. The fear of reprisals against witnesses and their reluctance to give evidence in public or to see the defendant has led to a number of steps to protect witnesses in giving evidence. In rape trials, a victim cannot be cross-examined by the alleged rapist. The Youth Justice and Criminal Evidence Act 1999 provided for 'special measures' to be taken in the case of vulnerable and intimidated witnesses. (The protection was extended to ASBO applications by the Serious Organised Crime and Police Act 2005.) Special measures provide for a range of steps that can be taken in courts to limit the pressure that might be felt by especially vulnerable witnesses, for example children or those with a disability, or those who are intimidated or fearful. These measures include:

- Giving evidence from behind screens, so the witness does not see the defendant.
- Giving evidence by live video link – allowing a witness to give evidence from outside the courtroom.
- Giving evidence in private – clearing the court of most people.
- Removal of wigs and gowns in the Crown Court.
- Pre-recorded testimony as **evidence in chief** – so that the witness only has to be cross-examined and then only if necessary.

However, in some cases these special measures have not been felt to be sufficient or applicable. In March 2005, four black youths were found guilty at Leicester Crown Court of the murder by shooting of Charlene Ellis, 18, and Letisha

Shakespeare, 17, outside a hairdresser's salon in Birmingham, and of seriously injuring Cheryl Shaw and Sophie Ellis. The allegations centred round gang rivalry. The evidence from the witnesses had to be presented to the defence – a requirement of the trial disclosure rules – while also preserving the anonymity of the key witnesses. One witness who was at the scene of the crime was referred to throughout the trial as Mark Brown.

The practice of giving witnesses anonymity was challenged by the House of Lords in June 2008 in the case of *R* v. *Davis* [2008] UKHL 36. This was an appeal to the House of Lords after a murder conviction based on anonymous witnesses who stated they were in fear of their lives if their identities were known.

The trial judge had allowed:

- The witnesses to give evidence under a pseudonym.
- The withholding of addresses and personal details.
- The appellant's counsel to ask the witnesses no question which might enable any of them to be identified.
- The witnesses to give evidence behind screens so that they could be seen by the judge and the jury but not by the defendant.
- The witnesses' natural voices to be heard by the judge and the jury but mechanically distorted so as to prevent recognition by the defendant.

A female witness was called and subject to these protections, whom the appellant believed to be the girlfriend who had a grudge against him. Although it was doubtful whether she was the girlfriend, anonymity meant the defendant could not explore this point. In deciding that the trial had not been fair, the House of Lords stated:

> . . . it is axiomatic that the common law is capable of developing to meet new challenges. But threats of intimidation to witnesses and the challenge which they pose to our system of trial are anything but new. In theory, the common law could have responded to that challenge at any time over the last few hundred years by allowing witnesses to give their evidence under conditions of anonymity. But it never did – even in times, before the creation of organised police forces, when conditions of lawlessness might have been expected to be far worse than today . . . while I am very conscious of the problems confronting the authorities which have led them to adopt these measures, in my view it is not open to this House in its judicial capacity to make such a far-reaching inroad into the common law rights of a defendant as would be involved in endorsing the procedure adopted in the present case. Similarly . . . the appellant's trial did not meet the standard required by article 6 of the European Convention [on Human Rights] . . .

As a result of the decision in the above case, a number of trials for serious offences were abandoned and the government, taking heed of the statement by the House of Lords that it was for Parliament to change the law, did so under an emergency timetable leading to the Criminal Evidence (Witness Anonymity) Act 2008.

The Act provides for the making of a witness anonymity order so that specified measures such as those used in *Davis* could be used on the order of the court. Conditions are laid down as to how the court is to balance the needs of a fair trial before such steps can be taken. The Coroners and Justice Act 2009 allows for the police to apply for an anonymity order for witnesses providing evidence in such cases of gang-related murder or manslaughter involving the use of a firearm or a knife, providing that the suspect was aged between 11 and 30 at the time of the crime. This is intended to help protect informants who have important information relating to the crime, but who are afraid of reprisals from street gangs.

For many defendants, the key to their protection is the assistance of someone who understands the issues and the legal system. Everyone is entitled to be represented by a lawyer if they wish. The cost of legal representation will be met in whole or in part by public funding (legal representation order) if it is in the 'interests of justice', and additionally in magistrates' cases if the defendant meets a financial (means) test which assesses income and liabilities within defined guidelines. The interests of justice test means that the defendant must show for example that the case might result in loss of liberty or livelihood, or that the case would involve expert cross-examination, or tracing of witnesses or the argument on a point of law.

The current arrangements for public funding in criminal cases are administered in accordance with the Access to Justice Act 1999 by the **Criminal Defence Service (CDS)**, established by the Legal Services Commission. The Criminal Defence Service, which started operating on 2 April 2001, is the quality control mechanism for criminal defence work, and also the funding body. The CDS has also piloted a Public Defender Service in four areas: Cheltenham, Darlington, Pontypridd and Swansea, and a telephone helpline (CDS Direct) piloted in 2005 in Liverpool and Boston, Lincolnshire. Public funding can cover the cost of:

- legal advice and assistance;
- free legal advice at the police station during questioning;
- preparation for and representation at court hearings.

The Legal Aid, Sentencing and Punishment of Offenders Act 2012 abolished the Legal Services Commission, whose work was subsumed by the Ministry of Justice as of 2013. Much defence work is undertaken through the duty solicitor scheme, which is an important way in which those accused, arrested or appearing in court can seek legal advice and representation. The duty solicitor scheme has two aspects: the police station advice scheme for suspects being interviewed, and the court scheme to assist defendants, which covers magistrates' courts. The scheme provides financial assistance, in that legal representation or advice is provided free of charge (without any means testing). The system depends on a rota of local solicitors. At the police station, PACE provides for a 24-hour duty solicitor advice scheme for those being questioned by the police, whether arrested or attending the police station voluntarily. The solicitors involved will attend calls on a rota basis and will be members of a locally appointed panel.

At court, a defendant can seek advice from the member of the duty solicitor panel in attendance that day. Again this system is free and is not subject to any means or interests-of-justice test. Representation is, however, limited to those in custody, or at risk of custody, or charged with an imprisonable offence. The solicitor can give advice on straightforward matters to enable defendants to deal with cases themselves, or can represent clients in court on simple matters such as first bail application and pleas in mitigation after a guilty plea. The court scheme does not apply to very minor incidents such as most motoring matters. While it is an important right that individuals should have access to free legal representation, and thus access to justice, in appropriate cases concerns have been expressed that apparently wealthy individuals before the courts have been given legal aid at the taxpayers' expense. Recent amendments to the provision of legal aid in criminal **litigation** cases were brought in under the Legal Aid, Sentencing and Punishment of Offenders Act 2012, which affect the eligibility of litigants. Those wishing to claim legal aid to help them with advice and assistant or court representation whether in the magistrates' court or the Crown Court are now subject to a means test which assesses individuals' incomes, savings and benefits payments. Legal aid for cases in the magistrates' court is only available to those with dependents or those without dependents earning less than £22,325 a year. Legal representation for cases heard in the Crown Court is made available as a matter of course in the interests of justice, but those in possession of a disposable income of £283.17 per month will be required to make contribution payments towards their representation. Those in possession of an income of £37,500 or higher (2014 figure) who are found guilty may be asked to pay a contribution from their capital. Anyone found not guilty will have their costs refunded. The Ministry of Justice publishes online a Criminal Legal Aid Manual and a Criminal Eligibility Calculator. Table 10.3 sets out the costs of services funded by the Criminal Defence Service in the year 2011/12. Over 2,000 solicitors' firms have contracts for defence work with the CDS. Reforms to the operation and cost-effectiveness of legal aid were suggested in the Carter Review (2006).

A convicted defendant will often have to contribute to his legal costs even if given legal aid.

Table 10.3 Criminal Defence Service Funded Support 2011/12

Type of service	Total claimed (£000)
Services to suspects prior to charge	169,960
Courts duty solicitors' sessions	23,224
Representation orders	188,985

Source: *Legal Services Commission Annual Report 2011/12*, Statistical Information Tables CDS1 and 2 (HMSO)

10.6 Evidence

Objective 6

Discuss the different types of evidence used in court and its role in the trial

Visitors to courts are often surprised by the significance attached to, and the time taken by, matters of procedure. This may be particularly noticeable at the pre-trial stage, but may loom large also at the trial stage. Procedure can have immense significance for the outcome of a trial and, even where it does not directly affect the outcome, knowledge of the structure and format of legal procedure is necessary to understand the context and significance of criminal proceedings. Rules of evidence, which are in part procedural and in part substantive legal rules, very often play a decisive role. The significance of procedural rules is partly practical – cases should finish within a reasonable time and impose a recognisable pattern on the trial process. Procedural rules are also affected by jurisprudential considerations, such as the need to seek justice by the even-handed application of rules. The system has its critics, and there is much legal and public debate over whether changes in the procedure of criminal trials could remedy perceived shortcomings. The adversarial system, in which two opposing sides contest the evidence, also affects the procedure of the trial with the emphasis on the oral testimony of witnesses in court.

This procedure and its justification was examined in the Auld Report: 'Our system of trial is dominated by the principle of orality, namely that evidence as to the matters in issue should normally be given by oral testimony of witnesses in court, speaking of their own direct knowledge.' The Association of Chief Police Officers (ACPO) presented an argument to Auld that '. . . the "adversarial dialectic" and the "principle of orality" have been elevated to ends in themselves rather than as a means to get at the truth' (**Auld 2001: 516**). Thus greater weight is typically given to what is said in court by a witness under cross-examination than to a written statement or oral or videotape statement made shortly after the event. The importance of hearing from a 'live' witness also justifies the exclusion of information described as hearsay because it is a statement about what another person had said and is not subject to direct examination in court. Auld quotes from John Spencer, 'that the weakness of the principle of relying solely or mainly on oral testimony is that it requires us: "to accept two remarkable scientific propositions: first, that memory improves with time; and secondly, that stress enhances a person's powers of recall"' (ibid.: 548).

The focus on partisan information is also considered in Auld. He quotes from Ian Dennis:

> . . . witnesses will not generally be questioned by anyone involved in the proceedings in a spirit of free impartial inquiry. Partisan, controlled questioning is the norm, and free report by the witness is the exception. This point helps to explain why some witnesses find the process of testifying at best bewildering, because they are unable to tell their story in their own way, or at worst traumatic, because of 'robust' cross-examination which may have the effect of making them feel that they themselves are on trial.
>
> (Auld 2001: 526)

Thus the Auld Report proposed that the English law of criminal evidence 'should, in general, move away from technical rules of inadmissibility to trusting judicial and lay fact finders to give relevant evidence the weight it deserves' (ibid.: 547). In other words, it should allow more information into the trial and allow the judge, magistrates and jury to decide how relevant and significant it is. This was to lead to reform: the Criminal Justice Act 2003 made important changes to evidential rules relating to the use of hearsay and information about previous convictions of the defendant. These two areas had been previously governed by perhaps the most difficult to understand, and difficult to justify, rules of evidence. The current law (explained below) is a more coherent, if no less complex, set of provisions.

The main stages in procedure will be outlined below, but it is important to note that, as indicated above, there are some differences between the magistrates' court and the Crown Court. The differences in procedure between magistrates' courts and the Crown Court reflect a functional difference: while juries are not trained in any way for their role, even lay magistrates have considerable training and, of course, regular experience on the bench.

The structure of a trial in the magistrates' court highlights the adversarial nature of the trial process, with magistrates acting as independent arbiters, not investigators involved at first hand in the proceedings. Whether the offence is only triable summarily, or a decision has been made to try a triable either way offence summarily, the first stage is that the charges are read to the accused, and the defendant then pleads guilty or not guilty to each charge.

Where the defendant pleads not guilty, the prosecution outlines the case and calls evidence in support of it. After the prosecution evidence has been called and challenged, if desired, by the defence, the defence will call the evidence in support of its case. This can be challenged by cross-examination on behalf of the prosecution. Cross-examination of either side is seen as the essential way of testing the truthfulness of a witness. At the end the defence will make a closing speech, putting any argument on the facts and the law to the magistrates. The prosecution may reply only on matters of law. When all the evidence has been heard, and all arguments made, the magistrates will reach a verdict.

Where a lay bench is sitting, the members will usually retire to discuss their views. Where there is a disagreement, the majority view prevails, but normally magistrates will try to come to a unanimous decision. Whether the decision is unanimous or by a majority, the verdict is announced without qualification. If the verdict is guilty, the accused is said to have been convicted and will then be sentenced to some form of punishment, even if it is only a token form such as an absolute or conditional discharge. If the verdict is not guilty, the accused is acquitted. In recent years magistrates have begun to give reasons for all their decisions and so will now explain the basis of their decision, including the points at issue and how they have been decided and including references to evidence they found compelling.

When a defendant decides to enter a plea of guilty, the prosecution outlines the facts and information is provided on the background of the offender, including any previous convictions. The defence can make a **plea in mitigation** and then the court proceeds to sentence, often after an adjournment in more serious cases to receive a pre-sentence report (PSR).

Trials in the Crown Court have a similar format to trials in the magistrates' court, but some differences reflect the presence of the jury as the fact-finding body, and of the judge as the arbiter of legal issues and procedure such as the admissibility of evidence. The most significant differences are that both prosecution and defence make closing speeches after all the evidence, and that the judge will thereafter sum up to the jury. In the summing-up the judge will direct the jury members on the law and remind them of the evidence. The jury members will then retire to consider their verdict and return to court to deliver it when they have agreed.

The format and structure of the trial process is affected by the rules of procedure. The content is affected by the rules of evidence, discussed below.

As we have seen, defendants can only be convicted on the basis of evidence. A criminal trial is founded on the presentation of admissible evidence with a view to persuading the tribunal of fact, that is the magistrates or the jury, of the soundness or otherwise of the prosecution's case. A trial determines whether or not the defendant is guilty as charged on the basis of evidence. Rules of evidence determine what must be proved, what can and cannot be used as evidence, along with who must prove the issues and to what standard. These rules will be referred to later, but it is important first to consider what is meant by the word evidence.

> Evidence is any material which tends to persuade the court of the truth or probability of some fact asserted before it.
>
> (Murphy 1992: 1)

Thus evidence can take many forms, and can be described in different ways, either in terms of how it is presented to the court, in terms of the legal rules applicable, or in terms of the function it fulfils. In relation to how the evidence is given in court, it can include the following:

- Oral testimony of witnesses.
- Documentary evidence in, for example, business records and witness statements, and computer print-outs.
- *Real* evidence such as exhibits of items to be displayed in court – for example, a murder weapon, fingerprints and other forensic items.
- Evidence of video and audio tapes and photographs.

As far as identifying its nature and persuasiveness, evidence is often described in the following ways:

- Eye-witness evidence from an observer of the facts.
- Evidence of alibi, indicating that the defendant could not have been at the place claimed at the relevant time.
- A confession from the accused, usually obtained when they are interviewed by the police.
- Character evidence about a witness's history and background.
- Opinion evidence from an expert to interpret specialist matters to the court.
- Hearsay (a reference to a statement made out of court advanced by a witness in the trial to establish the truth of what was stated – e.g. 'X told me before she died that Jones had stabbed her').
- Circumstantial evidence from which inferences can be drawn about matters relevant to the case.

Circumstantial evidence can be very weighty. It refers to deductions which can reasonably be made from the circumstances. For example, if there is evidence that a person accused of murder was in the habit of wearing a distinctive item of clothing, and that such an item was found at the scene of the crime, then that is some evidence of involvement. That someone was near the scene of a crime at the relevant time, or had a clear motive to commit the crime, is circumstantial evidence. Several items of circumstantial evidence can amount to a very compelling case.

Rules relating to the admissibility of evidence mean that much material is not permitted to be put before the court. Hearsay evidence (whether oral statements or those contained in a document) is less reliable because its truth cannot be checked in court by cross-examination. Before the CJA 2003 it was rarely admissible, but that Act provides a wider framework for admissibility. Evidence of the previous convictions of the accused is considered potentially very damaging and is generally admissible only with permission from the judge.

The law of evidence is concerned with the rules governing such issues. It is a body of procedural law (also known as adjective law), in contrast with what is termed substantive law – for example, the law of crime or contract. It should not be thought that rules of evidence constitute a dry body of regulations unrelated to the social context of law – the development of evidential rules over the years has reflected social and moral concerns with the protection of the defendant, the delimitation of police powers and notions of justice as well as purely theoretical legal concepts. Fears that evidence may be unreliable or concocted have strongly influenced the development of the law of evidence – the hearsay rule in particular has developed to minimise the danger of unreliable evidence. This rule has been continuously refined, especially in relation to confessions, because of concerns over methods of police interrogation. In addition, many rules have developed out of fears that the jury might be unfairly prejudiced against the defendant.

These rules reflect the due process model of criminal justice. Recently, crime control concerns have gained some ascendancy: the fear that the prosecution is hampered by technical rules from proving guilt has found support in the argument that even lay participants in the trial can properly and fairly examine the value or weight to be given to different types of evidence.

The Auld Report suggestion, referred to above, that 'the law should in general move away from technical rules of inadmissibility to trusting judicial and lay fact finders to give relevant evidence the weight it deserves' has been reflected in some of the provisions in the Criminal Justice Act 2003 (the admissibility of hearsay evidence, subject to safeguards, and the admissibility of evidence of previous convictions in certain situations).

Evidence should not be confused with proof. Evidence is the means by which some fact is proved or disproved or rendered more or less likely. Neither evidence nor proof should be confused with truth: as we have already seen, the court aims to establish guilt beyond reasonable doubt in the light of the evidence presented at the trial.

When considering evidence, three basic principles need to be considered:

- relevance;
- admissibility; and
- weight.

The relevance of a piece of evidence is determined largely as a matter of common sense but tempered by legal rules for the protection of defendants. Nothing can be admitted in evidence unless it is relevant to a matter before the court. But some relevant evidence may be inadmissible because of a procedural rule. Such evidence is often excluded to protect the defendant or to prevent the jury being misled. For example, evidence of opinion, unless of an expert, is usually not admitted. It also means that a jury or magistrates will not normally be told about any previous convictions of the defendant – at least not unless and until the defendant is found guilty.

The weight or cogency of evidence is not normally related to its admissibility, but to its reliability or credibility – how persuasive it is likely to be. A jury or magistrates, when assessing the weight to be attached to evidence of a witness in court, may, for instance, consider whether they believed the witness, whether the witness's memory was likely to be reliable, whether the witness had a reason to fabricate the evidence or to misinterpret an incident. They are thus assessing the weight to be attached to that evidence. Similarly, where two witnesses give conflicting evidence, the jury will need to assess the weight to be attached to each witness in order to determine whether they prefer one witness to the other. Oral witnesses may often give a version which contradicts documentary evidence – the jury will need to consider whether the documentary evidence is preferable to the oral evidence, which might be affected by how well the witness can remember an event that may have involved traumatic circumstances.

As we have seen, the criminal law determines that in order to prove theft, it must be established that the defendant:

> ... dishonestly appropriated property belonging to another with the intention of permanently depriving that other of it.
>
> (Theft Act 1968, s 1)

If Mrs Smith is charged with stealing a frozen chicken from a supermarket, the prosecution must prove that Mrs Smith (and not someone else) is guilty as described above. The prosecution may be able to bring evidence from a store detective that Mrs Smith was seen taking the chicken from the display and hiding it inside her coat, and leaving the supermarket without paying for it.

In the absence of a credible explanation, the prosecution, if the above evidence is believed, will be able to show an appropriation of property (the chicken) belonging to the supermarket. What of dishonesty? That can be assumed or inferred from the action: who hides a frozen chicken in their coat if they are not dishonest? What of intention to permanently deprive? Intention is one of the most difficult elements to establish – as it is known only to the defendant. But intention too can be inferred from conduct. We can infer or deduce that Mrs Smith intended to take the chicken for herself or others by the very fact of removing the chicken from the shop. In other cases, for example in murder, it must be proved that the defendant intended to kill or seriously injure and that death resulted. If the accused is shown to have shot the deceased at point blank range in the head, it is easy to infer intention – provided the defendant knew the gun was loaded.

The criminal law defines what must be proved; the law of evidence determines how that can be done, with rules concerning the admissibility of evidence and the burden and standard of proof. Many of our rules of evidence have been developed over the years, often by the courts, to protect the defendant in a criminal trial, and especially to ensure that the jury is not misled by weak or irrelevant evidence. While many support these approaches, fears have been raised in some quarters that rules such as preventing a jury from knowing about the previous convictions of a defendant allow the guilty to go free. Again the crime control and due process models come into conflict and the restriction of information in the adversarial system stands in contrast to the wider focus of the inquisitorial system on knowing what happened.

As previously mentioned, defendants are not compelled to give evidence on their own behalf. However, there are circumstances where their failure to do so, or their failure to give explanations at an early stage, can be construed against them at trial. This means that, when defendants are on trial, evidence can be given to the court that when they were arrested for an offence they failed to answer questions in any of the following matters:

- why they were at the place where and when the offence was committed;

- why they had in their possession items (such as tools that could be used in burglary, or scales usable for drug dealing) relevant to the offence in question;

- why they had in their possession substances (such as acid that might inflict property or personal damage) that could relate to the offence;

- why at the place of arrest there were items (such as drugs) relevant to the offence;

- why there were bodily marks (for example, traces of dirt gained in a burglary, or cuts gained in a fight) that could relate to the offence.

In any of the above cases, or at trial, where a defendant:

- uses an excuse that could have been mentioned when first interviewed or charged, but was not, or

- does not give evidence at all, or

- fails to conform to the disclosure provisions of the Criminal Procedure and Investigations Act 1996,

then the court (that is, the jury or magistrates) can take that into account with other evidence in deciding whether or not they find the defendant guilty. In doing so they must consider whether the defendant could or should have explained. Was there a good reason not to explain at the time? Was the defendant hiding some other, non-criminal, behaviour? Were they too ill or too frightened or too drunk to explain? Did they not know enough about the accusation? The mere fact that a solicitor advises a client not to answer police questions in interview will not of itself be sufficient reason to prevent an 'adverse inference' from being drawn (*R* v. *Condron* 1997).

▶ Presentation of evidence

These are rules governing the order in which witnesses are called and evidence produced. As the prosecution must prove the case, the prosecution starts the proceedings and the defence responds, or decides not to respond to the prosecution case. After outlining the case, the prosecution calls its witnesses in the order that enables the case to be presented most coherently. The defence are then entitled to call witnesses but need not do so. If the defendant is to give evidence, he or she will appear before any other defence witnesses. Each witness will be asked questions initially by the counsel who has called them. They may then be cross-examined by the opposing side, to elicit inconsistencies or weaknesses, and may also be re-examined by the original questioner. Although, as has been stated above, evidence can be in documentary or real form, the most common type of evidence is oral evidence given in the witness box and referred to as testimony. Most of the discussion below refers to testimony. In order to appreciate the process by which evidence is advanced, we will first examine the course of evidence and consider how the trial process takes place.

In the course of producing evidence, each side must be aware of what evidence is inadmissible. As has been previously mentioned, two areas of evidence which have been subject to significant changes under the Criminal Justice Act 2003 are the rules in relation to hearsay and bad character evidence.

The hearsay rules come into effect when a witness states in court what someone else had told them. The rules are applied when a witness refers to a statement, comment or opinion made by another person. The other person may not be available to give evidence, for a variety of reasons: for example, because they have since died or become ill or could not be traced – or because they are afraid to give evidence. Alternatively, the person may not in fact exist, or may have been lying or be unreliable. But the hearsay rules also apply to where witnesses are available, but where evidence is being given of what they said, by someone else. The reason for the hearsay rule is because, unlike the person in the witness box, the originator of the statement is not available to be cross-examined on the accuracy of the statement.

In criminal cases, hearsay evidence was normally inadmissible. An important exception relates to confession or admissions of guilt made out of court. It has long been recognised that, as confessions constitute very powerful evidence against any defendant, the desire on the part of the police to obtain this evidence may result in defendants being pressured into making confessions. There is also an awareness that some people do confess when they are in fact innocent. A series of measures are in place to avoid this: PACE provides that confessions will only be admissible if the prosecution can show that they were not obtained by oppression, or in consequence of anything said or done that would render that confession unreliable (s 76). If the way in which the confession was obtained is called into question, the prosecution must establish beyond reasonable doubt that it was not obtained in contravention of the Act. Breaches of the Codes of Practice under PACE are often relied on in arguments based on the potential unreliability of a confession.

In the case of R v. *Paris and Abdullah* in 1992, the defendants were being interviewed by the police about the murder of a prostitute in Cardiff. One defendant denied being involved over 300 times before eventually confessing. The Court of Appeal ruled that the confession should have been excluded because it was obtained by using oppressive methods. It castigated the police officers for their manner of interview and the accused's legal representative who had been present at the interviews and allowed it to continue.

Other non-confession kinds of hearsay – for example, documentary evidence and other out-of-court statements where the original speaker is not available are made more easily admissible in criminal proceedings subject to certain safeguards to allow the defence to challenge them.

Hearsay refers to a statement made by a witness about what someone else has done or said, and that person is not available to confirm or deny the statement. It is in a sense a third party's account of an event based on what someone else told them, and that other person, who is the original source of the information, is not available to confirm or deny or clarify what they said.

The reasoning for the historical exclusion of such evidence was based on the danger of concoction and the inability of the court to examine whether the original speaker was telling the truth. Over the years, although a number of exceptions have been developed (including exceptions in relation to confessions), the rules became both complicated and mysterious.

The Criminal Justice Act 2003 tried to rationalise the position, bringing into force in April 2005 a new set of provisions designed to clarify and simplify the position while still preventing a jury being misled. The Act provides for four groups of exceptions where hearsay will be admitted:

- under a statutory rule; or
- under a preserved common law exception (i.e. an exception developed in previous cases);
- where all parties agree to the use of hearsay;
- where the court decides it is in *the interests of justice* to allow hearsay.

It is the fourth provision which is probably the most important, and which is seen as both a victory for common sense and a way through some of the previous technicalities.

One of the most hotly debated evidential reforms under the CJA 2003 concerns the bad character provisions. Evidence of bad character relates to evidence of criminal or discreditable conduct, other than that of the defendant in relation to the current case. Before the CJA, although such evidence was admissible in some circumstances, the situations were limited and had given rise to technical and confusing procedures and sometimes complex and potentially confusing instructions to juries. Evidence of previous bad character, especially of a defendant, is powerful evidence. The arguments over its admission have concerned two simple opposing principles. First, the defendant should not be unfairly prejudiced, and the fear of prejudice arises because a jury (or magistrate) may believe that because they know the defendant committed a crime before, so he must be guilty of the charge. On the other hand, cases often arose where it seemed nonsensical not to alert the court to previous convictions. The effect of hearing about the previous convictions of the defendant is well illustrated by the case of *R* v. *Bills* (set out in the box) where it appears that the jury members' minds were changed after hearing the defendant's previous convictions. This led to the unusual situation – and subsequent appeal – described.

Jury changed verdict after hearing antecedents
Regina v Bills

Before Lord Justice Russell, Mr Justice Hooper [Judgement February 17]

Although there was no fixed rule of principle or of law that once the jury had been allowed to reconsider their verdicts, it could not be considered safe for them to reconsider when they had heard evidence of the defendant's previous convictions.

The Court of Appeal, Criminal Division, so held in allowing the appeal of Adrian Mark Bills against his conviction in April 1994 at Wolverhampton Crown Court (Judge Malcolm Ward and a jury) of wounding with intent to do grievous harm, contrary to section 18 of the Offences Against the Person Act 1861, for which he was sentenced to three and a half years' imprisonment.

Mr Patrick Darby, assigned by the registrar of Criminal Appeals, for the appellant; Mr Michael H J Grey for the Crown.

LORD JUSTICE RUSSELL, giving the judgment of the court, said that the defendant had been charged with an offence of wounding with intent to cause grievous harm, contrary to section 18 of the 1861 Act, but the jury had acquitted him of that offence and had convicted him of the lesser offence of unlawful wounding, contrary to section 20 of the 1861 Act.

After the trial judge had accepted that verdict, and while the jury remained in the jury box, prosecuting counsel dealt with the defendant's previous convictions which included other offences of violence, such as assault occasioning actual bodily harm and robbery. The jury were then discharged. What happened thereafter was unique in the experience of the court.

It appeared that immediately upon leaving court a juror spoke to the court usher and told him that the jury foreman had given the wrong verdict. The judge was informed. He decided to reconvene the jury and invited them to explain themselves. They indicated that the wrong verdict had been returned. The judge clarified the three possible verdicts and the unanimous altered verdict of guilty of the more serious offence was given and recorded.

It seemed to their Lordships that the original verdict was plain and unequivocal and they were abundantly satisfied that no adequate explanation had been put forward as to the jury's change of mind. It could not be gainsaid that the jury had heard material which they had no right to hear, namely the previous convictions of the defendant.

Wherever the truth lay, that course of action had led to a verdict which was unsafe and unsatisfactory and the appropriate course would be to reinstate the jury's original verdict of guilty of the section 20 offence and to alter the sentence to one of 30 months.

Solicitors: CPS, Midlands.

('Jury changed verdict after hearing antecedents *Regina v Bills*', *The Times*, 1 March 1995, Times Newspapers Ltd., © NI Syndication Limited, 1995.)

The CJA provides for what are known as 'gateways' for the admission of bad character evidence. If the evidence falls within one of the gateways it can be admitted. There is, however, a power given to judges to exclude evidence if, despite it being within a gateway, it would be unfair to admit it.

The gateways are:

- All parties agree to the evidence being admissible.
- The defendant brings forward the evidence himself (for example if the defence wishes to explain his suspicious behaviour because he was involved for example with drug dealers of whom he was afraid).

- It is important explanatory evidence. The evidence must be both important *and* explanatory, in that without it, the court or jury would find it impossible or difficult properly to understand other evidence in the case, and its value for understanding the case as a whole is substantial.
- It is relevant to an important matter where the defendant and the prosecution give differing accounts.
- It has substantial probative value in relation to an important matter of difference between the defendant and a **co-defendant**.
- To correct a false impression given by the defendant.
- If he has made an attack on another person's character.

The debate about admission of such evidence reflects the conflict between the crime control and the due process model. To some, including Lord Justice Auld, it is a change to allow more, rather than less, information about a case to be made available to the judge, magistrates and jury based on an inclusionary presumption rather than an exclusionary one. Auld writes:

> The need and form of reform of the rule against hearsay should be approached from the fundamental standpoints that rules of evidence should facilitate rather than obstruct the search for truth and should simplify rather than complicate the trial process. Inherent in a search for truth is fairness to the defendant and his protection from wrongful conviction – but it should not be forgotten that the present rule can operate unfairly against a defendant as well as the prosecution.
>
> (Auld 2001: 560)

Although the rules of evidence may be complex, the crucial task for those charged with determining the facts, who are usually lay people, is to assess the evidence submitted. This means they must decide whether they believe the evidence, and, if so, what it tells them about the facts in issue. This may involve weighing up the reliability of witnesses: whether they could observe, interpret and remember key incidents, whether they could identify participants, whether they had a reason to lie. Where witnesses give evidence they may support each other or conflict: could one or both be mistaken? Often, direct evidence of what a witness perceived gives only half the story: it is circumstantial evidence. What inferences or deductions can be made from those circumstances? Sometimes expert witnesses will be called to assist the court on matters outside the court's knowledge. Doctors, engineers, forensic scientists or psychiatrists might be called to explain the significance of evidence to the jury or to magistrates: this might result in the fact-finders being 'blinded by science' rather than being helped to determine the facts.

In 2002, governmental and public concern arose when expert evidence in proceedings involving children was found flawed and the convictions of Angela Canning and Sally Clark for killing their children were overturned. In 2005, the conviction of Donna Anthony was similarly overturned on the same basis. The expert evidence upon which the trial court had concluded that the mothers had caused the deaths of their children, perhaps because they were suffering from

Munchausen's Syndrome by proxy, was discredited. Much of the expert evidence was based on a theory that multiple cot-deaths (Sudden Infant Death Syndrome) did not occur in one family. The cases had far-reaching effects, not only on criminal convictions, but in cases where children deemed at risk were taken into care or adopted on the basis of the same expert approach, and a government review of all cases affected was instituted. This led to a number of convicted defendants being written to and invited to appeal to the Court of Appeal. In the course of the appeal Lord Justice Gage 'reminded judges, practitioners and experts of the obligations of an expert witness' and made the following points.

Lord Justice Gage on expert witnesses

- Expert evidence should be, and be seen to be, the independent product of the expert.
- An expert witness should provide independent assistance with objective, unbiased opinion in relation to matters within his expertise and should never assume the role of advocate.
- An expert witness should state the basis for his opinion and should consider material which detracts from his concluded opinions.
- An expert should make it clear when a particular matter falls outside his expertise, where he lacks information and where he changes a view based on new information.

(*R* v. *Faulder and ors* [2005] EWCA Crim 1980)

Suzanne Holdsworth, 37, was freed from prison in May 2008, and her conviction quashed in November 2008, three years after being jailed for life for murdering two-year-old Kyle Fisher, a neighbour's child whom she had been babysitting at her home in Hartlepool. Three judges at the Court of Appeal in London ordered a retrial in light of medical evidence that suggested the child could have suffered from an epileptic seizure. Referring to the use of medical evidence in the case, Lord Justice Toulson said that 'today's orthodoxy may become tomorrow's outdated learning'.

The challenging of these particular cases on the basis of flawed expert evidence brings us to the consideration of the system's processes for challenging decisions: the appeals system.

10.7 Appeals system

Objective 7

Outline the appeals system

There are provisions for the defendant to appeal against most of the decisions made in the court process, and against decisions such as those relating to bail and legal aid, but the most significant areas for appeal are the two decisions that most directly affect the offender: the decision to convict and the decision on sentence. Numbers of appeals in 2011 are set out in the box. The prosecution has generally only limited rights of appeal in these matters: against acquittal, only to challenge a point of law. Any subsequent decision does not affect the defendant's acquittal; and on sentence, against unduly lenient sentences in a limited number of more serious cases. In October 2009, the United Kingdom Supreme Court (UKSC) replaced the Appellate Committee of the House of Lords as the highest court in the UK so the figures from August to December 2009 are for the UKSC. Table 10.4 shows the number of referrals of sentences by the Attorney General to the Court of Appeal as unduly lenient from 2008 to 2011 and the number and percentage of sentences increased as a result.

Numbers of appeals 2011

- 77 appeals were made from the Court of Appeal (Criminal Division) to the UK Supreme Court

- 7,475 applications to the Court of Appeal (Criminal Division) were made from the Crown Court, of which 1,535 were against conviction and 5,623 against the sentence imposed

- 13,479 appeals were made from the magistrates' court to the Crown Court against conviction and sentence

(*Source*: Compiled from *Judicial and Courts statistics 2011* (2012))

The Criminal Justice Act 2003 section 75 introduced a new provision allowing retrial after an acquittal for certain very serious offences such as murder, where new evidence had come to light. This was introduced to reflect the ability of modern science to provide new evidence even some years after an event that was not available at the original trial. The case for the prosecution of the murderers of Stephen Lawrence famously made use of this provision in 2011. Two of the five suspects, some of whom were originally acquitted in 1996, faced retrial in 2011 after new DNA evidence linking them to the murder was discovered following a cold-case review, and were convicted in April 2012.

A defendant convicted after a trial in the magistrates' court can always appeal to the Crown Court against conviction and/or sentence. After a guilty plea the appeal is only against sentence. The appeal must be lodged within 21 days or any extended period granted by the Crown Court. The appeal takes the form of a fresh trial in the Crown Court, but the format is that of a summary trial, so there is no jury: the verdict is reached by the judge sitting with two lay magistrates. Their powers are to make any order that the original magistrates had power to impose.

Table 10.4 Referrals of unduly lenient sentences to Court of Appeal by A-G, 2008/11

Year	Total referrals	Sentences increased
2008	57	52 (91%)
2009	77	71 (92%)
2010	65	60 (92%)
2011	97	94 (97%)

Source: Attorney General's Office for England and Wales (2011)

This means that a defendant can be more severely punished by the Crown Court on appeal and is a factor that may deter some appellants. Alternatively, an appeal arguing that a procedural error took place goes to the Queen's Bench Division of the High Court.

Appeals from Crown Court trials are generally made to the Court of Appeal, Criminal Division, against either sentence or conviction or both. Before a person can appeal they must obtain permission to do so. This permission can be given by the trial or sentencing judge granting a certificate that the case is fit for appeal, or by the Court of Appeal granting leave to appeal. The former is rare, except where a novel point of law is involved and both sides accept that the matter would inevitably need resolution by a higher court, and the vast majority of cases are dealt with by the Court of Appeal first as applications for leave. The court will allow an appeal against conviction only if it is felt that the conviction is unsafe (Criminal Appeal Act 1995). If the appeal is allowed, the Court may quash, that is overturn, the conviction, convict the defendant on another lesser offence or order a retrial in the Crown Court. Where the appeal is against sentence (except where the prosecution has used the special procedure to appeal against an unduly lenient sentence), the Court may not impose a more serious sentence than the original sentence appealed against. If leave is granted, appeals from the Court of Appeal are made to the United Kingdom Supreme Court (UKSC) (although prior to October 2009 they were made to the House of Lords) by either side if leave is granted, or a certificate that a point of general public importance is involved. The UKSC sits in the Middlesex Guildhall in Westminster.

Despite the appeal system, there are occasions when an injustice may still occur and a 'safety-net' system was set up in 1997 to provide an additional mechanism of challenging court decisions. This is the Criminal Cases Review Commission.

10.8 Criminal Cases Review Commission (CCRC)

Objective 8

Describe the history and role of the Criminal Cases Review Commission

Under the Criminal Appeal Act 1995, an independent body was established to review suspected miscarriages of justice. This was established in response to the Report of the Runciman Commission in the aftermath of several notorious miscarriage of justice cases, including that involving the Birmingham Six. The Commission recommended the establishment of an independent body:

- to consider suspected miscarriages of justice;
- to arrange for their investigation where appropriate; and
- to refer cases to the Court of Appeal where the investigation revealed matters that ought to be considered further by the courts.

The Commission was set up and started its work on 31 March 1997 with the duties set out above and also with the power to advise the Home Secretary on the granting of Royal Pardons. By the end of June 2013, the CCRC had received in total 16,458 referrals, as set out in Table 10.5 (which also shows the results of the cases).

Many cases were ineligible to be heard by the Court, but of those submitted to the Court of Appeal nearly two-thirds resulted in the conviction being quashed (that is, overturned).

Some of the cases dealt with were historic or infamous cases, such as those involving Derek Bentley (whose conviction for murder was quashed in 1998), James Hanratty (referred to Court of Appeal by CCRC in 1999 – see box); Ruth Ellis (whose campaigners' appeal for a posthumous pardon, for Ellis's conviction for murdering her lover 48 years earlier, was rejected by the Court of Appeal in 2003) or Stephen Downing (whose murder conviction was quashed in 2002); others concern less public cases but provide a mechanism for righting wrongs that the 'normal' appeal system failed. Controversy has arisen over the handling of historic cases brought by relatives seeking a pardon for someone for murder. In the case of Ruth Ellis, the Court of Appeal questioned whether such investigations were any longer in the public interest.

The majority of the work of the Commission relates to cases which do not attract a huge amount of media interest, and Table 10.5 relates to examples of cases where procedures – due process – may have gone wrong.

Table 10.5 Total of CCRC case reviews (to 30 June 2013)

Total applications:	16,458
Cases waiting to be dealt with	608
Cases under review	545
Completed:	15,305 of which 530 were referred
Heard by Court of Appeal	498 (results: 341 quashed; 145 upheld; 2 reserved)

Source: Criminal Cases Review Commission, 2013

Miscarriage of justice? The hanging of James Hanratty

James Hanratty, aged 25, was hanged at Bedford Prison on 4 April 1962 for the murder of Michael Gregson and the rape and attempted murder of Valerie Storie. The murder was carried out in Gregson's car at Deadman's Hill in a layby on the A6 in Bedfordshire. Despite being shot five times, Valerie Storie survived. They had been lovers and had been abducted from Dorney Common in Berkshire in Gregson's car. The victims were shot at close range. The gun turned up in a London bus.

Hanratty claimed he was innocent and the case became a cause célébre: there was a petition signed by 28,000 people; campaigning journalist Paul Foot, Lord Russell of Liverpool, Louis Blom Cooper and the members of the Bootleg Theatre Company doubted that

justice had been done. Foot pointed to another potential suspect: Peter Alphon.

During the trial Hanratty changed his alibi, at first claiming he was in Liverpool at the time of the murder but during the trial he changed his story and claimed he was in Rhyl in North Wales. Even if the change of alibi was discredited, the trial judge made the point about the burden of proof and told the jury: 'He does not have to prove his alibi. The failure or otherwise of the alibi does not make him guilty. You do not have to rely on it.' (Quoted in **Goldman and Sherrard 2008: 99**.)

His defence barrister Michael Sherrard suggested that the evidence for the prosecution was flawed but the jury in Bedfordshire Crown Court found Hanratty guilty after 10 hours of deliberation following the longest murder trial – up until then – of 4 weeks.

Below is an extract based on the biography of Hanratty's defence barrister.

It turned out that the evidence was retained, frozen, to await the new technology that was eventually used: Valerie Storie's knickers; Hanratty's handkerchief. When the 2002 forensic results came through, confirming that there was a 1:2.5 million chance of the DNA on the handkerchief and knickers not being from Hanratty, one of the actors from the Bootleg Theatre Company telephoned Michael.

'So, do you think he did it?'

Michael gave him the only answer he could. 'I think the court is going to think so.'

'What shall we do?' he asked.

Michael was puzzled. He could not think that these DNA results would affect the actor.

He explained: 'All our livelihood is in the play. We thought it would run forever.'

Perhaps they had to change the ending . . .

The evidence that confirmed Hanratty's guilt, so far as the appeal process is concerned, is the DNA. But who would have thought that, for 31 years, the police would have kept, on ice, Valerie Storie's knickers and the handkerchief that wrapped the gun? Or exhumed him for DNA matches?

(Goldman and Sherrard 2008: 103–4)

Conclusion

In this chapter we have outlined the stages and participants in the trial and the principles and procedures followed, consistent with the due process model of criminal justice. It is clear that while the trial is central to the due process model, judgements about what is due process and how due process and crime control should be reconciled are difficult to make, leading to the controversy over changes such as to the right to silence, and the admissibility of hearsay evidence. Due process also demands an effective way of challenging decisions which, because dependent on human judgement, will inevitably be wrong on occasion. In general, pressures for cost-effectiveness may also conflict with those for crime control, just deserts and due process.

We have discussed in this chapter some of the reforms proposed by the Auld Report in 2001, and introduced by the Criminal Justice Act 2003. That Act also provided for significant changes to the sentencing powers of the courts. Some of these ideas have been abandoned even before implementation, reflecting many of the same conflicts between due process, bureaucratic efficiency and offender management as have been referred to in this chapter. The sentencing stage is the subject of the next chapter.

Review questions

1. Does the trial in England and Wales establish the innocence of the defendant?

2. Why do rules of procedure and evidence exist?

3. What is meant by the terms 'burden' and 'standard of proof'?

4. Below are six examples of evidence presented during a criminal trial.

   a. Classify them using the following categories of evidence:

      1. Character evidence

      2. Alibi evidence

      3. Eye-witness identification evidence

      4. Computer evidence

      5. Expert evidence

      6. Real evidence

   b. Classify them in terms of whether they are types of oral or documentary evidence or used as an exhibit:

      1. Mrs Green states in the witness box that she recognised the defendant coming out of the shop where the robbery took place.

      2. A report from a professor of mechanical engineering is presented to the court, setting out the damage to a car and explaining the likely speed of impact.

      3. A till roll from an electronic checkout machine is presented showing there was no entry in respect of items found in Mr Brown's shopping basket.

      4. A quantity of white powder, found in the defendant's car, is produced.

      5. Mr White says that the defendant has worked for him for 10 years and has always been a model of probity.

      6. Miss Scarlet states in her evidence that Rhett, the defendant accused of arson, was with her the whole of the night during which the offence is alleged to have taken place.

Discussion questions

1. Is there an acceptable alternative to the jury system?

2. What are the arguments for and against the admission of evidence about the previous convictions of the defendant in a criminal trial? Are there different arguments dependent on the type of conviction?

3. Should the public purse fund the defendants' costs of criminal trials?

4. Should witness identity be protected?

Further reading

Allen C (2008) *A Practical Guide to Evidence* (4th edn), Routledge-Cavendish Publishing: London

Ashworth A and Redmayne M (2010) *The Criminal Process* (4th edn), Oxford University Press: Oxford

Auld, Lord Justice (2001) *Review into the Workings of the Criminal Courts in England and Wales*, Home Office: London

Mathews R, Hancock L and Briggs D (2004) 'Jurors' perception, understanding, confidence and satisfaction in the jury system: a study in six courts', Home Office Research Findings 227

Sanders A and Young R (2006) *Criminal Justice* (3rd edn), Oxford University Press: Oxford

Weblinks

Criminal Cases Review Commission: **www.ccrc.gov.uk/**

Court statitstics: **www.gov.uk/government/publications/court-statistics-quarterly-july-to-september-2013**

Judicial and Court Statistics Annual Report 2011: **www.gov.uk/government/publications/judicial-and-court-statistics-annual**

Jury Summoning Bureau: **www.gov.uk/jury-service**

Legal Services Commission: **www.legalservices.gov.uk/**

CRIMINAL JUSTICE PROCESS: PENAL SYSTEM

Chapter 11

Sentencing aims and process

Learning objectives

After reading the chapter you should be able to:

1. Define the six main aims of sentencing
2. Describe the different types of sentence available in the courts
3. Outline sentencing procedures
4. Discuss the factors that influence sentencing decisions
5. Analyse the logic, structure and outcomes of sentencing decisions

Key statistics

- In the 12 months ending September 2012, 1.86 million individuals received an out-of-court disposal or were proceeded against in court
- Of the 1.23 million offenders sentenced during the 12-month period ending September 2012, 97,500 offenders were sentenced to immediate custody
- Of the 1.23 million offenders sentenced during the 12 months ending September 2012, 97,500 were sentenced to immediate custody
- A total of 310,233 offenders were sentenced for indictable offences in 12 months ending 2012 – this represents a 9.5% decline from the previous year.
- The most common disposal given in the latest year for offenders committing an indictable offence with no previous criminal history was a caution, with this accounting for 77% of juveniles in this group and 60% of adults. (*Source: Criminal Justice statistics update to June 2013*, Ministry of Justice, November 2013)

- In the 12 months ending September 2012, the Average custodial sentence length for indictable offences was 14.9 months.

- In the 12 months ending September 2012, 50,025 juveniles were sentenced by criminal courts in England and Wales, of which 66% received *Community Sentence* and 6% were sentenced to *Immediate Custody*

- In the 12 months ending 2012, 39.2 per cent of offenders sentenced for indictable offences with 15 or more previous convictions or cautions were sentenced to *Immediate Custody* and 19.9 per cent received *Community Sentence*

- 'Cases coming before the courts are becoming more serious, with three offence groups, violence against the person (VATP), drug offences and sexual offences, having the largest impact on increasing the prison population.' (*Story of the Prison Population: 1993 – 2012 England and Wales*, Ministry of Justice, January 2013: 24)

- Since 2001, the number of offenders imprisoned for fine defaulting has remained relatively steady at around an average of 100 per day

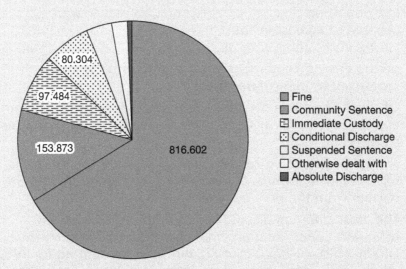

80.304

97.484

153.873

816.602

□ Fine
■ Community Sentence
▤ Immediate Custody
▦ Conditional Discharge
□ Suspended Sentence
□ Otherwise dealt with
■ Absolute Discharge

Figure 11.1 Types of sentences and distribution for ALL offences in the 12 months ending September 2012

Source: https://www.gov.uk/government/publications/criminal-justice-statistics--2

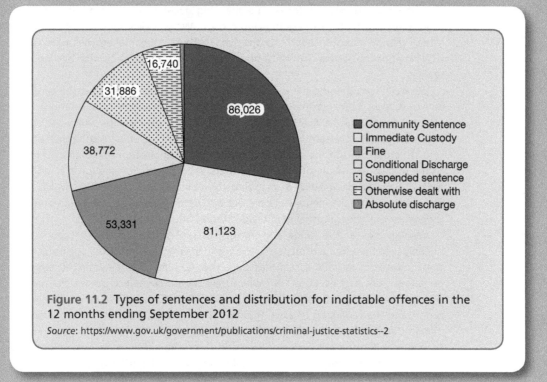

Figure 11.2 Types of sentences and distribution for indictable offences in the 12 months ending September 2012

Source: https://www.gov.uk/government/publications/criminal-justice-statistics--2

Introduction

Sentencing is a key function of the criminal justice process and brings together the objectives of protecting the public, defining public morality in practice and at the same time providing justice for defendants and victims. Reconciling these different goals in a consistent manner is a challenge to any criminal justice system. The models of criminal justice explored in previous chapters indicate some of the issues to be addressed by an examination of sentencing decisions and policy. Should sentences aim to punish or rehabilitate the individual offender or protect society from the risk posed by particular offenders? Should sentencing perform a broader role of expressing the community's condemnation of particular kinds of behaviour as the denunciation model suggests? Can or should the criminal justice process attempt to reduce crime, either by devising sentences aimed at individual offenders or at potential offenders in the general population? Can any criminal justice system reasonably aim to do all of these things, or should the purpose of sentencing be more restricted? Should sentences be individually tailored to the needs of, or risks posed by, an offender, or is consistency of disposal more important? As with other aspects of the process, a balance must be sought between the often conflicting pressures of different goals.

In this chapter, we will focus on sentencing decisions and the mechanisms and procedures which affect the sentencing process. We will also point to the increasing rate of change in sentence formats and availability as policy makers seek to reconcile shifting penal objectives with fiscal pressures, public (or media) opinion and political reality.

We start by examining the multiple aims of sentencing which affect the choice of sentence: a choice increasingly curtailed by statutory and other considerations.

The Criminal Justice Act 1991 (CJA 1991) was the first statute which set out to provide a coherent theoretical approach to sentencing including a coherent sentencing structure, placing the main types of disposal in an ascending hierarchy relating to the seriousness of the offence. Since then, various amendments (both minor and radical) have been introduced, including the Criminal Justice Act 2003 which set a different set of goals – denunciation is out and deterrence is back, and a greater role is given to the rehabilitation and incapacitation of persistent offenders.

We will look at the range and pattern of sentences given by the courts. It is unlikely that there is a jurisdiction in the world in which judges and magistrates have the choice from as wide a range of penalties. Coming to grips with the range of penalties is not easy as, since 1997 when New Labour came into power, the pace of change has been considerable with the introduction of a range of new sentences and orders and the renaming of existing ones. Thus in 2000, probation orders were re-named **Community Rehabilitation Orders** (CROs), community service orders became **Community Punishment Orders** (CPOs) and the combination order was re-branded as the **Community Punishment and Rehabilitation Order** (CPRO). The names and structure of community penalties for adults were changed again with the implementation of the Criminal Justice Act 2003. Several new disposals were introduced: action plan order, detention and training order, drug treatment and training order, drug abstinence order, referral order and reparation order. Some of these have been since removed by the Criminal Justice and Immigration Act of 2008 (see below).

The Criminal Justice Act 2003 (CJA 2003) made fundamental changes to the nature of sentences. All adult **community sentences** came under the generic term of a community order, with a range of possible requirements such as curfew, electronic monitoring, supervision, unpaid work and drug treatment. The Act also provided for shorter custodial sentences, to be served as intermittent custody (e.g. weekend gaol) and reform of custodial sentences of under 12 months(termed custody plus and custody minus). These two reforms were never implemented and have been repealed, as has the indeterminate sentences introduced by the CJA 2003, by the Legal Aid, Sentencing and Punishment of Offenders Act 2012 (LASPO).

These repeated changes have often been driven by the desire for modernisation and greater effectiveness (see the Halliday report published in 2001, *Making Punishments Work*). Their impact on offending rates is unclear, particularly as the rate of change gives little opportunity for evaluation. Some changes are driven by the desire for greater efficiency and cost saving, and others (including name changes for example) for the desire to increase public understanding or approval.

The choice among so many sentences and orders, while providing flexibility to meet the various objectives referred to above and explained below, gives rise to a concern about disparities; when similar crimes, committed in similar circumstances, are given different sentences. To this end, since the last third of the twentieth century various reforms have been introduced to achieve a more uniform approach among sentencers. Thus, statutory constraints, in terms of limits, maximum and minimum sentences, and 'gate keeping' criteria were added to the existing appeal process as measures to promote consistency. The appellate process was enhanced by Court of Appeal guideline rulings on different types of crime and the Attorney General's right of appeal against unduly lenient sentences. Added to this has been the widespread adoption of guidelines for use by magistrates, firstly developed through their own Association and used voluntarily and subsequently enhanced and extended by the Sentencing Guidelines Council and given statutory force. The Sentencing Council is the latest body created, in 2010, to give guidance and promote consistency, and was formed as a result of the CJA 2003. It built on the work previously undertaken by the Sentencing Advisory Panel and the Sentencing Guidelines Council.

The next section will examine other less obvious influences on sentencing decisions, some of which have caused concern on the grounds of alleged bias or inconsistency. The developments referred to above have been overtly driven by desires for consistency in sentencing: a goal not easily achieved in terms of individual circumstances of cases and complex life histories of offenders but made doubly difficult in the context of political pressures to respond both to crime control issues and an escalating prison population.

11.1 Aims of sentencing

Objective 1

Define the six main aims of sentencing

In 2012, 1.2 million offenders were sentenced by the criminal courts in England and Wales (see Table 11.3). To discover more about why all these people were sentenced in the way that they were, we need first to distinguish between the aims of sentencing, the justification for sentences and the distribution of sentences.

The *aim* of sentencing is the purpose or objective that the sentencer or policy maker is seeking to achieve. Does the sentence aim to rehabilitate, punish, or deter an individual offender or mark the seriousness of offences in some way? The *justification* for sentencing involves considering why the aims are desirable, especially where sentences aim at some beneficial consequences. The justification for sentencing policy may be that it can reduce crime, prevent private vengeance, or mark unacceptable behaviour. The *distribution* of punishment allows us to examine who is punished, and how they are – or should be – punished. Should the convicted criminal in a particular case be executed, locked away or made to pay a penalty? How long should they be locked away for? How much should they be required to pay if fined?

A sentence might involve some form of *punishment*, and a key feature distinguishing criminal from other branches of law is that it involves the possibility of the state imposing a punishment on an offender. Such punishment, however, must follow a finding of guilt in accordance with due process. This distinguishes state punishment from private vengeance. One definition of punishment in this context is provided by **H L A Hart (1968)**.

- Punishment must involve pain or other consequences normally considered unpleasant.

- It must be for an offence against legal rules.

- It must be of an actual or supposed offender for an offence.

- It must be intentionally administered by human beings other than the offender.

- It must be imposed and administered by an authority constituted by a legal system against which the offence is committed.

Through punishment it is often hoped to achieve one or more sentencing aims, often described as theories of sentencing. Six main theories are found in most jurisdictions, although the balance between different theories varies according to the prevailing sentencing policy of any individual system, which may place a greater emphasis on one aim or on a particular combination. The six theories are **retribution, incapacitation, rehabilitation, deterrence, denunciation** and **restitution**.

These theories affect what the sentencer hopes to achieve by a sentence and what considerations should be taken into account. Thus, if the aim is to rehabilitate, the needs of the offender must be considered; if to protect the community through incapacitating dangerous offenders, the risk of future danger must be calculated. If the aim is to deter, an evaluation of what will make an impact on those considering criminal acts in the future must be made; if to denounce, the moral expectation of the community must be signalled; if to seek retribution, the right balance must be found between the seriousness of the offence and the severity of the sanction.

The theories can be distinguished in terms of what they wish to achieve. Three of the objectives are sometimes described as offender-instrumental in that they aim to affect the future behaviour of individual offenders. Rehabilitation aims to change future behaviour through counselling, treatment and training. Deterrence aims to make the potential offender think again through the anticipation of future sanctions. Incapacitation seeks to restrain offenders physically to make it impossible for them to re-offend. However, the impact on the offender is just one aspect of sentencing, for there is another audience: the public and its desire to see criminals punished and to be protected from physical injury and loss of personal property. This is reflected in the aims of retribution, denunciation and incapacitation. Restitution seeks directly or indirectly to recompense the victim for the harm suffered.

Thus, sentences may be individualised, that is based on a consideration of their impact on individual offenders. This means that the circumstances of the offender and the risk they pose must be taken into account. On the other hand, sentences may be based primarily on the seriousness of the offence in that they aim to reflect public disapproval or attempt to punish in proportion to the seriousness of the offence, taking account of its actual or potential harm. In addition, it is often seen as desirable that sentences should be concerned with justice for, and fairness to, individual offenders, as implied by the due process model. Thus, if different sentences are given for similar offences to offenders with similar circumstances and background, they could be seen as unjust or unfair. This is known as sentencing disparity, and is more likely to happen, according to Andrew Ashworth, when the sentencer can draw on any one or any combination of the six theories to justify a decision. Different sentencers may have different aims and different conceptions of distribution, producing little consistency of approach. Therefore, unless a priority is established and agreed, individualised sentences will lead to disparities. Ashworth argues that 'unless decisions of principle are taken on priorities among two or more sentencing aims, the resultant uncertainty would be a recipe for disparity' (**von Hirsch and Ashworth 1993: 258**).

Turning penal aims into sentencing policy is not, however, easy, especially as most jurisdictions attempt to combine elements of the six theories so that sentencing policy simultaneously seeks to:

> denounce the wrongful, deter the calculating, incapacitate the **incorrigible**, rehabilitate the wayward, recompense the victim and punish only the culpable.
>
> (Davies 1989: 6)

In addition, different theories may be more influential at different times and the shifting balance between them is apparent not only in England and Wales but in other jurisdictions. These shifting penal paradigms will be examined in detail in **Chapter 12**. It is helpful, however, when exploring the influences on sentencing aims and practice, to look at policy pronouncements on these issues. In the 1990 White Paper *Crime, Justice and Protecting the Public*, which led to the CJA 1991, the following balance between objectives was articulated:

> The first objective for all sentences is the denunciation of and retribution for the crime. Depending on the offence and the offender, the sentence may also aim to achieve public protection, reparation and reform of the offender, preferably in the community. This approach points to sentencing policies which are more firmly based on the seriousness of the offence, and just deserts for the offender.
>
> (Home Office 1990a: 6)

Although regarding the two goals of denunciation and retribution as primary, the statement makes it clear that they are not the exclusive aims of sentencing and it also refers to public protection, reparation and reform of the offender (**Home Office 1990a: 6**). Note the absence of a reference to deterrence.

Subsequent reports have lost any reference to denunciation and restored deterrence as an overt aim of sentencing (cf. **Halliday 2001** and **Auld 2001**). The White Paper *Justice for All* (**Home Office 2002, para. 5.8**) referred to the purpose of sentencing in the following terms: sentences should 'first and foremost protect the public, act as a punishment and ensure the punishment fits the crime, reduce crime, deter, incapacitate, reform and rehabilitate, and promote reparation'.

The CJA 2003 was the first statute to spell out in detail the multiple aims of the sentencing system. The same goals for the sentencing of young offenders were reiterated in the CJIA 2008 (**see Chapter 8**). The term, incapacitation, is subsumed under protecting the public. The goals in relation to adult offenders (set out in s 142(1)) are:

a. the punishment of offenders;

b. the reduction of crime (including its reduction by deterrence);

c. the reform and rehabilitation of offenders;

d. the protection of the public; and

e. the making of reparation by offenders to persons affected by their offences.

As we see above, the objectives of sentencing can change over time, with different priorities being given by policy makers. The courts have the task of translating those objectives into sentencing disposals. There is rarely agreement among policy makers about the ideal form of sentencing. Translating sentencing objectives into a range of penalties and disposals for the courts, and providing a framework of principles to apply, is no easy task because of the multiple aims we simultaneously seek to achieve through sentencing. While philosophical, criminological and legal principles are important, they are not the only considerations. The CJA 1991 introduced the concept of unit fines. This was a method of calculating fines, in cases where it was decided by the court that a financial penalty was appropriate, to give a fairly precise reflection of both the seriousness of the offence, and the means of the offender. The repeal of this provision after a very short time shows the importance of not losing either the confidence of the judiciary or the public on such matters. Even if we devise a tariff of penalties and disposals within a just deserts framework, and ignore other claims, we would still have problems as the tariff cannot be derived from the scientific calibration of seriousness of a crime or the severity of a sanction, as the tariff is not a fixed currency but moves with the public mood.

The CJA 1991 was passed following a period of unparalleled consultation and planning, yet it was subject to fundamental amendments by the CJA 1993 after only six months of operation. Since then, further alterations to the CJA 1991 have followed in the Criminal Justice and Public Order Act 1994, the Crime (Sentences) Act 1997, the Crime and Disorder Act 1998, the Youth Justice and Criminal Evidence Act 1999, the Powers of Criminal Courts (Sentencing) Act 2000, the Criminal Justice Act 2003, the Courts Act 2003, the Criminal Justice and Immigration Act 2008, the Children and Young Persons Act 2008, the Coroners and Justice Act 2009, and the Legal Aid, Sentencing and Punishment of Offenders Act 2012. Sentencing policy, perhaps more than any other aspect of the criminal justice system, is constantly being re-examined and reflected upon in terms of 'Does it work?' and 'Is it credible?'

The history of sentencing policy is a history of changing emphases on the six sentencing goals, which we will now examine in turn.

▶ Retribution

As we have seen, many theories see the purpose of sentencing as to reduce crime or change offenders' behaviour or attitudes. Retributionists do not use this rationale. The purpose of retribution is to seek vengeance upon a blameworthy person because they have committed a wrongful act. While some versions of retributive theory sought to justify punishment by talk of redressing the moral balance or atonement for wrongs committed, the more straightforward versions merely state that some acts are wrong and deserve to be punished, thus punishment is an end in itself.

This theory is sometimes referred to as an 'eye-for-an-eye', but if taken literally this would require the duplication of the offence as the punishment. Thus proponents of capital punishment use the phrase 'a life for a life'. However, punishment based on the literal duplication of the crime could be seen as unethical, especially where the crime was a particularly cruel murder. It is also impractical for most other crimes. For instance, what would be the eye-for-an-eye for offences such as burglary or handling stolen goods? Even more problematic would be deciding what punishment should be given to a serial killer, a rapist or a child molester. The eye-for-an-eye is more helpful as a metaphor to suggest that there should be some balance between the wrong done by the offender and the pain inflicted on that offender in the form of a punishment, popularly expressed as 'let the punishment fit the crime'.

In a retributive approach, the calculation of punishment depends on two factors: first, culpability or blameworthiness. Retributionists insist that only blameworthy offenders should be punished. Therefore, as seen in earlier chapters, children and the mentally ill are absolved of blame for their criminal conduct and need not be punished. We have also seen that a crucial element in criminal liability is not only the *actus reus* but the *mens rea*. Thus before convicting for murder, the court must establish whether the defendant is blameworthy or, as in a case of self-defence, acted in an acceptable way and is, therefore, not culpable of murder. Also, different defences and mitigating factors are used to absolve the defendant, or reduce the level of culpability (as we saw in **Chapter 2**).

Once culpability is established the retributionist will look at the seriousness of the offence to determine the deserved penalty. In this respect retributive theory refers to commensurate punishment, a concept not used so much today because it implies a notion of equivalence. The term 'proportionate sentence' is preferred because this suggests that offences and penalties can be ranged from more to less severe without any suggestion that there can be an exact measurement of equivalence. Thus what is generally referred to as a tariff of penalties is notionally arranged in order of severity. There is no assumption, however, that they are somehow equivalent to the harm done by the offender.

▶ Incapacitation and public protection

We have already seen how considerations of public protection influence all stages of the criminal justice process. These underlie the aim of incapacitation, the purpose of which is to impose a physical restriction on offenders which makes it impossible or reduces the opportunities for them to reoffend. The most common way of incapacitating offenders is through long periods of imprisonment justified on the grounds that they prevent persistent or serious offenders from re-offending. Thus, the Prevention of Crime Act 1908 introduced a new measure of preventative detention to deal with 'habitual criminals' who made a career from crime. Section 10 of the 1908 Act allowed an addition of 5–10 years' detention on top of the original sentence for the current offence. The term applied to those who were persistently leading a life of crime and had three convictions since the age of 16. The extended sentence which replaced preventative detention in the Criminal Justice Act 1967, the discretionary life sentence and the retention in the CJA 1991 of discretionary parole for offenders sentenced for over four years in custody, were similarly justified in terms of public protection. The Crime (Sentences) Act 1997 provides minimum sentences for repeat offenders in drug trafficking and a mandatory life sentence for some serious offences.

There are other ways of incapacitating offenders. Disqualification of drivers convicted of serious motoring offences aims to stop them driving; and company directors convicted of serious fraud and other business offenders may also be incapacitated by disqualifications or by withdrawing licences which make it impossible for them to carry on in business. Offenders convicted of mistreating animals can be banned from owning them. Normally, incapacitation is linked to the type of crime committed but a generally incapacitative sentence was introduced by the Crime (Sentences) Act 1997 under which a driving disqualification can be imposed for any offence. More recent 'high-tech' forms of control, including electronic surveillance by the use of electronic tags and curfew orders, have an incapacitative element. The common justification for these approaches is that they prevent a future offence from being committed and thereby protect the public. Indeterminate sentences for public protection (IPP) and extended sentences for sexual and violent offenders were introduced by the CJA 2003 with explicit reference to incapacitation and public protection but only for violent and sexual offences. The IPP was replaced by the Extended Determinate Sentence (EDS) by LASPO Act 2012. These and the subsequent amendments to their operation are discussed below.

In the United States, public protection was the justification given for the 'three strikes and you are out' policy of incapacitation of those criminals convicted of three felonies. In 1994, in some US jurisdictions legislation was introduced to make a mandatory prison term applicable after the third similar offence – whatever the mitigation. This same incapacitative logic is to be found in the justification of the reforms found in the Crime (Sentences) Act 1997.

Incapacitation and retribution are often contrasted in terms of sentencing aims and effects. Retribution relates to punishment for the wrong done, whereas incapacitation relates to the prevention of future wrong where exceeding any notion of proportionate sentencing is justified on the grounds that the offender is a continuing risk. The contrast is often articulated as 'deservedness versus dangerousness' (**von Hirsch 1986**), and both ideas are given as criteria for imprisonment in the CJA 1991 and the Powers of Criminal Courts (Sentencing) Act 2000. One of the major problems with incapacitation lies in how offenders are selected for extended periods of imprisonment or other forms of incapacitation. As this involves longer and more severe sentences than would be considered appropriate by other theories, it raises issues not only of fairness, but of how accurate predictions of the risk of further offending are likely to be. The indeterminate IPP was a sentence specifically to address these matters.

Incapacitation seems to have been uppermost in Mr Justice Butterfield's mind when he sentenced Victor Farrant for murder and attempted murder in January 1998. On passing the mandatory life sentence for murder and 18 years for the attempt, committed within weeks of being released after serving 7 years of a 12-year rape sentence, the judge said:

> This murder was so terrible and you are so dangerous that in your case the sentence of life should mean just that – you should never be released. You have devastated the lives of many people. The opportunity to do so again should not be allowed to you.
>
> (*The Independent*, 30 January 1998)

▶ Rehabilitation

We have seen in previous chapters how the rehabilitative model affects not only the sentencing process – it permeates the entire criminal justice process. As a sentencing goal, rehabilitation is concerned with the future behaviour of an offender and aims to reduce the likelihood of future re-offending. Thus the use of welfare and treatment strategies is targeted at individual offenders. The justification for this is that, if successful, fewer people will be future victims of offences committed by these offenders.

In the twentieth century, the emergent social sciences appeared to hold out the hope that crime could be reduced humanely. It was believed that through the application of science the causes of crime, which was seen as a kind of illness, could be diagnosed and treated. Criminals, therefore, were in need of treatment rather than punishment. Rehabilitative sentences, therefore, must consider the needs of the offender rather than issues of morality, the seriousness of the offence or criminal responsibility. Thus sentences with a rehabilitative aim may be very different from those indicated by other approaches. Rehabilitation could justify a longer sentence than the seriousness of the offence might suggest, so that a programme of treatment could be carried out, or alternatively might suggest treatment outside institutions, although this would mean less protection for the public. Rehabilitative ideals have strongly influenced penal policy in many jurisdictions and led to the development of social work and psychiatry in the penal system and of special institutions to cater for offenders considered to be in need of psychiatric help. In particular, the desire to rehabilitate young offenders and thus prevent them developing into career criminals is much in evidence with the specific re-naming of the generic community order for young offenders as the Youth Rehabilitation Order (**see Chapter 8**).

Rehabilitation thus necessitates a sentencing policy that allows for the sentence to fit the individual rather than the offence. To this end, rehabilitative sentencing policies require the following:

- *Monitoring and classification.* Pre-sentence reports are required by the courts to assess needs prior to sentencing, and constant monitoring is required during a sentence to establish progress.

- *Individualisation.* A flexible range of sanctions and resources should be available so as to be able to respond to the individual needs of each offender in the hope of changing their future behaviour. Some offenders will need counselling with regard to drug dependency; others will need social skills training.

Table 11.1 Time before a conviction is spent

Sentence	Time before the conviction is spent Adults	Time before the conviction is spent under 18 at date of conviction
Custody over 4 years	Never	
Custody between 30 to 48 months	7 years beginning with the day on which the sentence (including any licence period) is completed	42 months beginning with the day on which the sentence (including any licence period) is completed
Custody between 6 to 30 months	48 months beginning with the day on which the sentence (including any licence period) is completed	24 months from the day on which the sentence (including any licence period) is completed
Custody between 6 months or less	24 months beginning with the day on which the sentence (including any licence period) is completed	18 months beginning from the day on which the sentence (including any licence period) is completed
Fine	12 months from the date of the conviction	6 months from the date of the conviction
Compensation order	The date on which the payment is made in full	The date on which the payment is made in full
Community or youth rehabilitation order	12 months beginning from the last day on which the order is to have effect	6 months beginning from the last day on which the order is to have effect

Source: https://www.gov.uk/government/news/reforms-to-help-reduce-reoffending-come-into-force

- *Indeterminacy.* If the offender has committed a sufficiently serious offence, or is deemed a danger to the public, institutional containment in prisons or hospitals might be necessary. However, rehabilitative and treatment needs mean that the length of such incarceration should be flexible, to allow for the response of the offender, now classified as an inmate, client or patient, to a treatment programme. Thus, sentences may be indeterminate, where the amount of time is not fixed at the time of sentence but is dependent on the progress of treatment.

- *Spent periods following a conviction or caution.* This was introduced by the Rehabilitation of Offenders Act 1974, to help offenders to move on with their lives, following a set period of time, a conviction or caution can be effectively ignored for most official purposes (exclusions relate to those working with children or the vulnerable). The term 'spent' is used. Prison sentences of up to 30 months could not ever be spent under the 1974 Act but this was repealed by LAPSO 2012 which extended the period from 30 to 48 months. Thus, sentences to imprisonment over 48 months are never spent.

The rehabilitation period for a sentence is the period beginning with the date of the conviction and ends at the time listed in Table 11.1 in relation to that sentence.

▶ Deterrence

The object of deterrence is to reduce the likelihood of crimes being committed in the future by the threat of punishment. It is based on the assumption that offenders, fearing punishment, will refrain from criminal behaviour. Deterrent policies may be aimed at individual offenders, thus we talk of individual deterrence, or may aim to affect the behaviour of others who may be contemplating committing a crime, known as general deterrence. Deterrence is used in everyday life – it is, for example, the theory underpinning a threat issued to encourage people to comply with rules or refrain from infringing them, and is a principle well known to most parents: 'if you do that again I will . . . (threat), or you won't . . . (reward)'.

Deterrence, like rehabilitation and incapacitation, aims to reduce the likelihood of an offence being committed in the future. Thus they are described as 'consequentialist' theories as the focus is on the consequences of sentencing. Deterrent theory is not concerned with issues of fairness and justice but with the question of effectiveness. Does it work? This question can be looked at theoretically and empirically.

At a theoretical level the theory makes certain assumptions. It assumes that before engaging in criminal acts criminals calculate how unpleasant a sentence might be. This involves three other assumptions: first, that crimes occur as a result of individuals exercising free will and acting out of choice; second, that these individuals consider the consequences of their acts and the likelihood of being caught; and third, that the potential criminal regards the potential sentence as undesirable.

Objections might be made that many criminal acts do not match these assumptions. In particular, the most serious crimes such as homicide are not always carried out after calculation, but result from anger, fear or a momentary loss of control. Other, and possibly most, offenders do not expect to be caught – so the likely sentence is far from their thoughts. Some serious crimes may be affected – offenders may, for example, think about the repercussions when deciding whether to use a weapon in a robbery. At the other end of the offending scale, in road traffic matters, deterrence has apparently had some effect. Sir Paul Condon, the then Metropolitan Police Commissioner, is reported as commenting that 'fatalities on stretches of roads in West London are down by one-third since the introduction of law-enforcement cameras' (**Condon 1994**).

Although, as we have seen, deterrence was not given much credence in the 1990 White Paper, Court of Appeal judges continued to use it to justify sentencing decisions. In May 1993 the Court of Appeal reduced a 12-month custodial sentence for Nicholas Decino to 10 months. Mr Decino had a 10-month suspended sentence for burglary and possession of drugs activated after he was convicted of theft from a telephone kiosk. The Court of Appeal thought this was sufficiently serious to justify a prison term but made it run **concurrently** so that the total term would be 10, not 12 months. Lord Justice Beldam explained the sentence of the court:

> . . . this was the kind of offence which was capable of depriving members of the public of the use of the public telephone which, to many people, was a lifeline. Of necessity telephone boxes were left unprotected. It was a matter of public policy to deter thefts from such boxes.
>
> (Law Report, *The Times*, 10 May 1993)

While evidence of the efficacy of the deterrent aspect of sentencing is often hard to prove, it is a combination of a deterrent approach, sometimes combined with the next sentencing aim we shall consider, that of denunciation, that underpins such statements as that made by Prime Minister Gordon Brown in June 2008, responding to a spate of stabbings of and by young people in London:

> We have to send out a message and reinforce it with immediate action. It is completely unacceptable to carry a knife. Young people need to understand that carrying knives doesn't protect you, it does the opposite – it increases the danger for all of us, destroys young lives and ruins families. Recent tragic events have reminded us of that. I am pleased to see the Police and the Courts working with us to tackle this and make the streets safe in all our communities.

The response of sentencers following the riots in England in 2011 was to give tough deterrent penalties to rioters, looters and those who benefitted from the riots by buying stolen goods, who were charged with handling stolen goods. Even those who did not take part in riots but encouraged others to do so via the internet were given tough penalties for incitement. Many of these were appealed but in the Blackshaw *et al.* Court of Appeal Guideline cases of 18 October 2011, the appeal judges upheld the prison sentences handed down using a deterrent logic.

> Those who deliberately participate in disturbances of the instant magnitude, causing injury, damage and fear to even the most stout-hearted of citizens, and who individually commit further crimes during the course of the riots were committing aggravated crimes. They have to be punished accordingly, and the sentences should be designed to deter others from similar criminal activity.
>
> (*R* v. *Blackshaw and other appeals* [2011] All ER (D) 144 (Oct))

❯ Denunciation

The denunciation model stresses the role of the criminal justice system in publicly expressing society's condemnation. Thus sentences can be used to underline the community's outrage at the particular offence and crime in general. Denunciation is concerned with the impact of the sentence on the community and how this in turn affects the demarcation of the moral boundaries of society. Thus by identifying what behaviour is unacceptable, societies define themselves.

Under denunciation theory, sentencing is an act of official disapproval and social censure. It shares with retribution a focus on the morality of the act, but unlike retribution it looks beyond what should happen to the offender and examines the impact of a sentence on the community. It thus brings to centre stage issues of morality and how community perceptions of crime and punishment may conflict with those of the state and the law.

> The impact of punishment is not a private matter between offender and victim, for it also involves the community's expectations about appropriate standards of behaviour . . . The criminal provides us with a living example of our moral boundaries: by our outrage we come to recognise our shared fears, rules of communal living and mutual interdependency. We collectively define what sort of people we are by denouncing the type of people we are not.
>
> (Davies 1993: 15)

Thus, one of the key functions of sentencing is to portray, however impressionistically, the public's mood about unacceptable behaviour, and to represent a collective expression of right and wrong in response to offensive behaviour. Judges, in passing sentence, sketch the official portrait of public morality but the community's response to sentencing decisions provides the fine detail. Sentencing decisions are on some occasions unpopular and judicial pronouncements are criticised as too avant garde or too dated.

Sentencing decisions have become the focus of public debate about the society we live in as they draw attention to the offence committed and the response. Of course, not all sentencing decisions evoke a moral debate; many, if not most, go unnoticed. However, occasionally sentences receive considerable publicity and criticisms of their appropriateness. In more routine cases the audience for the moral drama may only be the jury, victim and witnesses or their neighbours, friends and relatives. The message they receive may be distorted by their limited understanding of criminal procedure and law. But they will form an impression of the state of public morality, which, while affecting them only directly, will influence their perception of the type of community they live in.

Everyday morality is constructed, in part, in this way. In a more individualistic and pluralistic society, the attempt to express the community's view becomes more difficult but even more important as an effort to identify commonly held expectations about how we should behave towards each other. If unacceptable behaviour is not acknowledged and assumed morality is not reinforced by the courts, it might be concluded that there is no shared definition of unacceptable behaviour. This could enhance individualistic responses to crime and break down collective expectations, thus creating unpredictability and uncertainty and undermining the basis of citizenship. It is also likely to encourage people to take action themselves against crime by, for example, acts of vigilantism. This latter point has led to recent suggestions that there is possibly a further aim of sentencing – to maintain law and order and prevent such private responses to crime.

▶ Restitution or reparation

Increasing concern with the interests of victims has led to a growth of interest in reparation and restitution which aim to compensate the victim of crime usually through a financial payment or services provided. Prior to the implementation of LASPO 2012 an offender could have been ordered to make financial compensation to individual victims through a court ordered Compensation Order in addition to the main sentence. The Compensation Order is an example of an ancillary order.

Table 11.2 The rate of Victim Surcharge in 2014 for those aged over 18 years

A conditional discharge	**£15**
A fine	**At 10% of the fine value with a £20 minimum and a £120 maximum (surcharge should be rounded up or down to the nearest pound)**
A community sentence	**£60**
An immediate custodial sentence	**6 months and below – £80 Over 6 months and up to and including 2 years – £100 Over 2 years – £120 (only in Crown Court)**
A suspended sentence	**6 months and below – £80 Over 6 months and up to and including 1 year – £100**

Source: http://sentencingcouncil.judiciary.gov.uk/sentencing/victim-surcharge.htm

In addition to the Compensation Order, that is compensation to a specific victim made by the individual offender, a more general type of financial support for victims of crime in general is provided by a Victim Surcharge (see Table 11.2). Introduced in 2007 as an additional cost for those given a fine, it was extended from October 2012 to all sentences. The money raised goes to local charities organised to help victims of crime such as local rape centres, distributed through the Witness and Victim General Fund.

The potential effect of reparation is greatest perhaps with property crime and in circumstances where victims are willing to participate and offenders can make some kind of meaningful reparation. Their application is less appropriate in cases of serious violent crime, where it is unlikely that the offender can make any meaningful reparation. A symbolic form of reparation underlies some other sentencing options, as it can be argued that there is a notion of reparation in community service, in that the offender is in some way giving something back to the community.

In recent years, the label **restorative justice** has often been applied to schemes that seek to reconcile the victim and offender and make a form of actual or emotional reparation.

Victims may also claim for a compensatory payment from a government agency for physical injuries as a result of a criminal offence by applying to the Criminal Injuries Compensation Authority (CIPA).

Having looked at the theories underlying sentencing, we will now outline the main sentences available to the courts and, in general terms, ask which of the sentencing aims may be fulfilled by them.

11.2 Types of sentence

Objective 2

Describe the different types of sentence available in the courts

Four main categories of sentence – discharges, financial penalties, community orders and custodial sentences – are available to the courts. All are available to both magistrates' courts and the Crown Court but the magistrates' court has an upper limit for financial and custodial sentences. In addition, the court may bind over a defendant, defer sentence or impose a range of ancillary orders.

▶ Distribution of sentences

In 2011 the magistrates' courts sentenced over a million offenders (1,197,087) and the Crown Court 102,164. Tables 11.3, 11.4 and 11.5 show the numbers of sentences given to offenders. Taking the figures for 2011, in total 1,299,251 were sentenced. The tables show the range of sentences available and the frequency of their use by judges and magistrates. Magistrates gave 82,456 offenders a conditional discharge and sent 46,035 to prison. The Crown Court gave 2,511 offenders a conditional discharge and sent a total of 56,663 adults to prison. Of all offenders, 66 per cent left the court with a fine, which is the most often used sentence (71 per cent in the magistrates' courts and 2 per cent in the Crown Court).

▶ Discharges

There are two main forms of discharge. An absolute discharge in effect means that, although the conviction is recorded, nothing will happen to the offender. A conditional discharge means that if, for the duration of the order (a specified period of up to three years), offenders are not found guilty of any other offence, they will receive no punishment. If, however, during the period of the discharge, they are sentenced by a court for another offence, they may be sentenced not only for the new matter, but also for the offence for which they were originally discharged. Under the Powers of Criminal Courts (Sentencing) Act 2000 (PCC(S)A 2000) a court may impose a conditional or absolute discharge where it is of the opinion it is 'inexpedient to inflict punishment'. LASPO 2012 have also expanded the court's youth sentencing powers to grant a conditional discharge to be instituted following a guilty plea to a first time offence.

A discharge is thus a sentence that does not seek to punish. The main sentencing aim that would appear relevant, therefore, is denunciation – merely acknowledging that an offence has been committed – but in the circumstances it is accepted that it is unnecessary to punish. The conditional discharge also has a deterrent purpose: 'Do this again and you will be punished.' It is used in a wide variety of circumstances, but most commonly for first offenders who commit a less serious offence.

▶ Financial penalties

A fine is the most common penalty given by the courts (see Table 11.5). In 2011, 851,607 offenders were fined, mostly in the magistrates' courts, and this is the most likely result for summary offences and many triable either way (TEW) offences heard in the magistrates' court.

There has been a steady decline in the use of fines in magistrates' courts and the Crown Court. In 1977 the fine was used in over half of all sentences given in Crown and magistrates' courts for those convicted of an indictable offence. By 2011 this had been reduced to 15 per cent of all this group of offenders, i.e. indictable only and TEW (see Figure 12.1).

Table 11.3 Magistrates' courts: offenders sentenced 2001–2011 (numbers in 000s)

	2001	2002	2003	2004	2005	2006	2007	2008	2009	2010	2011
Absolute discharge	15,094	18,905	18,737	14,871	13,088	11,812	10,973	9,666	8,886	8,766	7,969
Conditional discharge	98,823	95,959	100,384	95,507	90,311	85,173	91,529	85,144	81,384	87,350	82,456
Fine	927,571	970,384	1,030,918	1,080,236	1,022,710	959,394	939,046	887,976	943,844	891,420	849,575
SSO*	1,122	1,013	1,159	1,300	7,081	23,274	25,471	23,705	25,408	26,191	26,229
Community sentence	145,469	164,864	168,328	178,696	181,844	173,605	181,607	174,832	179,729	170,083	156,344
Immediate custody	61,868	64,913	63,396	61,384	57,250	53,431	51,172	50,348	48,429	48,904	46,035
Otherwise dealt with	26,479	27,378	30,842	39,104	34,428	37,296	33,438	41,565	24,635	30,682	28,479
Total	1,276,426	1,343,417	1,413,764	1,471,098	1,406,712	1,343,985	1,333,236	1,273,236	1,312,315	1,263,396	1,197,087

*SSO 5 suspended sentence order
Source: Criminal Justice Statistics, December 2011.
Note: The sentencing data above is aggregate data for all age groups, and males and females.

Table 11.4 Crown Courts: offenders sentenced 2001–2011 (numbers in 000s)

	2001	2002	2003	2004	2005	2006	2007	2008	2009	2010	2011
Absolute discharge	87	75	74	67	52	67	55	68	83	6782	97
Conditional discharge	2,448	2,464	2,758	2,805	2,434	2,269	2,553	2,578	2,575	2,2693,160	2,511
Fine	2,550	2,353	2,699	2,454	2,354	2,141	2,488	2,320	2,302	2,511	2,032
SSO	1,633	1,506	1,558	1,555	1,585	10,235	15,217	17,446	19,749	21,927	21,569
Community sentence	19,528	21,656	23,094	22,807	22,403	17,232	14,817	15,339	16,174	19,238	17,090
Immediate custody	44,405	46,694	44,274	44,938	43,986	42,586	44,034	49,177	51,802	52,609	56,663
Otherwise dealt with	1,417	1,443	1,606	1,628	1,927	2,056	1,606	1,900	1,905	2,424	2,202
Total	72,068	76,191	76,063	76,254	75,741	76,586	81,506	88,828	94,590	101,951	102,164

Source: Criminal Justice Statistics, December 2011.
Note: The sentencing data above is aggregate data for all age groups, and males and females: and the totals are subject to revision.

Table 11.5 All Courts: offenders sentenced 2001–2011 (numbers in 000s)

	2001	2002	2003	2004	2005	2006	2007	2008	2009	2010	2011
Absolute discharge	15,181	18,980	18,811	14,938	13,140	11,879	11,028	9,734	8,969	8,848	8,066
Conditional discharge	101,271	98,423	103,142	98,312	92,745	87,442	94,082	87,722	83,959	90,510	84,967
Fine	930,121	972,737	1,033,617	1,082,690	1,025,064	961,535	941,534	890,296	946,146	893,931	851,607
SSO	2,755	2,519	2,717	2,855	9,666	33,509	40,688	41,151	45,157	48,118	47,798
Community sentence	164,997	186,520	191,422	201,503	204,247	190,837	196,424	190,171	195,903	189,321	173,434
Immediate custody	106,273	111,607	107,670	106,322	101,236	96,017	95,206	99,525	100,231	101,513	102,698
Otherwise dealt with	27,896	28,821	32,448	40,732	36,355	39,352	35,780	43,465	26,540	33,106	30,681
Total	1,348,494	1,419,608	1,489,827	1,547,352	1,482,453	1,420,571	1,414,742	1,362,064	1,406,905	1,365347	1,299,251

Source: Criminal Justice Statistics, December 2011.
Note: The sentencing data above is aggregate data for all age groups, and males and females: and the totals are subject to revision.

Where a case is sentenced in the magistrates' court, the maximum fine is governed by the statutory maximum for that offence. Prior to LASPO 2012, fines for summary offences ranged from level one (maximum £200) to five (maximum £5,000). LASPO 2012, however, removed the maximum fine limit of £5,000 for an adult following conviction for a summary offence. Some trading and environmental offences carry a penalty of up to £20,000 or £50,000. In the Crown Court fines are 'at large', which means there are no limits. Fines must be assessed in relation to the seriousness of the offence, and it has long been a principle of sentencing that the level of fine imposed on an individual should take into account the offender's means and income, and the court will vary the fine accordingly. The fine, therefore, can be accurately adjusted in terms of proportionality, and is usually thought of as a deterrent or retributive sentence. Some would urge that a fine can also have an incapacitative effect in limiting an offender's opportunities, perhaps by preventing the offender from buying alcohol when the offence is drink related.

Compensation must be considered by a court when dealing with a case that has resulted in personal injury or property damage. It can be ordered instead of, or in addition to, another order (PCC(S)A 2000). If the court fails to order compensation in such circumstances, it must state its reasons. If a compensation order is made, it means that the offender should pay a stated amount to the person harmed by the offence. A compensation order is the prime reparative disposal.

The total financial impact on an offender being sentenced by directly ordered costs ordered by the courts can include: fines, compensation order (this is an example of an ancillary order, ie in addition to the main penalty), the Victim Surcharge, plus a contribution to the prosecution costs.

Costs are also frequently ordered against offenders and may represent a substantial part of the financial effect of a court order. Costs may be awarded against any convicted offender, but rank after compensation, victim surcharge and fines in order of payment: if the offender's means are insufficient to meet all three, compensation to the victim takes priority.

▶ Community sentences

Sentencing reforms have been very pronounced in the area of community penalties, ranging from changes in the names of orders to adding new orders and reorganising their availability and implementation. As discussed above, in 2000 the names of orders were changed, and new disposals introduced. The Criminal Justice Act 2003 restructured all community sentences as a single community order with a range of requirements such as curfew, electronic monitoring, supervision, unpaid work, drug or alcohol treatment, mental health treatment, prohibited activities, and exclusion or an attendance centre or residential requirement. For young people the equivalent youth rehabilitation order was introduced in 2008 (see Chapter 9).

Community sentences have been the success story in the last 30 years in terms of usage, and they are now the most frequently given penalty for those sentenced in all courts for indictable offences, i.e. indictable only and TEW crimes. In 1977, the courts sentenced 15 per cent of this category of offender to a community penalty (see Figure 12.1). By 2007 this had increased to 34 per cent, but by 2011 the percentage had fallen slightly to 29 per cent of all sentences, possibly as a result of greater use of suspended sentence orders (SSOs).

The criteria for the imposition of a community sentence were first laid down by the CJA 1991, and later, as we have seen, amended by the CJA 1993. These criteria have been reaffirmed in the CJA 2003 and clarified for the generic community order in the CJIA 2008. Consequently, a community order can generally be only imposed if:

* the offence is imprisonable (s 11 CJIA);
* the offence or offences being dealt with are serious enough to warrant its imposition;
* the combination of orders is suitable for the offender; and
* the restriction on liberty of the offender is commensurate with the seriousness of offending.

An exception to the seriousness criterion was introduced by section 151 of the CJA 2003 to deal with persistent minor offenders. This provides that, where a person who is over 18 is before the court for sentence and has previously been fined on at least three occasions (after attaining the age of 16), the court can impose a community sentence if it is in the interests of justice so to do.

A pre-sentence report must be obtained before assessing whether or not the offender is suitable for an order, unless the court considers it unnecessary to do so. A pre-sentence drug test may also be ordered before a community sentence is passed.

Community order: range of possible requirements

The requirements which can be imposed under a community order are:

* supervision for the period of the order;
* unpaid work (between 40 and 300 hours of work within 12 months at the direction of the Probation Service);
* specified activities;
* prohibited activities;
* accredited programmes (which might involve participation in groups addressing the offending behaviour);
* curfew for a specified period of between 2 and 16 hours a day for a maximum of 12 months, sometimes supported by electronic tagging;
* exclusion which prohibits for a period up to two years an offender from entering a designated area;
* residence at a required address;
* mental health treatment;
* drug rehabilitation for a minimum of 6 months;
* alcohol treatment for a minimum of 6 months;
* attendance centre requirement if the offender is under 25 for a total of between 12 and 36 hours;
* prohibition of foreign travel to a country or countries outside of British Islands;
* alcohol abstinence and monitory requirement for a maximum of 120 days (conditional).

Sentencers may give any combination of the 14 requirements listed but in practice they would rarely give a combination of more than three requirements, and most have only one requirement (48 per cent in 2011 (*Offender Management Statistics Quarterly, January to March 2012*, Ministry of Justice: London)). The most frequently given requirement is supervision, followed by unpaid work and an accredited programme. Very little use is made of residential, exclusion, or prohibited activity requirements.

An unpaid work requirement simultaneously meets many penal objectives. It includes a symbolic element of reparation, if not to the individual victim, then at least to the community. It also involves denunciation, particularly if the imposition of the sentence is followed by a visible performance of the work, and the restriction on liberty is intended to have a punitive impact so as to deter and punish offenders. Others point to the rehabilitative effect of doing valuable work for the community. Other orders may concentrate solely on rehabilitation, such as the supervision requirement, or on a mixture of objectives. Requirements can be combined to tailor the order specifically to the particular case. Electronic monitoring is a relatively new technological approach to the monitoring of community sentences and is delivered by the private sector.

The Legal Aid, Sentencing and Punishment of Offenders Act 2012 made several changes to the conditions, originally set out in the Criminal Justice Act 2003, which previously had to be met before courts could make use of community order requirements.

- Section 66 gives courts a duty to specify when a community order should come to an end, and gives them the power to extend an order by up to six months should the courts see reason to do so, or in the event of a breach of any of the terms of the order.

- Section 67 gives the courts two new options for dealing with a breach of a community order: either to take no action, or to fine the offender up to £2,500.

- Section 70 makes it easier for courts to impose programme requirements by removing certain conditions that previously had to be met before a programme requirement could be imposed.

- Section 71 increases the maximum curfew which courts can impose from 12 to 16 hours a day and increases the maximum duration or the curfew order from six to 12 months.

- Section 72 allows courts to impose a foreign travel prohibition requirement as part of a community sentence or suspended sentence order.

- Section 73 removes the condition that a court can only impose a mental health treatment requirement on the evidence of an approved registered mental health practitioner, although the offender must still express a willingness to comply with it.

- Sections 74 and 75 remove the minimum treatment and testing period for drug rehabilitation and alcohol treatment requirements.

- Section 76 introduces a new 'alcohol abstinence and monitoring requirement' for those convicted of an offence contributed to by alcohol but who are not alcohol-dependent and who have not been given an alcohol treatment requirement. Sobriety will be monitored by breath, urine sweat and blood tests, although this section also makes provision for the possible future use of electric monitoring bracelets – 'an alcohol tag' or 'sobriety bracelet' – which will test the level of alcohol in the wearer's sweat.

* Section 77 provides for the piloting of alcohol abstinence and monitoring programmes.

A consultation paper on community sentences and probation was published by the Ministry of Justice in 2012, entitled *Punishment and Reform: Effective Community Sentences* (Cm 8334), it included proposals intended to reduce re-offending for those released from community orders, improve public confidence in community sentences, and improve on extraction rates for all fines. Some of its aims have already been facilitated by provisions included in LASPO 2012. The proposals recommended in the consultation paper included:

* a dedicated punitive element in every community order to reassure the public of the credibility of community sentences and to increase the element of deterrence;
* developing a more creative use of financial penalties alongside community orders, ensuring that they are set at the right level and effectively enforced;
* from 2013 onwards, increasing the maximum weekly deduction that can be made from benefits as payment towards fines from £5 to £25;
* increasing the use of restorative justice practices (with the victim's consent and input), possibly by introducing an individually tailored restorative requirement to the community order;
* increasing the proportion of non-custodial sentences that attract compensation orders;
* increasing the number of work placements available to offenders upon release from community sentences;
* increasing incentivisation for work programme providers to produce low reoffending rates by expanding 'payment by results' pilots;
* focusing on developing specific interventions, services and requirements for female offenders, whose needs tend to be more complex than those of male offenders;
* exploring options for intensive community based treatment for offenders with drug dependency or mental health problems.

▶ Custodial sentences

Before an offender can be given a custodial sentence the sentencer must identify one of the following reasons:

* the sentence is fixed by law;
* the offence is so serious that only a custodial sentence is justified;
* the offence is a specified violent or sexual offence and the offender poses a risk of serious harm;
* the offender refuses to comply with the terms of a community order.

There are a range of custodial sentences available for younger offenders (**see Chapter 8**). For adults there are the following:

- Determinate or fixed prison sentences for a specific term established by the sentencer but subject to early release provisions. This means that a person not classified as a dangerous offender will be released half way through their sentence.

- Life imprisonment. A life sentence is the most severe penalty available. It is a mandatory sentence for those found guilty of murder, and thus the judge has no choice. It is also a discretionary maximum sentence for those convicted of serious indictable crimes such as manslaughter, arson, rape, robbery, aggravated burglary, causing grievous bodily harm, wounding with intent, supplying class A drugs and kidnapping. Under the Firearms Act 1968 crimes of assault, theft, arson and resisting arrest carry a maximum sentence of life if the offender is carrying a gun. The Powers of Criminal Courts (Sentencing) Act 2000 introduced automatic life sentences for second serious offences such as rape or grievous bodily harm (unless exceptional circumstances applied). Whole life orders can be imposed where retributive and deterrent purposes can only be served by the offender remaining in prison for the whole of their life.

- Indeterminate prison sentences are those where the date of release from custody is not fixed in advance by the court but typically requires a decision made by a parole board (see Figure 11.3). Indeterminate prison sentences were introduced in the CJA 2003 for dangerous sexual or violent offenders who could be

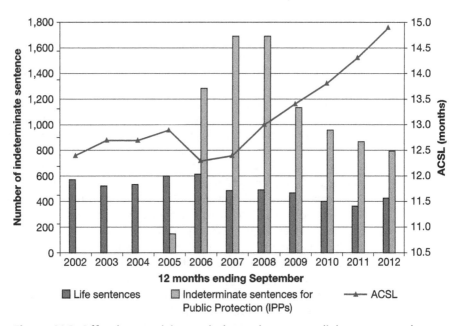

Figure 11.3 Offenders receiving an indeterminate custodial sentence and average custodial sentence length for all offenders; 12 months ending September 2002 to 12 months ending September 2012

Source: Criminal Justice Statistics – Quarterly Update to September 2012, Ministry of Justice, 2013

given a sentence of Imprisonment for Public Protection (IPP) or an extended sentence (EPP). These were introduced by the CJA 2003 but were subsequently abolished by LASPO 2012, which introduced another new custodial sentence called the Extended Determinate Sentence (EDS). The Court of Appeal has made it clear that offenders who constitute a particularly serious threat to public safety should be given a discretionary life sentence, where the stature provides for this, such as with rape where the maximum sentence is life imprisonment. The new EDS consists of a custodial term (to reflect the seriousness of the offence) but is followed by an extended licence period which is determined by the court on the basis of what the court considers necessary to protect the community from future serious harm. The maximum extended licence period is limited up to five years for a violent offence, and eight years for a sexual offence. The sum of the custodial term and the extended licence must not exceed the maximum penalty for the offence as set out in the statute. Prisoners serving an IPP or EPP sentence imposed prior to 3 December 2012 will continue to be released as before under the provisions of the Crime (Sentences) Act 1997 and the CJA 2003.

Further attempts to change the custodial sentencing structure were also provided for in the CJA 2003 which sought to limit the use of custodial sentences of less than 12 months with the introduction of two new types of sentence, called custody plus and **intermittent custody**, which would have enabled offenders to spend part of their sentence in prison and part in the community, and increased maximum powers of sentence for magistrates from 6 to 12 months' custody for a single offence, but these were never implemented and were repealed by LASPO 2012.

The CJA 2003 revived the suspended prison sentence, now called the Suspended Sentence Order (SSO). Suspended sentences of imprisonment have long been available, but they were seen as anomalous, as being available where the offence merited custody, but being suspended meaning that 'nothing happened'. A new suspended sentence order was introduced by the Criminal Justice Act 2003 for adult offenders, coming into force on 4 April 2005, and replaced the previous fully suspended sentence. During the suspension period the same requirements available under community orders may be attached, providing rehabilitative or punitive elements alongside the sentence.

Following a period after the CJA 1991 when the suspended sentence was only permitted where exceptional circumstances existed, justifying suspension, the new version of the order has regained popularity with sentencers (see Table 11.5). In 2004, 2,855 sentences were suspended under the old CJA 1991 law, but orders have grown steadily to 47,798 by 2011.

The SSO allows the court to impose a prison term of between 14 days and 2 years, and this may be suspended for any period specified in the order (called the operational period of the order). Prior to LASPO 2012, the court must have also made one or more requirements from the same list of the requirements available for a community order. As with the Community Order the most frequently used requirements were supervision, unpaid work and undertaking an accredited programme.

Of those given an SSO in 2011, 23 per cent were given an unpaid work requirement, 11 per cent a supervision order, 7 per cent a supervision order combined with an accredited programme, 5 per cent a supervision order combined with drug treatment, and 2 per cent a supervision order, unpaid work and accredited programme requirement. A further 26 per cent were given other combinations of requirements (*Offender Management Statistics Quarterly, January to March 2012*, Ministry of Justice: London). Thus the order at once recognises the serious level of offending, passing the 'custody threshold', allows its non-implementation in the specific circumstances, but ensures the defendant undergoes some element of punishment.

The LASPO Act 2012 increased the maximum length of custodial sentence eligible for suspension orders from one year to two, and introduced the option of imposing a fine of up to £2,500 for breach of a suspended sentence order instead of the custodial sentence. In addition, it is no longer mandatory for the courts to impose a community requirements with SSOs.

Custodial sentences can be justified by most of the major theories of sentencing. A prison sentence can be seen as a deterrent and it is still commonplace to argue that prisons should be austere places which should not provide comforts not generally available outside. The forbidding nature of prisons also underlines society's disapproval of inmates. The essential punishment involved in imprisonment is the deprivation of a person's liberty, and thus a prison sentence can be retributive, with the length of a sentence being determined by the seriousness of the offence. Prisons also take offenders out of society and thus protect the public and, as we have seen, they are the main form of incapacitative sentence. Furthermore, a major influence on penal policy and on the development of prison regimes throughout the twentieth century has been the belief that offenders can be rehabilitated while in prison (**as will be seen in Chapter 12**). The suspended sentence has a clear deterrent objective within its structure, and, since the introduction of the SSO, also often involves rehabilitation. The impact of these sentencing objectives on the shifting penal paradigms is discussed further in **Chapter 12**.

Sentencers also have various ancillary orders available, including orders allowing the confiscation of the proceeds of crime, the forfeit of money or property associated with offences and the destruction of items such as weapons or drugs. Other penalties relating specifically to motoring offences are worthy of note: the imposition of penalty points and disqualification from driving. Advertising campaigns, particularly over the Christmas period, focus on the potential harm caused by driving with excess alcohol, to enhance the denunciatory effect and stress the impact of the penalty, i.e. disqualification from driving, highlighting the deterrent element of the sentence.

▶ Enforcement of sentences

Each type of sentence brings with it particular problems in relation to dealing with the offender who fails to comply. For some sentences the approach is simple: it is an offence to escape from prison and an escaped prisoner will be given an additional sentence. Committing an offence during the currency of a conditional discharge means that the offender can be sentenced for the original offence as well as the new offence.

Community penalties and fines pose particular problems. During the period of a community penalty two problems may arise. First, failure to comply; for example, by behaving badly, failing to attend for unpaid work or doing it poorly, or not attending supervision meetings. Second, the offender may commit further offences during the period covered.

The courts' approach to a breach of the terms of any community order or of the commission of further offences during the period of an order was rationalised by the CJA 1993 and subsequently amended by the CJA 2003. It stated that for breach of a community order the courts must either:

- alter the original order and impose more onerous terms, or
- revoke the original order and re-sentence in some other way for the offence.

However, the LASPO Act 2012 amended the range of options available so that sentencers could alternatively choose to:

- take no action;
- extend the period of the order for up to six months further;
- fine an offender of up to £2,500 in relation to breach.

Enforcement of fines perhaps causes the most difficulty, not least because it is the most used sentence. Much time and cost are spent chasing recalcitrant payers: some who are well able to pay but are simply avoiding payment; others who are financially inept; others who are genuinely in difficulty or who find that their finances worsen after the imposition of the fine.

When imposing a fine magistrates must take into account the offender's means as measured in terms of income and expenses. However, circumstances may change and the offence and the sentence may lead to a worsening of the offender's financial situation: a drink driver might not be able to get to work after disqualification, or might lose their job; a man who assaults his wife might have to find alternative accommodation; an employee who steals from an employer will usually lose their job.

- If the offender cannot pay immediately, time to pay can be, and usually is, allowed. If the offender still falls behind, a number of measures to obtain payment can be used. To assist collection, since the Courts Act 2003 the fining courts must make a collection order in almost every case at the time of imposing the fine detailing the amounts and terms of payments and whether the person is already a fine defaulter. Where someone does default, or in any case with his consent, the courts can make:
- an attachment of earnings order, where a specified sum is deducted monthly or weekly from the earnings by the employer and sent to the court; or
- an application for benefit deduction to take a specified sum from benefit payments at source.
- Where further default is made, the fines can be collected administratively by a fines officer who must notify the defaulter of an intention to take 'further steps', i.e. issuing a distress warrant, registering the sum as a judgment debt and taking enforcement proceedings in a civil court, clamping a car (after which a court can order its sale), or may refer the matter back to the magistrates' court.

Since the Crime (Sentences) Act 1997 other measures for responding to fine default have been introduced:

- curfew;
- an unpaid work requirement;
- driving disqualification of up to 12 months.

Other measures available to deal with outstanding fines include:

- overnight detention in a police station in lieu of a fine;
- remission of fines, by reducing the original fine because of subsequent hardship or new information;
- imprisonment where the offence for which the fine was imposed is itself punishable by imprisonment and the offender is able to pay and refuses to do so. Maximum periods of imprisonment for default are 7 days for up to £200, rising to 12 months for defaults of over £10,000. For a fine defaulter who is imprisoned for a separate offence the fine can be disposed of by serving days in lieu of payment. This is normally served concurrently, so in effect, no extra days are served in prison. In 2011, there were 1,133 **receptions** into prison of fine defaulters with an average daily population of 100 fine defaulters in prison (*Offender Management Statistics 2011*).

Proposals included within the *Punishment and Reform* consultation paper make clear the government's intentions to increase the proportion of fines that are collected by ensuring that they are set at the right level and more effectively enforced, and, from 2013 onwards, by increasing the maximum weekly deduction that can be made from benefits as payment towards fines from £5 to £25.

Despite difficulties of enforcement, the fine is by and large a simply administered sentence and gains revenue. Additionally, effectiveness of fine collection is easily measurable in terms of amount and percentage successfully recovered and the time-scale involved. Thus fine enforcement can be identified as a measure of performance of courts and recovery agencies and has been identified for performance improvement in magistrates' courts. In 2004, a 'blitz' on fine defaulters called 'Operation Payback' was launched in 42 Magistrates' Areas. The aim was twofold: first to draw attention to the problem of fine dodgers; and, second, to make a concerted effort to recoup some of the £354.4 million outstanding in financial penalties at the end of 2003.

The fine is an infinitely flexible punishment – as a result it can be used in a wide variety of cases and is popular with policy makers.

11.3 Sentencing procedure

Objective 3
Outline sentencing procedures

Between the determination of guilt and decision on sentence there are various stages to go through, including a hearing of the mitigation the defendant may wish to offer in an attempt to reduce the severity of the sentence. Only in the most serious and the most trivial of cases will sentencing be carried out immediately after the decision on guilt. There is, as we have seen, a mandatory life sentence in cases of murder, and for many petty offences a discharge or small fine is likely and can be imposed immediately.

If the sentence follows a trial, the facts will have been presented. If there has been a guilty plea, the facts must be presented to the court by the prosecution. Occasionally there may be a dispute over the facts which affect the plea; for example the defendant may admit to an assault with fists, but deny kicking the victim. If the dispute is likely to affect the sentence, the sentencer must either sentence on the basis of the facts most favourable to the defence, or there must be what is called a 'Newton' hearing. This is like a mini-trial, where evidence is taken, but only on the specific issue involved.

The defendant may ask for offences to be **taken into consideration** (TIC). This means that the court takes them into consideration when sentencing, although there has been no formal conviction. This procedure is often used where a number of related offences have been committed, but the police may have been unable to prosecute them successfully – for example, where the defendant has confessed to a number of thefts from cars, or several cheque frauds. They may also form part of the plea negotiations.

There is no statutory basis for the TIC procedure, but it is recognised by the courts. Lord Goddard described the process as:

> simply a convention under which, if a court is informed that there are outstanding charges against a prisoner, the court can, if the prisoner admits the offences and asks that they should be taken into account . . . give a longer sentence than it would if it were dealing with him only on the charge mentioned in the indictment.
>
> (*R* v. *Batchelor* [1952], 36 Cr App R 64)

The effect of having offences taken into consideration does not mean that the defendant is convicted of them. Strictly, a defendant can be charged with the offence taken into consideration, but no additional penalty can be imposed. In practice, once an offence has been taken into consideration by a court, it is not the subject of later charges.

Whether or not there are offences to be taken into consideration, the court will then need to know whether the offender has any previous convictions and whether they are in breach of any existing orders.

The defendant, personally or through an advocate, may then put forward any mitigation in respect of the offence or their own circumstances. This is known as making a plea in mitigation, and is the opportunity for the defence to put the offending behaviour into the best possible light in order to gain the lightest sentence. This is the point at which financial information may also be given to the court. Financial details are relevant not only to show why a defendant may have committed an offence, but also because the court must take the means of the offender into account when imposing a financial penalty. Apart from the details of the case, such as that the defendant played a small part, sentence mitigation will include factors such as that the defendant pleaded guilty, especially if the guilty plea was entered early (PCC(S)A 2000 s 152), and that they were of previous good character (i.e. have no previous convictions). Defence counsel may argue, for example, that in some way the offender was pr.encing decisions the offence by financial or family problems. They may argue committing admitted the offence and can offer no defence, nevertheless t. they have the harm done and the offence occurred almost by accident, with. t intend forethought. This is especially the case where the offence is one of s.ning or which does not require intent, or where the offence has involved an ability do something. Thus, defendants may claim that they simply forgot to n to licence, but had always intended to do so or that they forgot to tell the Re. a and Customs about their earnings from a part-time job. Others may claim at they did not anticipate driving home after going to the pub. These mitigating factors attempt to reduce the culpability of the offender and thus seek to influence the eventual sentence (as seen in **Chapter 2**).

Before proceeding to sentence the court may require further information about the offender's circumstances, including their physical or mental health. In many cases before the Crown Court and in the more serious cases in magistrates' courts, a pre-sentence report is required. For adults, this is provided by the Probation Service and its preparation typically involves an adjournment of three weeks. The report contains information considered relevant by the probation officer and may cover such matters as home life, medical, psychiatric details, criminal background and schooling or employment. In the report the probation officer or social worker is asked to make an assessment of the seriousness of the offence, the risk of further offending and to consider the impact on the victim, although information on victims is often not available (**see Chapter 3**). In addition it should consider the possible sentences and the likely impact of such sentences on the offender. Before sentencing, the judge or magistrates will hear from the convicted person's defence counsel to remind the court of any mitigating circumstance and will also consider the pre-sentence report. This double exposure of mitigation before sentence has led to the criticism that it focuses too heavily on the circumstances, background and personality of the convicted person and insufficiently on the offence. The courts will also receive a victim impact statement, which allows the victim's voice to be heard (**see Chapter 3**).

11.4 Factors influencing sentencing decisions

Objective 4

Discuss the factors that influence sentencing decisions

Many factors influence sentencers' decisions. In respect of a particular case, the judge or magistrate must consider how serious the particular offence is in relation to other similar offences and assess whether or not the offence had any particular mitigating or aggravating factors. For example, if the offence has involved harm to a particularly vulnerable group, such as the elderly, this would be an aggravating factor, whereas absence of direct physical harm to a victim is more likely to be seen as a mitigating factor. Additionally, as seen above, the defendant may provide information about mitigating factors. Sentencers are also likely to take into account the previous convictions and record of an offender, and the recommendations in the pre-sentence report. Influences on sentencing can be grouped under the following headings:

• case-specific factors: case facts and offender circumstances and previous record of offending;
• statutory constraints;
• appellate process;
• judicial training, guidance and guidelines including those from the Sentencing Council.

Case factors refer to the individual case before the courts and sentencers must always address the information provided in the case papers available to them about the offender and the circumstances of the offence. However, the response to individual case facts is determined by legislation, the appeal process and guidelines that reflect the prevailing policy on sentencing.

First, there are the **statutory requirements**, i.e. responses to crime that are set out in legislation. We have a mandatory life sentence in the case of murder. All offences have **statutory maximum sentences**, such as 14 years for burglary of a domestic dwelling, even though this maximum is rarely, if ever, used. It provides an indication, however, of Parliament's view of the seriousness of the offence and so helps to set the sentencing tariff. There are a few minimum sentences for first offences, for example offenders convicted of driving with excess alcohol will receive a minimum period of 12 months' disqualification. Where a person is convicted of causing death by dangerous driving when under the influence of drink or drugs, or driving with excess alcohol, or driving while unfit, or failing to provide a specimen, and they have a previous conviction for any of these offences, then an obligatory driving ban of three years must apply. Section 111 of the Powers of Criminal Courts (Sentencing) Act 2000 provided that a minimum custodial period of three years must be imposed by the court where an offender aged 18 or over is convicted of a third domestic burglary.

The Crime (Sentences) Act 1997 introduced a mandatory minimum seven-year sentence for a third conviction for drug trafficking in class A drugs. For serious violent and serious sexual offences such as murder, manslaughter, rape or robbery with a firearm, an offender aged over 18, convicted of one of these offences for a second time, will be given a compulsory life sentence unless there are exceptional circumstances. In 2010 a new minimum tariff of 25 years for murders committed with a knife was introduced via the Criminal Justice Act 2003 (Mandatory Life Sentence: Determination of Minimum Term) Order 2010.

Statutes can provide limitations on sentencing in other ways: for example, the limitation on sentences given to young offenders of different ages (see **Chapter 8**). They can also limit sentencing powers by providing statutory criteria for the use of certain powers such as custody. The statutory criteria for the use of imprisonment were first set out in the CJA 1991 with respect to adults, although this had previously applied since 1982 for young persons.

Other **jurisdictions** use legislation to indicate more precisely the power of sentences. In California the 1976 Uniform Determinate Sentencing Act specified the prison terms that a judge could give with respect to each criminal offence. Thus, at that time, although subsequently amended upwards, the sentence for rape would be three, four or five years. The judge would choose which of these three terms to give depending on the aggravating and mitigating factors of the case. The middle term would be used in typical cases. Thus, a system of presumptive or expected, sentences was established and these sentences were determinate, that is fixed in length by statute.

In the magistrates' courts, sentencing decisions have increasingly been influenced by guidelines issued by the Magistrates' Association. These were originally issued in the 1970s in respect of motoring offences in an effort to curb complaints of inconsistency between benches. These had some success, especially for offences which could be easily compared – thus, a speeding offence on the M1 is very similar to a speeding offence on the M25. Their use, after consultation with the Justices' Clerks' Association and the Lord Chancellor's Department, was extended in 1989 to most offences dealt with in the magistrates' courts. More guidelines were issued to clarify the implementation of the CJA 1991 and reflected not only the framework of that Act but also the move towards more structured decision making, discussed in the next section of this chapter. The guidelines were re-issued in 1993 to reflect the changes in the CJA 1993 (in particular, the abolition of unit fines) and again in April 1997. Changes in the law and adjustments to the tariff were reflected in this edition, published as a section in a new publication, *The Magistrates' Court Bench Book*, under the auspices of the **Judicial Studies Board** in 2004. In 2008, the guidelines were further expanded and issued by the Sentencing Guidelines Council (now the Sentencing Council) and thus became part of the framework of guidance issued by that body and to which all courts had by the CJA 2003 to have regard. For the first time, therefore, the guidelines have statutory authority.

Both the layout and structure of the guidelines have changed over time to reflect legislation and good practice. The advice has also changed to reflect differing views of sentence range. The 1993 guidelines, for example, indicated a community sentence as the likely sentence or entry point for the offence of actual bodily harm. In 1997 custody was indicated. In 2008 the 'range' varies between community order and committal to the Crown Court.

One of the major changes in the latest version of the guidance is the introduction of ranges and bands of offending. Examination of the examples in Figure 11.4 will demonstrate both how the guidance should be used and the structured approach to sentencing, which is further discussed below.

A major influence on sentences in the Crown Courts in England and Wales is the appeal system. In 1907 the Court of Criminal Appeal was established to promote some degree of judicial self-regulation. Renamed the Court of Appeal (Criminal Division) in 1966, this court deals with appeals from the Crown Court against conviction and sentence. Most appeals are, however, against sentence. In 2011, there were 7,457 appeals to the Court of Appeal (Criminal Division): 5,623 against sentence and 1,535 against conviction; 1,386 were successful appeals against sentence (*Judicial and Court Statistics 2011*).

Since the 1980s, the Court of Appeal has issued guidance to sentencers with a series of guideline cases. These include *Bibi* in 1980 on the use of custody, *Roberts* in 1982 and *Billam* in 1986 on rape; *Barrick* in 1985 and *Price* in 1993 on theft. For drug dealing a number of guideline sentencing cases include *Aramah* in 1983, *Aranguren* in 1994 and *Warren and Beeley* in 1996.

Court of Appeal Guidelines for burglary were established in *R* v. *Brewster and others* (1998), *R* v. *McInerney and Keating* on 18 December 2002, and reviewed again in *R* v. *Saw et al.* in January 2009. The appellants in *R* v. *Saw* lost their appeal to have their sentences reduced. The judges confirmed the seriousness of burglary and set out the following aggravating factors.

From Court of Appeal judgment 16 January 2009 – aggravating factors when sentencing burglary

- Force used on, or threatened against, the victim, and especially if physical injury is caused – such cases will often be charged as robbery or as offences against the person;
- Trauma to the victim beyond the normal inevitable consequence of intrusion and theft;
- Pre-meditation and professional planning/ organisation in the execution – this may be indicated by burglars working in a group or when housebreaking implements are carried;
- Vandalism of the premises;
- Deliberate targeting of any vulnerable victim (including cases of 'deception' or 'distraction' of the elderly);

- Deliberate targeting of any victim, for example out of spite or upon racial grounds;
- The particular vulnerability of the victim, whether targeted as such or not;
- The presence of the occupier at home, whether the burglary is by day or by night;
- Theft of or damage to property of high economic or sentimental value;
- Offence committed on bail or shortly after the imposition of a non-custodial sentence;
- Two or more burglaries of homes rather than a single offence;
- The offender's previous record.

The Court of Appeal sentencing guidelines play a decisive part in fixing the appropriate tariff for an offence. Guideline cases are those where the appeal court has taken the opportunity to lay down detailed guidance to assist courts in sentencing. For example, in 1986 in *Billam*, the Lord Chief Justice both made a general statement of principle – that rape should be followed by a custodial sentence – and laid down a list of aggravating features which would call for a longer sentence than the norm, which he set at five years. Similarly, in the case of *Barrick*, which involved theft in breach of trust (e.g. from an employer), guidelines as to the length of a custodial sentence were given in terms both of the amount stolen, and the degree of trust broken. In the case of *Aramah*, and subsequent cases, guidelines were set out in terms of street value and class of drugs imported or supplied.

While these cases are an important and influential guide for lower courts in sentencing – and indeed for defendants and those advising them as to the likely sentence in a given case – they have limitations. First, the Court of Appeal can respond only to cases brought before it: therefore no systematic approach to offences or a certain range of offence can be made. While, as has been seen in the case of burglary referred to above, guidelines can change to reflect changing circumstances, the Court can only respond to cases before it. Second, the cases that come before the Court of Appeal have, until recently, only been a result of appeals against sentence on behalf of the defence.

The prosecution has only limited rights to appeal against unduly lenient sentences by virtue of section 36 of the Criminal Justice Act 1988. This gave the Attorney General the right to refer to the Court of Appeal sentences that seem unduly lenient. Despite this system of reference on unduly lenient sentences, the Court of Appeal is mostly concerned with lengthy custodial terms, as defendants receiving community sentences are not likely to appeal. It is comparatively rare, therefore, for short custodial or non-custodial sentences to be considered.

The **Sentencing Advisory Panel** (SAP) was created by the Crime and Disorder Act 1998 and was introduced to provide a means to develop a more systematic approach to sentencing guidelines. It takes a particular crime such as rape or a sentencing factor such as discounts for guilty pleas, and reviews the current approach and makes recommendations to the Court of Appeal. The Court may then incorporate its views and give legal effect to the recommendations. After the introduction of the Sentencing Guidelines Council (SGC) which came into effect in April 2004, SAP makes recommendations through the SGC. The SAP and the SGC were amalgamated into one body by the Coroners and Justice Act 2009 and renamed the Sentencing Council.

The four factors identified above are recognised constraints on sentencing decisions. As with any other discretionary process, however, informal factors also play a role. As we have seen, sentences may be directed towards different aims and many different considerations affect the decision. How, therefore, do sentencers approach individual decisions?

In a detailed review of sentencing decisions in the Court of Appeal, David Thomas identifies a twofold sentencing process. In the first, or primary, sentencing decision, judges decide on the basis of the individual case whether a 'tariff' sentence, primarily a retributive deterrent sentence, is appropriate or whether the sentence should be individualised – that is, based primarily on rehabilitative grounds (**Thomas 1979**). Individualised sentences may also be based on incapacitative and deterrent considerations with respect to the individual offender before the court, and will depend on an assessment of the likelihood of their reoffending and the danger they may be to the public. The secondary decision is which sentence will be imposed. Factors affecting the primary decision include both the personal characteristics of the defendant such as age, sex and previous history along with relevant personal circumstances and the seriousness of the offence. Where sentences are individualised it is extremely difficult to discern whether or not they are consistent as so many factors may affect the individual case (ibid.).

Sentencers themselves may have their own individual approach, or philosophy, based on a mixture of the theories of sentencing outlined above. They may also be affected by the attitudes and opinions prevailing on their own bench.

All these influences undoubtedly contribute to the variations found throughout the country which have caused so much concern. They may also, arguably, produce disparities not only when individual offenders are compared but when groups of offenders are compared. There has been criticism, for example, about the fairness of sentencing policy in relation to women and ethnic minorities. Concerns about the treatment of both unemployed and white-collar offenders raise issues of how far socio-economic status affects sentencing decisions. The next section will look briefly at these issues.

▶ Race and sentencing

Data for 2009/10 shows the proportion of offenders at various stages of the criminal justice system in terms of their ethnic identity. The base proportions are provided by Population Estimates by Ethnic Group, based on the 2001 census and examination of population trends, and if accurate and true in 2009/10 show an over-representation of ethnic minority people in terms of stop and searches, arrests, Crown Court trials and in prison, but because of the unknown numbers of illegal immigrants and visitors in the country it is difficult to make an accurate estimate or conclusion.

As we have seen in respect of earlier stages in the process, many other factors may account for this over-representation, indeed earlier stages of the process may affect sentencing outcomes. The legal and procedural factors which affect sentencing may account for many of the differences. Thus sentences are affected by the nature of the offence, the characteristics of individual offenders and whether or not defendants have pleaded guilty. We have already seen, for example, that more black offenders elect Crown Court trial and plead not guilty. This means that if convicted they would receive sentences that would not include a discount given for a guilty plea.

A Home Office research study of sentencing (**Flood-Page and Mackie 1998**) highlights one of the difficulties of research into difference of sentencing patterns for racial groups:

> . . . it needs to be borne in mind that the fairly crude ethnic breakdowns used in most studies (including this one) simplify a complex picture. Among the 'Asian' group are a number of ethnic minorities who differ in their socioeconomic position (e.g. Pakistanis and Bangladeshis suffer higher rates of unemployment than Indians and East African Asians) and there is some evidence that, while the proportion of Indians and Bangladeshis in prison is the same as in the general population, there are a disproportionately high number of Pakistanis in prison . . . There are also important differences between black people of Caribbean origin (most of whom are British citizens) and Africans (some of whom are temporarily in the UK).
>
> (Flood-Page and Mackie 1998: 118–120)

In their sentencing study based on 3,000 cases in 25 magistrates' courts and 1,800 in 18 Crown Court centres, Flood-Page and Mackie conclude:

> Asian men were significantly more likely to be sentenced to custody than would have been expected on the basis of their offence and other factors. However, variables such as the type and number of offences, their plea, whether they were subject to a court order when they committed the offence, being mentally ill or whether the offence was premeditated explained more of the variations in custody rates than ethnic origin . . .
>
> That ethnic minority males were not significantly more likely to receive custodial sentence than white males when other factors were taken into account was confirmed by further analysis. The differences in custody rates were explained by variables such as the type and number of offences, their plea, whether they were subject to a court order when they committed the offence, being mentally ill or whether the offence was spontaneous.
>
> (Flood-Page and Mackie 1998: 118–120)

▶ Sentencing women

Females make up just over half of the population but are below this proportion at all stages of the criminal justice process. There are many explanations; one being that women are less likely to commit crimes compared to males, and when they do they commit crimes they are less likely to generate a high level of public concern, and are less likely to generate a strong reaction from law enforcement agencies and the courts. Hedderman and Gelsthorpe's study in 1997 found that women were more leniently treated than men. However, the situation was complicated because the courts fined women less frequently than men, and were more likely to impose a discharge. Overall comparisons are difficult because in general women tend to commit less serious crimes than men and to commit fewer – therefore more women who are convicted are first offenders. These factors have, therefore, to be taken into account as shown in the studies below. As a consequence, repeat female offenders were more likely to be given a community penalty for subsequent offences.

Ministry of Justice statistics on women and the criminal justice system published in November 2012 show that, in 2011, there were still clear differences in the way that men and women were sentenced, such as:

- a higher proportion of female defendants received fines than males (77% compared with 61%);
- lower proportions of female offenders received community sentences than male defendants (10% compared with 15%), suspended sentences (2% compared with 4%), and immediate custody (3% and 10% respectively);
- average length of an immediate custody sentence for indictable offence was lower for females (at 11.6 months) than males (at 17.7 months).

Home Office researchers who conducted a study of 3,000 sentencing cases in the magistrates' courts and 1,800 in the Crown Court commented:

> Even allowing for their much lower rate of offending, females are much less likely to be prosecuted: in 1995, 59 per cent of women convicted or cautioned for indictable offences were cautioned, compared to 37 per cent of men . . .
>
> In this study a higher proportion of male first offenders received a custodial sentence than female first offenders in the Crown Court. So few first offenders received custodial sentences in the magistrates' courts sample that the difference was not significant. Men with previous convictions were four times as likely to receive a custodial sentence than women who were repeat offenders in magistrates' courts. In the Crown Court male repeat offenders were one-and-a-half times as likely to receive a custodial sentence as women.
>
> Further analysis confirmed that men had a significantly higher probability of receiving a custodial sentence than women even when other factors were taken into account.
>
> (Flood-Page and Mackie 1998: 121–2)

Table 11.6 Percentage of males and females sentenced for all offences in 2011 in England and Wales

Disposal	Females	Males
Absolute or conditional discharge	7.3%	7.4%
Otherwise dealt with	1.4%	1.4%
Fined	76.6%	60.6%
Community Sentence	9.6%	15.1%
Suspended Sentence	2.5%	4.2%
Immediate Custody	2.7%	9.9%
Total	297,938	948,382

Source: *Statistics on Women and the Criminal Justice System 2011*, Ministry of Justice, 2012

In respect of the sentencing of women, one question is to ask whether they are sentenced more leniently or harshly. Another issue is to consider the differential impact of sentences on men and women. Answers reveal that issues of justice are hard to resolve and come down to whether it should be the offender or the offence that provides the primary focus when determining sentence. It may well be reasonable for sentencers to refrain from sending women to prison to avoid adverse effects on their children, but this is scarcely fair on fathers and their families.

▶ Socio-economic status

The effects of both gender and ethnicity may also be related to the socio-economic circumstances of offenders. Thus, it is more likely to be women in adverse socio-economic circumstances who end up in prison and, as seen above, many black offenders are unemployed. Thus, the potential effect of socio-economic status on sentencing must be explored.

This can be seen in the situation of the unemployed, which provides a clear example of indirect and 'unintentional' discrimination. It is routinely stated in mitigation for offenders that they are in employment and that imprisonment would lead to the loss of such employment. Such employment is generally regarded as being a sign of good character (**Cavadino and Dignan 1997**) and a factor that might help promote good habits and so reduce the likelihood of future offending, and thus appeal to sentencers seeking a rehabilitative approach. On the other hand, the unemployed, having less to lose, may be more likely to end up in prison. It is also more difficult to fine unemployed offenders.

The situation of the unemployed offender contrasts starkly with that of the middle-class and particularly the white-collar offender. Many such offenders, for example, may plead in mitigation that they have much to lose – that a prison sentence would harm their innocent families and they might lose their house and their 'standing' in the community. Again, while it may be fair to take such factors into account, it may discriminate, albeit unintentionally, against offenders who have little to lose, let alone any 'standing' in the community (see, e.g., **Croall 2001; Levi 1989**). Few studies have, however, found that social status or class alone affects sentencing outcomes. Indeed, judges, concerned to be fair and seen to be fair, may be conscious of any likely partiality on the grounds of class. Thus, Mr Justice Henry, on refusing leave to appeal against a £5 million fine levied on one of the Guinness defendants, commented that:

> . . . punishments are after all intended to be punitive and the court must ensure that a man's wealth and power does not put him beyond punishment.
>
> (*The Guardian*, 3 October 1990; quoted in Croall 2001: 131)

At the same time, however, few offenders could pay a massive fine and the ability of wealthier offenders to pay both large fines and substantial compensation may make a financial penalty more likely. In addition, they are better able to employ legal representation, which may affect how they present their case. Other factors may operate to reduce the severity of sentences for white-collar offenders. The absence of direct victimisation in many white-collar offences and in some the apparent lack of intent may also lead to less severe sentences (**Croall 2001**).

On a more general level, lower-class offenders may appear in court to be less likely cases for sympathy. As indicated above, sentencers may make judgments based on the demeanour and bearing of offenders and look for evidence of character, remorse and an acceptance of the courts' authority. Decisions earlier in the criminal justice process may also demonstrate a differential approach, where the police may be more likely to caution middle-class youths – a decision which may reflect home circumstances and the employment of parents (**Cavadino and Dignan 1997**).

Taken together, consideration of the effects of ethnicity, gender and socio-economic status on sentencing decisions reveals how difficult it is to determine whether any discrimination exists on the part of sentencers. Nevertheless, at the end of the criminal justice process there are differences in the proportions of some groups of offenders who receive different sentences. These raise important questions about the calculation of 'just deserts', which will be discussed in **Chapter 12**.

11.5 Structuring sentencing decisions

Objective 5

Analyse the logic, structure and outcomes of sentencing decisions.

We can see from the above that a variety of factors directly and indirectly influence sentencing decisions, and these tend to reflect two different goals in respect of sentencing policy and practice:

- the need for consistency so that justice is even-handed and disparities are avoided (disparity occurs when similar case facts about the offence and the offender result in different sentences);
- the need for flexibility so that sentences can be matched to the individual circumstances of the case.

These concerns have generated a desire to achieve a more consistent approach to sentencing without creating too much of a straitjacket. Consistency has at least three dimensions: across place (is there consistency across different courts?), time (is the approach of the courts consistent with what they did before?) and cases (are similar facts of a case dealt with in the same way?). There have accordingly been various attempts to encourage a structured approach to sentencing decisions.

The 1990 White Paper which preceded the CJA 1991 pointed out that 'there is still too much uncertainty and little guidance about the principles which should govern sentencing . . . The Government is therefore proposing a new and more coherent statutory framework for sentencing' (**Home Office 1990a: 1**). The White Paper goes on to argue that 'to achieve a more coherent and comprehensive consistency of approach in sentencing, a new framework is needed for the use of custodial, community and financial penalties' (ibid.: 5). The CJA 1991 sought to provide a firm basis for such consistency. Magistrates' training has increasingly focused on a structured approach following a systematic path to the sentence, ensuring that factors are considered in the appropriate order.

Examples of the Sentencing Guidelines are shown in Figure 11.4. The structured decision-making approaches can easily be identified – and followed – by using the guidelines and the nine-step approach as set out by the Sentencing Council.

First, sentencers consider the seriousness of the offence in terms of harm and culpability, taking account of the guidelines, to locate the offence with its starting point. A selection of ranges of seriousness are given, all based on someone with no previous convictions who had pleaded not guilty. Second, they consider any aggravating or mitigating factors of the offence, some of which are listed in the guidelines, including any previous convictions of the defendant, whether the offence was committed on bail or was more serious by having a racially motivated element. A provisional sentencing decision is thereby reached. The third stage is to consider whether there is any mitigation in favour of the defendant, such as remorse, and to consider a reduction if the offender has pleaded guilty. The next stage requires consideration of any ancillary order such as costs or compensation. Then the final sentence can be decided upon, and reasons formulated.

▶ Sentencing Council

The introduction of bodies such as guidelines councils and sentencing commissions have been set up to achieve a number of aims: consistency in sentencing decisions, developing a policy framework in an expert setting, providing a barrier to populist political intervention or public opinion, and incorporating resource constraints.

The use of sentencing commissions has been popular in some states in the United States and Figure 11.5 shows the Minnesota sentencing grid to show how sentences are arrived at in that state. The two axes of the grid represent the main factors of seriousness of offence and the offender's previous criminal history.

The bold line represents the in/out, or custody or not, presumption set out by the sentencing commission. Below the line incarceration is presumed; above it the judge may substitute a community penalty. But if they decide to give a custodial sentence above or below the line, the range of sentences is set out for all categories of crime except for first-degree murder.

The Sentencing Commission in Minnesota ranked felony level offences into 11 severity levels, ranging from low (Severity Level I) to high (Severity Level XI). The criminal history index measures the offender's prior record and consists of four measures involving a weighted measure of:

- prior felony sentences;
- prior **misdemeanour** sentences;

Domestic or dwelling house burglary is a triable either way offence.

Sentencing

- Maximum when tried summarily: Level 5 fine and/or 26 weeks' custody
- Maximum when tried on indictment: 14 years' custody (Theft Act 1968)
- Offence range: Community order – 6 years' custody
- Provision for repeat offenders:

    Where sentencing an offender for a qualifying third domestic burglary, the Court must apply Section 111 of the Powers of the Criminal Courts (Sentencing) Act 2000 and impose a custodial term of at least three years, unless it is satisfied that there are particular circumstances which relate to any of the offences or to the offender which would make it unjust to do so.

STEP ONE
Determining the offence category

The court should determine the offence category using the table below.

Category 1	Greater harm **and** higher culpability
Category 2	Greater harm **and** lower culpability **or** lesser harm **and** higher culpability
Category 3	Lesser harm **and** lower culpability

The court should determine culpability and harm caused or intended, by reference **only** to the factors below, which comprise the principal factual elements of the offence. Where an offence does not fall squarely into a category, individual factors may require a degree of weighting before making an overall assessment and determining the appropriate offence category.

Factors indicating greater harm	Factors indicating higher culpability
Theft of/damage to property causing a significant degree of loss to the victim (whether economic, sentimental or personal value)	Victim or premises deliberately targeted (for example, due to vulnerability or hostility based on disability, race, sexual orientation)
Soiling, ransacking or vandalism of property	A significant degree of planning or organisation
Occupier at home (or returns home) while offender present	Knife or other weapon carried (where not charged separately)
Trauma to the victim, beyond the normal inevitable consequence of int rusion and theft	Equipped for burglary (for example, implements carried and/or use of vehicle)
Violence used or threatened against victim	Member of a group or gang
Context of general public disorder	**Factors indicating lower culpability**
Factors indicating lesser harm	Offence committed on impulse, with limited intrusion into property
Nothing stolen or only property of very low value to the victim (whether economic, sentimental or personal)	Offender exploited by others
Limited damage or disturbance to property	Mental disorder or learning disability, where linked to the commission of the offence

Figure 11.4 Burglary Offences Definitive Guideline for Domestic Burglary which is an offence under the Theft Act 1968 (s 9)

Source: Burglary Offences Definitive Guideline, Sentencing Council

STEP TWO
Starting point and category range

Having determined the category, the court should use the corresponding starting points to reach a sentence within the category range below. The starting point applies to all offenders irrespective of plea or previous convictions.

Where the defendant is dependant on or has a propensity to misuse drugs and there is sufficient prospect of success, a community order with a drug rehabilitation requirement under section 209 of the Criminal Justice Act 2003 may be a proper alternative to a short or moderate custodial sentence.

A case of particular gravity, reflected by multiple features of culpability or harm in step 1, could merit upward adjustment from the starting point before further adjustment for aggravating or mitigating features, set out below.

Offence Category	Starting Point (*Applicable to all offenders*)	Category Range (*Applicable to all offenders*)
Category 1	3 years' custody	2–6 years' custody
Category 2	1 year's custody	High level community order – 2 years' custody
Category 3	High Level Community Order	Low level community order – 26 weeks' custody

The table below contains a **non-exhaustive** list of additional factual elements providing the context of the offence and factors relating to the offender. Identify whether any combination of these, or other relevant factors, should result in an upward or downward adjustment from the starting point. **In particular, relevant recent convictions are likely to result in an upward adjustment**. In some cases, having considered these factors, it may be appropriate to move outside the identified category range.

When sentencing **category 2 or 3** offences, the court should also consider the custody threshold as follows:

- has the custody threshold been passed?
- if so, is it unavoidable that a custodial sentence

Factors increasing seriousness	Factors reducing seriousness or reflecting personal mitigation
Statutory aggravating factors:	Offender has made voluntary reparation to the victim
Previous convictions, having regard to a) the nature of the offence to which the conviction relates and its relevance to the current offence; and b) the time that has elapsed since the conviction*	Subordinate role in a group or gang
	No previous convictions **or** no relevant/recent convictions
Offence committed whilst on bail	Remorse
Other aggravating factors include:	Good character and/or exemplary conduct
Child at home (or returns home) when offence committed	Determination, and/or demonstration of steps taken to address addiction or offending behaviour
Offence committed at night	Serious medical conditions requiring urgent, intensive or long-term treatment
Gratuitous degradation of the victim	
Any steps taken to prevent the victim reporting the incident or obtaining assistance and/or from assisting or supporting the prosecution	Age and/or lack of maturity where it affects the responsibility of the offender
Victim compelled to leave their home (in particular victims of domestic violence)	Lapse of time since the offence where this is not the fault of the offender
Established evidence of community impact	Mental disorder or learning disability, where not linked to the commission of the offence
Commission of offence whilst under the influence of alcohol or drugs	Sole or primary carer for dependent relatives
Failure to comply with current court orders	
Offence committed whilst on licence	
Offences Taken Into Consideration (TICs)	

Figure 11.4 (*cont'd*)

STEP THREE

Consider any factors which indicate a reduction, such as assistance to the prosecution

The court should take into account sections 73 and 74 of the Serious Organised Crime and Police Act 2005 (assistance by defendants: reduction or review of sentence) and any other rule of law by virtue of which an offender may receive a discounted sentence in consequence of assistance given (or offered) to the prosecutor or investigator.

STEP FOUR

Reduction for guilty pleas

The court should take account of any potential reduction for a guilty plea in accordance with section 144 of the Criminal Justice Act 2003 and the *Guilty Plea* guideline.

Where a minimum mandatory sentence is imposed under section 111 Powers of Criminal Courts (Sentencing) Act, the discount for an early guilty plea must not exceed 20 per cent.

STEP FIVE

Dangerousness

A burglary offence under section 9 Theft Act 1986 is a serious specified offence within the meaning of chapter 5 of the Criminal Justice Act 2003 if it was committed with the intent to (a) inflict grievous bodily harm on a person, or (b) do unlawful damage to a building or anything in it. The court should consider whether having regard to the criteria contained in that chapter it would be appropriate to award imprisonment for public protection or an extended sentence. Where offenders meet the dangerousness criteria, the notional determinate sentence should be used as the basis for the setting of a minimum term.

STEP SIX

Totality principle

If sentencing an offender for more than one offence, or where the offender is already serving a sentence, consider whether the total sentence is just and proportionate to the offending behaviour.

STEP SEVEN

Compensation and ancillary orders

In all cases, courts should consider whether to make compensation and/or other ancillary orders.

STEP EIGHT

Reasons

Section 174 of the Criminal Justice Act 2003 imposes a duty to give reasons for, and explain the effect of, the sentence.

STEP NINE

Consideration for remand time

Sentencers should take into consideration any remand time served in relation to the final sentence at this final step. The court should consider whether to give credit for time spent on remand in custody or on bail in accordance with sections 240 and 240A of the Criminal Justice Act 2003.

Figure 11.4 (*cont'd*)

IV. SENTENCING GUIDELINES GRID
Presumptive Sentence Lengths in Months

Italicized numbers within the grid denote the range within which a judge may sentence without the sentence being deemed a departure. Offenders with non-imprisonment felony sentences are subject to jail time according to law.

SEVERITY LEVEL OF CONVICTION OFFENSE (Common offenses listed in italics)		CRIMINAL HISTORY SCORE						
		0	1	2	3	4	5	6 or more
Murder, 2nd Degree (intentional murder; drive-by-shootings)	XI	306 *261-367*	326 *278-391*	346 *295-415*	366 *312-439*	386 *329-463*	406 *346-480²*	426 *363-480²*
Murder, 3rd Degree Murder, 2nd Degree (unintentional murder)	X	150 *128-180*	165 *141-198*	180 *153-216*	195 *166-234*	210 *179-252*	225 *192-270*	240 *204-288*
Assault, 1st Degree Controlled Substance Crime, 1st Degree	IX	86 *74-103*	98 *84-117*	110 *94-132*	122 *104-146*	134 *114-160*	146 *125-175*	158 *135-189*
Aggravated Robbery, 1st Degree Controlled Substance Crime, 2nd Degree	VIII	48 *41-57*	58 *50-69*	68 *58-81*	78 *67-93*	88 *75-105*	98 *84-117*	108 *92-129*
Felony DWI	VII	36	42	48	54 *46-64*	60 *51-72*	66 *57-79*	72 *62-84²*
Controlled Substance Crime, 3rd Degree	VI	21	27	33	39 *34-46*	45 *39-54*	51 *44-61*	57 *49-68*
Residential Burglary Simple Robbery	V	18	23	28	33 *29-39*	38 *33-45*	43 *37-51*	48 *41-57*
Nonresidential Burglary	IV	12¹	15	18	21	24 *21-28*	27 *23-32*	30 *26-36*
Theft Crimes (Over $5,000)	III	12¹	13	15	17	19 *17-22*	21 *18-25*	23 *20-27*
Theft Crimes ($5,000 or less) Check Forgery ($251–$2,500)	II	12¹	12¹	13	15	17	19	21 *18-25*
Sale of Simulated Controlled Substance	I	12¹	12¹	12¹	13	15	17	19 *17-22*

☐ Presumptive commitment to state imprisonment. First-degree murder has a mandatory life sentence and is excluded from the guidelines by law. See Guidelines Section II.E., Mandatory Sentences, for policy regarding those sentences controlled by law.

▨ Presumptive stayed sentence; at the discretion of the judge, up to a year in jail and/or other non-jail sanctions can be imposed as conditions of probation. However, certain offenses in this section of the grid always carry a presumptive commitment to state prison. See, Guidelines Sections II.C. Presumptive Sentence and II.E. Mandatory Sentences.

¹One year and one day

²M.S. § 244.09 requires the Sentencing Guidelines to provide a range for sentences which are presumptive commitment to state imprisonment of 15% lower and 20% higher than the fixed duration displayed, provided that the minimum sentence is not less than one year and one day and the maximum sentence is not more than the statutory maximum. See, Guidelines Sections II.H. Presumptive Sentence Durations that Exceed the Statutory Maximum Sentence and II.I. Sentence Ranges for Presumptive Commitment Offenses in Shaded Areas of Grids.

Effective August 1, 2008

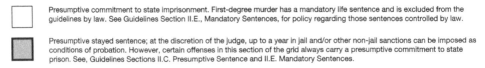

Figure 11.5 Minnesota sentencing grid

- prior serious juvenile record; and
- 'custody status' which indicates if the offender was under supervision when the current offence occurred.

The Minnesota Sentencing Guidelines are updated regularly and a commentary added. The latest version is found in the *Minnesota Sentencing Guidelines and Commentary: 1 August 2013:*

> The presumptive sentence for any offender convicted of a felony committed on or after May 1, 1980, is determined by locating the appropriate cell of the Sentencing Guidelines Grids. The grids represent the two dimensions most important in current sentencing and releasing decisions – offense severity and criminal history.
>
> . . .
>
> The offense of conviction determines the appropriate severity level on the vertical axis of the appropriate grid. The offender's criminal history score, computed according to section B above, determines the appropriate location on the horizontal axis of the appropriate grid. The presumptive fixed sentence for a felony conviction is found in the Sentencing Guidelines Grid cell at the intersection of the column defined by the criminal history score and the row defined by the offense severity level. The offenses within the Sentencing Guidelines Grids are presumptive with respect to the duration.
>
> . . .
>
> Criminal History: A criminal history index constitutes the horizontal axis of the Sentencing Guidelines Grids. The criminal history index is comprised of the following items: (1) prior **felony** record; (2) custody status at the time of the offense; (3) prior **misdemeanor** and gross misdemeanor record; and (4) prior juvenile record for young adult felons.
>
> The classification of prior offenses as petty misdemeanors, misdemeanors, gross misdemeanors, or felonies is determined on the basis of current Minnesota offense definitions and sentencing policies . . .

Sentencing commissions are used in several US states as well as for sentencing in the federal courts. Michael Tonry, writing for the National Institute of Justice, commented:

> The Minnesota and Washington experiences suggest that the combination of sentencing commissions and presumptive guidelines is a viable approach for achieving consistent and coherent jurisdiction-wide sentencing policies. However, the experiences in Maine, New York, Pennsylvania, and South Carolina counsel that the sentencing commission approach won't necessarily succeed. Six jurisdictions are too few to support any but the most tentative generalizations about success and failure. Still, it is clear that most local legal and political cultures shape the environments in which the commissions work.

Minnesota and Washington, for example, are both relatively homogeneous states with reform traditions. In neither state were criminal justice issues highly politicized. New York and Pennsylvania, by contrast, are heterogeneous states in which criminal justice issues are highly politicized and law-and-order sentiment is powerful. In some states, especially where trial judges are elected, judges may vigorously resist efforts to limit their discretion. Perhaps the only generalization that can be offered concerning political and legal culture is that the potential and the effectiveness of a sentencing commission will depend on how it addresses and accommodates constraints imposed by the local culture.

(Tonry 1987: 59)

It seems, therefore, that the legal and political culture of the jurisdiction contributes to the success or failure of such an approach. This point was reflected in the United Kingdom in the consultation leading up to the CJA 1991, when the idea of a sentencing council was rejected. John Patten, then a junior minister at the Home Office in 1991, identified the traditions of the criminal justice system as a reason why he thought the idea of a sentencing council would not work in England and Wales. In a letter to *The Times*, he wrote:

Sentencing councils are the most fashionable nostrum these days for how much that advice (on sentencing) might be formalised. There seems to be almost as many recipes as there are cooks, producing councils, commissions or whatever; they vary in how much guidance or instruction should be given to the courts on sentencing and by whom it should be given.

At the end of this road stands Minnesota in the United States. There, I am told, the local sentencing commission has produced tight numerical guidelines for prison sentences, which have taken the form of a 'sentencing grid'. Two axes determine the presumptive sentence. Along one side are the offence categories and along the other categories of 'criminal history'. So the ultimate sentence really depends on where the points along each axis occupied by the offender meet in the middle . . .

Those who ponder sentencing councils must not ignore that which is already in place, potentially providing so much of what they want to see, but in a way that works with the *grain of the criminal justice traditions* in this country. For there is a fast developing framework for judges and magistrates.

In no particular order, first, there is the coherent statutory framework for sentencing in the new criminal justice bill, as we do not think that Parliament has said enough about the principles that govern sentencing decisions. Second, there is the power for the Attorney-General to refer cases to the Court of Appeal, where sentences are allegedly over-lenient. Third, the powerful effect of guideline judgments with the Court of Appeal is self-evident. Last, the work of the Judicial Studies Board seems to be of ever-increasing importance in training and guiding the sentencers in their work.

(*The Times*, 5 February 1991; emphasis added)

The New Labour Government in England and Wales on coming to power established two sentencing bodies to provide advice and guidance: the Sentencing Advisory Panel and the Sentencing Guidelines Council.

The Sentencing Advisory Panel (SAP) was an independent public body set up by the Crime and Disorder Act 1998. It had 14 members and the inaugural chair was Professor Martin Wasik. It initially provided advice direct to the Court of Appeal. The prime aim was to achieve consistency in sentencing but other policy goals gradually became apparent such as reducing the use of custody.

In Scotland, where sentencing has been characterised by a very strong tradition of judicial discretion and the Court of Appeal has not, unlike the situation in England and Wales, issued guideline judgments, a Sentencing Commission, headed by Lord MacLean, was set up. This examined: the scope to improve consistency of sentencing; the effectiveness of sentences in reducing reoffending; the arrangements for early release from prison and supervision of short-term prisoners on their release; and the basis on which fines are determined. Its work completed it was wound up although the Scottish Government has suggested a new sentencing council.

The Criminal Justice Act 2003 introduced the Sentencing Guidelines Council. The SAP submitted its advice to the new body. The review by and recommendations of SAP have covered specific offences such as murder, burglary, sexual, racial and drug-related offences, manslaughter by provocation and it has considered specific sentencing factors such as the discount for a guilty plea and principles determining seriousness.

The Coroners and Justice Act 2009 duly replaced the SAP and the SGC with a single body, the Sentencing Council. Its president in 2012 is the aptly named Lord Judge, and the chairman is the Lord Justice Leveson (the man whose name has become synonymous with the investigation into the 2011 *News of the World* phone hacking scandal). It largely continues the work of the SAP and SGC but within a more unified structure. The Sentencing Council's job is to consult on and set sentencing guidelines, conduct research and analysis, and maintain public confidence in the criminal justice system.

The Coroners and Justice Act 2009 places a number of obligations on the Council with regard to monitoring and data analysis. To fulfil these statutory obligations the Council must be responsible for its own independent statistical analysis, impact assessments and research to support its functions.

In 2012, the Sentencing Council listing its research and analysis priorities as:

* Crown Court Sentencing Survey – collecting and analysing information on factors taken into account when sentencing;
* Magistrates' courts sentencing data – the Council will consider how best it might collect information from magistrates' courts on the factors taken into account when sentencing;
* Producing resource assessment documents and analysis and research bulletins;
* Testing the effect of proposed changes to guidelines.

The Sentencing Council is also concerned to increase the quantity and quality of information and engagement available to the public on sentencing, in order to raise public confidence in sentencing. It is especially concerned to respond to those who are directly affected by sentencing, particularly as victims and witnesses. Methods for achieving this include:

- holding public consultations;
- developing its website;
- working with victims organisations;
- utilising traditional and social media to help explain sentencing to the public;
- supporting local projects to get the public more engaged with the sentencing process.

One means of encouraging members of the public to engage with sentencing set up by the Sentencing Council is via an online game called 'You be the Judge'. It is operated by the Ministry of Justice on behalf of the Council and consists of a virtual court room in which real-life cases are re-enacted by actors, and visitors to the site can participate by hearing the evidence, considering the sentences available, and finally impose their own sentence, then see how it compared to the original sentence that was handed down. It has proved very popular with law students in particular.

The Sentencing Council is there to offer advice to judges and magistrates where there are ambiguities or conflicting principles, and set out the relevant aggravating and mitigating factors established by Court of Appeal Guideline cases to identify different levels of seriousness within an offence. Essentially the perennial difficulty remains – a multitude of objectives and the conflict between the desire to individualise cases, taking account of personal circumstances, character and history, always unique to the offender, and the desire to have a consistent approach so that similar cases are dealt with in the same way, in the interests of fairness, just deserts and due process.

Conclusion

This chapter has indicated the many issues involved in sentencing decisions. In the first place, the different theories of punishment embody the different aims which sentencers may take into account. The changes in range and detail of sentences available to the court reflect these different aims, and many sentences may be directed to achieve a combination of these aims. Before the CJA 1991 and other reforms attempted to impose greater consistency in sentencing policy, sentencers could in effect choose between a range of different sentences in what has been described as a 'cafeteria' approach (**Ashworth 1989**). The tradition of judicial independence and the tendency of both magistrates and judges to judge each case on its merits may produce the disparities which have caused so much concern. As **Ashworth (1994b: 852)** comments: 'unstructured discretion leaves leeway to the personal preferences of the judge, and if the concept of the "rule of law" has any stable meaning, it must exclude such preferences'.

As we have seen, therefore, there have been a variety of attempts to encourage a more consistent approach to sentencing, including the use of statutory criteria, voluntary and now mandatory use of guidelines and Court of Appeal guideline cases. The CJA 2003 introduced a more coherent approach by identifying sentencing objectives and establishing the Sentencing Guidelines Council, and, in contrast to the CJA 1991, reflected a changing emphasis on the different aims of sentences. The Coroners and Justice Act 2009 replaced the SAP and the SGC with the Sentencing Council in the interests of establishing a clearer purpose and greater consistency and transparency in sentencing decisions.

Review questions

1. Contrast the six major theories of punishment in terms of the following:

   a. What do they seek to achieve?

   b. Which are concerned primarily with the impact of the sentence on the offender before the court? Which are concerned with the impact on the public at large?

   c. Which aim to reduce crime in the future?

   d. If the judge or magistrates wish to achieve two objectives with the same sentence, which of the theories are compatible and which are not?

2. Consider the following statements, which are quotations from judges who are describing their approach to sentencing dwelling-house burglars (Davies and Tyrer: Research with Crown Court Judges: unpublished). Identify the sentencing objectives that are illustrated in the judges' remarks about sentencing burglars. Which quote is an example of:

   - retribution

   - denunciation

   - deterrent (there are two examples below)

   - incapacitation?

   a. 'I think all these are instances of one thing, which is giving expression to society's reaction to this particular crime . . . whether or not it actually works in a particular way.'

   b. 'While he is inside he can't do it to anybody else.'

   c. 'I believe the primary purpose for this kind of offence . . . is to show that there is a risk of something unpleasant happening to you if you commit this type of offence.'

   d. 'The reason . . . is because everyone needs to know that those who invade the privacy of others in order to steal their property – an all too prevalent offence in our area nowadays – must know that, when they are brought to book, they will be properly punished.'

   e. 'If we were not sending domestic burglars to prison, I would be quite satisfied in my mind that there would be many more . . . burglaries committed . . . you can see it in a totally different context if you look at the fact that it is generally known that if you exceed the speed limit by more than 30 miles an hour you are in danger of being disqualified . . . A fear of the consequences I am certain is a motivating factor in a significant number of peoples' minds.'

3. What are the main sentences available to the court? How can they be related to each of the major aims?

4. List the major constraints and influences which will determine the way the sentencers reach a sentencing decision. Which factors are likely to produce disparity?

5. Describe and evaluate the differing attempts to achieve a more structured approach to sentencing. How is this achieved in England and Wales?

6. The term 'offender-instrumental' sentencing strategies encompasses three sentencing theories (**set out in section 11.1 of this chapter**). Name the three theories concerned with the impact of a sentence on the future criminal behaviour of the offender.

7. What is meant by the following terms: culpability, proportionality and tariff? What sentencing theory uses these concepts?

8. In the following three extracts from Court of Appeal decisions on sentencing cases, identify the aims of sentencing (i.e. an example of a deterrent statement) that are referred to by the court. Identify the statement and indicate which theory it represents.

Extract 1

Kiosk theft justifies jail: *Regina* v. *Decino*

The offence of theft of money from a telephone kiosk was capable of being so serious that only a custodial sentence could be justified, within the terms of section 1(2)(a) of the Criminal Justice Act 1991.

The Court of Appeal (Lord Justice Beldam, Mr Justice Connell and Mrs Justice Ebsworth) so held on April 21 when allowing an appeal by Nicholas Decino against a sentence of 12 months' imprisonment imposed on January 8, 1993 by Mr Recorder Williams at Cardiff Crown Court, following his conviction on December 8, 1992 at West Berkshire Magistrates' Court of theft of £40.20 from a telephone kiosk.

For that offence he was sentenced to two months, and suspended sentences totalling ten months for burglary and possession of a controlled drug were activated consecutively.

The sentences were made concurrent, reducing the total to ten months.

LORD JUSTICE BELDAM said that this was the kind of offence which was capable of depriving members of the public of the use of the public telephone which, to many people, was a lifeline. Of necessity telephone boxes were left unprotected. It was a matter of public policy to deter thefts from such boxes.

There was evidence that the appellant and two other young men provided themselves with the necessary tools and went on a deliberate expedition to rob telephone boxes of their contents.

In their Lordships' view it was, as the recorder has said, an offence capable of being so serious that only a sentence of custody could be justified for it.

(*Source*: 'Kiosk theft justifies jail', *The Times*, 10 May 1993, Times Newspapers Ltd., © NI Syndication Limited, 1993)

Extract 2

Sentencing in cases of incest: *Regina* v. *Meggs*

(Before Lord Lane, Lord Chief Justice, Mr Justice Kennedy and
Mr Justice Hutchinson. [Judgment February 21])

Cases of incest varied so enormously the one from the other that it was very difficult to derive any assistance from the previous instances which had appeared before the Court of Appeal.

The Lord Chief Justice so stated when giving the judgment of the court on an appeal by Eric William Meggs, aged 50, against prison sentences totalling 10 years passed at the Central Criminal Court by Sir James Miskin, QC, the Recorder of London, on pleas of guilty to specimen counts of incest with two of his daughters, extending, in the case of the elder, for more than 22 years. Sentence of three years on one count, which had been made **consecutive**, was ordered to run concurrent with the other sentences, totalling 7½ years.

Mr William Clegg, assigned by the Registrar of Criminal Appeals for the appellant.

THE LORD CHIEF JUSTICE said that, having made the elder girl pregnant twice the appellant caused her to have abortions. For a time they had lived as a married couple which, according to Mr Clegg, was what the neighbours thought they were.

The elder daughter became pregnant by her boy friend but the appellant did not desist from having sexual intercourse with her throughout.

The appellant, throughout interviews with the police, denied that anything improper had occurred.

Such cases varied so enormously from one to the other that it was very difficult to derive any assistance from the previous instances which had appeared before the court.

The court had to mark its disapproval and the disapproval of the community of such behaviour. It had to endeavour to deter other men from behaving in such a way.

It had to punish the appellant for using his two daughters, in particular his elder daughter, simply as a chattel to satisfy his own sexual appetite, regardless of the damage he might do to her welfare and happiness and, perhaps most important of all, her ability to enjoy a happy married life herself.

Mr Clegg submitted that insufficient regard was given to the plea of guilty and that overall the totality was too great despite the horrifying features of the case.

He pointed out that the appellant was disowned by his family, which was not surprising, but the effect was that he received no visits and was serving his sentence isolated to a great extent from his fellow prisoners.

They were all matters to be taken into account and their Lordships had concluded that Mr Clegg was correct in stating that the totality was too high.

There was nothing wrong with the individual sentences but their Lordships were concerned with the overall total and the proper course was to order that the sentence on a count ordered to run consecutively should, instead, run concurrent, so that the sentence was reduced by three years.

(*Source*: 'Sentencing in cases of incest', *The Times*, 22 February 1989, Times Newspapers Ltd., © NI Syndication Limited, 1989)

Extract 3

Punishment for perjury: Regina v. Knight (Colin)

(Before Mr Justice McCowan and Mr Justice Leggatt.
[Judgment delivered 26 January])

Punishment for **perjury** had to be condign and commensurate with the gravity of the offence to prevent conviction of another for which the perjury was committed. The Court of Appeal so stated in dismissing an appeal by Colin Charles Knight, aged 32, against a three-year prison sentence passed at the Central Criminal Court by Sir James Miskin, QC, Recorder of London on a plea of guilty to perjury in that, being lawfully sworn as a witness on the trial of a man called Tobin at the Central Criminal Court, the appellant knowingly falsely described a man who jumped down from a crane.

Mr C Y Nutt, assigned by the Registrar of Criminal Appeals, for the appellant.

MR JUSTICE LEGGATT said that the crane was driven by Tobin into the back of a security van to gain access to it by a group of professional armed robbers. The jury disagreed at his first trial.

At the second trial the appellant, not called at the first trial, gave perjured evidence in saying that he had been in the area at the time of the robbery and described a man different from Tobin getting down from the crane. In the event Tobin was convicted.

In mitigation of the appellant's offence it was suggested that there had been some inducement and threat by an intermediary.

In passing sentence on the appellant, Sir James Miskin had said that armed robbery, planned with exquisite skill by intelligent, determined men for high profit, was one of the most serious crimes known to the courts and there was a great deal too much of it. Those who intentionally gave false testimony on behalf of such men did so intending to mislead the jury into returning a verdict contrary to true justice and the evidence.

Not having seen one whiff of what had happened and for reward the appellant had entered the witness box and told a whole string of purposive lies. Account was taken of the plea of guilty and good character and implicit show of steel on the part of the intermediary. However, perjury was difficult enough to detect and much more difficult to prove. When it occurred it demanded instant prison.

Three years was imposed so that the appellant might be seen to be punished and, even more importantly, so that every single person in this age who contemplated events like giving false evidence in any case, let alone a serious one, or was minded to tamper with a jury, might know it would always be met by immediate, condign punishment.

Their Lordships agreed with every word of the judge in sentencing and, in particular, that punishment had to be condign. The purpose of the appellant's perjury was to avoid conviction for a grave offence. The punishment had to be commensurate with the gravity of that offence. The maximum penalty was seven years' imprisonment. The judge having made such allowance as could have been made for the appellant's antecedents and plea of guilty, the sentence was unimpeachable. The appeal was dismissed.

(*Source*: 'Punishment for perjury', *The Times*, 4 February 1984, Times Newspapers Ltd., © NI Syndication Limited, 1984)

Discussion questions

1. Identify recent sentences that have been reported in the press and consider the stated or apparent objectives of the judge in the sentence imposed (the objectives of sentencing are set out on pages 393–404).

2. Is controlling the future behaviour of the offender more important than punishing for the harm caused by a past offence?

3. How would you explain the recent growth in the use of Suspended Sentence Orders since 2005?

Further reading

Ashworth A (2007) 'Sentencing', in Maguire M, Morgan R and Reiner R (eds) *The Oxford Handbook of Criminology* (4th edn), Oxford University Press: Oxford

Ashworth A (2010) *Sentencing and Criminal Justice (Law in Context)* (5th edn), Cambridge University Press: Cambridge

Easton S and Piper S (2008) *Sentencing and Punishment: the Quest for Justice* (2nd edn), Oxford University Press: Oxford

Mair G, Cavadino P and Dignan J (2013) *The Penal System: An Introduction* (5th edn), Sage: London

Ministry of Justice (2013) *Story of the Prison Population: 1993–2012 England and Wales*, Ministry of Justice: London

Wasik M (2001) *Emmins on Sentencing* (4th edn), Oxford University Press: Oxford

Weblinks

Magistrates' Courts Sentencing Guidelines: **www.sentencing-guidelines.gov.uk/docs/ magistrates_court_sentencing_guidelines_update.pdf**

Ministry of Justice: **www.gov.uk/government/organisations/ministry-of-justice/about**

Criminal Justice Statistics: **www.gov.uk/government/uploads/system/uploads/ attachment_data/file/220090/criminal-justice-stats-sept-2012.pdf**

Sentencing Council: **sentencingcouncil.judiciary.gov.uk/index.htm**

You be the Judge **ybtj.justice.gov.uk/**

Chapter 12

Punishment philosophies and penal paradigms

Key statistics

- Fines are the most common sentence passed at court, accounting for around two-thirds of all sentences handed out by the criminal courts (66.5% in the 12 months ending September 2012)
- Of the 1.23 million offenders sentenced during the 12 months ending September 2012, there were 97,500 persons sentenced to immediate custody; 153,900 people (or 12.5% of those sentenced) were given a Community Sentence; and, 44,400

people (or 3.6% of those sentenced) were given a Suspended Sentence Order

- At the end of March 2013, the prison population stood at 83,842, the lowest recorded since December 2010
- The reduction in the number of juveniles who are first time entrants is down 71.5% between September 2007 and September 2012
- The riots of August 2011 had an immediate impact of around 900 on the prison population
- At the end of June 2013, almost half of the total prison population constituted of individuals aged 25 to 39; a record high level for the 60 and over age group was recorded in the same period, accounting for 4% of the total prison population

Introduction

We saw in **Chapter 11** that policy makers, judges and magistrates have sought to find a balance between the six major theories of sentencing, and the twenty-first century has seen a change in the emphasis given to these goals in the Criminal Justice Act 2003. This chapter will focus on these shifting penal paradigms, that is, ways of thinking about the causes and consequences of crime and how we should respond to them. The beginning of the twentieth century witnessed a growth in what was seen as a modern or progressive approach which believed that punishment could be replaced with treatment and welfare stratagems to cure criminals through a rehabilitative approach. This was to give way to the back-to-justice approach of the late 1960s as disenchantment with the rehabilitative model set in.

This chapter will start by looking at the history of penal reforms in terms of innovations in the form of new sentences and institutions and the abolition of certain other types of sanctions. It will then consider the ways of thinking about punishment, the penal paradigms, that influenced sentencing reforms and penal practice in the twentieth and into the twenty-first century. First, we will trace the influence of rehabilitative penal objectives, and then explore the justice approach based on 'just deserts' ideas of punishment and fairness. The impact of imprisonment on offenders will be considered and we will discuss whether imprisonment works and whether it can deter. Finally, we will examine the question that arises at the sentencing stage, namely who is sentencing for?

12.1 Sentencing trends and reforms in the twentieth and twenty-first century

Objective 1

Outline the main sentencing trends and reforms in the twentieth and twenty-first century

By the beginning of the twentieth century the prison was the dominant penal sanction. Transportation had been formally abolished in 1867 and the number of offences that warranted the death penalty had been reduced to four (arson in Her Majesty's Dockyards, treason, piracy and murder) and it was primarily used for murder. The Royal Commission on Capital Punishment (1949–53) recorded that for the decade 1900 to 1909, 257 men and 27 women were sentenced to hang; 103 of the men and 22 of the women were reprieved. In contrast, in one year alone (in 1900), there were 149,397 offenders of both sexes and of all ages given a custodial sentence by the courts. By 1910 the number had risen to 179,397, whereas the number of adult and younger offenders, both male and female, given a custodial sentence in 2007 was 95,206.

The term 'custody' covers a variety of sentences given different names over the century, which includes for adults:

> imprisonment, life sentence, corrective training (1949/67), preventive detention (1908/67), extended sentences (1967/91), partially suspended sentence (1982/92), imprisonment for public protection (IPP 2005/12), extended sentence for public protection (EPP 2005/12), and extended sentences (2012).

and for younger offenders:

> borstal training (1908/83), those children sentenced under s 53(1) and s 53(2) of the Children and Young Offenders Act 1933 for murder and grave offences (1933 onwards), approved school order (1933/70), detention centre order (1953/88), youth custody order (1983/8), detention in a young offender institution (1988 onwards), secure training order (1998 onwards), detention and training order (1998 onwards), detention for public protection (2005), extended sentence of detention (2005), detention for life.

Over the twentieth century, the absolute and relative use of custody by the courts for sentencing declined:

> In 1894, the total number of convicted criminals sent to prison in that year was 156,466, which represented 526 persons per 100,000 of population . . . In 1994, the number given an immediate custodial sentence was 60,800 . . . representing 118 persons per 100,000 of population.
>
> (Davies *et al.* 1996: 75)

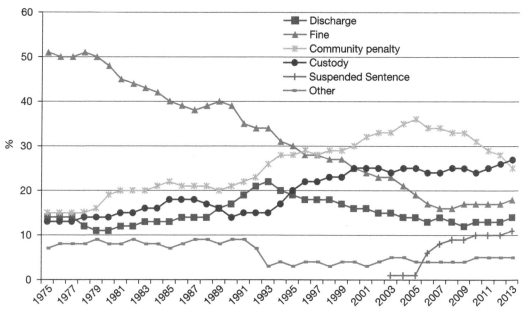

Figure 12.1 Sentencing Patterns 1975 to 2013

Source: Compiled from Annual Sentencing Statistics from 1975 to Sentencing Statistics 2013 England and Wales, Ministry of Justice Statistics Bulletin, November 2013; Tables 1.3, 1.4, 1.5 and 4.5

By 2009, the prison rate in England and Wales was 152 prisoners per 100,000 members of the population, a rate that is four times less than 100 years ago. Even though there has been an increase in use of custodial sentences since 1993, the trend across the last century has been to rely less on custody and to make greater use of fines and community sentences and more recently, since 2005, of the suspended sentence order (see Figure 12.1). The decline in the use of custody began during the 1914/18 war. By 1920 the number sent to custody had fallen to 35,439. After the 1939/45 war the numbers sentenced to custody began to rise again and they rose from a total number sentenced to custody of 33,875 in 1950 to a high of 83,300 by 1985. The trend from 1986 to 1993 was downwards, with 58,400 sentenced by the courts to immediate custody in 1993, since when it has risen to 102,698 in 2011 (*Criminal Justice Statistics, Quarterly Update to December 2011*, Ministry of Justice Statistics bulletin, May 2012).

The use of physical or corporal punishments was reformed and then stopped during the twentieth century. In 1908 a person under the age of 16 could no longer be executed. This was raised to 18 by the Criminal Justice Act 1948 and this reform led to one of the prolonged controversies about the death penalty when Derek Bentley was hanged in 1953 and his more culpable 16-year-old accomplice escaped the death penalty. The Criminal Justice Act 1948 also abolished hard labour, and abolished corporal punishment as a sentence of the court, although it was still allowed as a punishment within penal establishments until the Criminal

Justice Act 1967. The Murder (Abolition of the Death Penalty) Act 1965 abolished capital punishment for murder, and the last execution for murder took place in 1964. The Criminal Damage Act 1971 abolished the death penalty for arson in Her Majesty's Dockyards. The death penalty existed for the offence of high treason and piracy with violence until the Crime and Disorder Act 1998, although the last person executed for treason was William Joyce, in 1946, who made pro-German wireless broadcasts during the 1939/45 war.

The sentence most often given by the courts is the fine. Its use grew throughout the first half of the twentieth century so that by the 1970s it was used for half of all indictable offenders sentenced by the courts. Although its use has declined (see Figure 12.1) with indictable offenders since 1978, it is still the most frequently used sentence and was given in 83 per cent of summary offences in 2011 in the magistrates' courts. The reduction in the use of the fine for those convicted of indictable offences (indictable only and TEW) is one of the more dramatic shifts in usage, with over 50 per cent receiving a fine in 1977 compared to 17 per cent by 2011.

The use of community sentences has grown over the century as new types of sanctions have become available. These, with the date of introduction, include the following:

- probation (1887 and 1907);
- attendance centre orders (1948);
- community service order (1972);
- curfew orders for younger offenders (1982);
- combination orders (1991);
- curfew orders for adults (1991);
- reparation orders (2000);
- action plan orders (2000);
- drug treatment and testing orders (2000);
- referral orders (2002);
- generic community order with up to 14 possible requirements (2003);
- youth rehabilitation order (2010).

In 2011, of those sentenced for indictable offences, 29 per cent received community penalties and these were used more frequently than immediate custody, which was used for 25 per cent of those sentenced for indictable offences, although suspended sentence orders, which increased sharply in popularity when re-introduced in 2005. They straddle the divide between community sentences and custody (intermediate sanctions), were handed out in 10 per cent of indictable cases (for trends in sentencing for indictable offences, 1975–2007, see Figure 12.1).

In recent decades, there have been more efforts through sentencing to include measures that benefited victims, such as compensation orders and schemes involving reparation to victims and the community. The shift away from offender-instrumental theories was also evident as new orders were introduced to prevent offenders benefiting from their crime, as with forfeiture orders (from 1983) and confiscation orders, introduced under the Drug Trafficking Act 1986.

12.2 The era of rehabilitation

Objective 2

Describe the changing elements of the rehabilitative approach to sentencing

During the twentieth century, penal policy throughout Europe and the United States was strongly influenced by the theory of rehabilitation. This moved away from earlier emphases on retribution and deterrence which were less concerned with the causes of crime and its treatment than with the justification for and distribution of punishment. Crime was seen as an immoral act that was in need of punishment, which was justified primarily on deterrent or retributive grounds. To rehabilitationists, however, crime, like any other social problem, could be studied scientifically to establish its causes. In what came to be described as a medical model, crime was likened to an illness which could be diagnosed and treated, and, through work with individual criminals and social reform, eventually cured. Thus, from the start of the twentieth century experts from the world of medicine, the growing professions of psychiatry and social work, educational specialists and social reformers became increasingly involved in the courts and penal system. Rehabilitation offered the promise that crime could be almost eradicated by these scientific and professional approaches – an orthodoxy which dominated penal policy until the 1960s.

There were many different views on how rehabilitation could be achieved, which led to a variety of different strategies. First, the medical model stressed the need to diagnose, treat and cure criminals. This led to a growing involvement of doctors and psychiatrists in the criminal justice process, providing medical and psychiatric reports to the courts and working in prisons and other institutions. Second, others believed in the value of discipline and work, and advocated methods such as industrial and vocational training to encourage offenders to develop self-discipline and good work habits. Unlike medical and psychiatric treatment these measures aimed not to reform offenders from within but to equip them with better skills which would, it was hoped, keep them from committing crimes. Third, the growing profession of social work advocated the use of case work and counselling for offenders both inside prisons and through the work of the probation service. This led to the widespread use of pre-sentence reports outlining the circumstances of offenders, and also influenced the growth of aftercare provision for ex-prisoners. Fourth, many believed in the power of moral awakening, either through religion or, more recently, by confronting the offender with the harm they had done. Early prison regimes encouraged offenders to contemplate on their wrongdoing, and religion has always played a role in prisons. Fifth, others welcomed rehabilitative strategies as a more humane way to treat prisoners, which ameliorated the degrading and brutalising aspects of prison life. Thus penal reformers, who had for long sought to improve the conditions of prisoners and who felt that prison could make people worse, supported rehabilitative measures enthusiastically. Lastly, rehabilitation was linked to the ideas of social engineers who identified social deprivation as the root of all social problems and put their faith in growing affluence and the welfare state.

In England and Wales, the rehabilitative paradigm was officially recognised in 1895 in the report of the Home Office Departmental Committee on Prisons chaired by Herbert Gladstone (**Home Office 1895**). The committee found that 'the moral condition in which a large number of prisoners leave the prison, and the serious number of re-committals have led us to think that there is ample cause for a searching inquiry into the main features of prison life'. It went on to state, 'we start from the principle that prison treatment should have as its primary and concurrent objects deterrence and reformation', and, in what became one of the most influential statements about the aims of prison, continued that:

> . . . prison discipline and treatment should be more effectually designed to maintain, stimulate or awaken the higher susceptibilities of prisoners, to develop their moral instincts, to train them in orderly and industrial habits, and whenever possible to turn them out of prison better men and women, both physically and morally, than when they came in.
>
> (Home Office 1895: 8)

The first decade of the twentieth century saw the development of many rehabilitative policies such as the introduction of probation in 1907, of Borstal in 1908, special provision for child offenders in 1913 and new arrangements for the mentally deficient offender in 1914. Welfare officers, psychiatrists and psychologists were recruited into the Prison Service and in 1919 the prison warder was replaced by the prison officer, a title which marked a changing role. The annual reports of prison commissioners revealed a new mood in which prisons were increasingly seen not negatively, as institutions for incarcerating the bad, but positively, as institutions which could act as agencies of human change.

Although our focus here is on penal philosophy, the growth of rehabilitative policies, especially in prisons, was strongly influenced by individuals. One particularly influential individual was Alexander Paterson, who was involved in social work with the Oxford Medical Mission in Bermondsey where he also worked as an elementary school teacher. Although never chairman of the Prison Commission he was its most dominant figure and his liberal reform values were evident in penal documents from 1921 until his death in 1947. This was a period in which the approach embodied in the Gladstone Report began to crystallise into the dominant penological paradigm. Thus Lionel Fox commented that 'it was in 1921 that gusts of fresh air began to blow through the pages of the reports of the prison commissioners' (**Fox 1952**). The 1930s were characterised as an age of optimism in penal reform (**Hood 1974**).

This spirit of optimism is illustrated in extracts from Paterson's evidence to the 1931 Persistent Offenders Committee. This committee also provides a good example of how changing views about the role of prisons legitimated the participation of medical experts. Of the 68 people who gave evidence to the committee, 13 were drawn from the medical world, working within the system as medical superintendents in prisons or in psychiatric hospitals. The growing influence of the medical model and the treatment approach is confirmed in Paterson's evidence. Thus:

... The English Courts today, facing a young offender under 21 in the dock, are not concerned like their predecessors to weigh out a dose of punishment appropriate to the proved offence, but exercised rather to diagnose his condition and to prescribe the right form of training or treatment for the condition. This more thoughtful, sensible and expensive way of dealing with the young offender has inevitably resulted in a marked fall in the number of professional recidivists.

(Evidence to Persistent Offenders Committee 1931: vol. 3: 669)

The significance to rehabilitation of other measures was also noted. Thus Paterson comments:

... There has ensued in the last 25 years a whole series of changes in law and practice. The Children's Courts have been established to discover and check the potential tendency of the child offender; the probation system has emerged as a commonsense alternative to the imprisonment of the first offender of any age; the reformatories and industrial schools are no longer convict prisons for turbulent children, but take their place among other educational agencies, as special schools for the backward and the forward; the adolescent offender is sent in increasing proportion for training in a Borstal Institution rather than confinement in a prison.

(Evidence to Persistent Offenders Committee 1931: vol. 3: 669)

Paterson was well aware of some of the problems and what have come to be called the 'pains' of imprisonment and the full impact on the individual offender and their families of a period of imprisonment.

Imprisonment is to be avoided whenever possible. It is often but a clumsy piece of social surgery, tearing a man away from the social fabric of home and work and club and union that has woven round himself, causing distress to others and rendering his replacement in social and industrial life a matter of grave difficulty.

(Evidence to Persistent Offenders Committee 1931: vol. 3: 675)

He wished to abolish prisons, and replace them with other institutions which were primarily concerned with reform – thus he also wrote:

I propose to abolish all prisons.

I propose to replace the prison commission with a Board of Welfare, whose members shall under a director administer:

a. Probation and Aftercare

b. Reformatory and Industrial Schools

c. Borstal Institutions

d. Examination Clinics

e. Training Centres

f. Places of detention

There shall be no more place s called prisons.

(Evidence to Persistent Offenders Committee 1931: vol. 3: 675)

While Paterson's ambition to abolish prisons was not achieved, his thinking, and the goal of rehabilitation, was paramount in the penal approach. However, the result of rehabilitative policies may have had a surprising outcome: an increase in prison sentence lengths. One implication of rehabilitative theory is that sentence lengths should be flexible and responsive to the needs of the offender (**as we saw in Chapter 11**). From this came the argument that sentences should be indeterminate, along with the idea that offenders needed to be sent to prison for a sufficient time for treatment and training to take effect. Thus Paterson said, 'if we are concerned to train him, a few weeks in prison will be an idle pretence' (**Paterson 1927**). This was a view clearly held by those running the prison system in the inter-war years. Thus the Report of the Commissioners of Prisons for 1925/6 stated:

. . . the short sentence remains an outstanding defect in our penal system and difficulty in prison administration. Repetition on this point is not amiss.

The highest administrative and judicial authorities have taken the same view, and have drawn attention to the uselessness of the short sentence. The International Penitentiary Congress in August 1925 passed a resolution to the same effect. There is no doubt but that the prospect of prison has a strong deterrent effect on those who have never yet passed its gates; nor that, once the disgrace of imprisonment has been incurred, much of that effect has been lost. It can also be readily understood that an impediment to the development of a sound system of prison training is the presence of a number of men who only come in for a few days, and cannot therefore be taught any work other than the simplest. The difficulty, of course, is to find proper alternatives. The most hopeful prospect lies in the development of the probation system. A point may be reached where many offenders can be so well supervised in the open that, if they fail, a period of custodial training of substantial length will be justified.

(Paterson 1927: xiii)

This extract makes it clear that the prison commissioners did not seek longer sentences for all prisoners. Indeed they advocated non-custodial alternatives for less serious offenders. However, if offenders were to go to prison, the logic was clearly that short sentences would not allow sufficient time to treat and train them to lead a good and useful life. The Prison Rules, first introduced in 1949, took the view that the task of the Prison Service was to 'encourage and assist the inmate to lead a good and useful life'. In their Annual Report for 1949, the commissioners repeated the need for longer sentences in the context of discussing the new Criminal Justice Act 1948. Thus they argue, 'the purpose of the Act was not to provide some new form of training but to give the courts power to pass sentences long enough to enable the methods of training already developed in training prisons to be effectively applied'. This can be contrasted vividly, as we shall later see, with theories based on punishment and deterrence where the 'short sharp shock' or the 'clang of the prison gates' is urged as the most effective part of imprisonment. The effect of this policy is shown in Table 12.1 (a) and (b), which shows prison terms from 1913 to 1975 in absolute and percentage figures.

Table 12.1(a) Length of prison sentence imposed 1913/75

	1913	1938	1948	1958	1968	1975
Up to 2 weeks	80,961	8,820	3,366	3,030	2,932	3,161
Over 2 weeks up to 5 weeks	30,359	7,475	5,595	4,922	3,765	5,069
Over 5 weeks up to 3 months	16,862	7,043	8,925	8,398	6,930	10,126
Over 3 months up to 6 months	5,070	3,947	6,447	6,710	7,801	7,483
Over 6 months up to 12 months	2,873	1,881	4,775	4,843	5,858	7,418
Over 12 months up to 18 months	1,033	694	2,361	2,085	3,179	4,546
Over 18 months up to 3 years	774	581	2,478	2,906	4,059	6,197
Over 3 years up to 5 years	231	158	617	733	1,086	1,749
Over 5 years	120	47	123	348	364	532
Life	13	14	30	40	95	153

Table 12.1(b) Length of prison sentences expressed as percentages

	1913	1938	1948	1958	1968	1975
Up to 2 weeks	58.6	28.7	10.0	8.9	8.1	6.0
Over 2 weeks up to 5 weeks	21.9	24.4	16.7	14.5	10.5	10.9
Over 5 weeks up to 3 months	12.2	23.0	24.7	24.7	19.2	21.8
Over 3 months up to 6 months	3.7	12.9	18.3	19.7	21.6	16.1
Over 6 months up to 12 months	2.1	6.1	14.3	14.2	16.2	16.0
Over 12 months up to 18 months	0.7	2.3	7.1	6.3	8.8	9.8
Over 18 months up to 3 years	0.5	1.9	7.4	8.5	11.3	13.3
Over 3 years up to 5 years	0.2	0.5	1.0	2.1	3.0	3.8
Over 5 years	0.1	0.2	0.4	1.0	1.0	1.2
Life	–	–	0.1	0.1	0.3	0.3

Note: The data includes periods imposed in cases of fine default but excluding sentences of corrective training or preventive detention. The data also includes male and female offenders.
Source: Home Office (1977) Prisons and the Prisoner: 157–8

Table 12.1 shows that sentence lengths increased between 1913 and 1975. This is partly explained by the increasing use of non-custodial sentences from 1913 which meant that fewer petty criminals were sent to prison for short periods of time – thus increasing the average sentence length. The figures also include offenders of all ages, and are therefore affected by the growing use of Borstal and detention centres for those under 21, and by statutory restrictions on sending younger offenders to prison. A major factor in the increase, however, is the influence of the rehabilitative arguments outlined above. By 1975, over 28 per cent of offenders sentenced to custody received terms of imprisonment of over 12 months, compared with less than 1.5 per cent in 1913. Thus, policies based on rehabilitation appear to have contributed towards the demand for longer prison sentences. This same debate is being re-run in the first decade of the twenty-first century as penal reformers claim that short prison sentences do not allow an opportunity for prisoners to take part in programmes to address the offenders' behaviour.

The 1979 May Report on the prison service also noted the link between sentences and rehabilitation and commented:

> However, confidence in the treatment model as it is usually called has now been waning throughout the Western world for some years. The drive behind the original borstal ideas has fallen away and there is now no belief that longer sentences may be justified because they make actual reformative treatment more possible.
>
> (Home Office 1979: 63)

This last quote indicates that, certainly by 1979, the influence of rehabilitation had waned: the reasons for this will be discussed below.

▶ Rehabilitation reassessed

Rehabilitation fell out of favour largely because its promise was not achieved – it became a faith dashed on the rocks of the unprecedented rise in recorded crime in the post-war years. As this coincided with the growing post-war affluence of the 1950s, it also challenged reformers' claims that crime would be reduced with the growth of social welfare. Thus, a 1959 White Paper, *Penal Practice in a Changing Society*, lamented:

> It is a disquieting feature of our society that in the years since the end of the war, rising standards in material prosperity, education and social welfare have brought no decrease in the high rate of crime reached during the war: on the contrary, crime has increased and is still increasing.
>
> (Home Office 1959)

There were several main sources of the declining influence of rehabilitation. The medical model, whose influence has been illustrated above, began to come under considerable criticism. By the 1960s it was apparent that it could justify a range of treatments which seemed far from humane. Many feared the development, for example, of the use of surgery and drug treatment which could readily be used to produce docile inmates. When medical intervention took these more dramatic forms many of the liberal reformers, who supported rehabilitation as a more humane approach, came to realise that punishment might be a better alternative. In addition, the increase in sentence lengths mentioned above, along with the use of indeterminate sentences, made rehabilitative treatments appear harsher than those which would be justified by retributive approaches. Hence, the support from liberal and civil rights groups in the 1970s for the back-to-justice movement, to be discussed below.

A further problem with rehabilitation was its link, seen most clearly in the medical model, with a view that criminality resulted from the pathologies of individual offenders. Yet despite a large volume of research attempting to discover how the characteristics of individual offenders could be related to their criminality, the pathological causes of crime proved hard to identify and apply in individual cases. There were also many other approaches to explaining crime, and many offenders possess no clearly identifiable pathology (as seen in **Chapter 2**). In addition, from a labelling perspective, excessive intervention risked increasing crime, and adherents advocated the use of minimal intervention (**Schur 1973**). Thus the promise to diagnose and therefore to devise suitable treatments for offenders was never fulfilled.

One of the greatest problems with the rehabilitative strategies was that they failed to live up to the claim that they would reduce recidivism. The lesson that prisons were not likely to reform offenders was slow to be learnt. The results of research seeking to establish the impact of rehabilitative measures led to the gloomy conclusion that 'nothing works' (**Lipton *et al*. 1975**). During the 1960s, the coalition of interests that made up the rehabilitative lobby in Europe and North America began to fall apart. The debate about 'what works' to reduce recidivism continues and the 1997 New Labour Government showed an interest in identifying effective offender programmes. This focus on effectiveness measured in offender-instrumental terms was reflected in the title of the Halliday report (2001), *Making Punishments Work*; and reflects the new Offender Management Model of criminal justice (**see Chapter 1**).

By the 1980s Prison Service policy documents had abandoned the ambitious mission statements of previous penal epochs, and referred to the much more basic functions of prison. Thus in 1988, a statement by the Prison Service contained the message that 'Her Majesty's Prison Service serves the public by keeping in custody those committed by the courts'. They had not abandoned, but diluted, the rehabilitative aspirations of the prison and strengthened the concern with humane conditions. 'Our duty is to look after them (inmates) with humanity and to help them lead law-abiding and useful lives in custody and after release' (**Prison Service 1988**).

By the 1980s, the view was established that if rehabilitation was to be achieved then imprisonment was not a suitable location: 'it made bad people worse', to summarise the prevailing orthodoxy. While not claiming that prisons should give up their attempts to rehabilitate inmates, the argument prevailed that if rehabilitation was the primary aspiration of the court at the time of sentence then it would be better to leave the offender in the community. Thus, community sentences and the Probation Service became the main focus of rehabilitative ambitions.

By 2003, this view had been amended to incorporate the idea that to be effective with recidivists there needed to be greater integration between programmes in prisons and on release into the community and this logic led to the idea of establishing the National Offender Management Service (NOMS) in 2004 whereby probation and prisons became an integrated service.

By 2000, the search for effective rehabilitation programmes was back on the agenda of government initiatives for those involved with youth justice and the correctional services. However, these schemes (now and throughout the twentieth century) were not without criticism. First, from a retributive sentencing perspective, there is criticism on the grounds that sentences which stress the primacy of changing offenders' behaviour are likely to be insufficiently punitive. This conflict is seen in the way that community sentences have been presented. When, for example, community service was introduced during the 1960s, discussions referred to 'treatment in the community'. In the 1990s, however, the predominant phraseology was 'punishment in the community': for example, the Green Paper issued by the Home Office in 1995 was entitled *Strengthening Punishment in the Community*.

Thus, by 1990, the rationale for community penalties had moved on from an alternative-to-custody approach towards an intermediate sanction rationale in which success would be measured in terms of just deserts and denunciatory goals. By 2003, the pendulum had swung somewhat in the other direction with the search for more effective sentences as measured in terms of recidivism.

Many of the new types of sentences introduced from the 1960s onwards, such as the Community Service Order, were presented as alternatives to custody. That is, they were to be regarded as equivalent to custody, and imposed only in circumstances where a prison sentence would have been considered. This implies that the sentences can be substituted for prison and are equivalent; and indeed the Court of Appeal established that 190 hours of community service were equivalent to 9–12 months of imprisonment (*R* v. *Lawrence* (1982)). When the Community Service Order was originally introduced, courts were enjoined to indicate whether the order was a direct alternative to custody or not, and to record that fact in the court register (**Home Office 1986: 43**).

The problem with this kind of approach is that many sentencers and the public simply do not see community penalties as in any way equivalent to prison. Thus, there was a tendency for the new, so-called alternatives to prison to be used instead as alternatives to probation. In addition, the mixed rationales underlying the Community Service Order made it difficult to approach in terms of the tariff – how, for example, did such sentences match the seriousness of the offence? If, however, the use of imprisonment was to be reduced while at the same time maintaining a notion of tough sentences, new approaches to community sentences were necessary.

Such new approaches were influenced by the justice model. The logic of just deserts and proportionality implied that penalties should be differentiated according to the severity of the crime and the culpability of the offender. In practice, prison terms are measured in terms of the degree of restriction on the offender's liberty. Community sentences could also, it was argued, be justified in this way. It was suggested that community penalties could be made tougher. This could be done by increasing sentencing options and introducing tougher penalties between probation and prison, thus producing a continuum or gradation of penalties which would reflect sentencers' needs for sanctions proportionate to the seriousness of the offence.

The Criminal Justice Act 1991 made community sentences part of a framework of sentences based on a just deserts approach. These sentences, as revised by the Act, provided for a range of community penalties, with some being more demanding than others. They were no longer merely alternatives to prison but intermediate sentences, a sentence in punitive terms somewhere between prison and probation, and became sentences in their own right with specific aims.

Despite the new role for community penalties as 'intermediate sanctions', research suggests that some magistrates perceived community penalties as insufficiently demanding to provide the structured steps in a hierarchy of punitiveness between probation and prison. This is illustrated by the following comments from magistrates about the implementation of community service orders:

> To me it's not structured enough. They come and go as they please.
>
> I wouldn't say it was terribly demanding necessarily, only the discipline of having to be there and doing it . . . I wouldn't think they'd break out in a sweat.
>
> I think they tend to lose credibility with me when we have breach hearings and you hear how often the administrator has really bent over backwards to accept their excuse.
>
> The underlying view I think of probation officers would not be to divert people from crime but to divert people from prison.
>
> (Davies *et al.* 1996: 94–5)

These comments reflect in part the ambiguity about the role of community sentences and also the continued debate about the position of the penal objective of rehabilitation: though it was given a secondary role within a sentencing framework established by just deserts and denunciation in the Criminal Justice Act 1991, the Criminal Justice Act 2003 has restored its role to one of five primary objective of sentencing.

More recently, the Legal Aid, Sentencing and Punishment of Offenders Act 2012 (LASPO) increased the powers available with community sentences by introducing new options – in addition to the original 12 requirements – of attaching a foreign travel prohibition, a new alcohol abstinence ban, and extended home curfew periods from a maximum of 6 months to 12. Further changes to community sentences were recommended following a public consultation document in 2012 entitled *Punishment and Reform: Effective community sentences*, included an explicitly punitive element in every community sentence handed down, to demonstrate to the offender that they have done wrong, and to explore the introduction of a 'robust and intensive punitive community disposal' for use on offenders who merit a significant level of punishment, but for whom prison would be unsuitable.

12.3 Just deserts and the justice model

Objective 3

Explain the concepts that underpin the just deserts and the justice models of punishment

The declining faith in rehabilitation along with the continuing rise in recorded crime led to a reappraisal of sentencing aims in the late 1960s and 1970s. Extremely influential in this process was what came to be known as a back-to-justice policy which affected legislation throughout the 1980s, and most particularly the Criminal Justice Act 1991. There was no one single and comprehensive formulation of the justice model, but it developed out of a number of publications by American academics such as **Davis (1969)**, **Fogel (1975)**, **Frankel (1973)** and **von Hirsch (1976)**. In the United States, where the justice model developed and influenced policy more directly, it was influential in shaping reforms of the juvenile courts and the introduction of determinate sentencing laws in California in 1976. These reforms were strongly influenced by the problems of rehabilitative sentencing policies. The long and seemingly harsh sentences associated with rehabilitation and the uncertainty produced by indeterminate sentences and the individualisation of sentences were seen to conflict with the rights of offenders to receive predictable and proportionate sentences. Thus the justice model argues that sentencing should be fair and not aim to achieve anything other than punishing offenders in proportion to the harm they have done. It developed directly out of a critique of rehabilitation and, as **Messinger and Johnson (1978)** comment, 'it represented . . . an outright rejection of previous sentencing policy and seems to be based on the opposite assumptions in every respect'.

The justice model is often linked to, and is not logically incompatible with, retributive theories; however, it emphasises fairness while retribution is often popularly distorted to support demands for vengeance or harsher sentences. Thus, while the justice model stresses punishment as an end in itself it was not called 'back-to-punishment', and **von Hirsch (1976)** described it as 'vengeance with fairness'. This approach is incompatible with rehabilitation as a primary goal of punishment. It can, however, be included as a secondary aspect of sentencing provided it does not distort the length or type of sentence in terms of the principles of just deserts. There is no clearly articulated theory of just deserts; however, there are four main sets of assumptions and principles that can be identified. These include assumptions about human behaviour, the objective of punishment, the distribution of punishment, and the extension of due process into the prisons.

❱ Assumptions about human behaviour

To advocates of the justice model, individuals are responsible for their own behaviour. Criminal behaviour therefore, like any other, is thus a result of conscious decisions made by responsible, autonomous, self-determined individuals. Thus the rehabilitationist notion that criminality results from some individual pathology or is attributable to the offender's social, economic or personal circumstances was rejected. While it was accepted that these factors could affect behaviour, the view should not be disregarded that human action is primarily attributable to individual choice. Thus offenders have made a free choice to commit crime, and should therefore be punished. Where they have not been able, for example, because of age or mental disability, to make a free choice, they are not fully responsible for their actions and need not be punished.

▶ The objective of punishment

Punishment is seen as an end in itself and a just and **condign** reward for morally wrong behaviour. It does not have to be justified by social protection or on the grounds that it is likely to reduce the future likelihood of crime. It should therefore be based simply on the notion of just deserts: culpable criminals should be punished in amounts proportional to or commensurate with the seriousness of the harm done.

This raises important questions. By whom, and how, is culpability to be assessed? What constitutes the proportionate level of punishment for each offence and who should determine this? Thus there can be moral and political objections to this approach. In unequal or unjust societies, just deserts may be determined by those in power and may be far from just to those at the receiving end. In addition, in pluralist societies, cultural differentiation makes shared agreement as to what is right or wrong difficult to assess. Decisions as to how serious a crime is and what its 'just' punishment should be may open up a wider debate on moral, social and political issues. It might not be easy, for example, to distinguish between different offences in terms of seriousness. How can the respective seriousness of rape, burglary or tax fraud be assessed? As we have seen, the public may have very different views over what should be criminalised, and how to rank crime in terms of seriousness. Disagreements are inevitable when citizens are asked to consider the harmful consequences of crime, and the merits of different modes of punishment. However, even if agreement cannot be reached as to what is 'just', it does keep the debate about punishment associated with issues of morality and justice. This point is made by C S Lewis:

> The humanitarian theory removes from punishment the concept of Desert. But the concept of Desert is the only connecting link between punishment and justice. It is only as deserved or undeserved that a sentence can be just or unjust . . . we may very properly ask whether it is likely to deter others and to reform the criminal. But neither of these two last questions is a question of justice.
>
> (Lewis 1953)

Von Hirsch, discussing the twin objectives of deterrence and deserts, makes it clear that the deserts principle is more important for decisions about the distribution of punishment. Thus he argues:

> . . . we think that the commensurate deserts principle should have priority over other objectives in decisions about how to punish. The disposition of convicted offenders should be commensurate with the seriousness of their offences, even if greater or less severity would promote other goals.
>
> (von Hirsch 1976)

▶ The distribution of punishment

Once culpability is established the main determinant of the type or amount of punishment will be the seriousness of the offence. A secondary consideration once this has been established is the degree of responsibility. Thus both mitigating and aggravating circumstances in relation to both the offence and the offender form part of the consideration of the sentence to be given.

Proponents of the justice model aimed to reduce individualised sentencing strategies, which, as we have seen, underlie sentencing disparities, and to eradicate indeterminacy. Thus they wished to see fixed and determinate sentencing with an established tariff for each offence, and uniformity of sentences for offenders committing the same offence in similar circumstances. Hence the move towards more constraints on judicial discretion at the sentencing stage throughout much of the United States and the United Kingdom.

▶ Legalism: the extension of due process

Indeterminate prison sentences created a situation whereby the length of a prison sentence depended on discretionary decisions made within the prison. This led to many problems, which, especially in the United States, were associated not only with increasing sentence lengths and thus an increase in the prison population, but also with unrest within prisons. Prisoners could not predict how long their sentences were to last, nor could they always predict what they had to do to ensure an early release. This could also lead to a situation where release dates and parole decisions could be used as a means of control within the prison system. It also led to apparent injustices as offenders sent to prison for similar offences could in effect serve very different lengths of sentence. This not surprisingly led to much discontent and feelings of inequity. Thus a major argument of the justice model was to extend the principles of due process into the prison system. The clearest impact on prison regimes was achieved by David Fogel, who, as Commissioner for Prisons in Minnesota from 1971 to 1973, attempted to apply the principles of the justice model to prisons. He advocated reforms which would involve more due process: greater openness in decision making and accountability according to the demands of natural justice. His reforms emphasised prisoners' rights and a belief that in the world of the prison community there should be an atmosphere of justice and fairness. This view was later echoed in the Woolf Report 1991 (**Home Office 1991a**) into prison disturbances in 1990 (**which will be discussed in Chapter 13**).

In the United Kingdom the justice approach made its mark in a more diffuse way than in the United States. By the end of the 1970s aspects of prison policy were being scrutinised by the courts and greater attention was paid to prisoners' rights. The indeterminate sentence of Borstal training was replaced by the determinate sentence of youth custody in 1982. Also, increasing guidance was given to courts to reduce sentence disparity (**as we have seen in Chapter 11**). The 1990 White Paper and the subsequent legislative reforms in the Criminal Justice Act 1991 gave the clearest message that just deserts should be the primary principle for sentencing decisions in England and Wales.

The post-1997 approach to sentencing objectives has eroded the dominance of the justice approach with its emphasis on the seriousness of the offence, and we now have a penal paradigm that gives greater emphasis to the offender-instrumental goals that seek to reduce crime.

12.4 Prison reductionists: limiting the use of imprisonment

Despite the good intentions of penal reformers, prisons had not achieved the goals claimed by their protagonists in the 1920/50 era in that they were not likely to rehabilitate offenders. Prisons are primarily justified by notions of retribution and denunciation, the uncertain impact of deterrence and a claim to incapacitate. The existence of violence, gangs and drug use within prisons means that even the claim to incapacitate is only partially true.

In addition, prisons are costly institutions and there have been recurrent concerns over the overcrowding of existing prisons and conditions within them. Many prisons in the United Kingdom were built in Victorian times and have few modern facilities. Concerns about overcrowding, on the part of the Prison Officers' Association, were evident in Britain as early as the 1940s and the Prison Commissioners' Annual Reports repeated the warning from 1955 until their demise in 1964. The degrading conditions within prisons also caused considerable concern and were described as an 'affront to civilised society' by the Director General of Prisons in the Annual Report of the Prison Department in 1980.

Out of these concerns grew what came to be known as the 'prison reductionist' movement. Some focused on degrading conditions and overcrowding, while others focused on the adverse effects of prisons and claimed that sentencers were sending too many people to prison. By the 1970s liberal and welfare-orientated groups who had supported rehabilitation came to argue for a reduction in the use of prison. Their message was underlined by media stories of overcrowded cells, antiquated conditions and incidents of unrest in prisons.

Of course, one solution to problems of overcrowding and degrading conditions would be to build more prisons. Moreover, the argument that sentencers send 'too many people' to prison is a difficult one to evaluate given the different aims underlying a prison sentence. Nonetheless, the argument of the reductionists, who shared a common view that the size of the prison population should be reduced, became an influential one. A key part of this argument was that, as prisons could no longer be seen to rehabilitate and indeed could have an adverse effect on prisoners, their use should be curtailed.

This influence was evident in the parliamentary debate on the 1967 Criminal Justice Bill. Roy Jenkins, the then Home Secretary, echoed the reductionist position in his speech on the bill in which he stated that 'the main range of the penal provision of the bill revolves round the single theme, that of keeping out of prison those who need not be there . . . the overstrain upon prison resources, both of buildings and men, is at present appalling'.

From the 1960s, official documents started to move away from the grander claims made during the heyday of rehabilitation and towards an acceptance that prisons were not appropriate places to reform individual inmates. It began to be argued that prisons had an adverse effect on inmates, making them reliant on institutional life, and could further deepen their commitment to crime as they mixed freely with other criminals: the prison as the university of crime. In addition, ex-prisoners might face considerable stigma, making it more difficult for them to gain housing or employment. Thus a more limited rehabilitative rationale emerged in arguments that, if rehabilitation was sought by sentencers, it was not likely to be achieved in prison. This was made most apparent in the arguments in the Green Paper *Punishment, Custody and the Community* (**Home Office 1988a**) and the subsequent White Paper of 1990 (**Home Office 1990a**).

During the late 1980s and early 1990s the reductionist message was paramount. The arguments of those who wished to see prisons reduced on the grounds that they were ineffective and inhumane were echoed by more pragmatic reductionists concerned with the costs, efficacy and the strains caused by the numbers in the system. Thus, from the 1980s onwards, as we have seen, successive legislation and policy initiatives aimed to encourage more consistency in sentencing; imposed limitations on the use of imprisonment, such as the introduction of statutory criteria on the use of prison in the Criminal Justice Acts 1982, 1988 and 1991. This led to the establishment of a Sentencing Guidelines Council in the CJA 2003.

In 1990, explicit recognition was given in a White Paper to the idea that imprisonment has a limited role to play in penal policy (**the report is discussed in Chapter 13**). Changing prison regimes alone, however, could not alleviate the problems of the prison system and the White Paper argued that prison over-crowding could not be solved in isolation from sentencing policy. Hence the search for sanctions which could be used instead of prison, not necessarily to act as an alternative sentence, but to rank on the tariff below prison. These sentences should, it was argued, be less severe than imprisonment, but be demanding enough to encourage sentencers to use them for the less serious offences that had previously attracted a prison term.

During Michael Howard's period at the Home Office, the prison reductionist view was challenged by the claim that prisons work. This, of course, depended on what prisons were expected to deliver and we discuss this debate in a later section of this chapter.

By 1997, the Labour Party were back in government and there was to be a shift in policy whereby the rhetoric accepted the argument that prisons were overused and simultaneously the prison population continued to increase to record levels. Custody, in the words of *Justice for All*, has an important role in punishing offenders and protecting the public, but it is expensive and should be limited to 'dangerous, serious and seriously persistent offenders and those who have consistently breached community sentences'.

Reductionism took on a new lease of life when Lord Woolf was appointed Lord Chief Justice in 2000. His report on prison riots in the 1980s had established his liberal credentials and his subsequent actions were based on a view that less use should be made of imprisonment. The controversial decision of the Court of Appeal case on not sending burglars to prison was mainly inspired by the views of Lord Woolf, despite this view being out of touch with his fellow judges, the public at large and the recommendations of the Sentencing Advisory Panel on domestic burglary. In the *McInerney and Keating* Court of Appeal Guideline case (December 2002), he rejected the stepped tariff approach of the Criminal Justice Act 1991, claiming that short prison sentences were ineffective (as selectively measured by recidivism rates) and argued the sentence for burglars should 'ensure the sentence is (a) an effective punishment and (b) one which offers action on the part of the Probation Service to tackle the offender's criminal behaviour and (c) when appropriate, will tackle the offender's underlying problems such as drug addiction'. The emphasis on rehabilitation and changing behaviour had not been so pronounced since the optimistic decade of the 1930s with the belief in science and the medical metaphor of 'cure' and the optimism about the ability to change offenders' conduct.

Another aspect of the prison reductionist case, used by Lord Justice Woolf, is based on the apparent over-punitiveness of the English courts when contrasted to other jurisdictions around the world. Libya was quoted at one stage but more regularly we are referred to what is happening among our European Union partners. The crude prison rate of prisoners per population shows England and Wales with more prisoners per head of population than the rest of Europe; but the question is whether the comparison of prison rates should be based on population or related to the amount of crime. Comparing populations with different age profiles and crime rates would not be meaningful, whereas comparisons with the amount of crime in general or, more importantly, with the amount of serious crime are more useful in determining whether the judges are more punitive in one jurisdiction than another.

Table 12.2 compares the number of prisoners in 2010 to the size of the population as well as the number of recorded crimes across the western members of the

Table 12.2 The rate of imprisonment in the European Union, 2010

Country	Prison population	Prisoners per 100,000 pop	Estimated country population (thousands)	Recorded crimes per 100,000 population	Recorded crimes	Prisoners per 1,000 recorded crimes
EU Average		126				18.3
England and Wales	85,002	154	62,042	6,689	4,150,097	20.4
Northern Ireland	1,469	82	1,810	5,803	105,040	13.9
Scotland	7,853	152	5,295	6,101	323,060	24.3
Austria	8,597	99	8,415	6,366	535,745	16.0
Belgium	10,968	96	11,007	9,541	1,050,235	10.4
Denmark	3,965	68	5,569	8,459	471,088	8.4
Finland	3,189	62	5,357	8,057	431,623	7.3
France	66,532	102	65,460	5,379	3,521,256	18.8
Germany	70,103	88	81,758	7,257	5,933,278	11.8
Greece	12,590	108	11,645	2,868	333,988	37.6
Ireland (Eire)	3,556	78	4,588	–	–	–
Italy	67,961	106	60,419	4,338	2,621,019	25.9
Luxembourg	669	137	472	6,461	30,532	21.9
Netherlands	14,289	87	16,697	7,143	1,192,640	11.9
Portugal	11,613	105	10,608	3,984	422,587	27.4
Spain	73,929	163	47,151	4,873	2,297,484	32.1
Sweden	6,891	74	9,360	14,641	1,370,399	5.0

Note: Figures from Eurostat 'Trends in Crime and Criminal Justice, 2010', Table 1: Crimes recorded by the police: Total Crime: http://epp.eurostat.ec.europa.eu/cache/ITY_OFFPUB/KS-SF-13-018/EN/KS-SF-13-018-EN.PDF; Table 9: Prison Population: http://epp.eurostat.ec.europa.eu/cache/ITY_OFFPUB/KS-SF-13-018/EN/KS-SF-13-018-EN.PDF
Source: Civitas website: civitas.org.uk

EU jurisdictions. Looking at prisoners against the amount of crime, the average across the European countries listed is 18.3 prisoners for every 1,000 crimes: and the figure for England and Wales is 20.4. Measured in this way the English and Welsh courts do not appear to be as punitive as when using the prisoner to population ratio where we have the highest ratio of 154 inmates per 100,000 of population.

(The shifts and complexities of the penal paradigm are explored in Section 12.5.)

12.5 Shifting penal paradigms

Objective 5

Outline recent changes and define the concept of a penal paradigms

By the 1980s, therefore, many factors suggested that there was a need for a review of penal policy. It had been largely recognised that the individualised sentencing associated with rehabilitation had produced disparities and what were seen by proponents of a justice model as injustices. It had become associated with longer and indeterminate sentences, far out of proportion to the crime committed. The belief in the positive rehabilitative effects of custody may have produced a rise in the prison population. However, there were strong arguments in favour of substantially reducing the use of imprisonment, on the grounds of the relative ineffectiveness of prison in terms of rehabilitation, and also on the grounds of its cost-effectiveness. At the same time, however, public concern over rising crime rates, particularly in offences of violence, suggested that reducing the use of imprisonment could be seen as paying insufficient regard to the protection of the public. Community sentences lacked credibility. These issues were reflected in a series of discussion documents and government papers (notably the 1988 Green Paper, *Punishment, Custody and the Community*, and the 1990 White Paper, *Crime, Justice and Protecting the Public*) preceding the Criminal Justice Act 1991, which promised to be one of the most thorough overhauls of sentencing policy. We have already outlined many of the changes brought about by this legislation, some to be quickly overturned in the Criminal Justice Act 1993. This section will place these changes in the context of the shifting penal paradigms outlined in this chapter.

The difficulties of the deterrent approach to sentencing was developed in the White Paper:

> Deterrence is a principle with much immediate appeal. Most law abiding citizens understand the reasons why some behaviour is made a criminal offence, and would be deterred by the shame of a criminal conviction or the possibility of a severe penalty. There are doubtless some criminals who carefully calculate the possible gains and risks. But much crime is committed on impulse, given the opportunity presented by an open window or unlocked door, and it is committed by offenders who live from moment to moment; their crimes are as impulsive as the rest of their feckless, sad or pathetic lives. It is unrealistic to construct sentencing arrangements on the assumption that most offenders will weigh up the possibilities in advance and base their conduct on rational calculation. Often they do not.
>
> (Home Office 1990a: 6)

According to Ashworth, 'The origins of the new law were in the government's white paper of 1990, which stated that desert should be the primary aim of sentencing, that rehabilitation should not be an aim of sentencing but should be striven for within proportionate sentences, and that deterrence is rarely a proper or profitable aim for a sentencer' (**von Hirsch and Ashworth 1993: 285–6**). The White Paper rejected deterrent sentencing and, while it saw a role for rehabilitation, rejected any notion that rehabilitation should be a primary goal. Denunciation was also seen as significant: thus the 1990 White Paper stated that 'the first objective for all sentences is denunciation of and retribution for the crime' (**Home Office 1990a: 6**). The emphasis on just deserts meant that the seriousness of the offence was to be the primary criterion for determining the sentence, and it was also envisaged that it should limit the severity of a sentence. This can be seen in the following extract:

> . . . the severity of the sentence in an individual case should reflect primarily the seriousness of the offence which has been committed. While factors such as preventing crime or the rehabilitation of the offender remain important functions of the criminal justice process as a whole, they should not lead to a heavier penalty in an individual case than that which is justified by the seriousness of the offence or the need to protect the public from the offender.
>
> (Home Office 1991b: 1)

This extract also shows that, while just deserts is a major principle, the protection of the public is also important; thus the Criminal Justice Act 1991 contained an important incapacitative element. What is often known as bifurcation or a twin-track approach was introduced on the principle that for most offenders the sentence was to be based on the seriousness of the offence, except in circumstances where, as, for example, with sexual and violent offenders, incapacitation was seen to be necessary. This was described largely in terms of distinguishing property offences from those involving violence. While the courts were to be encouraged to use non-custodial sentences for property offenders where possible, prison terms, and terms longer than the offence itself merited, could be used for violent offenders.

One controversial provision of the Criminal Justice Act 1991 (CJA 1991) provided that previous convictions should not be looked at when assessing seriousness (s 29), the only exception being where earlier offences were taken as aggravating features of the current offence. The offender was to be sentenced on the basis of the current offence and not previous convictions. Another controversial section, referred to as the 'two offence rule', meant that regardless of the number of offences only one offence (the most serious) and only one other would be considered to determine the sentence in typical cases. This was, as had been intended, given a very narrow interpretation by the courts. Both provisions were heavily criticised as limiting the powers available to courts when sentencing the persistent offender whose offences taken individually were not counted as 'so serious'. The Criminal Justice Act 1993 altered this position by repealing these two sections, allowing judges to consider previous offences and the number of offences when sentencing.

A second implication of the approach was that any restriction on liberty should be commensurate with the seriousness of the offence. This applied to both custodial and community sentences. As we have seen, the 1990 White Paper made it clear that imprisonment should not be used for rehabilitative or deterrent motives but might be justified in particular cases on retributive, denunciatory and incapacitative grounds. This is the significance of the statutory criterion to restrict the use of imprisonment, particularly aimed at property offenders. Just desert principles, to reflect the seriousness of the crime, were also used to determine lengths of custodial sentences.

In addition, the element of indeterminacy implied by parole was also changed with the introduction of provisions to clarify release dates from prisons with the reform of the system of parole and remission to automatic release dates for all offenders given a determinate sentence to the halfway point of sentence, minus time spent on remand in custody.

The CJA 1991 also changed the role, function and organisation of community sentences. Indeed the 1990 White Paper devoted four out of nine chapters to exploring the role of community penalties. To make changes that were acceptable to the public meant that they had to be tied into the just deserts approach, and had to be credible punishments in their own right. Thus the 1990 White Paper referred to a continuum of penalties involving an increasing degree of restriction on the offender's liberty, with custody at one end and probation at the other and with a range of intermediate punishments in the community. This new approach was based on the assumption that the punishment was to be the degree of restriction on the offender's liberty.

Thus it was argued that imprisonment should be retained as the means of punishment for the most serious offences, and fines and discharges for the least serious offences. The Green Paper clarified this point: 'Liberty under the law is highly valued by all of us. The deprivation of liberty is the most severe penalty available to the courts' (**Home Office 1988a: 8**). Apart from financial penalties, most court disposals place restrictions on offenders' freedom of action. The degree of restriction on offenders' freedom of action thus provides the link between community-based forms of punishments and imprisonment. Custody is at one end of the continuum of restrictions on offenders' freedom of action:

> The effect of custodial sentences is to restrict offenders' freedom of action by removing them from their homes, by determining where they will live during the sentence, by limiting their social relationships and by deciding how and where they will spend the 24 hours in each day.
>
> (Home Office 1988a: 3.3)

Thus the CJA 1991 was a logical development in the context of the shifting penal paradigms explored above. In addition, it stated, more clearly than before, the main principles to be used by sentencers, and thus hoped to encourage consistency. Consequently an editorial in the *Criminal Law Review* on the introduction of the

Act commented that 'it can be claimed that the 1991 Act differs from its predecessors in one significant respect: its sentencing provisions have some fairly coherent themes' (**Ashworth 1992: 229**). Ashworth comments, 'it introduced a primary rationale for English sentencing (desert) and clarified the extent to which other "aims" such as public protection, rehabilitation and deterrence should play a part' (**Ashworth 1994b: 853**).

The aims and principles of the CJA 1991 were welcomed by many, although the details of its implementation – for instance, the system of unit fines – led to opposition in some quarters. Of course, not everyone accepted a sentencing policy based primarily on a just deserts approach which fitted sentences to the seriousness of the offence. One of the problems was that the Act gave little guidance on how this seriousness is to be assessed. There is an assumption, for example, that violent and sexual offences are more serious than property ones, but in practice the delineation of seriousness is far more complex, and perhaps leaves space for individualisation in terms of judging offence seriousness.

Some argued that just deserts policies can lead to an increase in the tariff. This is not inevitable, however – just deserts models have led to more severe sentencing approaches in California (**Davies 1989**), but not in Scandinavian countries (**Ashworth 1997; Davies et al. 1996; Hudson 1993**). Much depends on exactly how maximum sentences are conceived and how actual sentencing lengths are determined in practice.

The shift in the penal paradigm was apparent with the changes initiated by the New Labour Government from 1997. It became evident that a number of trends were simultaneously at work and the logic of the sentencing framework of the CJA 1991 was to change away from a primary focus on deserts and denunciation. One important new emphasis was a belief that rehabilitation rates could be improved. Under New Labour, the offender-instrumental goals were to be given a heightened and interrelated role, so that more programmes should be in place to help rehabilitate offenders both in and out of prisons, to assist greater monitoring of those left in the community; and the prisons were to be used for punishment, deterrence, incapacitation of recidivists and the attempted rehabilitation of prisoners. The fashionable view by 2001 was that there was little penal value in the short prison sentence, which would do little to reduce recidivism – reminiscent of the views of the Prison Commissioners in the 1920s and 1930s. Furthermore, prisons were overused. However, at the same time the use of custody by judges and magistrates was increasing.

These views were found in the Halliday Report (2001) entitled *Making Punishments Work*. The message from the foreword to the White Paper *Justice for All* (July 2002) that preceded the Criminal Justice Act 2003 was on the need to be tough and effective.

The White Paper commented, under the heading of 'What is not working', 'Half of all prisoners discharged in 1997 were reconvicted within 2 years' (2002: 24). What was missing was the fact that an equal proportion of offenders given community sentences are reconvicted after two years; so, although they claimed to be evidence-based, they had in effect accepted the prison reduction lobby's views (at least about the problems of prisons) even if the judges were still sending more criminals to prison – although the judicial leadership under Lord Chief Justice Woolf did what it could to change this.

The beginning of the twenty-first century saw another departure from the logic that prevailed in 1990 and the CJA 1991. In the Criminal Justice Act 2003 the aims of sentencing have been set out in the statute and 'deterrence' is included but 'denunciation' excluded (**see Chapter 11**).

In contrast to the logic of the Just Deserts Model of the 1991 CJA, where the sentence was to be based primarily on the seriousness of the offence, the New Offender Management Model (**see Chapter 1**) requires more offender-instrumental intervention, which includes a wide range of offender modification strategies such as drugs and alcohol programmes but also more monitoring and testing that might extend beyond the sentence, as in the case of those on the sex offenders register. This more ambitious attempt to monitor and control the future behaviour of past offenders also requires more inter-agency cooperation and sharing of information.

The overall purpose was set by the Ministry of Justice in 2009 – note in their Objectives that there is little reference to punishment or just deserts but a clear offender management logic.

> Protecting the public and reducing reoffending is central to our whole purpose. We are increasing prison capacity and an independent working group will be reporting on better ways to align supply and demand through the sentencing framework. We are committed to offender management reforms and delivering more effective community penalties that reflects the needs of local people. We are also working more collaboratively across government to protect the public and reduce reoffending.
>
> (Ministry of Justice departmental strategic objectives, 2009)

Crucial to this whole strategy is the additional monitoring of individual offenders seen as posing a continuing risk. The work of the Multi-Agency Public Protection Arrangements, MAPPA, is central to this.

How does MAPPA work?

The figures below are as recorded on 31 March 2011. This provides a one-day snapshot of the numbers of MAPPA-eligible offenders in specific categories and levels, rather than the total numbers registered during the previous 12 months.

There are four key features within MAPPA:

1. Identifying offenders to be supervised under MAPPA

This is generally determined by the offender's offence and sentence, but also by assessed risk.

There are three formal categories:

1. Category One: Registered Sex Offenders (37,225 offenders)

2. Category Two: Violent or other sex offenders (13,785 offenders)

3. Category Three: Other offenders (479 offenders)

On 31 March 2011 there were a total of 51,489 MAPPA-eligible offenders. This is an increase of 7% when compared with 31 March 2010, but it is important to note that many sexual offenders are required to register for long periods of time, with some registering for life, and this has a cumulative effect on the total number of offenders required to register at any one time.

2. Sharing of information about offenders

MAPPA promotes information sharing between all the agencies, resulting in more effective supervision and better public protection.

For example:

- Police will share information with offender managers that they have gathered about an offender's behaviour from surveillance or intelligence gathering
- Local authorities will help find offenders suitable accommodation where they can be effectively managed.

It is very important that victims' needs are represented in MAPPA, with the result that additional measures can be put into place to manage the risks posed to known victims.

3. Assessing the risks posed by offenders

Most MAPPA offenders do not present a risk of serious harm to the public: the MAPPA enable resources and attention to be focused on those who present the highest risks.

4. Managing the risk posed by individual offenders

MAPPA offenders should be managed at one of three levels. While the assessed level of risk is an important factor, it is the degree of management intervention required which determines the level.

- **Level One: involves normal agency management**

  Generally offenders managed at this level will be assessed as presenting a low or medium risk of serious harm to others. On 31 March 2011, 48,650 offenders – 94.5% of MAPPA offenders were being managed at this level.

- **Level Two: often called local inter-risk agency management**

  Most offenders assessed as high or very high risk of causing harm. In 2011, 2,649 (or 5.1%) of MAPPA offenders were managed at this level.

- **Level Three: known as Multi-Agency Public Protection Panels (or MAPPPs)**

  Appropriate for those offenders who pose the highest risk of causing serious harm or whose management is so problematic that multi-agency cooperation and oversight at a senior level is required with the authority to commit exceptional resources. In 2011, 190 – or 0.4% – of MAPPA offenders were managed at this level.

The offender management approach also requires an ability to identify highly prolific and future recidivists and hence the need for effective risk analysis. Probation departments in England and Wales use an electronic Offender Assessment System (OASys) which shares information on individual offenders with other probation departments across the country. It is a structured assessment tool which uses the following measures:

- the offending-related factors relevant to the offender
- the risk of serious harm the offender presents
- the offender's sentence plan
- a summary sheet – informed by the offender's
  - criminal history
  - current offence details
  - accommodation situation
  - education, training and employability

- financial management and income

- relationships

- lifestyle and associates

- any drug misuse details

- any alcohol misuse details

- emotional well-being

- thinking and behaviour

- attitudes

- self-assessment questionnaire

- information not to be disclosed to the offender.

A study in 33 probation districts indicates the problems of the inconsistency in applying this risk analysis across different parts of the country and also indicates the contrasting confidence among probation staff about some of the indicators of risk (*Can OASys deliver consistent assessments of offenders? Results from the inter-rate reliability study*, Sarah Morton, 2009 (Research Summary 1/09, Ministry of Justice)).

Whereas there was general agreement that the sections on accommodation, lifestyle, associates and drug misuse were reliable indicators, there was less confidence in aspects of the risk test which covered financial management, alcohol misuse, thinking and behaviour, and risk of serious harm. Questions to do with education, training and employability, relationships, emotional wellbeing, and attitudes, were regarded as moderately reliable guides to predicting future offending.

OASys was revised in 2009 after reviews highlighted problems with the scoring system. For example, it did not feature a score for age or gender, although being young and male were found in fact to be strongly predictive of future recidivism. It also used the same measures of risk analysis across all offence groups, despite some measures being more strongly associated with some kinds of offences, such as violence, whereas other measures were more strongly associated with other offences, such as theft or drugs offences.

To resolve this, the revised OASys now features two sets of predictors: the OASys Violence Predictor (OVP) and the OASys General reoffending Predictor (OGP). It also has a 'Full' and a 'Standard' version for use with offenders of different risk levels, both of which are shorter than the original OASys, which has produced a 'modest time saving', while dispensing with some need measures which were not proving useful (Howard P, *Recent thinking and results from OASys*, London: NOMS).

12.6 Does prison work?

Objective 6

Analyse and provide an answer to the question of 'Does prison work?'

Penal reform groups, prison reductionists and policy makers in the 1990 White Paper claimed that a deterrence approach to sentencing is an unrealistic policy because it assumes that criminals make calculations about the likelihood of being detected, arrested and punished and mostly they do not, as most crime is opportunistic or carried out by people who do not make estimates of the likely consequences of their actions. Further, as very few offences result in a sentence (**see Chapter** 2) it is assumed that not many people are affected by sentences. In addition, reconviction rates show that the majority of imprisoned offenders will be reconvicted of a new offence in the two-year period following their release from prison. Thus prisons, it would seem, neither deter nor rehabilitate the majority of offenders who are sent there. These points add up to a view that prisons do not work and that the deterrent theory of imprisonment is invalid. The 1990 White Paper claimed that, 'It was unrealistic to construct sentencing arrangements on the assumption that most offenders will weigh up the possibilities in advance and base their conduct on rational calculation' (**Home Office 1990a: 6**).

For other critics of imprisonment the question is not whether prison works but whether there are more effective ways of using resources. If the reconviction rates of those sent to prison and those given community sentences are similar, they would argue that it is better to use the cheaper option. Other critics of the use of imprisonment recognise its value for locking up only potentially dangerous offenders.

However, the problem with these different criticisms of prison – that it does not work, or it works but is too costly, or that it should be reserved for dangerous offenders only – is that they focus exclusively on offender-instrumental considerations as if sentencing is only about the consequences on the future behaviour of those already convicted of crimes. These critics ignore the impact on other participants in, or audiences for, the sentence: the public and the victims. The public will include potential offenders who may well be influenced by the general deterrent effect of the sentence and do make estimates as to whether the potential risks of offending are outweighed by the possible gains; and also includes the law-abiding who wish to be reassured that offending does not pay and that the rules of the community are being respected, and that when they are not, a person pays for this in the hard coinage of punishment. Thus a concern with general deterrence, retribution and denunciation means that prisons may well play an effective part in maintaining a stable and law-abiding society.

It can be argued that prisons do not need to be justified in terms of whether they rehabilitate or deter the offenders sent to them, but in terms of the impact on those who do not go to prison. Prisons, it is argued, can work for the following sentencing reasons: first, on retributivist grounds, because they are regarded by the bulk of the public as suitable institutions for punishing people who have done wrong and have been convicted of a sufficiently serious crime such that the offence cannot be ignored and is considered worthy of a serious punishment such as incarceration; second, on denunciatory grounds, because they underline society's commitment to defining rules about the appropriateness of certain types of behaviour and censuring others as unacceptable; and third, on grounds of incapacitation, in that certain dangerous and sometimes persistent offenders need to be locked up to protect the public. There is a fourth justification based on a general deterrence view that prisons deter crimes from happening because of the fear of punishment. As we have already seen, there is a strongly held view among policy makers that crime is often opportunistic and not based on premeditated calculations of potential gains and losses. However, not all crimes are spontaneous and it is likely that the calculations about the chances of being discovered and punished may well deter some people who contemplate crime. Testing this idea is difficult because it requires a measure of why people do or do not act in a criminal manner.

Let us look at some data about the possible impact of imprisonment, which are part of the debate as to whether prisons work. There are three ways that prisons are considered to be effective: recidivism rates, incapacitation and deterrence.

The reconviction rate for adult prisoners subsequently convicted for offences within a two-year period since they were discharged was 58 per cent (**Spicer and Glicksman 2004: 6**). Thus over half of adult prisoners reoffend. This is an underestimate as the data excludes those sentenced to fines and discharges. Accurate reconviction rates for community penalties are also difficult to obtain but they also suggest that over half of adults given a community sentence will re-offend. The rate for all types of community sentences was 51 per cent, with considerable variation in the rate – 60 per cent of offenders given a CRO reoffending in contrast to 38 per cent of those given a CPO.

Let us look at some data on the idea of incapacitation. The Halliday Report, *Making Punishments Work* (2001), quoted a **self-report survey** of offenders admitted to prison in 2000, which revealed that the average offender admitted to committing 140 offences in the year before they were caught, and offenders who had a drug problem admitted on average to committing 257 offences per year. Thus, on average, for each 1,000 offenders imprisoned for a 12-month period the incapacitation effect would be to reduce offending by 140,000.

The case for the general deterrent effect of custody is difficult to measure with certainty. But one international comparative study, by **Langan and Farrington (1998)**, contrasted six crimes (murder, rape, robbery, assault, burglary and motor vehicle theft) in the United States with England and Wales between 1981 and 1996. They contrasted the amount of crime based on crime surveys, with a combined index that brought together the chances of being caught and convicted and the sentence. They were thus able to assess what happened to crime over a 16-year period and assess the likelihood of an average offender being convicted and sent to prison.

Langan and Farrington (1998) found that in England and Wales in the early 1990s, criminals faced a lower risk of conviction and punishment compared with the United States. Between 1981 and 1995 an offender's risk of being caught, convicted and imprisoned increased in the United States for all six crimes but fell for all crimes in England and Wales except for murder. For burglary there were 5.5 imprisoned burglars for every 1,000 alleged burglars in the United States, increasing to 8.4 in 1994. In England and Wales there were 7.8 in 1981 but this dropped to 2.2 by 1995.

This decline in England and Wales was due to an increase in the use of cautions and unrecorded warnings; greater procedural safeguards for the accused; the growth in discontinuance of cases by the Crown Prosecution Service; the policy exhortations to judges and magistrates to make less use of prison; and the downgrading of the crime of theft of a motor vehicle in 1988 in England and Wales to a less serious offence category.

Another theorist who has taken up the issue of the deterrence role of imprisonment is Charles Murray, who challenges the liberal orthodoxy of the prison reductionists in *Does Prison Work?* Murray states the case for the theory of general deterrence and the impact of imprisonment, concluding that policy directions have been taken since the 1950s that have helped to promote rather than inhibit the growth of crime. Murray argues that, 'incarcerating people will not, by itself, solve the crime problem . . . But if the question is "How can we deter people from committing crimes?" then . . . prison is by far the most effective answer short of the death penalty' (**Murray 1997: 20**).

He shows that the chances of a convicted criminal going to prison have fallen dramatically in the period from 1954 to 1994. The prison reductionist claim about the overuse of custody is unconvincing when one contrasts, as Murray does, the steady but slow rise in prison population figures (doubled in 40 years) with the far more dramatic growth in crime over the period. Murray concludes over the period, 'The risk of going to jail if you commit a crime was cut by 80 per cent' (ibid.: 1). By contrasting the number of recorded crimes for a particular offence against the numbers given custody in the form of prison or borstal, he concludes:

> The reduction varied from crime to crime. In 1954, the number of people sentenced to prison or borstal for felonious wounding represented one out of five such felonious woundings; in 1994, one out of eight – a drop of 45 per cent. For rape, the number of people sentenced to custody went down from one out of three to fewer than one out of twelve – down 77 per cent. For burglary, from one out of ten to one out of a hundred – down 87 per cent. For robbery, from one out of three to one out of twenty – down 86 per cent.
>
> (Murray 1997: 1)

The evidential basis of his views relates to statistics on offenders sentenced for indictable offences and total crimes recorded, taken from *Criminal Statistics England and Wales*. These official statistics can be misleading (**see Chapter 2**), but Murray argues that the upwards trend in recorded crime from the 1950s represents a real growth in crime. This interpretation is confirmed by data from the British Crime Survey from 1982 onwards. Other evidence for the thesis is given in Figure 12.2, which shows the number of recorded crimes from 1950 to 2007 and the numbers of offenders given a custodial sentence of any form (see the list at the beginning of this chapter for a description of types of custodial sentence) in all courts for men and women of all ages. Figure 12.2 shows a tenfold growth in recorded crime over the 50-year period but a far less dramatic rise in the use of custody, which provides a small proportion of all those sentenced over the same period.

Murray argues that the reduced risk of imprisonment was part of a deliberate policy to switch away from reliance on custody and towards diversion. This approach is illustrated by the policies as regards younger offenders. 'For more than three decades, English criminal justice policy has taken successive steps to make the criminal justice system less punitive towards youngsters. The motives were noble, but the effect has been that young offenders can be confident that not much is going to happen to them for any offence short of a major felony' (**Murray 1997: 25**).

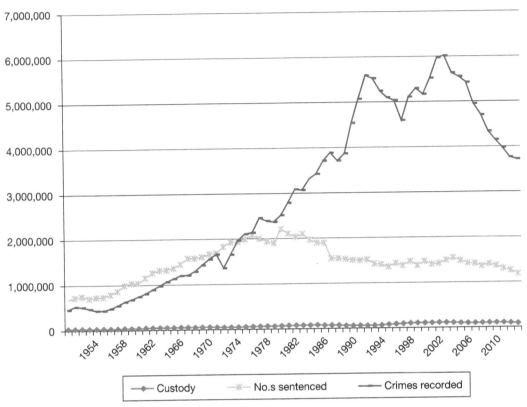

Figure 12.2 Crime and Sentencing Trends 1950 to 2013

Source: Sentencing Statistics, 2013 England and Wales, Ministry of Justice Statistics Bulletin, November 2013; Tables 1.1–1.5

Murray also argues that something can be done about crime and that 'the public is not upset about the crime problem only because the crime rate has gone up. Much of the public's anger and anxiety arises from two other aspects of the crime problem: a breakdown in lawfulness and a breakdown in public civility' (**Murray 1997: 23**).

Prison is one part of a strategy to reduce crime and restore public confidence, built on a deterrence and just deserts approach. Murray believes that public confidence is likely to be undermined in a system of criminal justice if lawlessness is tolerated such that crime is ignored or criminals go unpunished. To help restore public confidence he argues that we need to discard 'most of the system's sympathy for the offender' (ibid.: 26). The criminal justice system is not primarily designed to engage in social work solutions. It is first and foremost designed around the principles of retribution to establish the culpability of the accused for the offence. In an adversarial system this puts the offender into the limelight. But after conviction there is no logical reason why offender-instrumental considerations should have priority over the interests of either the victim or the community.

In addition to the deterrence and retributive functions of imprisonment, Murray identifies the denunciatory functions of sentencing. He says:

> The court . . . is a stage in the never-ending morality play. It is a public forum in which the peaceful members of the community assert their superiority over the outlaws. It dispenses just deserts.
>
> (Murray 1997: 24)

The combination of denunciation and deterrence was central to the government's White Paper about tackling youth crime, *No More Excuses* (**Home Office 1997a**). 'Punishment is necessary to signal society's disapproval when any person – including a young person – breaks the law and as a deterrent' (ibid.: 18). In the final section of this chapter we will be looking in more detail at a penal paradigm which, by the end of the twentieth century, had incorporated a concern for public confidence as well as about the impact of sentencing on the law breakers, both real and potential.

12.7 Sentencing for whom?

Objective 7

Discuss the issue of who is the main target or audience for sentencing decisions

We have seen above how penal policy has changed, and how new policies and the philosophies underpinning them are based on criticisms of the policies they replace. Shifts in the penal paradigm usually represent a change in the balance between the claims of many different theories and considerations. One of the questions that highlights the differences between the theories of punishment is, 'Who is sentencing for – the offender, the victim or the public?' A related and crucial issue is how the different expectations of offenders, victims and public are to be reconciled in practice.

The dilemmas of sentencing policy are often popularly encapsulated as seeking a balance between the offender and the offence. Thus should the punishment fit the crime or should punishment fit the offender? Many discussions of sentencing policy focus on the individual offender or on the individual offence, as is evident in the just deserts approach. But denouncers and those who stress public protection would argue that this focus neglects the wider role of sentencing policy in expressing the public's disapproval of crime and recognising their need for protection. Others see the victim as a forgotten player in the drama of crime and punishment (**see Chapter 3**).

It is not surprising that a criminal justice system based on adversarial principles should produce a sentencing policy that is geared towards the individual offence, offender and the circumstances of the case. The criminal justice system is after all primarily concerned with implementing the rules which determine criminal liability, and it deals with individual cases and individual offenders. Thus as Judge Rhys Davies comments, 'Judges . . . must look at the person before them, and all the circumstances, and do what they know to be right conscientiously. That's their duty' (*The Times*, 28 June 1994). To sentencers, therefore, what is fair in the individual case is likely to take priority over abstract principles of justice. This is compounded by the case law tradition of English law in which, as we have seen, there are no penal codes stating general principles but a tendency to judge each case on its merits.

The individualisation of sentencing has also, of course, been justified by the offender-instrumental approach which argues that sentences should aim to prevent further criminality. Also, in the adversarial system, defendants have the opportunity as required by due process to present factors in mitigation. All of this encourages a focus on the circumstances of the convicted criminal.

This individualisation, however, neglects a key person in many offences – the victim. While there is a focus on the harm done, the victim would appear to be little involved in sentencing other than as the potential recipient of a compensation order. As we have seen, some argue that there should be a victim impact statement and others have gone so far as to argue that victims' opinions should be sought. This might seem fair in some respects but is often rejected – also on the grounds of fairness and justice. It is, for example, regarded as a key part of criminal law that punishment is undertaken by the state on behalf of the general public (see, e.g., **Ashworth 1997**). An offence, unlike a civil dispute, is not a private matter; it is a public one. Therefore, the victim should have no role in sentencing, other than when compensation or reparation is considered. In addition, such victim involvement might further compound disparities when different sentences are given to similar offenders on the basis of victim participation. This would add yet further individualised circumstances, this time based on the opinion of the victim, and could produce highly unpredictable sentencing decisions, further undermining any notion of fairness.

In terms of considering fairness, therefore, current discussions focus on fairness to individual offenders and fairness in terms of the sentence being proportionate to the crime. In recent years the balance has shifted, with more weight being given to the seriousness of the offence and less to the needs and risks of individual offenders. However, the justice approach does restrict the severity of sentencing and encourage consistency, thus increasing justice to offenders. A major advantage of including in the aims of sentencing the retributivist concern with just desert is that it sets, in principle, limits on that system as to how and when it can act, against whom, and thus provides the justification for civil rights within the criminal justice system.

However, as we have seen, fairness to individual offenders is not easy to achieve. How much, for example, should their individual circumstances be a factor in sentencing? And how might this lead to other kinds of inequities in sentencing? This can be seen when we looked at the sentences given to those from different socio-economic backgrounds (**as in Chapter 8**). Thus offenders' domestic, financial, and social circumstances may mean that they are judged favourably or adversely by the court. They may affect how they can present themselves, whether or not they can pay a fine, and the kind of mitigating factors they may put forward. In addition, sentences may have an unequal impact on these different groups.

Some of the above points indicate that sentencing policy cannot hope to include what some would see as the root causes of crime if these lie in social inequalities and the individual circumstances. This brings us back to the limitations of current offender-instrumental approaches to make much of an impact on the volume of crime. To what extent, therefore, can the public be protected or reassured through sentencing policy?

In answer to this it could be argued that tougher policing and tougher sentencing policies are only likely to have a marginal effect on crime prevention if we consider only the impact on offenders before the court. This is because, as we have seen, only a minority of cases reaches the courts in comparison with the totality of crime. In 2011, there were 148,250 cases heard in the Crown Court, a fall from a high of 152,336 in 2010, whereas the British Crime Survey suggests that around 10 million crimes are committed each year. Even if the police force caught twice as many criminals, the courts could only be dealing with less than 1 per cent of known crimes. Of these cases, only a small minority results in a conviction, and of these the overwhelming majority are offences that do not result in a prison sentence. Thus the offender-instrumental approach can at best have only a marginal impact on the amount of crime that the community is subject to. Furthermore, as we have seen, the promise of rehabilitation that crime could be cured and the arguments of deterrent theorists are open to question.

Thus, the criminal justice process appears to have an intrinsically limited role to play in reducing or preventing crime. What implication does this have for sentencing policy, particularly in respect of its credibility with the public? The furore caused by unpopular sentencing decisions and the unit fines introduced by the CJA 1991 illustrates, however, that the public do perceive sentencing policy as important. To the denunciation model, as we have seen, punishment is not only a matter for offenders and victims but also involves the community's expectations about standards of behaviour and appropriate punishment. The criminal endangers their civil liberties by threatening their property, physical wellbeing and shared values.

The CJA 1991 also recognised the denunciatory role of punishment. Thus the 1990 White Paper stated that, 'Punishment can effectively denounce criminal behaviour and exact retribution for it. The sentence of the court expresses public repugnance of criminal behaviour and determines the punishment for it' (**Home Office 1990a: 5**). The CJA 1991 therefore could be seen as advocating what has been described as a denunciatory-retributivist perspective which by focusing on the morality of the act looks at the consequences of punishment for society as a whole rather than on the convicted criminal (**Davies 1993**).

Sentencing, after all, is a judgement about an appropriate sentence for a wrong done and is in effect morality in action. The judge condemns the offender in the name of the community and so re-enforces standards of morality. Thus, a denunciatory-retributivist approach to sentencing recognises the moral censuring role of sentencing; and that in a democracy the tariff of sentencing should reflect and articulate the moral concerns of the community as well as ensuring fairness to the individual offender before the courts.

Denunciation could add a more positive dimension to a sentencing policy which in many ways has accepted the rather gloomy prognostication that 'nothing works'. One strength of rehabilitative and deterrent arguments was that they appeared to do something positive; they focused on the future rather than on the past. Just deserts focuses on the harm done in the past and therefore could be seen as negative – punishment, however fair, for its own sake. Denunciation, on the other hand, stresses the key role of punishment in focusing public attention on to issues of morality and right and wrong. This in turn draws attention to the social function of punishment. Thus David Garland comments:

> In designing penal policy we are not simply deciding how to deal with a group of people on the margins of society – whether to deter, reform, or incapacitate them and if so how. Nor are we simply deploying power or economic resources for penological ends. We are also and at the same time defining ourselves and our society in ways which may be quite central to our cultural and political identity. An important part of a society's penal rhetoric is taken up with the suggestion of a social vision.
>
> (Garland 1990)

Thus the importance of punishment for community and society should be recognised. The values embodied in the criminal law demonstrate a society's moral views of right and wrong; and those who breach the laws are doing more than just the physical and financial damage they do to the individual victim, they are challenging the values of society, and threaten the individual's definition of normality. Justice Minister Nick Herbert, in a speech about the Government's White Paper *Swift and Sure Justice*, in July 2012, argued that following the example of some police forces of publishing the identity of convicted local criminals on their websites, 'the next step will be the widespread naming of offenders online so that communities have confidence that justice has been done'. The aim is to reinforce the values for which justice stands for, by giving concrete examples of anti-social behaviour that has been dealt with by the police and courts. The purpose of punishment for the denouncer is not directed at the criminal act or the criminal actor, but at the values which define the rules embodied in the criminal law. The audience is neither the criminal nor the victim but the public at large.

Thus the link between punishment and the public involves more than protecting individual citizens from individual criminals, though it is one essential role of the criminal justice system. Crime does more than threaten the individual; it is a threat to the community itself. 'The real significance of crime', wrote Joseph Conrad, 'is in its being a breach of faith with the community of mankind.'

Conclusion

This chapter has looked at how sentencing policy must be placed within the context of changing views about the causes of crime and the role of the penal system, especially prison. Thus the rehabilitative model was based on the idea that the problems which caused crime could be established and therefore alleviated. A sentence of imprisonment could be likened to a period of hospital treatment, an approach which had great appeal to reformers who also saw it as more humane. After decades of influence, however, the key ideas of rehabilitation were challenged. Rehabilitative policies were criticised as inhumane and inefficient. To some indeed they represented another way in which the powerful in society could enforce their values on others. Where, for example, did rehabilitation stop and enforced conformity, 'thought reform' or brainwashing begin? Did offenders who were effectively sentenced to be helped not have rights? Were these sentences fair?

The justice model aimed to provide an answer to the many problems of rehabilitation and other offender-instrumental policies. Punishment should not aim to do good, but to do as little harm as possible. Harsher sentences on the grounds of rehabilitation or deterrence could be limited by an approach which stressed linking the sentence to the harm done by culpable offenders. Yet, as we have seen, the application of the justice model raises questions about what is meant by justice and fairness in relation to sentencing.

A key feature of sentencing policy has also been an acceptance of the prison reductionist's aim, whether for idealistic or practical reasons, to reduce the use of imprisonment. This involved stressing the punitive nature of community sentences so as to make them credible to the police and sentencers. Whether or not this has been successful either in terms of reducing the use of imprisonment or making community penalties acceptable as a punishment, is still debatable. An initiative in 2009 asks the public to comment via the Ministry of Justice website on the type of work that those on community orders should undertake, such as picking up litter, when they are given a an unpaid work requirement.

Changes in penal policy reflect the efforts of policy makers to find a balance between the various aims of sentencing as well as the aims of the criminal justice process as a whole. There is a constant tension between the need for due process, which extends beyond conviction to the sentencing process and the penal system, and the often conflicting claims of public protection. While the CJA 1991 defined the primary aim of sentencing as just deserts it also, with the twin-track approach, allowed for incapacitation through larger sentences for some violent and sexual offences. Incapacitation may conflict with the interests of due process, particularly where an assessment needs to be made of the circumstances in which a particular offender is assessed as dangerous enough that a sentence out of proportion to just deserts is justified.

The revival of rehabilitation and deterrence as part of a wider offender-instrumental penal strategy in the Criminal Justice Act 2003 required a re-evaluation of existing sentencing practices and penal sanctions. How, for example, might this affect prisons? How will the new emphasis on punishment in the community affect the operation of community sentences previously seen as rehabilitative and offender focused? Some of these issues will be taken up in the next two chapters. **Chapter 13** will look at prisons and **Chapter 14** will explore developments in community sentencing.

Review questions

1. Explain why the principles of individualisation and indeterminacy followed from a rehabilitative approach to sentencing.

2. What is meant by the term 'disparity'? Explain how it is affected by individualistic strategies of sentencing.

3. What are the main elements of a justice approach to sentencing?

4. Explain the difference between a rationale for community penalties that aims to achieve an 'alternative to custody' and a rationale that seeks an intermediate sanction.

Discussion questions

1. Anne Owers, the Chief Inspector of Prisons, commented on a BBC *Law in Action* programme broadcast in 2007 that 'the overwhelming problem in prison is over-crowding'. She was then asked by presenter Clive Coleman, how many prisoners she thought our gaols should contain. She replied, 'That's not a question you can answer: it is less than it is now . . . and the question is what else we can provide, rather than saying it's always got to be prisons.'

   a. Discuss this issue in the light of the sentencing data provided in this chapter to answer the question, 'Is prison the first choice of sentence for most sentencers?'

   b. If the claim is that there are 'too many in prison', is it a legitimate question to ask what should be the number of people in prison and how would that be calculated?

   c. How would you deal with a key aspect of this question in that prisons, and those sent there, do not exist in a vacuum but are part of the process of criminal justice that starts with a crime, then an arrest, conviction and a sentence?

   d. If too many offenders are sent to prison, then are we entitled to assume that there are magistrates and judges who are sentencing inappropriately?

Further reading

Ashworth A (2007) 'Sentencing' in *The Oxford Handbook of Criminology* (4th edn), Oxford University Press: Oxford

Cavadino P and Dignan J (2002) *The Penal System: An Introduction* (3rd edn), Sage: London

Davies M (1993) *Punishing Criminals: Developing Community-based Intermediate Sanctions*, Greenwood: Connecticut

Easton S and Piper C (2008) *Sentencing and Punishment: The Quest for Justice* (2nd edn), Oxford University Press: Oxford

Weblinks

www.gov.uk/government/publications/prison-population-figures-2014

www.gov.uk/government/organisations/ministry-of-justice/about/statistics

Chapter 13

Prisons

Learning objectives

After reading the chapter you should be able to:

1. Understand the origins of the penitentiary
2. Describe the prisons and prison system in England and Wales
3. Explain the components and shifts in the prison population of England and Wales
4. Analyse the impact that imprisonment has on inmates
5. Distinguish and discuss the different aims and measures of performance of the Prison Service in England and Wales

Key statistics

- There were 81,371 males and 3,966 females in prison in England and Wales in November 2013 (*Monthly Prison Population Briefing*, 8 November 2013, Ministry of Justice)
- The main offence committed by sentenced prisoners of all ages and sex were: violence against the person (27%), sexual offences (15%), drugs offences (14%), robbery (13%), burglary (10%), theft and handling stolen goods (6%)
- 80% of the population in custody in 2013 were sentenced males aged over 18 and 13% were remand prisoners of either sex awaiting trial or sentence
- The remand population in prison has fallen from 24% in 1993 to 13% in 2013
- 14,279 prisoners were on indeterminate sentences (mainly IPPs) on 30 June 2012 (this offence was abolished in December 2012 under the LASPO Act 2012
- Juvenile and young adults population in custody has fallen between 2002 and 2013; over the same period the number of prisoners aged 60 and over has doubled (*Prison Population Statistics*, 29 July 2013, House of Commons Library)

Introduction

Despite efforts of the prison reductionists to declare prisons as vestiges of a past era, prisons in the early twenty-first century are thriving around the world. They must, therefore, be useful for some purposes but there appears to be no consensus in England and Wales on what is the primary purpose of imprisonment. The answer to the question 'Do prisons work?' depends on what is considered to be their primary purpose.

In October 1993, in a speech to the Conservative Party Conference, the Home Secretary, Michael Howard, stated that:

> Let us be clear. Prison works. It ensures that we are protected from murderers, muggers and rapists – and it makes many who are tempted to commit crime think twice.

The considerable public debate which followed demonstrated conflicting views about the role, aims and functions of prison along with continuing concerns about aspects of prison regimes, conditions and security. In general terms, prisons have credibility with the public as an institution for punishment – the punishment being loss of liberty. This serves a retributive and denunciatory purpose. Prisons are also seen as a potential deterrent for the general public, and they incapacitate dangerous and persistent offenders for the period of time they are incarcerated. Whether prison could rehabilitate **inmates** or deter them from committing further offences is far less obvious in the light of statistics on recidivism. Indeed, some argue that it may increase the likelihood that offenders will continue their life of crime – not only have prisons been characterised as schools of crime but they remove offenders from the stabilising effect of their families and the likelihood of obtaining gainful employment. Yet others feel that the prison experience is insufficiently punitive and makes little difference to those with a criminal lifestyle.

In less than a decade, the New Labour agenda on crime control shifted to focus on offender management, a return to the belief that the primary objective was on controlling the criminal rather than the deserved punishment in response to the seriousness of a crime. The current debate is not polarised into a simple punishment versus reform of the criminal, but the new post-1997 agenda has restored a fresh commitment to the corrections penal paradigm with its aim to reduce recidivism by offender change. Phil Wheatley, Director General of the Prison Service, refers to this objective and to the new joined-up agency concerned with offender management:

> ...From June 2004, the Prison Service is operating within the new National Offender Management Service framework, which in itself brings fresh challenges for the Service. We cannot be complacent, but I believe that these results show that we are well equipped to operate efficiently and competitively within the new arrangements to help drive down reoffending.
>
> (Annual Report and Accounts 2003/4)

This objective for prisons derives from the recommendation in the Halliday Report of 2001 to find more effective punishments defined in offender-instrumental terms, and the Home Office aims 'to deliver effective custodial and community sentences to reduce reoffending and protect the public'. The newly restored corrections discourse is seen in the White Paper *Justice for All* (2002), reflecting the New Labour penal paradigm and the prison reductionist logic that sees prisons as 'not working' to reduce recidivism, blames prisons for the break-up of families and the acquiring of criminal skills, and sees the record numbers in prison as undesirable (with female numbers doubling between 1993 and 2002). **Chapter 12** commented on some aspects of the prison reductionist case that underpins New Labour's strategy on prisons, and we will look at other claims in this chapter.

The challenges facing the correctional services require an enhanced focus on reha-bilitative work with offenders but with the edge that greater surveillance and tougher penalties are promised for those who do not comply. Clearly reflecting a shift away from the offence-focused system of the Criminal Justice Act 1991 (CJA 1991) to a focus on controlling offenders, the Criminal Justice Act 2003 (CJA 2003) introduced a new **indeterminate custodial sentence**. Under the CJA 1991 there was no supervision following release for prisoners sentenced to less than 12 months.

Since May 2007 the Prison Service, along with the Probation Service (**see Chapter 4**), came under the new Ministry of Justice – they were previously under the Home Office – the logic being to achieve a greater coordination between prison and probation and to achieve through-care and enhanced and coordinated supervision of offenders released back into the community. The role of National Offender Management Service (NOMS) is to achieve this greater integration.

This chapter will explore many of these issues. It starts by examining the origins of the **penitentiary**, and how the use and aims of prison have developed over the last century. The current organisation of the prison system in England and Wales will be outlined, and the numbers and characteristics of the prison population will be con-sidered, followed by examination of the experience of imprisonment, the aims of prisons, and an exploration of the issues involved in assessing whether or not prison can be said to work (**see also Chapter 12**).

Finally, there will be consideration of the question of how to balance the primary purposes of imprisonment (restriction of liberty as a punishment; and protection of the public by incapacitation) consistently with other objectives so as to provide 'humane containment' while seeking to reduce the likelihood of inmates committing further crimes on their release from prison.

To those who run prisons, the day-to-day problems of security (ensuring that pris-oners do not escape) and control (attempting to prevent riots and violence) may well take precedence over more abstract goals of rehabilitation or deterrence.

13.1 Origins of the penitentiary

Objective 1

Understand the origins of the penitentiary

The prison as we know it today is a relatively recent exper-iment which began 200 years ago. Before that time people were not usually given a sentence of imprisonment. The prisons, dun-geons and gaols were owned by a variety of municipal and private bodies, and were used to hold debtors or people who had been arrested and were awaiting trial at the quarter sessions (quarterly sittings of the court). They also held those awaiting the implementation of a sentence. For serious offenders, transportation or execution was the main punishment. For lesser offenders, prison was used to encourage a person to pay a fine and short periods of confinement were prescribed for offenders too poor to pay a fine.

John Howard, in his survey of prisons in the 1770s, estimated a prison population of 4,084. His census of 1776 calculated that the prison population was made up of debtors (59.7 per cent), felons awaiting trial, transportation and execution, along with a few serving a prison sentence (24.3 per cent), and petty offenders (15.9 per cent). Howard was appointed to the post of High Sheriff for Bedfordshire in 1773. One of his duties, usually neglected by other sheriffs, was to report on the prisons in his county. The conditions he encountered so shocked him that he undertook a more widespread review of prison conditions that was printed in 1777, entitled *The State of the Prisons*.

Punishment in the eighteenth century for those convicted of misdemeanours consisted of the stocks, corporal punishment or fines. For serious offenders the sanction was the death penalty, or a substitute. During the eighteenth century, the number of capital offences rose from 50 to 225, and the death penalty became the prescribed punishment for most offences classified as felonies. Juries, however, were often reluctant to convict a person knowing that the person would be executed. 'Pious perjury', according to William Blackstone, became more popular after 1750. By re-evaluating the value of goods stolen to less than a shilling, juries convicted offenders for petty larceny rather than the capital offence of grand larceny. Despite the growth in the number of capital offences, the number of executions declined over the century and transportation became the typical sentence by the end of the eighteenth century. As Table 13.1 shows, in the five years from 1765 to 1769, 70 per cent of criminals sentenced at the Old Bailey were transported.

The Transportation Act 1717, providing for transportation to the American colonies as a punishment, was introduced with the purpose of deterring criminals and supplying the colonies with much-needed labour. It became common practice to commute a death penalty to transportation. Although transportation did not stop immediately with the American Revolution of 1776, prisoners began to

Table 13.1 Distribution of punishments, Old Bailey 1760/94

Year	Per cent death sentence	Per cent transported/hulks	Per cent whip/brand/fine	Per cent imprisoned
1760/64	12.7	74.1	12.3	1.2
1765/69	15.8	70.2	13.4	0.8
1770/74	17.0	66.5	14.2	2.3
1775/79	20.7	33.4	17.6	28.6
1780/84	25.8	24.1	15.5	34.6
1785/89	18.5	50.1	13.2	13.3
1790/94	15.9	43.9	11.7	28.3

Source: Ignatieff (1975: 81)

be housed in hulks which were permanently moored ships. A House of Commons Committee review of transportation in 1779 recommended the continued use of hulks and that two new penitentiaries be built. The idea of the penitentiary was therefore seen at this time as a way forward, even though alternative locations were also being examined to permit the continuation of transportation.

Transportation came under scrutiny because some felt it was not a sufficient deterrent. Indeed, despite the health hazards of the journey it was said that some committed crime in order to be transported. A Transportation Act was passed in 1784 at a time when there was nowhere to send convicts, although the Beauchamp Committee of 1785 reported favourably on the practice and cited its potential for reform, its cheapness and the advantages to the colonies of a convict workforce. Alternatives considered included Algiers, Tristan da Cunha and sending convicts down the coal-mines, but Australia was preferred.

Transportation to Australia reached its peak in the 1830s and 1840s with between 4,000 and 5,000 convicts being sent each year. There were also periods in the early nineteenth century when 70 per cent of convicted felons were imprisoned in hulks. The use of hulks and transportation declined after the prison building programme of the 1840s. By 1853, the idea of penal servitude as a substitute for transportation was introduced for those sentenced to under 14 years. In 1857 the last prison hulk went out of service and transportation formally ended in 1867.

Ideological and practical considerations changed the conditions within, and the function of prison. Among the new penal ideas that emerged at the end of the eighteenth century, the penitentiary style of prison was advocated as a place that could change criminals' behaviour by making them penitent. Places of detention were to be transformed from gaols for holding criminals into penitentiaries for transforming them into law-abiding citizens. This new ideology was influenced by a combination of ideas about religious salvation, humanitarian concern with the conditions of prisons and control concerns about the growing urban population. The penal ideology of the era was also shaped by theories of rehabilitation (**discussed in Chapter 12**). These involved isolating the offender from the bad influences of the community in '**total institutions**' (**Goffman 1961**) which cut off the inmate from the environmental sources that were considered by some to be the cause of crime (**Rothman 1980**). This penal ideology also focused on the importance of surveillance and styles of discipline which could transform prisoners into self-disciplined workers (**Bentham 1791; Foucault 1977**).

These new ideas were prevalent across the emerging industrial societies of Europe and the United States. They were embodied in reforms influenced by Quaker thinkers in Pennsylvania and prison reformers such as John Howard and Elizabeth Fry in England (**Rothman 1980**). They also represented a shift in views about how to control problem groups in the community (**Scull 1977**). By the end of the eighteenth century not only prisoners, but orphans, mentally ill, sick and unemployed persons were being assigned to new style institutions such as prisons, orphanages, asylums, hospitals and workhouses. The grand Georgian and late Victorian style of institutions were invented at this time as the solution to deal with 'problem' categories of the population.

The Penitentiary Act 1779 provided the first indication of the new role for prisons as institutions to reform and deter criminals. The influence of John Howard,

Sir William Blackstone and William Eden was apparent in the new direction to penal policy. This positive role for prisons was re-echoed in the report of the May Committee on prisons as late as 1979, and in the statements of the Chief Inspector of Prisons in the 1990s, Judge Stephen Tumim. Many ideas on prisons and their roles were utopian – such as Jeremy Bentham's panopticon, a model discussed below (see Figure 13.1). However, these ideas offered a way forward for a penal system which faced three main practical problems.

First, there was concern about growing numbers of migrants coming to the cities in search of work. The old-style welfare system, based on parish relief, was no longer viable as the new factory system needed a more mobile labour force. It was no use having large pools of unemployed workers in isolated rural areas away from the new sources of work; hence, the problem of how to care and control those who were moving to rapidly expanding urban areas. This encouraged the search for innovative solutions and the invention of new institutions to cope

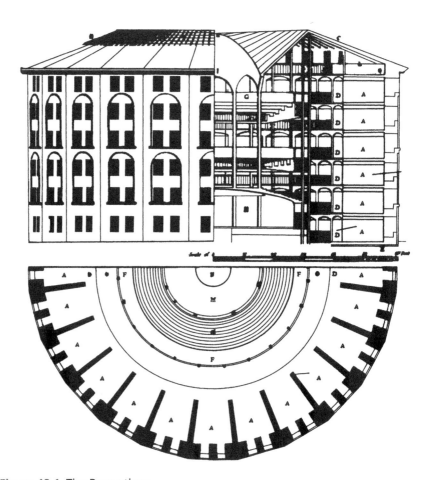

Figure 13.1 The Panopticon

Source: *The works of Jeremy Bentham, IV* (Bowering J, 1843: 172–3), The British Library, © The British Library Board (X9/4127)

with those deemed to be either a threat or inadequate – thus the workhouse, asylum and orphanage as well as the penitentiary.

Second, there was the practical problem after 1776 that transportation to the colony of Virginia was no longer available as a result of the American Revolution. Third, there was growing disquiet among reformers and thinkers such as Blackstone, Romilly and Beccaria about the large numbers of capital offences. The ideas of Cesare Beccaria, the Italian professor of political economy, about the use of the death penalty influenced debates in the House of Commons. He attacked the widespread use of **capital punishment**, arguing that the death penalty brutalised rather than deterred the population. His views were espoused by William Eden in the reform debates in Britain. Eden's book, *Principles of Penal Law*, was published in 1771. Sir Samuel Romilly took the lead in the parliamentary campaign to reduce the number of capital offences. He realised that to relinquish one mode of punishment the public and Parliament would need to be reassured that a satisfactory alternative was available. Thus, some promoters of the penitentiary argued that it was a more humane alternative to the death penalty, not that it was more efficient, as Bentham and Howard were to argue.

It took 50 years for prisons to become the main mode of punishment used by the criminal courts in Britain. The views of Howard and Bentham influenced prison policy for the next two centuries. Prison became not merely a substitute for the death penalty and transportation but a positive institution in which regimes, if sufficiently constructive, could rehabilitate those sent to them. Regimes were also to be sufficiently austere to deter future lawbreakers. The principle of 'less eligibility' implied that prison conditions were not to be more favourable than those found in the homes of the honest poor lest it encouraged crime.

The most celebrated of the novel ideas for bringing about constructive rehabilitation of convicts was the panopticon design proposed by Jeremy Bentham. The panopticon style prison involved a central viewing tower with rings of cells on each floor facing inwards to be visible to the observation tower. Observation and inspection were the keys to Bentham's approach to a more humane and effective mode of punishment. The panopticon would permit surveillance to allow prison officials to make assessments of prisoners' rehabilitation by constantly monitoring their behaviour.

The coliseum style and circular design of the panopticon was to prove difficult to build and was also inefficient. Pentonville was opened in 1842, and became the model for most Victorian prisons. It had stacked galleries on landings along a central straight corridor. Each corridor met at a central location in a fan-shaped floor plan with a central control and observation point permitting uninterrupted observation of each wing.

This systematic approach to prison design and administration reflected a growing interest in penal reform, which was wider than that of mere philanthropy. As the nineteenth century progressed, a growing number of professional experts such as architects and doctors began to take an interest in penal affairs. The intervention of central government into penal policy meant that resources were made available to those who appeared to offer a solution to the problems of crime. Government involvement had been spurred by the problems of where to ship those sentenced to transportation. Having resorted to housing increasing numbers of prisoners in the hulks, it was then necessary for the government to find them work such as river dredging.

For the next 200 years, the government became increasingly concerned in the administration of prisons. The second half of the nineteenth century saw the gradual transfer of responsibility for monitoring conditions and the administration of prisons to central government. This process began with the Gaol Act 1823, in which Peel's administration set out the first comprehensive statement of principles about the running of local prisons. The Act imposed health requirements; required inspection by visiting justices; banned the consumption of alcohol and demanded the classification of inmates and the segregation of different categories. There were to be five classes of inmates, with male separated from female prisoners; and an annual report on the prison had to be submitted to the Home Secretary.

In 1877, all prisons were nationalised in a Prison Act which brought all prisons under central government control. The government established the Prison Commission to run prisons and the first of a number of influential chairmen of the commissioners was appointed, Sir Edmund Du Cane. Some commissioners led the debate on penal reform and were strong advocates of a modern penology based on better prison conditions and strategies to achieve the rehabilitation of inmates. They represented the age of optimism (**documented in Chapter 12**) about the positive aspects of penal institutions as places of reform. This commitment to the belief that through positive regimes inmates could be encouraged to lead good and useful lives was given official recognition in the Gladstone Committee of 1895 and became one of the leading principles of the Prison Service when incorporated into the Prison Rules in 1949. This states that the purpose of imprisonment was 'to encourage and assist the inmate to lead a good and useful life'.

During the 1930s, the treadmill and arrows on convict uniforms were abolished. During this period also experiments with open prisons for adults were started at Wakefield Prison in 1936, when selected inmates from the prison slept in non-secure accommodation at New Hall Camp. In 1963, the Prison Commission was abolished and prisons were run by the Prison Service, a branch of the Home Office. The aim was to allow penal policy to be more fully integrated into a more general approach to crime control. This view was to be echoed in the rationale for integration of the Prison and Probation Service.

Events in the 1990s within prisons caused a review of all aspects of prison regimes and staffing. In 1990, prisoners rioted at Strangeways, a local prison in Manchester. It took 25 days for the prison authorities to gain control of the prison. The damage to the prison was valued at £30 million. Rioting spread to other institutions and an independent public inquiry was established under the chairmanship of Lord Justice Woolf to look at the causes of these riots and to make recommendations. The report *Prison Disturbances, April 1990* was published in 1991 (see **Home Office 1991a**). The first half of the report, written by Lord Justice Woolf, examined the causes of the riots. The second half of this extensive 600-page report was written by Lord Justice Woolf and Judge Stephen Tumim, Her Majesty's Inspector of Prisons. It provided an overview of prison conditions, made 204 specific proposals aimed to reduce future conflicts between inmates and the prison authorities and listed the following 12 key recommendations:

- Closer cooperation between the different parts of the criminal justice system. For this purpose a national forum and local committees should be established.

- More visible leadership of the Prison Service by a Director General who is and is seen to be the operational head and in day-to-day charge of the service. To achieve this, there should be a published 'compact' or 'contract' given by ministers to the Director General of the Prison Service, who should be responsible for the performance of that 'contract' and publicly answerable for the day-to-day operations of the Prison Service.

- Increased delegation of responsibility to governors of establishments.

- An enhanced role for prison officers.

- A 'compact' or 'contract' for each prisoner setting out the prisoner's expectations and responsibilities in the prison in which he or she is held.

- A national system of accredited standards, with which, in time, each prison establishment would be required to comply.

- A new prison rule that no establishment should hold more prisoners than are provided for in its certified normal level of accommodation, with provisions for Parliament to be informed if exceptionally there is to be a material departure from that rule.

- A public commitment from ministers setting a timetable to provide access to sanitation for all inmates at the earliest practical date, not later than February 1996.

- Better prospects for prisoners to maintain their links with families and the community through more visits and home leaves and through being located in community prisons as near to their homes as possible.

- A division of prison establishments into small and more manageable and secure units.

- A separate statement of purpose, separate conditions and generally a lower security categorisation for remand prisoners.

- Improved standards of justice within prisons involving the giving of reasons to a prisoner for any decision which materially and adversely affects him; a grievance procedure and disciplinary proceedings which ensure that the governor deals with most matters under his present powers; relieving Boards of Visitors of their adjudicatory role; and providing for final access to an independent Complaints Adjudicator.

(Home Office 1991a: para. 15.5)

In response, Kenneth Baker, the then Home Secretary, had already begun to introduce some of the proposals to improve conditions within prisons. An increase in visits, letters and access to telephones was implemented together with the start of a programme of works to meet the Woolf deadline of February 1996 for ending the practice of slopping out. The planning and building of new prisons also continued in order to reduce the overcrowding described in the Woolf Report. By early 1994, the Prison Service could claim that there were no cases of three inmates having to share a prison cell designed for one. Sentencing planning for inmates was introduced on 1 October 1992 for those serving four years and over, and for Category A inmates. For inmates serving between 12 months and less than 4 years the scheme started on 1 November 1993. The CJA 1993 removed the disciplinary powers of the Board of Visitors in line with the recommendations of the Woolf Report; and National and Area Criminal Justice Consultative Councils were established. However, there has been less development with regard to community prisons and a national system of accredited standards.

A second significant incident led to further reviews and reports that considered prison regimes. On 9 September 1994, six prisoners escaped from the high-security prison at Whitemoor. An inquiry was conducted by Sir John Woodcock into that escape and, following the publication of his findings in December 1994, the Home Secretary announced a review of 'physical security and security procedure in the prison service in England and Wales'. This was to be conducted by General Sir John Learmont. In the month in which the inquiry team started, Frederick West committed suicide in Winson Green Prison on 1 January 1995 and on 3 January three prisoners escaped from Parkhurst Prison on the Isle of Wight. Whitemoor and Parkhurst were **dispersal prisons** with regimes designed to prevent the escapes of inmates regarded as a danger to the public. The inquiry found that one of the Parkhurst prisoners was a sheet-metal worker who was given access to workshops where he made the key used in the escape. The inquiry focused primarily on security in dispersal prisons.

The Learmont Report (**Learmont 1995**), *Review of Prison Service Security in England and Wales and the Escape from Parkhurst Prison on Tuesday 3rd January 1995*, made 127 recommendations regarding security in dispersal prisons, including the following:

- a daily audit of tools and materials used in workshops;
- visitors to be subject to rub-down searches and X-ray checks and efforts made to prevent smuggling;
- 360-degree CCTV surveillance in visiting rooms;
- an end to family visits in dispersal prisons;
- the volume of inmates' possessions should be limited to that which would fit into two transit boxes;
- the statement of purpose of the Prison Service should be revised to make custody the primary purpose;
- key performance indicators should be reviewed to show progress towards preventing escapes rather than just measuring the number of escapes, and the degree of success at dealing with the drug problem in prison;
- the concept of drugs-free wings and of drug testing should be implemented where appropriate;
- early release should be a privilege earned through good behaviour;
- all prisoners should be offered meaningful work and wages;
- television in the cells should be an aspect of the privileges schemes and earned through good behaviour.

While the outcomes of these two major reports centred on detailed management within prisons, other recent reviews have focused on the ethos and organisation of the service as a whole. The current organisation, management and monitoring of the Prison Service are discussed in the next section.

13.2 Prisons in England and Wales

Objective 2
Describe the prisons and prison system in England and Wales

As part of the restructuring of the Home Office and the Department of Constitutional Affairs, the Prison Service was moved from the Home Office to become part of the new Ministry of Justice. Within the new Ministry, the Prison Service forms part of the National Offender Management Service (NOMS). Its role is described thus:

> The Service contributes to the NOMS purpose and aims as well as playing a key role in 'Protecting the public and reducing reoffending', which is one of the Ministry of Justice's four Departmental Strategic Objectives (*DSOs*).
>
> (*Prison Service Annual Report and Accounts 2007/8*)

The original institutional divide between prison and probation and the consequences of this for offender management has been challenged with the organisational restructuring of the two services and the introduction of the National Offender Management Service. The Prison Service has the responsibility of operating the prison system in England and Wales, including the prisons operated by private companies. The Prison Act 1877 had created a state monopoly and brought under the control of the Prison Commissioners all those prisons that had previously been in local and private control. On 1 April 1993 the Prison Service became an executive agency of the Home Office, giving it some degree of independence from Home Office control of daily operations and responsibility for budget and expenditure. With the changes to departmental roles, control over prisons was removed from the Home Office in May 2007 and given to the Ministry of Justice. In 2012 there were 131 prisons in England and Wales, of which 14 were contracted out (privately run) prisons. As described below, with contracted out prisons, the Prison Service lost in 1988 the monopoly on operating prisons it was granted in 1877.

The range of prisons reflects the variety of tasks they are used for. Some need to be near criminal courts in urban areas to house those remanded in custody while awaiting trial or sentence. Others deal with specialist populations such as young offenders or females. (In 2012 there were 11 female prisons.) Some hold inmates for relatively short periods, while others need to offer a regime for those prisoners who might spend the rest of their life inside a prison. Some can pay less attention to security because they house prisoners who have shown they can be trusted, while others must contain inmates convicted of serious violent offences who would be a danger to the public if they were to escape, and remain a danger to those inside prison while they are there. The Prison Service classifies prisons as local, training and dispersal prisons, young offender institutions, **remand centres**, juvenile institutions and women's prisons. Closed prisons have most security and surveillance to prevent escapes, whereas **open prisons** have more relaxed security. Open prisons include Ford near Worthing and Leyhill near Bristol. They have little, if any, perimeter security and house Category D prisoners posing a minimal risk to the public. Ford is renowned for the celebrities and white-collar criminals who have spent time there, including George Best who served three months for a drink-driving offence, Jeffrey Archer, Lord Brockett (the insurance fraudster) and the Guinness trio of Gerald Ronson, Ernest Saunders and Anthony Parnes.

Local prisons are used to hold those remanded in custody awaiting trial or sentence. After conviction and sentence to a period of incarceration, the observation, classification and allocation unit in the local prison carries out an initial assessment and classification. This determines which prison the prisoner will be sent to, depending on security categorisation, the length of sentence and the training, medical and other needs of the inmate.

Those sentenced to a short period in prison will probably stay in the local prison. This is usually near to where they live and so helps facilitate family visits. The local prisons tend to be the older prisons built in the Victorian era and found in urban built-up areas. A new local prison, Belmarsh in East London, was opened in 1991, but this is unusual as most expenditure on prison building went on new training prisons. These are convenient for proximity to the courts and to the prisoners' families but are often the most overcrowded with the oldest facilities.

Remand wings and centres are used in addition to local prisons for holding remand prisoners either in separate remand centres or in parts of local prisons with adult remand wings. Remand centres were created specifically for young offenders in response to growing concerns about mixing young remand prisoners with adults and, in particular, about the level of suicides and self-inflicted harm among remand prisoners under the age of 21.

Dispersal prisons are high security prisons which have regimes designed to ensure no escapes, as they hold prisoners with the maximum security classification. All sentenced prisoners on arrival in a prison are given a security rating. This ranges from **Category A**, for those whose escape would constitute a serious risk to the public, to Category D, for those who can be sent to open prisons.

The escape of the Soviet spy, George Blake, from Wormwood Scrubs prison in 1965 led to an inquiry by the Mountbatten Committee (**Home Office 1966**). Their report in December 1965 recommended that all high-risk inmates be held in one maximum security prison. This recommendation was not approved and, after a further proposal from a committee chaired by Professor Leon Radzinowicz which reported in 1968 (**Home Office 1968**) it was decided that high-security prisoners should be dispersed among a number of prisons with maximum security facilities; hence the term 'dispersal prisons' of which there were eight in 2012 holding on average a daily population of 6,123 prisoners. Three of these have special security units for those Category A inmates most likely to try to escape.

The need for security classifications was another of the recommendations of the Mountbatten Report. Initial classification is based on the crime committed and the reports made by the assessment unit in the local prison. These categories are reassessed at regular intervals and most inmates are reclassified downwards during their prison term. Category A is for prisoners whose escape from custody would be highly dangerous to the public or to the security of the state. Category B is used to classify inmates who do not constitute such a serious risk. Category C is applied to prisoners who cannot be trusted in open prisons but are deemed unlikely to make an effort to escape, and category D is for prisoners who can be trusted to serve their time in open prisons where the security aspect of the regime is minimal. Women's and young offender institutions are only classified as open or closed.

Training prisons hold long-term inmates. There are 71 training prisons and they can be open or closed. They provide training facilities, vocational courses and the opportunity to work in the prison industries. At Coldingley Prison, a closed prison, inmates can work making motorway signs or in the large industrial laundry that has a contract with hospitals in the region. Grendon Underwood, opened in 1963, offers a specialist regime based on the therapeutic community concept pioneered by Maxwell Henderson in psychiatric hospitals.

Young offender institutions (YOIs) hold young adult offenders aged between 18 and 20 and juvenile offenders aged 15 to 17. Juveniles may be kept in custody for remand orders and as a consequence of being given a detention and training order (DTO), which replaced previous custodial sentences for juveniles in 2000. The DTO, for 12–17-year-old offenders, varies between four months and two years, with half of the period spent in custody and the other half under supervision by a youth offending team. Juveniles sentenced to custody under a DTO may not be sent to a YOI as there is also the option of being sent to a **secure training centre** (STC) or a **local authority secure children's home** (LASCH).

Places for incarcerating younger offenders have changed over the years since the Victorian era when the first efforts to separate younger inmates from adults were made with the introduction of reformatories and industrial schools. Borstals were introduced in 1901 and made fully available after the Prevention of Crime Act 1908. Detention centres were introduced in the Criminal Justice Act 1948. Chapter 8 described the changes since 1982 to the name of institutions holding younger offenders. The names may have changed more rapidly than the nature of the regimes that the changes were supposed to signify.

In April 1998 Medway Secure Training Centre was opened near Rochester, Kent. It is the first of a new type of custodial institution for 12–14-year-olds who have committed serious offences. The offenders, called trainees, spend between three months and a year in a regime designed to rehabilitate and punish. Trainees are required to attend educational courses and programmes to address offending behaviour. It is run by a private firm, Rebound ECD, which is owned by G4S (Group 4). This type of secure accommodation for younger offenders is not a Prison Service institution and comes under the supervision of the Youth Justice Board established by the Crime and Disorder Act 1998.

Female establishments are only classified in security terms as either open or closed. The female prison population is under 4,000 and these are housed in 13 women's prisons in England. These are: Askham Grange, Bronzefield (private), Drake Hall, Downview (small unit currently under review), East Sutton Park,

Eastwood Park, Foston Hall, Holloway, Low Newton, New Hall, Peterborough (private operated by Sodexo and houses both female and male prisoners in separate units), Send and Styal.

A mother and baby unit (MBU) enables mothers to have their children with them in prison. There are currently seven MBUs, located at Styal, New Hall, Eastwood Park, Holloway, Askham Grange, Peterborough and Bronzefield.

Young women prisoners aged between 18 and 21 live in units that are separate from adult prisoners. Young women prisoners aged under 18 are held in Young Women's Units, which are separate units within women's prisons. There are three dedicated units – the Jospehine Butler Unit at Downview, the Mary Carpenter Unit at Eastwood Park and the Rivendell Unit at New Hall.

Special hospitals are used for offenders who need treatment for mental disorders under conditions of special security because of their violent or criminal behaviour. These offenders can be sent to one of three special hospitals: Broadmoor, Rampton or Ashworth. These have maximum security facilities similar to a dispersal prison. Special hospitals are run by the Department of Health. All the other types of prisons mentioned above are the responsibility of the Prison Service.

The Prison Service is not the only agency allowed to run prisons. The Criminal Justice Act 1988 allowed for private companies to take over the operation of remand prisons, a sector of the prison establishment where the worst conditions were usually found. Since then companies such as G4S have been involved in operating prisons but the Prison Service has overall responsibility for the 'contracted-out' prisons run by the private sector. All contracted-out prisons have a prison service controller of Governor grade to monitor the delivery of the contract with the Prison Service, and to undertake adjudications for prisoners charged with offences against disciplinary rules.

Contracted-out prisons: The first to open was The Wolds private remand centre near Hull. Now there are 10, including Blakenhurst near Redditch, and Doncaster which opened in June 1994. The then Conservative Government's aim to break down the Prison Service monopoly in this area was not only influenced by its ideological belief in the virtues of competition. Two other factors played a part: first, a desire to inject new ideas into the running of remand prison regimes; and second, after a series of industrial disputes, a determination to undermine the powerful trade union, the Prison Officers' Association.

The influence of the Prison Officers' Association has been apparent in a number of industrial disputes over the years. The Labour Government of James Callaghan established an inquiry chaired by Mr Justice May after a long period of deteriorating industrial relations in prisons in England and Wales. It examined the prison population, objectives and regimes, the organisation of the system, resources, the roles of prison officers and governors, pay and allowances, industrial relations and working conditions. The resulting Home Office report was published in 1979 (*The Report of the Committee of Inquiry into the UK Prison Service*, Cmnd 7673). It concluded that 'Central administration ought to have shown itself more responsive to growing feelings of dissatisfaction with the organisation and management and service as a whole, especially in the field of personnel management.' With reference to the importance of having clear and agreed aims for prisons (**discussed later in this chapter**) it commented:

> A great deal of the evidence we received maintained that at the present time these objectives (of imprisonment) were unclear or confused or both, and that this had brought about or contributed not only to a lack of incisive and purposeful leadership but also to indecision, frustration and the consequent lowering of morale throughout the prison service.
>
> (Home Office 1979: 1961)

The May Report found that over one-quarter of junior prison officers were working more than 60 hours' overtime a week, boosting a modest basic salary into reasonably high average earnings. In response to these staffing costs, a new higher basic wage for a 39-hour working week was introduced for prison officers in exchange for abandoning some of the expensive shift work practices. Fresh Start, as the initiative was called, was introduced in 1987 in an attempt to overcome these staffing costs.

Industrial disputes were not overcome by the Fresh Start programme and the government sought other ways of curtailing the influence of the Prison Officers' Association. The introduction of 'contracting out' of prison service work to private companies should be seen in this context. The Criminal Justice and Public Order Act 1994 curtailed the right of prison officers and governor grade staff to go on strike.

Employee costs are the major contributor to the cost of imprisonment. In 2011, the Ministry of Justice calculated that the average direct cost per prisoner was £26,978 per inmate per year, and the average overall cost per prisoner was £37,163. These costs ranged from a high end of £62,698 for male YOIs, to £18,565 for male open prisons.

However, this does not mean that sending one person fewer to prison would save this amount, as most of these costs are relatively fixed. Three-quarters of prison service expenditure is attributable to staffing costs: the Prison Service had 30,821 employees in December 2012, representing a ratio of under three inmates per officer. This is a very generous ratio of officers to prisoners compared with prison services around the world.

The Prison Service is open to inspection by the Inspectorate of Prisons (HMIP), established by statute in 1982 after a recommendation in the 1979 May Report. Members of HMIP can make unannounced visits as well as having a number of scheduled visits to certain prisons each year. After a visit a report is made highlighting the strengths and weaknesses of the establishments visited. Some reports have been very damning about conditions in prison establishments and the treatment of prisoners.

Independent Monitoring Boards (IMBs) took over the role of the Board of Visitors in 2003 and perform a vital 'watchdog' role on behalf of Ministers and the general public in providing a lay and independent oversight of prisons. In total there are over 1,800 lay members of these boards. Each Board is independent of the prison it monitors and reports each year to the Home Secretary. Board members can visit the prison at any time in order to talk to the staff, inmates or detainees, hear their concerns and check on the conditions they are living and working in. Boards have achieved significant changes through the work of their members.

Until 1992, the Board of Visitors adjudicated on matters of discipline where an inmate might be liable to lose remission for disciplinary offences. As a result of the CJA 1991 prison governors have the right to order up to 14 'added days' for disciplinary offences. The Board of Visitors at Wandsworth prison in the 1980s was among the first to publish a public report, describing the insanitary conditions associated with slopping out and the health hazards of a cockroach infestation near the kitchen area.

These independent Boards produce annual reports, and in some prisons they have played a critical role and offer an insight and sometimes a warning about the regime. In April 1994, the Board of Visitors at Whitemoor prison in March, Cambridgeshire, published a report about the conditions and regime in the prison, which held 514 inmates, 20 per cent of whom were classified as Category A. These included Dennis Nilsen and IRA terrorists. Another 20 per cent were life sentence prisoners. It was in this prison that Leslie Bailey, a paedophile convicted of serious sexual offences against children, was found strangled in his cell in October 1993. The report described the prison as dirty and the Board of Visitors condemned the illegal brewing of 'hooch' by inmates. The main concern expressed by the Board in its report was that management had lost control of the situation and it quoted a governor who was of the opinion that the prisoners and not the staff were virtually in control of the prison – an allegation that was to be prescient in the light of the subsequent escape attempt in September 1994 by five convicted IRA prisoners in which one prison officer was shot and wounded. All the prisoners were recaptured within hours of the escape. In the same month, quantities of the explosive Semtex were found at Whitemoor. These incidents raised many questions about why no action had been taken and led to demands for the resignation of the Home Secretary, as did the escape in January 1995 of three Category A offenders from another dispersal prison, Parkhurst, on the Isle of Wight.

Each IMB publishes an annual report, most of which are made public. The reports indicate matters for action both by the prison and the minister but also record improvements and matters for commendation within the prison.

13.3 Prison population

Objective 3

Explain the components and shifts in the prison population of England and Wales

The daily population in prison varies depending on the time of year. It usually drops in December and rises to a high point in March. The prison population rose to 50,000 by 1988 and then fell until 1993, since when it has steadily risen. The number of people in prison was 81,371 in November 2013, a fall from the high point of 86,634 in 2012.

To measure the degree of overcrowding, the prison population is compared with the **Certified Normal Accommodation** (CNA). In October 2011 the average occupancy level across all prisons was 112 per cent. This varies considerably between categories of prisons. In July 2012, HMP Kennet, a male local category C prison, was overcrowded by 93 per cent, whereas some institutions were under capacity, such as open young offender institutions, two of which (HMYOI Hindley and HMYOI Ashfield) were only 53 and 56 per cent occupied during the

Table 13.2 Total prison estate population 1980–2013 as average of monthly totals

Year	Total
1980	42,264
1990	44,975
1997	61,114
1998	65,299
1999	64,770
2000	64,602
2001	66,301
2002	70,843
2003	73,038
2004	74,657
2005	75,980
2006	78,145
2007	80,437
2008	82,636
2009	83,585
2010	84,725
2011	85,951
2012	86,634
2013	84,392

Source: Ministry of Justice, Prison Population Figures, www.justice.gov.uk/statistics/prisons-and-probation/prison-population-figures

same month. The annual averages of the population in custody over the period from 1980 to 2013 are given in Table 13.2.

Prison capacity was increased by 20,000 places between 1997 and 2009, but to cope with overcrowded prisons, the New Labour Government announced plans in 2009 for a number of new prisons and extensions to existing ones plus three super large prisons called Titan prisons, each housing 2,500 offenders to take the CNA from 76,191 in 2009 to 96,000 by 2014. In April 2009 the then Justice Secretary Jack Straw announced that these plans would be abandoned in favour of five smaller prisons each housing 1,500 at a total cost of £4 billion. When the Coalition Government took over in 2010, the legacy of the prison expansion programme did not sit comfortably with either the Conservative or Liberal Democrat manifesto promises of reducing the prison population and reducing reoffending, and the plans were amended to allow for the building of two new prisons, HMPs Thameside and Oakwood, together housing a total of 2,505 prisoners, which opened in 2012, while closing three other prisons due to the cost of running them. Nationally, the total usable operational capacity stood at 90,914 in September 2012, an increase of more than 2,000 on the previous September when the capacity stood at 88,628.

In speeches and legislative changes, Kenneth Clarke proved to be unstinting in his opposition to further prison building plans; his approach was to focus on reducing the use of prison and on stabilising – and ultimately reducing – the prison population, by changing sentencing policy, expanding the use of custody alternatives, and improving the reoffending rates associated with rehabilitation programmes and alternatives to custody. He promised a 'rehabilitaion revolution'.

However, Kenneth Clarke was deposed from his role as Justice Secretary in the Cabinet reshuffle of September 2012 and replaced by Chris Grayling, whose personal stance on justice is generally considered to be more 'hard line', but whose priorities were limited as the Ministry of Justice is under pressure to further reduce its spending bill (of which just under a third is spent on running the prison and probation service) to make savings of 26 per cent by 2014, and that a 'rehabilitation revolution' to cut re-offending was named the number one priority for the department in its three-year business plan published in May 2012 (*Business Plan 2012–2015*, Ministry of Justice).

▶ International comparisons

It is often claimed in the press and in broadcasts that the courts in England and Wales make more use of custody than other countries. Comparisons with other western European Union countries is given in the last chapter in Table 12.2, while Table 13.3 shows some comparisons with other prison populations in other advanced industrial countries, some with adversarial legal systems similar to that in England and Wales.

Both tables show average daily populations plus the rate per size of population. In Table 12.2 the number of prisoners per crimes recorded is also shown. There are difficulties in ensuring the data is directly comparable; however, the main question to ask is 'what comparisons make most sense?' Should we compare the prison population against the total size of the population or the amount of crime? Populations vary and we would not expect a country with a larger proportion of infants or elderly citizens to have the same crime problem as others. The problem with comparisons based on the population is that it takes no account of the amount of crime committed, which is, after all, the main reason why people go to prison. The demographic comparative data does not take into account the differences in usage of imprisonment or the risk of imprisonment because of the age of

Table 13.3 International comparison of estimated prison populations in some countries outside Europe 2001 and 2010/12

Country	2001	2010/12	Rate per 100,000 population in 2010/12
England and Wales	67,056	86,708	154
Australia	22,458	29,106	129
Brazil	233,859	514,582	260
China	1,428,126	1,640,000	121
Egypt	56,587	66,000	80
India	313,635	368,998	30
Iran	158,000	250,000	333
Israel	N/A	17,700	236
Japan	63,415	69,876	55
New Zealand	5,887	8,433	190
Russia	923,765	722,200	505
South Africa	174,893	157,375	310
USA	1,961,247	2,266,832	730

Source: Kings College ICPS World Prison Brief, www.prisonstudies.org/world-prison-brief

criminal responsibility. Thus, it is suggested that a better comparison would be to compare prison populations against crime problems. However, even if this were to be done, we should still ask whether there is any utility in such a comparison because crime definitions and sentencing policies can vary, reflecting different cultures and the different political significance of certain crimes. The cultural significance of types of crime, and modes and the scale of punishment, is unlikely to be the same in all countries around the globe.

▶ Categories of prisoner

Not all inmates held in Her Majesty's Prisons are of the same status. Some defendants are remanded in custody in prison before and during trial. These unconvicted prisoners have rights distinguishing them from other inmates such as daily access to visitors. There are also those who have been convicted but have not yet been sentenced. These remand prisoners constitute approximately one-fifth of the average prison population. Offenders aged under 21 cannot be sentenced to prison for any reason, but may be remanded in custody in prison for trial or sentence. Young adults aged 18 to 20, if sentenced to a custodial sentence by the courts will be sent to a Young Offender Institution.

▶ Fine defaulters in prison

Although there are many ways in which a fine can be enforced by the courts, the ultimate sanction for non-payment of fines or compensation orders is imprisonment, as indeed it is for non-compliance with community sentences. Fine defaulters are not, however, automatically sent to prison as Mark Romer, a Metropolitan Stipendiary Magistrate, explained in a letter to *The independent*:

> Fine defaulters are not imprisoned because they cannot pay their fines but because, often after many attempts to get them to pay, they will not. Magistrates are forbidden by law to imprison fine defaulters unless either they refuse to pay or, having had the means to pay and other methods of enforcing payment (e.g. by a bailiff's warrant) having failed, they do not pay.
>
> (*The Independent*, 5 March 1995)

'The fine defaulter population decreased rapidly to very low levels which have been stable since 2001' (*Story of the Prison Population: 1993–2012 England and Wales*, Ministry of Justice, January 2013). The average daily population of fine defaulters in prison is 30. The yearly figures over a 12-month period are shown in Table 13.4.

The drop in recent years is in part because of a Queen's Bench judgment on 28 November 1995 (*R v. Oldham Justices and Another, ex parte Cawley*) that the courts must consider all other methods of enforcing the fine before committing a fine defaulter to prison. The Magistrates' Association and the Justices' Clerks' Society produced guidelines that required the magistrates to take each enforcement

Table 13.4 Fine defaulters annual receptions 1997/2012

1997	6,336	2005	2,038
1998	5,374	2006	1,904
1999	3,727	2007	1,475
2000	2,476	2008	1,378
2001	1,453	2009	1,528
2002	1,192	2010	1,041
2003	1,250	2011	1,257
2004	1,835	2012	1,412

Source: Ministry of Justice Offender Management Statistics Quarterly

measure in turn to consider whether each measure is appropriate or not. Good practice guidance notes were issued to the courts in July 1996 regarding the enforcement of financial penalties. Under the Criminal Procedure and Investigations Act 1996 the method of initiating an attachment of earnings order, in the case of fine default, was changed to allow justices' clerks to take proceedings without reference to the magistrates.

▶ Life sentence inmates

In contrast to those who enter prison for a week or two, the offender given a life sentence has a very different situation to face. Life sentence prisoners spend some time after sentence at a life sentence unit to undergo counselling and preparation for their future life in prison or on licence. They have no entitlement to automatic release but are eligible to apply for *release on licence*. This is discretionary, and if released, the person is on licence for the rest of his or her life and may be recalled to prison at any time. The reason why the courts give some offenders a life sentence is shown in the list below:

For adults aged over 21 the following sentences result in a life sentence:

- Mandatory Life Sentence for persons found guilty of murder.

- Discretionary Life Sentence may be imposed as the maximum penalty for grave offences, e.g. manslaughter, attempted murder, rape, armed robbery or arson.

- Automatic Life Sentence re-introduced by section 122 LASPO 2012 for offenders over the age of 18 and who were convicted after 3 December 2012. The life sentence will be imposed where the court would otherwise have imposed a 10-year sentence or more and the offender sentenced had a previous conviction for which he received 10 years or more, or a life sentence with a minimum tariff of 5 years.

- Imprisonment (or Detention) for Public Protection (IPP) was an indeterminate sentence introduced in the CJA 2003 and applied to offenders who were convicted of a specified sexual or violent offence carrying a maximum penalty of 10 years' imprisonment or more, and who were considered by the court to pose a 'significant risk to members of the public, of serious harm'. As of May 2012, with the introduction of the Legal Aid, Sentencing and Punishment of Offenders Act (LASPO), IPPs were abolished and replaced by the new Extended Determinate Sentence (EDS), which consists of a custodial term (custodial sentence the court would have imposed for the offence if the offender was not deemed to be 'dangerous') and an extended licence period (additional extension period for the purpose of protecting the public from the risk of the offender committing a further violent or sexual offence). However, the new EDS sentence, which is not indefinite, cannot be treated as a direct replacement for the old IPP. The main differences between EDS and previous extended sentences is that EDS can be imposed both on adults and juveniles and the prisoner must serve at least two-thirds of the custodial term before they may be released.

For those aged under 21, the following terms refer to the equivalent of a life sentence:

- Custody for life for those aged 18–20 convicted of murder or another life sentence offence.
- Detained during Her Majesty's pleasure under section 90 of the Powers of Criminal Courts (Sentencing) Act 2000 is a mandatory sentence for those convicted of murder who are aged over 10 but under 18 at the time of the offence.
- Detention for life under section 91 of the Powers of Criminal Courts (Sentencing) Act 2000, is a discretionary life sentence. This sentence is available for persons aged over 10 but under 18 convicted of offences other than murder, for which a life sentence may be passed on an adult.

A youth in the Crown Court may receive an Extended Determinate Sentence under s 226(b) LASPO 2012 if he meets the criteria for 'dangerousness' under s 229, i.e.:

- the offender is convicted of a sexual or violent offence (listed in Schedule 15 to the CJA 2003);
- the court considers the offender to be dangerous;
- the current offence merits a determinate sentence of at least four years (after discount of guilty plea is applied).

In June 2012, there were 13,754 adult prisoners serving indeterminate sentences in prisons in England and Wales: 13,360 of these were men, 394 were women. There were 269 young adults, and 31 were aged 15–17 (*Offender Management Statistics Quarterly, January–March 2012*, Ministry of Justice). The average time served by mandatory life sentence prisoners released in 2011 was 16 years, up from 9 years in 1965 (*Offender Management Statistics Quarterly, 2011 Annual Tables*, Ministry of Justice).

Every life sentence prisoner or offender sentenced to IPP had to serve a minimum term of imprisonment to act as a deterrent and for retribution. All minimum terms, called the tariff, were set by the trial judge in open court. After tariff expiry, a life sentence prisoner or those sentenced to IPP may have been released if the Parole Board was satisfied that they were not a risk to the public. The LASPO Act abolished the use of IPPs with immediate effect in May 2012, but the Parole Board is still responsible for reviewing the cases of those IPP prisoners who are still in the system. On 30 June 2012, out of 6,078 IPP prisoners in England and Wales still in custody, the tariff date of 3,531 prisoners was known to have already passed.

Males over 21 will be sent to a local prison for assessment, risk analysis and to develop a Life Sentence Plan. 'First stage' lifer prisons vary and depend on the security risk or threat to public safety. Those classified as a Category A prisoner will be sent to a dispersal prison. Progress and behaviour in prison will determine who moves to a 'second stage' prison, and lifers normally need to reach a 'third stage' open prison before they will be considered by the Parole Board.

After tariff expiry, release on licence is dependent on a prisoner showing that the risk to the public has been reduced to a minimum. The Parole Board takes this decision on the basis of reports prepared by Prison and Probation staff and others as appropriate, depending on the prisoner's progress in custody. The Parole Board must consider the likely risk to other people when considering the release of a person on licence and the extent to which he or she has complied in the past or is likely in the future to comply with the conditions of a licence. Life licensees can be recalled to prison at any time if they commit an offence or otherwise fail to comply with the conditions of their licence.

The time served before release on licence varies depending on the nature of the crime and the perceived risk to the community of releasing a life sentence inmate. Some inmates may never be released. Such is likely to be the situation of Ian Brady, the Moors murderer, convicted with Myra Hindley in 1966 at Chester Assizes for the murder of Lesley Anne Downey, aged 10, and Edward Evans, aged 17. Hindley, who died in prison in 2002, confessed to her role in the murder of three other children.

The responsibility for determining the time to be served under a life sentence and whether this should be a political or judicial decision has occasioned much criticism, and the matter came before the European Court of Human Rights in *Dennis Stafford* v. *United Kingdom* (2002) and the House of Lords in *R* v. *Secretary of State for the Home Department, ex parte Anderson and Taylor* (2002). As a result of these cases, legislation allowing the Home Secretary to set the minimum period to be served under a life sentence was declared incompatible with the Human Rights Act 1998 and the CJA 2003 introduced new provisions with effect from December 2003. These provide guidelines for the courts in assessing the tariff for mandatory life sentences and an extensive list of aggravating and mitigating factors which must be taken into account. Whole life tariffs were introduced for multiple and some child murders as well as for murder committed for political or religious causes. Other guideline tariffs are set at 30 years (e.g. for the murder of a police or prison officer, or a murder committed for gain) and at 15 years where none of the aggravating features listed are present. Different considerations are in place for those under the age of 18.

▶ Female prisoners

The number of female prisoners has increased in the last decade. Table 13.5 shows the percentage of female inmates as a proportion of all prisoners over the last 100 years – the table gives data on five-year intervals (except for 2012) from 1900 to 2012 and shows that, despite the recent rapid growth in female imprisonment in absolute terms, current proportions are not as high as in the first half of the twentieth century.

Other data showing the numbers of female prisoners per 100,000 of the whole population over a hundred years indicate a decline from a high of 20 female

Table 13.5 Female prisoners as a percentage of the prison population in England and Wales 1900/2012

Year	Male	Female	Total	Females as a proportion (%)
1900	14,459	2,976	17,435	17.1
1905	18,398	3,127	21,525	14.5
1910	18,323	2,581	20,904	12.3
1915	9,244	2,067	11,311	18.3
1920	9,573	1,427	11,000	13.0
1925	9,635	874	10,509	8.3
1930	10,561	785	11,346	6.9
1935	10,587	719	11,306	6.4
1940	8,443	934	9,377	10.0
1945	13,180	1,528	14,708	10.4
1950	19,367	1,107	20,474	5.4
1955	20,156	978	21,134	4.6
1960	26,198	901	27,099	3.3
1965	29,580	841	30,421	2.6
1970	38,040	988	39,028	2.5
1975	38,601	1,219	39,820	3.1
1980	40,748	1,516	42,264	3.6
1985	44,701	1,532	46,233	3.3
1990	43,378	1,597	44,975	3.6
1995	48,983	1,979	50,962	3.9
2000	61,252	3,350	64,602	5.2
2005	71,512	4,467	75,979	6.1
2010	80,489	4,236	84,725	5.0
2012	82,481	4,154	86,634	4.8

Sources: Prison Statistics England and Wales 2002, Offender Management Statistics Quarterly January–March 2012, Ministry of Justice website, and House of Commons Library Prison Population Statistics, 2013

prisoners per 100,000 of population in 1902. The proportion of female prisoners stabilised from 1929 to 1996 between 3 and 7 per cent. In 2009 the proportion of female inmates was 5.2 per cent.

The White Paper Justice For All under the heading 'What is not Working' states, 'The number of female prisoners more than doubled between 1993 and 2001' (Home Office 2002: 85). While it identifies a trend towards a higher proportion of women prisoners, any claim that this constitutes evidence that the system is not working is unusual because female offenders are sent to prison by judges and magistrates in response to their crimes. Is there a 'correct' percentage of female prisoners and, if so, what is it?

▶ Minority ethnic prison population

The prison population in England and Wales on average in 2011/2012 was 72 per cent White, 13 per cent were Black or Black British, 7 per cent were Asian or Asian British, 4 per cent were of mixed ethnicity and 1 per cent from Chinese or other ethnic groups (see Table 13.6).

Table 13.6 Ethnic identity of prisoners: analysis of the average prisoner population 2011/2012

Total	86,813
White	62,409
Asian or Asian British	6,444
Black or Black British	11,469
Chinese or Other	994
Mixed	3,194
Not stated	142
Unrecorded	2,162

Source: *Offender Management Statistics Quarterly*, January–March 2012, Ministry of Justice website

The picture is sometimes confusing because of the number of non-resident overseas criminals who are in prison plus some non-criminal inmates who might be awaiting deportation. On 30 June 2012, there were 10,861 foreign inmates. Some, but not all, of these will be liable to automatic deportation upon reaching the end of their sentences or, when accepted by the recipient country, up to 270 days before their release date under the Early Removal Scheme. The automatic deportation provision for foreign nationals was introduced by the UK Borders Act 2007 on 1 August 2008 in response to general controversy in 2006 when it emerged that many foreign prisoners, released following a prison term for a serious offence were not automatically considered for deportation. The Act provides that any foreign national serving a custodial sentence of 12 months or more should face automatic deportation, except in specific circumstances including those where deportation would breach the person's human rights (as Abu Qatada's solicitors claimed was the case when their client faced post-release deportation in 2012) and those cases in which the offender was under 18 when convicted.

In 2012, the LASPO Act introduced further power for the Secretary of State to remove from the UK foreign prisoners once they have served the minimum term set by the court without the consent of the Parole Board. Any such prisoners who subsequently returns to the UK is liable under the provisions of this Act to be detained and re-incarcerated for the duration of their original sentence.

In October 2011, a UK Border Agency Inspection Report revealed that 4,200 foreign national prisoners were deported from the UK in 2007. In 2010, two years after the introduction of the automatic deportation scheme, 5,235 foreign national prisoners were deported. In May 2011, there were 3,775 foreign national prisoners in the community who had not been removed at the end of their custodial sentence. The UK Border Agency (UKBA) cannot deport all the foreign national prisoners who should be removed, according to the criteria, because of difficulties with obtaining travel documents and because of claims regarding their human rights on such matters as a right to a family life under Article 8 of the Human Rights Act (HRA) 1998.

❯ Time served

The time served in prison is not usually the amount of time imposed by the judge or magistrate, for the following reasons: first, time is deducted for pre-sentence periods while on remand in custody awaiting trial or sentence; second, because prisoners are entitled to 50 per cent remission or 'automatic release'; third, because of parole; fourth, because of early release under the Home Detention Curfew scheme; and fifth, for Release on Temporary Licence (ROTL). The Prison Act 1898 allowed the use of remission of part of the sentence for the good conduct of inmates. The maximum remission, for those given penal sentences, was one-quarter for men and one-third for women. In the 1940s, this was changed to one-third for all inmates. Parole was introduced in 1967 and allowed inmates to apply for early release in addition to remission. This was a discretionary element and, unlike remission, was not automatic. Prior to the changes brought about by the CJA 1991, parole release time was in addition to the one-third deduction from sentence length for remission. Thus with remission (one-third) and parole eligibility starting at the one-third stage of the sentence, before the changes brought about by the CJA 1991, an inmate might be released soon after the one-third stage of their sentence.

Sentence calculations changed with the abolition of the terms 'remission' and 'parole' by the CJA 1991. All inmates were to serve one-half of their sentence, with full allowance for time held on remand in custody. For breaches of prison rules an inmate may serve up to 14 'added days'. Three sets of rules govern release as a consequence of the CJA 1991:

- *Those serving a sentence of under 12 months* are automatically released at the 50 per cent stage as before. This is referred to as 'automatic unconditional release' (AUR). In 2015, with the implementation of the CJA 2003, prisoners sentenced to under 12 months are to be supervised in the community after their release.

- *Those sentenced from 1 to 4 years* serve 50 per cent of the time but on release will be supervised in the community until the three-quarters period of time. So a person sentenced to 2 years will be released after 1 year, allowing for time spent on remand in custody, and supervised for a further 6 months. This is known as 'automatic conditional release' (ACR).

- *Those sentenced to 4 years and over* must serve half their sentence, with an allowance for time spent in custody while on remand. But they must still apply after the 50 per cent stage of sentence for release. This is a discretionary decision. They might not be successful, in which case they will serve up to the two-thirds stage of sentence time. Whether they are released at the earliest opportunity (50 per cent stage) or serve all their time to the two-thirds stage, the released prisoner will be supervised in the community after release until the three-quarters stage.

Thus, a prisoner sentenced to 10 years who had spent 6 months awaiting trial and sentence would, from the time of sentence, be able to apply for release after a further 4 years 6 months. If successful the prisoner would be supervised on release in the community for a further 2 years and 6 months, i.e. to the three-quarters stage. If unsuccessful in a bid for early release the prisoner would be released finally at the two-thirds stage, i.e. at 6 years 8 months minus the 6 months served on remand. The prisoner would then be supervised in the community for a further 1 year and 4 months, i.e. a total period either in prison or under supervision in the community of 7 years 6 months for a sentence of 10 years.

The CJA 2003 created some new types of custody called Custody Plus and Intermittent Custody (**as discussed in Chapter 11**) which were due to affect the early release provisions, but which were never implemented and were subsequently repealed by the Legal Aid, Sentencing and Punishment Act 2012. Previously, the Labour Government had already begun phasing out the early release scheme in order to meet with public approval in time for the 2010 General Election – a move which is said to have resulted in an increase of the daily prison population in England and Wales by 1,200 – and in his White Paper, *Breaking the Cycle: Effective Punishment, Rehabilitation and Sentencing of Offenders*, of December 2010, Kenneth Clarke pledged the Coalition Government's approval, promising 'we will not introduce any early release schemes', but gave explicit support to Home Detention Curfew, which allows an approved prisoner to be security tagged and released on strict conditions up to four and a half months before reaching the halfway mark of their sentence.

▶ Home detention curfew

The home detention curfew (HDC) applies to prisoners who are serving a fixed sentence of between 3 months and under 4 years. It allows prisoners to live outside prison prior to release at the half way point of their sentence. The scheme was introduced throughout England and Wales in January 1999. It refers to an additional form of early release for those sentenced from 3 months to 4 years when they are within 135 days of release (after serving half their sentence). The HDC, originally for 2 months, was extended to 3 months in 2002 and by the CJA 2003 to 135 days. It is not used with those convicted of violent or sexual crimes.

The scheme uses electronic tagging to monitor the released prisoner for periods of curfew. The prisoner released under this scheme would be given specific conditions as to the number of days of electronic surveillance, with a minimum of 14 days. The curfew applies for a minimum of 9 hours and a maximum of 12 hours a day, normally 7 p.m. to 7 a.m.

In 2002, of 55,370 prisoners eligible to apply for the HDC scheme, 20,525 (37 per cent) were released early and 1,478 were recalled to prison because of new charges (16 per cent), breach of release conditions (54 per cent) and change of circumstances (26 per cent). In 2010, 11,532 prisoners were released on the HDC scheme, of whom 413 (3.6 per cent) reoffended while on license, committing a total of 668 offences, equivalent to 1.62 offences per offender (*Compendium of reoffending statistics and analysis*, Ministry of Justice Statistics Bulletin, July 2012). In 2011, a total of 12,727 prisoners were released early on home detention curfew. They spent an average of 2.8 months of their sentences on HDC (*Offender Management Statistics Quarterly Bulletin*, January to March 2012, England and Wales, 2012).

▶ Release on temporary licence (ROTL)

Some inmates are also released for short periods of time on a temporary licence such as to visit a dying relative or to prepare for release by attending an interview. Reasons for granting a temporary licence include:

- For personal reasons: inmates can apply for a *Special Purpose Licence*. This allows them for exceptional personal reasons to visit a dying relative, attend funerals, for marriage or religious services, to receive medical treatment and to attend court, tribunal or inquiry proceedings.

- Rehabilitation: inmates can apply for a *Resettlement Day Release Licence* that will allow them to participate in reparative and community service projects, maintaining family ties, housing, employment, life and work skills training/education courses.

- Rehabilitation: for a longer period, allowing the inmate to stay out overnight, they can apply for a *Resettlement Overnight Release Licence*. Reasons for this include the above and these are also used nearing the release date, again for family reasons but also to make arrangements for accommodation, work or training.

- Mothers: Particularly for inmates who are mothers, the *Childcare Resettlement Licence* is designed for those who have responsibility for children under 16.

▶ Parole

Parole was introduced in the Criminal Justice Act 1967: the first releases under the scheme took place in 1968. It allowed a prisoner to be released early, for in addition to the one-third off for remission, after 1967 they could apply for parole at the one-third point of their sentence. Those released on parole were supervised by the Probation Service. Before 1967 they would have been released at the two-thirds stage. Introduced as part of a prison reductionist strategy, the parole system provided for an indeterminate element in a sentence between the one-third and two-thirds stage. The decision about suitability for release was made by a Local Review Committee who dealt with short-term prisoners and made recommendations for other prisoners, including life sentence prisoners eligible for release on licence, which went to the Parole Board for consideration and finally to the Home Secretary who could veto a recommendation. The Parole Board was composed of criminologists, judges, probation officers, psychiatrists and independent members. All were part-time.

The system was changed by the CJA 1991, which allowed for automatic release at the 50 per cent stage of sentence for all prisoners serving under four years. The Local Review Committee was abolished. The Parole Board was left to consider all cases of prisoners sentenced to four years and over. It makes the decision in the case of prisoners serving four to seven years and sends recommendations in the case of those sentenced to over seven years to the Home Secretary. There are now full-time officials in addition to the part-time members. Following recommendations in a review of parole by the Carlisle Committee in 1988, the CJA 1991 introduced a more complex criteria system to be used by the Parole Boards when reviewing cases. For prisoners serving sentences of up to 15 years the Parole Board makes the final decision. For longer sentence prisoners it makes recommendations to the Home Secretary.

Offenders released under the conditions of parole are supervised in the community by a probation officer up to the three-quarters point of those with a determinate sentence. In 2011/12 the Parole Board received 878 requests for release from determinate prisoners, of which 22 per cent were considered eligible for parole by the Board.

Under the Criminal Justice Act 2003, the Parole Board, which previously had an advisory role, became the main decision-making body on the release or recall of inmates. From 2005, parole was made automatic for those prisoners serving determinate sentences of more than 12 months. These prisoners are now automatically released at the half-way point of their sentence and are on licence supervision until the end of their sentence. If the Probation Service decides to recall an inmate on licence, it is the role of the Parole Board to review the decision.

The Parole Board also has responsibility for assessing the suitability for discretionary early release (DCR) of all prisoners serving more than 4 years whose offence was committed before 4 April 2005 and prisoners given extended sentences for public protection (EPP) for offences committed on or after 4 April 2005. Prisoners serving EPPs were required to serve a minimum of two-thirds of their sentences rather than the usual half before having their cases reviewed by the Parole Board.

The Parole Board also had the responsibility for the release of those given an indeterminate sentence of Imprisonment for Public Protection (IPP) and had to decide whether it was safe to release a prisoner after they have served their tariff time. Since the abolition of indeterminate sentences (both the EPP and IPP) by the Legal Aid, Sentencing and Punishment of Offenders (LASPO) Act 2012, offenders receiving the new Extended Determinate Sentence (EDS) must serve a minimum of two-thirds of the custodial term and if such term is less than 10 years, release is automatic at the two-thirds point. If sentenced to 10 years or more than release takes place between two-thirds and end of the custodial term, and this decision is at the discretion of the Parole Board.

Prisoners already serving EPP or IPP sentences imposed before commencement of LASPO provisions – 3 December 2012 – will continue to be subject to the same release provisions as before (under the Crime Sentences Act 1997 and the Criminal Justice Act 2003), which have not been changed by LASPO.

Parole Board caseload in 2011/12

Total cases dealt with in the year: 25,436

- There were 4,216 oral hearings

- 878 determinate sentence cases were considered by paper panels during the year – this is down from 1,381 in 2010/11 and 7,857 in 2006/7, a steep drop which is due to the phasing out of the use of discretionary conditional release

- There were 14,977 recall cases considered by the board

- Parole was granted in 22% of all determinate sentenced cases

- 5 determinate sentence prisoners were recalled from parole during the year following an allegation of a further offence

- Following an oral hearing, 16% of applications for life licences from inmates on a life sentence were granted

- 116 prisoners on life licence were recalled in 2011 for all reasons including re-offending

Source: The Parole Board for England and Wales Annual Report and Accounts 2011/12

The length of time served is one calculation that the sentenced inmate will be keen to work out soon after reception. However, other considerations will affect the nature of the prison experience that the inmate will face during his or her prison term. Having explained the quantity of time that an inmate will have to serve, what factors influence the quality of time served?

13.4 Impact of imprisonment on inmates

Objective 4

Analyse the impact that imprisonment has on inmates

For 200 years, since the introduction of the penitentiary, the impact of prison life on the inmate has been debated, some believed that prison life could provide a positive and constructive experience that would rehabilitate, while others argued that the consequence of imprisonment is to lock an offender further into a life of crime (**see Chapter 12**). The 1990 White Paper, *Crime, Justice and Protecting the Public* (**Home Office 1990a**), made it clear that the effect of imprisonment is unlikely to be beneficial in rehabilitative terms. It is important to bear in mind, however, that individual inmates vary in character and that generalisations about the impact of prison regimes will not hold for every inmate. Empirical studies of how inmates experience and adapt to prison help to shed light on the consequences of being incarcerated, and explain why they have not matched the good intentions of those who saw prison as a means of resocialising inmates. Toleration of life in prison varies from inmate to inmate. Some will feel their conviction or sentence was unjust, others will accept it, and others will be grateful that the sentence length was no longer. Each prisoner will bring a range of pre-existing impressions and knowledge of prisons. The National Prison Survey 1991 showed most (57 per cent) sentenced inmates had been in prison before (**Walmsley *et al*. 1993**).

The physical aspects of the regime such as food, overcrowding, the time locked up in a cell, access to bath and toilet facilities, and staff attitudes are vital to the trouble-free running of a prison, as was shown in the section of this chapter which considered the findings of the Woolf Report on the riots in 1990.

❱ Regimes, sentence planning and privileges

A framework of privileges and incentives was introduced into prisons in 1995. Intended by the then Home Secretary, Michael Howard, to ensure greater discipline, the scheme allows for a greater number of visits, more disposable cash and community visits for those who comply with the regimes. There are three levels based on the facilities provided:

- *Basic:* the minimum level of facilities to which the prisoner is entitled by law regardless of performance and behaviour of the prisoner.
- *Standard:* set above the legal minimum requirements.
- *Enhanced:* at this level prisoners become eligible for additional privileges.

The aims of the scheme were to ensure that privileges for prisoners are earned through good behaviour and are removable if prisoners fail to maintain acceptable standards of responsible behaviour. The scheme encourages hard work and rewards participation in constructive activity by prisoners. The scheme also enhances the role of sentence planning. Finally, the scheme has a control function in that it seeks to create a more disciplined, better controlled and safer environment for prisoners and staff.

The earnable privileges include:

- access to private cash above a set minimum;
- extra visits;
- eligibility to take part in enhanced earning schemes;
- community visits for Category D inmates;
- permission to wear one's own clothing;
- time out of cell in association.

Sentence planning was introduced in 1992, following the recommendations of the Woolf Report, to encourage inmates to identify a way of progressing throughout their time in prison so that they might acquire skills and attempt to address their offending behaviour. Following discussion between staff and the inmate, targets are set which aim to reduce future reoffending by agreement to undertake training programmes and activities such as drug counselling or the sex offender treatment programme. At the start of the sentence, information is put together about the inmate's community and family ties, prior training and educational attainments. Information is collected about substance abuse, criminal history and self-harm history. During the period of incarceration comments are kept on file about how the prisoner cooperated with the wing or unit's routines, and how he or she related to other inmates and staff. This information is open to inmates to read and challenge if they regard it as inaccurate.

▶ Inmate adaptation to prison life

How do people cope with being deprived of their liberty? Prisoners do not have the same degree of freedom to decide their daily routines, eating habits, social contacts and sleeping arrangements. Studies of how inmates adapt to prison life illustrate its impact on the inmate and how this is likely to affect their potential for successful rehabilitation. These sociological and psychological studies of prison life give clues about the causes of prison disturbances and riots that we discussed earlier in this chapter (**Cohen and Taylor 1972; Fitzgerald 1977; King and Elliott 1977**).

How people cope with prison depends on a number of factors. First, if they have had prior experience of prison, they will have some understanding of the routines of prison life. For the novice, initial acquaintance with prison life might be overwhelming and intimidating. Erving Goffman uses the term 'mortification', to describe the induction process in which supports for the person's individuality such as personal name, clothing and hairstyle are replaced by a prison number, uniform and hygiene requirements (**Goffman 1968**). This can be lessened and some prison administrators have introduced regimes to normalise some aspects of prison life by, for example, less insistence on uniforms and fewer restrictions on what might be allowed in a cell, although this might conflict with the needs of containment and security, as was suggested in the case of the IRA prisoner escape from Whitemoor Prison.

Prisoner adaptation, whether the inmate is an 'old hand' or a novice, will depend on individual circumstances. Most important is the length of sentence. The nature of the crime committed also influences the prison experience. Thieves, fraudsters and robbers are often regarded with relative degrees of respect and contempt by other inmates, but they will not suffer the fear felt by those convicted of sexual crimes, especially those where the victim was a child. To avoid attacks from other inmates, the 'nonces', as they are called in prison argot, often request to be housed in vulnerable prisoner units and segregated for their own protection under **Prison Rule 45** (formerly Rule 43), which states:

> Where it appears desirable for the maintenance of good order or discipline or in his own interest, that a prisoner should not associate with other prisoners, either generally, or for particular purposes, the governor may arrange for the prisoner's removal from association.

Another factor influencing prisoners' adaptation is relationships in the outside world. One of the realities of prison life is that inmates are cut off from ordinary routine interactions with the outside world. Goffman calls prisons, along with other institutions such as monasteries, mental hospitals and boarding schools, 'total institutions'. They are 'total' in that all aspects of life such as sleeping, eating, working and leisure are conducted within the one organisation (ibid.). This means that the array of contacts and opportunities is severely confined and the impact of the outside world is limited. However, this does not mean that there is no outside contact and weekly visits, access to telephones for prisoners and outside visits in pre-release schemes have all been extended in recent years. Of course, the main leisure activities such as watching television, listening to the radio and reading newspapers and magazines mean that inmates in prison can keep up with events that interest them. Regimes will vary between prisons and some, such as open prisons, allow inmates two days a month out of the prison for 'town visits'.

The loss of daily contact with the home or workplace is no hardship for some inmates. Others suffer mental anguish when they think about their outside lives, homes and families. The shame of imprisonment on the family and themselves will have an impact on some of those sentenced to imprisonment. Some argue that these factors are of particular significance to women prisoners, especially where they have children (**Eaton 1993**), and on family life in general.

Justice for All claimed that prison can 'break up families, impede resettlement and place children at risk of an inter-generational cycle of crime' (**Home Office 2002: 85**), with over 40 per cent of sentenced prisoners claiming to have lost contact with their families since entering prison. Other research from the Social Exclusion Unit (SEU) states, 'Research shows that prisoners are six times less likely to reoffend if contact with their families is maintained' (**Social Exclusion Unit 2002: 106**). David Green comments on this:

There are two main problems with this statement. First, it is not true that simply reinstating family contacts will reduce offending. The SEU reported in 2002 that 43% of prisoners had other family members who had been convicted (compared with 16% of the general population) and 35% had a family member who had been in prison. In such cases the family may be a bad influence . . . while it is true that people with strong family ties are less likely to be criminals, it does not follow that *all* people with strong family ties are law abiding . . .

Second, it is not true that prison always causes the breakdown of family contacts. Many criminals had few, if any, close family ties before admission to prison. The SEU report shows that 47% of male prisoners had run away from home as a child, and 27% had been in care (compared with 2% of the general population). Some 81% were unmarried prior to imprisonment, nearly 5% were sleeping rough before admission, and 32% were not living in permanent accommodation prior to their imprisonment. Moreover, when their family disowns them or a wife leaves them, it is often because they disapprove of the prisoner's self-chosen conduct.

(Green 2004)

A further factor shaping the way in which inmates adapt to prison life is their attitude towards their offence and sentence. While some accept their guilt and feel ashamed, others feel no remorse. This might be because they are professional thieves who have made a career out of criminal activity and regard imprisonment as an occupational hazard. Those incorrectly convicted are entitled to feel outrage and anger. Others are outraged because of the type of person they are. Some are resigned to their fate and 'do their time'. Others will be influenced by the type of company they come into contact with in the prison. Although there is no one factor that determines how a prisoner responds, a number of research studies have indicated patterns of adaptation (**Cohen and Taylor 1972**).

Some theories accounting for offender adaptation have stressed the importance of institutional traditions and opportunities, particularly focusing on the impact of inmate subcultures and the deprivations associated with a 'closed' institution. Theorists in this tradition include Donald Clemmer, Gresham Sykes and Erving Goffman. Other theorists have focused on the 'importation' model, where the prisoners' adaptations will depend on their pre-institutional careers and lifestyles (**Schrag 1944**). Schrag's work showed how the social role adopted in prison depended on the inmate's previous lifestyle before imprisonment.

John Irwin's study, *The Felon* (**Irwin 1970**), found three types of response among inmates in California prisons: 'jailing', 'doing time' and 'gleaning'. These responses tended to reflect the prisoner's personal history, although Irwin makes the caveat that inmates did not always fit into only one response model and that the three main response patterns did not cover every inmate. Thus, 'jailing' was characteristic of 'state raised youth' who had prior institutional contacts from an early age and knew how to exploit the opportunities in a total institution to achieve maximum benefits and status through the rackets and gangs. Prison was not too burdensome for them as they usually had little status outside the institution other than in gang life, which continued in prison. The professional and more mature thieves who were career criminals adopted a different response. Their predominant aim was to get through their sentence as quietly and as quickly as possible. Therefore, they were not interested in the rehabilitative programmes of the institution except where it meant an easier life inside or the chance to get out of prison more quickly. Nor were these inmates interested in campaigning or confrontation with the authorities, as were the 'jailing' inmates. The third pattern of adaptation described by Irwin was 'gleaning'. These inmates engaged in the opportunities offered by education, counselling, therapy and work programmes to increase their opportunities of being granted parole and of changing their lifestyles.

In a later study, *Prisons in Turmoil* (**Irwin 1980**), Irwin points out that the models of inmate subcultures were easier to identify in the traditional style of penitentiary with more rigid and authoritarian regimes. Clemmer's study in 1940 found a very distinctive and conformist prisoner culture, with an inmate code, defined and enforced primarily through the inmates (**Clemmer 1958**). Since that time, the nature of the prison experience has become more diversified, as new types of inmate and values have been brought into prison. The commitment to rehabilitative strategies in the 1950s brought about more liberal regimes with less emphasis on the convict culture found in many prisons before 1950. The new mix of inmates also undermined the single inmate culture. In the United States in the 1960s, as with the British prisons during the period of the 1914–18 war, political prisoners objecting to the war generated a more articulate and politically sophisticated inmate. In the United States the black power movement created another form of politically orientated inmate. Younger inmates convicted of drug and gang-related crimes were not so easily impressed by either the formal or informal cultures of prison life and had their own support and reference groups as gang and drug activities meant that prison contacts became an extension of street life.

More recent theorists and studies have stressed the greater diversity of inmate culture as less strict regimes and more diverse pre-institutional lifestyles have become more apparent in prison in the 1990s and into the twenty-first century.

13.5 Aims and performance of the Prison Service

Objective 5

Distinguish and discuss the different aims and measures of performance of the Prison Service in England and Wales

Does prison work, as Michael Howard asserted in the quote at the beginning of this chapter? To answer this it is necessary to ask what the goals of imprisonment are. In clarifying these goals we must distinguish between the function of imprisonment within the criminal justice system (i.e. to carry out the sentence of the court) and the specific goals of prisons as institutions.

Thus, prisons work in one sense if they deprive offenders of their liberty for the period of time specified by the court. Hence, the main purpose of imprisonment is in terms of sentencing goals. When assessed in terms of whether prisons fulfil this function, they are successful if general deterrence, denunciation and just deserts goals are achieved; and at the minimum they fulfil an incapacitative function of keeping away from the community offenders who would, and will, when released, continue criminal activities.

However, the Prison Service has its own institutionally specific goals reflecting the penal paradigms explored in **Chapter 12**. In 1979 the report of the May Committee referred to the loss of faith in the treatment objective in prison and recommended the rewriting of Prison Rule 1 and adopting the idea of custody which is both 'secure and yet positive'. 'Positive custody' was defined in four ways (**Home Office 1979: 67**). It should:

- create an environment which can assist them (the inmates) to respond and contribute to society as positively as possible;
- preserve and promote their self-respect;
- minimise, to the degree of security necessary in each particular case, the harmful effects of their removal from normal life;
- prepare them for and assist them on discharge.

In the 1990s, the Prison Service set out the following goals of imprisonment in its mission statement:

> Her Majesty's Prison Service serves the public by keeping in custody those committed by the courts. Our duty is to look after them with humanity and help them lead law-abiding and useful lives in custody and after release.

The Ministry of Justice (*Prison Service Annual Report and Accounts 2007/8*) identified the goals of prison in 2008, indicating that, in addition to protecting the public, they expect rehabilitative aims to be achieved via NOMS. They have introduced seven pathways to reducing reoffending which focus on:

- education, training and employment;
- mental and physical health;
- drugs and alcohol;
- finance, debt and benefits;
- children and the families of offenders;
- attitudes and behaviour.

In terms of the institutional goals the Prison Service has set itself, prisons can be assessed as to their effectiveness by monitoring their success at achieving the objectives set. Key performance indicators (KPIs) were introduced for this purpose. In 2004, the objectives and KPIs were as follows.

Prison Service objectives and KPI targets

The blend of containment, concern with conditions and capacity, rehabilitative aspirations and non-prison-specific objectives associated with the organisational culture are evident in this statement of objectives set out in the Prison Service's Corporate and Business Plan 2003/4:

- maintain security and prevent escapes;
- ensure safe and decent conditions for prisoners;
- improve prisoners' prospects on release;
- provide capacity;
- increase diversity and equality;
- improve performance;
- introduce organisational development and change.

These objectives are turned into targets through key performance indicators (KPIs). The *Prison Service Annual Report 2007/8* measures its performance against the KPIs:

- There were 5 escapes from prisons and prison escorts. This represents a rate of 0.01%. The target rate was 0.05% of average daily prison population, and there have been no Category A escapes since 1995.
- 511 absconded, mainly from Open Prisons. There was only one escape from escort per 39,377 prisoners, compared with the target of one escape from escort per 20,000 prisoners.
- The average staff sickness rate was 11.7 days against a target of 11 working days.
- The rate for timely delivery of prisoners to court (a new KPI) was 82% against a target of 81%.
- In the resettlement sphere, 27.3% at discharge had an employment opportunity. The target was 25%.
- 85.4% of inmates had accommodation to go to on release (target 74%).
- 6.2% of staff were from a minority ethnic group, not meeting the target of 6.3%.
- 6,960 offending behaviour programmes were completed, with a target of 6,360, and 1,037 sex offender treatment programmes were completed (the target was 1,035).
- There were 7,412 completed drug treatment programmes against a target of 6,595.
- 51,623 inmates were tested for drugs and 4,586 proved positive. The rate of positive mandatory drug tests was 8.9% against the target of 10%.
- There were 83 suicides. The rate of self-inflicted deaths was 115.5 per 100,000 prisoners against a target of 112.8.
- Overcrowding target was 24% of capacity and the actual rate of overcrowding was 24.6%, with a major impact in male local prisons where the rate of overcrowding was 51.4%.
- There were 900 serious assaults on fellow prisoners and 164 on staff. The rate of serious assaults was 1.67% against a target of 1.47%.

Table 13.7 NOMS performance outcomes in 2010/11 compared with 2011/12

Measure	2010/11	2011/12
The percentage of orders and licences successfully completed	75.8%	76.3%
The percentage of prisoners held in overcrowded accommodation across the prison system	23.8%	23.9%
The rate of self-inflicted deaths per 100,000 prisoners (3-year rolling average)	70	70
The rate of drug misuse in prisons as reflected by those testing positive in mandatory drug tests	7.1%	7.0%
The number of Category A escapes	0	1
The number of escapes from prison and prison escorts	2	4
The rate of escapes from prison and prison escorts as a proportion of the average prison population	0.002%	0.005%
The number of escapes from contractor escorts	10	13
The rate of escapes from contractor escorts as a proportion of the throughput of prisoners	1 in 99,577 prisoner movements	1 in 72,510 prisoner movements
The percentage of offenders in employment at the end of their sentence, order or licence	37.6%	37.9%
The percentage of offenders in settled or suitable accommodation at the end of their sentence, order or licence	86.7%	87.2%
The average number of working days lost through sickness absence in public prisons and probation trusts	9.78	9.75
The proportion of black and minority ethnic staff in NOMS Agency	9.2%	9.1%

Source: NOMS Annual Report of 2010/11

In general debates about the role and success of prisons, the details of KPIs are subsumed under more general issues as to whether those sent by the courts are retained until the proper release date and whether this represents adequate punishment for the crime, and the possibility of rehabilitation within the prison.

After the change of government in 2010, there was a general shift away from centrally imposed KPIs in favour of locally identified priorities, and in the National Offender Management Service (NOMS) Business Plan of 2012–13 (which replaced the annual publications by the Prison Service and Probation Service with one unified organisational plan) there is no mention of KPIs. Rather, the plan specifies eight broad areas as 'business priorities':

Transformation

1. Rehabilitation – Breaking the Cycle
2. Re-balancing capacity
3. Commissioning and Competition
4. Organisational Restructure

Operational Delivery

5. Delivering the punishment and orders of the courts
6. Security, Safety and Public Protection
7. Reducing Reoffending
8. Improving efficiency and reducing costs

Under each priority, the plan outlines how NOMS expects to achieve its aims. The NOMS Annual Report of 2010/11 gives greater insight into how it measures its own performance. Below is a table comparing outcomes for different measures against those of the previous year.

▶ Rehabilitation and offender management

Since 2004, rehabilitation has become one of the primary concerns of both the Prison Service and the Probation Service. The objective of integrating the two under NOMS was to ensure that by following a unified management plan for all offenders throughout the whole of their sentences, whether in custody or in the community, the offender stands a better chance of receiving the rehabilitation services he or she requires.

Another project that concentrates on integrating prisoners into the community is the 'Restorative Prison' which applies the principles of restorative justice in the prison. The North East Restorative Community Partnership project started in 2000 and is based on the idea of the community prison referred to in the Woolf Report. The community prison is based on the principles of restorative justice: prisoners work with victims, prisoners work for the benefit of the community, and an approach to resolving conflicts in prison that avoids formal and adversarial process and uses mediation procedures. The claim is that this will result in a better atmosphere in prison, with prisoners feeling better about themselves; prison is boring, so this gives them something to do; and work done in public parks is giving something back to the community.

The project to link prisoners with the community and to instil civic values is also evident in the campaign to give prisoners the vote, in relation to a 2004 decision of the European Court of Human Rights, with the aim of making them more responsible citizens (see the question at the end of this chapter and the arguments produced by the Prison Reform Trust in 2004). In April 2009, the Ministry of Justice indicated that the right to vote would be given to offenders sentenced to less than four years' imprisonment.

> We will ensure . . . the most serious and dangerous offenders held in custody will not be able to vote. Prisoners sentenced to more than four years' imprisonment will not be permitted to vote in any circumstances.
>
> We believe this is compatible with the court's judgement and reflects the expectation of the British public that those guilty of the most serious offences should not be entitled to vote while in custody.

This restored optimism in the rehabilitative role of imprisonment is in contrast to the pessimism of the previous decades. The 1990 White Paper concluded they were counter-productive in this regard:

> It was once believed that prison, properly used, could encourage a high proportion of offenders to start an honest life on their release. Nobody now regards imprisonment, in itself, as an effective means of reform for most prisoners . . . however much prison staff try to inject a positive purpose into the regime, as they do, prison is a society which requires virtually no sense of personal responsibility from prisoners. Normal social or working habits do not fit. The opportunity to learn from other prisoners is pervasive. For most offenders, imprisonment has to be justified in terms of public protection, denunciation and retribution. Otherwise it can be an expensive way of making bad people worse.
>
> (Home Office 1990a: 6)

The Green Paper *Punishment, Custody and the Community* cited the many unintended consequences of imprisonment which made them counter-productive in rehabilitative terms. Paragraph 1.1:

> . . . they are not required to face up to what they have done and to the effects on their victim.

Paragraph 1.1 commented further:

> . . . if they are removed in prison from the responsibilities, problems and temptations of everyday life, they are less likely to acquire the self-discipline and self-reliance which will prevent reoffending in the future.

Paragraph 1.6:

> . . . Imprisonment is likely to add to the difficulties which offenders find in living a normal and law-abiding life. Overcrowded local prisons are emphatically not schools of citizenship.

Paragraph 2.15:

> ... [With regard to young offenders] Even a short period of custody is quite likely to confirm them as criminals, particularly if they acquire new criminal skills from more sophisticated offenders. They see themselves labelled as criminals and behave accordingly.
>
> (Home Office 1988a)

The mood a decade on was that more could be done to reduce the recidivism rates of prisoners. One aspect of this strategy was to challenge the efficacy of the short prison sentence on rehabilitative grounds. *Justice for All* noted that prisoners given short sentences were reconvicted at a higher rate than those who served longer sentences. **David Green (2004)** comments on this argument that it 'implies that a prisoner's subsequent conduct is determined by his short time in jail. Consider someone aged 20 who has been a regular offender and only just been caught. How likely is it that 3 months in jail will become the main cause of his later conduct? It is more likely that the attitudes acquired in the previous 20 years continue to exert a powerful influence.'

The University of Maryland's review of What Works evidence concluded that there was no evidence that prison increased the likelihood of future recidivism. 'The evidence seems to point to an overall picture of criminals, particularly property criminals, generally "returning to work" after their time in prison' (**Murray 2003: 9**).

Part of the new emphasis has been based on a faith in cognitive skills programmes with prisoners to make them more aware of what they were doing when they committed a crime. Two evaluations have been published by the Home Office about the impact of cognitive skills programmes with prisoners. In July 2003, *Findings* 206 (**Falshaw *et al.* 2003**), acknowledged, 'This evaluation found no differences in the two-year reconviction rates for prisoners who had participated in a cognitive skills programme between 1996–1998 and a matched comparison group. This contrasts with the reduction in reconviction shown in the previous evaluation of cognitive skills programmes for prisoners, delivered between 1992 and 1996.'

The test of the success of working with prisoners is primarily through reconviction rates as an indicator of recidivism. **Chapter 12** showed that the average re-offending rate following imprisonment is the same as that for community sentences. The two-year recidivism rates measure the proportion of offenders re-convicted for a further offence in a two-year period from release. These figures show that imprisonment is likely to be related to future reoffending. However, they also show that non-custodial sanctions are not much better at reducing the likelihood of re-offending.

Perhaps sentencing an offender, whether to prison or in the community, has little to do with the influences on offending behaviour. If it is difficult to establish the proposition that prisons work to reduce the criminality of offenders following their release, the value of imprisonment should be assessed in terms of its functions other than those concerning its effect on individual offenders (**see Chapter 12**).

So the answer to the question of whether prisons work is that it depends on what we expect of them. The failure to meet the original high expectations of those pioneering the penitentiary as an institution to change offenders into law-abiding citizens is apparent. But prisons meet other demands, particularly as the most credible way to achieve retribution, denunciation, general deterrence and incapacitation.

Finally, no doubt the 'success rate' of imprisonment, in terms of any of its aims, could be improved if more money is spent on the prison system. What would be the cost of ensuring no escapes? Would the taxpayer wish to pay this cost? For those who think prison has failed in all or most respects, the onus is on them to say what they would put in its place as the major institution symbolising punishment.

Conclusion

This chapter has shown that prisons have been expected to perform many functions. The rehabilitative paradigm influenced the design, organisation and regimes of prisons from their inception to around the 1960s. Thus prisons were seen not as degrading and punitive institutions but as institutions where inmates should be encouraged and assisted to lead a good and useful life through a regime of treatment and training. These ideals, however, were not achieved, and some of the reasons why prisons may not be able to achieve rehabilitation have been noted. They are, after all, institutions in which inmates are deprived of their liberty, which may have an adverse effect on their sense of individuality and purpose. Some prisoners are wedded to a life of crime; others, particularly those serving long sentences, may simply wish to forget the outside world and see no hope for the future.

Intermittent custody, introduced in the Criminal Justice Act 2003, attempts to reduce the negative outcomes that can accompany even short periods of full-time custody, such as loss of employment, loss of accommodation, and family disintegration.

The demise and resuscitation of rehabilitative goals, however, has a profound effect on the institutions making up the prison system. One attraction of rehabilitative goals to penal reformers was that they held out the promise of treating prisoners with humanity. With its demise, these conditions also declined, some training programmes ceased and prisoners were locked up for longer periods in their cells. These conditions arguably contributed to the disturbances in the early 1990s.

It is important to distinguish between the aims of sentencers in sending offenders to prison and the aims of the prison system itself. Thus while sentencers and policy makers focus on punishment, incapacitation and the deprivation of liberty, these do not provide constructive goals for the institutions who must carry out these aims. Reducing the goal of prison to that of keeping offenders from escaping until they are due to be released ('warehousing') might further distance staff from inmates and undermine programmes aimed at reforming them.

Prisons must deal with those whom the courts send to them and attempt to prevent them escaping and creating disturbances. Yet the interests of security and control may run counter to positive regimes and humane conditions in a cost-conscious climate. The debate over the balance between security, control, costs and changing offender behaviour in prison is likely to continue. In the end the debate often comes down to the question of: what is the purpose of imprisonment?.

Review questions

1. What are the different security categories of prisons run by the Prison Service in England and Wales?

2. Calculate the actual amount of time served by an inmate if he or she is sentenced to: (a) 8 months; and (b) 2 years?

3. What are the different aims of imprisonment? What kind of evidence should be examined to explore whether or not these aims are being achieved?

Discussion questions

1. What arguments are involved in considering whether more prisons should be built or greater efforts should be made to reduce the prison population?

2. Using the information in Table 12.2, showing the comparative use of imprisonment in western European countries, consider:

   a. where England and Wales is ranked among the countries and jurisdictions listed, in terms of the numbers of prisoners in 2010;

   b. where England and Wales is ranked among the countries listed, in terms of the numbers of prisoners per 100,000 of the population in 2010;

   c. where England and Wales is ranked among the countries listed as a proportion of the number of crimes recorded in 2010;

   d. which of the comparisons (the total numbers in prison, the numbers compared with the population as a whole, or the numbers compared with the amount of recorded crime) do you regard as most useful for assessing claims about the overuse of custody in England and Wales?

3. Would giving prisoners a vote in elections re-integrate them into the community as responsible citizens or has their offending behaviour caused them to forfeit their rights? Search the Prison Reform Trust website using the search term 'vote' for information on the Trust's views.

Further reading

Berman G and Dar A (2013) *Prison Population Statistics*, House of Commons Papers 29 July 2013: London

Cavadino M and Dignan J (2007) *The Penal System: An Introduction* (4th edn), Sage: London

Falshaw L, Friendship C, Travers R and Nugent F (2003) 'Searching for "What Works": an evaluation of cognitive skills programmes', Home Office Findings 206, Home Office: London

Jewkes Y (ed.) (2007) *Handbook on Prisons*, Willan Publishing: Devon

Liebling A and Maruna S (eds) (2006) *The Effects of Imprisonment*, Willan Publishing: Devon

Morgan R (2007) 'Imprisonment', in Maguire M, Morgan R and Reiner R (eds) *The Oxford Handbook of Criminology* (4th edn), Clarendon Press: Oxford

Weblinks

Independent Monitoring Board: **www.imb.gov.uk/**

Ministry of Justice: **www.justice.gov.uk**

HM Inspectorate of Prisons annual reports: **www.justice.gov.uk/publications/corporate-reports/hmi-prisons**

Prison Service: **www.gov.uk/government/organisations/hm-prison-service**

Chapter 14

Probation Service and community penalties

Learning objectives

After reading the chapter you should be able to:

1. Outline the development of community sentences
2. Describe the functions and services provided by the Probation Service
3. Analyse the question of 'What Works' and why and explain recent initiatives in community sentences
4. Evaluate the effectiveness of community sentences

Key statistics

- 35 Probation Trusts employed 16,297 staff in 2013 (In 2007 there were 21,000 full time probation staff)
- 149,328 or 12.2% (13% in 2011) of all those sentenced by the courts in 2012 received community orders
- 44,644 or 3.6% of all those sentenced received Suspended Sentence Orders (SSOs) in 2012
- 50% of community orders had only one requirement
- 42% of Suspended Sentence Orders had two requirements
- The most popular requirements for Community Orders and Suspended Sentence Orders were *unpaid work* and *supervision*

Introduction

In this chapter, we will discuss the work of the Probation Service and look in more detail at community sentences.

The development of community sentences reflects the search in England and Wales for non-prison punishments. The desire for such punishments has been justified by arguments based on cost-effectiveness, on a just deserts philosophy (in terms of an intermediate sanction) and on the basis of the need for reform and rehabilitation rather than punishment of offenders.

The role and function of community penalties have changed considerably since their inception in the late nineteenth century, changing particularly rapidly in the last decade. First seen as largely rehabilitative, probation orders (and later community service orders) were a key part of attempts to divert offenders from custody. At times some community orders were specifically described as 'alternatives to prison' and at other times as 'punishment in the community' and as an intermediate punishment: between prison and probation (**see Chapter 12**).

Probation was affected severely by the pessimism of the 'nothing works' era, but a new optimism has surrounded recent emphases on 'What Works' in community sentences, and on implementing programmes aimed at reducing the likelihood of an offender re-offending, signalling a return to rehabilitative methods on the grounds that they can best have an impact on recidivism. This has been accompanied by rapid changes in the structure and organisation of one of the main agencies involved in community sentences, that is the Probation Service, which was under the authority of the Home Office. Since 2007 it now forms, along with the Prison Service, part of the National Offender Management Service (NOMS) under the authority of the Ministry of Justice. The delivery of probation services is organised by 35 Probation Trusts.

This chapter will start by outlining the development of community sentences, illustrating many of these changes and highlighting their fluctuating objectives. It will then describe the role of the Probation Service. Thereafter, the text will explore current thinking about how community sentences can be delivered effectively. Finally, some of the ways in which the effectiveness of community sentences can be evaluated will be considered.

Before this, it is important to define what is meant by community sentences – which in theory can encompass all sentences of the court where the offender is left in the community and not sent to prison. Community sentences or penalties are usually defined as 'court ordered punishments . . . structurally located between custody, on the one hand, and financial or nominal penalties (fines, compensation and discharge) on the other' (**Bottoms *et al.* 2001: 1**). They can be distinguished from fines and discharges as in these sentences no further intervention is made. In community sentences, however, some contact takes place, whether by way of attendance in a programme of counselling or treatment as in a community rehabilitation order (the renamed probation order), a programme of unpaid work in the community as in a community punishment order (the renamed community service order), or active surveillance as in electronic monitoring and the curfew order.

14.1 The development of community sentences

Objective 1

Outline the development of community sentences

The idea that offenders can be dealt with in the community has a long history. In the late nineteenth century many juvenile offenders were 'saved' from prison by police court missionaries who agreed to be responsible for them – the forerunners of the Probation Service. The historical development of probation was linked to reforms brought about by the Summary Jurisdiction Act 1879, which introduced conditional discharge for younger and first-time offenders. The court could add the requirement of supervision. Volunteers and friends offered to supervise, and from this developed the role whereby people, sometimes police officers, supervised and acted as mentors to offenders. The Probation of First Time Offenders Act 1887 specified the term 'probation' and outlined its role. The Probation of Offenders Act 1907 provided that the courts could appoint and pay probation officers and defined their duties, which were seen as being to 'advise, assist and befriend offenders'. The Criminal Justice Act 1925 formalised the role and required each petty sessional division (the geographical area that came under the jurisdiction of a magistrates' court) to employ at least one probation officer.

After this the work of the Probation Service expanded considerably. Probation officers became responsible not only for work in the criminal courts but also for civil work involving divorce. They provided social enquiry reports to the court giving information about offenders' circumstances and attitude to offences and gave the court advice about what sentence would be appropriate. They also began to work with ex-prisoners, reflected in the use of the term Probation and After-care Service. Their role was strongly linked to the rehabilitative philosophies outlined in **Chapter 12**, and the service became professionalised. In the twentieth century most probation officers were trained as social workers and worked according to a treatment model and practised what was described as social casework (**Raynor and Vanstone 2002**).

Some features of probation in this era were of considerable importance both to the rehabilitative philosophy and to the role of probation within the penal system. Originally, probation was not in itself a sentence but a release according to conditions – a period quite literally of probation. Offenders who breached the conditions of supervision, and who re-offended, could in theory be taken back to court and sentenced for the original offence, although this was in practice relatively rare. Offenders had to agree to be placed on probation, as it was felt that rehabilitation and supervision had to be voluntarily accepted rather than seen as a punishment which was imposed – thus setting the tone of the relationship between caseworker and offender.

The legitimacy of probation was challenged during the disillusionment with rehabilitation which followed and the 'nothing works' pessimism outlined in **Chapter 12**. In addition, there was little demonstrable evidence of the effectiveness of probation in making any real impact into offenders' lives – once on probation, some argued, nothing much else happened. Offenders saw probation officers at intervals, sometimes as little as once a month. While there were some experiments with more intensive supervision these were not fully evaluated for their effect on offenders, with whether or not the offender had completed a period of supervision normally being taken to be the benchmark of success.

Probation did, however, constitute an alternative to custody and growing concerns over rates of imprisonment led many to see the primary role of community sentences as being to reduce the prison population. These arguments influenced the introduction of new measures during the 1960s and 1970s. Parole and the suspended sentence were introduced in 1967 and the Criminal Justice Act 1972 introduced Community Service Orders (CSOs), made available nationally in 1975. Community Service Orders proved popular because they combined several sentencing aims. They could be seen as a form of retributive punishment by depriving offenders of their free time – as a 'fine on time' which in itself could also be construed as a deterrent. The element of unpaid work, often with voluntary organisations, could be seen as a form of reparation, and it was also assumed that working with community organisations could contribute to rehabilitation. Their popularity meant that by 1988 they accounted for 8 per cent of all sentences for indictable offenders. This may have been due to their 'Jack of all Trades' image, although in practice their role has been affected by 'philosophical confusion' (**Gelsthorpe and Rex 2004: 230**). While the legislation itself made no specific reference to their use for those who would otherwise have been sent to prison, they were in 1972 expected to be used primarily as an alternative to prison but more realistically by the CJA 1991 became justified as intermediate sanctions, positioned on the tariff as between prison and probation.

During the 1970s and 1980s, new elements were added to community sentences. In 1973 provisions were made that offenders on probation could be required to attend day training centres. The Criminal Justice Act 1982 provided that courts could require full-time attendance at day centres for a maximum of 60 days. Day centres were viewed with concern by many probation officers who saw their use as increasing their control function (**May 1994**). Other policies during the 1970s involved targeting selected offenders for intensive probation supervision, and during the 1980s some schemes involved tracking offenders. There were, however, considerable local variations in provision and, despite the addition of new strategies, community sentences could be seen as a 'soft option' to those calling for tougher punishment.

Throughout the 1980s, Home Office policy sought to reduce local variations and to increase the punitive elements of sentences. There was an attempt to exert greater control over community sentences, the strong welfare orientation within the Probation Service being seen as an impediment (ibid.). In 1984 a Statement of National Objectives for Probation (SNOP) was issued which stated that the priorities of the Probation Service were to provide alternatives to custody and prepare social enquiry reports for the court. A major theme was that offenders with a high risk of imprisonment were to be targeted, signalling a shift away from the traditional role of the service as dealing with less serious offenders who would benefit from treatment, help or support (ibid.). In 1988, an Action Plan called on every local probation area to develop its own strategy for targeting more intensive supervision on young adult offenders.

Changes were also made to Community Service Orders. In 1989, a set of national standards for community service was introduced which encouraged the adoption of more exacting procedures for dealing with lateness, non-compliance and unsatisfactory behaviour (*National Standards for the Supervision of Offenders in the Community*). A strong preference for manual labour was indicated, laying emphasis on tasks such as cleaning up graffiti. Following the Criminal Justice Act 1991 (CJA 1991) and the influence of 'just deserts' policies, the emphasis was laid on the amount of restriction of liberty being commensurate with the offence. This criterion was in addition to the criterion for the imposition of a community sentence itself: that the offence or offences were 'serious enough' for the imposition of a community penalty. Thus the choice of specific penalty had also to reflect seriousness and just deserts. This created a notional ranking of the punitiveness of the sentences involved, and their variability in terms of lengths and intensity. To further increase this range and in response to criticisms, the combination order was introduced to enable the combination of the punishment aspects of community service with the rehabilitative aspects of probation in the CJA 1991. A probation order could be combined with additional specified requirements, under which the court could order that the offender undergo particular programmes, or treatment.

Initially, it was a prerequisite of most community sentences that the offender give his consent to the order. Failure to consent was a ground for imposing a custodial penalty. This provision was thus criticised on two grounds: first, that it was conceptually bizarre to ask an offender to consent to the sentence, and second, that asking for consent with the threat of prison in the event of a refusal was nonsensical. The requirement for consent was removed in most cases, therefore, by the Crime (Sentences) Act 1997.

Although the reparative and reintegrative effects of orders were stressed in the CJA 1991, its practical effect was, as **Gelsthorpe and Rex (2004)** argued, to intensify the distinction between probation as rehabilitation and community service as punishment. The intention was thus to clarify community orders as an intermediate sanction.

Probation, too, was increasingly affected in the 1990s by the frustration with a disposition which was not regarded as punishment and was not seen as successful at reducing reoffending rates. Following considerable controversy surrounding the perceived laxness of community sentences typified in press reports of offenders being sent to holiday camps as part of their order, the Home Secretary, addressing the annual conference of the Central Probation Council in May 1994, commented that 'probation services are working with offenders but for the community and not the other way round'. The courts and the public, he went on to say, must have confidence in community sentences as punishment, and, while he was in favour of programmes making demands on offenders, they should not be given 'privileged access to opportunities which law-abiding members of the community cannot afford'. While community sentences had for many years been described as 'treatment in the community', the new emphasis on just deserts and punishment were associated with a new terminology – 'punishment in the community' – as used, for example, in the title of a Green Paper issued by the Home Office in 1995, *Strengthening Punishment in the Community*. Less emphasis was thus placed on *diversion* from custody, but rather a community sentence was considered as a rigorous and punitive sentence in its own right that was less severe than custody; hence an intermediate sentence in the tariff. The turn in policy was signalled by the then Home Secretary Michael Howard's claim that 'prison works' and a consequent lessening of the desire to use community sentences as merely diversions from custody.

The desire to gain judicial and public acceptance of community punishments was accompanied by a range of measures aimed at 'toughening up' the delivery of community sentences. In August 1994 the government announced new national standards which included a ban on safari and domestic holidays and requirements that work on community sentences should be demanding and usually physical in nature.

Before the imposition of a community penalty, courts had usually been required to obtain a social enquiry report from the Probation Service. In the CJA 1991 these were renamed pre-sentence reports, which in part re-focused their purpose as an aid to the sentencer. This heralded a different approach to the preparation of the pre-sentence report and underlined the role of probation officers as officers of the court, responsible for helping the court assess the risk of re-offending. Criticisms that probation officers had often made unrealistic suggestions as to the appropriate sentence were answered by making probation officers assess offending seriousness in the same way that a court might.

This reflected the range of changes which arguably altered the role of the probation officer and the nature of probation supervision. From 1991 onwards, probation orders had become a sentence in their own right with a place in the tariff, rather than an order *instead* of a sentence. In the mid-1990s the requirement that probation officers be qualified social workers was abolished, which many see as a change that symbolised the changing function of probation – from a social work service providing welfare and rehabilitation to offenders to a law enforcement, 'correctional' agency (**Raynor and Vanstone 2002; Robinson and McNeill 2004**). As mentioned above, in 1997 the requirement that offenders consented to an order was withdrawn, making it more like an imposed punishment than a voluntary contract. There was also a successive tightening up of requirements for law enforcement should offenders breach the requirements of their order. Hitherto, probation officers had had considerable discretion whether to take the offender back to court for breaching their order, but this discretion was successively removed. To many this further signalled a move towards law enforcement, raising the spectre of armed parole officers (as in the United States) who have rights to drug-test released offenders under supervision and pursue and arrest those who do not comply. Discussions of electronic monitoring of community orders further underlined this trend. In 2004, the transition became complete with the Probation and the Prison Services jointly considered as correctional services and managed together under the National Offender Management Service.

Nonetheless, attention to rehabilitation was still prominent, and the legitimacy of probation could be strengthened by evidence that it could make a difference to reducing offending through effectively intervening in offenders' lives to encourage them to stop offending. This in turn could be justified by appeals to public protection as offenders were turned away, if the intervention was successful, from committing crimes in the future. Attention turned to what works in relation to offending behaviour, an agenda which has become prominent in the early twenty-first century, and which will be discussed below. While this received some criticism (**Mair 2004**), it has provided a considerable source of optimism for some and has arguably provided a new *raison d'être* for the Probation Service.

The most recent changes to the work of probation officers are the result of reforms to community sentences in England and Wales brought in by the CJA 2003 (**outlined in Chapter 11**) and those brought in by the LASPO Act 2012. The CJA 2003 provided for the introduction of a generic community order with up to 12 requirements, which could be combined in a myriad of ways, effectively encompassing and replacing the range of individual community penalties that existed before. Thus the 'community punishment order' became a 'community order with the requirement of unpaid work'. If the Probation Service were to provide supervision of the offender, then it was called a 'community order with a supervision requirement'. The LASPO Act 2012 brought in additional requirements for use under community orders (**as detailed in Chapter 11**), one of which enables the courts to prohibit foreign travel and the other of which allows the courts to impose a 'sobriety order' on an offender whose offence is deemed to be alcohol-related. These will require probation officers to run regular tests to detect alcohol consumption on relevant offenders at specific times.

In practice, the magistrates and judges tend to use this wide range of potential requirements sparingly, even though the logic of the new generic community order was to allow the sentencer to tailor the requirements to individual offender needs and risk. Reviews of community orders, which preceded the LASPO Act, revealed that sentencers were often deterred from using some of the requirements such as those requiring offenders to undertake a specified activity or to undergo treatment for mental health, drug or alcohol problems due to the availability of such facilities. As a result the LASPO Act removed the obligation for sentencers to establish the availability before using these requirements, making it easier for sentencers to make use of a wider range of requirements in the future. The actual number of requirements given per offender is shown below based on data from 2006–2008:

For every 100 offenders given a community order in 2012:

- 50 were given 1 requirement
- 36 were given 2 requirements
- 14 were given 3 or more requirements

Community penalties have been a recent success story in terms of frequency of use by the courts (see Figure 12.1). The use of community orders in magistrates' courts when sentencing indictable offenders rose from 29 per cent in 1997 to 39 per cent by 2007. With the numbers being sentenced by the court being in decline the numbers in recent years has been falling. In 2012, 138,700 persons received a community order in a magistrates' court and over the last decade, the proportion of all offenders sentenced at the magistrates' court who receive a community order has ranged from 11.8 to 13.9 per cent. In 2012, 15,100 persons received their sentence at the Crown Court: 16.3 per cent of all those sentenced. Community orders have declined in use since 2005 as the Crown Court has made more use of Suspended Sentence Orders (a type of community order).

In 2011/2012, of the 331,745 offenders sentenced in all courts for indictable offences, 29 per cent received a community order compared to 25 per cent given a custodial order. Over the same period, 153,900 juvenile offenders were sentenced by the Youth Courts to a Youth Rehabilitation Order (YRO was introduced in November 2009) representing 45 per cent of all the sentences handed down by the Youth Court.

14.2 The Probation Service

Objective 2

Describe the functions and services provided by the Probation Service

In 2001, the implementation of the Criminal Justice and Courts Services Act 2000 meant that the Probation Service in England and Wales became a national service, divided into 42 local services matching police force boundaries for the first time. In organisational terms this completed the move to co-terminous boundaries for the main criminal justice agencies: police, CPS and probation. Having moved from the status of voluntary activity in the nineteenth century, probation became a national public service in the twentieth century. In the twenty-first century reform by the Offender Management Act 2007 allows for private companies and voluntary groups to compete with the public Probation Service in the delivery of programmes.

In January 2008, the National Audit Office *Value for Money Report – The supervision of community orders in England and Wales* reported that, 'the Probation Service's total annual offender caseload has increased 32 per cent between 2001 and 2006, while staff increased by 35 per cent over the same period'. The range of tasks undertaken by the Probation Service are listed below, and Table 14.1 gives the annual caseload of offenders given a community sentence that involves probation supervision, and offenders on licence following release from prison for the years 2002 to 2012. The main functions are:

* *Writing pre-sentence reports for courts:* the preparation of a full Pre-Sentence Report (PSR) or a fast-track version.
* *Supervision of court-ordered community sentences and suspended sentences:* since the implementation of the CJA 2003 the community order with supervision requirements means the offender must meet regularly with a probation officer. The newly introduced suspended sentence order also demanded a minimum of one requirement, and this would usually involve a supervision requirement along with an unpaid work requirement.
* *Pre- and post-release supervision:* probation was at one time called Probation and After-Care to indicate the continued supervision of the offender following release from prison. Since the CJA 2003, all prisoners are supervised following release from prison.
* *Contacting victims:* since 2000, the Probation Service has a statutory duty to consult and inform victims in relation to the release arrangements of certain offenders.
* *Hostels for bail and probation requirements:* the Service runs hostels which cater for those on probation or bail with a condition of residence in a hostel, and those on licence after release from prison.
* *Advice and training:* providing support for offenders in need in areas such as housing, basic skills and employment.

Table 14.1 Caseload for the Probation Service 2002 to 2012: supervision of those on community sentences and inmates released from prison; and total number of pre-sentence reports written for the courts

	2002	2003	2004	2005	2006	2007	2008	2009	2010	2011	2012
Supervision – Total	**191,394**	**199,237**	**209,461**	**224,094**	**235,029**	**242,722**	**243,434**	**241,504**	**238,973**	**234,528**	**224,823**
Court orders	116,125	120,734	128,217	137,377	146,532	145,179	146,725	140,951	134,746	125,444	114,234
Pre- or post-prison release supervision, (e.g. parole, HDC, post-release supervision)	77,235	803,199	83,408	89,438	90,740	94,459	98,477	102,022	105,413	110,437	111,859
Court Reports – Total	**213,768**	**201,871**	**204,821**	**189,600**	**209,525**	**215,358**	**216,353**	**217,853**	**212,484**	**204,631**	**192,728**
All PSRs	185,275	163,265	161,525	142,997	154,250	147,016	135,499	114,512	94,324	78,208	61,174
All Fast Delivery PSRs	28,493	38,606	43,296	46,603	55,275	68,342	80,854	56,046	118,160	126,423	131,554

Source: Compiled from Offender Management Statistics Quarterly, Annual Probation Tables 2012, Ministry of Justice Statistics Bulletin, Tables A 4.13 and A 4.27

Table 14.2 Offenders starting court order and pre-release supervision by the Probation Service by sentence type; England and Wales, 2005/2012

Type of sentence	2005	2006	2007	2008	2009	2010	2011	2012
All court orders	140,430	155,614	162,648	164,873	166,837	163,268	156,713	145,218
All community sentences	136,130	128,336	125,369	126,170	127,012	122,174	115,940	106,339
Community order	53,248	111,752	117,860	120,743	122,796	118,696	112,571	103,759
All pre CJA orders	93,925	19,530	8,625	6,248	4,864	1,842	348	171
Youth rehabilitation order	..	..	..	..	..	1,797	3,026	2,323
Other sentences	5,952	33,111	44,991	46,087	47,430	48,486	48,103	45,779
Deferred sentence	104	384	570	585	533	584	582	504
Suspended sentence order	5,848	32,727	44,421	45,502	46,897	47,902	47,521	45,275

Source: Compiled from *Offender Management Statistics Quarterly, Annual Probation Tables 2012*, Ministry of Justice Statistics Bulletin, Table A 4.1

Table 14.3 Offenders starting Community Order and Suspended Sentence Order supervision by number of requirements; England and Wales, 2005/2012

	2005	2006	2007	2008	2009	2010	2011	2012
Community Orders	53,248	111,752	117,860	120,743	122,796	118,696	112,571	103,759
1	25,913	53,042	57,699	60,503	61,260	59,195	56,685	52,129
2	18,137	40,132	41,235	42,428	43,070	42,077	39,836	37,597
3	7,836	15,854	16,033	15,073	15,441	14,409	13,218	11,875
4	1,198	2,381	2,542	2,393	2,591	2,581	2,429	1,853
5 or more	164	343	351	346	434	434	403	305
Average (mean) number of requirements	1.7	1.7	1.7	1.7	1.7	1.7	1.7	1.7

Source: Compiled from *Offender Management Statistics Quarterly, Annual Probation Tables 2012*, Ministry of Justice Statistics Bulletin, Table A 4.8

Once on a community order, offenders face a variety of experiences. These may include a programme of meetings with their supervising officer or attendance at counselling or therapy sessions for alcohol and drug abuse or anger management. Some will require help finding accommodation and work, others with welfare and social security applications. Others may participate in a variety of projects: for example, motor projects which provide offenders who have been involved in car crime with an opportunity to drive and work with cars legitimately. Other offenders are sent on programmes involving physical exercise to improve their ability to use leisure time constructively and cooperate within teams and groups.

The range of programmes can vary across the country and reflects demand and resources. The joint approach to programmes that aim to change offending behaviour is shown in the common aspirations – set out in the document,

Table 14.4 Number of requirements commenced under Community Orders and Suspended Sentence Orders by type; England and Wales, 2005/2012

	2005	2006	2007	2008	2009	2010	2011	2012
Community Orders	**96,133**	**211,905**	**223,511**	**226,234**	**231,444**	**223,227**	**211,335**	**192,732**
Unpaid Work	29,947	66,937	74,779	74,629	76,699	73,797	69,674	61,639
Supervision	34,741	76,234	78,102	77,777	77,769	72,998	67,332	61,434
Specified Activity	2,638	7,706	8,763	9,639	13,476	15,189	19,663	21,421
Curfew	3,209	9,615	12,608	15,526	16,479	17,476	17,279	14,930
Accredited Programs	17,440	34,287	30,143	26,483	23,442	20,444	16,448	13,430
Drug treatment	5,853	11,895	12,145	13,153	12,087	11,996	9,866	9,290
Alcohol treatment	1,356	2,439	3,267	4,664	6,485	5,949	5,873	5,971
Attendance Centre	94	287	430	523	787	947	1,367	1,338
Prohibited Activity	130	483	847	1,116	1,376	1,491	1,258	931
Exclusion	195	510	845	1,029	1,106	1,135	1,021	962
Residential	268	762	930	956	929	1,062	899	816
Mental Health	262	750	652	739	809	743	655	570

Source: Compiled from *Offender Management Statistics Quarterly, Annual Probation Tables 2012*, Ministry of Justice Statistics Bulletin, Table A 4.9

Reducing Re-offending National Action Plan – of the Ministry of Justice, NOMS and the Home Office:

> Reducing crime and public protection are top priorities for the Government. Crime can have a devastating effect on the lives of victims, families and communities with extraordinary costs to society as a whole. The cost of reoffending by ex-prisoners alone is at least £11 billion per year and reoffending by those serving sentences in the community adds to the burden which victims and communities face.
>
> The Reducing Re-offending National Action Plan fulfils the Government's commitment to reduce re-offending through greater strategic direction and joined-up working. It aims to address concerns raised in a number of important reports on this issue, such as the Social Exclusion Unit's report on reducing re-offending by ex-prisoners.
>
> ... takes forward two important Government manifesto commitments: to ensure that punishment and rehabilitation are both designed to minimise re-offending; and to improve the education of those offenders in custody.
>
> Over 60 national action points have been agreed across Government, covering all the key areas, or pathways, to support the rehabilitation of offenders, in a concerted effort to reduce reoffending.
>
> (*Reducing Re-offending National Action Plan*, Home Office 2004)

There were seven key action areas, or pathways, set out in the 2004 document to identify the priority areas where intervention strategies and programmes should focus their work on reducing offender behaviour. These were:

- accommodation;
- education employment and training;
- mental and physical health;
- drugs and alcohol;
- finance, benefits and debt;
- children and families of offenders;
- attitudes, thinking and behaviour.

The priority established by government was reducing offender behaviour, which generally means to reduce recidivism among criminals and in particular, means reducing the reconvictions of those who have been previously sentenced. Along with this demand of government policy, the Probation Service will have to balance the other objectives of community sentences. The increasing emphasis on cost-effectiveness monitoring and the deprivation of liberty may have an impact on how offenders respond to some schemes. For example, pressures of cost-effectiveness may lead to offenders being placed on a scheme that happens to be available in a locality that might not always be appropriate to a particular offender's needs. Thus resource constraints and competing objectives make probation work difficult to carry out and difficult to evaluate.

Along with other criminal justice agencies, in keeping with the trend to managerialism, the National Probation Service is subject to targets and inspection. HM Inspectorate of Probation reports to ministers in relation to Probation Service achievements. In addition the Prisons and Probation Ombudsman investigates complaints from those subject to probation supervision (as discussed in **Chapter 4**).

Efforts to define a key role for probation by the beginning of the twenty-first century led to the search for multi-purpose community penalties that seek to monitor the offender more closely while in the community as well as aiming to meet punishment and rehabilitative goals. Ideally these penalties have to be credible with the public and sentencers, contribute to reducing the prison population, and achieve the crime reduction targets set by the government. In the White Paper *Justice for All*, the search was on for a third way, for 'tough community sentences' that are a 'credible alternative to custody', with multiple conditions like tagging, reparation and drug treatment and testing. A new model of criminal justice was launched – offender management – which focused on offenders and sought to punish, control and rehabilitate through more demanding and multi-purpose community sentences (**see Chapter 1**).

14.3 'What Works' and why, and recent initiatives in community sentences

Objective 3

Analyse the question of 'What Works' and why and explain recent initiatives in community sentences

It was seen above that probation practice is influenced by what has been described as a 'What Works' agenda. What worked in terms of changing offender behaviour had not been so prominent in the 1980s/early 1990s when efforts were being made to identify a punishment role for community sentences. It re-emerged with the emphasis on evidence-based policy of the New Labour Government and, in particular, in June 1998 with a circular entitled *The Effective Practice Initiative: National Implementation Plan for the Supervision of Offenders* (**Mair 2004: 1**). Early work revealed that there was considerable variation in programmes, with little clear evidence of success, and a Pathfinder project was set up which contained several cognitive behavioural programmes which were to be closely evaluated. The accreditation of programmes increased and a Joint Prison/Probation Accreditation Panel was formed in 1999 which favours cognitive behavioural approaches.

The What Works programmes vary in focus. Some emphasise the importance of cognitive behavioural therapy, which focuses on addressing the 'risk factors' associated with offending which include habits of thinking ('cognition'), and patterns of behaviour which are identified with deficiencies in skills – such as, for example, 'social skills'. Cognitive skills courses encourage offenders to change attitudes. The 'change' element includes teaching educational skills, both general and vocational, and providing 'offending behaviour programmes' inspired by cognitive-behavioural therapy. They are based on the belief that criminals carry out crimes because of misperceptions, so that they think that no one gets hurt, e.g. victims of property crimes are assumed to be insured, or they perceive innocent actions as confrontational, for example, by aggressive responses such as 'What are you looking at?'.

In the 1990s, much effort went into finding out what works. Meta-analyses of a number of studies pointed to shared findings about what interventions were likely to be successful, and research on programmes with offenders considered to be at a 'high risk' of reoffending found that interventions of various kinds could make a difference to offenders' propensity to reoffend.

Iain Murray (2003: 15–16) develops the framework of Andrews, **Bonta and Hodge (1990)** to identify effective recidivism-reducing strategies:

- *Risk*: programmes must differentiate between the risk of reoffending of individual offenders.
- *Needs*: programmes must address the specific crimogenic (e.g. drug use) and non-crimogenic needs (e.g. low self-esteem) of the offender.
- *Responsiveness*: the offender's willingness to participate and join in the programme is crucial.
- *Professional discretion*: staff must be allowed to vary activities in response to the individual offender they are dealing with.
- *Programme integrity*: there must be a well-resourced and properly implemented programme.

In the United Kingdom, another meta-analysis claimed that some forms of intervention could produce reductions in offending, it was claimed, of between 10 and 20 per cent. **Raynor and Vanstone (2002: 88)** provide a useful summary of elements that are included in the most effective programmes, being those which:

- target high-risk offenders who are otherwise considered likely to reoffend (they are less successful with low-risk offenders who gain little benefit or are harmed);
- focus on 'criminogenic need' – the circumstances or characteristics of offenders held to have contributed to their offending;

- follow a tight structure which makes clear demands and follows a logical sequence;
- use a directive working approach so that those involved are clear about what they are meant to be doing;
- use cognitive behavioural approaches to provide opportunities to learn new thinking and behaviour;
- are located in the community, although they can also be used in prison;
- have programme integrity, with clear procedures;
- are implemented by appropriately trained staff;
- are adequately resourced;
- are evaluated, preferably by external researchers.

The optimism about community sanctions in England and Wales was built in part around a faith in the multi-dimensional features of Intensive Supervision and Surveillance Programmes (ISSP) which was introduced for offenders aged 10 to 17 in 2001. A similar intensive community sentence called the Intensive Control and Change Programme (ICCP) scheme was introduced in 2003 as a direct alternative to custody for young adult offenders aged 18 to 20.

The target group for these programmes, being the most serious and prolific young offenders, was thought to be responsible for a quarter of all youth crime. The programmes are available for convicted young offenders and also aim to prevent persistent young offenders on bail from committing more crimes while awaiting trial. They subject the offender to intensive surveillance and monitoring for up to 24 hours a day, seven days a week, if necessary. Electronic tagging and telephone voice verification can be used in addition to police and probation surveillance. The minimum requirement is for two surveillance checks per day. In addition, for rehabilitative purposes, offenders are subject to a structured programme of activities for 25 hours a week for the first three months, after which the supervision continues at a reduced intensity (a minimum of five hours per week) for a further three months. The Criminal Justice Act 2003 replaced the ISSP and the ICCP, along with the other myriad community sentences available for juveniles, young adults and adult offenders with a far simpler Youth Rehabilitation Order (YRO) for juveniles, and a generic Community Order for adults and young adults. This change came into effect in April 2005, and it allows sentencers to tailor a community sentence that is appropriate for the offender, recommending a single requirement or, less frequently, a combination of requirements from up to 12 non-custodial interventions such as supervision by the Probation Service, a curfew, compulsory unpaid work, a specified activity (such as making reparations or attending an educational course) or a drug or alcohol treatment programme.

The evidence about what works in terms of community sentences is still unclear; in government, prison reductionist pressure groups and some academic circles in the United Kingdom there have also been signs of a growing confidence that community service can contribute to reducing recidivism (**Gelsthorpe and Rex 2004; McIvor 2004**). Some studies have found lower reconviction rates than would be expected for those sentenced to community service, and there is some evidence that some features of it do have reintegrative and rehabilitative potential.

However, recent overviews of re-offending rates for adults and juveniles sentenced to custody or community sentences, published by the Ministry of Justice in 2011 and 2012 showed slightly higher reoffending rates for those sentenced to community penalties or no statistically significant difference, compared with those sentenced to custody (*2011 Compendium of re-offending statistics and analysis*, London: Ministry of Justice, 2011; and *2012 Compendium of re-offending statistics and analysis*, London: Ministry of Justice, 2012).

One meta-analysis of over 500 evaluation studies of What Works in terms of reducing recidivism was produced by the University of Maryland in 1997 for the US Congress, *Preventing Crime: What Works, What Doesn't and What's Promising*. While the original thesis of Martinson that 'nothing works' in 1974 had been modified, the subsequent evaluation trials had not come up with much that supports the level of optimism that was to be found in the 1997/2003 period in the United Kingdom. The study found some programmes that were promising but had not been fully evaluated. The conclusion seems to be that any specific programme is unlikely to deliver a large reduction in recidivism because of the complexities that affect the life opportunities and choices of offenders. Responding to the risk factors of individual offenders might offer a more realistic chance of reducing recidivism.

In 2008, the National Audit Office (NAO) commissioned RAND Europe to conduct a review of research around the world to provide a summary of the evidence available about the effectiveness of community orders in reducing re-offending (**Davis *et al.* 2008**).

The report focused on 10 features commonly found in community sentences: unpaid work, mental health treatment, education/skills training, drug treatment, anger management, alcohol treatment, programmes for perpetrators of domestic abuse, regular probation, intensive probation and cognitive/behavioural programming. Despite the absence of totally reliable evidence to demonstrate unambiguous conclusions, there are two features – cognitive/behavioural programming and drug treatment – 'where rigorous research exists which points to a reduction in the odds of re-offending. In four other areas – programmes for domestic abuse perpetrators, unpaid work, education and basic skills training and intensive probation – existing studies have not suggested that the programmes have a positive effect on recidivism. Finally, in four areas – anger management, probation, and alcohol and mental health treatment – the question of impact on re-offending remains unsettled' (ibid.).

However, there is scepticism about the evidence supporting What Works programmes and in the way in which 'what works' research has been interpreted and implemented in practice – often focusing on a more narrow concept of cognitive skills rather than on the wider social and economic needs of offenders (**Mair 2004**).

Some have questioned the strength of the 'evidence' base on which claims about effectiveness are made – many are based on local initiatives and on inconsistent findings about the effectiveness of programmes on different groups of offenders, and there have been concerns that the growth in accredited programmes has preceded the collection of evidence. Indeed, even supporters of the initiatives accept that the evidence base in Britain is still small (**Raynor and Vanstone 2002**), and one critic comments that the 'foundations of What Works in England and Wales cannot be said to be neat, evidence based, carefully considered and well planned' (**Mair 2004: 21**). In addition there have been problems in implementation, some of which are attributable to a shortage of qualified staff across the National Probation Service along with a lack of administrative support and difficulties in ensuring adequate evaluation.

What works? Aspects of community programmes that have evidence of being able to reduce reoffending rates

There is strong evidence that these aspects of community programmes work in reducing recidivism

- *Cognitive behavioural programming* that aims to change dysfunctional attitudes and ways of thinking

- Drug treatment programmes

Available evidence suggests that some community-based interventions have no positive effects in reducing recidivism

- Domestic violence programs

- Basic skills training and education

- Unpaid work
- Intensive probation supervision

Evidence inconclusive in the case of the following interventions associated with community sentences

- Anger management
- Probation
- Alcohol treatment programmes
- Mental health treatment programmes

Source: Synthesis of Literature on the Effectiveness of Community Orders, Rand Europe, prepared for the NAO, London, 2008

Resource issues, such as the lack of programme provision in some areas, were picked up by the National Audit Office Value for Money Report, *The Supervision of Community Orders in England and Wales, 2008.* It states:

> Some requirements, such as NHS-funded alcohol and mental health treatment, are not available in all Probation Areas, which could limit the effectiveness of an order if offending behaviour cannot be addressed.
>
> . . .
>
> Some Community Order requirements, for example alcohol treatment which is largely funded by the National Health Service and delivered in partnership with other agencies, are not available or rarely used in some of the 42 Probation Areas (this is despite strong links between alcohol and offending behaviour). This means orders may not be addressing the underlying causes of offending behaviour as fully as they could.

To some critics, the emphasis on cognitive behavioural approaches implies a return to the medical model of deviance, with its assumptions that offenders are somehow 'different' and 'deficient' and that they are to be treated as 'others' – which can become exclusive rather than inclusive (**Mair 2004**). This in turn may be related to the way in which What Works research has been implemented in England and Wales – in terms which stress individual responsibility and cognitive skills rather than taking a more 'holistic' view of the broader personal and social problems which offenders face. For offenders faced with pressures of unemployment and homelessness, it could be argued, programmes to encourage them to learn social skills may not provide sufficient motivation to cease offending and indeed the pressures of their circumstances may impede attendance at programmes. In Scotland – where there is more emphasis on social inclusion and a welfare approach – what works can potentially include a broader approach focusing on the wider factors which affect desistance, which may include personal problems, feelings of confidence, employment, education and feelings of achievement, suggesting the importance of a more personalised approach (**Robinson and McNeill 2004; McIvor 2004**).

14.4 The effectiveness of community sentences

Objective 4

Evaluate the effectiveness of community sentences

There have been many pressures for community sentences to establish their effectiveness. Yet we have also seen that, given the different functions accorded to community sentences, it may be difficult to assess what is meant by effectiveness. Is their effectiveness to be judged in terms of how well they provide an alternative to prison? Or in terms of how many offenders are diverted from further crime? Alternatively, given the high costs of imprisonment and pressures for cost effectiveness, should we subject community sentences to a cost–benefit analysis? Finally, irrespective of any of these measures, should we look at the extent to which offenders are helped by these schemes, whether or not they reoffend?

In relation to the first question – their effectiveness as alternatives to prison – evidence is mixed. To start with, in what sense are community sentences an alternative to prison (i.e. an equally valid option)? In just deserts terms this was not considered credible. (The cost and effectiveness of comparing imprisonment and community sentences were discussed in **Chapters 12 and 13**.) The prison population has continued to rise despite the introduction of measures which in part were aimed at reducing it; and it appeared that the so-called alternatives to prison acted instead as alternatives to existing non-custodial sentences. This may even have resulted in more people being sent to prison – if, for example, an offender failed to comply with an order or committed further offences, they could be sent to prison, thus moving more rapidly up the tariff than they might otherwise have done. Another possible reason was that the courts, viewing community sentences as too soft, were not prepared to use them for offenders that they would otherwise have sent to prison.

There are two obvious advantages to the offender and their family of community penalties in that the offender is able, if in employment, to continue to go to work. This point is made in the National Audit Office's Value for Money Report, *The Supervision of Community Orders in England and Wales*, 2008. It concluded:

In addition to punishment, community orders offer benefits to the community and offenders. Community orders enable offenders to stay with their families and in their jobs while they serve their sentence and avoid additional pressure on the prison system (although this is not one of their primary purposes). A comparison between the actual reconviction rate and a predicted rate shows community sentences can reduce reconvictions proportionally more than a custodial sentence, although more evidence is required on the effectiveness of individual requirements (for example supervision).

It is clear that a *qualitative* case, as stated above, can be made for community penalties; however, given the policy makers are operating in a political context where the fear of crime is high on the agenda of public concerns, it is the *quantitative* case that is looked at to see if there are important differences in offender-instrumental terms, particularly around future reoffending and recidivism rates. Effectiveness is primarily measured in terms of reconviction data, typically based on the number of recorded convictions that follow in a two-year period after start of a community penalty. The problems of reliance on such measures are obvious for those who have understood the huge under-reporting of crime discussed in **Chapter 2**, and the barriers to convicting offenders of crime in an adversarial system (as seen in **Chapter 10**).

Effectiveness may be measured by looking at the number of offenders who complete their sentence rather than being returned to court for **breaching** orders. The initial enthusiasm of the judges and magistrates for the Drug Treatment and Testing Order (DTTO) when it was first introduced was not supported by the initial evidence with regard to completion rates. The first evaluation by the **National Audit Office (2004: 26)**, *The Drug Treatment and Testing Order: Early Lessons*, found that the majority of drug offenders did not complete their community sentence and just 28 per cent did. This figure included those with orders that expired while offenders were waiting formal revocation by the courts.

DTTOs, like other former community interventions, have now been replaced with the more generic Community Order, which may include a drug treatment requirement alongside other requirements. The non-completion of a community sentence may result in a breach and a return to court. In 2011, only 55 per cent of all offenders on Community Orders completed their sentences, with a further 11 per cent being allowed to terminate their sentences early for good behaviour. Of the remaining 34 per cent, 14 per cent were unable to complete their sentence due to non-compliance with the terms of the order and 10 per cent due to committal of another offence. While these figures might be regarded as a success by those familiar with the problems of dealing with offenders, from another perspective they represent a failure of offenders to complete the sentence given by the court; a sentence usually proposed in the pre-sentence report by the Probation Service.

The major test of effectiveness preferred by the government and the prison reductionists is what is described as the 'proven re-offending' rates. Proven re-offending is defined as any offence resulting in a court conviction, caution, reprimand or warning committed in a one year period following either: release from custody;

Table 14.5 Male and female annual proven reoffending rates (within 12 months) 2000 to 2010

Years	Males – number of offenders in cohort	Males – percentage who reoffend%	Females – number of offenders in cohort	Females – percentage who reoffend%	Total number of offenders	Total percentage who reoffend%
2000	396,727	27.5	80,971	19.9	477,698	26.2
2002	410,147	29.0	85,517	21.2	495,664	27.6
2003	430,126	28.2	90,534	20.7	520,660	26.9
2004	419,878	26.8	92,722	19.2	512,600	25.5
2005	433,844	26.5	98,201	17.8	532,045	24.9
2006	460,479	26.2	104,175	17.3	564,654	24.6
2007	479,023	26.3	109,666	17.3	588,689	24.6
2008	483,404	27.0	109,296	17.9	592,700	25.4
2009	472,147	26.8	106,629	17.6	578,776	25.1
2010	455,116	26.8	103,107	17.5	558,223	25.1

Note: For the years 2006/2010 inclusive, the statistics refer to the 12 months ending in September of the relevant year.
Source: *Proven Re-offending Statistics Quarterly Bulletin*, October 2009 to September 2010, England and Wales, Ministry of Justice, 24 July 2012

or, from the date when an offender is given a non-custodial sentence; or, from the date when an offender is given a caution, reprimand, warning or a positive test for opiates or cocaine. Proven reoffending rates may be useful for comparing success with certain types of offenders, or certain types of offence, but do not provide a full picture of reoffending as they naturally do not include those offences which go undetected, unrecorded or unreported.

Table 14.6 shows indictable offences dealt with by reprimand, warning, caution or conviction broken down by the number of previous offences in the offenders' histories between 2001 and 2012. It shows that the majority of offenders sentenced for indictable offences over the past 10 years are repeat offenders. Only 10 to 12 per cent had no previous cautions or convictions, whereas a consistently high proportion (between 20 and 25 per cent) of these offenders have between 3 and 6 previous convictions or cautions. In 2012, 10 per cent had no previous offences, 58.2 per cent of offenders had between one and 14 previous offences; while 31.8 per cent of the cohort had 15 or more previous offences. These offenders are known as serial recidivists, and the statistics shows below suggest that the proportion of offences committed by this group have leapt over the past 10 years from just over 18 per cent in 2002 to nearly 32 per cent in 2012.

Thus different sentencing strategies will be required for these different offender profiles. The problem of interpreting these figures is not simple, as the measurement of reconviction rates does not take account of the original risk of re-offending. Risk of re-offending may be affected by age, sex, previous history of offending, type of offence, as well as by the sentence imposed. For offences committed in 1999, the two-year reconviction rate varied between under 30 per cent for those whose original conviction was for sex offences, to 80 per cent for offenders whose original conviction was for theft from a vehicle. Additionally, the criminal justice system can itself affect the statistics as some of the 'reconvictions' are for offences dealt with after the original one but committed before (pseudo-reconvictions – see Lloyd *et al.* 1994).

Table 14.6 Offenders sentenced for indictable offences by number of previous offences in the 12 months up to March each year from 2002 to 2012

Years	Re-offending rates%					
	No previous convictions	1–2 previous convictions	3–6 previous convictions	7–10 previous convictions	11–14 previous convictions	15 or more previous convictions
2002	11.7	19.9	25.0	15.2	10.0	18.3
2003	11.1	19.0	24.0	14.9	10.3	20.6
2004	10.9	18.3	23.2	14.5	10.4	22.7
2005	11.5	18.2	22.5	13.9	10.1	23.9
2006	11.6	18.5	22.5	13.3	9.7	24.3
2007	11.1	18.7	22.8	13.2	9.4	24.9
2008	10.6	18.1	22.6	13.3	9.4	25.9
2009	10.3	17.4	21.6	13.1	9.5	28.1
2010	10.6	17.6	21.7	12.7	9.3	28.1
2011	10.4	17.0	21.3	12.7	9.2	29.5
2012	10.0	15.9	20.6	12.5	9.2	31.8

Source: *Criminal Justice Statistics, Quarterly Update to March 2012*, Ministry of Justice Statistics Bulletin, September 2012

Finally, there is not only the one measure of effectiveness based on reconviction data. This measure assumes that sentencing is concerned primarily with the aim of changing offender behaviour. The six theories of sentencing discussed in **Chapter 11** show that there are other interested parties in a sentencing decision; and that includes the victim and future victims of crime. Some offenders who are under the supervision of the Probation Service, either as those sentenced to community penalties or those on licence following release from prison, go on to commit very serious crimes. This questions the effectiveness of community sentences because while in prison the public are at least protected from the potential criminal (incapacitative logic). These issues are starkly raised in, for example, the case of the banker John Monckton (49) who was stabbed to death by Damien Hanson (aged 24) when he answered his front door to his Chelsea home. Hanson was also convicted of the attempted murder of Monckton's wife. Hanson had been released three months previously from prison after serving six years of a 12-year sentence for attempted murder. The effectiveness of the Probation Service was questioned in two ways: first, Hanson at the time of the murder was living in a probation hostel in Streatham; and second, had been released following a parole board hearing where the risk assessment on his potential for re-offending was ranked as low.

The Independent newspaper reported in 2008 on the number of grave crimes committed, including 120 murders, over the two years from 2006 to 2008, by those under the supervision of the Probation Service.

Criminals under the supervision of the probation service have committed more than one murder every week in the past two years, the Ministry of Justice said today.

Figures show offenders on probation were convicted of more than 1,000 serious violent or sexual offences in the two years from April 2006.

Those included 120 murders, 103 rapes and 80 kidnappings. But the figures are likely to rise as nearly 400 criminals have been charged with serious crimes and are still awaiting trial.

Criminals on probation received 44 manslaughter convictions in the two-year period, and 49 were convicted of arson attacks where they hoped to seriously hurt someone.

(The Independent, 28 Oct 2008)

Conclusion

This chapter has shown that the Probation Service and the particular sentences with which they are involved have undergone considerable changes since their inception in the early twentieth century. In the last 20 years we have seen a re-interpretation of the role of community sentences, whether seeing them as primarily a rehabilitative measure, a diversionary measure or as part of the higher tariff sentences of the criminal justice process, concerned more with public protection and punishment. There has also been the reawakening of an interest in rehabilitation, seen in the increasing attention paid to what works and the use of cognitive therapy, and a recognition of the personal, social and economic circumstances of offenders which might impede efforts to make them less likely to re-engage with crime. An important issue with community sentences has always been their credibility and legitimacy, with many seeing them as a 'soft option'; in part, the increasing emphasis on What Works and an evidence base can be taken as an attempt to address this issue. The recent development of a multi-purpose and intensive intervention with high-risk offenders justifies our inclusion of the new model of criminal justice we introduced in **Chapter 1**.

Review questions

1. List the main arguments for increasing the use of community sentences.

2. Consider the range of community programmes described in this chapter. In what way and to what extent are they restrictive of liberty?

3. How has the Probation Service changed from a service to befriend and support offenders to a service to manage offenders?

4. What are the problems of relying on reoffending rates that follow up convictions after a one-year period as a measure of 'What Works'?

Discussion question

1. What's in a name? What are the implications of having probation as part of:
   a. the correctional services;
   b. the National Offender Management Service?

Further reading

Bottoms A, Gelsthorpe L and Rex S (eds) (2001) *Community Penalties: Change and Challenges*, Willan Publishing: Devon

Davis R, Rubin J, Rabinovitch L, Kilmer B and Heaton P (2008) *A Synthesis of Literature on the Effectiveness of Community Orders*, Technical Report Summary, RAND Corporation: Cambridge

Gelsthorpe L and Morgan R (eds) (2007) *Handbook of Probation*, Willan Publishing: Devon

Mair G (ed.) (2004) *What Matters in Probation*, Willan Publishing: Devon

Mair G and Burke L (2009) *A Short History of Probation*, Willan Publishing: Devon

Raynor P and Vanstone M (2002) *Understanding Community Penalties: Probation, policy and social change*, Open University Press: Buckingham

Winstone J and Pakes F (2005) *Community Justice: Issues for Probation and Criminal Justice*, Willan Publishing: Devon

Weblinks

Ministry of Justice: **www.justice.gov.uk/publications/docs/**

National Probation Service: **www.gov.uk/government/organisations/national-probation-service**

HM Inspector of Probation: **inspectorates.homeoffice.gov.uk/hmiprobation/**

Chapter 15

Conclusion

The early years of a new century provide an opportunity to take stock of the developments over the past one and to speculate about the trends that provide clues to the future. In 1900, it is unlikely that we would have found a commentator who would have predicted the extent of changes in the field of criminal justice. Some changes were unforeseeable: the impact of information technology and its ability to process a mass of information and to generate horrific images of atrocities which can be sent almost instantly around the world; the development of the computer and its contribution to the phenomenon called globalisation. World news and international travel are aspects of life in wealthy Western society, which is taken for granted at the beginning of the twenty-first century. Whilst enhanced travel and career opportunities are thus provided, so are opportunities for international crime, be it international terrorism or trafficking in illegal drugs, weapons or people, or the opportunities for cyber crime via computer technology to facilitate fraud, theft and pornography.

What conclusions can be made concerning the frenetic pace of reform in the United Kingdom since 1997, which has left no agency or aspect of criminal justice untouched, in the name of effectiveness, evidence-based reforms and modernisation? Partly this is a response to the heightened public anxiety about crime. No rationalisation in terms of moral panics can fully explain the level of public concern and fear of crime. By 2000, it appeared that some aspects of middle-range crime – burglaries for instance – were responding to focused targeting. However, this did not allay public anxiety as everyday street-level incivilities and yobbishness meant people felt threatened when using public transport or visiting town centres once the bars, pubs and vicinity were taken over by alcohol- and drug-fuelled rowdy youths. The increase in crime as a result of the economic recession, as predicted by some criminologists, has not occurred. The crime rates have gone down over during a period of economic austerity, since 2010.

Then came the new nightmare of the twenty-first century as, around the world, people witnessed the unthinkable as passenger aircraft were flown into the twin towers of the World Trade Center in New York City on 11 September 2001. The fear of terrorist actions in busy urban areas provided the new paranoia, which turned, in a short period of time, to reality for those affected by terrorist bombs in Nigeria, Madrid, Istanbul, Bali, London, Mumbai and Paris. The impact of such incidents have been significant and as a result many anti-terrorist policies have been since implemented.

At the same time other fundamental changes were taking place in matters previously taken for granted and vital in dealing with crime. Membership of the European Union was changing the nature of sovereignty and the role of the nation state. New rules, regulations and institutions were introduced and others proposed. New crimes were being defined in Brussels and Strasbourg and new cross-European arrangements were introduced. The United Kingdom's place within the European Union will continue to provide a major source of change to the criminal justice system in the foreseeable future.

Even so, in the first decade of the twenty-first century we are aware that in England and Wales there is a system that has slowly evolved over a thousand years, built on the key principles of the rule of law. Societies that go through periods of lawlessness, such as, in recent times, Rwanda, Congo, Afghanistan and Syria, quickly learn the consequences of living in fear of other people and the unpredictability of everyday life when there is no rule of law.

In England and Wales, crime policy became part of the political debates partly in response to rising crime and partly as a result of the reform era of the 1960s and 1970s. Social change in this period was to shift the cultural roots and social arrangements of people undertaking everyday activities in the home, the community and at work. The 1970s seemed to be a different country from the drearily austere and conformist post-1939–45-war Britain of the 1950s. Change and consequent uncertainty was apparent in the debates about the causes of crime and the role of criminal justice agencies. In the 1990s human rights reforms and data protection legislation were to cause further uncertainty; with tragic consequences in the case of the latter when the Humberside police did not keep effective records about allegations of sexual offences by Ian Huntley, who went on to murder Holly Wells and Jessica Chapman in Soham in 2003.

The theme of sexual crimes was to become very pronounced during the period of the Coalition Government in the UK from 2010 to 2015. Ancient allegations going back 50 years were raised and prosecutions followed of radio and TV celebrities, particularly disc jockeys who were alleged to have abused their status to sexually exploit females. The BBC and the activities of Jimmy Savile was one of several notorious incidents raised by complainants who had felt that their experiences had been ignored.

The other unexpected criminal event during the period of the Coalition Government was the riots of August 2011. It may have been sparked by a real or imagined community issue but it soon became an excuse for widespread lawlessness and anarchy on the streets that reminded us in these sophisticated times in terms of theories of crimes and the developments in human rights of the basic right that Thomas Hobbes identified following the era of English Civil War in the seventeenth century, that of the right to live in a society with law and order. The riots, or civil disturbances as the authorities preferred to call them, reminded us that law and order cannot be taken for granted and that criminal justice systems that cannot deliver law and order are falling down in their primary duty to their citizens.

Terrorism at home and globally was to generate much concern during the Coalition period of government with British Muslims leaving to take part in the civil wars in Syria and Iraq in 2013 and 2014. This raised the debate about British traditions and the freedom to travel as some potential fighters were detained and passports withheld. Arguments referring to traditional British freedoms concerning the rights of suspects and the new challenge of dealing with violent terrorists who could act globally were evident in the repeal of control orders for foreign terrorist suspects. Unpredictable violence with bombings, kidnapping and mass murder in northern Nigeria illustrated the global nature of the conflict. The issue of law and order was again confronted with the difficulties of achieving this in a society driven by a human rights agenda, and by terrorists who had little respect for British values, whether ancient or modern.

In fact, few of the traditional institutions have remained untouched (particularly during the New Labour era), as laws provided new rights, and intervened into spheres previously regarded as private, such as the home. The pre-1960s political consensus on crime was to become polarised as reformers imposed changes which were not necessarily subject to consensus. The abolition of capital punishment was one such example, the establishment of a British Supreme Court was another.

Change and uncertainty were rife in many aspects of everyday life, and crime policy was no exception. Therefore, it was no surprise when in July 2004 a new five-year plan was announced by the government for more action against anti-social behaviour, with more police community support officers and community wardens on the beat, a better deal for victims and tougher and focused action against the prolific offenders who seem immune to the interventions of the current system.

In an ambitious attempt to do something about the persistent offender, the New Labour Government shifted the focus from the CJA 1991, with its just deserts approach, to achieving a standardised and proportionate response to the crime committed, and adopted an 'offender-management' model with its many-layered interventions which seek to be part rehabilitative, part surveillance and also part punishment. Thus the offender and not the crime became the new emphasis of the criminal justice system. Prison overcrowding since the mid-1990s has led to increasing emphasis on community sentences. The budget deficit and world-wide recession which greeted the Coalition Government in 2010 forced politicians to focus on cost-effective criminal justice policies.

This textbook has considered aspects of the criminal justice system in terms not only of the work and effect of the agencies involved, but also the policy and political contexts in which they operate and the often conflicting pressures and objectives that influence their operation. By using various models for considering the criminal justice system the text has highlighted how processes can be analysed to put them into a wider context. It has identified how change in one area can impact on another.

The first sections of this text examined the changing nature of what is considered a crime and differing approaches to key players: note was taken of the increased focus on victims of crime and on desires to include them in the criminal process as well as to make amends for the crimes committed against them.

Varying political approaches to the 'crime problem' and the initiatives under New Labour and the Coalition to curtail crime by an offender-management approach have been considered, including, in this context, the impact of the desire for cost-effective, measurable outcomes and monitoring of achievements by targets and KPIs. A combination of cost-effectiveness and political considerations has affected the continuing move towards privatisation, and the new move to give incentives to fine collecting by the courts.

The increasing focus on cost-effectiveness may conflict with other influences on penal policy. Governments face a dilemma in pursuing strategies, often seen as politically desirable, which stress being tough on crime while at the same time taking account of economic considerations. Tougher and more punitive policies may involve higher costs of prosecution and an increasing use of imprisonment. This has led to a tendency towards bifurcation, whereby tougher policies are reserved for more serious offences and offenders, while others are diverted from the system at various stages. Some may be diverted before prosecution by the use of cautions and victim–offender mediation schemes and diverted from prison by the greater use of community sentences. This can, of course, conflict with notions of just deserts and denunciation and with the interests of victims who see their offenders going unpunished.

Many of the strategies to make the system more effective have been accompanied or based on new technologies both for the management of systems and the control of the offenders within it. More offenders can be kept out of prison if they are monitored by what is popularly known as electronic 'tagging', and many town and city centres and other public spaces are subject to surveillance by closed-circuit television. Despite the obvious success of CCTV in identifying suspects and providing evidence for the prosecution offenders, there has been a counterview shared across the factions in the Coalition Government to reduce the extent of CCTV and electronic monitoring, as seen with the reduction in the number of functioning speed cameras on British roads since 2010.

There has also been an enormous growth of what is often described as 'private' policing. Local authorities increasingly employ security companies and many have their own municipal security – as in, for example, parks – and some have extended this to council property, housing estates and public places. There has also been a growth of auxiliary police and community wardens, and a general wish to include the community in policing and crime prevention.

The processes and changes in court procedure and particularly the criminal trial have also been considered, with examination of the tensions between due process and bureaucratic efficiency models. Diversionary strategies referred to above, including the rise of penalty notices in lieu of prosecution, can increase efficiency in the court process but can lead to public disquiet on the grounds that offenders may be perceived as being 'let off too lightly', and denunciationists argue that offenders should be publicly prosecuted.

The 'what works' debate had dominated the agenda about prisons and probation. The prison reductionist arguments about the high cost of prison and the recognition that prisons have only a limited rehabilitative potential raise important questions for the prison system. Should a steady increase in the prison population be accepted, or should steps be taken to reduce numbers in prison? If they are increasingly to be used for more serious, hard-core offenders, for largely incapacitative purposes, how should regimes be organised and what should they aim for? If there are few goals other than security and control, popularly expressed as 'keeping them in and keeping them quiet', do they become, as **Cohen (1985)** argues, effectively 'human warehouses'.

From 1997, legislative reforms proceeded apace and were indicative of the all-encompassing approach of New Labour to modernisation and the pursuit of change. The most all-encompassing is the Criminal Justice Act 2003. This Act, building on the reports by Auld and Halliday, though not implementing all their suggestions, is one of the most far-reaching pieces of criminal justice legislation in modern times. Its impact relates to bail, police conduct, composition of the jury, the conduct of criminal trials, rules of evidence, sentencing, appeals, prison and probation.

It is clear, therefore, that in the twenty-first century the criminal justice system faces considerable change and continuing dilemmas. The different models of criminal justice outlined in **Chapter 1** continue to influence thinking and remain significant, although the limitations of the system in reducing or preventing crime are more widely recognised. It is, more than ever, clear that criminal justice policy and agencies must be seen in a wider social, cultural, economic, national and international context.

Glossary of criminal justice terms

Absolute discharge: A sentence of the court in which no further action is taken.

Acceptable Behaviour Contract (ABC): An arrangement under which a police officer and a representative of the Local Authority housing department meet with the young person and their parents and together agree a contract specifying how the young person should behave.

Accused: The person suspected and accused of committing a crime.

Acquittal: Finding of not guilty.

Action Plan Order: A three-month community sentence for a child or young person (10–17) convicted of any offence other than one for which the sentence is fixed by law. It provides an early opportunity for targeted intervention to help prevent further offending.

Actual bodily harm (ABH): An offence of violence (assault occasioning actual bodily harm) where assault results in physical or mental injury. More serious than common assault but less serious than grievous bodily harm (GBH).

Actus reus: A Latin phrase referring to the acts (the guilty act) constituting a criminal offence. It refers to the part of a definition of a criminal offence that relates to the activity or consequence. For example the *actus reus* of murder is 'causing the death of a living person'.

Adjudication: To act like a judge and to make a decision in judicial proceedings by following due process.

Adversarial justice: The system of justice based in criminal cases on the assumption that the prosecution must prove the guilt of the person accused of committing a crime by presenting admissible evidence that demonstrates the guilt of an offender beyond reasonable doubt. It is open to the defence to challenge this evidence.

Affidavit: A sworn statement made that is signed, witnessed and made under oath.

Anti-Social Behaviour Orders (ASBOs): A civil order made by a magistrates' court on the application of the police or the Local Authority. They prohibit the individual from specified anti-social acts or from entering particular areas. Breaching an ASBO is a criminal offence.

Appeal: To ask for a higher court to re-examine the decisions of a lower court, usually on matters of conviction or sentence.

Arraignment: An early stage of court proceedings requiring an appearance in court by the defendant to hear the charges read out by the clerk.

Arrest: An action whereby a suspect is lawfully detained, usually by the police, but in certain circumstances by any individual. (The latter is sometimes called a 'citizen's arrest'.)

Arrest warrant: Issued by the magistrates to arrest a suspect for an indictable charge or when an accused, or defendant, or witness has not attended court.

Assault: The intent element of the offence of causing harm and criminal physical injury.

Asset Recovery Agency (ARA): This agency set up to recover assets generated as a result of crime was abolished and its work incorporated into SOCA.

Association of Chief Police Officers (ACPO): An organisation of chief officers of the Police Service.

Association of Police Authorities: A body that works to represent local government and the police authorities in England, Wales and Northern Ireland.

Attorney General: The government Minister answerable for prosecution policy and the CPS in Parliament.

Automatism: A criminal defence on the basis that the actions of the defendant took place without the defendant being aware of them, as in sleep-walking but not drunkenness.

Autopsy: An examination of a corpse undertaken by a pathologist to provide evidence to the coroner to establish the cause of death.

Bail: Release of a suspect or defendant before the conclusion of a case, under an obligation to return at a specified time to the police station or court, where failure to do so can result in punishment.

Bail Information Scheme: To assist the court make a bail decision the Probation or Prison Service provides information about the accused or defendant regarding their risk of harm to the public and other relevant information.

The Bar: A term used to refer to practising barristers collectively, or to the profession of being a barrister: being 'at the bar'.

Barrister: A professional lawyer who acts as an advocate in the courtroom who can only be instructed by a solicitor.

Basic Command Unit: Is a police operational unit covering a population the size of a town or city borough (c. 200,000).

Battery: Is the effects following an assault resulting in harm done.

Borstal: A type of custodial institution which, from 1908 to 1982, sought to rehabilitate young offenders aged from 16 to 21.

Brief: Instructions to a barrister from a solicitor regarding an appearance in court; and also used as a slang term to refer to a defence barrister.

British Crime Survey (BCS): The Home Office Crime Victimisation Survey covering England and Wales carried out annually.

Burglary: The criminal offence of illegally entering premises and committing or intending to commit acts such as theft, serious assaults and criminal damage. Referred to in Scotland as housebreaking.

Capital punishment: The death penalty as a sentence.

Case law: Decisions made following appeal about legal cases that establish details regarding the interpretation and usage of the law in particular instances that provides a body of precedents that is used to clarify and encourage consistency in subsequent similar cases.

Category A: One of four security classifications that relate to the security risk of an inmate.

Caution: (1) A formally worded statement made at the time of arrest by the police warning the suspect that whatever he or she says or does not say may be referred to as evidence in court. The caution also advises suspects that failure to reveal information may harm their court defence in certain circumstances.

(2) An official caution in lieu of conviction and sentence is a means by which offenders who admit their guilt may be given an official warning by the police and are not sent to court for trial. It is a means of diversion. Cautions given to younger offenders are called reprimands and warnings. Conditional cautions were introduced by the CJA 2003 and can lead to prosecution if the conditions are breached.

Caution Plus: As above in 1 but with a condition or additional element such as a fine.

Central Jury Summoning Bureau (CJSB): Communicates and provides information about the jury process.

Certified mentally ill: A person certified as not criminally liable because of the state of his or her mental health.

Clear-up rate: The detection rate expressed as a ratio of crimes cleared up as a percentage of crimes recorded by the police. A crime is cleared up if a person has been charged, cautioned or summonsed, or if an offender asks for crimes to be taken into consideration, or if a prisoner admits to a crime, or no further action (NFA) is taken because the criminal is below the age of criminal liability.

Closed circuit television (CCTV): A photographic system used as a means of security and surveillance.

Co-defendant: A person charged in the same case as another.

Committal: A stage in pre-trial proceedings whereby a case is sent from the magistrates' court to the Crown Court for trial or sentence; since 2014 only for sentence.

Common law: Law established by the decisions of judges in real cases and not derived from a codes or statutes. These provide precedents that would guide and offer a degree of consistency for future similar cases.

Community Punishment Order (CPO): Sentence of the court providing for an offender to do unpaid work for the community for between 40 and 240 hours over the course of one year.

Formerly named Community Service Order. Replaced under CJA 2003 by an unpaid work requirement for 40 to 300 hours

Community Punishment and Rehabilitation Order (CPRO): Sentence of the court combining CPO and CRO in specified ways. Formerly named Combination Order. Replaced under CJA 2003 by combination of requirements.

Community Rehabilitation Order (CRO): Sentence of the court providing for rehabilitation by way of supervision by the Probation Service. Formerly named Probation Order. Replaced under CJA 2003 by a community order with a supervision requirement for up to three years. Minimum period is six months. Replaced under CJA 2003 (see Community sentence).

Community sentence: A community sentence can be made up of a range of different orders, which under the Criminal Justice Act 2003 includes a variety of requirements (such as unpaid work, activity or treatment requirements). Prior to the introduction of these orders, community sentences included Community Punishment Orders, Community Rehabilitation Orders, Community Punishment and Rehabilitation Orders, Curfew Orders and Attendance Centre Orders.

Compensation Order: A monetary payment ordered by the court to be paid by the offender to the victim.

Concurrent sentence: Following conviction for multiple offences the different prison sentences given to an offender are to be served at the same time, rather than consecutively, one after another.

Condign: Merited or deserved as in a sentence.

Conditional Cautioning: An alternative to prosecution. Failure to comply with the conditions could result in prosecution for the original offence.

Conditional discharge: A sentence of the court that results in no further action for the current offence, but which allows the court to sentence in some other way if another offence is committed within the time specified.

Consecutive sentence: Prison sentences that are to be served sequentially.

Conviction: Formal ascription of guilt in a criminal court.

Coroner's court: A tribunal to investigate sudden or violent deaths presided over by a coroner.

Correctional Services Board: A board responsible for setting the overarching strategy for the prison, probation and youth justice agencies.

Corroboration: Evidence that confirms other statements or information about the facts of an investigation.

Counsel: Synonymous with barrister.

Court of Appeal: The court to which appeals from the Crown Court against conviction or sentence generally go.

Cracked Trial: Term applied to a trial that has been listed as a contested trial following a not guilty plea but does not proceed, either because the defendant pleads guilty to the whole or part of the indictment or an alternative charge, or because the prosecution offers no evidence.

Crime and Disorder Reduction Partnerships: Partnerships between the police, Local Authorities, Probation Service, health authorities, the voluntary sector, and local residents and businesses. The aim is to produce a strategy for tackling crime and disorder in their area.

Crime control model: An objective, or model, of criminal justice which stresses the aim of reducing crime.

Crime Reduction Programme (CRP): Local authority and agency initiated projects funded by central government to reduce crime.

Crimes without victims: Crimes that do not have an obvious or direct victim so they are less likely to be reported to the police, for example, prostitution, gambling, drug taking.

Criminal Cases Review Commission (CCRC): An independent body established under the Criminal Appeal Act 1995, to review and investigate suspected miscarriages of justice. It refers appropriate cases to the Court of Appeal.

Criminal Defence Service (CDS): Provides legal advice and representation to those suspected or accused of crimes through a mix of contracts with private lawyers and salaried defenders.

Criminal Injuries Compensation Authority (CICA): A non-departmental public body that administers a system of financial compensation in the form of payments for those injured as a result of criminal activities.

Criminal Justice Unit (CJU): A unit in which police and CPS staff work together to prepare cases for the magistrates' courts and are usually located in a police station.

Criminal liability: Legal responsibility for an offence.

Criminal Records Bureau (CRB): Was established by the Police Act 1997 to provide information on criminal records to organisations in the public, private and voluntary sectors when making recruitment decisions that involve working with children or vulnerable adults.

Criminal statistics: Officially published statistics of crimes recorded by the police.

Crown Court: The higher criminal court that replaced the Assize and Quarter Sessions in 1972 where trials on indictment take place before a judge and jury.

Crown Prosecution Service (CPS): The agency that, since 1986, has been responsible for prosecuting most criminal offences.

Culpability: Responsibility of an offender for a crime. Blameworthiness.

Curfew: a) A sentence that requires the person to remain in a specified place such as his or her home between specified times. b) A condition of bail to the same effect.

Custody: A sentence of imprisonment, or, for those aged 21 and under, detention in a young offenders' institution.

Custody plus: Sentence introduced by CJA 2003 for short-term custodial sentences where a term of custody is followed by release under supervision. Not implemented.

Defendant: The person in the trial who has been accused of committing an offence.

Deferred Cautioning: A diversion strategy for adult drug users arrested for the first time for possessing small amounts of Class A or Class B drugs. The offender is not cautioned at once but placed on police bail, and the decision whether or not to caution is deferred to allow them to get help from a drug agency. If the offender cooperates with the agency, and shows good progress, the police take no further action.

Delinquent: A criminal who is not an adult.

Denunciation: An objective of sentencing and punishment where the aim is to reinforce community values by indicating that certain behaviour is regarded as reprehensible and will not be tolerated.

Deposition: A written out-of-court statement based on oral answers to questions produced during an investigation.

Designated Case Worker (DCW): A CPS employee who is not a qualified lawyer who has taken an accredited training course. They review and present straightforward and less serious cases, including early guilty pleas in the magistrates' court. They have now been renamed as Associate Prosecutors.

Detention and Training Order: Custodial sentence for young offenders.

Determinate sentence: A prison sentence with a fixed term.

Deterrence: An objective of sentencing and punishment the purpose of which is to reduce the likelihood of a crime being committed in the future by the threat or anticipation of a penalty.

Disclosure: Pre-trial procedure whereby the prosecution shows to or informs the defence of all the material that has been gathered during the investigation which is relevant to the case but is not intended to be used at the trial.

Discontinuance: A term used by the CPS to indicate a case is not continuing following a review of the case files after it has started. This can be either on the grounds of insufficient evidence or the public interest. Discontinuance is governed by the Code for Crown Prosecutors.

Discovery: The stage of a case before the trial when information collected by the prosecution is revealed to the defendant.

District Judges (magistrates' courts): Legally qualified and paid magistrate, appointed from solicitors and barristers of at least seven years' standing. Formerly called stipendiary magistrate.

Director of Public Prosecutions (DPP): The appointed head of the CPS answerable to the Attorney General.

Dispersal Prison: Type of prison designed for high risk, Category A prisoners.

Disposal: Another term for a sentence of the court.

Diversion: Using strategies such as cautioning to keep offenders out of the criminal justice system.

DNA: Deoxyribonucleic acid, a component of all living matter present in blood, hair, bones, fingers, nails and bodily fluids which is used for identification purposes in criminal investigations and at a trial.

Doli incapax: The Latin term used to describe children who are deemed in law incapable of committing an offence because they are regarded as being too immature to appreciate the wrongfulness of their actions.

Double jeopardy: At risk of being punished twice for the same matter.

Drug Action Teams: Multi-agency groups set up to coordinate local action on drug misuse with representatives of agencies from the health, local authority, police, probation, social services, education, youth services and the voluntary sector.

Due process: The term used to describe the legally required procedure so as to ensure that a criminal investigation and the trial is conducted in a fair manner and is regarded as protecting the civil liberties of the defendant.

Duress: A defence referring to serious threats made to a person who commits a crime as a result. It does not apply to murder or treason.

Educational Supervision Orders (ESO): Can be applied for by a Local Education Authority to place a child of compulsory school age who is not being properly educated under the supervision of the Local Education Authority.

Either-way Offence: Triable either way is a category of criminal offence that can be tried in either the magistrates' court or in the Crown Court.

Evidence in Chief: The initial evidence given by a witness, in answer to questions asked by their 'own side' before being cross-examined by the other party.

Evidential Sufficiency: One of the two criteria the CPS must apply in reviewing all cases before they may proceed to trial to ensure that sufficient and appropriate evidence has been collected by the police.

Extradition: Formal process of transferring a suspect or criminal from one country to another.

Family Liaison Officers: A police officer who is responsible for maintaining communication with the victim's family.

Felony: A major crime contrasted with a misdemeanour. A term relating to categories of crime that was abolished in the UK since the Criminal Law Act 1967.

Final Warning scheme: Police caution for young offenders.

Forensic Science Service (FSS): Provides scientific support in the investigation of crime and expert evidence to the courts.

Green Paper: A preliminary discussion paper issued by a government department inviting comment on proposed changes to the law.

Grievous bodily harm (GBH): A crime of assault with serious harm such as broken ribs.

Habeas corpus: A court order that commands an official to bring the prisoner or detained person to court. Latin for show us the body.

Her Majesty's Inspectorate of Constabulary (HMIC): Responsible for monitoring and reporting on individual police forces in England and Wales.

Her Majesty's CPS Inspectorate (HMCPSI): Responsible for inspection, evaluation and reporting on the CPS and the 42 CPS Areas.

Her Majesty's Inspectorate of Prisons (HMIP): An independent inspectorate which reports on conditions for and treatment of those in prison, young offender institutions and immigration detention facilities.

Her Majesty's Inspectorate of Probation: An independent Inspectorate, funded by the Ministry of Justice, and reporting to the Secretary of State on the effectiveness of work with individual offenders, children and young people aimed at reducing reoffending and protecting the public.

Hidden figure of crime: Sometimes referred to as the dark figure; the number of crimes that go unrecorded.

Home Affairs Committee (HAC): A select committee of the House of Commons that monitors criminal justice issues.

Home Office: The government department responsible for law and order policies and the overall responsibility for the police, probation and prison services.

Homicide: Offences involving the unlawful killing of a person, for example, murder, manslaughter, infanticide.

Hooliganism: Rowdy and disorderly behaviour, usually in a group, that is regarded as threatening by others.

Incapacitation: Sentencing or punishment strategy that makes it impossible for the criminal to reoffend by imposing physical restraints on him or her such as imprisonment.

Incorrigible: An offender who refuses to change his or her criminal behaviour; unmanageable; unable to be reformed.

Independent Police Complaints Commission: Body established from April 2004 and funded by the Home Office, but independent of the police to deal with complaints about the police. Replaced Police Complaints Authority.

Indeterminate sentence: A sentence that is not fixed in length, such as a life sentence.

Indictable: A criminal offence that may be tried in the Crown Court. Indictable offences are thus those that can only be tried in the Crown Court and triable either way offences.

Indictable-only Offence: An indictable-only offence is a category of criminal offence that can only be tried in the Crown Court.

Indictment: The formal document that contains the charges against a defendant for Crown Court trial.

In loco parentis: Acting in place of a parent with regard to an underage defendant or suspect.

Inmate: A person kept in prison or in a mental hospital.

Intensive Supervision and Surveillance Programme (ISSP): An intensive intervention available for young offenders who can be monitored for up to 24 hours a day, seven days a week and are subject to a highly structured programme of activities for 25 hours a week for three months.

Intermittent custody: Court sentence introduced under CJA 2003 allowing a custodial sentence to be served over longer periods of time, not on consecutive days such as at weekends. Not implemented.

Joyriding: A popular term for the criminal offence of aggravated vehicle taking.

Judicial Appointments Commission (JAC): Makes judicial appointments in England and Wales.

Judicial Studies Board (JSB): Provides training and instruction for judges in England and Wales.

Jurisdiction: The geographical and legal extent of the powers of an agency or court.

Jury: The 12 adults who are selected to decide, in Crown Court trial, whether from the evidence they have heard the accused is guilty or not. A jury (7–11 people) is also used in the Coroner's Court.

Jury vetting: Examining the jury list before trial to exclude jurors with extreme political views: only possible in terrorist and national security trials.

Just deserts: Sentencing approach in which the sentence should be appropriate for the offence.

Justice Gap: The gap between the number of crimes committed and the number of crimes solved.

Justice model: Punishment model based on just deserts.

Juvenile Court: Renamed the Youth Court after the Criminal Justice Act 1991 and extended its jurisdiction from 16 to 17 year olds.

Labelling: The process of identifying, categorising and stereotyping social groups such as delinquents.

Law Commission: The Law Commission Act 1965 established this body to review and reform the law.

Law Society: The professional body for solicitors in England and Wales.

Lay magistracy: Voluntary Justices of the Peace.

Legal Services Commission (LSC): Responsible for legal aid and the Criminal Defence Service.

Litigation: Using the courts to pursue a legal remedy.

Local Authority Secure Children's Home: Provide placements for remanded and sentenced juveniles to provide security with education.

Local Criminal Justice Boards (LCJBs): There are 42 Criminal Justice Boards which will coordinate the efforts to deliver the targets of the National Criminal Justice Board.

Lord Chancellor's Department or Department for Constitutional Affairs: The government department formerly responsible for the courts and the appointment of magistrates and judges. Now replaced by Ministry of Justice.

Magistrates: The men and women appointed to decide matters in the magistrates' courts: District Judges (magistrates' courts) and lay magistrates.

Magistrates' court: The lower of the two criminal courts that try criminal cases.

Mandatory: Something that must happen as set down by legislation, for example, mandatory sentences: the court has no choice.

Manslaughter: A criminal offence of causing death without the *mens rea* necessary to be guilty of murder, or where murder is reduced to manslaughter because of provocation or diminished responsibility.

Mens rea: A Latin term meaning guilty mind, used to cover the various levels of the mental element (eg intention or recklessness) in the definition of an offence. For example, in the case of murder the *mens rea* is the intention to kill or to cause grievous bodily harm.

Metropolitan Police: The police force for London and the surrounding area.

Miscarriage of justice: A term commonly used to describe a case where a defendant, after serving a term of imprisonment, is later found to be not guilty or is acquitted on the grounds that the conviction is unsafe. It might, but does not necessarily, mean they are innocent. The term is rarely used in respect of mistaken acquittals, i.e. where a guilty person is found 'not guilty' following a trial.

Misdemeanour: A crime category that distinguished less serious crimes from those classified as felonies.

Mitigation: Factors that reduce an offender's culpability for a crime without being a defence and thus are used in decisions about sentences.

Mode of trial: The way a defendant is tried, i.e. summarily or on indictment: an allocation decision (previously called a mode of trial decision) is required for triable either way cases.

Moral panic: An alarmed reaction to a social problem. The media is blamed for over-reacting to a type of crime and making it appear more serious or prevalent than it is.

Mugging: A commonly used word to refer to a street robbery.

Murder: Causing the death of another human being intending to cause death or intending to cause grievous bodily harm.

National Criminal Justice Board: The body responsible for overseeing and directing the work of the local Criminal Justice Boards.

National Policing Improvement Agency (NPIA): Its aim is to develop a more coordinated approach to police reform, training and standards in terms of operational policing on matters such as leadership training; identify good practice and propose plans for a more effective poling structure with regard to matters of technology and communications. (2007–2012.)

Negligence: The failure to act with reasonable care that could lead to criminal charges.

Neighbourhood Watch Association: Voluntary community schemes of local people that liaise with the police at neighbourhood level to prevent and respond to crime.

Nolo contendere: A plea indicating that the issue in a trial or legal proceedings will not be contested or disputed by the person charged with an offence.

Notifiable offences: These are offences recorded by the police and broadly refers to most indictable (including triable either way) offences, although a few summary offences are included such as unauthorised taking of a motor vehicle. Not as extensive as the List of Standard Offences.

Organised crime: Refers to the serious crimes of organised gangs and criminal syndicates.

PACE: Police and Criminal Evidence Act 1984. Refers to the codes used to regulate police encounters with the public when dealing with crime.

Paradigm: A way of thinking about a subject of study or professional practice.

Parenting Orders: An order to help and support parents or guardians in addressing anti-social or offending behaviour.

Parole Board: Body responsible for decisions about the release, and recall of prisoners on licence.

Penitentiary: A prison. In earlier use in the United States it was a prison committed to rehabilitative aims.

Perjury: An offence committed during judicial proceedings when a witness gives false testimony. Perjury Act 1911.

Plea: The answer of the accused to the question of whether he or she is guilty or not to the crime of which he or she has been accused.

Plea bargaining: Process of a defendant pleading guilty to certain lesser charges when more serious charges are dropped or an indication of a likely sentence is given.

Plea before venue: Name given to magistrates' court procedure where plea to a triable either way offence is taken before a decision is made as to whether the case is tried in the magistrates' court or Crown Court.

Plea in mitigation: Argument on behalf of an offender after conviction with the aim of reducing the sentence.

Police Complaints Commission: See Independent Police Complaints Commission.

Police Federation: Representative body for police officers below the rank of Superintendent. It was established by the Police Act 1919 to provide the police with a means of bringing attention to their views about matters of employment and conditions of service because the police may not join a trade union.

Police National Computer (PNC): The national computer that records police information on those arrested and prosecuted for crimes.

Positivism: Application of scientific methods to the study of crime.

Post-mortem: The examination of a dead body to establish the causes of death.

Preparatory Hearing: A pre-trial hearing to assist in the management of certain fraud trials and other complex and lengthy cases.

Pre-sentence report (PSR): A report, prepared by the Probation Service in the case of those over 16 and the social services for those under 16 (or Youth Offending Team for young offenders) describing the background and circumstances of the offender with a view to providing information that might be useful in the sentencing decision. It replaced the social enquiry report (SER) in 1992. In some circumstances obtaining a PSR is mandatory.

Presumption of innocence: The principle that governs the conduct of a trial, and puts the entire burden of proving guilt onto the prosecution. The accused is not required to give any explanation or defence. The outcome of the trial does not lead to the conclusion that the accused is innocent but that he or she has not been proved to be guilty.

Presumptive sentences: Sentencing guidelines that are not mandatory but give a strong suggestion as to the sentence appropriate for different types of offences and offender histories.

Pre-trial Hearing: A hearing held before the trial begins, to assist the management of the trial.

Prima facie: On the face of it. Is there a case.

Prison: Certified Normal Accommodation (CNA): The designed capacity of a prison.

Prison: open: A prison with minimum security arrangements, in contrast to a closed prison.

Prison: receptions: The annual total of people sent for whatever reasons into the prison system.

Prisoners' Aid Society: Founded by Lord Shaftesbury in 1854 to help released prisoners to find work and provide welfare support for their families.

Proactive policing: The police initiating enquiries without relying on citizen complaints.

Probation: breach: Failing to comply with the terms of a probation order.

Probation Order: see also Community Rehabilitation Order. Since CJA 2003 called a Community Order with a requirement for supervision.

Procurator Fiscal: A Scottish official responsible for charging and prosecuting criminals in Scotland; and is a much older prosecuting agency than the CPS.

Professional crime: Crimes committed by a career criminal.

Public interest criterion: The second criterion (see also evidential sufficiency) that the CPS must apply in determining whether a case should be started or continued. Contains a list of specific questions that have to be considered in making such a decsion, such as age or ill health.

Queen's Counsel (QC): A senior barrister appointed by letters patent from the reigning monarch to be one of 'Her [or His] Majesty's Counsel learnt in the law'.

Rape: Having sexual intercourse with a man or a woman without his or her consent.

Reactive policing: The police responding to citizens' reports of crime in contrast to preventative or proactive policing.

Recidivist: A persistent repeat offender.

Recorder: A part-time judge who presides in the Crown Court; also certain judges with specific administrative responsibilities or traditional duties such as the Recorder of London.

Referral Orders: The primary sentence for young people coming before the court with no previous convictions, who plead guilty and do not warrant a custodial sentence or an absolute discharge. A Youth Offender Panel will agree a programme with the young person to tackle the underlying causes of their offending behaviour, including reparation and to repair the harm done.

Reformatory: A custodial training institution for younger offenders (1854/1933).

Rehabilitation: Sentencing objective concerned with the reform of the offender.

Remand centre: Place of detention for those remanded in custody before a criminal case is completed.

Remand in custody: Detention of a suspect/defendant in custody pending the next stage in his or her case.

Remand on bail: Release of defendant pending the next stage in his or her case under compulsion to return to court or police station.

Reparation: Making amends for a wrong done; repairing the damage. A sentencing objective to achieve this.

Requisition: Document accompanying written charge requiring suspect to appear in magistrates' court. Not yet implemented.

Resident Judges: A senior judge at a Crown Court Centre and who has particular administrative functions.

Restitution: Compensation for the victim of a crime; sentencing objective to achieve this.

Restorative justice: Refers to schemes and initiatives to bring together offenders, victims, family, and local community representatives to deal with an offender with the aim of raising awareness in the offender of the consequences of their actions, and offering help to prevent re-offending. Particularly considers the impact on the victim and encourages reparation.

Retribution: A purpose of sentencing and punishment to exact vengeance for wrongdoing. Just deserts.

Right of Audience: The right to speak in court.

Robbery: An offence that involves the theft of property through the use or threat of violence.

Rule 43/45: The Prison Rule that allows a prisoner to be held in isolated accommodation for his or her own protection, or because they are disruptive.

Safer Communities Initiative: Local anti-crime initiatives to combat crime hot spots in communities, based on the recognition that crime tends to involve repeat victims and persistent offenders.

Secure Training Centres: Hold remanded and sentenced young people aged 12–17 and provide a constructive regime which focuses on education, vocational training, and tackling offending behaviour and are operated by private contractors under the supervision of the Youth Justice Board.

Self-report study: A survey which asks the respondents about how many offences they have committed.

Sentencing Advisory Panel: Advisory body on sentencing in conjunction with the Sentencing Guidelines Council.

Sentencing Guidelines Council (renamed Sentencing Council): Chaired by the Lord Chief Justice it sets guidelines for sentencing individual criminal offences and also provides general guidelines on approaches to sentencing generally. Established in 2010.

Serious Organised Crime Agency (SOCA): National Police agency to combat organised and international crimes such as drug, firearm and people trafficking; money laundering; and attempts to recover the proceeds of crime.

Sex Offender Order: Introduced in the Crime and Disorder Act 1998, they are applied for at court by the police in order to restrict the behaviour of certain offenders who present a risk. It can for example prevent offenders going to certain areas, for example those frequented by children. Breach is punishable by up to five years' imprisonment.

Silk: Synonymous with Queen's Counsel (QC).

Solicitor: A lawyer who can be approached directly by the public with rights of audience mainly in the magistrates' court, though some have 'Higher rights'.

Special Constables: Special Constables work part-time and on a voluntary basis alongside the regular police force and have the same legal powers.

Standard List Offences: A list of offences for which the name of the offender and details of each sentence have been collected by the Home Office. Covers all indictable only, triable either way and some summary offences such as assault on a police constable, and criminal damage under £5,000. Data from this is used for the Offender Index and for reconviction studies. More comprehensive than the List of Notifiable Offences.

Stare decisis: To look at previous cases to establish the Authority for making a decision in a case before the courts. Use of precedents.

Street Crime Initiative: Launched in 2002 the initiative is designed to identify and implement ways of effectively tackling street crime.

Statutory law: The law set out in Acts of Parliament.

Statutory sentence: A sentence provided for by Act of Parliament.

Stipendiary magistrate: see district judge.

Strict liability offence: A crime not requiring any intention or other mental element.

Subpoena: A court document requiring the attendance of a witness to appear to give testimony before a court.

Summary offence: A category of criminal offences (one of three). Offences that can be tried in the magistrates' court only.

Summary trial: Trial in the magistrates' court.

Summons: A written notice to appear in court on a specified date to answer a criminal charge.

Superintendents' Association: Sole representative body of police officers of superintending ranks in England and Wales.

Taken into consideration (TIC): Offences taken into consideration, i.e. not specifically charged but which the court takes account of when sentencing.

Theft: Dishonest appropriation of property belonging to another with the intention of permanently depriving that other of it (stealing).

Total institutions: A sociological term for an institution such as a prison in which the entire round of life is conducted within the one place with the same people, isolated from the rest of society.

Triable either way (TEW): A category of criminal offence (one of three). These offences may be tried either in the magistrates' court or the Crown Court.

Trial: Contesting liability in a court.

Trial Unit: Operational unit of the Crown Prosecution Service, responsible for the preparation and presentation of Crown Court prosecutions. Criminal Justice Units handle magistrates' court cases.

Vandalism: The offence of criminal damage.

Verdict: A formal finding by a jury in a trial.

Victimology: The study of victims of crime.

Victim Personal Statements: Statements that give victims an opportunity to inform the court and other criminal justice agencies of the effect of the crime on them. Used in sentencing process.

Victim Support: Voluntary organisation concerned with giving advice and support to victims of crime.

Victim survey: A survey, such as the BCS, which asks people about their experiences as a victim.

Virtual Unified Case File: Virtually Unified Case File (VUCF) refers to a project to make available data held on computers by the different agencies so as to provide users across the CJS with seamless access to case information.

Warrant: An order of the court; for example, an arrest warrant which gives power to the police to arrest someone; a search warrant allows the police to search a property without the owner's consent.

White-collar crime: A term referring to crimes relating to business or professional activities.

White Paper: A report published prior to legislation indicating the policy direction of reforms from a government department such as the Home Office.

Witness Liaison Officer (WLO): An officer at each Crown Court centre to provide a link with the other criminal justice agencies and the Witness Service.

Young Offender Institution: A custodial institution for those aged between 15 and 21.

Younger offender: Defined as child (offender aged 10–14); juvenile or youth (offender aged 14–17); and young adult (offender aged 18–21).

Youth Court: The name since 1992 of the part of the magistrates' court that deals with younger offenders aged under 18 and previously known as the Juvenile Court.

Youth Justice Board for England and Wales (YJB): An executive Non-Departmental Public Body (NDPB) established in September 1998 to provide leadership and coordination to Youth Offending Teams and the youth justice system as a whole. The Board advises the government on youth justice service provision, standards for service delivery and the performance of the youth justice system.

Youth Offending Teams (YOTs): Multidisciplinary teams responsible for local delivery of community-based intervention and supervision for young offenders and work with young offenders at risk of offending.

Youth Offender Panels: Panel to which young offenders are referred under a referral order. The panel agrees a contract with the young offender that includes reparation to the victim and a programme of activity to address the risk of reoffending.

Zero tolerance: A crime prevention strategy of not tolerating or ignoring breaches of the law no matter how trivial.

Appendix Practical Exercises

Exercise 1: Crime data exercise

You should consider how crime is defined. Look at various sources of information about crime, particularly at the media and official sources. Why are some kinds of crime seen as more serious than others? To understand the creation and interpretation of official data about crime, you will need to examine the processes underlying the reporting of crime – by the public, victims and the police. The reliability of official criminal statistics will depend upon these factors.

Interpreting crime statistics

Consult extracts from the criminal statistics and answer the following questions, illustrating your answers with figures taken from statistics. Specify your source of information. Give the title of the publication you consulted and indicate which year the data covers:

Title: ....

Year: ....

(a) By how much has the total volume of crime known to the police increased, or decreased, in recent years?

....

....

....

(b) What percentage of all crimes reported to the police do the following constitute?

    murder   ....

    rape   ....

    robbery   ....

    theft   ....

    fraud   ....

    car theft   ....

559

Consider which crimes are likely to be proportionately over-represented and why?

....

....

Which crimes are likely to be under-represented and why?

....

....

(c) Give examples of the variations in the rate at which different kinds of crimes are 'cleared up' by the police.

....

....

What does it mean to say that a crime is 'cleared up'?

....

....

Why are some offences more likely to be 'cleared up' than others?

....

....

(d) Which groups in the population are most 'at risk' from 'personal crime'?

....

....

Should we be more afraid of strangers, acquaintances or family? Why?

....

....

(e) What percentage of known offenders are male?

....

....

Taking into account the process of 'creating' statistics – how accurate do you think the ratio of male to female known offenders is?

Exercise 2: Victim survey

You should use the following 'Crime Victim Questionnaire' and interview eight people (four male, four female). Note their age. Try to include a range of people.

Consider the following:

1. Which offences are respondents most/least likely to be the victims of? Are there any significant age/gender differences?

2. Which offences are more likely to be reported?

3. What reasons do victims give for not reporting crimes?

Crime victim questionnaire

In the last two years, how many times have you been the victim of the following crimes?	*If so, was this reported to the police?*	*If not reported, why not?*
Theft:		
of a motor car		
from a motor car		
of a bicycle		
at work		
from your person		
Burglary		
Assault:		
with injury		
no injury		
Robbery:		
in street		
in bank/post office		
Insulted/bothered:		
by strangers		
Any other?		
describe briefly		

Exercise 3: Magistrates' court observation report

We recommend you observe a morning session of a magistrates' court, which will normally start at 10 a.m. and go on until lunchtime. If you are unable to attend during the week it may be possible to find inner urban courts that sit on Saturday and there is at least one evening court in the London area.

1. Name: ....

   Location of magistrates' court: ....

   Date of visit: ....

   Time of arrival: ....

   Time of departure: ....

2. Before you go give some impression of what you expect to see in a magistrates' court.

   ....

   ....

3. How many courtrooms were there?   ....

   How many cases were scheduled to be heard in each?

   ....

   ....

4. After 10 minutes, from your time of arrival at the magistrates' court, describe your initial impressions.

   ....

   ....

5. Can you identify the following (*please tick*):

   Bench ☐

   Clerk's desk ☐

   Advocates' seats ☐

   Dock ☐

   Witness box ☐

   Press box ☐

   Usher's seat ☐

   Public seating ☐

   Seating for defendants on bail or summons ☐

6. Personnel in the courtroom.

    How many magistrates were there? ....

    Name the other functionaries.

    ....

    ....

    Who else was in the court?

    ....

    ....

7. Defendants

    How many defendants appeared while you were in the court?

8. What sort of cases did you observe (*please tick*)?

    a remand   ☐
    a decision as to mode of trial   ☐
    an adjournment   ☐
    a decision to grant bail   ☐
    a remand in custody   ☐
    a community order being made   ☐
    a disqualification from driving being ordered   ☐
    a guilty plea being entered   ☐
    a trial   ☐
    a fine being imposed   ☐

9. How would you describe the types of defendants you saw?

    ....

    ....

10. Were there some defendants who seemed unable to understand the proceedings?

    ....

    ....

11. Outcomes

    How many cases were disposed of, from plea to sentence? ....

    How many defendants were remanded in custody? ....

How many defendants were given bail with conditions? ....

How many defendants were given bail without conditions? ....

How many defendants were sent for trial to the Crown Court? ....

How many cases were adjourned to a future date? ....

If they were adjourned, give the reasons why.

....

....

12. What were your impressions of the performance of the Crown Prosecutor?

....

....

13. What was your impression of the magistrates?

....

....

14. What was your impression of the defence lawyer?

....

....

15. Using keywords, describe your general impression of the magistrates' court.

....

....

16. What time did the court commence business? ....

17. Was the conduct of the court efficient in your view? If not explain why not.

....

....

18. Are there any other comments you wish to make about your observations?

....

....

Bibliography

Agnew R (2012) *Toward a Unified Criminology: Integrating Assumptions About Crime, People and Society – New Perspectives in Crime, Deviance and Law*, New York, NY: New York University Press.

Aitchison A and Hodgkinson J (2003) 'Patterns of Crime', in Simmons J and Dodd T (eds) *Crime in England and Wales 2002/3*, London: Home Office National Statistics.

Alderson J (1978) *Communal Policing*, Exeter: Devon and Cornwall Constabulary.

Allen C (2004) *A Practical Guide to Evidence* (3rd edn), London: Cavendish.

Allen C (2008) *A Practical Guide to Evidence* (4th edn), London: Routledge-Cavendish Publishing.

Amir M (1971) *Patterns of Forcible Rape*, Chicago, IL: University of Chicago Press.

Anderson S, Kinsey R, Loader I and Smith C (1994) *Cautionary Tales: Young People, Crime and Policing in Edinburgh*, Aldershot: Avebury.

Andrews D, Bonta J and Hodge R (1990) 'Classification for Effective Rehabilitation', *Criminal Justice and Behaviour*, **17**: 19–52.

Ashworth A (1989) 'Criminal Justice and Deserved Sentences', *Criminal Law Review*: 340–55.

Ashworth A (1992) *Sentencing and Penal Policy* (2nd edn), London: Weidenfeld & Nicolson.

Ashworth A (1994a) *The Criminal Process*. Oxford: Clarendon Press.

Ashworth A (1994b) 'Sentencing', in Maguire M, Morgan R and Reiner R (eds) *The Oxford Handbook of Criminology*, Oxford: Clarendon Press.

Ashworth A (1997) 'Sentencing', in Maguire M, Morgan R and Reiner R (eds) *The Oxford Handbook of Criminology* (2nd edn), Oxford: Clarendon Press.

Ashworth A (1998) *The Criminal Process* (2nd edn), Oxford: Clarendon Press.

Ashworth A (2000) 'Victims' Rights, Defendants' Rights and Criminal Procedure', in Crawford A and Goodey J (eds) *Integrating a Victim Perspective within Criminal Justice*, Aldershot: Ashgate/Dartmouth.

Ashworth A (2002) 'Sentencing', in Maguire M, Morgan R and Reiner R (eds) *The Oxford Handbook of Criminology* (3rd edn), Oxford: Clarendon Press.

Ashworth A (2003) *The Criminal Process* (3rd edn), Oxford.

Ashworth A (2007) 'Sentencing', in Maguire M, Morgan R and Reiner R (eds) *The Oxford Handbook of Criminology* (4th edn), Oxford: Oxford University Press.

Ashworth A (2010) *Sentencing and Criminal Justice* (5th edn), Cambridge: Cambridge University Press.

Ashworth A (2013) *Positive Obligations in Criminal Law*, Oxford: Hart Publishing.

Ashworth A and Horder J C N (2013) *Principles of Criminal Law* (7th edn), Oxford: Oxford University Press.

Ashworth A and Redmayne M (2005) *The Criminal Process* (3rd edn), Oxford: Oxford University Press.

Audit Commission (2004) *Youth Justice 2004: a Review of the Reformed Youth Justice System*, London: Audit Commission.

Auld Report (2001) *Review into the Workings of the Criminal Courts in England and Wales*, London: Home Office.

Ayres, Murray and Fiti (2003) *Arrests for Notifiable Offences and the Operation of Certain Police Powers under PACE*, Home Office Statistical Bulletin, 17/03.

Baldwin J and McConville M (1979) *Jury Trials*, Oxford: Clarendon Press.

Barclay G (ed.) (1995) *Digest 3: Information on the Criminal Justice System in England and Wales*, London: HMSO.

565

Bennett T (1990) *Evaluating Neighbourhood Watch*, Aldershot: Gower.

Bennett T (1994a) 'Community Policing', *Criminal Justice Matters*, No 17, Autumn 1994: 6–7.

Bennett T (1994b) 'Recent Developments in Community Policing', in Stephens M and Becker S (eds) *Police Force, Police Service: Care and Control in Britain*, London: Macmillan.

Bennett T and Lupton R (1992) 'A National Activity Survey of Police Work', *Howard Journal of Criminal Justice*, **31** (3): 200–23.

Bentham J (1791) *Panopticon: or the Inspection House*, London: Payer.

Blumberg A (1967) *Criminal Justice*, Chicago: Quadrangle Books.

Bonta J, Wallace-Capretta S and Rooney J (1999) *Electronic Monitoring in Canada*, Ottawa: Solicitor General Canada.

Bosworth M F and Hoyle C (2012) *What is Criminology?*, Oxford: Oxford University Press.

Bottoms A, Gelsthorpe L and Rex S (eds) (2001) *Community Penalties: Change and Challenges*, Cullompton: Willan Publishing.

Bowling B (1998) *Violent Racism, Victimisation, Policing and Social Context*, Oxford: Oxford University Press.

Bowling B and Foster J (2002) 'Policing and the Police', in Maguire M, Morgan R and Reiner R (eds) *The Oxford Handbook of Criminology* (3rd edn), Oxford: Clarendon Press.

Bowling B and Phillips C (2003) 'Policing Ethnic Minority Communities', in Newburn T (ed.) *Handbook of Policing*, Cullompton: Willan Publishing.

Bowling B and Phillips C (2007) 'Ethnicities, racism, crime and criminal justice', in Maguire M, Morgan R and Reiner R (eds) *Handbook of Criminology* (4th edn), Oxford: Oxford University Press.

Boyd E (2012) *Policing 2020: What kind of police service do we want in 2020?*, London: Policy Exchange.

Brand S and Price R (2000) 'The Economic and Social Costs of Crime', Home Office Research Study 217, Economics and Resource Analysis, Research, Development and Statistics Directorate, London: Home Office.

Bratton W (1997) 'Crime is Down in New York City: Blame the Police', in Dennis N (ed.) *Zero Tolerance: Policing a Free Society*, London: IEA.

Brookman F (2005) *Understanding Homicide*, London: Sage.

Brooks G and Gross C (1996) *British Retail Consortium Retail Crime Costs 1994/5 Survey*, London: BRC Retail Crime Initiative.

Brown D (1997) *PACE Ten Years On: A Review of the Research*, Home Office Research Study No 155, London: Home Office.

Brown J M (ed.) (2014) The Future of Policing, Oxford: Routledge.

Bullock S (2007) *Police Service Strength – England and Wales*, Home Office Statistical Bulletin: London: Home Office.

Cain M (1973) *Society and the Policeman's Role*, London: Routledge & Kegan Paul.

Calvert-Smith, Sir D (2003) *The Police Service in England and Wales – final report of formal investigation by CRE*, London: CRE.

Carrabine E *et al.* (2004) *Criminology: A Sociological Introduction*, London: Routledge.

Carter P R (Lord) (2006) *Legal Aid: a Market-based Approach to Reform*, London: Home Office.

Cashmore E (2001) 'The experiences of ethnic minority police officers in Britain: under-recruitment and racial profiling in a performance culture', *Ethnic and Racial Studies*, **24** (4): 642–59.

Cashmore E (2002) 'Behind the Window Dressing: Ethnic Minority Police Perspectives on Cultural Diversity', in *Journal of Ethnic and Migration Studies*, **28** (2): 327–41.

Cavadino P and Dignan J (1997) *The Penal System: An Introduction* (2nd edn), London: Sage.

Cavadino P and Dignan J (2002) *The Penal System: An Introduction* (3rd edn), London: Sage.

Cavadino, M and Dignan, J (2007) *The Penal System: An Introduction* (4th edn), London: Sage.

Chibnall S (1997) *Law and Order News*, London: Tavistock.

Civitas Crime Factsheets (2014) *Policing in England and Wales*, London: Civitas.

Clarke (1980) 'Situational Crime Prevention: Theory and Practice', *British Journal of Criminology*, 20: 136–47.

Clarke R and Hough M (1984) *Crime and Police Effectiveness*, Home Office Research Study 79, London: HMSO.

Clarke R V G (2005) 'Seven misconceptions of situational crime prevention', in Tilley N (ed.) *Handbook of Crime Prevention*, Cullompton: Willan Publishing.

Clemmer D (1958) *The Prison Community*, New York, NY: Holt, Rinehart& Winston.

Cloward R and Ohlin L (1960) *Delinquency and Opportunity: A Theory of Delinquent Gangs*, New York, NY: Free Press.

Cohen S (1980) *Folk Devils and Moral Panics*, Oxford: Martin Robertson.

Cohen S (1985) *Visions of Social Control*, Cambridge: Polity Press.

Cohen S and Taylor L (1972) *Psychological Survival*, Harmondsworth: Penguin.

Coleman C and Moynihan J (1996) *Understanding Crime Data: Haunted by the Dark Figure*, Buckingham: Open University Press.

Coleman C and Norris C (2000) *Introducing Criminology*, Cullompton: Willan Publishing.

Collison M (1996) 'In Search of the High Life: Drugs, Crime, Masculinities and Consumption', *British Journal of Criminology*, 36 (3): 428–44.

Condon P (1994) Address to meeting of British Society of Criminologists, London, January 1994.

Conway G (1997) *Islamophobia: A Challenge for Us All*, London: Runnymede Trust.

Copes H and Pogrebin M (2012) *Voices from Criminal Justice: Thinking and Reflecting on the System (Criminology and Justice Studies)*, London: Routledge.

Crawford A (1998) *Crime Prevention and Community Safety: Politics, Policies and Practices*, London: Longman.

Crawford A (2007) 'Crime Prevention and Community Safety', in Maguire M, Morgan R and Reiner R (eds) *The Oxford Handbook of Criminology* (4th edn), Oxford: Clarendon Press.

Crawford A and Goodey J (eds) (2000) *Integrating a Victim Perspective within Criminal Justice: International Debates*, Aldershot: Ashgate.

Crime in England and Wales 2006/7: A Summary of the Main Figures (Home Office RDS 2007 available from www.homoffice.gov.uk/rds/pdfs07/crime0607summ/pdf).

Croall H (2001) *Understanding White Collar Crime*, Buckingham: Open University Press.

Croall H (2003) 'Combating Financial Crime: Regulatory versus Crime Control Approaches', *Journal of Financial Crime*, 11: 144–55.

Croall H (2007) 'Victims and Social Exclusion', in Davies P, Greer C and Francis P (eds) *Victims, Crime and Society*, London: Sage.

Crown Prosecution Service (annually) *Annual Report*, London: HMSO.

Davies M (1989) 'An Alternative View: Square Deal Punishment in the Community: It is Cheaper But Who Will Buy It?', in Rees H and Hall Williams E (eds) *Punishment, Custody and the Community: Reflections and Comments on the Green Paper*, Suntory Toyota International Centre for Economics and Related Disciplines.

Davies M (1993) *Punishing Criminals: Developing Community-based Intermediate Sanctions*, Connecticut: Greenwood.

Davies M (1997) 'Sentencing Trends and Public Confidence', in Murray C, Davies M, Rutherford A and Young J (eds) *Does Prison Work*, London: IEA and *Sunday Times*.

Davies M, Takala J-P and Tyrer J (1996) *Penological Esperanto and Sentencing Parochialism*, Aldershot: Dartmouth.

Davies P (2003) 'Crime Victims and Public Policy', in Davies P, Francis P and Jupp V (eds) *Victimisation: Theory, Research and Policy*, Basingstoke: Palgrave/Macmillan.

Davies P, Francis P and Jupp V (eds) (2003) *Victimisation: Theory, Research and Policy*, Basingstoke: Palgrave/Macmillan.

Davis K (1969) *Discretionary Justice: A Preliminary Inquiry*, Baton Rouge, LA: Louisiana State University Press.

Davis R, Rubin J, Rabinovich L, Kilmer B and Heaton P (2008) *A Synthesis of Literature on the Effectiveness of Community Orders – Technical Report Summary*, Cambridge: RAND Europe.

Department for Constitutional Affairs (2003) *Judicial Appointments Annual Report 2002/3*, London: DCA.

De Lint W, Marmo M and Chazal N (2014) *Criminal Justice in International Society*, London: Routledge.

Dicey A (1959) *Introduction to the Study of the Law of the Constitution*, London: Macmillan.

Dignan J (2004) *Understanding victims and restorative justice*, Milton Keynes: Open University Press.

Dignan J (2007) 'The Victim in Restorative Justice', in Walklate S (ed.) *Handbook of Victims and Victimology*, Cullompton: Willan Publishing.

Dignan J and Wynne A (1997) 'A Microcosm of the Local Community', *British Journal of Criminology*, 37 (2): 184.

Ditton J and Duffy J (1983) 'Bias in the Newspaper Reporting of Crime News', *British Journal of Criminology*, 23: 129.

Ditton J and Short E (1999) 'Yes, it works – no, it doesn't: compare the effects of open-street CCTV in two adjacent town centres', *Crime Prevention Studies*, 10: 201–23.

Duff A and Garland D (1994) *A Reader on Punishment*, Oxford: Oxford University Press.

Durkheim E (1970) *Suicide*, London: Routledge & Kegan Paul.

Easton S and Piper C (2008) *Sentencing and Punishment: The Quest for Justice*, (2nd edn), Oxford: Oxford University Press.

Easton S and Piper C (2012) *Sentencing and Punishment: The Quest for Justice* (2nd edn), Oxford University Press.

Eaton M (1986) *Justice for Women?*, Milton Keynes: Open University Press.

Eaton M (1993) *Women after Prison*, Milton Keynes: Open University Press.

Eden W (1777) *Principles of Penal Law*, London: B White & T Cadell.

Ekblom P (2001) 'Situational Crime Prevention', in McLaughlin E and Muncie J (eds), *The Sage Dictionary of Criminology*, London: Sage.

English R (2010*) Terrorism: How to Respond*, Oxford: Oxford University Press.

Ernst and Young (2000) 'Reducing Delay in the Criminal Justice System: Evaluation of the Indictable Only Initiative', London: Home Office.

Evans R and Wilkinson C (1990) 'Variations in Police Cautioning Policy and Practice in England and Wales', *Howard Journal of Criminal Justice*, 29 (3): 155–76.

Eysenck H J (1977) *Crime and Personality*, London: Routledge & Kegan Paul.

Falshaw L, Friendship C, Travers R and Nugent F (2003) Searching for 'What Works': an evaluation of cognitive skills programmes, Home Office Findings 206, London: Home Office.

Felson M (2002) *Crime and Everyday Life* (3rd edn), London: Pine Forge.

Fielding N, Kemp C and Norris C (1989) 'Constraints on the Practice of Community Policing', in Morgan R and Smith D (eds) *Coming to Terms with Policing*, London: Routledge.

Finch E and Fafinski S (2012) *Criminology Skills*, Oxford: Oxford University Press.

Fitzgerald M (1977) *Prisoners in Revolt*, Harmondsworth: Penguin.

Fitzgerald M (1999) *Searches in London under Section 1 of the Police and Criminal Evidence Act*, London: Metropolitan Police.

Fitzgerald M and Hale C (1996) *Ethnic Minorities: Victimisation and Racial Harassment: Findings from the 1988 and 1992 British Crime Surveys*, Home Office Research Study No 154, London: Home Office.

Fletcher G and Allan J (2003) 'Perceptions of and Concerns about Crime in England and Wales', in Simmons J and Dodd T (eds) *Crime in England and Wales 2002/3*, London: Home Office National Statistics.

Flood-Page C and Mackie A (1998) *Sentencing practice: an examination of decisions in magistrates' courts and the Crown Court in the mid-1990's*, Home Office Research Study No. 180, London: Home Office.

Flood-Page C, Campbell S, Harrington V and Miller J (2000) *Youth Crime: Findings from the 1998/99 Youth Lifestyles Survey*, Home Office Research Study 209, London: Home Office Research, Development and Statistics Directorate Crime and Criminal Justice Unit.

Fogel D (1975) *We are the Living Proof: The Justice Model for Corrections*, Cincinnati, OH: WH Anderson.

Foster J (1989) 'Two Stations: An Ethnographic Study of Policing in the Inner City', in Downes D (ed.) *Crime and the City*, London: Macmillan.

Foster J (2003) 'Police cultures', in Newburn T (ed.) *Handbook of Policing*, Cullompton: Willan Publishing.

Foucault M (1977) *Discipline and Punish*, Harmondsworth: Penguin.

Fox L (1952) *The English Prison and Borstal System*, London: Routledge & Kegan Paul.

Frankel M (1973) *Criminal Sentences: Law Without Order: The American Friends Service Committee 1971 Struggle for Justice*, New York, NY: Hill & Wang.

Garland D (1990) *Punishment and Modern Society*, Oxford: Oxford University Press.

Gelsthorpe L and Morgan R (eds) (2007) *Handbook of Probation*, Cullompton: Willan Publishing.

Gelsthorpe L and Morris A (1994) 'Juvenile Justice 1945–1992', in Maguire M, Morgan R and Reiner R (eds) *The Oxford Handbook of Criminology*, Oxford: Clarendon Press.

Gelsthorpe L and Rex S (2004) 'Community Service as reintegration: exploring the potential', in Mair G (ed.) *What Matters in Probation*, Cullompton: Willan Publishing.

Gill M and Mawby R (1990) *Volunteers in the Criminal Justice System: A Comparative Study of Probation, Police and Victim Support*, Milton Keynes: Open University Press.

Gilling D (2001) 'Community Safety and Social Policy', *European Journal on Criminal Policy and Research*, 9: 381–400.

Gleeson E and Bucke T (2006) *Police Complaints: Statistics for England and Wales 2004/5*, London: IPPC.

Goffman E (1961) *Asylums: Essays on the Social Situation of Mental Patients and Other Inmates*, Golden City, New York, NY: Doubleday.

Goffman E (1968) *Stigma: Notes on the Management of Spoiled Identities*, Harmondsworth: Penguin.

Goldman L and Sherrard M (2008) *Wigs and Wherefores: A biography of Michael Sherrard*, London: Wildy Simmonds & Hill Publishing.

Goldsmith A and Lewis C (2000) *Civilian Oversight of Policing*, Oxford: Hart.

Goldson B and Muncie J (eds) (2006) *Youth Justice*, London: Sage.

Goodey J (2004) *Victims and Victimology: Research, Policy and Practice*, London: Pearson Longman.

Gower Davies J (2012) *Mind-forg'd Manacles: Murder, Macpherson and the (Metropolitan) Police*, London: Civitas.

Graham J and Bennett T (1995) *Crime Prevention Strategies in Europe and North America*, Helsinki: Heuni.

Graham J and Bowling B (1995) *Young People and Crime*, Home Office Research Study No 145, London: Home Office.

Green D (ed.) (2000) *Institutional Racism and the Police: Fact or Fiction?*, London: Civitas.

Green, D (2004) 'Crime Reduction: Are Government policies likely to achieve its declared aims?', www.civitas.org.uk.

Gross H (1979) *A Theory of Criminal Justice*, New York, NY: Oxford University Press.

Hagell A and Newburn T (1994) *Persistent Young Offenders*, London: Policy Studies Institute.

Hall S and Winlow S (2012) *New Directions in Criminological Theory*, Routledge.

Halliday Report (2001) *Making Punishments Work: Review of the Sentencing Framework for England and Wales*, London: Home Office.

Hannibal M and Mountford L (2002) *The Law of Criminal and Civil Evidence*, Harlow: Pearson.

Harding C, Hines B, Ireland R and Rawlings P (1985) *Imprisonment in England and Wales*, Beckenham: Croom Helm.

Harman H and Griffith J (1979) *Justice Deserted: The Subversion of the Jury*, London: NCCL.

Hart H L A (1968) *Punishment and Responsibility*, Oxford: Clarendon Press.

Hartless J, Ditton J, Nair G and Phillips S (1995) 'More Sinned Against than Sinning: A Study of Young Teenagers' Experience of Crime', *British Journal of Criminology*, **35** (1): 114.

Hawkins K (1984) *Environment and Enforcement: Regulation and the Social Definition of Pollution*, Oxford Socio-Legal Studies: Clarendon Press.

Hayward K and Young J (2007) 'Cultural Criminology', in Maguire M, Morgan R and Reiner R (eds) *The Oxford Handbook of Criminology* (4th edn), Oxford: Clarendon Press.

Heal K and Laycock G (1986) *Situational Crime Prevention: From Theory to Practice*, London: Home Office.

Hedderman C and Moxon D (1992) *Magistrates' Court or Crown Court? Mode of Trial and Sentencing Decisions*, London: Home Office.

Heidensohn F (1992) *Women in Control? The Role of Women in Law Enforcement*, Oxford: Oxford University Press.

Henham R (2013) *Sentencing: Time for a Paradigm Shift (Key Ideas in Criminology)*, London: Routledge.

Hentig H von (1948) *The Criminal and his Victim*, New Haven, CT: Yale University Press.

Hickey T J (2013) *Taking Sides: Clashing Views in Crime and Criminology*, Columbus, OH: McGraw-Hill.

Higgins N and Budd S (2007) 'Geographic Patterns of Crime', in *Crime in England and Wales* 2007/7.

Hirsch A von (1976) *Doing Justice – The Choice of Punishment*, New York: Hill & Wang.

Hirsch A von (1986) *Past or Future Crimes*, Manchester: Manchester University Press.

Hirsch A von and Ashworth A (eds) (1993) *Principled Sentencing*, Edinburgh: Edinburgh University Press.

HM Prison Service (2004) *Annual Report and Accounts 2003/4*, London: HMSO.

HM Prison Service (2008) *Annual Report and Accounts 2007/8*, London: The Stationery Office.

HMIC (2007) *Beyond the Call: Thematic Report*, London: Home Office.

Hobbs D (1991) 'A Piece of Business: the Moral Economy of Detective Work in the East of London', *British Journal of Sociology*, **42** (4).

Hobbs D (2013) *Lush Life: Constructing Organised Crime in the UK (Clarendon Studies in Criminology)*, Oxford: Oxford University Press.

Hoffmann J P (2011) *Delinquency Theories: Appraisals and applications*, London: Routledge.

Holdaway S (1983) *Inside the British Police*, Oxford: Basil Blackwell.

Holdaway S (1997) 'Some Recent Approaches to the Study of Race in Criminological Research', *British Journal of Criminology*, **37** (3): 383–400.

Holdaway S and Barron A (1997) *Resigners? The Experience of Black and Asian Police Officers*, London: Macmillan.

Home Office (1895) *Report from the Departmental Committee on Prisons* (chaired by Herbert Gladstone), London: Home Office.

Home Office (1959) *Penal Practice in a Changing Society*, London: Home Office.

Home Office (1966) *Report of the Inquiry into Prison Escapes and Security* (chaired by Earl Mountbatten), London: HMSO.

Home Office (1968) *Report on the Regime for Long-term Prisoners in Maximum Security* (chaired by Sir Leon Radzinowicz), London: HMSO.

Home Office (1977) *Prisons and the Prisoner*, London: HMSO.

Home Office (1979) *The Report of the Committee of Inquiry into the UK Prison Service* (chaired by Mr Justice May), Cmnd (for 1956 to Nov 1986) 7673, London: HMSO.

Home Office (1984) *Criminal Justice: A Working Paper*, London: Home Office.

Home Office (1986) *The Sentence of the Court*, London: HMSO.

Home Office (1988a) *Punishment, Custody and the Community*, Cm 424, London: HMSO.

Home Office (1990) *Crime, Justice and Protecting the Public*, London: Home Office.

Home Office (1991a) *Prison Disturbances, April 1990*, Report of an inquiry presented to the Home Office by Lord Justice H Woolf and Judge Stephen Tumim, Cm 1456, London: HMSO.

Home Office (1991b) *A General Guide to the Criminal Justice Act 1991*, London: HMSO.

Home Office (1991c) *Custody, Care and Justice: The Way Ahead for the Prison Service in England and Wales*, Cm 1647, London: HMSO.

Home Office (1994) *Home Office Research Findings*, No 14, London: HMSO.

Home Office (1996) *Victims Charter*, London: Home Office.

Home Office (1997a) *No More Excuses – A New Approach to Tackling Youth Crime in England and Wales*, Cm 3809, London: Home Office.

Home Office (1997b) *Getting to Grips with Crime – A New Framework for Local Action*, London: HMSO.

Home Office (1997c) *Review of Delay in the Criminal Justice System* (chaired by M Narey), London: HMSO.

Home Office (1998) *Statistical Bulletin 7/98*, London: Home Office.

Home Office (2000) *Complaints against the Police – Framework for a New System*, London: Home Office.

Home Office (2000) *Feasibility of an independent system for investigating complaints against the police*, Police Research Series Paper 124: London: Home Office.

Home Office (2000) *Victim Respect: ensuring the victim matters*, London: Home Office.

Home Office (2001) *Religious Discrimination in England and Wales*, Home Office Research Study 220: London: Home Office.

Home Office (2002) *Race and the Criminal Justice System*, London: Home Office.

Home Office (2002) *Mobile Phone Theft*, Home Office Research Study 235, London: Home Office.

Home Office (2002) *Justice for All*, London: Home Office.

Home Office (2003) *Prison Population Brief*, London: Home Office.

Home Office (2003) *Respect and Responsibility – taking a stand against anti-social behaviour*, London: Home Office.

Home Office (2003) *Statistics on Women and the Criminal Justice System 2003*, London: Home Office.

Home Office (2004) *Building Communities, Beating Crime: A Better Police Service for the 21st Century*, Norwich: The Stationery Office.

Home Office (2004) *Building Communities, Beating Crime*, London: Home Office.

Home Office (2004) *National Policing Plan 2005–2008*, London: Home Office.

Home Office (2004) Occupation of Prisons, Remand Centres, Young Offenders Institutions and Police Cells England and Wales (monthly), London: Home Office.

Home Office (2004) *One Step Ahead: A 21st Century Strategy to Defeat Organised Criminals*, London: Home Office.

Home Office (2005) *Neighbourhood Policing: Your Police; Your Community; Our Commitment*, London: Home Office.

Home Office (2005) *Statistics on Race and the Criminal Justice System 2004: A Home Office Publication under section 95 of the Criminal Justice Act 1991*, London: Home Office.

Home Office (2006) *Allocation of Specific Grant to Police Authorities in England and Wales for 2007/08 (Written Ministerial Statement)*, London: Home Office.

Home Office (2006) *Review of the Partnership Provisions of the Crime and Disorder Act*, London: Home Office.

Home Office (2007) Modernising Police Powers, A review of PACE: consultation document.

Home Office (2008) *From the neighbourhood to the national: policing our communities together*, London: Home Office.

Home Office (2008) *Statistics on Race and the Criminal Justice System – A Home Office publication under section 95 of the Criminal Justice Act 1991*, London: Home Office.

Home Office (2008) *Youth Crime Action Plan*, London: Home Office.

Home Office (annually) *Criminal Statistics England and Wales*, London: Home Office.

Home Office (annually) *Judicial Statistics* . . .

Home Office (annually) *Prison Statistics England and Wales 2000*.

Home Office (annually) *Prison Statistics England and Wales 2002*.

Home Office (annually) *Probation Statistics* . . .

Hood R (1965) *Borstal Re-assessed*, London: Heinemann.

Hood R (ed.) (1974) *Crime, Criminology and Public Policy*, London: Heinemann.

Hope T (1997) 'Inequality and the future of community crime prevention', in Lab S P (ed.) *Crime Prevention at a Crossroads*, American Academy of Criminal Justice Sciences Monograph Series, Cincinnati, OH: Anderson Publishing.

Hope T (2000) 'Inequality and the Clubbing of Private Security', in Hope T and Sparks R (eds), *Crime Risk and Insecurity*, London: Routledge, pp 83–106.

Hope T (2001) 'Crime victimisation and inequality in risk society', in Matthews R and Pitts J (eds) *Crime, Disorder and Community Safety*, London: Routledge.

Hopkins Burke R (2009) *An Introduction to Criminological Theory* (3rd edn), London: Routledge.

Hough M and Mayhew P (1983) *The British Crime Survey: First Report*, London: HMSO.

Howard J (1777) *The State of Prisons*.

Hoyle C and Zedner L (2007) 'Victims, Victimization and Criminal Justice', in Maguire M, Morgan R and Reiner R (eds) *The Oxford Handbook of Criminology*, (4th edn), Oxford: Clarendon Press.

Hudson B (1993) *Penal Policy and Social Justice*, London: Macmillan.

Hughes G (2002) 'Crime and Disorder Partnerships: The Future of Community Safety?', in Hughes G, McLaughlin E and Muncie J (eds) *Crime Prevention and Community Safety: New Directions*, London: Sage.

Ignatieff M (1975) *A Just Measure of Pain: The Penitentiary in the Industrial Revolution 1750–1850*, London: Macmillan.

Innes M (2005) 'Why "soft" policing is hard: on the curious development of reassurance policing, how it became neighbourhood policing and what this signifies about the politics of police reform', in *Journal of Community and Applied Social Psychology* **15** (3): 156–69.

Innes M (2006) 'Reassurance and the "New" Community Policing', *Policing and Society* **16** (2): 95–8.

Interpol (2008) *Interpol: An overview*, available from: www.interpol.int/Public/ICPO/FactSheets/GI01.pdf.

Irwin J (1970) *The Felon*, Englewood Cliffs: Prentice Hall.

Irwin J (1980) *Prisons in Turmoil*, Toronto: Little, Brown & Co.

Jackson R, Jarvis L, Gunning J and Breen-Smyth M (2011) *Terrorism: A Critical Introduction*, Basingstoke: Palgrave Macmillan.

Jaishankar K and Ronel N (2013) *Global Criminology: Crime and Victimisation in a Globalised Era*, Boca Raton, FL: CRC Press.

Jansson K, Povey D and Kaiza P (2007) 'Violent and sexual crime', in Nicholas S, Kershaw C and Walker A (eds) *Crime in England and Wales 2006/7*, London: Home Office, pp 49–72.

Jefferson T (1990) *The Case Against Paramilitary Policing*, Milton Keynes: Open University Press.

Jewkes Y (2004) *Media and Crime*, London: Sage.

Jewkes Y. ed. (2007) *Handbook on Prisons*, Devon: Willan Publishing.

John T and Maguire M (2004) *The National Intelligence Model: Key lessons from early research*, available from: www.homeoffice.gov.uk/rds/pdfs04/rdsolr3004.pdf

Jones T and Newburn T (1994) *How Big is the Private Security Industry?*, London: Policy Studies Institute.

Joutsen M (1990) *The Criminal Justice System of Finland: A General Introduction*, Helsinki: Ministry of Justice.

Jowell R, Curtis J, Lindsay B, Ahrendt D with Pork A (eds) (1994) *British Social Attitudes, 11th Report*, Aldershot: Dartmouth Publishing Co.

Karmi G (2001) 'The new British anti-terrorist legislation', The Council for the Advancement of Arab-British Understanding, *Focus*, 7 (2).

Kaye C and Howlett M (eds) (2008) *Mental Health Services Today and Tomorrow*, Oxford: Radcliffe Publishing.

Kershaw C, Nicholas S and Walker A (eds) (2008) *Crime in England and Wales 2007/8*, London: Home Office.

King M (1981) *The Framework of Criminal Justice*, London: Croom Helm.

King R and Elliott K (1977) *Albany: The Birth of a Prison, the End of an Era*, London: Routledge & Kegan Paul.

Langan P and Farrington D (1998) *Crime and Justice in the United States and in England and Wales 1981–96*, Washington DC: US Department of Justice.

Lavranos N (2003) 'Europol and the fight against terrorism', *European Foreign Affairs Review*, 8: 259–75.

Lea J and Young J (1992) *What is to be Done about Law and Order?* (2nd edn), London: Pluto Press.

Learmont J (1995) *Review of Prison Service Security in England and Wales and the Escape from Parkhurst Prison on Tuesday 3rd January 1995*, Cm 3020, London: HMSO.

Legal Services Commission, *Annual Report 2002/3*, London: HMSO.

Leishman F, Loveday B and Savage S (eds) (1998) *Core Issues in Policing* (2nd edn), London: Longman.

Leng R, McConville M and Sanders A (1992) 'Researching the Discretions to Charge and to Prosecute', in Downes D (ed.) *Unravelling Criminal Justice*, London: Macmillan.

Levi M (1987) *Regulating Fraud: White Collar Crime and the Criminal Process*, London: Tavistock.

Levi M (1989) 'Suite Justice: Sentencing for Fraud', *Criminal Law Review*: 420–34.

Levi M (2002) 'The Organisation of Serious Crimes', in Maguire M, Morgan R and Reiner R (eds) *The Oxford Handbook of Criminology* (3rd edn), Oxford: Clarendon Press.

Levi M, Burrows J, Fleming MH and Hopkins M et al. (2007) *The Nature, Extent and Economic Impact of Fraud in the UK*, Report for the Association of Chief Police Officers' Economic Crime Portfolio, available from www.acpo. police.uk/asp/policies/Data/Fraud%20in%20 the%20UK.pdf

Lewis C S (1953) 'On Punishment', *Res Judicatae*, 6: 1952–4.

Liberty (2000) *An Independent Police Complaints Commission*, available from: www.liberty-human-rights.org.uk/publications/6-reports/police.pdf

Liebling A and Maruna S (eds) (2006) *The Effects of Imprisonment*, Devon: Willan Publishing.

Lipton D, Martinson R and Wilks J (1975) *Effectiveness of Correctional Treatment*, Springfield, MA: Praeger.

Lockyer K (2013) *Future Prisons: A radical plan to reform the prison estate*, London: Policy Exchange.

Loeber R and Welsh B C (2012) *The Future of Criminology*, Oxford: Oxford University Press.

Lombroso Cesare (1897) *L'Uomo Delinquente* (5th edn), Torino: Bocca.

Lovbakke J (2007) 'Public Perceptions', in Nicholas S, Kershaw C and Walker A (2007) (eds) *Crime in England and Wales: A Summary of the Main Figures 2006/7* (Home Office RDS 2007, available from www.homeoffice.gov.uk/rds/pdfs07/crime0607summ/pdf).

Loveday B (1992) 'Right Agendas: Law and Order in England and Wales', *International Journal of the Sociology of Law*, 20: 297–319.

MacPherson W (1999) *The Stephen Lawrence Inquiry: Report of an Inquiry by Sir William MacPherson*, London: Home Office.

Maguire M (2002) 'Criminal Statistics: the "Data Explosion" and its Implications', in Maguire M, Morgan R and Reiner R (eds) *The Oxford Handbook of Criminology* (3rd edn), Oxford: Clarendon Press.

Maguire M (2003) 'Criminal Investigation and Crime Control', in Newburn T, *Handbook of Policing*, Cullompton: Willan Publishing.

Maguire M (2004) 'The Crime Reduction Programme in England and Wales: Reflections on the vision and the reality', *Criminology and Criminal Justice*, **4** (3): 213–38.

Maguire M, Morgan R and Reiner R (eds) (1997) *The Oxford Handbook of Criminology* (2nd edn), Oxford: Clarendon Press.

Maguire M, Morgan R and R Reiner (eds) (2012) *Oxford Handbook of Handbook of Criminology* (5th edn), Oxford: Oxford University Press.

Maguire M and Pointing J (eds) (1988) *Victims of Crime: A New Deal?*, Milton Keynes: Open University Press.

Mair G (ed.) (2004) *What Matters in Probation*, Cullompton: Willan Publishing.

Mair G and Burke L (2009) *A Short History of Probation*, Cullompton: Willan Publishing.

Mathews R, Hancock L and Briggs D (2004) 'Jurors' perception, understanding, confidence and satisfaction in the jury system: a study in six courts', Home Office Research Findings 227.

Mawby R (2007) 'Public Sector Services and the Victim of Crime', in S Walklate (ed.) *Handbook of Victims and Victimology*, Cullompton: Willan Publishing.

Mawby R C and Wright A (2003) 'The Police Organisation', in Newburn T (ed.) *Handbook of Policing*, Cullompton: Willan Publishing.

May T (1994) 'Probation and Community Sanctions', in Maguire M, Morgan R and Reiner R (eds) *The Oxford Handbook of Criminology*, Oxford: Clarendon Press.

Mayhew P, Clarke R, Sturman A and Hough J (eds) (1976) *Crime as Opportunity*, Home Office Research Study No 34, London: HMSO.

Mayhew P, Elliot D and Dowds L (1989) *The 1988 British Crime Survey*, London: HMSO.

McCabe S (1988) in Findlay M and Duff P (eds) *The Jury Under Attack*, London: Butterworth.

McConville M and Wilson G (2002) *The Handbook of the Criminal Justice Process*, Oxford: Oxford University Press.

McIvor G (2004) 'Getting Personal: developments in policy and practice in Scotland', in Mair G (ed.) *What Matters in Probation*, Cullompton: Willan Publishing.

McLaughlin E and Muncie J (eds) (2005) *The SAGE Dictionary of Criminology*, London: Sage.

McNeill and Batchelor S (2004) 'Persistent Offending by Young People: Developing Practice', *Issues in Community and Criminal Justice*, Monograph 3.

Merton R K (1938) 'Social Structure and Anomie', *American Sociological Review*, **3**: 672–82.

Messinger S and Johnson P (1978) 'California's Determinate Sentencing Statute History and Issues', in *Determinate Sentencing: Reform or Regression*, National Institute of Law Enforcement and Criminal Justice, Washington, DC: Government Printing Office.

Ministry of Justice (2008) Singer L and Jones A, *Statistics on Race and Criminal Justice System 2006/7*, London (July): Ministry of Justice.

Ministry of Justice (2008) *Statistics Bulletin*, 4 September, London: Ministry of Justice.

Ministry of Justice (2009) *Statistics Bulletin, Population in Custody*, February 2009.

Ministry of Justice (January 2009) *Statistics on Women and the Criminal Justice System*, London: Ministry of Justice.

Ministry of Justice *Criminal Statistics* (Annual), London: Ministry of Justice.

Ministry of Justice *Judicial and Court Statistics* (Annual), London: Ministry of Justice.

Ministry of Justice Offender Management Caseload Statistics (NS) (2006), London: Ministry of Justice.

Mirrlees-Black C, Mayhew P and Percy A (1996) 'The 1996 British Crime Survey: England and Wales', *Home Office Statistical Bulletin*, Issue 19/96, London: HMSO.

Mitchell H and Babb P (2007) 'Crimes Detected in England and Wales', *2006/7 Home Office Statistical Bulletin* 15/07.

Morgan J and Zedner L (1992) *Child Victims: Crime, Impact, and Criminal Justice*, Oxford: Clarendon Press.

Morgan R (1989) 'Policing by Consent: Legitimating the Doctrine', in Morgan and Smith (eds) *Coming to Terms with Policing: Perspectives on Policy*, London: Routledge.

Morgan R (1997) 'Imprisonment', in Maguire M, Morgan R and Reiner R (eds) *The Oxford Handbook of Criminology* (2nd edn), Oxford: Clarendon Press.

Morgan R (2007) 'Imprisonment', in Maguire M, Morgan R and Reiner R (eds) *The Oxford Handbook of Criminology* (4th edn), Oxford: Clarendon Press.

Morgan R and Jones T (1992) 'Bail or Jail?', in Stockdale E and Casales S (eds) *Criminal Justice Under Stress*, London: Blackstone.

Morgan R and Newburn T (1997) *The Future of Policing*, Oxford: Clarendon Press.

Morgan R and Russell N (2002) 'Survey on Public View on Residential Burglary', in Sentencing Report to the Court of Appeal (2002) *Domestic Burglary*, London: Sentencing Advisory Panel.

Morgan J and Zedner L (1992) *Child Victims*, Oxford: Oxford University Press.

Morris A and Giller H (1987) *Understanding Juvenile Justice*, London: Croom Helm.

Morton S (2009) *Can OASys deliver consistent assessments of offenders? Results from the inter-rater reliability study* (Research Summary 1/09), London: Ministry of Justice.

Moss B (2004) 'Coming Soon to a Court Near You', *Counsel*, June: 22.

Muir R and Lodge G (2008) *A new beat, options for more accountable policing*, London: Institute for Public Policy Research.

Muncie J (1999) *Youth and Crime: A Critical Introduction*, London: Sage.

Muncie J (2003) 'Youth, Risk and Victimisation', in Davies P, Francis P and Jupp V (eds) *Victimisation: Theory, Research and Policy*, Basingstoke: Palgrave Macmillan.

Muncie J (2005) 'The globalisation of crime control – the case of youth and juvenile justice', *Theoretical Criminology* 9 (1): 35–64.

Muncie J, McLaughlin E and Langan M (eds) (1999) *Criminological Perspectives*, London: Sage.

Murphy P (1992) *A Practical Approach to Evidence*, London: Blackstone Press.

Murray C (1997) *Does Prison Work?*, London: IEA and *Sunday Times*.

Murray I (2003) 'Making Rehabilitation Work', www.civitas.org.uk.

National Audit Office (2004) *The Drug Treatment and Testing Order: Early Lessons*, London: NAO.

National Audit Office (2009) *Administration of the Crown Court*, London: NAO.

National Audit Office (2009) *National Offender Management Information System*, London: NAO.

Newburn (2002) 'Young People, Crime and Youth Justice', in Maguire M, Morgan R and Reiner R (eds) *The Oxford Handbook of Criminology*, (3rd edn), Oxford: Clarendon Press.

Newburn T (2003a) *Crime and Criminal Justice Policy* (2nd edn), London: Longman.

Newburn T (ed.) (2003b) *Handbook of Policing*, Cullompton: Willan Publishing.

Newburn T (2007) *Criminology*, Cullompton: Willan Publishing.

Newburn T (2007) 'Youth Crime and Youth Culture' in Maguire M, Morgan R and Reiner R (eds) *The Oxford Handbook of Criminology* (4th edn), Oxford: Oxford University Press.

Newburn T (2008) *Criminology*, Cullompton: Willan Publishing.

Newburn T (ed.) (2008) *Handbook of Policing*, (2nd edn), Cullompton: Willan Publishing.

Newburn, T (2012) *Criminology* (2nd edn), Oxford: Routledge.

Newburn T and Neyroud P (eds) (2007) *The Dictionary of Policing*, Cullompton: Willan Publishing.

Newburn T and Reiner R (2007) 'Policing and the police', in Maguire M *et al.* *Oxford Handbook of Criminology*, Oxford: Oxford University Press.

Newburn T and Souhami A (2005) 'Youth Diversion', in Tilley N (ed.) *Handbook of Crime Prevention*, Cullompton: Willan Publishing.

Newman O (1972) *Defensible Space: Crime Prevention Through Urban Design*, New York, NY: Collier-Macmillan.

Nicholas S and Wood M (2003) 'Property Crime', in Simmons J and Dodd T (eds) *Crime in England and Wales 2002/3*, London: Home Office National Statistics.

Nicholas S, Kershaw C and Walker A (2007) (eds) *Crime in England and Wales* 2006/7, London: Home Office.

Norris C and Armstrong G (1997) *The Unforgiving Eye: CCTV Surveillance in Public Space*, University of Hull: Centre for Criminology and Criminal Justice.

Norris C and Armstrong G (1999) *The Maximum Surveillance Society: The Rise of CCTV*, Oxford: Berg.

Open Society Institute (2005) *British Muslims – Discrimination, Equality and Community Cohesion*, available from: www.eumap.org/reports/2004/britishmuslims/report/equality/6_Equality.pdf.

Owen J (2013) *Riots and Public Disorder: Law Enforcement, Policy and Civil Society (Library of Crime and Criminology)*, London: I. B. Tauris.

Packer H (1968) *The Limits of the Criminal Sanction*, Stanford, CA: Stanford University Press.

Pain R (2003) 'Old Age and Victimisation', in Davies P, Francis P and Jupp V (eds) *Victimisation: Theory, Research and Policy*, Basingstoke: Palgrave/Macmillan.

Painter K (1998) *Lighting and Crime – The Edmonton Project*, Enfield: Middlesex Polytechnic.

Painter K and Farrington D (1998) 'Marital Violence in Great Britain and its Relationship to Marital and Non Marital Rape', *International Review of Victimology*, **5**: 257–76.

Parker H, Sumner M and Jarvis G (1989) *Unmasking the Magistrates*, Milton Keynes: Open University Press.

Paterson A (1927) *Report of the Prison Commission*, London: HMSO.

Pease K (2002) 'Crime Reduction', in Maguire M, Morgan R and Reiner R (eds) *The Oxford Handbook of Criminology* (3rd edn), Oxford: Clarendon Press.

Peay J (2002) 'Mentally Disordered Offenders', in Maguire M, Morgan R and Reiner R (eds) *The Oxford Handbook of Criminology* (3rd edn), Oxford: Clarendon Press.

Phillips C (2002) 'From Voluntary to Statutory Status: reflecting on the experience of three partnerships established under the Crime and Disorder Act 1998', in Hughes G, McLaughlin E and Muncie J (eds) *Crime Prevention and Community Safety: New Directions*, London: Sage.

Phillips C and Bowling B (2002) 'Racism, Ethnicity, Crime and Criminal Justice', in Maguire M, Morgan R and Reiner R (eds) *The Oxford Handbook of Criminology* (3rd edn), Oxford: Clarendon Press.

Porter M (1997) *Tackling Cross Border Crime*, Home Office Research Report, London: Home Office.

Povey D and Allan J (2003) 'Violent Crime', in Simmons J and Dodd T (eds) *Crime in England and Wales 2002/3*, London: Home Office National Statistics.

Prison Commissioners (1925) *Annual Report*, London: HMSO.

Prison Service (1988) *Briefing*, November, London: HMSO.

Prison Service (annually) *Annual Report and Accounts 2000.*

Quinton P, Bland N, and Miller J (2000) *Police Stops, Decision-making and Practice*, Police Research Series Paper No. 130, London: Home Office.

Quraishi M (2005) *Muslims and Crime: A Comparative Study*, London: Ashgate.

Raynor P and Vanstone M (2002) *Understanding Community Penalties: Probation, policy and social change*, Buckingham: Open University Press.

Reeves H and Mulley K (2000) 'The New Status of Victims in the UK: Opportunities and Threats', in Crawford A and Goodey J (eds) *Integrating a Victim Perspective within Criminal Justice*, Aldershot: Ashgate/Dartmouth.

Reiner R (2000) *The Politics of the Police*, London: Harvester Wheatsheaf.

Reiner R (2010) *The Politics of the Police* (4th edn), Oxford: University Press.

Reisig M D and Kane R J (2014) *The Oxford Handbook of Police and Policing*, Oxford: Oxford University Press.

Robertson G, Pearson R and Gibb R (1995) *The Mentally Disordered Offender and the Police*, Home Office Research Findings, No 21.

Robinson G and McNeill F (2004) 'Purposes matter: examining the "ends" of Probation', in Mair G (ed.) *What Matters in Probation*, Cullompton: Willan Publishing.

Rock P (1998) *After Homicide*, Oxford: Clarendon Press.

Rothe D L and Friedrichs D O (2014) *Crimes of Globalisation – New Directions in Critical Criminology*, London: Routledge.

Rothman D (1980) *Conscience and Convenience: The Asylum and its Alternatives in Progressive America*, Boston, MA: Little, Brown.

Runciman, Lord (1993) *The Report of the Royal Commission on Criminal Justice* (chaired by Lord Runciman), London: HMSO.

Rutter M (1985) 'Family and school influences on behavioural development', *Journal of Child Psychology and Psychiatry* **26**: 349–68.

Ryan M (2003) *Penal Policy and Political Culture in England and Wales: Four essays on policy and process*, Winchester: Waterside Press.

Sanders (2002) 'Prosecution Systems', in McConville M and Wilson G (eds) *The Handbook of the Criminal Justice Process*, Oxford: Oxford University Press.

Sanders A and Jones I (2007) 'The victim in court', in Walklate S (ed.) *Handbook of Victims and Victimology*, Cullompton: Willan Publishing.

Sanders A and Young R (1994) *Criminal Justice*, London: Butterworth.

Sanders A and Young R (2006) *Criminal Justice* (3rd edn), Oxford: Oxford University Press.

Sanderson J (1992) *Criminology Textbook*, London: HLT.

Schlesinger P and Tumber H (1994) *Reporting Crime: The Media Politics of Criminal Justice*, Oxford: Clarendon Press.

Schrag C (1944) 'Social Types of a Prison Community. Quoted in Ditchfield J (1990)', *Control in Prisons: A Review of the Literature*, London: HMSO.

Schur E (1969) *Our Criminal Society*, Englewood Cliffs: Prentice Hall.

Schur E (1973) *Radical Non-Intervention. Rethinking the Delinquency Problem*, Englewood Cliffs: Prentice Hall.

Scottish Executive (2003) 'Criminal Proceedings in Scottish Courts, 2001', Scottish Executive Statistical Bulletin Cr/2002/9.

Scull A (1977) *Decarceration: Community Treatment and the Deviant – A Radical View*, Englewood Cliffs: Prentice Hall.

Shapland J, Willmore J and Duff P (1985) *Victims and the Criminal Justice System*, Aldershot: Gower.

Shawcross (Lord) (1951) House of Commons Debate, Vol 483, 29 January 1951.

Sheptycki J W E (2014) *Transnational Organised Crime*, London: Sage.

Simmons, J and Dodd T (eds) (2003) *Crime in England and Wales 2002/3*, London: Home Office National Statistics.

Skolnick J (1966) *Justice Without Trial*, New York, NY: Wiley.

Smith D J (1997) 'Race, Crime and Criminal Justice', in Maguire M, Morgan R and Reiner R (eds) *The Oxford Handbook of Criminology* (2nd edn), Oxford: Clarendon Press.

Smith D J and Gray J (1985) *Police and People in London: the PSI Report*, Aldershot: Gower.

Smith G (2004) 'Rethinking Police Complaints', *British Journal of Criminology*, **44** (1): 15–33.

Smith R (2007) *Youth and Crime* (2nd edn), Cullompton: Willan Publishing.

Social Exclusion Unit (2002) *Reducing Re-offending by Ex-prisoners*, London: Office of Deputy Prime Minister.

Soothill K (1993) 'Sex Crime in the News Revisited', Unpublished paper presented to the British Criminology Conference, Cardiff, July 1993.

Soothill K and Walby S (1991) *Sex Crime in the News*, London: Routledge.

Spalek B (2004) 'Islam and Criminal Justice', in Muncie J and Wilson D (2004) *Student Handbook of Criminal Justice and Criminology*, London: Cavendish Publishing.

Spencer S and Stern B (2002) *Reluctant Witness*, London: NCCL.

Spicer K and Glicksman A (2004) Adult reconviction: results from the 2001 cohort, Home Office Online Report 59/04, London: Home Office.

Sprack J (2004) *Emmins on Criminal Procedure* (10th edn), London: Blackstone Press.

Sprack J (2008) *A Practical Approach to Criminal Procedure* (12th edn), London: Blackstone Press.

Starmer K (2009) 'A prosecution service for the 21st century', speech to the CPS, 9 January 2009.

Taylor P, Hoare J and Murphy R, 'Property Crime', in Nicholas S, Kershaw C and Walker A (eds) *Crime in England and Wales* 2006/7, London: Home Office, pp 73–94.

Taylor, Lord Chief Justice (1993) *17th Leggatt Lecture – What do we want from our Judges?*, Guildford: University of Surrey.

The Institute for Public Policy Research (November 2006), *Freedom's Orphans: Raising Youth in a Changing World*, London: IPPR.

Thomas D A (1979) *Principles of Sentencing*, London: Heinemann.

Thomas C with Balmer N (2007) *Diversity and Fairness in the Jury System*, Ministry of Justice Research Series 2/07, June.

Thorpe K, Robb P and Higgins N (2007) 'Extent and Trends', in Nicholas S, Kershaw C and Walker A (2007) (eds) *Crime in England and Wales: A Summary of the Main Figures 2006/7* (Home Office RDS 2007, available from www.homeoffice.gov.uk/rds/pdfs07/crime0607summ/pdf).

Tilley N (1993) 'Crime Prevention and the Safer Cities Story', *Howard Journal of Criminal Justice*, **32** (1): 40–57.

Tilley N (2002) 'Crime Prevention in Britain, 1975–2010: breaking out, breaking in and breaking down', in Hughes G, McLaughlin E and Muncie J (eds) *Crime Prevention and Community Safety: New Directions*, London: Sage.

Tilley N (2003) 'Community Policing, problem-oriented policing and intelligence-led policing', in Newburn T (ed.) *Handbook of Policing*, Cullompton: Willan Publishing.

Tombs S and Whyte D (2006) 'Community Safety and Corporate Crime', in Squires P (ed.) *Community Safety: Critical Perspectives on Policy and Practice*, Cambridge: Polity Press, pp 155–68.

Tonry M (1987) *Sentencing Reform Impacts*, Washington, DC: US Department of Justice.

Tuffin R (2007) 'Neighbourhood Policing', in Newburn T and Neyroud P (eds) *The Dictionary of Policing*, Cullompton: Willan Publishing.

Utting D, Bright J and Henricson C (1993) *Crime and the Family: Improving Child Rearing and Preventing Delinquency*, Occasional Paper 16, Family Policy Studies Centre.

Van Dijk JJM and de Waard J (1991) 'A Two-dimensional Typology of Crime Prevention Projects: with a bibliography', *Criminal Justice Abstracts*, **23**: 485–503.

Vennard J (1985) 'The Outcome of Contested Trials', in Moxon D (ed.) *Managing Criminal Justice*, London: HMSO.

Victim Support (1995) *The Rights of the victims of crime*, London: Victim Support.

Victim Support (2003) *Insult to Injury: How the criminal injuries compensation system is failing victims of crime*, London: Victim Support.

Walby S and Allen J (2004) *Domestic Violence, Sexual Assault and Stalking: Findings from the British Crime Survey*, Home Office Research Study 276, London: Home Office, www.homeoffice.gov.uk/rds/pdfs04/hors276.pdf.

Walker C (2009) *Blackstone's Guide to the Anti-Terrorism Legislation* (2nd edn), Oxford: Oxford University Press.

Walker M (1987) 'Interpreting Race and Crime Statistics', *Journal of the Royal Statistical Society A*, **150**, Part 1: 39–56.

Walker N and Padfield N (1996) *Sentencing: Theory, Law and Practice* (2nd edn), London: Butterworth.

Walklate S (1989) *Victimology: The Victim and the Criminal Justice Process*, London: Unwin Hyman.

Walklate S (2007) *Imagining the Victim of Crime*, Milton Keynes: Open University Press.

Walmsley R (2003) *World Prison Population: List* (5th edn), Home Office Findings, London: HMSO.

Walmsley R, Howard L and White S (1993) *The National Prison Survey 1991: Main Findings*, Home Office Research Study No 128, London: HMSO.

Wasik M (1993) *The Magistrate*, October.

Wasik M (2001) *Emmins on Sentencing* (4th edn), Oxford: Oxford University Press.

Wasik M and Taylor R (1994) *Criminal Justice Act, 1991*, London: Blackstone.

Watson L (1996) *Victims of Violent Crime Recorded by the Police, England and Wales, 1990–1994*, Home Office Statistical Findings, Issue 1/96, London: HMSO.

Webb B and Laycock G (1992) *Tackling Car Crime: The Nature and Extent of the Problem*, Home Office Crime Prevention Paper No 32.

Wells C (1988) 'The Decline and Rise of English Murder: Corporate Crime and Individual Responsibility', *Criminal Law Review*: 789–801.

West D J and Farrington D (1973) *Who Becomes Delinquent?*, London: Heinemann.

West D J and Farrington D (1977) *The Delinquent Way of Life*, London: Heinemann.

Whitelaw W (1989) *The Whitelaw Memoirs*, London: Arum Press.

Wikstrom P H, Treiber K H, Oberwittler D and Hardie B (2012) *Breaking Rules: The Social and Situational Dynamics of Young People's Urban Crime (Clarendon Studies in Criminology)*, Oxford: Oxford University Press.

Wilson J Q and Kelling G (1982) 'Broken Windows', *Atlantic Monthly*, March: 29–38.

Windlesham Lord (1993/2001) *Responses to Crime* (4 vols), Oxford: Clarendon Press.

Winlow S and Atkinson R (2012) *New Directions in Crime and Deviancy*, London: Routledge.

Wright A (2002) *Policing: An introduction to the concepts and practice*, Cullompton: Willan Publishing.

Wright R (2000) 'Financial Markets at Risk: The Threats to Stability and Integrity of the Financial Order and the Good Governance of the Financial Services Industry', speech delivered to the 18th International Cambridge Symposium on Economic Crime, 11 September 2000.

Young J (2003) 'Merton with energy, Katz with Structure: the sociology of vindictiveness and the criminology of transgression', *Theoretical Criminology*, 7 (3): 389–414.

Zalman M and Carrano J (2013) *Wrongful Conviction and Criminal Justice Reform: Making Justice*, London: Routledge.

Zander M (2003) *The Police and Criminal Evidence Act 1984* (4th edn), London: Sweet & Maxwell.

Zedner L (2002) 'Victims', in Maguire M, Morgan R and Reiner R (eds) *The Oxford Handbook of Criminology* (3rd edn), Oxford: Clarendon Press.

Zimbardo P (1969) 'The human choice', Nebraska Symposium on Motivation **17**: 237–307.

Zito Trust (1997) Community Care Homicides, London: Zito Trust.

Index

Page references to Figures or Tables will be in *italics*, while references applicable to Glossary entries are in **bold**